Mass Media
and
American Politics

Mass Media
and
American Politics

Fifth Edition

Doris A. Graber
University of Illinois at Chicago

A Division of Congressional Quarterly Inc.
Washington, D.C.

Copyright © 1997 Congressional Quarterly Inc.
1414 22nd Street, N.W., Washington, D.C. 20037

Printed in the United States of America

Cover design: Naylor Design Inc.

Library of Congress Cataloging-in-Publication Data

Graber, Doris A. (Doris Appel)
  Mass media and American politics / --5th ed.
   p. cm.
  Includes bibliographical references and index.
  ISBN 0-87187-768-6
  1. Mass media--Social aspects--United States. 2. Mass media--Political aspects--United States. I. Title.
HN90.M3G7   1996   96-32482
302.23'0937--dc20   CIP

To
Jack, Jim, Lee, Susan, Tom —
my very special students

Contents

Tables and Figures   xi

Preface   xv

c h a p t e r   o n e

Media Power and Government Control   1

    Political Importance of Mass Media   2
    Functions of Mass Media   5
    Effects of Mass Media   13
    Who Should Control Newsmaking?   18
    Models of the News-Making Process   23
    Summary   28

c h a p t e r   t w o

Ownership, Regulation, and Guidance
of Media   33

    Control and Ownership: Public and Semipublic   34
    Patterns of Private Ownership   39
    Government Regulation of the Media   47
    Summary   54

c h a p t e r   t h r e e

Press Freedom and the Law   58

Access to the Media   59
Access to Information   68
Individual Rights Versus the Public's Right to Know   76
Summary   86

c h a p t e r   f o u r

News Making and News Reporting Routines   93

Profile Sketch of American Journalists   94
Gatekeeping   99
Effects of Gatekeeping   116
Appraising the News-Making Process   124
Summary   128

c h a p t e r   f i v e

Reporting Extraordinary Events   135

Four Crises   136
Media Responses and Roles   138
Covering Pseudo-Crises   150
Summary   152

c h a p t e r   s i x

The Media as Policy Makers   156

Manipulative Journalism in Perspective   157
Muckraking Models   159
Beyond Muckraking: Journalists as Political Actors   166
Agenda Building   168
Documentaries and Docudramas   177
Methods: Fair and Foul   179
Summary   183

c h a p t e r   s e v e n

Media Impact on Attitudes and Behavior   188

Differential Effects of Print and Broadcast News   189
The Role of Media in Political Socialization   191
Patterns in Socialization   195
Choosing Media Stories   197
Learning Processes   202
Learning Effects: Knowledge and Attitudes   204
Learning Effects: Behavior   212
Summary   218

c h a p t e r   e i g h t

Elections in the Television Age   228

The State of Research   229
The Consequences of Media Politics   230
Media Content   243
Media Effects   257
Summary   263

c h a p t e r   n i n e

The Struggle for Control: News from the Presidency and Congress   269

The Adversarial Relationship   270
The Media and the Executive Branch   272
The Media and Congress   288
Summary   300

c h a p t e r   t e n

Covering the Justice System and State and Local News   306

The Media and the Courts   306
Covering State and Local Affairs   313

The Contents of Subnational News   322
Summary   333

c h a p t e r   e l e v e n

Foreign Affairs Coverage   339

The Foreign News Niche   340
Making Foreign News   341
Appraising Foreign Newsmaking   365
Impact on Public Opinion   367
Exporting News   368
Summary   371

c h a p t e r   t w e l v e

Trends in Media Policy   380

Dissatisfaction with the Media   381
The Impact of New Technologies   388
The Shape of the Future   400
Summary   405

Index   411

Tables and Figures

Tables

1-1	Contrasting Assumptions about Press Mission	21
2-1	Income Sources of Public Broadcasting Systems: 1992	38
4-1	Roles Deemed "Extremely Important" by Journalists	99
4-2	Sources of Front-Page News Stories	101
4-3	Police Versus Newspaper Crime Reports: Chicago, 1994	107
4-4	Frequency of Mention of News Topics: June 1, 1995, to July 20, 1995	110
4-5	Network Coverage of State News: August 1994 to July 1995	112
4-6	Coverage of News Elements in National and Local Broadcasts	126
5-1	Principal Sources of Disaster Information	138
7-1	Rankings of Top Twenty-five Content Categories and Average Ratings Across Ten Markets	199
7-2	Reasons for Attention or Inattention to News Stories	200
7-3	Network Television News Characteristics	211
8-1	Distribution of Coverage Areas in the 1983 Chicago Mayoral Primary and General Elections	247
8-2	Source Orientation in the 1983 Chicago Mayoral Primary and General Elections	249
8-3	Candidate Evaluations in Post–Labor Day Network Television News: 1984	252

8-4 Median Number of Local Newspaper Paragraphs
Mentioning Selected Themes in Fourteen Tight Congressional Races: September 27 to November 7, 1978   256

8-5 Presidential Qualities Mentioned by the Public and by
Newspapers   258

8-6 Comparison of Percentage of Mention of Issues and Events
by Newspapers, Television, and Survey Responses   259

9-1 Evening Network News Coverage of the Three Branches
of Government: August 1994 to July 1995   271

9-2 Evening Network News Coverage of the Three Branches
of Government in Percentage of Network Time:
August 1994 to July 1995   272

9-3 How Network Sources Rated President Clinton's Policies:
January 20, 1993, to June 20, 1994   277

9-4 Top Ten Issues on Network Evening News about
the President and Congress: August 1994 to July 1995   290

9-5 An Evaluation of Press Coverage of Congress   297

10-1 Political News in New York State Papers   322

10-2 Regional Focus of Network News Coverage:
August 1994 to July 1995   324

10-3 State Distribution of Network News Attention,
Ten Leaders and Trailers: August 1994 to July 1995   325

10-4 News Choice Preferences   326

10-5 Distribution of Television News Story Topics:
June 1, 1995, to July 20, 1995   327

10-6 Senate Committee Coverage, National Versus Local
Priorities: 1979 to 1985   329

11-1 Distribution of Foreign Correspondents: 1991   344

11-2 Distribution of U.S. Foreign Correspondents Serving
Major News Outlets   345

11-3 Network Coverage of World Regions: March 1993 to
February 1994   353

11-4 Soviet News Story Topics in the U.S. Press: January 1945
to January 1991   357

Figures

2-1   The Diverse Holdings of the General Electric Company   41

6-1   How Scientists Rate Media Portrayals of Cancer Risks   173

8-1   News Coverage of the Republican Contenders in *Time* and
    Newsweek in Early Stages of 1988 Nominating Contest   233

8-2   Issue Focus on ABC and CNN News: January to
    October 1992   262

12-1 The Cable TV Explosion   396

Preface

THE MASS MEDIA PLAY A CENTRAL and ever-growing role in the conduct of American politics. They mold the thinking and actions of political leaders as well as of ordinary citizens. The primary reasons for the growth in media influence are "new media" technologies such as cable and satellite television transmission, business mergers involving the electronic media and newspaper chains, and the deregulation of the communications industry from the 1980s onward. Recent years have also witnessed a sharp escalation of the battle between journalists and politicians for control over news content. The mainstream media have provided the chief battleground, but the struggle has also spilled over into some of the new media that have become prominent.

To report and analyze the flow of major changes and its impact on politics and political news requires revision of this book at frequent intervals. This fifth edition features up-to-date knowledge about the current media scene, including important advances in the study of media influence on social values and public policies. Many of the new data come from my own research on television's bearing on politics. Research on media impact on political actors, events, and issues has been updated, and fresh examples have replaced older ones throughout. The book's approach is interdisciplinary and objective, offering a variety of viewpoints on controversial issues. The language has been kept simple and clear to suit the needs of novices in this area of knowledge, without sacrificing the scholarly depth, documentation, and precision that more advanced readers require.

Much has changed in the media and in politics since the original publication of *Mass Media and American Politics* in 1980. Still, the basic features of the interrelation between mass media and American politics have remained the same—testimony to the maturity of the relationship. The primary emphasis of the book remains on news produced by television and newspapers, because these are the chief sources of current information for people in public and private life. Other mass media play a distinctly subordinate role. Nonetheless, this edition devotes more space than earlier ones to radio in the form of talk shows; to cable television, especially the Cable News Network (CNN); and to the impact of the Internet and the World Wide Web.

Most political communication research continues to emphasize the relationship between media and politics during elections, although the scope of research has broadened over time as the references in the text and at the end of each chapter indicate. The fifth edition of *Mass Media and American Politics,* like prior editions, takes a broader approach, encompassing the entire media landscape because media scholars can no longer afford to ignore how all the pieces of the media/government puzzle fit together. Understanding these complex interrelationships requires a comprehensive, up-to-date text that provides an overview of the entire media field from a political perspective, yet steeped in an intimate knowledge of the U.S. media system. *Mass Media in American Politics* fills that need.

Chapters 1 and 2 examine the mass media as institutions in the U.S. political system and contrast the U.S. situation with those in other societies. I show how the media are influenced by governmental structures and functions and, in turn, influence government. The recent wave of media consolidations is discussed, as well as new developments in the wake of the 1996 Telecommunications Act. Chapter 3 completes the discussion of the legal and political framework in which American media operate. It describes the legal rights of ordinary citizens, public officials, and newspeople to obtain and publish information and to seek protection from damaging publicity.

Chapter 4 deals with newsmaking under ordinary circumstances, with a focus on media structures, personnel, and operations. I also report on "Public Journalism," which has become a major media reform movement. Chapter 5 describes news patterns under extraordinary circumstances, such as natural disasters and wars. What happens when newspeople take an exceptionally active role in politics, such as investigating business scams or misbehaviors by public officials and the influence of these reports on public policy, is the main focus of Chapter 6. In Chapter 7, I explore the wealth of information about political learning and opinion formation along with theories about media-induced asocial and prosocial behavior. Much of this material is based on my own ongoing research and on earlier research undertaken jointly with Maxwell E. McCombs, currently at the University of Texas at Austin, and David H. Weaver, currently at Indiana University.

The powerful influence of the media in a variety of political situations is the subject of Chapters 8 through 11. These situations include media coverage of elections (Chapter 8) and the interplay between the media and major political institutions such as the presidency and Congress (Chapter 9). The media's role in the judicial system and at state and local levels is discussed in Chapter 10. Chapter 11 details the growing impact of news media on the conduct of foreign policy. The book concludes with a discussion of policy trends and the new technologies and political forces shaping them (Chapter 12).

Political and technological events, new mass media studies, and suggestions from colleagues and students who have used the book have guided most of the changes in this new edition. The contributions made by readers of the book and other colleagues and friends are deeply appreciated. The fifth edition has also benefited greatly from extensive, careful critiques by Greg Diamond of George Washington University; Virginia Relph of Indiana/Purdue University, Fort Wayne; and an anonymous reviewer who contributed seven single-spaced pages of immensely valuable commentary. I have tried to heed most of these scholars' suggestions.

I am also indebted to my research assistants, especially LaVonne Downey, who played a major role in updating the tables and tracking down many elusive references and other data. Lynn Akin at Harvard University's Kennedy School of Government did yeoman service in producing a clean manuscript from innumerable scattered revision notes. Much of the revision was finished in airplanes and airport lounges during a winter and spring of commuting between the University of Illinois at Chicago and the Kennedy School of Government, where I held a visiting chair. While there, I was able to sharpen my insights into the media and politics connection by listening to and talking with knowledgeable colleagues and a parade of visiting politicians and media stars. The problems created by my hectic revision schedule were skillfully allayed by Debbie Hardin, who edited the final version of the manuscript. Brenda Carter, acquisitions editor for CQ Press, and the editorial team at CQ provided their usual invaluable support that greatly eased the many chores entailed in book production. The concern and friendship of the CQ crew have been real morale boosters.

My family, as always, has given me support and encouragement to complete yet another revision. Their patience is legendary, as are their love and understanding. I thank them for this precious gift.

Doris A. Graber

Mass Media
and
American Politics

c h a p t e r   o n e

Media Power
and Government Control

ON JUNE 17, 1994, A WHITE BRONCO CARRYING football star O. J. Simpson traveled along a Los Angeles freeway with police as well as media in pursuit. Was Simpson trying to elude the police fearing their questions about the murder five days earlier of his ex-wife Nicole Brown Simpson and her friend Ronald Goldman? Millions of television viewers around the world wondered. They continued to wonder about the unfolding Simpson case for the next sixteen months, and they watched it move from the chase to a grand jury first degree murder indictment of Simpson, a lengthy criminal trial, and finally acquittal in October 1995.

Coverage of the Simpson case by print and electronic media throughout the world was enormous. For example, in the six months preceding the trial, the major U.S. television networks devoted close to fourteen hours on the evening news to the case, exceeding the time spent all year on either health care reform or the U.S. midterm elections.[1] When testimony began in the Simpson case in January 1995, network coverage averaged 50 percent more than coverage given to President Bill Clinton. Audiences complained that they were tired of the trial, but nationwide polls showed that almost two thirds of the public paid attention to the case on a daily basis, often at the expense of paying attention to important political news.[2] Only 13 percent of news viewers said that they had seen none of the Simpson television coverage.

When the so-called *trial of the century* ended in acquittal, many Americans were shocked to discover the wide opinion cleavages that existed along racial lines. Many African Americans hailed the acquittal as a victory for the presumption that Americans accused of crime are innocent unless

1

Reprinted by permission: Tribune Media Services.

proven guilty beyond a reasonable doubt or as a case of jury nullifica-
tion—a jury sending a political message rather than judging the accused.
Many whites viewed it as a miscarriage of justice. (Of course, not all
African Americans approved of the verdict and not all whites disapproved
of it.) The media's close-ups of judicial maneuvering in the courtroom
also disenchanted many viewers, who felt that the case demonstrated the
corruption of the American criminal justice system. Images of police inep-
titude, petty bickering by high priced lawyers, a judge incapable of controlling the case, and jury members eager to profit from their experience
all contributed to a sense that justice had been served poorly, if at all.

Political Importance of Mass Media

The impact of television on opinions about societal cleavages, the
merits of the criminal justice system, and the quality of television coverage
of major crime stories are examples of how mass media, in combination
with other political factors, can influence American politics. How journal-

ists cover stories often plays a crucial part in shaping the perceptions of reality of millions of people in all walks of life. News stories take Americans to the battlefields of the world in Eastern Europe or Central Africa. They give them ringside seats for space shuttle launches or basketball championships. They provide the nation with shared political experiences, such as watching presidential inaugurations or congressional investigations, that then undergird public opinions and unite people for political actions.[3]

Print, audio, and audio-visual media often serve as attitude and behavior models. In the process of image creation, the media indicate which views and behaviors are acceptable and even praiseworthy in a given society and which are unacceptable or outside the mainstream. Audiences can learn how to conduct themselves in ordinary social and work situations, how to cope with personal crises, and how to evaluate major social institutions like the medical profession or the police. Media stories also indicate what is deemed important or unimportant by various groups of elites, what conforms to prevailing standards of justice and morality, and how events are related to each other.[4] In the process the media present a set of cultural values that their audiences are likely to accept in whole or in part as typical of American society. The media thus help to integrate and homogenize American society.

The mass media also serve as powerful guardians of political norms because the American people believe that a free press should keep them informed about the wrongdoings of government. Media images are especially pervasive when they involve aspects of life that people experience only through the media. The personal and professional lives of politicians, revolutions in distant lands, frenzied trading at stock exchanges, tornadoes in the Middle West, or earthquakes in California are not generally experienced firsthand. Rather, popular perceptions of these activities are shaped largely by the images portrayed in news and fictional stories in print and electronic media. For example, prime-time television exaggerates the likelihood of becoming a victim of crime. Heavy viewers, therefore, fear crime more and take more protective measures than do light viewers.[5] Attention to the mass media is all-pervasive among twentieth-century Americans. The average high school graduate today has spent more time in front of a television set than in school, and much of this time is spent during preschool and elementary school days. Even in school much learning about current events is based on information provided by the media. An average adult American spends nearly half of her or his leisure time watching television, listening to the radio, or reading newspapers and magazines. Averaged out over an entire week, this amounts to more than seven hours of exposure per day to some form of mass media news or entertainment. Television, relayed over the air, via cable or videotape recorder, occupies three fourths of this time. Despite considerable reported dissatisfaction with the quality of television programs, television is the primary source of news and entertainment for the average American. It is also the most trusted source of information.

On a typical day, nearly half the country's population is watching television between 8:00 P.M. and 9:00 P.M. If a "special" is broadcast, 75 million to 80 million people may watch it in the United States, not to mention millions of foreign viewers.[6] The ability to attract such vast audiences of ordinary people, as well as political elites, constitutes a major ingredient in the power of the mass media and makes them extraordinarily important for the individuals and groups whose stories and causes are publicized.

Politically relevant information is often conveyed through stories that are not concerned explicitly with politics. In fact, because most people are exposed far more to nonpolitical information, make-believe media, such as movies and entertainment television, have become major suppliers of political images.[7] Entertainment shows on television, for example, portray social institutions, such as the police or the schools, in ways that convey esteem or heap scorn on them. They also express social judgments about various types of people. For instance, in the past television often depicted African Americans and women as socially inferior and limited in abilities. This type of coverage conveys messages that audiences may accept at face value, even when they distort real-world conditions. Audience members may think that social conditions and judgments shown on television are widely accepted and socially sanctioned and therefore ought to be maintained.

Not only are the media the chief source of most Americans' views of the world, but they are also the fastest way to disperse information throughout the entire society. News of the assassination of President John F. Kennedy and the attempt on the life of President Ronald Reagan spread with incredible speed. In both cases more than 90 percent of the American people heard the news within ninety minutes of the event, either directly from radio or television or secondhand from other people who had received mass media messages.[8]

All of the mass media are politically important because they can reach large audiences. However, their impacts vary, depending on the characteristics of each medium, the nature and quantity of the political messages that it carries, and the size of the audience that it reaches. Print media need readers who are literate at appropriate levels. Large segments of the U.S. population lack the skills. Readers enjoy the luxury of choosing what portion of content they wish to examine and to review. Users of electronic media find it more difficult to exclude portions of undesired content. Aside from recording and replaying the broadcast, or hearing a repeat broadcast, they cannot review what has been presented. However, many people who lack reading skills can extract meaning from broadcasts. That includes even very young children. The intonations available from the spoken word and meanings conveyed by nonverbal sounds and by visuals in telecasts provide additional information that is largely lacking from printed messages.

Print media excel in providing factual details and explanations involving abstract ideas. Electronic media, especially television, provide a greater sense of reality, which explains why some audiences find electronic media more credible than print media. Electronic media also convey physical images, including body language and facial expressions, much more effectively than print media, and they are especially well suited to engage the viewers' emotions. Many people find it easier to gather insights on events and issues through the electronic media. The nature of each technology has implications for the political purposes for which it is useful. Therefore, political images transmitted by different types of media may vary substantially in substance, sophistication, manner of presentation, and the political consequences they are likely to generate.

Functions of Mass Media

What major societal functions do the mass media perform? Political scientist Harold Lasswell mentions (1) surveillance of the world to report ongoing events, (2) interpretation of the meaning of events, and (3) socialization of individuals into their cultural settings.[9] To these three, a fourth function should be added: deliberate manipulation of politics. The manner in which these four functions are performed affects the political fate of individuals, groups, and social organizations, as well as the course of domestic and international politics.

Surveillance

Surveillance involves two major tasks. For the political community at large, *public* surveillance throws the spotlight of publicity on selected people, organizations, and events. This publicity then may make them matters of concern to politicians and to the general public. It may determine which political demands are exposed and which are kept hidden. It also may force politicians to respond to situations on which their views would not have been aired otherwise. For individual citizens in their private capacities, *private* surveillance informs them about current events.

Although it may lead to political activities, its primary functions are gratification of personal needs and quieting of anxieties. The media, as Marshall McLuhan has observed, are "sense extensions" for individuals who cannot directly witness most of the events of interest to them and their communities.[10]

Public Surveillance.   Newspeople determine what is *news*—that is, which political happenings will be covered and which will be ignored. Their choices are politically significant because they affect who and what will have a good chance to become the focus for political discussion and action.[11] Without media attention the people and events covered by the news might have no influence, or reduced influence, on decision makers. Conditions that may be tolerated if these people or events remain obscure may become intolerable quickly in the glare of publicity. This is why politicians, who seek to garner or avoid publicity, time and structure events with media coverage in mind.

The following example illustrates the power of publicity to produce public action. On April 30, 1995, in the glare of television lights, a sobbing, frightened four-year-old boy, clutching his adoptive mother's shoulder, was handed to his biological father. The transfer, watched by millions of Americans, was the climax of a three-year-long battle over the child who had been legally adopted after his unmarried biological mother had surrendered parental rights to her infant son. Initial attempts by the father to invalidate the adoption had been rejected by Illinois courts until the Illinois Supreme Court reversed the adoption and granted him immediate custody.

The extensive coverage of the unfolding case on television as well as in the print media in the summer of 1994 captured public interest throughout the United States. The court's final order to transfer the four-year-old child to a family that he had met only an hour earlier angered many journalists and other citizens as well as public officials. Illinois Governor James Edgar called the decision heartbreaking and disgusting. The Illinois legislature, which was equally appalled by the decision, passed the Baby Richard Law in an emergency session just prior to the transfer; the law provided that the best interests of children must be considered before adoptions can be annulled and birth parents can reclaim their offspring. Despite the legislative intent to apply the law to the Baby Richard case, the Illinois Supreme Court ordered the transfer to proceed, arguing that the law could not apply to a pending case.

The events reported in this story are not unique. Many young children who have been legally adopted or have lived in long-term foster care have been restored to their biological parents. The objections of their caretakers have received little official attention. The fact that the Baby

Richard case engendered legislative action as well as protests by political leaders was a result of the extensive publicity that the case received.

Not all media publicity spurs beneficial reaction, of course. In many instances, misperceptions and scares created by media stories have undermined confidence in good policies and practices, good people, and good products. The human and economic costs have been vast. For example, stories of dubious validity that questioned the safety of chemically treated apples and cranberries caused millions of dollars of losses in the affected industries.

Major effects of public surveillance may spring from impressions created by news stories. If media stories dwell on crime and corruption in the inner city, residents may move to the suburbs, leaving the inner city deserted and even less safe and deprived of tax revenues. Speculation that international conflicts or economic downturns are in the offing may scare investors and produce fluctuations in domestic and international stock markets and commodity exchanges. Serious economic (and hence political) consequences may ensue. Fear of publicity can be as powerful a force in shaping action as actual exposure. Politicians and business leaders know what damage an unfavorable story can create and act accordingly, either to avoid or conceal censurable behaviors or to atone for their misdeeds by public confessions of guilt and regret. Thus, when marijuana use became an issue during the 1988 and 1992 presidential election campaigns, a parade of officials openly confessed to similar sins or vowed publicly that they had never indulged.

The media can doom people and events to obscurity by inattention as well. When the information supply exceeds the media's capacity to transmit it, many stories remain untold. Constraints are most stringent on television and radio newscasts. Newspeople also ignore matters that do not seem "newsworthy" by accepted journalistic criteria or that fail to catch their attention. Conscious attempts to suppress information for ideological or political reasons are another, less frequent reason for lack of coverage.

For many years left-wing social critics have faulted mainstream American journalists for using their news selection power to strengthen white middle-class values and suppress socialist viewpoints. They claim that these choices are made deliberately to perpetuate capitalist exploitation of the masses, in line with the ideological preferences of media owners. Critics also claim that the media have intentionally suppressed the facts about dangerous products, such as alcohol and tobacco, and about the socially harmful activities of large corporations, which may be responsible for water and air pollution or unsafe consumer goods.[12] By the same token, right-wing critics complain that the media give undue attention to the views of the enemies of the established social and political order in hopes of undermining it. Each camp can cite a long list of stories to support its contentions.[13]

Media people deny these charges. They disdain political motives in news selection and defend their choices on the basis of general criteria of newsworthiness (treated more fully in Chapter 4). They can muster a lot of evidence from news stories to support their claims. At the heart of controversies over the ideological bias of the media lie two basic questions that cannot be answered conclusively. The first concerns people's motivations. How can one prove what motivates journalists to act in certain ways? And is it fair to ascribe motivations to them in the face of their denials? The second question relates to story effects. To what degree can media stories produce the goals owners of print and electronic media and news professionals are allegedly seeking?

Besides calling attention to matters of potential public concern, the media also provide cues to the public about the degree of importance of an issue. Important stories are covered prominently—on the front page with big headlines and pictures or as a major television or radio feature. Less important matters are buried in the back pages or given brief exposure on television or radio. However, nearly all coverage, even though it is brief and comparatively inconspicuous, lends an aura of significance to publicized topics. Through the sheer fact of coverage the media can confer status on individuals and organizations. They "function essentially as agencies of social legitimation—as forces, that is, which reaffirm those ultimate value standards and beliefs, which in turn uphold the social and political status quo."[14]

Television made African American civil rights leaders and their causes household names. Martin Luther King, Jr., and Jesse Jackson became national figures in part because of television. A political candidate whose efforts to win an election are widely publicized, a social crusader whose goals become front-page news, or a convicted murderer or terrorist who wins a hearing on radio or television often becomes an instant celebrity. Their unpublicized counterparts remain obscure and bereft of political influence.

Because the attention of the media is crucial for political success, actors on the political scene deliberately create situations likely to receive media coverage. Daniel Boorstin has labeled events arranged primarily to stimulate media coverage "pseudo-events."[15] They may range from news conferences called by public figures even when there is no news to announce to physical assaults on people and property designed to dramatize grievances. Newspeople who must cover such events may feel manipulated and resent it.

When events are exceptionally significant or have become widely known already, or when the story is reported by competing media, decisions about what to publish and thereby put on the agenda for public discussion and possible action are beyond the discretion of media personnel. For example, professional considerations demand reporting of news about prominent persons and major domestic or international events.[16] Beyond such unavoidable events, there remains an extremely wide range of persons and events for which coverage is optional.

The power of the media to set the civic agenda is a matter of concern because it is not controlled by a system of formal checks and balances as is power at various levels of government. It is not subject to periodic review through the electoral process. If media emphases or claims are incorrect, remedies are few. Citizens can be protected from false advertising of consumer goods through truth in advertising laws, but there is no way in which they can be protected from false political claims or improper news selection by media personnel without impairing the crucial rights to free speech and a free press. Media critic Jay Blumler expressed the dilemma well:

> Media power is not supposed to be shared: That's an infringement of editorial autonomy. It is not supposed to be controlled: That's censorship. It's not even supposed to be influenced: That's news management! But why should media personnel be exempt from Lord Acton's dictum that all power corrupts and absolute power corrupts absolutely? And if they are not exempt, who exactly is best fitted to guard the press guardians, as it were?[17]

Private Surveillance.   Average citizens may not think much about the broader political impact of the news they read, hear, and watch. They use the media primarily to keep in touch with what they deem personally important. The media are their eyes and ears to the world, their means of surveillance, which tell them about economic conditions, weather, sports, jobs, fashions, social and cultural events, health and science, and the public and private lives of famous people.

The ability to stay informed makes people feel secure, whether or not they remember what they read or hear or see. Even though the news may be bad, at least they feel that there will be no startling surprises. News reassures them that the political system continues to operate despite constant crises and frequent mistakes. Reassurance is important for people's peace of mind. But it also tends to keep them politically quiescent because there is no need to act if political leaders seem to be doing their jobs. For good or ill, the public's quiescence helps to maintain the political and economic status quo.[18]

Other significant private functions that the mass media fulfill for many people are entertainment, companionship, tension relief, and a way to pass the time with minimal physical or mental exertion. The mass media can satisfy these important personal needs conveniently and cheaply. People who otherwise might be frustrated and dissatisfied can participate through the media vicariously in current political happenings, in sports and musical events, in the lives of famous people, and in the lives of families and communities featured in the news.[19]

Interpretation

Media not only survey the events of the day and make them the focus of public and private attention, but they also interpret their meanings, put them into context, and speculate about their consequences. Most incidents lend themselves to a variety of interpretations, depending on the values and experiences of the interpreter. The kind of interpretation that is chosen affects the political consequences of media reports. For example, since 1962 the way in which the media interpret the legal and social significance of abortions has changed considerably. Abortion almost universally used to be considered murder. The abortionist was the villain and the pregnant woman was an accomplice in a heinous crime. Now abortion is often cast into the frame of women's rights to control their bodies in order to protect their physical and mental health.

The situation that spawned the switch in media interpretation and eased the change in public attitudes toward abortion involved television personality Sherri Finkbine. She had taken thalidomide during her pregnancy before the drug's tragic effects on the unborn were known. Once she learned of the potential harm, she feared a severely malformed baby and underwent an abortion in 1962.

Instead of reporting the action as murder, as had been the custom, news media throughout the country defended Finkbine's decision to terminate her pregnancy. To steer clear of the negative connotations of the word *abortion,* journalists used a new vocabulary to put the act into a different light. They talked of "surgery to prevent a malformed baby," of "avoiding the possibility of mothering a drug-deformed child," and of the necessity of inducing a miscarriage to spare a child from loathing "its own image and crying out against those who might have spared it this suffering."[20]

Numerous circumstances influenced the type of interpretation that the Finkbine story received. In the end, it hinged on journalists' decisions, made independently or in response to pressures, to stress a particular image and to choose available informants and facts accordingly. Journalistic concerns play a large role in determining how the news will be framed, which in turn determines its likely impact.

By suggesting the causes and relationships of various events, the media may shape opinions even without telling their audiences what to believe or think. For example, linking civil strife in Central America to the activities of Soviet and Cuban Communist agents ensured that the American public would view the situation with considerable alarm. Linking the hostilities to poverty and social oppression would have put the problems into a far less threatening light.

There are countless ways in which news presentations can predetermine the conclusions that people are likely to draw.

> We [journalists] can attribute any social problem to official policies, the machinations of those who benefit from it, or the pathology of those who suffer from it. We can trace it back to class or racial inequalities, to ideologies such as nationalism or patriotism, or to resistance to the regime. We can root the problem in God, in its historic genesis, in the accidental or systematic conjuncture of events, in rationality, in irrationality, or in a combination of these or other origins. In choosing any such ultimate cause we are also depicting a setting, an appropriate course of action, and sets of virtuous and evil characters, and doing so in a way that will appeal to some part of the public that sees its own sentiments or interests reflected in that choice of a social scene.[21]

The items that media personnel select to illustrate a point or to characterize a political actor need not be intrinsically important to be influential in shaping opinions and evaluations. During the 1988 presidential election campaign, the *Miami Herald* reported that a young woman had spent the night at the home of candidate Gary Hart while his wife was absent. Pictures of the young woman sitting in the candidate's lap during a boat trip circulated in the press. Hart was then the front-runner among Democratic candidates. Although the story shed little light on his political capabilities, Hart believed that it had done such harm to his campaign that he eventually abandoned the race. A brief reentry into the campaign several months later demonstrated that his chances for winning the presidential nomination had been irreparably damaged.

Socialization

The third major mass media function mentioned by Lasswell is political socialization (discussed more fully in Chapter 7). It involves the learning of basic values and orientations that prepares individuals to fit into their cultural milieu. Prior to the 1970s, studies largely ignored the mass media because parents and the schools were deemed the primary agents of socialization. Research in the 1970s finally established that the media play a crucial role in political socialization.[22] Most information that young people acquire about the nature of their political world comes directly or indirectly from the mass media. The media present to the young specific facts as well as general values, teaching them which elements produce power, success, and dominance in society, and they provide young people with models for behavior. Young people use such information to develop their opinions because they lack established attitudes and behavior patterns.

Research indicates that most of the new orientations and opinions that adults acquire during their lifetime also are based on information supplied by the mass media. People do not necessarily adopt the precise attitudes and opinions that may be suggested by the media. Rather, mass media information provides the ingredients that people use to adjust their existing attitudes and opinions to keep pace with a changing world. The mass media must be credited, therefore, with a sizable share of continuing adult political socialization and resocialization. Examples of resocialization—the restructuring of established basic attitudes—are the shifts in sexual morality and racial attitudes that the American public has undergone since mid-century and the changing views on relations with mainland China and with Russia.[23]

Manipulation

In the post-Watergate era direct manipulation of the political process by the media has become increasingly common. Many journalists are major players in the game of politics, rather than acting in their traditional role as chroniclers of information provided by others. Political manipulation often takes the form of investigative journalism. Major print and electronic media now operate their own investigative units. Feature articles and television shows such as "60 Minutes" and "20/20," devoted primarily to revealing the results of investigations, are very popular.

The purpose of such investigative shows is to *muckrake*. President Theodore Roosevelt was the first to apply the term to journalists who conducted their own investigations into corruption and wrongdoing in order to stimulate governmental action to clean up the "dirt" they had exposed. The term comes from a rake designed to collect manure. Muckraking today may have several different goals.[24] The journalist's primary purpose may be to write stories that expose misconduct in government and produce reforms. Or the chief purpose may be to present sensational information that attracts large media audiences and enhances profits. Other manipulative stories may be designed primarily to affect the course of politics in line with the journalist's political preferences. The various forms that manipulation can take are discussed in Chapter 6.

Effects of Mass Media

The public believes that the media have an important impact on the conduct of politics and on public thinking. Politicians act and behave on the basis of the same assumption. But many studies conducted by social scientists fail to show substantial impact. Why is there such a discrepancy between many social science appraisals of mass media effects and the general impression, reflected in public policies, that the mass media are extremely influential?

There are three major reasons. First, many studies, particularly those conducted during the 1950s and 1960s, have taken a narrow approach to media effects, looking for only a few specified effects, rather than all possible effects. Second, theories about the ways in which people use newspapers, television, radio, and other mass media have enhanced the belief that media have minimal effects because people are disinclined to learn from the media. Third, social scientists have encountered great difficulties in measuring effects because media make their impact as part of a complex combination of social stimuli.

Early Studies

American social scientists began to study the effects of the mass media primarily in one narrow area: vote change as a result of media coverage of presidential elections. Among these early studies, several are considered classics. *The People's Choice* by Paul Lazarsfeld, Bernard Berelson, and Hazel Gaudet, all of Columbia University, reported how people made their voting choices in Erie County, Pennsylvania, in the 1940 presidential election. Sequels to the study followed in short order. The best known are *Voting: A Study of Opinion Formation in a Presidential Campaign, The Voter Decides,* and *The American Voter.*[25]

Focus on Vote Choices. The early voting studies were based on the assumption that a well-publicized campaign presumably changed votes. If it did not, this indicated that the media lacked influence. Subsequent studies have shown that this reasoning is faulty. There may be measurable media influence even when vote choice remains stable. Besides, media effects vary, depending on the office at stake and the historical period. At the time of the early voting studies, change of vote choice was quite uncommon because most voters adhered closely to party lines, regardless of media coverage. In recent years party allegiance has weakened substantially among many voters, so that the opportunities for media influence on vote choice are far greater.

Had the investigators concentrated on other settings, such as judicial or nonpartisan elections (for which few voting cues outside the media are available), they also might have discovered greater media-induced change in attitude. Substantial media influence might have been found even in presidential elections if changes in people's trust and affection or knowledge about the candidates and the election had been explored. The early studies largely ignored all media influences that did not result in easily measurable behavior and attitude changes. Yet such changes constitute important media influences that are crucial components of a variety of political behaviors aside from voting decisions.

The early voting studies focused almost exclusively on effects at the individual level and failed to trace effects on the social groups to which individuals belong and through which they influence political events. Farm workers in California might not change their votes after hearing a candidate attack illegal immigrants. But they might use their union to testify against legislation favored by the candidate. They might even participate in violence in the wake of the news stories about illegal immigrants. In turn, these activities might affect U.S. relations with other nations. Yet the early studies of media effects totally ignored such impacts on the entire political system and its component parts.

The findings that media effects were minimal were so pervasive in early research that social science research into mass media effects fell to a low ebb after an initial flurry in the 1940s and 1950s. Social scientists did not want to waste time studying inconsequential effects. Despite seemingly solid evidence of media importance, they did not care to swim against the stream of established knowledge. As a consequence, in study after study dealing with political socialization and learning, the mass media were hardly mentioned as important factors.

Learning Theories.   The early findings were all the more believable because they tied in well with theories of persuasion. Mass media messages presumably miss their mark because they are impersonal. They are not tailored to the interests of specific individuals, as are the messages of parents, teachers, and friends. They do not permit immediate feedback, which then allows the sender to adjust the message to make it more suitable for the receiver. Furthermore, there is no compulsion to listen to mass media messages and no need to answer. Hence it is easy to ignore them.

Although there is a lot of truth to these claims, they fail to consider that television can simulate intimate personal settings. Audiences frequently interact with the television image as if what appears on screen were actually present in front of them. They may look on television commentators and actors as personal friends. Children often imitate people and situations on television, just as if they were part of it.

Further support for the minimal effects findings came from various cognitive consistency theories. They postulate that average individuals dislike being presented with information that is incompatible with cherished beliefs. To avoid this painful experience and the necessity to change established beliefs, people expose themselves to the media selectively. Social scientists have evidence that people are indeed selective in their use of the media and search for information that reinforces what they already believe and know. But, as will be discussed more fully in Chapter 7, the phenomenon is quite limited.

Recent Research

When researchers resumed their investigations of mass media effects in the wake of persistent evidence of strong media impact, they cast their net more broadly. They began to look beyond media effects on voting to other effects during elections and in other types of political events. In this vein, researchers have examined media impact on factual learning, on opinion formation, and on the satisfaction of a variety of human needs. They also have looked beyond the individual to effects on political systems and subsystems, a search that promises to be highly rewarding. But despite improvements in research designs and techniques, research into mass media effects has remained hampered by serious measurement problems.

Measuring Complex Effects. Mass media effects are difficult to measure, both at the level of the individual and at the societal level, because they are highly complex and elusive. The most common measuring device at the individual level—self-assessment of impact elicited during a poll—is notoriously unreliable. Researchers lack tools to measure human thinking objectively. Even when thoughts lead to overt behavior, they cannot judge accurately what prompted the thoughts. Moreover, actions spring from a variety of motivations, so that it is difficult to isolate the part played by media.

Assessing the impact of particular news stories is especially difficult because mass media audiences already possess a fund of knowledge and attitudes that they bring to bear on new information. Because researchers rarely know precisely what this information is, or the rules by which it is combined with incoming information, they cannot pinpoint the exact contribution that particular mass media stories have made to an individual's cognitions, feelings, and actions. To complicate matters further, the impact of the mass media varies depending on the subject matter. For instance, media impact is greater on people's perceptions of unfamiliar issues than on their perceptions of issues that they have faced personally.

It is even more difficult to establish effects at the societal level. A good example is the *CNN effect* that was widely credited as propelling President George Bush to dispatch U.S. troops to Somalia in 1992. The term *CNN effect* refers to the fact that news media, particularly the extensive news coverage of breaking events by the Cable News Network (CNN), directly inflame public opinion with gripping pictures of major events. The public's clamor for action then forces an unprepared government to take hasty action. Media decisions become the dogs that wag the public policy tails.

In the Somalia case, reports and pictures of widespread starvation and devastation had been aired widely by CNN and other television networks in the summer months of 1992. It was largely believed that these pictures inflamed the public and aroused pressure groups that forced members of the Bush administration, against their better judgment, to airlift relief supplies and later to dispatch American troops to Somalia. The rescue effort ultimately failed, and American lives were lost.[26]

Political scientists Steven Livingston and Todd Eachus reached a different conclusion about the respective roles of the news media and the Bush administration in determining U.S. policy in Somalia. After examining a variety of sources, including *New York Times* and *Washington Post* stories about U.S. humanitarian relief policies and after interviewing key government decision makers and long-term relief personnel in Somalia, they concluded that plans for relief efforts had been under way for more than a year prior to CNN coverage of the tragedy. Government officials, including concerned members of Congress who had traveled to Somalia, rather than television news stories, had been the spur to action. The Somalia case did not reflect the CNN effect.

Despite persuasive evidence that extensive media coverage of the tragedy followed, rather than preceded, President Bush's announcement of the military airlift and other relief measures on August 14, 1992, many observers still argue that media mobilization of public opinion was an essential prerequisite for the Somalia intervention. It is impossible to prove that the administration would have abstained from relief measures in the absence of media coverage of the tragedy because graphic media coverage is credited so often with providing the impetus for action or serving as the last straw that tips the decision scales. Inability to prove mass media impact beyond a doubt has made social scientists shy away from assessing media influence on many important political events. In fact, social scientists often go to the other extreme and deny that effects exist simply because these effects defy measurement. This is unfortunate because many effects that cannot be measured precisely can be observed in the field and studied in the laboratory.

Ignoring Unanticipated Effects. Measurement of media effects also has suffered because unanticipated effects are frequently ignored. For example, when ABC television broadcast a highly publicized television drama about the horrors of nuclear war in 1984, the sponsors and social scientists expected that many of the 80 million viewers would become more concerned about nuclear war. When the anticipated reaction did not occur, most researchers reported that there were no effects. They failed to notice several unexpected important consequences of the broadcast discovered by one research team that asked different questions. The percentage of people who previously had criticized President Reagan for pursuing policies believed likely to lead to war dropped sharply from 57 percent before the broadcast to 43 percent afterward. Opposition to the military policies of the Reagan administration thus had decreased sharply. The broadcast also made people more conciliatory toward the Soviet Union and more supportive of general arms limitation agreements between the superpowers.[27]

Statistical Versus Political Significance. Social scientists also have been rather rigid in interpreting the significance of media influence when it has been established. They have falsely equated statistical significance with political significance, despite the fact that media impact on a small number of individuals can have great political consequences. For example, during an election only 1 or 2 percent of the voters may change their votes because of media stories. That is a statistically negligible effect. From a political standpoint, however, the impact may be major, because many important elections, including several presidential elections, have been decided by a margin of 2 percent of the voters. If an extra 2 percent of the vote had gone to the losing candidate in the 1976 presidential race, Gerald Ford would have stayed in the White House and Jimmy Carter would have remained a peanut farmer. Moreover, 2 percent of the voters sounds like a small number, but when translated into actual numbers in 1976 it amounted to more than a million people.

Even on a much smaller scale, if a broadcast of details of a race riot attracts a few listeners to the riot site and stimulates some to participate, the situation may escalate beyond control. In the same way, the impact of a single news story may change the course of history if it induces one assassin to kill a world leader or convinces one world leader to go to war.

Influencing Elites. Another major problem with social science research on mass media effects is that it has concentrated on measuring the effects on ordinary individuals rather than on political elites. The average individual, despite contrary democratic fictions, is fairly unimportant in the political process. Mass media impact on a handful of political decision makers usually is vastly more significant than similar impact on ordinary individuals. In addition, the impact on decision makers is likely to be far more profound because mass media information relates more directly to their immediate concerns. They may pay closer attention to stories in which the public is not interested and that the public often fails to understand. And they may spend considerable time and effort to generate media coverage that promotes their interests.

For example, in the summer of 1983 a *Washington Post* story noted that there had been little public reaction to reports that a campaign briefing book prepared for President Carter had fallen into the hands of the Reagan campaign staff and used to brief Reagan for his debate with Carter. The story caught the eye of two influential members of Congress.[28] The upshot was a major congressional investigation.

In light of what we have discussed thus far, it seems totally unrealistic to deny that the media are important in setting the stage for ongoing political developments, in shaping the views and behaviors of political elites and other selected groups, and in influencing the general public's perception of political life. As Theodore White put it, albeit with some exaggeration:

> The power of the press in America is a primordial one. It sets the agenda of public discussion; and this sweeping political power is unrestrained by any law. It determines what people will talk and think about—an authority that in other nations is reserved for tyrants, priests, parties, and mandarins.
>
> No major act of the American Congress, no foreign adventure, no act of diplomacy, no great social reform can succeed in the United States unless the press prepares the public mind.[29]

Even if one argues that the media are nothing but conduits of information over which they have no control, one cannot deny that people throughout the world of politics consider the media to be powerful and behave accordingly. This is why governments everywhere, in authoritarian as well as democratic societies, try to control the flow of information produced by the media lest it thwart their political objectives.

Who Should Control Newsmaking?

Attempts by governments to control and manipulate the media have been universal because public officials everywhere believe that media are important political forces. This belief is based on the assumption that institutions that control public information can shape public knowledge and behavior and thereby determine the support or opposition of citizens and officials to the government and its policies. That is why Emperor Napoleon claimed that "Four hostile newspapers are more to be feared than a thousand bayonets."

Although control occurs in all societies, its extent, nature, and purposes vary. There are several reasons. Political ideology is one of them. In countries in which free expression of opinion is a paramount value and in which dissent is respected, the media tend to be comparatively unrestrained. The right of the press to criticize government also flourishes when the accepted ideology grants that governments are fallible and often corrupt and that average citizens are capable of forming valuable opinions about the conduct of government. Finally, freedom of the press, even when it becomes a thorn in the side of the government, is more easily tolerated in governments that are well established and politically and economically secure. In developing nations, for instance, in which governments are unstable and resources limited, it may be difficult to tolerate press behavior that is apt to topple the government or retard its plans for economic development.

Nowhere are the media totally free from formal and informal government and social controls, even in times of peace. On the whole, authoritarian countries control more extensively and more rigidly than nonauthoritarian ones, but all systems represent points on a continuum of control. There are also gradations of control within nations, depending on the current regime and political setting, regional and local variations, and the nature of news. Common types of controls used in authoritarian and nonauthoritarian societies will be described without giving details about any particular country.[30]

Authoritarian control systems are of two types: those that are nonideological and simply represent a desire by the ruling elites to control media output tightly so that it does not interfere with the conduct of government and those that are based on a totalitarian ideology (for example, communism). The latter type actively controls and uses the media to support ideological goals. Examples of nonideological authoritarian control can be found in states ruled by military governments or in which constitutional guarantees have been suspended. Examples of control based on communism are found in Cuba and the People's Republic of China.

There are also two types of *nonauthoritarian approaches to control*, although they are not linked to differences in political ideology. Rather, these types are linked to differences in philosophies about the role that the media ought to carve for themselves in countries in which they enjoy a great deal of freedom. The two types of nonauthoritarian approaches have been labeled *libertarian* and *social responsibility*. When journalists in democratic societies subscribe to the libertarian philosophy, they feel free to report whatever they wish as long as public tastes are satisfied. By contrast, when social responsibility philosophies prevail, newspeople expect to contribute to the betterment of society, spurring media audiences to behave in socially responsible ways. Journalists in the United States and Western Europe furnish examples of both of these philosophies. Often libertarian and social responsibility journalism occur simultaneously, or they may alternate during successive historical periods.[31]

In today's world, authoritarian systems of media control prevail in the majority of countries, although many governments profess a desire for democratization and are struggling to move in that direction. Nonetheless, their attempts to control internal and external news flows persist. Several members of the United Nations Educational, Scientific, and Cultural Organization (UNESCO) have opposed freedom of reporting about their countries in foreign media. They contend that only news that supports the established regime should be permitted and that all newspeople should be subject to supervision by officials of the country whose affairs they report. This story is told more fully in Chapter 11.

Role of Media in Authoritarian Regimes

What basic assumptions underlie authoritarian and nonauthoritarian philosophies of media operation, and what types of governmental structures and practices have been invented to implement these philosophies? As Table 1-1 suggests, authoritarian systems operate on the assumption that the government knows and represents the best interests of the people. Therefore, the mass media must not interfere with the operations of the government or endanger its survival. The press may point out minor deficiencies or corruption of low-level officials and suggest adjustments in line with prevailing policies, but criticism of the basic system or its rulers is considered inappropriate.

In most authoritarian political systems the mass media are expected to take positions that firmly support the government. News must engender support for major policies and must echo official stands about who the country's domestic and international friends and enemies are. Beyond that, the media are free to choose the stories they wish to publish, as long as they do not hurt the state or interfere with public policies.

In totalitarian societies the role of the media is more stringently defined. The likely political and social effects of a story—rather than its general significance, novelty, or audience appeal—determine what will be published and what will be buried in silence. For instance, news about accidents, disasters, and crimes is often suppressed because it does not contain socially useful information that is apt to strengthen people's allegiance to the political system. Even entertainment programs, such as music and drama performances and even cartoon shorts in movie theaters, must carry appropriate social messages or have historical signifi-

TABLE 1-1   Contrasting Assumptions about Press Mission

Authoritarian regime assumptions	Democratic regime assumptions
Government knows and respects people's best interests	Governments are fallible and often corrupt
Press should not attack the government and its major policies	Press should attack the government when officials and policies seem flawed
News should engender support for major policies	News should stimulate critical thinking about major policies
News and entertainment programs should be selected for their social values	News and entertainment programs should be selected for audience appeal

SOURCE: Compiled by author.

cance. The government supports such entertainment financially because it serves the important public purpose of shaping people's minds in support of the system.

Role of Media in Nonauthoritarian Regimes

The basic assumptions underlying mass media control in democratic countries contrast sharply with those of authoritarian societies, as Table 1-1 indicates. In democracies, governments are viewed as fallible, potentially corrupt, servants of the people. As a result, they must be watched constantly to guard against mistakes and misbehaviors.

Journalists are regarded as the public's eyes and ears who scrutinize government performance and report their findings. In that way, they provide the feedback that democratic systems need to remain on course. If, as the result of their scrutiny, governments fall and public officials are ousted, this is as it should be.

While this is the theory behind the role of media in democratic societies, the practice is less clear-cut. In the United States, for example, neither newspeople nor government officials are completely at ease with the media's watchdog role. The media limit their criticism to what they perceive as perversions of fundamental social and political values or noteworthy examples of corruption and waste. They rarely question the fundamentals of the political system. Because journalists depend heavily on established elites as their sources of news, their links to the existing power structures are strong. They may even share information with government agencies, including policing bodies such as the Federal Bureau of Investigation (FBI) and the Central Intelligence Agency (CIA). When disclosure might cause harm, reporters in a democratic society occasionally withhold important news at the request of the government. This has happened repeatedly during terrorism incidents when the lives of hostages were at stake and in the advance stages of military interventions. In an effort to keep their images untarnished by media attacks, government officials may try to control the media through regulatory legislation or through rewards and punishments. These tactics are described more fully in Chapter 9.

The chief obligation of the mass media in free societies is to provide the general public with information about significant current events and with entertainment. According to the libertarian philosophy, anything that happens that seems interesting or important for media audiences may become news. It should be reported quickly, accurately, and without any attempt to convey a particular point of view. Subjects with the widest audience appeal should be stressed, even if that means heavy doses of sex and violence. Audience appeal is then expected to translate into good profits for media owners. Although audiences may learn important things from the media, libertarians believe that teaching is not the media's chief task. Nor is it their task to question the truth, accuracy, or merits of the information supplied to them by their sources. Rather, it is left to the news audience to decide what to believe and what to question.

By contrast adherents to social responsibility tenets believe that news and entertainment presented by the mass media should reflect social concerns. Media personnel should be participants in the political process, not merely reporters of the passing scene. As guardians of the public welfare, they should foster political action when necessary by publicizing social evils, such as the dumping of nuclear waste or child abuse. In a similar vein, undesirable viewpoints and questionable accusations should be denied exposure, however sensational they may be. If reporters believe that the government is hiding information that should be made public, they should try to discover the facts and publish them.

Social responsibility journalism and totalitarian journalism have some philosophical resemblances. Both approaches advocate using the media to support the basic ideals of their societies and to shape people into more perfect social beings. They are convinced that their goals are good and would not be achieved in a media system dominated by the whims of media owners or audiences.

But the similarities should not be exaggerated. Social advocacy in nonauthoritarian systems lacks the fervor, clout, and single-mindedness it has in systems in which media control is monopolized by the government. Social responsibility journalism rarely speaks with a single uncontested

voice throughout the entire society. Nevertheless, it frightens and antago-
nizes many news professionals and news audiences. If one agrees that the
media should be used to influence social thought and behavior for "good"
purposes, it becomes difficult to determine which purposes deserve to be
included in that category. Critics of social responsibility journalism point
out that journalists do not have a public mandate to act as arbiters of
social values and policies in a society without a single vision of truth and
goodness. Newspeople lack the legitimacy that in a democracy comes only
from being elected by the public or appointed by duly elected officials.

Whatever the merits or faults of these arguments may be, at the present time social responsibility journalism is popular with a sizable proportion of the news profession.[32] Pulitzer prizes and other honors go to journalists who have successfully exposed questionable practices in the
interest of social improvement. The most prominent "villains" targeted for
exposure are usually big government and big business.[33]

Models of the News-Making Process

Beyond the basic concerns reflected in the philosophies of libertarians and social responsibility advocates, there are many other guiding principles for reporting events. For example, scholars have identified four distinct models of the news-making process: *the mirror model, the professional
model, the organizational model,* and *the political model.* Each represents judgments about the major forces behind news making and each profoundly
affects the nature of news and its political impact.

Proponents of the *mirror model* contend that news is and should be a
reflection of reality. Newspeople observe the world around them and
report what they notice as accurately and objectively as possible. "We don't
make the news, we merely report it," is their slogan. The implication is
that newspeople reflect whatever comes to their attention; they do not
shape it in any way.

Critics of the mirror model point out that this conception of news
making is unrealistic. Millions of significant events take place daily, forcing journalists to choose which they wish to observe and report. Events
that are publicized inevitably loom larger than life, distorting the picture
that the real world presents. Events that are ignored routinely vanish into
nothingness. Even films and photographs deceive the eye. A small group
of demonstrators may look like an invading army when cameras zoom in
on them.

In the *professional model,* news making is viewed as an endeavor of
highly skilled professionals who put together an interesting collage of

events selected for importance, attractiveness to media audiences, and balance among the various elements of the news offering. There is no pretense that the end product mirrors the world. Because audience appeal is the most important consideration for economic reasons, the audience becomes the ultimate judge of which stories pass scrutiny and which will be ignored.

The *organizational model* is based on organizational theory. Its proponents contend that determination of what items will become news emerges from the pressures inherent in organizational processes and goals. Pressures springing from interpersonal relations and professional norms within the news organization are important, as are constraints arising from technical news production processes, cost–benefit considerations, profit orientations, and legal regulations.

The *political model* rests on the assumption that news everywhere reflects the ideological biases of individual newspeople, as well as the pressures of the political environment in which the news organization operates. High-status people and approved institutions are covered by the media; people and events outside the dominant system or remote from the centers of power are generally ignored. Supporters of the prevailing system are pictured as good guys, opponents as bad guys.

In the 1990s, yet another role model has emerged. Variously called *public journalism* or *civic journalism,* it arose from widespread concern that average citizens shun participation in public affairs and have become distrustful of government and the news media. Proponents of the new model believe that the press can ascertain citizens' concerns and then write stories that help audiences to play an active and successful role in public life.[34] Journalists must articulate and explain available public policy choices in readily understandable language. They must facilitate a public dialogue that encourages and respects diversity of views. After consensus has been reached among the clients of a particular news channel, that enterprise then must vigorously champion appropriate public policies.

None of these models fully explains the news-making process; rather, the process reflects all of them in varying degrees. Because the influences that shape news making fluctuate, one needs to examine individual news-making situations carefully to account for the factors at work. Organizational pressures, for instance, vary depending on the interactions of people within the organization. Audience tastes change or are interpreted differently. Perceptions of "facts" differ, depending on reporters' dispositions. Moreover, the precise mix of factors that explains news making in any particular instance depends to a large degree on chance factors and on the current needs of a particular news medium.

Control Methods

Four types of controls of the press are widely used: *legal, normative, structural,* and *economic.*[35] All governments have laws to prevent press misbehavior such as publishing deliberate falsehoods. All societies also have social norms that the press dare not defy. For example, in a religiously conservative country, ridiculing sacred concepts would lead to social condemnation. The way media organizations are structured and operated also shapes their product, as is clear when one compares the policy discretion enjoyed by publicly and privately owned media. Finally, economic support in the form of direct and indirect subsidies can be used to influence media performance.

The combination of methods by which governments control the media varies, and so do the major objectives of control. Authoritarian societies use legal, structural, and economic means to restrict access to mass communications to voices friendly to the regime and to ensure that news stories remain supportive of most government policies. By contrast, nonauthoritarian regimes rarely make formal attempts to deny foes of the regime access to the media. However, they often use normative pressures to avert publicity that endangers the national defense or violates widely held social norms.

In many authoritarian societies control over media content is established by limiting entry into the media business. For example, the government may require franchises for entry and grant them only to people who fully support the government. Franchises often bestow monopoly control. Control through franchise is quite common for electronic media, even in democratic countries, because the government assigns broadcast channels. But democratic countries use this power less frequently to shut out political opponents. Entry to the mass media business is usually open to people representing a wide spectrum of political views. Newspapers generally need no licenses in democratic societies. In the United States, for instance, anyone with sufficient money can start a newspaper or newsletter. No permits are necessary.

Authoritarian countries frequently control publications through subsidies to favorite publishers or favoritism in the allocation of tightly controlled paper stocks for printing newspapers and magazines. Newspaper publishers whose activities displease the government may find themselves out of business because they cannot obtain paper. These types of economic controls may be imposed informally on disliked publishers or they may be invoked through formal rationing and subsidy schemes.

Media also may be controlled through manipulating access to news. For instance, the government may release information only to favored publications, in effect putting less favored ones out of business. Although such practices are common in authoritarian societies, they occasionally happen on a smaller scale in more open societies. In 1993, President Bill Clinton barred reporters from easy access to the White House communication office by closing off a connecting hallway to the press room.[36]

In addition to controlling the news business through franchises and restraints on access to news, authoritarian governments often limit what information may be published. In some countries nothing can be printed or broadcast until it has been approved by the government censor, who can suppress any story deemed objectionable. At times deletions are made after papers or magazines have been prepared for printing or already printed. This leaves tantalizing white spaces or missing pages. Television and radio scripts often are written or edited directly by government officials and must be broadcast without editorial changes.

Authoritarian societies frequently use treason and sedition laws to control media output. *Treason* and *sedition* usually are defined broadly in these countries so that anything that is critical of the government is potentially treasonable or seditious. People judged guilty of these crimes may be removed from the media business, sentenced to prison, or even executed. Such severe punishments are extremely strong deterrents to publishing stories that attack the government. Accordingly, disobedience is rare. Most journalists avoid difficulties with official censors and with treason and sedition laws by refraining from using material that is likely to be objectionable. Government censorship then becomes replaced largely by self-censorship.

In totalitarian regimes, media control is simplified because the government owns and operates all mass media, fully determining their output. In addition, totalitarian countries frequently block out all unapproved communications from abroad. This includes jamming foreign broadcasts and prohibiting the import of foreign printed materials. The strictness with which these controls are applied waxes and wanes, depending on the country's relations with other powers. But even during friendly interludes, totalitarian regimes rigidly control any information from abroad that might undermine their political system. They view such censorship as an intellectual quarantine that must be imposed to keep evil influences from undermining a beneficial political system.

In democratic societies official control of the content of mass media is deemed largely unnecessary. The First Amendment to the U.S. Constitution, which provides that "Congress shall make no law ... abridging the freedom of speech, or of the press," has given the media an exceptionally strong basis for resisting government controls in the United States. The courts have ruled, however, that the protection is not absolute. On occasion, it must give way to social rights that the courts consider to be superior.

Competition among privately owned papers, magazines, and television and radio stations presumably generates a variety of viewpoints. If some media attack the government, other media will support it. The underlying, intriguing, but questionable assumption is that positive and negative as well as correct and incorrect information will somehow balance out and that the audience will be able to extract the truth from these conflicting reports.

A limited number of controls, such as regulatory laws, court decisions, and informal social pressures, guard against excesses by the media. In the United States the courts generally have ruled that these controls may be enforced only after media misbehavior has occurred. Courts have been loath to impose prior restraint such as granting injunctions that would stop publication of information on the grounds that it would cause irreparable harm. But informal social and political pressures and the fear of indictments after publication have restrained presentation of potentially damaging stories.

Controls in nonauthoritarian societies generally fall into four categories: guarding state survival through treason and sedition laws, shielding sensitive governmental proceedings, protecting individual reputations and privacy, and safeguarding the prevailing moral standards of the community. All societies find it necessary to have treason and sedition laws that prohibit publication of information that would endanger the nation's survival. The difficulty is to determine the point at which secrecy is so essential that freedom to publish must give way. In democratic societies media and the government are in perennial disagreement about the exact location of this point. Governments lean toward protection; the media lean toward disclosure.

There is little argument that treason and sedition are beyond the boundaries of unrestricted publication, even in an open society. More controversial are curbs on publication of government secrets—so-called *classified information*. Governments try to establish controls over the publication of material that they deem harmful to themselves or to individuals. For instance, confidential reports about the performance of government agencies, records of bidding on public jobs, and conversations during closed meetings generally are shielded from publicity. Finally, most governments also have laws protecting the reputations of individuals or groups and laws against obscenity. The merits of these controls on publication are discussed more fully in Chapter 3.

Defining the limits of government control over information dissemination raises difficult questions for democratic societies. Does official censorship, however minimal, open the way for the destruction of free expression? What guidelines are available to determine how far censorship should go? What types of material, if any, can harm children? Or adults? Should prejudicial statements be prohibited on the ground that they damage the self-image of minorities? The answers are controversial and problematic.

In addition to formal control of potentially damaging news in authoritarian and nonauthoritarian societies, many informal restraints exist. As we shall see in Chapter 9, all governmental units, and often many of their subdivisions, have their own information control systems by which they determine what news to conceal or release and how to present it.

The limitations on the freedom of publication in democratic societies raise questions about the actual differences in press freedom in nonauthoritarian and authoritarian societies. Is there really a difference, for example, in the independence of government-operated television networks in France and in North Korea? The answer is a resounding "yes." The degree of restraint varies so sharply that the systems are fundamentally different. In authoritarian societies the main objective of controls is to support the regime in power. In democratic societies the media are usually free to oppose the regime, to weaken it, and even to topple it. Although they rarely carry their power to the latter extreme, the potential exists. It is this potential that makes the media in nonauthoritarian societies a genuine restraint on governmental abuses of power and a potent shaper of governmental action.

Summary

The mass media are an important influence on politics because they regularly and rapidly present politically crucial information to huge audiences. These audiences include political elites and decision makers, as well as large numbers of average citizens whose political activities, however sporadic, are shaped by information from the mass media.

Decisions made by media personnel determine what information becomes available to media audiences and what remains unavailable. By putting stories into perspective and interpreting them, media personnel assign meaning to the information and indicate the values by which it ought to be judged. At times, newspeople even generate political action directly through their own investigations or indirectly through their capacity to stimulate pseudo-events.

Although many social scientists have remained somewhat skeptical about claims of large-scale media impact on politics, governments everywhere are keenly aware of the political importance of the media. Governments therefore have developed philosophies about the political role to be played by the media in their societies and about the proper ways to control the impact of the media on government activities. These philosophies have been implemented by constitutional and legal rules as well as by a host of informal arrangements. In this chapter we have described briefly how the basic philosophies, constitutional arrangements, and legal provisions differ in authoritarian and nonauthoritarian regimes.

Notes

1. "1994—The Year in Review," *Media Monitor* 9(1) (January/February 1995): 9.
2. "Did O. J. Do It?" Times Mirror Center for the People and the Press, News Release, April 6, 1995.
3. For a brief overview of current knowledge about mass media effects, see Dean E. Alger, *The Media and Politics* (Belmont, Calif.: Wadsworth, 1996); and W. Lance Bennett, *News: The Politics of Illusion* (White Plains, N.Y.: Longman, 1996).
4. The clues that mass media stories supply to the culture of their societies are discussed by George Gerbner, "Toward 'Cultural Indicators': The Analysis of Mass Mediated Public Message Systems," in *The Analysis of Communication Content*, ed. George Gerbner, Ole R. Holsti, Klaus Krippendorff, William J. Paisley, and Philip J. Stone (New York: Wiley, 1969), 123–132.
5. George Gerbner, Larry Gross, Michael Morgan, and Nancy Signorielli, "Charting the Mainstream: Television's Contributions to Political Orientation," *Journal of Communication* 32 (1982): 106–107.
6. Ray Hiebert, Donald Ungarait, and Thomas Bohn, *Mass Media VI* (White Plains, N.Y.: Longman, 1991), chap. 11.
7. Michael Parenti, *Make-Believe Media: The Politics of Entertainment* (New York: St. Martin's, 1992); S. Robert Lichter, Linda S. Lichter, and Stanley Rothman, *Watching America: What Television Tells Us about Our Lives* (New York: Prentice Hall, 1991).
8. Walter Gantz, "The Diffusion of News about the Attempted Reagan Assassination," *Journal of Communication* 33 (Winter 1983): 56–65.
9. Harold D. Lasswell, "The Structure and Function of Communication in Society," in *Mass Communications*, ed. Wilbur Schramm (Urbana: University of Illinois Press, 1969), 103.
10. Marshall McLuhan, *Understanding Media: The Extensions of Man* (New York: McGraw-Hill, 1964).
11. Chapter 4 gives a more detailed definition of news. Evidence that the media set the agenda for national issues is presented in Donald L. Shaw and Maxwell McCombs, *The Emergence of American Political Issues: The Agenda-Setting Function of the Press* (St. Paul, Minn.: West, 1977), and in sources cited there. See also the essays in Sidney Kraus and Richard M. Perloff, eds., *Mass Media and Political Thought* (Beverly Hills, Calif.: Sage, 1985); and Maxwell McCombs, Edna Einsiedel, and David Weaver, *Contemporary Public Opinion: Issues and the News* (Hillsdale, N.J.: Lawrence Erlbaum, 1992).

12. Examples of such criticism can be found in Bennett, *News: The Politics of Illusion;* and Michael Parenti, *Inventing Reality: The Politics of the News Media,* 3d ed. (New York: St. Martin's, 1993).

13. An example of a conservative Washington-based media analysis group is Accuracy in Media (AIM). It publishes periodic reports of its media investigations. For claims that journalists in the elite media are ultraliberal, see S. Robert Lichter, Stanley Rothman, and Linda S. Lichter, *The Media Elite* (New York: Adler and Adler, 1986).

14. Jay G. Blumler, "Purposes of Mass Communications Research: A Transatlantic Perspective," *Journalism Quarterly* 55 (Summer 1978): 226.

15. Daniel Boorstin, *The Image: A Guide to Pseudo-Events* (New York: Atheneum, 1971).

16. Criteria of what constitutes *news* are discussed fully by Bernard Roshco, *Newsmaking* (Chicago: University of Chicago Press, 1975), chap. 3.

17. Blumler, "Purposes of Mass Communications Research," 228.

18. The results of reassuring publicity are discussed by Murray Edelman, *The Symbolic Uses of Politics* (Urbana: University of Illinois Press, 1964), 38–43, reprinted 1985.

19. Robert Kubey and Mihaly Csikszentmihalyi, *Television and the Quality of Life: How Viewing Shapes Everyday Experience* (Hillsdale, N.J.: Lawrence Erlbaum, 1990), chaps. 5 and 7.

20. Marvin N. Olasky and Susan Northway Olasky, "The Crossover in Newspaper Coverage of Abortion from Murder to Liberation," *Journalism Quarterly* 63 (1986): 31–37.

21. W. Lance Bennett and Murray Edelman, "Toward a New Political Narrative," *Journal of Communication* 35 (1985): 156–171.

22. The early writings include David Easton and Jack Dennis, *Children in the Political System: Origins of Political Legitimacy* (New York: McGraw-Hill, 1969); Fred I. Greenstein, *Children and Politics* (New Haven, Conn.: Yale University Press, 1965); Richard Dawson and Kenneth Prewitt, *Political Socialization* (Boston: Little, Brown, 1969); and Robert D. Hess and Judith Torney, *The Development of Political Attitudes in Children* (Chicago: Aldine, 1967). Examples of the studies in the 1970s are Sidney Kraus and Dennis Davis, *The Effects of Mass Communication on Political Behavior* (University Park: Pennsylvania State University Press, 1976); Steven H. Chaffee, "Mass Communication in Political Socialization," in *Handbook of Political Socialization,* ed. Stanley Renshon (New York: Free Press, 1977). Also see Ellen Wartella, ed., *Children Communicating: Media and Development of Thought, Speech and Understanding* (Beverly Hills, Calif.: Sage, 1979).

23. Benjamin I. Page and Robert Y. Shapiro, *The Rational Public: Fifty Years of Trends in Americans' Policy Preferences* (Chicago: University of Chicago Press, 1992); Shanto Iyengar and Donald Kinder, *News that Matters: Television and American Opinion* (Chicago: University of Chicago Press, 1987); and Doris A. Graber, *Processing the News: How People Tame the Information Tide,* 2d ed. (Lanham, Md.: University Press of America, 1993).

24. David L. Protess et al., *The Journalism of Outrage: Investigative Reporting and Agenda Building in America* (New York: Guilford Press, 1991), 8–12.

25. Paul Lazarsfeld, Bernard Berelson, and Hazel Gaudet, *The People's Choice* (New York: Columbia University Press, 1944); Bernard Berelson, Paul Lazarsfeld, and William McPhee, *Voting: A Study of Opinion Formation in a Presiden-

tial Campaign (Chicago: University of Chicago Press, 1954); Angus Campbell, Gerald Gurin, and Warren E. Miller, *The Voter Decides* (Evanston, Ill.: Row, Peterson, 1954); and Angus Campbell, Philip E. Converse, Warren E. Miller, and Donald Stokes, *The American Voter* (New York: Wiley, 1960).

26. This account is based on Steven Livingston and Todd Eachus, "Humanitarian Crisis and U.S. Foreign Policy: Somalia and the CNN Effect Reconsidered," *Political Communication* 12(4) (1995): 413–429.

27. William C. Adams, Dennis J. Smith, Allison Salzman, Ralph Crossen, Scott Hiber, Tom Naccarato, William Vantine, and Nine Weisbroth, "Before and After *The Day After:* The Unexpected Results of a Televised Drama," *Political Communication and Persuasion* 3 (1986): 191–213. See also Stanley Feldman and Lee Sigelman, "The Political Impact of Prime-Time Television: 'The Day After,' " *Journal of Politics* 47 (May 1985): 556–578.

28. *New York Times,* July 13, 1983.

29. Theodore White, *The Making of the President, 1972* (New York: Bantam, 1973), 327.

30. The discussion is modeled on Fred Siebert, Theodore Peterson, and Wilbur Schramm, *Four Theories of the Press* (Urbana: University of Illinois Press, 1963).

31. For a brief account of media history in the United States, see Bernard Roshco, *Newsmaking* (Chicago: University of Chicago Press, 1975), 23–57; see also James K. Baughman, *The Republic of Mass Culture: Journalism, Filmmaking, and Broadcasting in America since 1941* (Baltimore: Johns Hopkins University Press, 1992).

32. David H. Weaver and G. Cleveland Wilhoit, *The American Journalist in the 1990s: U.S. News People at the End of an Era* (Mahwah, N.J.: Lawrence Erlbaum, 1996).

33. See, for example, Bernard Rubin, *Media, Politics, Democracy* (New York: Oxford University Press, 1977); and Erik Barnouw, *The Sponsor: Notes on a Modern Potentate* (New York: Oxford University Press, 1978).

34. Daniel Yankelovich, *Coming to Public Judgment: Making Democracy Work in a Complex World* (Syracuse, N.Y.: Syracuse University Press, 1991).

35. Michael Gurevitch and Jay G. Blumler, "Linkages between the Mass Media and Politics: A Model for the Analysis of Political Communications Systems," in *Mass Communication and Society,* ed. James Curran, Michael Gurevitch, and Janet Woolacott (Beverly Hills, Calif.: Sage, 1979), 283.

36. John Anthony Maltese, *Spin Control: The White House Office of Communication and the Management of Presidential News,* 2d ed. (Chapel Hill: University of North Carolina Press, 1994), 232–233.

Readings

Bennett, W. Lance. *News: The Politics of Illusion.* White Plains, N.Y.: Longman, 1996.

Graber, Doris A., ed. *Media Power in Politics.* 3d ed. Washington, D.C.: CQ Press, 1994.

Hess, Stephen. *News and Newsmaking.* Washington, D.C.: Brookings Institution, 1996.

Lichter, S. Robert, Linda S. Lichter, and Stanley Rothman. *Prime Time: How TV Portrays American Culture.* Washington, D.C.: Regnery, 1994.

Schudson, Michael. *The Power of News.* Cambridge, Mass. and London: Harvard University Press, 1995.

Smith, Leslie, Milan Meeske, and John W. Wright II. *Electronic Media and Government: The Regulation of Wireless and Wired Communication in the United States.* White Plains, N.Y.: Longman, 1995.

Spitzer, Robert J., ed. *Media and Public Policy.* Westport, Conn.: Praeger, 1993.

Thomas, Erwin K., and Brown H. Carpenter, eds. *Handbook on Mass Media in the United States: The Industry and Its Audiences.* Westport, Conn. and London: Greenwood, 1994.

Ownership, Regulation, and Guidance of Media

THE BREAKUP OF THE SOVIET UNION IN 1991 into a series of independent states produced a scramble for control of the media formerly owned and operated by the USSR. Boris Yeltsin, the new leader of the Russian Republic, immediately appropriated all printing presses hitherto owned by the communist party. He dismissed top-level media personnel whom he considered political opponents. When the new Russian-controlled media ran into serious economic difficulties a few months later, the Yeltsin government—despite its own fiscal problems—promptly came to their rescue. Government leaders knew that a friendly press was essential in a period of political and economic instability and wanted to make sure that their political allies in the media would remain in control. To emphasize the high priority given to media enterprises, the Russian minister of information, a former editor of *Moscow Pravda* and a close friend of Yeltsin's, was promoted to vice premier. The Russian republic's strenuous efforts to put control of the media into the hands of political supporters is a contemporary version of the classic battle for control of the information communicated to political elites and the general public.

Concern about who will wield media power has been a central issue in American politics since colonial days. It has become particularly important in the twentieth century because many new public policy issues have been raised by new technological and economic developments. In this chapter the pros and cons of public and private control and of big business influence in the media industry will be weighed. The impact of internal and external pressures on the industry, including those arising from economic constraints and from citizen lobbies, will be assessed also. The public policy issues involved in media control are so complex, so intertwined with political predispositions and preferences, that no control system stands out clearly as "best." It therefore is no wonder that attempts to legislate have produced clashes of views, litigation, and little agreement on what the laws should be.

Control and Ownership: Public and Semipublic

The various forms of control and ownership of the media affect not only media economics but also the substance of media output.

Forms of Control: Pros and Cons

The old adage, "He who pays the piper calls the tune," expresses one major concern about media control and ownership: People who fear government and its policies are likely to disapprove of direct operation of the media by government. They also are apt to be leery about extensive government regulation of privately operated media. By contrast, people who are afraid of the business ethics of private individuals and corporations would not want unfettered media control in private hands or directly influenced by large corporate enterprises.

Public policy issues raised by the debate over the merits of public versus private ownership of television illustrate the pros and cons. When governments own and operate major television channels, programming tends to reflect governmental policies closely, even in democratic countries. France, Israel, and Sweden are examples. However, Britain's experience with operating radio and television through the British Broadcasting Corporation (BBC) shows that governments can keep programming reasonably free from direct political interference.

Big business control of television, if divided among various large corporations, is likely to bring more conflicting interests into play than would government control. For instance, a conglomerate heavily involved in export industries will not share the same views on tariffs as a conglomerate interested primarily in domestic manufacturing. Even within conglomerates, the interests of various components may clash, thus moderating the stands of the general management and lessening the chances that specific business interests will dominate programming. Nonetheless, the prevailing values reflected in the choice of broadcasts are likely to be mainstream and middle class.

Although there is more chance for diversity of political outlooks when business rather than government controls programming, the pressures springing from profit considerations lead to homogeneous program types. Media offerings must be structured so that they yield financial returns to the private owners of media enterprises. Small fees must be collected from audiences or large fees from advertisers and other sponsors. The latter want to attract large numbers of viewers, particularly the eighteen- to forty-nine-year-old age group, which holds the bulk of purchasing power. Mass appeal, rather than any social or cultural concerns, becomes the primary goal. Governments are free from such pressures because they can use tax money to finance whatever programs they believe to be in the public interest. They must consider intragovernment power struggles, but they do not need to concern themselves with the economic consequences of the size of their audiences.

Given the pros and cons of government and business control, which is the better system? The answer depends on one's assessment of the motivations of the public and private sectors and one's beliefs about the proper role of the media. At present, when distrust of government is high and people view "big media" as a counterfoil to "big government," private control is the option preferred by most Americans. Thanks to this choice the bulk of television fare is geared to simple, emotion-laden programming that attracts large, diverse audiences. It also means shying away from controversial or troublesome issues that may antagonize and deplete media audiences and diminish advertising revenues.

Although "light-weight" programming draws the wrath of many people, particularly intellectual elites, one can argue that their disdain constitutes intellectual snobbery. Who is to say that the mass public's tastes are inferior to those of elites? The contention that people would choose educational programs over fluffy entertainment, if they had the chance, is false. Proof is plentiful that the mass public does indeed prefer light entertainment to more serious programs.[1] In print news, for example, magazines featuring sex or violence far outsell journals that treat political and social issues seriously. In fact, scholarly political journals frequently require subsidies to remain in print. Huge crowds are willing to pay heavily in time and money to see movies featuring heinous crimes and explicit sex. The most popular pay television channels show what is euphemistically called "adult entertainment," whereas channels devoted to highbrow culture languish and often perish.

Related to the concerns about domination of the media by government or private business interests is the fear of undue concentration of power if control over the nation's media is concentrated in just a few giant organizations. Diversity of media ownership presumably encourages the expression of a great variety of views, which, to many Americans, is the essence of democracy. The marketplace into which ideas and opinions flow must be wide open. But there is no agreement on exactly how diverse ownership must be to ensure sufficient diversity.[2] Americans appear to be more concerned about the concentration of media ownership in comparatively few hands than about control of media by business. Social reformers, however, are more concerned about business control, claiming that it caters to the lowest levels of taste and suppresses discussion of pressing social problems.

Public Control

In the United States outright government ownership and control over media has been comparatively limited. However, it is growing as more and more local governments own cable television systems or operate channels on privately owned systems. Government ownership raises serious unresolved questions about the limitations, if any, to be placed on the government's rights to use these outlets to further partisan political purposes.[3]

The federal government currently is most heavily involved in broadcasting, with local governments in second place. Abroad the federal government controls broadcasts to American military posts and owns various types of foreign propaganda outlets. Most programs broadcast by these propaganda agencies, such as the Voice of America, are barred from the domestic airwaves because Congress has been reluctant to expose American audiences to deliberate propaganda.

A substantial proportion of the radio broadcast spectrum, ranging from 50 percent in the pre-Carter years to 25 percent thereafter, belongs to the federal government, which uses it for radio services supplied by the executive branch. Another 40 percent of the space is shared by the government and private interests, leaving only 35 percent for the exclusive use of the private sector.[4] Altogether, foreign and domestic federal broadcasts equal the volume of commercial broadcasts produced in the United States.

Semipublic Control

Media operation by semipublic institutions is another control option. The public broadcasting system is one example. It represents a mixture of public and private financing and programming and public and private operation of radio and television stations. Created through the Public Broadcasting Act of 1967, the public broadcasting system supports educational and public service television stations whose programs generally do not attract large audiences. These stations usually cannot find enough commercial sponsors to pay for their shows.

Roughly one fourth of American television stations participate in the public broadcasting system. In 1992 members included 352 noncommercial television stations and 400 noncommercial radio stations, the latter linked together as National Public Radio (NPR).[5] The administrative arrangements for the public broadcasting system, regulated now under the Public Telecommunications Act of 1978, have been complex. A Corporation for Public Broadcasting (CPB), staffed by political appointees, has handled the general administration, but it has been kept separate from the programming side of the operation to insulate public broadcasting from political pressures. A separate Public Broadcasting Service (PBS) has produced television programs, often in collaboration with state-supported foreign broadcast systems, like Britain's BBC or France's Antenne Deux or Japan's NHK. The Independent Television Service created by Congress in 1991 has awarded grants to independent producers for programs that "reflect regional, racial, ethnic or cultural issues otherwise unavailable on public television and programs that successfully explore aesthetic values, formats and genres."[6]

The attempt to keep the CPB from influencing programming has failed. The corporation does not tell public television stations what specific programs they should feature. Instead, it has guided programming by paying for some types of programs and refusing to pay for others. This has constituted effective purse-string control of programming by government. In the field of radio, NPR was created both to produce and distribute programs. Because cost considerations made it impossible to include all noncommercial radio stations, only the largest, best organized ones were included. Some 400 stations currently qualify and are eligible for CPB funding grants and participation in NPR programs.

Private foundations and big business enterprises and large corporations have poured money into the public broadcasting system. Table 2-1 lists their contribution as 22 percent of total income. The *Washington Post* gives a 36 percent figure for 1995, using a somewhat broader category for "foundations."[7] The Federal Communications Commission (FCC) during the Reagan years permitted PBS to engage in some commercial broadcasting of economic news and to accept a limited amount of advertising. All of these changes have enhanced corporate influence over programming. The general public also has influenced public broadcasting through donations that constitute nearly one quarter of the income of public broadcasting systems and through community advisory boards. Nevertheless, securing adequate financing is an enduring problem. Dependence

TABLE 2-1   Income Sources of Public Broadcasting Systems: 1992
(includes nonbroadcast income)

Income sources	Millions of dollars	Percentage of budget
Federal government	374	21
State/local government and colleges/universities	485	27
Subscribers and auction/marathons	404	23
Business and industry	300	17
Foundations	80	5
Other	148	8
Total income	1,791	100

SOURCE: Bureau of the Census, *Statistical Abstract of the United States, 1995* (Washington, D.C.: U.S. Government Printing Office, 1995), 576.

NOTE: Public broadcasting system includes 400 CPB-qualified public radio stations and 352 public television stations.

on public funds, even when these funds constitute only a fraction of total funding (down to 14 percent for the federal government by 1995), may mean subservience to government control, despite barriers to direct government influence.

Public television broadcasts are distinguished from commercial television primarily by an emphasis on experimental programs; cultural offerings such as plays, classical music, and ballet (which constitute 59 percent of program content); news; public affairs; educational programs (33 percent); and local programs (7 percent).[8] The nature and quality of programming varies widely because public television represents a decentralized bevy of local stations. The audience for public television, except for its children's programs, which represent less than one fifth of its programming time, has been small. Even minority groups, for whom a number of public broadcast programs presumably are tailored, prefer the entertainment provided by commercial stations. Because of the limited appeal of public broadcasting and pressures to reduce public expenditures, there have been demands to disband the system completely and reallocate its frequencies to commercial channels. Some of its programs then might be shown on commercial cable stations, possibly with federal subsidies.[9]

Supporters of the system contend that it should be viewed as a provider of needed special services that are neglected by commercial television precisely because they lack mass appeal or are commercially unattractive. They point out that innovations pioneered by public broadcasting have spread to commercial broadcasting. For example, public broadcasting played a leading role in developing captions for individuals with hearing impairment. Public radio and public television also were among the first to move to satellite distribution that made it possible to deliver multiple national programs to communities. Nonetheless, the ultimate fate of public broadcasting is in doubt.

Patterns of Private Ownership

The overarching feature of media control in the United States is that it is predominantly in private hands. Control arrangements range from individual ownership, where one person owns a newspaper or radio or television station, to ownership by huge corporate conglomerates. Owners include small and large business enterprises, labor groups, religious and ethnic organizations, and many other types of interests represented in American society. The facts about private media control patterns are relatively simple to explain, but there is much disagreement about their consequences.

Business Configurations

In the media business, there are *independents,* individuals or corporations that run a single media venture and nothing else. The publisher who owns one newspaper or one radio or television station is an example. However, their numbers are declining.

Multiple owners have become increasingly common. These are individuals or corporations who own several media of the same type—mostly radio or television stations or cable channels or newspapers. Because there are fewer than 1,800 daily newspapers in the entire United States and fewer than 1,200 commercial television stations, one might question whether society is well-served when a vast majority of these media are held by group owners.[10] Nevertheless, this has been the trend.

Crossmedia ownership has been less common than multiple ownership. It occurs when an individual or corporation owns several types of media, such as newspapers *and* television stations or newspapers *and* radio stations. Crossmedia ownership is most worrisome when one owner controls all media in the same location. Such monopolies have been prohibited since 1975, except where they were already established. However, crossmedia ownership dispersed over various locations is thriving. Gannett Company, for example, owns 93 daily newspapers, 15 television stations, and 19 radio stations following its 1995 merger with Multimedia Company.

A fourth pattern encompasses *conglomerates*—individuals or corporations own media enterprises along with other types of businesses. The General Electric Company (GE) is an example. Figure 2-1 illustrates the diversity of GE's interests. Conglomerates raise fears that their nonmedia business interests may color their news policies. If, for instance, there is a soundly based demand to reduce the size of the military or to oppose construction of a missile system, the management of a conglomerate such as GE, which holds many defense contracts, may not examine these questions open-mindedly.

In major urban centers most media fall into the multiple-owner, crossmedia, and conglomerate classifications. For instance, the *Chicago Tribune* is owned by the Tribune Company, which owns two dozen media enterprises and thirteen companies outside the media field.[11] The major television and radio stations in Chicago are owned by the national television networks and conglomerates or members of conglomerates. Radio and television stations that remain under single ownership for the most part are small with comparatively weak signals.[12]

The number of media outlets controlled by various entrepreneurs ranges widely. In 1995 Cox Broadcasting Corporation owned eleven radio stations, three television stations, four cable television systems, and nine newspaper companies; the New York Times Company owned thirty-six daily newspapers, eight weeklies, two radio stations, five television stations, and numerous magazines. Capital Cities/ABC, the American Broadcasting Company Network, owned seven television stations, seven radio networks serving more than 3,000 affiliated radio stations, eighteen radio stations, and seventy-five weekly newspapers, as well as numerous magazines and trade publications. It grew even larger after merging with the Walt Disney Company in 1995.[13] But one cannot judge the sweep of control exercised by any group merely by looking at the number of its outlets. Three additional factors need to be considered: *market size, competition within the market,* and *prestige of each media institution.*

Market Size

For purposes of assessing mass media performance and regulating electronic media, the country is divided into markets rather than states or regions. A *market* is the area in which a medium attracts a substantial audience. For instance, each television station has a signal that can be received clearly by people living within a certain radius of the station. All of the people within that radius who can receive the signal are considered to be within the market. This means that they can be expected to respond to advertising for products and services provided by program sponsors.

FIGURE 2-1   The Diverse Holdings of the General Electric Company

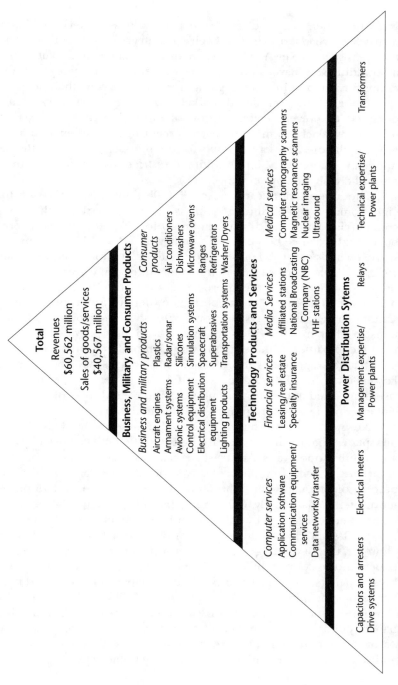

Total

Revenues
$60,562 million

Sales of goods/services
$40,567 million

Business, Military, and Consumer Products

Business and military products
Aircraft engines
Armament systems
Avionic systems
Control equipment
Electrical distribution equipment
Lighting products

Plastics
Radar/sonar
Silicones
Simulation systems
Spacecraft
Superabrasives
Transportation systems

Consumer products
Air conditioners
Dishwashers
Microwave ovens
Ranges
Refrigerators
Washer/Dryers

Technology Products and Services

Computer services
Application software
Communication equipment/ services
Data networks/transfer

Financial services
Leasing/real estate
Specialty insurance

Media Services
Affiliated stations
National Broadcasting Company (NBC)
VHF stations

Medical services
Computer tomography scanners
Magnetic resonance scanners
Nuclear imaging
Ultrasound

Power Distribution Sytems

Capacitors and arresters
Drive systems

Electrical meters

Management expertise/ Power plants

Relays

Technical expertise/ Power plants

Transformers

SOURCE: Standard and Poor's Corp., *Corporation Records*, 1994; General Electric, *Annual Report*, 1993.

Altogether, there are 420 newspaper markets in the United States and nearly 300 broadcast markets. Their sizes vary widely. In major metropolitan areas such as New York, Chicago, or Los Angeles, a market with a fifty-mile radius may have a population of several million people. The same radius for a station in Wyoming might cover more cows than people.

The FCC has considered market size only recently in its regulations designed to prevent concentration of ownership. It specifies that one owner may reach no more than 35 percent of the audience in a market. FCC regulations also set top limits for the numbers of stations that can be under the same ownership. Additional restrictions are imposed on multiple and crossmedia ownership.

The Telecommunications Act of 1996 limits an owner to a total of eight commercial AM and FM stations in a radio market with 45 or more commercial stations, with lower limits set for smaller markets. There must be a rough balance between the number of AM and FM stations under a single owner's control. For television stations, the top limit, established in 1992, is 12 television stations in a single market, but Congress has directed the FCC to reexamine the appropriateness of this number. Lifting previous restrictions, the 1996 Act permits owners of a network of broadcast stations to own a cable system as well. It also permits owners of cable systems to offer many services that were previously provided only by telephone companies. Although limitations on building media empires have been eased, regulations to enforce social policies have been enhanced. For example, the 1996 Act provides for special services for hearing- and vision-impaired audiences and puts curbs on the display of obscenity and violence in television programs accessible to minors.

Newspapers can enter an unlimited number of markets. As a result, newspaper chains can expand at will, up to the limits allowed by antitrust and antimonopoly laws. Antitrust regulations become operative when the eight largest firms in a particular type of business control more than 50 percent of the market and the twenty largest firms control 75 percent or more of the market. By 1994 more than 80 percent of America's daily papers were controlled by national and regional chains.[14] There are more than 100 such chains, but the majority control fewer than ten papers. However, the eleven largest groups controlled nearly half of all daily newspapers in the country in 1994. Thomson Newspapers has the most numbers of papers under its control: 110 daily papers. Gannett held the number two spot with 93 daily newspapers, followed by Knight Ridder, Newhouse, and Dow Jones. Most of these newspaper groups also own papers published less frequently, as well as radio and television stations. Although ownership figures are changing constantly as papers are bought and sold, the relative rankings remain fairly stable. The proportion of circulation controlled by chain-owned papers has been growing over the decades, but not by leaps and bounds. Although individual papers within chains generally enjoy editorial-page autonomy, they tend to be more uniform in political endorsements than are independently owned papers.[15]

Influence is even more concentrated for television. Three huge conglomerate-owned networks—National Broadcasting Company (NBC), Columbia Broadcasting System (CBS), and ABC—dominate roughly 54 percent of the television households in the nation.[16] Through their affiliates in the United States and abroad, their reach is even broader. ABC and its associated enterprises, for example, can reach nearly all U.S. households as well as audiences in Japan, Germany, France, and Luxembourg.[17]

In the past, the networks produced a limited number of television and radio entertainment programs for their own use. The bulk of entertainment programming came from other sources. That has changed drastically in the 1990s with the removal of FCC prohibitions, which previously barred the merger of program production enterprises with distribution enterprises.

To keep figures on media concentration in proper perspective, however, one must keep in mind that the three major television networks compete vigorously with each other for public favor and that they do not dominate programming completely for their affiliates. The three networks are also facing vigorous competition from the emerging fourth network, Fox Broadcasting Corporation, owned by media baron Rupert Murdoch, which seems to be cornering the child, teenage, and young adult audiences. It has arranged to have its programs carried by cable television, which has become a major contender for the television audience's attention. Cable television's share of the audience has been rising steadily, but it is split among dozens of more or less specialized channels. The broadcast networks remain the only gate to huge mass audiences.[18] By 1994, 62 percent of the nation's households—59 million altogether—were served by cable television.[19]

The capstone to the picture of narrowly held control over information outlets is supplied by the wire service companies. A huge share of the news stories appearing in nearly every newspaper in the country and featured on television or radio news originates from the wires of the Associated Press (AP). The roots of this organization go back to 1848, when six New York newspapers formed a cooperative association to share the cost of collecting foreign news. Out of this initial effort grew large organizations that employ reporters scattered throughout the world to collect and report news. News stories and bulletins are transmitted electronically to subscriber newspapers and radio and television stations. A handful of other wire services, such as those operated by the *New York Times, Los*

Angeles Times, and *Chicago Tribune,* serve their own papers, along with a smaller array of subscribers.

News stories and bulletins supplied by the wire services are used either verbatim or rewritten by their clients. Depending on the resources available to a particular news organization for gathering and writing its own news, the proportion of wire service stories used directly or in rewritten form may vary from less than 10 percent to 80 percent or more of all stories. For many newspapers, a look at the mix of stories carried by wire services on any particular day will foretell accurately the mix of stories carried by the paper. Wire service stories tend to predominate for foreign news and even for national news for smaller papers and stations that cannot afford their own correspondents. This means that a large share of news production in the United States is dominated by a small number of companies. However, none of the situations of limited competition that have been discussed thus far involve monopoly controls. Even in one-newspaper towns, there is usually some intermedia competition from television and radio stations. Unfortunately, the messages that competing media present are likely to be similar.

Intramarket Competition

Despite efforts by the FCC to increase intramarket competition, limited competition (oligopoly) conditions prevail in the majority of markets. Electronic media generally are owned in pairs, limiting the total number of media owners in the community. Intramarket newspaper competition also has become rare. Ninety-eight percent of all American cities have only one daily newspaper.[20] Newspaper competition is rare outside the largest cities. Suburban dailies, which flourish in a few major cities, do not alter the situation substantially because their coverage of major news stories usually is limited.

Prestige Leadership

Another reason for homogeneity in news supply is the consensus among journalists about the nature of news and the elements of good reporting. There are widely accepted standards of professionalism in journalism, just as there are in law or medicine or engineering. As part of this system of norms, certain members and products are accepted widely as models whose influence reaches far beyond their own organization. Critics call this the "jackal syndrome" or "pack journalism." In the political news field the *New York Times* is the lion whom the jackals follow. In television Dan Rather and Tom Brokaw are models for the profession. Other news professionals watch what information these sources present, how they present it, and what interpretations they give to it; they then adjust their own presentations accordingly. The upshot is that the multiplication of voices in the media marketplace has contributed relatively little to meaningful diversity in news. The newcomers quickly join the old chorus and hum the prevailing tunes.

Small Business Versus Big Business Control

The steady trend toward consolidation in the media industry increasingly has left control of information in the hands of a limited number of large organizations. Because concentration generally has stopped short of infringing antitrust and antimonopoly laws, these laws have been of little help in halting or reversing consolidation. As will be pointed out in Chapter 4, economic factors are largely responsible for consolidation. Production of television programs and worldwide news gathering are expensive. Only large, well-financed organizations, which are able to spread the costs over many customers, can provide the lavish media fare to which the American public has become accustomed.

Even when there is no infringement of antitrust and antimonopoly laws, is it sound public policy to allow the rapid pace of consolidation of media enterprises to continue? Is there a danger that centralized control, besides bringing undesirable uniformity, also will lead to neglect of local needs? Does the absence of newspaper competition in American cities prevent diverse viewpoints from reaching the public? The fears underlying these questions have been largely groundless, although there have been some troubling cases.[21] Neither is there solid evidence that the media giants routinely suppress diversity among the news outlets under their control, squelch antibusiness news, and stress antilabor, pro-Republican, and jingoistic stories. It is true that many important stories are not published, including some that would be poor publicity for big business, but there is no hard evidence that the choices that are necessary to cope with an oversupply of news conform predominantly to conservative political orientations.[22]

The charge that media owners pressure journalists into supporting the existing political system also is not borne out. American journalists in large organizations, like their colleagues in small, independently owned enterprises, are interested in appealing to their audiences. This is why their stories usually reflect the values of mainstream American society, regardless of the journalists' personal political orientations.[23] However, there is a real danger that serious news increasingly will be overwhelmed by "info-tainment" programs in the wake of the mergers of news enterprises with entertainment giants. If this happens, the quality of civic life in the United States may be impaired.[24]

What about the argument that small, individually owned enterprises would produce better programming, more suited to local needs? One way to test this assertion is to compare the news and other public service programs offered by various types of television stations. By and large, news and public service programming have been more plentiful on stations owned by big business and by conglomerates than on stations owned by individuals.[25] Network stations do best of all. In a similar way, radio stations and newspapers that have the best public service coverage, as judged by professional journalists, generally are controlled by large business enterprises or are part of a large network.

However, the contention that individually owned, small enterprises provide poorer public service than their larger, group-owned cousins is open to question. The measures of public service programming used by the FCC and most media studies are primarily quantitative. They gauge how much broadcasting time is spent on certain kinds of programs, but they do not analyze the quality of these programs. Small stations may make up in the quality of their public offerings what they lack in quantity.

It would not be surprising if big business control does indeed mean qualitatively superior programs. Large enterprises are able to absorb the losses that are often incurred in the production of documentaries and public service programs. They can spend more money on talented people, research, investigations, and costly entertainment shows. They can afford to send their leading reporters to all parts of the world to cover breaking stories firsthand. And they can pay their anchors multimillion dollar salaries.

On balance it seems that some of the arguments made against big business control of media are exaggerated. So are some of the arguments in favor of control by small enterprises. When FCC rules have forced small stations to spend time on non-network programs, they have been unable to afford costly original programs produced locally. Instead, they have filled their non-network hours with cheap canned movies or syndicated quiz or talent shows. The arguments concerning the respective merits of big and small media enterprises cannot be settled definitively until more thorough comparisons of the quality of programs have been made. In the meantime it is important to recognize that current policies designed to reduce media concentration and encourage local programming rest on questionable assumptions and have failed to meet their objectives. It is equally important to acknowledge that the media's mandate to serve the public interest of a democratic society remains only partly fulfilled.

Government Regulation of the Media

The federal government regulates private electronic media primarily through the FCC, a bipartisan body appointed by the president and confirmed by the Senate. The FCC was a seven-member body until the summer of 1984, when it was downsized to five commissioners to save money. In 1986 the appointment term was shortened from seven to five years, ensuring faster turnover of commission personnel and greater control by the president. In theory, the commission is an independent regulatory body. In practice, congressional purse strings, public and industry pressures, and presidential control over appointment of new members, including naming the chair, have greatly curtailed its freedom of operation. The commission's independence is weakened also because its rulings can be appealed to the courts, which frequently have overturned them. Conflicting political pressures from outside the agency as well as internal political pressures influence FCC policy making. As the authors of *The Politics of Broadcast Regulation* note:

> The broadcast policy-making system is usually modest in its goals, flexible in policy choices, sensitive to feedback, and prone to dealing with immediate problems through steps and options that are only incrementally different from existing policies.... A consequence of these characteristics is a reactive rather than an innovative system sluggish to respond to change in its environment, particularly to technological change that probably will be very rapid in the next decade or so. Clearly there are problems with this kind of policy-making system.[26]

FCC Rules

Its vague mandate under the Communications Act of 1934 and its 1996 counterpart to "serve the public interest, convenience, and necessity" has made it difficult for the FCC to identify the objectives that should guide its regulatory powers. It has had to determine what social, economic, and technical goals the communications industry should achieve. It also has had to deal with conflicts over the adoption of various technologies and with the philosophical issue of regulation versus deregulation. On balance, the FCC's record of setting goals and enforcing its rules has earned it the reputation at best of being an ineffective watchdog over the public interest and at worst an industry-kept, pressure-group-dominated lapdog.

FCC control is limited to electronic media that reach large audiences other than cable television, which has been treated largely as a carrier of broadcast messages rather than a broadcaster. Similarly, interactive computer broadcasting systems, such as the Internet and the World Wide Web, have been excluded from regulation, although a Computer Decency Act passed in 1996 seeks to enforce obscenity and indecency rules in cyberspace to protect minors. The constitutionality of this act will be tested in the courts.[27] The print media essentially are uncontrolled except for antitrust and monopoly laws. Despite these laws the Justice Department has permitted economically weak newspapers to combine their business and production facilities, free from antitrust and monopoly restraints, as long as their news and editorial operations are kept separate.

FCC control has taken four forms: (1) rules limiting the number of stations owned or controlled by a single organization, (2) examination of the goals and performance of stations as part of periodic licensing, (3) rules mandating public service and local interest programs, and (4) rules to guarantee fair treatment to individuals and to protect their rights. Although none of these rules deal directly with content, all of them were designed to increase the chances that content would be diverse and of civic importance.

Rules Limiting Station Ownership. As explained earlier, to prevent high concentrations of media ownership and ensure diversity of information sources, the FCC limits the number of stations that television and radio owners may control. It also limits the size of the audience that may be within the range of any one group of owners, allowing them no more than 35 percent market share. Nonetheless, networks with many affiliates, such as ABC, CBS, NBC, and Fox, are within reach of more than 90 percent of the nation's audiences.

Station ownership has been enormously profitable. This is why the Walt Disney Company was willing to spend $19 billion in 1996 to buy Capital Cities/ABC and Westinghouse raised nearly $11 billion to acquire and run CBS. However, profitability declined in the late 1980s. Television news units were especially hard hit. They were forced to slash budgets and lay off several thousand employees. Partial deregulation of the television industry, the rise of new networks, such as media mogul Ted Turner's Cable News Network (CNN), and the development of new technologies generated fierce competition. Independent television stations multiplied, as did cable systems, television satellites, videotape recorders, and similar services such as teletext and microfiche. Affiliates reduced their reliance on network programming by producing their own news shows or importing satellite programs. Network audience share dropped from 93 percent in 1977 to 54 percent in 1994, producing a drop in advertising rates. Advertising revenues also declined because the pool of large advertisers shrank in the wake of business mergers.[28]

Thus far, no initial investment has been required to get a license from the government, although pressures to change this are mounting. The FCC estimates that auctioning licensees to the highest bidder could yield the federal government $35 billion—more than the combined costs of operations of the Justice, Interior, State, and Commerce Departments in 1995.[29] Licenses of profitable stations can be sold for millions of dollars because government controls have limited the total numbers of licenses issued so that the demand exceeds the supply.

Licensing as Performance Control. By granting or refusing to grant a radio or television license initially or renewing it after eight years, the FCC determines who may own valuable communication properties. What performance standards does it use for license decisions? Communication law mandates that television and radio must "serve the public interest, convenience, and necessity."[30] But beyond requiring broadcasters to ascertain community needs and interests by talking with community leaders, there are no guides for interpreting these rules. Even the requirement to keep in touch with community leaders was dropped in 1984. In the absence of specific performance requirements, it has been nearly impossible to use the power to grant licenses initially and to renew them as a tool to foster high quality. When processing licenses, the FCC usually looks at the mix of programs, the proportion of public service offerings, and the inclusion of programs geared to selected groups. It does not scrutinize the subject matter of broadcasts in detail. This hands-off attitude has applied to both program inclusions and exclusions. However, the FCC has set limits on the amounts of advertising permitted in children's shows. Ads may not exceed twelve minutes per hour on weekdays and ten and a half minutes on weekends.

The FCC has used its power to grant new licenses to ensure service geared to the information needs of socioeconomic groups different from those already served by existing stations in a given area. When there are several qualified applicants for new broadcasting stations, the FCC may use a lottery that is tilted to favor applications by women, minorities, labor unions, and community organizations that are underrepresented in the ownership of telecommunications facilities. Once a license has been granted, owners hold it for good unless they engage in discriminatory or fraudulent practices or receive many complaints about poor programming. Owners may sell their licenses at will, earning huge profits on the sale.

Since the 1970s numerous civic groups have entered renewal hearings to protest the type of programming offered or omitted by a particular station. As a result of such pressures, the FCC reluctantly has withdrawn licenses from a few stations over the years. For example, a Chicago station lost its license in 1990 for neglecting informational programs and presenting obscene movies.[31] However, the 1996 Telecommunications Act makes license withdrawal more difficult. It specifically forbids the FCC from continuing its practice of comparing the merits of new applicants with those of existing license holders in license renewal applications.

Compared with regulatory agencies in other countries, even in Western Europe, Canada, and Australia, the FCC controls the electronic media with a light hand. The members of the FCC could, if they wished, rigorously define what constitutes "programming in the public interest." They could enforce the FCC rulings more strictly and verify station performance records at license renewal time. The threat of license withdrawal for rule violations could be used as a much more powerful deterrent to misbehavior and as a much stronger lever to guide programming. Part of the problem is that the FCC staff is much too small to cope with all the duties assigned to the agency. In fact, it is chronically behind schedule, even for routine matters such as publication of its annual reports.

Public Service and Local Programming. In the past the FCC stipulated the minimum time that ought to be devoted to public service programs on television. Under the 5-5-10 rule, which is no longer enforced, 5 percent of programming had to be devoted to local affairs, 5 percent to news and public affairs, and 10 percent to nonentertainment programs. Beyond checking a television station's log to ascertain that it recorded the minimum amount of public service programming, the FCC did not examine the nature and quality of programs labeled "public service." In 1991, as part of its regulations of children's television, the FCC directed stations to maintain a record of educational and informational programs for children. But it set no quality standards, even though the record is a requirement for license renewal.[32]

Fair Treatment Rules. The FCC also has made rules about access to the airwaves for candidates for political office and for people who have been subjected to media attacks. These types of controls are discussed in Chapter 3.

Control by Industry Associations and Advertiser Pressures

Industry lobbies are another means of controlling the mass media. Radio and television interests, especially the networks and their affiliated stations, are active lobbyists. Most belong to the National Association of Broadcasters (NAB), a powerful Washington lobby despite the diversity and often clashing interests of its members. A number of trade associations and publications, such as *Broadcasting* magazine, also engage in lobbying, often at cross-purposes to each other. For newspapers the American Newspaper Publishers Association (ANPA), now merged with several other press associations, has been one of the most prominent. These organizations try to influence appointments to the FCC and to guide public policies affecting new technologies that may threaten established systems or practices. For instance, the network lobbies for many years tried to stifle cable television and to acquire control over domestic satellites.

To forestall regulation by outside bodies, the industry has developed mechanisms for self-control. The NAB has had a radio code since 1929 and a television code since 1952 that set rules on program content and form. Both codes have been modernized periodically. Industry-wide codes have been supplemented and often are superseded by individual codes in major broadcast enterprises and by codes adopted by the Council of Better Business Bureaus. Print press self-policing has developed along similar lines. Scholars, too, have set forth codes of journalism ethics. Most codes are quite vague, such as the five principles advocated by Edmund Lambeth. Ethical behavior, he contends, requires telling the truth and heeding humanness above all. It also requires striving for fairness, striving for independence from power holders, and acting as responsible trustees for the public's interests.[33] What these principles mean in practice is left for decision in specific cases.

The impact of industry-wide codes always has been limited. NAB codes, for example, apply only to its members and then only if they explicitly choose to subscribe to them. In a typical year, one half of the members might not subscribe.[34] Penalties for code violations have been minimal. The worst penalty is withdrawal of a station's right to list itself as a subscriber to the code. Therefore, the code has exerted only a limited amount of moral pressure on the industry. It did serve to blunt demands by pressure groups for government intervention to set and enforce standards. Such intervention came nonetheless in 1996 when the Telecommunications Act required the installation of blocking devices in newly manufactured television sets to permit parents to bar their children from viewing excessively violent and sexually explicit shows. Television producers were urged to develop a rating system to guide parents and agreed to do so.

In the 1970s advertisers began to influence program content by actually withdrawing their commercials from programs they considered to be obscene or excessively violent. Sears Roebuck was one of the earliest and largest advertisers to do so. McDonald's, American Express, and AT&T refused to place commercials on such shows. Other companies, such as Procter and Gamble, the top television advertiser in the nation, retained consultants to seek out acceptable programs for their advertisements and avoid unacceptable ones. With advertisements on top-rated shows such as the Super Bowl yielding $36,000 per second of advertising time in 1995, threats of withdrawal constitute tremendous economic pressures.[35] In the wake of such pressures from advertisers, the number of programs featuring violence, particularly during prime-time hours, dropped temporarily. ABC, for example, canceled the sequel to a successful crime drama in 1989 after it failed to attract paid advertising. The program contained four reenactments of crime, including two stabbings, a shooting, and a murder in which a husband set fire to his wife.

There is deep concern, however, that advertisers, spurred by pressure groups, may become unofficial censors. For instance, General Motors' sponsorship of an Eastertime program on the life of Jesus was canceled because evangelical groups objected to the content. There were crippling withdrawals of advertising from a CBS documentary on gun control, opposed by the gun control lobby, and from a series of interviews featuring former president Nixon, which aroused the ire of Nixon foes. Islamic groups tried unsuccessfully in 1994 to stop PBS from showing "Jihad in America." The film focused on an Islamic terror network in the United States at a time when Islamic fundamentalists were on trial for a devastating bomb attack on New York's World Trade Center. Protesters feared a backlash against Muslims in the United States. The television networks, although not shy about saturating the airwaves with uninhibited sex in television dramas, have refused advertising designed to instruct viewers about the use of condoms for protection against unwanted pregnancies and acquired immune deficiency syndrome (AIDS). In these cases, fundamentalist religious groups have been the unofficial censors.

Citizen Lobby Control

Citizens' efforts to affect the quality of broadcasting began in earnest in 1966 when the Office of Communication of the United Church of Christ, a public interest lobby, challenged the renewal of a TV license for WLBT-TV in Jackson, Mississippi, accusing the station of discriminating against African American viewers.[36] African Americans then constituted 45 percent of the Jackson population. The challenge failed, but it was the beginning of efforts by many other citizens groups to use pressure tactics to challenge license renewals.

A major victory was won in 1975 when the FCC refused to renew licenses of eight educational television stations in Alabama and denied a construction permit for a ninth station because citizen groups had charged racial discrimination in employment at these stations. There also had been complaints that programs that dealt with affairs of the African American community had been unduly excluded.[37] Since then, numerous stations have yielded to pressure for increased minority employment and programming rather than face protracted legal action.

By permission of Mike Luckovich and Creators Syndicate.

The National Citizens' Committee for Broadcasting (NCCB), headed by former FCC commissioner Nicholas Johnson, became widely known for sharp attacks on the shallowness of broadcasting and the weakness of governmental controls at national and local levels. The committee has been absorbed into Ralph Nader's consumer protection organization. Other prominent national citizens' lobby groups include Accuracy in Media (AIM), a well-financed conservative media-monitoring organization; the Coalition for Better Television (CBTV), representing fundamentalist religious groups; Citizens for the American Way (CAW), a liberal media organization intent on blocking conservative lobbies; Action for Children's Television (ACT), which disbanded in 1992; the National Black Media Coalition (NBMC); and the National Latino Media Coalition (NLMC).

Despite substantial impact of such groups on FCC rule making and licensing procedures, citizens' national lobbying efforts declined in the 1980s.[38] One reason was the difficulty of sustaining citizen interest over long periods of time; another was lack of financial support and loss of leadership. The broadcast lobby defeated efforts to obtain public funding for citizens' lobby groups, and foundation support dried up. Many groups also were discouraged when the appeals courts reversed substantial victories won in the lower courts. Some of the energies of citizens groups have been redirected into lobbying at the local level to ensure that cable systems serve the interests of various publics at reasonable costs.

In addition to the more than sixty organizations concerned exclusively with media reform, other organizations, such as the Parent Teacher Association (PTA), the National Organization for Women (NOW), and the American Medical Association (AMA), have lobbied on a variety of media issues. These include concern about stereotyping, access to media coverage and to media employment and ownership, advertising on children's programs, and enforcement of FCC program regulations. The groups' tactics include monitoring media content, publicizing their findings, and directly pressuring broadcasters, advertisers, media audiences, and government control agencies. Protest by PTA members has pressured advertisers, who, in turn, have succeeded in reducing the number of violent programs shown in the early evening hours. Legal maneuvers have ranged from challenges of license renewals to damage suits for the harmful effects of media content.

It is difficult to assess the precise influence of these organizations because many of their goals overlap with other forces that affect media policy. Some of the causes for which they have worked have prospered over the years, however, and part of the credit undoubtedly belongs to them. The provisions of the 1996 Telecommunications Act designed to protect children from exposure to violence and pornography are among the most recent victories. Yet these groups have a long road to travel before they can match the clout and resources enjoyed by the broadcast lobby in protecting its interests even when they run counter to the concerns of large numbers of citizens.

Summary

In this chapter we have examined the most common types of ownership and control of the media. The national government owns and operates vast overseas radio and television enterprises. At home it partially controls a far-flung system of public television and radio broadcasting that provides an alternative to commercial programming.

For the average American these government-controlled systems are peripheral compared with privately owned print and electronic media enterprises. The major political problem in the private sector is concentration of ownership of media and concentrated control over news and entertainment programs. There has been great concern that the American public is ill-served because much of the media output is controlled by large business conglomerates, and newspaper competition is limited in most cities. Comparatively few potentially biased minds shape the news and entertainment supply that undergirds public perceptions of political issues.

We have looked into the structure of the media business and government regulations designed to avert the potential dangers of concentration. We also have tried to evaluate the impact of the existing system on the form and slant of news and entertainment. Many prevailing views about the interrelation between media structures and functions appear to be wrong. Business ownership has not led to programming dominated by business perspectives although it has enhanced the focus on entertainment. It has not shielded big business from harsh criticism. Coverage of local news has not withered, and large, rather than small, enterprises have excelled in providing news and entertainment. Because fears about the ill effects of the current structure seem misdirected, further research is needed to provide a sounder basis for public policies intended to ensure that American media serve the public interest.

Media operations and products are shaped not only by who owns them but also by industry lobby groups and citizens' lobbies. Given the diversity of influences that are brought into play when news and entertainment are produced, it is as yet impossible to assess the precise impact that each of these influences has on media content in general or even on a particular story. In the next chapter we will focus on legal aspects of news production for additional clues to the mystery of the mix of influences shaping the news.

Notes

1. Examples of the types of shows that attract the largest audiences are "Murphy Brown" (comedy), "E. R." (drama), and "60 Minutes," the popular investigative series that shares many qualities with popular detective shows. In addition, there are the ever-popular sports events such as the Super Bowl, entertainment industry awards presentations, and competitions such as the Miss America contest.
2. Ben H. Bagdikian, *The Media Monopoly,* 4th ed. (Boston: Beacon Press, 1992), 3–26. For a negative view of the "marketplace of ideas" concept, see Benjamin Ginsberg, *The Captive Public: How Mass Opinion Promotes State Power* (New York: Basic Books, 1986), 98–148.
3. "Despite the expressed insulation of public broadcasters from federal editorial domination, case law specifically allows broadcast program decisions to be dictated by political officials when the state is licensee. Therefore, potential conflict exists between First Amendment and political interests." William Hanks and Lemuel Schofield, "Limitations on the State as Editor in State-Owned Broadcast Stations," *Journalism Quarterly* 63 (Winter 1986): 798.

4. Erwin G. Krasnow, Lawrence D. Longley, and Herbert A. Terry, *The Politics of Broadcast Regulation*, 3d ed. (New York: St. Martin's, 1982), 23, 74.
5. *Statistical Abstract of the United States, 1995* (Washington, D.C.: U.S. Government Printing Office, 1995), 576.
6. *U.S. Government Manual 1995* (Washington, D.C.: Office of Federal Register), 673–675.
7. Thomas B. Edsall, "The Campaign to Turn Off Public Broadcasting," *Washington Post National Weekly Edition*, April 24–30, 1995, 15.
8. Steve Johnson, "Representative TV," *Chicago Tribune*, March 12, 1995.
9. Lawrie Mifflin, "Reprieve for PBS but Hunt for Funds Continues," *New York Times*, January 2, 1996.
10. *Statistical Abstract of the United States, 1995*, 571.
11. Besides media holdings, Tribune enterprises encompass the fields of energy, mining, trucking, paper, finance, and a major league baseball team. *Directory of Corporate Affiliations 1995* (New Providence, R.I.: Read Reference), 1696–1699.
12. Herbert H. Howard, "TV Station Group and Cross-Media Ownership: A 1995 Update," *Journalism Quarterly* 72 (Summer 1995): 390–401.
13. *Editor and Publisher International Yearbook, 1995* (New York: Editor and Publisher).
14. *Industry Survey*, Vol. 2 (New York: Standard and Poor's, 1994), M20.
15. Media critic Ben H. Bagdikian claims that quality deteriorates when papers are acquired by a chain. *The Media Monopoly*, 6–7, 84–89.
16. *New York Times*, December 31, 1995, 36.
17. Vincent J. Schodolski, "$19 Billion Betrothal," *Chicago Tribune*, August 1, 1995.
18. Lawrie Mifflin, "Cable TV Continues its Steady Drain on Network Viewers," *New York Times*, October 25, 1995.
19. Furthermore, nearly 79 million households owned video cassette recorders (VCRs) that permitted them to supplement over-the-air television fare. *Statistical Abstract of the United States, 1995*, 571.
20. Bagdikian, *The Media Monopoly*.
21. W. Lance Bennett and Timothy E. Cook, "Journalism Norms and News Construction: Rules for Representing Politics," *Political Communication*, special issue (Winter 1996); Robert M. Entman, "Newspaper Competition and First Amendment Ideals: Does Monopoly Matter?" *Journal of Communication* 35 (1985): 147–165; and Stephen Lacy, "The Effects of Intracity Competition on Daily Newspaper Content," *Journalism Quarterly* 64 (Summer/Autumn 1987): 281–290. For a contrary view see Bagdikian, *The Media Monopoly*.
22. Bennett and Cook, "Journalism Norms and News Construction."
23. For a discussion of journalists' political orientations and professional values, see Chapter 4.
24. Bill Kovach, "Big Deals with Journalism Thrown In," *New York Times*, August 3, 1995.
25. Gary A. Hale and Richard C. Vincent, "Locally Produced Programming on Independent Television Stations," *Journalism Quarterly* 63 (Autumn 1986): 562–568.
26. Krasnow, Longley, and Terry, *The Politics of Broadcast Regulation*, 284.
27. Peter H. Lewis, "Protests to Greet Communications Bill," *New York Times*, February 8, 1996.
28. Michael Arnott, "FCC Says TV Licenses Worth $35 Billion," *Chicago Tribune*, August 19, 1995.

29. *New York Times,* December 31, 1995, 36.
30. 47 U.S.C.A. §307(a), 1934.
31. Steven Morris, "FCC Denies WSNS-TV New Broadcast License," *Chicago Tribune,* September 20, 1990.
32. Many contradictory bills have been introduced in Congress to deal with news and public service programming requirements. Most of them die early in the game. *Congressional Quarterly Weekly Report* is an excellent source for tracking these legislative developments.
33. Edmund B. Lambeth, *Committed Journalism: An Ethic for the Profession* (Bloomington: Indiana University Press, 1986). See also Bruce A. Linton, "Self-Regulation in Broadcasting Revisited," *Journalism Quarterly* 64 (Summer/Autumn 1987): 483–490.
34. Joel Persky, "Self-Regulation of Broadcasting—Does it Exist?" *Journal of Communication* 27 (Spring 1977): 200–210.
35. *Media Week* 6(2) (January 8, 1996): 3.
36. *Office of Communication of the United Church of Christ v. FCC,* 359 F.2d 994 (D.C. Cir. 1966).
37. Krasnow, Longley, and Terry, *The Politics of Broadcast Regulation,* 54–62.
38. Ibid., 56–57.

Readings

Alger, Dean E. *The Media and Politics.* 2d ed. New York: Wadsworth, 1996.
Altschull, J. Herbert. *Agents of Power: The Media and Public Policy.* 2d ed. White Plains, N.Y.: Longman, 1996.
Bennett, W. Lance. *News: The Politics of Illusion.* White Plains, N.Y.: Longman, 1996.
Hoynes, William. *Public Television for Sale: Media, the Market and the Public Sphere.* Boulder, Colo.: Westview, 1994.
Krasnow, Erwin G., Lawrence D. Longley, and Herbert A. Terry. *The Politics of Broadcast Regulation.* 3d ed. New York: St. Martin's, 1982.
Parenti, Michael. *Inventing Reality: The Politics of the News Media.* 2d ed. New York: St. Martin's, 1993.
Snow, Marcellus S., ed. *Marketplace for Telecommunications: Regulation and Deregulation in Industrialized Democracies.* New York: Longman, 1986.
Tunstall, Jeremy. *Communications Deregulation: The Unleashing of America's Communications Industry.* London: Basil Blackwell, 1986.

Press Freedom and the Law

To SAFEGUARD AMERICAN DEMOCRACY the U.S. Constitution guarantees the freedom of the press from government control. What does press freedom mean in practice and how do constitutional guarantees affect what American mass media cover or neglect? When television anchor Dan Rather claimed that press freedom redounds to "the benefit of listeners and viewers and readers. The cause is America," was he correct?[1] Or has press freedom been the suit of armor that protects a powerful, privileged, and often arrogant press from taking responsibility for its frequent misbehaviors?

What press freedom has meant and should mean poses perplexing dilemmas for democratic societies. How can freedom of the press to report all news be reconciled with protection of society from the dangers of unrestrained publicity? How can an unfettered media establishment be kept responsive and responsible?

We will begin to answer these questions by probing the problems that arise when a free press claims the exclusive right to decide what to publish and, in the process, often clashes with demands by citizen groups for newspaper space and air time to publicize social and political causes. Then we will turn to difficulties the press faces in gaining access to information needed for a story when the government claims the right to conceal this information. Finally, we will examine barriers to publication that have been imposed by legislators and courts to safeguard private and public interests.

The First Amendment is the constitutional basis for press freedom in America. The amendment guarantees that "Congress shall make no law ... abridging the freedom of speech or of the press." This makes the press the only private enterprise in America that is granted a privileged status by the Constitution. The interpretations of the scope of this privilege, however, have fluctuated since the First Amendment was ratified in 1791, and similar clauses in state constitutions often have been construed in ways that differ from interpretations at the national level.[2]

America's Founders granted this special status to the press because they considered the right to express opinions and to collect and disseminate information free from government controls as the bedrock of a free society.[3] If restraints are needed to protect society from harmful publicity, they must come through the deterrent effects of fear of punishment after publication, not through "prior restraint." Publication can be prevented only if it "will surely result in direct, immediate, and irreparable damage to our nation or its people."[4] The belief in the political importance of a free press has stood the test of time and remains a cornerstone of American democracy. Therefore, anything that affects the interpretation or the scope of this basic right is a matter of major political significance.

Access to the Media

The notion of government "by the people" implies that the people have a right to make their voices heard. Practically speaking, this means that they must have access to the mass media to advocate their beliefs. Ralph Nader's consumer protection movement or the antismoking crusade that swept the country in the 1980s, to take two examples, never could have gathered widespread support without mass media publicity. Did the reformers have a *right* to mass media publicity for their views and for their organizing activities?

The answer is "no." In fact, it is difficult for most people, other than journalists or major public figures, to gain access to the media. In a book on the right of access to the mass media, Jerome Barron, a lawyer interested in civil liberties, accused journalists of fighting for broad rights of free expression for themselves while denying these same rights to the public.[5] Media personnel decide what stories to publicize and whose views to present, leaving many who want to proclaim their views without a suitable public forum.

Barron argued that the First Amendment right to publish freely should extend to all individuals and groups, not only to news professionals. If individuals have a special cause or think that mass media stories have been inaccurate or inadequate, they should have an opportunity to use the mass media to state their views. Without this right, they may be doomed to political ineffectiveness.

Non-Broadcast Media

What rights of access to the mass media do individuals in private and public life have? To answer this question accurately, a distinction must be made between non-broadcast and broadcast media. American courts usually have held that the freedom of the print media to determine what they will or will not print, and whose views they will present, is nearly absolute. The chances are good that interactive computer media, such as the Internet and the World Wide Web, will enjoy the same freedom, although this issue remains to be tested fully in the courts.[6] As long as non-broadcast media stay clear of deliberate libel and slander and do not publish top-secret information, their publishing decisions are unhampered by legal restraints. They may even publish false or misleading information.

The U.S. Supreme Court defined print press rights in the case of *Miami Herald Publishing Company v. Tornillo* (1974).[7] At issue was the constitutionality of a Florida statute that gave a right to immediate reply to candidates for public office who had been personally attacked by a newspaper. The rebuttal could match the format and placement of the attack. The law had been passed to deal with the problem of personal attacks published very late in a campaign, giving candidates little time to respond. The consequence might be loss of the election.

The case arose in 1972 when Patrick Tornillo, Jr., leader of the Dade County Teachers Union, was running for the Florida State Legislature. Just before the primary the *Miami Herald* published two editorials objecting to Tornillo's election because he had led a recent teachers' strike. Tornillo demanded that the paper print his replies to the editorials. The paper refused. After Tornillo lost the primary decisively, he brought suit against the paper.

In 1974 the case reached the U.S. Supreme Court, which ruled unanimously that newspapers can print or refuse to print anything they like. No one, including a candidate whose reputation has been damaged, has the right to obtain space in a newspaper. Therefore, the Florida right to reply statute was unconstitutional. The decision reaffirmed what had been the thrust of the law all along. Private citizens may request that a story or response to a personal attack be printed and that request may be granted, but they have no right to demand publication.[8]

Broadcast Media

The rules are different for the broadcast media, based on the now outdated view that limited spectrum space makes broadcast media semimonopolies. Unlike the print media business and interactive computer communications, which are open to anyone, entry into the broadcast media business requires a license from the government. In return for the privilege of broadcasting over the public airwaves, license holders are subject to government regulations. These include rules ensuring that the license holders respect the public's limited rights of access to the airways.

Based on Section 315 of the Communications Act of 1934 and its amendments and interpretations, the public's access rights to broadcast media fall under three categories: the *equal time provision,* the *fairness doctrine,* and the *right of rebuttal.* All of the regulations that mandate public access are subject to one important implicit condition: the rights arise only after a station has broadcast the information in question.

The Right to Equal Time. If a station gives or sells time to one candidate for a specific office, it must make the same opportunity available to all candidates for that office, including those with few backers. However, if the station refuses time to all candidates for the same office, none of them has a right to demand access under the campaign coverage provisions of Section 315. The rules exclude coverage provided through regular news programs and talk shows that have been specifically exempted.

Stations constrained by the all-or-none equal time rule often opt for "none," particularly for state and local offices and when many candidates are competing for the same office. This keeps many viable candidates off the air who might otherwise have gained exposure. But it saves stations from cluttering their programs with numerous campaign broadcasts that would be of little interest to their listeners and costly to the station in lost advertising revenues.

To make it possible to stage lengthy debates among mainline candidates for major offices without running afoul of the equal time provisions, Congress suspended these provisions in 1960 so that Kennedy and Nixon could debate. A different tactic was used in 1976 and 1980. To facilitate the Carter-Ford and Carter-Reagan debates, the FCC permitted them to be staged as public meetings, which could be covered by the news media like regular news, exempting them from the equal time rule. This was obviously a subterfuge to avoid the intent of the law.

Several minor party candidates, eager to be included in the debates, sued in 1976 claiming that this circumvention of equal time provisions was illegal. But the courts ruled against them. Finally, in November 1983, the FCC lifted its previous restraints, allowing radio and television broadcasters to stage political debates at all political levels among a limited array of candidates chosen in a nondiscriminatory way. Candidates who feel that they have been unfairly shut out may appeal to the FCC.[9]

The curbs on political dialogue other than debates remain and have led to widespread dissatisfaction with the equal time rule. They have blocked the public from receiving many important messages by current and prospective public officials. For instance, when President Ford set forth his farm policy in a speech to the Future Farmers of America during the 1976 campaign, the networks shied away from full-length coverage because it might involve them in an equal time allotment for the Democratic candidate. Normally, they would have broadcast a presidential speech outlining major policy proposals. Critics are also unhappy about public sanction of subterfuges to evade the rule such as allowing the League of Women Voters to sponsor debates so that the event can qualify as regular news. They believe the rule should be abandoned, rather than continuing the current practice of piecemeal legalized exceptions.

The Right to Fair Treatment. The fairness doctrine, which is currently in limbo, has had a broader reach than the equal time provision because it is not limited to candidates for political office. When the FCC abandoned the rule in the mid-1980s Congress passed a bill in the spring of 1987 to ensure its survival. President Reagan promptly vetoed the bill, arguing that, contrary to its intent to foster fairness, it had in fact resulted in "blandness" or "nothingness." Nonetheless, Congress has tried repeatedly to revive the rule, leaving its ultimate fate uncertain.

The fairness doctrine provided free air time for the presentation of issues of public concern and the expression of opposing views whenever a highly controversial public issue was discussed on television. Like the equal time provision, the fairness doctrine impoverished public debate by suppressing controversy, because the media frequently shied away from programs dealing with controversial public issues to avoid demands to air opposing views in place of regular revenue-producing programs. When controversial programs were aired, it was difficult to decide who, among many claimants for airtime, had the right to reply.

The media often bypassed fairness claims by including opposing views on controversial issues in their regular news programs. In general, the FCC and the courts sustained the media's contentions that these issues were aired fully in regular newscasts. The courts also have ruled against an automatic right to oppose statements made during presidential news conferences, as long as the media aired contrary views in news analyses immediately after the conferences.

The media always have retained control over the array of viewpoints that receive a hearing. Pressures and litigation, however, have made the media more receptive to featuring opposing views. It has become traditional to allow spokespersons for the opposition to offer rebuttals after presidential, gubernatorial, and mayoral messages covering major policy issues. The temper of the times has curbed editorial freedom, even though legal rights remain unchanged.

Is there a right of reply to contentious statements made in business commercials? The oil industry, conservationists, and the drug industry, among other groups, have used commercials to raise questions about controversial public policies. Commercial firms and public interest groups have asked for time to respond. The question about response rights arises because First Amendment protections do not extend automatically to commercial messages. In fact, free expression in such messages has been constrained severely through truth-in-advertising laws administered by the Federal Trade Commission. If the media must make time available to respond to commercial messages, must it be free of charge? The answer is unclear.

A landmark case in 1969 seemed to indicate that there was a right to reply to commercial messages. It concerned television advertisements for cigarettes before such commercials were banned from television. John W. Banzhaf III, then a young Manhattan lawyer and antismoking activist, accused the cigarette companies of promoting cigarette smoking as glamorous without mentioning its dangers. He demanded the right to present views opposed to smoking, which he characterized as a life-and-death public health issue. The networks countered that opposition to smoking had been presented adequately by commercials and publications from various health organizations. The Supreme Court sided with Banzhaf, concurring with the circuit court's decision that smoking involved such an extraordinarily important health issue that, contrary to usual rules, broadcasters must balance cigarette commercials with antismoking spots.[10]

This decision did not supply a yardstick to determine which issues are exceptional enough to warrant time for countercommercials. The case has turned out to be the exception rather than the rule. Subsequent requests for countercommercial time have been refused. The law remains unclear about the right to reply to commercial messages because the courts have spoken with forked tongues and media willingness to allow replies has been quite mixed.

The Right of Rebuttal. Individuals who are assailed on radio or television in a way that damages their reputations have the right of rebuttal. The landmark case *Red Lion Broadcasting Co. v. Federal Communications Commission* (1969)[11] established a rather broad scope for the right of reply. The case arose because a book about Barry Goldwater, a conservative senator, was attacked by the Rev. Billy James Hargis on a program conducted and paid for by the ultraconservative Christian Crusade. The book's author, Fred Cook, asked for rebuttal time, free of charge. The station was willing to sell him reply time but refused free time, disclaiming responsibility for the content of the programs prepared by private parties.

In the *Red Lion* case, to the delight of proponents of ready public access to the airwaves, the courts sided with the plaintiff. Cook was granted the right of rebuttal, at station expense, on the grounds that maligned individuals deserve a right to reply and that the public has a right to hear opposing views. The decision proved to be a hollow victory for supporters of free access, however, because stations fearful of rebuttal claims sharply curtailed air time available for controversial broadcasts.

The *Red Lion* case is also noteworthy as an example of political manipulation of the regulatory process. Cook's protest had been paid for and orchestrated by the Democratic National Committee as part of an effort to generate an avalanche of demands for rebuttals to conservative radio and television programs. The hope was that stations then would cancel these programs to avoid the costs of free rebuttal time.[12] This did, indeed, happen. By 1975 the Christian Crusade had been dropped by 300 of its 350 stations. Since 1969 the courts have retreated somewhat from their broad support for the right of rebuttal at station expense because of its chilling effects on controversial broadcasts. The flood of rebuttal requests also mired the FCC in a morass of claims and counterclaims that it could not process with its limited resources. Easing of the rules has been a boon to the many interactive radio and television talk show programs that have mushroomed in recent years.

Reform Proposals. To halt the deleterious effects on programming and the flood of FCC proceedings, strong demands have been voiced by members of Congress and many broadcasters and communication scholars to do away entirely with equal time and right of rebuttal provisions. The rationale is that broadcast media no longer are semimonopolies. In fact, print media, which are uncontrolled by government, face less competition in the age of one-newspaper towns than do broadcast media. Besides, the distinction between various types of media is becoming increasingly blurred because they use a mixture of technologies to disseminate their messages. Therefore, the argument goes, all media should be free from government interference in making publishing decisions.

Opponents of reform warn that removal of access protections will leave the public at the not-so-tender mercies of media gatekeepers. As Jerome Barron has lamented, "The myth says that if the press is kept 'free,' liberty of discussion is assured. But, in how few hands is left the exercise of 'freedom'!"[13] The vast influence of the electronic media on public perceptions requires safeguards stronger than ordinary market forces, others argue. If audience rights are paramount, as the *Red Lion* case affirms, should not the audience be protected from media unfairness and misjudgment?[14]

Problems of the Status Quo

Apart from the right to reply to a personal attack and the right of rival candidates to equal broadcast time, there are no access rights for individuals. Short of getting into the mass media business, there is no way to bring messages to public attention through the mass media if they are unwilling. Public television enjoys complete editorial freedom as well. A group of citizens had sued the Alabama Educational Television Commission and the University of Houston because they canceled the film "Death of a Princess" in response to protests by Saudi Arabia's royal family and threats of economic boycott. The citizens had charged unfair denial of their right of access to information and claimed that the cancelation constituted political censorship. The federal district court disagreed.[15]

Exclusive broadcast rights to major events increasingly are granted to a single network or station. This practice is another restraint on information dissemination. News outlets aside from the contract holder are precluded from covering the event.[16] Exclusive contracts have been negotiated even for public spectacles such as the rededication of the Statue of Liberty during its centennial. The television networks also have been very restrictive in allowing professionals outside their own organizations to air public information programs. In the same way, professional organizations frequently restrain the flow of news to the general public. For instance, when scientists discovered a treatment that could cut pneumonia deaths by AIDS patients by half, they felt constrained to withhold the news for five months until the *New England Journal of Medicine,* a highly regarded professional publication owned by the Massachusetts Medical Society, had first published their reports. The power of the journal to act as the gatekeeper for major medical news springs from the fact that scientists prize the prestige derived from publication of their work in the journal. If they violate journal rules by releasing data to the lay public prior to publication in a medical journal, their story may be rejected for publication.[17]

People in public office who want access to the mass media to explain their views face problems quite similar to those of private individuals. Although the media are likely to be more sympathetic to their requests, on many occasions coverage is denied. Several speeches by Presidents Nixon, Ford, Reagan, Bush, and Clinton were not broadcast at all because the media considered them partisan political statements or claimed that they contained nothing new. Others were carried by only a few stations, forcing the president to compete against regular broadcasts, reducing his audience sharply. On still other occasions broadcasts of presidential speeches have been deferred until late evening, denying the president access to prime-time audiences. Carter and Reagan tried to prevent such problems by tailoring their requests for media time to the needs of the media. In particular, they avoided schedule conflicts with major sports events.

The question of access rights to the airwaves also has been raised in connection with interest groups. Several groups have asked for more children's programs, even though they would be of little interest to the majority of adult listeners and viewers. The FCC has concurred that children constitute an important special audience whose needs for distinctive programming must be met. It has pressured stations to increase programming, often with a veiled threat that failure to oblige would lead to mandatory rules. Stations have been reluctant to add children's programs because revenues from them are comparatively low, particularly after the FCC reduced the amount of advertising permitted on children's programs. Curtailment of advertising was intended to spare immature viewers from the temptations offered by advertising.

Other audiences whose right of access to special programs has been recognized sporadically include African Americans, Hispanics, and lovers of classical music, to name a few. Occasional rulings have forced the electronic media to set aside time for broadcasts geared to such groups, whose needs might be ignored if the forces of the economic marketplace were allowed full rein. The FCC has further protected the interests of these groups by giving preference in license applications to stations whose output is likely to serve neglected clienteles. In light of the growing number of cable, television, and radio outlets, making access easier for everyone, government protection of special interest groups is declining. In 1981 the Supreme Court freed the FCC from any obligation to weigh the effects of alternative program formats on various population groups when making licensing decisions. The Court's ruling arose from a series of cases in which radio stations had changed their format, for instance, from all news to all music.[18]

Other Approaches to Media Access

Attempts to gain access to the mass media through independently produced programs, individual requests for air time, and FCC rulings that support the interest of minority audiences have been only moderately successful. Other routes to access are even less satisfactory. Letters to the editor and op-ed essays are examples. Due to lack of space, most papers publish few letters and opinion pieces. The *New York Times,* for instance, receives more than sixty thousand letters a year and publishes 4 to 5 percent of them, limiting length strictly. Even with these stringent controls, space devoted to letters equals space for editorials in the *Times*. Editors select the letters and op-ed essays to be published, using a variety of criteria that disadvantage those from average people. Messages that are unusual or are sent by someone well known are most likely to be printed.

Another avenue to access is the use of paid advertisements. Labor unions, business enterprises, lobby groups, and even foreign governments have placed advertisements on the air or in newspapers, such as the *New York Times* and *Wall Street Journal,* to present their side of disputes and public policy issues. Usually, only large companies, such as W. R. Grace and the Mobil Corporation, can afford the steep purchase price, which may run into thousands of dollars for full-page advertisements and national broadcast exposure. Even then print and electronic media occasionally have refused to print advertisements or sell air time when messages seemed to them too controversial — on topics such as the energy crisis and deficit spending, for example. Concern about the denial of advertising space has lessened in the wake of creation of the World Wide Web where space for home pages can be rented and used to disseminate messages to computer users around the world. However, access to these message systems remains limited largely to computer-savvy people.

When people who are eager to publicize their views cannot afford the high cost of paid messages, they may try to gain attention by creating a sensational event and inviting the media to witness it. A young Chinese dissident used the tactic in 1992 when he invited the media to watch his display of posters commemorating the brutal suppression of China's pro-democracy movement in Beijing's Tiananmen Square. The ensuing free publicity reached millions of people all over the world. Few publicity seekers meet with such success and many fail miserably, as happened to the man who invited the media to a self-immolation to protest unemployment in 1983. Camera crews filmed the action while the protester suffered life-threatening burns. The story received nationwide coverage, but the emphasis was on the callousness of the film crew that did not stop the burning. The unemployment issue was well-nigh ignored.[19]

The rise of lobby groups eager to ensure broad access rights to people with minority viewpoints, and the FCC's sympathy with their pleas, have made broadcasters more sensitive to pressures for access by political activists. But even if radio or television station management is willing to grant access to such people, especially when they have engaged in newsworthy activities, there still is the problem of insufficient time to air every claimant's views. Despite the multiplication of television and radio channels in the wake of technological advancements, there will never be enough channels or even newspaper pages to publicize all important views to large audiences. Even the creation of the World Wide Web does not guarantee everyone a hearing. Concerned citizens have neither the time nor the capacity to listen to all significant views and put them into proper perspective. In fact, the capacity to broadcast and publicize already far exceeds the audience's capacity to listen and assimilate. Studies of cable system users have shown that regardless of the number of channels available and the important stories that they may feature, the average viewer rarely taps more than six.

Access to Information

Access to information involves two major issues: *who* shall have access and *what* information must be open for public inspection.

Special Access for the Media?

The right to publish without restraint means little if information cannot be obtained. This raises questions about the media's right of access to places where they wish to gather information. Supreme Court decisions have denied that the media enjoy special rights in this regard. In *Zemel v. Rusk* (1965), for instance, the U.S. Supreme Court ruled that neither ordinary citizens nor media personnel have a right to gather information because a citizen's right to speak and publish does not entail an unrestrained right to gather information.[20] A similar ruling was handed down in *Branzburg v. Hayes* (1972), a case involving a journalist's right to refuse testimony before a grand jury because he wanted to protect his sources. "It has generally been held," noted the Court, "that the First Amendment does not guarantee the press a constitutional right of special access to information not available to the public generally."[21] The press had argued that its surveillance of the political scene on behalf of the public entitled it to special rights of access.

Without special access rights, journalists can be barred from many politically crucial events, thus depriving the public of important, albeit sensitive, information. Closed White House and State Department meetings provide examples. The media often are excluded from pretrial hearings and grand jury proceedings that determine the sufficiency of evidence of wrongdoing to justify indictments. Because grand jury proceedings frequently involve high political stakes, news about them repeatedly has been leaked to newspeople by participants. The press also has no right to attend conferences of the Supreme Court at which the justices reveal why they decided to hear certain cases and refused to hear others. Media people may be barred from attending sessions of legislative bodies closed to the general public. Such sessions ordinarily deal with secret information that may require protection or with matters that might prove embarrassing to legislators.

Newspeople have no right to be admitted to sites of crimes and disasters when the general public is excluded. Nor do they have the right to visit prisons and interview and film inmates, even for the purpose of investigating prison conditions and rumors of brutality. In many cases in which access has been denied, the Supreme Court has stressed that reporters could get the information they needed without special access privileges.[22] This may indicate that the Court is willing to grant access in situations in which information about prison conditions is totally lacking.

Many of the Supreme Court's decisions in the early 1970s regarding access to information were highly controversial, as shown by 5 to 4 divisions in *Branzburg v. Hayes* (1972), *Pell v. Procunier* (1974), and *Saxbe v. Washington Post Co.* (1974).[23] This clash of views among the justices has made media access rights a fluid and exciting area of legal development. A great deal of pressure also has been exerted on Congress to pass legislation that would clear up some of the uncertainties. Advocates of broadened access rights have been especially vocal.

By custom, although not by law, newspeople often receive preferred treatment in gaining entry to public events. Press passes ensure media access to the best observation points for inaugurations of chief executives, space shuttle landings, and political conventions. In many instances the media are admitted to the scene of events, such as accidents and crimes, while the general public is kept out. Access, however, is purely at the discretion of the public authorities in charge.

In wartime military officials often bar news personnel from combat zones. They keep them out by denying transportation to these areas or, as happened in Grenada in October 1983, by keeping invasion plans secret. Initial news accounts of American forces' invasion of this tiny Caribbean island were vague and often contradictory because the administration had banned the press. Two days after the invasion, fifteen reporters were allowed to visit for a few hours under strict military supervision. On subsequent days two larger groups followed. Press restrictions remained in force for a full week. The situation was the same during the buildup to the Persian Gulf War in 1990–1991 and during the war itself. Despite press protests and a suit filed by news outlets against President Bush and the Department of Defense (DOD) the government effectively throttled free access to news. Such news blackouts clearly exemplify denial of access to news without any legal recourse. Following the Gulf War the DOD issued new regulations to ease media access in similar future situations. Past experience suggests that the regulations will make little difference.

Access to Government Documents

Government documents are another extremely important source of political information to which access frequently is obstructed. The Freedom of Information Act, signed by President Lyndon B. Johnson on July 4, 1966, and amended in 1974 to make the act more enforceable, ostensibly opened many government files to the news media and the general public.[24] Burdensome application requirements and the costs of duplicating information, however, have limited its usefulness for news personnel. In recent years, the intricacies of scanning computerized records that were programmed in unfamiliar ways have raised additional access hurdles. Nonetheless, the act has led to important disclosures such as CIA involvement in political affairs in Chile and Cuba; illegal financial dealings by members of Congress; and the failure of government to protect the public from unsafe nuclear reactors, contaminated drinking water, and ineffective drugs. Most reporters, however, are content to cover readily available current news rather than use the Freedom of Information Act to dig into government files to unearth past misdeeds.

The act has been used by organized crime and narcotics traffickers to spot threats to their activities and by business firms to spy on competitors. To cope with these and other abuses, the act was amended again in 1986. Fees charged to businesses for information were raised to cover the full costs of inquiries. Fees were lowered for media enterprises to encourage their search for information. Although most of the changes garnered widespread approval, some First Amendment champions criticized provisions that broadened the right of government agencies to refuse requests for information.[25]

General Rules. Many types of public documents remain unavailable to reporters despite the pervasiveness of freedom of information laws at all levels of government. Most laws provide for access to *public records,* but political jurisdictions define *public records* differently. Laws obviously constitute a public record, but are citizens entitled to inspect the minutes of the meetings that preceded passage of a law, or tapes of the proceedings, or exhibits that a legislative committee considered before passing the law? In many states the term *public record* does not encompass any information about the genesis of laws and regulations.

Computerization of governmental records is raising many new issues about access. There is no common policy at either the federal or state level that specifies how computerized government information is to be disseminated. The courts have acknowledged that information stored in government computers constitutes a public record, but they have yet to decide definitively what access rights exist. For example, do journalists have the right to ask for specific data within a database, or does such a request entail the creation of a new "record" that public agencies are not required to supply? Must government agencies facilitate computer access by installing user-friendly programs? The *Congressional Record,* for example, could not be searched effectively until full text-searching facilities were developed. What about data stored in now obsolete files that current personnel cannot retrieve? It will take many years to find satisfactory answers to such questions and to develop reasonably uniform policies.

Applicants for information often must demonstrate a special need for a particular set of data. A journalist or private citizen cannot go into a record center and request to examine all records on public health matters or public housing or road repairs. Exactly what is wanted must be specified, which is difficult to do without knowing what is available. The kinds of need that must be demonstrated and the degree of specificity of information requests are determined by administrators.

A widely used rule of thumb about access to information is that disclosure must be in the public interest and must not do excessive harm. Access should be denied if the harm caused by opening records is greater than the possible benefit. Accordingly, a reporter's request for the records of welfare clients for a story on welfare cheating probably would be denied because it is embarrassing to many people to have others know that they need public assistance. Because there are no precise guidelines for determining what is in the public interest and what degree of harm is excessive, the judgments of public officials who control documents are supreme.

Many state legislatures are unwilling to leave access policies to the discretion of administrative officials. Therefore, they construct detailed lists of the kinds of records that may or may not be disclosed. That approach is unsatisfactory, too, because legislators cannot possibly foresee all types of records that may be kept. Release of records then may be forestalled simply because they are not mentioned specifically in the legislation.

Certain types of documents are barred routinely from disclosure. For example, examination questions and answers for various tests given by government agencies usually are placed beyond public scrutiny. If they were published, the value of these examinations might be totally destroyed. However, if the fairness and appropriateness of examination questions for public jobs are in doubt, public scrutiny of questions and answers might be beneficial. Favoritism in grading exams of the protégés of the powerful is a common abuse that also is difficult to expose without access to graded exams.

Other data frequently kept from media personnel are business records that could give advantage to competitors, such as bids for government contracts. Because corruption is common in awarding government contracts, reporters often are very interested in what has been bid or what promises have been made in return for contract awards. Without access to the records, investigative reporting of suspected fraud or corruption is impossible. However, secrecy is warranted because publicizing the details of a bid could give an unfair advantage to another firm to underbid the lowest bidder by a few dollars and clinch the contract.

Clearly, some restraints on access are essential to protect individuals, especially now when access to computerized government information can make the average citizen's life an open book with deleterious consequences for the exposed individual. Yet restraints may make betrayals of the public trust easier. The cloak of secrecy may conceal vast areas of corruption. Finding the right balance between protection of individuals and protection of the interests of the public through media access is an extremely difficult and controversial task.

Historical and National Security Documents. Access to the official and private records of major public officials is limited. They are usually unavailable to the media and the general public until twenty-five years after the death of the public official. The lengthy limit was selected to spare possible embarrassment to people whose private and public lives were entangled with that of the official.[26] When exceptions are made to the twenty-five year rule they frequently are contested in court. Former president Richard Nixon unsuccessfully sued to recover control of many of his records about the Watergate affair that had been released to the media.

The closure of the private records of public officials is part of the privacy protection afforded to all individuals, but it serves a public purpose as well. For uninhibited discussion in policy making, assurance of confidentiality is essential. Without it, people will posture for an audience rather than freely address themselves to the substance of the issues that are under consideration. The danger of inhibiting free discussion also explains why deliberations prior to legislative or judicial decisions are generally closed to public scrutiny.

Documents concerning matters of national security usually cannot be published. Examples are CIA intelligence data and information about prospective negotiations or sensitive past negotiations. News about specific new weapons adopted by the United States or stories indicating that security devices are not operating properly may be restricted also. In some cases, however, such information is available in open files and can be pieced together into a coherent story. This is how a Wisconsin magazine, *The Progressive,* was able to piece together and publish directions for making a hydrogen bomb. Government efforts to stop the publication of this kind of story have been unsuccessful in recent years, except when prohibitions about publication were a matter of law. In 1982, for instance, it became a crime to publish the names of covert intelligence agents, even when they were taken from public documents.

Of course, most instances of security censorship never reach the lawsuit stage, leaving an enormous number of documents concealed from the public. The National Archives estimated that they have 300 million to 400 million classified documents dating from the World War I era to the mid-1950s. That is a tiny fraction of the total body of classified information. More than 1 million documents are labeled as *classified* annually. Many more are placed beyond easy access because they contain information taken from previously classified documents. Added to these staggering statistics at the federal level are massive numbers of documents withheld by state and local officials.[27]

The most difficult aspect of security censorship is the determination of what information is truly sensitive and must be protected and what information should remain open to media personnel and the public. The media and, to a lesser degree, Congress have been trying to expand the range of information that is made available for publication. The president and executive agencies, charged with protecting national security, have bent over backward to protect information that might compromise security.

A graphic illustration of this perennial battle is the *Pentagon Papers* case. Daniel Ellsberg, a former aide to the president's National Security Council, claimed that foreign policy information contained in a DOD study of America's gradual entrapment in the Vietnam War had been classified improperly as top secret. Its release, he thought, would turn people against the war. He copied the information surreptitiously and gave it to prominent newspapers for publication. Because the war was still in progress, the executive branch considered this a criminal breach of security and sued Ellsberg and the media that printed the information.

In *New York Times Co. v. United States* (1971), the Supreme Court absolved the media, ruling that the government had been overly cautious in classifying the information as top secret.[28] In the Court's view publication did not harm the country. The government's case against Ellsberg for leaking the information was dismissed also because prosecutors had collected evidence through illegal means. Although the case cleared Ellsberg and the media of the specific charges brought against them, it left the government's contention unchallenged that officials may be prosecuted for jeopardizing national security by disclosing classified information to the press. Accordingly, Samuel Loring Morison, a naval intelligence analyst, was convicted in 1985 on espionage charges for providing a British military magazine with intelligence satellite photographs.[29]

The Supreme Court decision in the *Pentagon Papers* case and subsequent lower court rulings did not end the public controversy. Analysts still disagree about whether the disclosures from the *Pentagon Papers* damaged national security of the United States. Those who concur with the Court point out that much of the information released had been available already. Dissenters counter that the information had never been compiled in a single document and published in prominent sources such as the *New York Times* and *Washington Post*. They also refer to the dismay expressed by many European leaders about spotlighting events that they had deemed confidential.

Prior to the Nixon years, if a government agency decided that certain information needed to be kept from the media, the courts usually went along with the decision on the assumption that the agencies charged with guarding national security are infinitely better qualified to assess such matters than are judges whose training is narrowly legal. This has changed. Wise decisions about disclosure of national security information are particularly difficult because both the clamor of the media to obtain access and the government's contention that the information requires protection are often self-serving. What is dubbed "the public interest" may be simply the reporters' interest in furthering their careers, or the publishers' interest in making money, or the government's interest in shielding itself from embarrassment.

At times, security issues are resolved through informal cooperation between the government and the media or through self-censorship. For instance, during the 1979 Iranian hostage crisis, six American hostages were sheltered in the Canadian embassy in Teheran for several weeks. Prominent news organizations, such as NBC, CBS, *Time, Newsweek,* and the *New York Times,* were privy to this information. Following requests from the White House and State Department, they decided to withhold the news to protect the hostages, even though it meant foregoing an excellent story. The story surfaced early in 1980, after the six hostages had been smuggled out of Iran.[30] In a similar way, media have refrained from providing the public with details in a number of kidnapping incidents when news stories could have jeopardized delicate negotiations between kidnappers and the would-be rescuers of the victims. Information about these instances is hard to obtain because neither the media nor the government want to publicize their collaborative efforts to suppress news. If the information leaks out, it is often denied by all the collaborators.

Executive Privilege. The doctrine of executive privilege is deeply intertwined with the question of the limits of secrecy. Chief executives have the right to conceal information that they consider sensitive. This privilege extends to all of their personal communications to their staffs about public matters. Prior to the Nixon years the courts usually upheld executive privilege, but decisions since then suggest that the scope of the privilege is waning.

Silence by various government departments and agencies also sharply restricts political news available to the media. Undisclosed information frequently concerns failures, incidents of malfeasance, malfunctions, or government waste. Agencies guard this type of news zealously because disclosure might harm the agency or its key personnel. Chief executives at all levels of government often issue directives restraining top officials from talking freely to journalists. In March 1983 President Reagan even ordered lie detector tests for officials to check compliance with disclosure rules. In the face of opposition, the directive was later rescinded. Although not usually enforceable, directives that muzzle public officials tend to reduce the flow of information to the press and the public.

Except for the ever-present opportunity to get information through leaks, reporters find it difficult to penetrate the walls of silence erected by publicity-shy agencies. It is far easier to rely on press handouts or publicity releases supplied by the agency or on secondary reports from agency personnel. Handout information, however, usually reflects the sources' sense of what is news rather than the reporters' sense of what is news.[31]

Private Industry Documents

Although the problem of government secrecy as a restraint on information collection is formidable, it is small compared with the problem of access to news stories covering the private sector of society. Many enterprises whose operations affect the lives of millions of Americans as much as or more than many government agencies shroud their operations in secrecy. If asbestos companies or major tobacco companies want to exclude reporters from access to information about their business practices, they can do so with impunity. So can drug companies, repair shops, or housing contractors.

The Freedom of Information Act does not cover unpublished records of private businesses, except for the reports made to the government about sales or inventory figures or customer lists. As noted earlier, many of these reports are withheld from the public on the ground that business cannot thrive if its operational data are made available to its competitors. Moreover, the chances that withheld information will be disclosed through leaks are infinitely less in business than in government. Employees can be pledged to secrecy as a condition of employment and summarily dismissed if they break their vow.

Individual Rights Versus the Public's Right to Know

Thus far we have mainly considered barriers to the free flow of information imposed by the mass media to protect editorial freedom or by government or industry to shield potentially sensitive information. Next we will discuss barriers to circulation of information imposed by individuals or on behalf of individuals for the purpose of protecting the right to privacy, the right to an unprejudiced trial, the right to gather information freely, and the right to a good reputation.

Privacy Protection

How much may the media publish about the private affairs of people in public and private life without infringing on the constitutionally protected right of privacy? How much is excluded from public scrutiny because of privacy rights? The answers depend on the status of the people involved. Private individuals enjoy broad, though shrinking, protections from publicity; people who have become public figures because their lives are of interest to the public or because they are public officials do not enjoy such protections.

In general, state and federal courts have been fairly lenient in permitting the media to cover details about the personal affairs of people whose lives have become matters of public record. The right to publish has been upheld more often than the right to privacy. This trend is epitomized by a 1975 Georgia case involving a young woman who had been raped and murdered. To protect their privacy, the family wanted to keep the victim's name out of stories discussing the crime. The news media did not honor the family's request and published gruesome details of the crime and named the victim. The family sued for invasion of privacy, claiming that there was absolutely no need to disclose the name and that Georgia law prohibited the release of the names of rape victims. The U.S. Supreme Court disagreed and overturned the Georgia law. It held that crime was a matter of public record, making the facts surrounding it publishable despite protests by victims and their families.[32]

Circumstances may turn private individuals into public figures. This happened to Oliver Sipple, a young man in a crowd of people watching a public appearance by President Ford. Sipple prevented an assassination attempt on the president by grabbing the would-be assassin's gun. When newspeople checked his background they discovered that he was homosexual. Although this had nothing to do with his action in protecting the president, it was publicized and caused Sipple great personal difficulties. He brought suit for invasion of privacy, but the courts denied his claim, saying that he had forfeited his right to privacy and become an "involuntary public figure" by seizing the gun.

Individuals also may lose their right to privacy when they grant interviews to reporters. Once the interview is given, reporters are free to round the story out with observations that were not part of the interview but the journalists feel are "newsworthy." They are also free to publish those facts that were told to them in confidence, though they usually honor their pledge of keeping an interviewee's name confidential.[33] If reporters, without malice, misrepresent some of the facts, this, too, is tolerated. The rationale is that the public is entitled to a full story, if it gets any story at all, and that reporting should not be unduly inhibited by fears of privacy invasion suits.

Many privacy invasion cases involve unauthorized photographs of people in public life. Jacqueline Kennedy Onassis, the widow of President Kennedy, sued one particularly obnoxious photographer for taking photographs of her private life. The court ruled that even though she was no longer the first lady, she remained a public figure. Therefore, pictures could be taken and printed without her consent. The court, however, ordered the photographer to stop harassing her.[34] The courts have also permitted reporters to keep the homes of relatives of murder suspects under photographic surveillance and to film police officers during compromising sting operations.

To strengthen privacy protection, the courts in recent years have permitted subjects of unsolicited investigative reports to use trespass laws to stop the media. An example is the trespassing judgment won by the fashionable restaurant, *Le Mistral,* against CBS after reporters had entered the premises and filmed a story showing violations of New York's health code.[35] The courts also have been increasingly willing to protect people against willful inflictions of emotional pain by news media. However, the Supreme Court ruled unanimously in 1988, in a case brought by the Rev. Jerry Falwell against *Hustler* magazine publisher Larry Flynt, that the work of satirists and cartoonists enjoyed full First Amendment protection.[36] Falwell's plea for privacy protection and for compensation for emotional injury was denied.

Because relatively few cases of invasion of privacy are taken to the courts for decision, privacy protection rests primarily on news media sensitivity. In recent years, it has not been finely honed. Even mainstream newspapers now feature columns devoted to celebrity gossip, and tabloid papers and television shows of the same genre revel in this type of journalism. When *USA Today* informed former tennis star Arthur Ashe in 1992 that it was investigating rumors that he was infected with HIV/AIDS, Ashe knew that the story was destined to become front page news. Efforts to protect his privacy would be futile. Therefore, he chose to make a public announcement about his illness himself. Many journalists and members of the public condemned *USA Today* for the privacy invasion. But most agreed that in the current news climate it has become impossible to protect newsworthy individuals from the "feeding frenzy" of print and electronic tabloid journalists. Once the proverbial cat is out of the bag, all join the chase, including serious news professionals who do not want to ignore stories that draw large audiences.[37] Efforts by several states to prohibit privacy invasion when the news lacks "social value" are currently under judicial scrutiny to determine whether they violate the First Amendment.[38]

Fair Trial and the Gag Rule

The courts favor a broad scope of disclosure for most people in public life, but they insist on a limited scope of disclosure in their own bailiwick. The courts have guarded the right of accused persons to be protected zealously against publicity that might influence judge and jury and harm their cases. This has been true even though scientific evidence demonstrating that media publicity actually influences the parties to a trial is scant and contradictory.[39]

The stern posture of the courts in censoring pretrial publicity is weakening, however. In 1983 two Supreme Court justices refused to block a nationwide television broadcast about a sensational murder case scheduled for trial three weeks later. The trial involved seven white New Orleans police officers accused of the revenge slaying of four African American men suspected of participation in the murder of a white police officer. In the same vein, a federal court refused in 1983 to prevent television stations from showing tapes of a cocaine transaction incriminating John DeLorean, a well-known automobile maker and jet-set celebrity. DeLorean's attorneys had argued that the pretrial publicity would make it impossible to impanel an impartial jury. In another case the courts ruled that incriminating tapes used in a corruption trial of several members of Congress could be shown publicly, even though some of the defendants had not been tried as yet and the convicted defendants were appealing the case.[40] When prominent national political figures have asked to have their trials moved out of Washington because of prejudicial pretrial publicity, their requests almost invariably have been refused.[41]

The question of the permissible scope of media coverage of court cases was brought to wide public attention by two murder cases, *Shepherd v. Florida* (1951) and *Sheppard v. Maxwell* (1966).[42] In these cases the Court held that the defendants, convicted of murder, had not had a fair trial because of widespread media publicity. As Justices Robert H. Jackson and Felix Frankfurter put it in *Shepherd v. Florida,* "The trial was but a legal gesture to register a verdict already dictated by the press and the public opinion [it] generated."[43] The convictions therefore were overturned.

Judges have the right to prohibit the mass media from covering some or all of a court case before and during a trial, even when the public is allowed to attend courtroom sessions. Gag orders interfere with the media's ability to report on the fairness of judicial proceedings. They also run counter to the general reluctance of American courts to condone prior censorship. Nonetheless, the courts have upheld gag laws as a necessary protection for accused persons. As discussed in Chapter 10, judges may make rules restraining filmed coverage or may bar it completely without presenting evidence that the information covered by the gag order would impede a fair trial. Gag orders may extend even to judges' rulings that tell the media to refrain from covering a case. Thus the fact of judicial suppression of information may itself be hidden.

Numerous reporters have gone to jail and paid fines rather than obey gag rules because they felt that the courts were overly protective of the rights of criminal suspects and insufficiently concerned with the public's right to know. A 1976 decision, *Nebraska Press Association v. Stuart,* partly supports the reporters' views.[44] In that case the Supreme Court reversed a gag order in a murder trial. The Court declared that careless reporting that interferes with the rights of defendants should be forestalled by judicial maneuvers other than gag laws. For instance, trials can be moved to different jurisdictions if there has been excessive publicity locally. Suits also can be brought against media enterprises or individual reporters who act irresponsibly, such as publicizing testimony from closed sessions of the courts, taking unauthorized pictures, or bribing court personnel to leak trial testimony.

The policy on gag laws is still unclear, however. Some lower courts have failed to comply with Supreme Court directives or have evaded the spirit of decisions. For example, instead of gagging the press, judges have placed gags on all the principals in a case, including the plaintiffs and defendants, their lawyers, and the jury, to prohibit them from talking about the case, particularly to members of the press. In an increasing number of cases, judges have barred access to information by closing courtrooms to all observers during pretrial proceedings as well as trials. However, this has not stopped legal personnel, including prosecutors, from leaking information to the press when that seems advantageous.

During the 1980s, the Supreme Court struck down a number of these restrictions or limited their use by specifying the circumstances under which media access may be denied. In *Richmond Newspapers v. Virginia* (1980), the Court ruled that the public and the press had an almost absolute right to attend criminal trials.[45] In the same vein the justices declared in 1984 that neither newspeople nor the public may be barred from observing jury selection, except in unusual circumstances.[46] The Supreme Court appears to be moving closer to the notion that the public's access to judicial proceedings is part of the First Amendment rights guaranteed by the Constitution. However, a change in direction is possible following adverse public reaction to televising the murder trial of O. J. Simpson as if it were a soap opera serial.

Shield Laws

Digging into the affairs of public officials and other prominent citizens or exposing the activities of criminals or dissidents often requires winning the confidence of informants with promises to conceal their identities. Newspeople are hampered in their research if a court or legislative body has the right to know the identity of their sources, to examine unpublished bits of information, and to issue subpoenas for them. If reporters disclose such information, they break their word. Their sources are likely to dry up, whether these sources are public officials who have leaked confidential information or underworld informers.

However, failure to disclose information may allow criminals to go unpunished and innocent victims to be denied justice. This is why media organizations at times agree to comply with subpoenas fully or partially. For instance, the networks in 1985 agreed to surrender portions of unused film scenes from the hijacking of a TWA airliner that they deemed relevant for the prosecution of the hijackers.[47] In 1992, seven local television stations, the *Los Angeles Times,* and a *New York Times* photographer received federal grand jury subpoenas for unpublished pictures of crimes committed during the Los Angeles riots. They were expected to refuse; however, they were willing to surrender pictures that had been published already.[48] The use of subpoenas to compel testimony from news organizations has been increasing steadily. A 1993 survey of 900 news organizations by the Reporters Committee for Freedom of the Press showed that 52 percent of the organizations had received subpoenas at one time.[49]

Shield laws that protect reporters against inquiries have become particularly urgent whenever law enforcement agencies find it difficult to penetrate dissident and deviant groups. At such times these agencies are tempted to use subpoenas to compel testimony from journalists, making them unwilling agents of the government. Shield laws are needed also to protect the physical safety of sources who disclose the activities of organized criminals or terrorists.

The Supreme Court has ruled that newspeople, like ordinary citizens, generally do not have the right to protect their sources in the face of a subpoena. They have no special right to be warned about a court-approved search of their premises to uncover evidence that might reveal their sources and the information provided by them.[50] Nor may they shield records or editorial deliberations from judicial scrutiny if these records are needed to prove deliberate libel. However, if the needed information is available from unshielded sources, the judges often have excused journalists from disclosure.[51]

Recognizing the ill effects of these common law-based compulsory disclosure rules on investigative reporting of crime and corruption, more than half of the states have passed shield laws to protect reporters from forced testimony. Shield laws give journalists most of the rights enjoyed by lawyers, doctors, and clergy to shield their sources' identity and information. Shield laws also may bar searches of news offices to discover leads to crimes. The Privacy Protection Act of 1980 prohibits government authorities at all levels from conducting surprise searches of newsrooms, except in a few, clearly specified situations.[52]

Shield laws usually do not ensure absolute protection. For example, when the right of reporters to withhold the names of their sources clashes with the right of other individuals to conduct a lawsuit involving serious matters (such as gathering evidence for a murder or conspiracy trial or a libel suit), state shield laws and common law protections must yield. In 1983 the Maryland Supreme Court ruled that Loretta Tofani, a *Washington Post* reporter, must testify about prisoners in a suburban jail who had told her about committing rape and being rape victims. The reporter's articles had won a Pulitzer Prize.[53] Likewise, CBS News was required to give Gen. William Westmoreland the text of its in-house investigation of a 1982 television documentary that had allegedly libeled the general. The documentary on the Vietnam War had charged Westmoreland with falsifying enemy troop figures. In his libel suit Westmoreland contended that producers of the documentary had deliberately omitted information that exonerated him. The U.S. District Court in New York City rejected the network's contention that its in-house report was protected by First Amendment guarantees; the network had referred in court to findings contained in the report.[54]

Some journalists advocate a federal shield law to protect all newspeople throughout the country and to reduce the costs of litigation when they resist forced disclosure. Others, fearing that such a law would provide conditional shielding only, prefer to do without shield laws of any kind; they contend that the First Amendment constitutes an absolute shield. These differences of opinion have taken steam out of the pressure for a federal shield law.[55] Members of the judiciary also deny that shield laws are needed, but for different reasons. In the words of Justice Byron R. White, "From the beginning of our country, the press has operated without constitutional protection for press informants and the press has flourished." Hence absence of shield laws has "not been a serious obstacle to either the development or retention of confidential news sources by the press."[56]

Libel Laws

Libel laws are designed to provide redress when a person's reputation has been tarnished unjustly by published information. To win a libel suit, a plaintiff must prove that the defendant's negligence or recklessness led to publishing information that exposed the plaintiff to hatred, ridicule, or contempt. For years libel suits, even when they were lost in court, had a dampening effect on investigative reporting. That changed substantially in 1964 for cases involving public officials. An action for libel was brought by the police chief of Montgomery, Alabama. An advertisement in the *New York Times* had charged him with mishandling civil rights demonstrations. The Supreme Court absolved the newspaper, ruling in *New York Times v. Sullivan* that a public official who claims libel must be able to show that the libelous information was published "with knowledge that it was false or with reckless disregard of whether it was false or not."[57]

The *Sullivan rule* has made it very difficult for public officials to bring suit for libelous statements made about them. Malicious intent and extraordinary carelessness are hard to prove, especially because the courts give the media the benefit of the doubt. By the same token, the Sullivan rule has made it much easier for media to publish adverse information about public officials without extensive checking of the accuracy of the information prior to its publication.

Since its 1974 decision in *Gertz v. Robert Welch,* the Supreme Court has applied more restrictive interpretations of the meaning of *public figure.*[58] In that case the Court held that a prominent lawyer, whose name had been widely reported in the news, was not a public figure and therefore could sue for libel. A person who had not deliberately sought publicity, the Court ruled, would be deemed a public figure only in exceptional circumstances. What these circumstances are remains unclear.[59]

The battle between freedom of the press and the right of individuals to be protected from harmful publicity is full of confusing developments.[60] The courts have pulled back from the position that individual rights, except the right to a fair trial, are largely subordinate. They have done so by distinguishing the rights of private individuals from those of

By permission of Chip Bok and Creators Syndicate.

public figures and by construing the category of *public figures* more narrowly. This leaves private individuals with substantial rights to bar the media from publishing potentially libelous or embarrassing facts, so long as those facts are not a matter of public record. Whether libel suits may be brought to challenge expressions of opinions remains controversial after the Supreme Court ruled that opinions could be libelous if proof of their falsity was possible.[61]

By and large, laws and court decisions protecting private individuals have not greatly benefited people in public life. The principle that full publicity for the activities of public officials and institutions is essential has been reaffirmed repeatedly, most recently in the *Hustler v. Falwell* case, which strongly reaffirmed the Sullivan rule.[62] The Supreme Court has even discouraged libel suits by public figures by requiring that such suits be dismissed by the federal courts before trial if the evidence fails to suggest libel with "convincing clarity."[63] The best protection for public figures from unscrupulous exposure by the media is the informal and formal codes of ethics by which most journalists generally abide. The increasing number of suits by public figures against media people also have become a damper on careless reporting because these suits are costly in time and money, even when the media are exonerated. The emergence of the Internet has raised several new issues in libel law that remain to be settled. Most importantly, who bears responsibility when libels are published? Early decisions suggest that access providers, such as America OnLine or Compuserve, are not responsible for screening messages for libel.

The Libel Defense Resource Center, which tracks libel law, reported in 1991 that average libel awards in 1989 and 1990 ran just under $4.5 million. That was a tenfold increase over the average figures for the 1987 to 1988 period, when juries often failed to impose heavy fines. The Center estimated that 90 percent of all libel actions are dropped, settled, or dismissed prior to trial. Even without trials the cost to news organizations is enormous. When trials *do* occur, news organizations are the losers in two thirds of the cases. Individual judgments have run as high as $58 million awarded in a 1991 case against a Texas broadcast company, but such judgments have been routinely reduced sharply on appeal. Nonetheless, financially weak institutions cannot afford to risk multi–million-dollar judgments against them that would force them out of business.[64]

Other Restrictions on Publication

As discussed in Chapter 1, all governments prohibit the publication of certain information on the ground that the public interest would be harmed. The United States is no exception. Censorship is most prevalent in matters of national security involving external dangers, national security involving internal dangers, and obscenity. In each category there is general agreement that certain types of information should not be publicized. There is very little agreement, however, about where the line ought to be drawn between permitted and prohibited types of material. We have already discussed the controversy surrounding the release of the *Pentagon Papers* as well as the government's efforts to prohibit publication of a magazine article detailing, on the basis of available but dispersed information, how a hydrogen bomb might be manufactured. Additional examples involving external security will be presented in Chapter 11.

Internal security news primarily entails investigations of allegedly subversive groups and reports on civil disturbances. Several relevant cases are discussed in Chapter 5. Such news also involves media portrayal of asocial behavior that might lead to imitation. Various attempts to limit the portrayal of crime and violence, either in general or on programs to which children have access, are examples. They are discussed in Chapter 7.

Closely related to restraints on the depiction of crime and violence are restraints on publication of indecent and obscene materials and broadcasts that include offensive language or portray sexual matters or human excretion. It is feared that such broadcasts may corrupt members of the audience, particularly children, and lead to imitation of undesirable behavior. Although reports of the Presidential Commission on Obscenity and Pornography have cast doubt on the claim that such broadcasts are socially dangerous, many foes of obscenity and "dirty" words remain unconvinced.

In addition, proponents of obscenity restraints argue that publication of indecent and obscene materials, particularly in visual form, offends community standards and therefore should be prohibited by law. This argument rests on the notion that the public, as represented generally by self-selected spokespersons and organized protest groups, should have the right to prohibit the dissemination of material that offends the sense of propriety of many citizens. Despite the popularity of pornography, as shown by the millions of citizens who read pornographic magazines, go to pornographic movies and stage shows, and rent pornographic videos, laws in many places bar free access to such information. The FCC requires that indecent programming be featured only between midnight and 6:00 A.M., when children are unlikely to be watching television. Obscene programming is barred at all times. Indecent material has been defined by the FCC as "material that depicts or describes, in terms patently offensive by contemporary community standards for the broadcast medium, sexual or excretory activities or organs." Obscenity has been defined by the Supreme Court as "something that, taken as a whole, appeals to the prurient interest; that depicts or describes in a patently offensive way sexual conduct; and that lacks serious artistic, political and scientific value."[65] The Telecommunications Act of 1996 outlawed transmission over computer networks of sexually explicit and other indecent materials to minors under 18. The Supreme Court has repeatedly upheld these types of restrictions. Nonetheless, the prohibitions in the 1996 Act face numerous constitutional challenges as well as major enforcement problems.

Another example of protective censorship is the ban since 1971 on cigarette advertising on radio and television. It is designed to protect susceptible individuals from being lured into smoking by seductive advertisements. Pressures for additional areas of protective censorship have been considerable and range from pleas to stop liquor, sugared cereal, and casino gambling advertisements to requests to bar information dealing with abortion or drug addiction. Legislatures and courts have rejected most of them except when advertising on children's programs was involved. But the future is unclear. Some of these matters have become election issues. If candidates have committed themselves to censoring abortion or drug information, for example, they may be compelled to follow through on their promises by working for appropriate laws while in office.

So-called "hate" broadcasters also remain a gray area in broadcast law, which has achieved new prominence because hate messages abound on the Internet and World Wide Web. Contrary to the expressed public policy of the nation, many small over-the-air and cable stations or individual programs routinely attack racial, ethnic, and religious groups. As with broadcasts with obscene language, these attacks violate the sense of propriety of many citizens. Nevertheless, the FCC has been reluctant to withhold licenses from the offending parties because genuine freedom of expression includes "freedom for the thought we hate," as Supreme Court Justice Oliver Wendell Holmes said long ago.

The case of KTTL-FM, a small country-music station in Dodge City, Kansas, illustrates the dilemma. The station has attacked African Americans, Asians, Roman Catholics, Jews, public officials, the courts, and the Internal Revenue Service. It has suggested hanging public officials, "cleansing the earth" of "black beasts," and preparing militarily for an impending racial Armageddon. But despite protests to the FCC from Kansas lawmakers and members of the public, KTTL-FM's license is unlikely to be revoked as long as no actual violence can be linked to its broadcasts.[66] Although formal restraints remain few, informal restraints have mushroomed. Television and radio stations have disciplined or dismissed reporters and commentators who made comments offensive to groups such as African Americans, women, and homosexuals.

Summary

In a democratic society citizens have the right and civic duty to inform themselves and to express their views publicly. The press, as the eyes and ears of the public, shares these rights and must be protected against restraints that could interfere with its ability to gather information and disseminate it freely. In this chapter we have seen how these important basic principles have been modified to meet the realities of political life in the United States. Despite legislation such as the Freedom of Information Act of 1966, a great deal of information about government activities remains unpublished. Either it has been classified as secret for security reasons or it is not released to the public because it could embarrass individuals or lead to undesirable business practices. The public and press also are excluded from many executive sessions of legislatures, grand jury sessions, pretrial proceedings in the courts, and other official meetings if the participants so desire.

Nearly all of these exclusions have been challenged in the courts because they constitute restrictions on the right of access to information that may deserve publication. The courts have ruled that most of them are compatible with constitutional guarantees of free speech and press. They also have ruled, for the most part, that news professionals enjoy neither greater rights of access to information than does the general public nor, in the absence of shield laws, greater freedom to protect their access to information by refusal to disclose their sources.

The right to publish information is also limited. Here the public is most seriously restricted because newspeople claim the exclusive right to determine what to publicize and what to omit. The power of print media to refuse a forum to most citizens is nearly absolute, aside from social pressures mandating that stories of widely recognized public concern be published. Under current rules and regulations television must grant equal access to the air to political candidates for the same office. Although put to rest for the time being, the fairness rule requiring exposure of opposition views remains a lively ghost that may well rise again. The right of rebuttal is likely to share the fate of the fairness rule—either death is in the cards or a reincarnation in the form of congressional legislation.

Even when access to a media forum is ensured, the right to publish is not absolute. News has been suppressed because of public policy considerations, such as the need to safeguard external and internal security and the need to protect the moral standards of the community. The scope of permissible censorship has been the subject of countless inconclusive debates and conflicting decisions by the courts.

The right to publish also conflicts on many occasions with the rights of individuals to enjoy their privacy, to be protected from disclosure of damaging information, true or false, and to be safeguarded from publicity that might interfere with a fair trial. The courts have been the main forum for weighing these conflicting claims, and the scales have tipped erratically from case to case. Two trends stand out from the haze of legal battles: the right to a fair trial generally wins out over the freedom to publish, and private individuals enjoy far greater protection from publicity than do people in public life. Shifting definitions of what turns a private person into a public person have blurred this distinction, however.

When one looks at the massive restraints on the rights of access to information, the rights of access to publication channels, and the right to publish information freely, one may feel deep concern about freedom of information. Is there cause for worry? Taking a bright view, one can point out, as Justice White did in the 1972 *Branzburg* case, "the press has flourished. The existing constitutional rules have not been a serious obstacle" stopping the press from investigating wrongdoing.[67] The press as watchdog may be chilled by legal restraints, but it is not frozen into inaction. From the perspective of champions of First Amendment rights, that may be small comfort. Many current political and judicial trends, including the 1996 Telecommunications Act that is the new basic law for public communication, point toward greater restraints and greater public tolerance for restraints, especially when social and national security are involved. Constant vigilance is the price that will have to be paid to preserve the heritage of freedom of thought and expression.

Notes

1. Quoted in Lucas A. Powe, Jr., *The Fourth Estate and the Constitution: Freedom of the Press in America* (Los Angeles: University of California Press, 1991), 289.
2. Robert F. Copple, "The Dynamics of Expression under the State Constitution," *Journalism Quarterly* 64 (Spring 1987): 106–113.
3. For an analysis of how well these rights have been used, see Doris A. Graber, "Press Freedom and the General Welfare," *Political Science Quarterly* 101 (Summer 1986): 257–275.
4. Justice Potter Stewart in *New York Times v. United States,* 403 U.S. 713 (1971).
5. Jerome Barron, *Freedom of the Press for Whom? The Right of Access to the Mass Media* (Bloomington: Indiana University Press, 1973).
6. The courts have treated cable television as a common carrier and therefore free from broadcast content regulations.
7. 418 U.S. 241 (1974).
8. For a full discussion of the case, see Fred W. Friendly, *The Good Guys, the Bad Guys and the First Amendment: Free Speech vs. Fairness in Broadcasting* (New York: Random House, 1977), 192–198.
9. Phil Gailey, "F.C.C. Lets Broadcasters Hold Political Debates," *New York Times,* November 9, 1983.
10. *Banzhaf v. Federal Communications Commission,* 405 F.2d 1082 (D.C. Cir. 1968), *cert. denied,* 396 U.S. 842 (1969).
11. 395 U.S. 367 (1969).
12. Friendly, *The Good Guys,* 32–42.
13. Barron, *Freedom of the Press for Whom,* 5.
14. For a discussion of these issues, see Jonathan W. Emord, *Freedom, Technology, and the First Amendment* (San Francisco: Pacific Research Institute for Public Policy, 1991); Hugh Carter Donahue, *The Battle to Control Broadcast News: Who Owns the First Amendment?* (Cambridge, Mass.: MIT Press, 1989).
15. *Muir v. Alabama Educational Television Commission,* 688 F.2d 1033 (5th Cir. 1982). First Amendment problems encountered when governments own media are discussed by William Hanks and Lemuel Schofield, "Limitations on the State as Editor in State-Owned Broadcast Stations," *Journalism Quarterly* 63 (Winter 1986): 797–801. The right of public broadcasters to editorial-

ize was upheld in *League of Women Voters v. FCC,* 731 F.2d 995 (D.C. Cir. 1984).

16. Paula J. Lobo, "First Amendment Implications of Exclusive Broadcast Contracts," *Journalism Quarterly* 60 (Spring 1983): 41–47.

17. "AIDS Panel Delayed News of Treatment," *New York Times,* November 14, 1990.

18. *FCC v. WNCN Listeners Guild,* 450 U.S. 582 (1981).

19. W. Lance Bennett, Lynne A. Gressett, and William Haltom, "Repairing the News: A Case Study of the News Paradigm," *Journal of Communication* 35 (Spring 1985): 50–68.

20. *Zemel v. Rusk,* 381 U.S. 1 (1965). See also Louis A. Day, "Broadcaster Liability for Access Denial," *Journalism Quarterly* 60 (Summer 1983): 246–261.

21. *Branzburg v. Hayes,* 408 U.S. 665 (1972).

22. See, for instance, *Pell v. Procunier,* 417 U.S. 817 (1974); *Saxbe v. Washington Post Co.,* 417 U.S. 843 (1974); and *Houchins v. KQED,* 438 U.S. 1 (1978).

23. These and related cases are discussed more fully in John J. Watkins, "Newsgathering and the First Amendment," *Journalism Quarterly* 53 (Autumn 1976): 406–416. For more recent cases see T. Barton Carter, Marc A. Franklin, and Jay B. Wright, *The First Amendment and the Fourth Estate,* 6th ed. (Westbury, N.Y.: Foundation Press, 1996).

24. The act was an amendment to the 1946 Administrative Procedure Act—5 U.S.C.A. 1002 (1946)—which provided that official records should be open to people who could demonstrate a "need to know" except for "information held confidential for good cause found" (Sec. 22). The 1966 amendment stated that disclosure should be the general rule, rather than the exception, with the burden on government to justify the withholding of a document (5 U.S.C.A. Sec. 552 and Supp. 1, February 1975).

25. Linda Greenhouse, "Agencies Get New Power to Withhold Investigative Reports," *New York Times,* October 29, 1986.

26. Douglas Jehl, "Clinton Revamps Policy on Secrecy of U.S. Documents," *New York Times,* April 18, 1995.

27. Neil A. Lewis, "New Policy on Declassifying Secrets Is Debated," *New York Times,* January 4, 1994.

28. 403 U.S. 713 (1971).

29. Stuart Taylor, Jr., "Federal Judge Rules Espionage Laws Apply to Disclosures to Press," *New York Times,* March 15, 1985; *United States v. Morison,* 844 F.2d 1057 (4th Cir.), *cert. denied,* 488 U.S. 908 (1988).

30. Deirdre Carmody, "Some News Groups Knew of 6 in Hiding," *New York Times,* January 31, 1980. Also see Doris A. Graber, *Public Sector Communication: How Organizations Manage Information* (Washington, D.C.: CQ Press, 1992), 49–61.

31. Judy Van Slyke Turk, "Information Subsidies and Media Content: A Study of Public Relations Influence on the News," *Journalism Monographs* 100 (December 1986): 1–29; Donald Gillmor et al., *Mass Communication Law: Cases and Comment,* 5th ed. (St. Paul, Minn.: West, 1990), 307–310. For comparative views of government secrecy, see Itzhak Galnoor, ed., *Government Secrecy in Democracies* (New York: Harper and Row, 1977). Also see Graber, *Public Sector Communication,* 49–61.

32. *Cox Broadcasting Corp. v. Cohn,* 420 U.S. 469 (1975).

33. *Cohen v. Cowles Media Co.,* 501 U.S. 663 (1991). Also see Linda Greenhouse, "Justices Rule Press Can Be Sued for Divulging a Source's Identity," *New York Times,* June 25, 1991.

34. *Gallella v. Onassis,* 487 F.2d 986 (2d Cir. 1973).
35. *Le Mistral Inc. v. Columbia Broadcasting System,* 402 N.Y.S.2d 815 (1978).
36. *Hustler v. Falwell,* 485 U.S. 46 (1988). See also Robert E. Drechsel, "Mass Media Liability for Intentionally Inflicted Emotional Distress," *Journalism Quarterly* 62 (Spring 1985): 95–99.
37. Alex S. Jones, "News Media Torn Two Ways in Debate on Privacy," *New York Times,* April 30, 1992.
38. Linda Greenhouse, "National Enquirer Forces Trial on Invasion-of-Privacy Issue," *New York Times,* December 5, 1995.
39. Judges presumably can command jurors to strike improper information presented in court from their memory but disclaim the ability to wipe out media information that jury members might have received outside the courtroom.
40. See, for example, *U.S. v. Alexandro,* 675 F.2d 34 (2d Cir.), *cert. denied,* 459 U.S. 835 (1982); *U.S. v. Jannotti,* 673 F.2d 578 (3d Cir.), *cert. denied,* 457 U.S. 1106 (1982); *U.S. v. Myers,* 692 F.2d 823 (2d Cir. 1982); *U.S. v. Williams,* 705 F.2d 603 (2d Cir. 1983); and *U.S. v. Kelly,* 707 F.2d 1460 (D.C. Cir. 1983).
41. An example is Michael K. Deaver, a Reagan White House aide indicted for perjury. In his request for a change of venue, he presented the court with 471 hostile news clips from Washington, D.C. papers. Philip Shenon, "Like Others in the Past, Deaver Says Fair Trial Isn't Possible in Capital," *New York Times,* April 22, 1987.
42. 341 U.S. 50 (1951) and 384 U.S. 333 (1966).
43. 341 U.S. 50 (1951), at 69.
44. 427 U.S. 539 (1976).
45. 448 U.S. 555 (1980). The implications for the right of access are discussed in Roy V. Leeper, "*Richmond Newspapers, Inc. v. Virginia* and the Emerging Right of Access," *Journalism Quarterly* 61 (Autumn 1984): 615–622. Subsequent cases are discussed in Ann L. Plamondon, "Recent Developments in Law of Access," *Journalism Quarterly* 63 (Spring 1986): 61–68.
46. Glen Elsasser, "High Court Curbs Secret Jury Selection," *Chicago Tribune,* January 19, 1984. The controversy arose because the Riverside County, California, Superior Court closed jury selection in a rape and murder case. The Press-Enterprise Company of Riverside sued to gain access to the court proceeding and to the relevant transcripts.
47. Alex S. Jones, "CBS Compromises on Subpoena for Videotapes of Hostage Crisis," *New York Times,* July 27, 1985.
48. "Tapes and Photos of Riots Are Focus of Legal Struggle," *New York Times,* May 22, 1992.
49. William Glaberson, "Press," *New York Times,* March 27, 1995.
50. *Zurcher v. The Stanford Daily,* 436 U.S. 547 (1978).
51. *Anthony Herbert v. Barry Lando and the Columbia Broadcasting System Inc.,* 441 U.S. 153 (1979).
52. The impact of the law is discussed in Tony Atwater, "Newsroom Searches: Is 'Probable Cause' Still in Effect Despite New Law?" *Journalism Quarterly* 60 (Spring 1983): 4–9.
53. *Tofani v. State of Maryland,* 297 Md. 165 (1983).
54. "Westmoreland/CBS Controversy," *Historic Documents of 1983* (Washington, D.C.: Congressional Quarterly, 1984), 401–412. See also *Westmoreland v. CBS, Inc.,* 596 F. Supp. 7170 (S.D.N.Y. 1984).

55. Jonathan Friendly, "Prosecutors Increase Efforts to Make Press Name Sources," *New York Times,* November 26, 1983.
56. *Branzburg v. Hayes,* 408 U.S. at 699.
57. 376 U.S. 254, at 279–280 (1964).
58. 418 U.S. 323 (1974).
59. *Time Inc. v. Firestone,* 424 U.S. 448 (1976); *Hutchinson v. Proxmire,* 443 U.S. 111 (1979); *Wolston v. Reader's Digest,* 443 U.S. 157 (1979). Also see Robert L. Hughes, "Rationalizing Libel Law in the Wake of *Gertz:* The Problem and a Proposal," *Journalism Quarterly* 60 (Autumn 1985): 541–542.
60. On fact/opinion distinctions, see Harry W. Stonecipher and Don Sneed, "Libel and the Opinion Writer: The Fact-Opinion Distinction," *Journalism Quarterly* 64 (Summer–Autumn 1987): 491–498. The problem of proving damages is discussed in David A. Anderson, "Presumed Harm: An Item for the Unfinished Agenda of *Times v. Sullivan,*" *Journalism Quarterly* 62 (Spring 1985): 24–30.
61. Hughes, "Rationalizing Libel Law"; Linda Greenhouse, "Ruling in Libel Case, High Court Says Some Opinion Isn't Protected," *New York Times,* June 22, 1990.
62. *Hustler v. Falwell,* 485 U.S. 46 (1988).
63. *Anderson v. Liberty Lobby,* 477 U.S. 242 (1986). Also see *Bose Corporation v. Consumers Union of United States,* 466 U.S. 485 (1984).
64. Alex S. Jones, "Libel Study Finds Juries Penalizing News Media," *New York Times,* September 26, 1991, and Glaberson, "Press."
65. *Miller v. California,* 413 U.S. 5, at 15 (1973). Definition quoted in Irvin Molutsky, "F.C.C. Rules on Indecent Programming," *New York Times,* November 25, 1987.
66. Reginald Stuart, "F.C.C. Bars Penalty on Racism on Air," *New York Times,* April 29, 1985; Joseph A. Kirby, "The Right to Offend," *Chicago Tribune,* June 9, 1996.
67. *Branzburg v. Hayes,* 408 U.S. at 699.

Readings

Bittner, John R. *Law and Regulation of Electronic Media.* 2d ed. Englewood Cliffs, N.J.: Prentice Hall, 1994.
Branscomb, Anne Wells. *Who Owns Information: From Privacy to Public Access.* New York: Basic Books, 1994.
Carter, T. Barton, Marc A. Franklin, and Jay B. Wright. *The First Amendment and the Fourth Estate: The Law of Mass Media.* Westbury, N.Y.: Foundation Press, 1996.
Duncan, George T., Thomas B. Jabine, and Virginia A. de Wolf. *Private Lives and Public Policies: Confidentiality and Accessibility of Government Statistics.* Washington, D.C.: National Academy Press, 1993.
Garry, Patrick M. *Scrambling for Protection: The New Media and the First Amendment.* Pittsburgh: University of Pittsburgh Press, 1994.
Martin, Shannon E. *Bits, Bytes, and Big Brother: Federal Information Control in the Technological Age.* Westport, Conn.: Praeger, 1995.

Powe, Lucas A., Jr. *The Fourth Estate and the Constitution: Freedom of the Press in America.* Los Angeles: University of California Press, 1991.

Teeter, Dwight L., and Don R. LeDuc. *Law of Mass Communications: Freedom and Control of Print and Broadcast Media.* 8th ed. Westbury, N.Y.: Foundation Press, 1995.

chapter   four

News Making and News Reporting Routines

WHY ARE SOME EVENTS CHOSEN FOR EXTENSIVE nationwide coverage whereas others that seem as politically significant or even more so are slighted? What explains the uniformity of story types in America's print and electronic media? What stories should the media cover and how should they cover them?

This chapter focuses on how routine news is usually selected and reported. The discussion of news making during various types of crises is left to the next chapter. Speaking about news "making" does not mean that journalists concoct the stories they report. It does mean that they decide which of a myriad of events happening in a particular time period will be brought to public attention. The way they present these events determines the nature of the finished news product. It is, therefore, a manufactured creation and *not* a natural growth that journalists merely harvest.

No magical quality makes something "news." What is publishable in one setting for one medium is not necessarily appropriate for another. Newsworthiness of individual stories will vary from country to country, audience to audience, and time to time. Thus in 1903, when Orville and Wilbur Wright invited the press to Kitty Hawk, North Carolina, to cover their attempts to fly an airplane, not a single reporter came. Only seven American newspapers considered the first controlled and sustained flight newsworthy enough to print stories about it, and only two papers gave the feat front-page play. Now, nearly a century later, all facets of aviation fascinate the public. Flocks of reporters came to see a lone pilot, using human foot power, pedal above the English Channel in a lightweight aircraft called the *Gossamer Albatross*. The story received worldwide press and television coverage.

Profile Sketch of American Journalists

What determines journalistic choices and thus shapes the flow of news and entertainment? The question can be answered from three perspectives. *Personality theory* explains professional behavior in terms of personality and social background factors. *Organization theory* focuses on the impact of organizational goals and pressures on the behavior of members of news production organizations. *Role theory* maintains that depending on the professional role conceptions that media personnel adopt, their stories will vary. For instance, journalists who see themselves as impartial reporters of the news will behave differently from those who see themselves as partisan reformers.

Background and Personality Factors

Factors known to influence occupational performance include social background and traits that are idiosyncratic to particular individuals. Examples of background factors are level of education, race, and gender. Their precise impact on professional orientations remains a matter of heated scientific and political controversy. Idiosyncratic factors, which include artistic tastes, emotional outlook, and intellectual interests, explain why newspeople who have similar backgrounds will nonetheless prefer different stories or will give a different emphasis to the same news story or entertainment plot. Personality factors and organizational logic intertwine, with the latter setting the broad boundaries of what is acceptable news.

What are some of the personality and background factors that influence the substance and shape of news? Data collected by G. Cleveland Wilhoit and David H. Weaver for their study *The American Journalist in the 1990's* are helpful in answering this question. Other studies support these authors' findings, which are based on telephone interviews with 1,410 randomly selected newspeople in the United States working for 574 diverse daily and weekly newspapers, radio and television stations, and news services and magazines.[1]

Wilhoit and Weaver found that the social profile of newspeople resembled the profile of other professionals in the United States. Of the participants in their study, 92 percent were white, 66 percent were male, 54 percent were Protestant, and 82 percent had graduated from college.

Education appears to be the single most important background characteristic that shapes newspeople's general philosophy of reporting: 61 percent
had not majored in journalism, though many had taken some journalism
courses. People with more schooling are likely to be more liberal and have
a keener sense of social responsibility.[2]

At the time of Wilhoit and Weaver's poll in 1992, journalists were
more Democratic and less Republican than the general population. Of
the participants, 41 percent claimed to be Democrats, compared to 34
percent of the public; 16 percent called themselves Republicans, compared to 33 percent of the public; and 34 percent considered themselves
Independents, compared to 31 percent of the general population. The
political orientations of media personnel are reflected in the overall tone
of stories selected. Economic and social liberalism prevails, especially in
the most prominent media organizations, as does a preference for an
internationalist foreign policy, caution about military intervention, and
some suspicion about the ethics of established large institutions, particularly big business and big government. However, in deference to the
greater conservatism of media audiences, reporters restrain their liberalism somewhat.[3] Media personnel also treat the major parties fairly in most
election campaign coverage. Such evenhandedness is encouraged by
anticipation of scrutiny and criticism on that score. Media bias has rarely
been investigated outside the election context. Hence the extent to which
biased reporting based on party preferences is a problem in American
media is not fully known.[4]

Minority journalists and women have a different profile. For example, African American, Hispanic, and Asian journalists are more likely to
be women. Among Hispanics, Catholicism is the prevailing religion. Even
though the proportion of non-white journalists has risen, the proportion
of women has remained steady at roughly one third of the total. It is lowest in the wire services and television and highest in weekly newspapers
and news magazines. By contrast, non-whites have their highest representation in radio and television and their lowest representation in weekly
newspapers. Minorities and women are much more likely to call themselves Democrats than are white journalists and less likely to claim to be
Independents. Overall, non-white journalists constitute a little more than
8 percent of the journalism workforce at a time when non-whites represent 25 percent of the population. If demographically distinct groups are
uniquely qualified to assess their own needs, then racial, ethnic, and gender underrepresentation in the media is undesirable.

What effect do demographic characteristics have on the news product? The evidence is inconclusive, making it debatable whether adequate
coverage of the nation's problems requires media organizations that are a

microcosm of the larger society. For example, women do report more frequently on social issues of special concern to women, but they are no
more inclined than male reporters to quote females.[5] Most general media
emphasize established white middle-class groups and values and neglect
minorities and poor people and their concerns. They also stress urban
rather than rural affairs and focus heavily on male-dominated sports.
These patterns suggest either that news output reflects reporters' backgrounds and interests or that the patterns cater to the tastes of the kinds
of audiences that advertisers find most attractive.[6] In either case,
reporters' unique life experiences are important in shaping their stories.
It matters what personal contacts they are able to make. Washington-based
reporters, for instance, use friendships with well-connected government
officials to get important scoops. But, as a result of close personal ties with
these officials, they are apt to become captives of their sources' perspectives on the world.

Organizational Factors

Colleagues and settings strongly influence newspeople. Every news
organization has its own internal power structure that develops from the
interaction of owners, journalists, news sources, audiences, advertisers,
and government authorities. In most news organizations today, the internal power structure is slightly left of middle America yet predominantly
supportive of the basic tenets of the current political and social system.

When asked how much freedom they believed they had in choosing
the stories they reported, 44 percent of the respondents in the Wilhoit-
Weaver study reported that they had "almost complete freedom." This is a
significantly smaller percentage than the 60 percent who felt they enjoyed
wide discretion twenty-one years earlier. There was an even sharper drop
in the percentage of reporters who said they had "almost complete freedom" to decide which aspects of a story should be emphasized—76 percent in 1971 compared with 51 percent in 1992. When asked how much
editing their stories received, 23 percent said "none at all," a drop of 9
percentage points since 1971. Overall, it is clear that reporters feel
increasingly controlled by their news organizations. When others in the
news organization exercise such control, it often involves politically crucial matters and tends to condition reporters to stick closely to organizational norms.[7]

The feeling of shrinking reportorial autonomy was also reflected in
reporters' responses to an open-ended question about what they consider
to be "the most significant limits" on their "freedom as a journalist."
Roughly half of the respondents listed internal organizational constraints,

such as time and space limits, inadequate staffing, and, to a lesser degree, editorial control. The respondents also complained about the corrosive effects of stressing profits over quality and limiting travel in order to keep expenses low. One third cited external constraints from government officials unwilling to release information, hostile publics who fail to cooperate with members of the press and resent their probing, and pressure from advertisers who want news that attracts their potential clients. Only 8 percent mentioned professional standards, such as ethics, good taste, and objectivity as concerns.[8]

Organizational pressures begin to operate even before the job starts. Most people join news organizations and remain with them only if they share the organization's basic philosophy. To win approval from their colleagues, professional recognition, and advancement, reporters learn quickly which types of stories are acceptable and which are likely to be squelched—and they learn to react in ways that maximize receptiveness. Relationships with colleagues are particularly important within large, prominent news enterprises in which newspeople receive their main social and professional support from coworkers rather than from the community at large. The opposite holds true in small towns, in which newspeople often interact freely with community leaders and receive their support.

Which news media are used most widely by journalists when they select and write their stories? By and large, they are elite newspapers, such as the *New York Times,* the *Wall Street Journal, USA Today,* and the *Washington Post;* major news magazines such as *Newsweek, Time,* and *U.S. News & World Report;* and major magazines such as *National Geographic* and *Sports Illustrated.* Television, both local and national, is valued much less highly as an information source by members of the media. The most relied on media are located along the northeastern seaboard. This distribution supports the frequently heard claim that American journalism is intellectually dominated by a small slice of the Eastern press, which accounts for roughly 8 percent of the news profession. These *generative* media produce the news that *derivative* media distribute. The generative media are staffed by elite journalists whose social perspectives are left-liberal in contrast to the views characterized as "middle American."[9] Heavy reliance by newspeople throughout the country on eastern elite news sources fosters nationwide similarity in patterns of American news coverage. Regardless of regional and local differences that shape social and political views, Americans share most of their news. This provides a basis for nationwide public opinions that bear, to a marked degree, the imprint of the pacesetter media.

Despite the substantial evidence of media influence on American politics, most newspeople deny that they should be concerned about the impact of their stories. As self-appointed watchdogs of government and other social institutions journalists insist routinely and appropriately that government and business must take responsibility for the intended and unintended consequences of their actions. Yet they reject responsibility for the consequences of their work even while claiming to subscribe to social responsibility journalism. Journalists commonly argue that journalism is a craft and not a profession. Practitioners, they claim, are little more than conveyors of bits of information created by others for which these others are solely responsible.

Role Models

Although editors and reporters take many cues about story importance and interpretation from the Eastern elite media, they shape their basic news policies according to their own views about the role that media should play in society. The effects of the social responsibility role compared with libertarian stances have already been considered (see Chapter 1). News products also vary depending on whether newspeople see themselves largely as objective observers who must present facts and diverse views voiced by others or as interpreters who must supply meanings and evaluations. There are major differences on that score among reporters in Western democracies and among proponents of traditional and *civic* or *public* journalism.[10] The advocates of civic journalism believe that reporters must tailor the news so that it informs citizens about important happenings known to be of concern to them and helps them to take collective action to resolve problems.[11] Beyond turning reporters into interpreters of what the news means or should mean, it also turns them consciously into participants in the political process. Although this may be laudable in many instances, it sacrifices their role as the public's watchdog on guard against misbehavior by government officials.

Journalists' perceptions of the proper roles of reporters and media obviously shape news and are politically significant. Table 4-1 presents journalists' answers to questions about the importance of various journalistic roles. It shows that journalists, irrespective of the demographic differences noted earlier, take a broad view of their responsibilities. The watchdog role is designed as their primary obligation. Despite the general perception that reporters have transformed themselves from watchdogs to vicious attack dogs, fewer than one in four rates attacks on the government or on the bastions of capitalism as a high priority. In general, when one looks at various groupings, print journalists and African American and Asian journalists put the highest value on the adversary role.

TABLE 4-1   Roles Deemed "Extremely Important" by Journalists

Role	Percentage
Getting information quickly to the public	69
Investigating government claims	67
Analyzing complex problems	48
Being an adversary of government	21
Reaching widest audience	20
Being an adversary of business	14

SOURCE: Compiled from G. Cleveland Wilhoit and David H. Weaver, Preliminary Report, 1992, 10–14.

Readers who live in large cities or subscribe to out-of-town papers often can select the papers with the type of focus they want. They may choose a paper like the *Wall Street Journal,* which tailors its news to the tastes of business people, or like the *New York Times,* which emphasizes broad general coverage. In Chicago, citizens can subscribe to the conservative *Tribune,* the sensational *Sun Times,* or more specialized papers such as the *Herald,* which serves the southern part of the metropolitan area, or the *Defender,* which caters to African Americans. Most people, however, cannot pick and choose news sources representing particular role models so easily. They have only a single print source readily available and a few radio and television stations. They are, therefore, limited to the role models represented by these sources.

Gatekeeping

A small number of journalists have final control over story choices. They are often called "gatekeepers." Included are wire service and other reporters who initially choose stories, the editors who assign the reporters and accept or reject what they submit, disc jockeys at radio stations who present five-minute news breaks, and television program executives. In general, fewer than twenty-five people within a large organization are involved in the final decision of what news is used. On the three major networks the combined total editorial personnel responsible for choosing news number fewer than fifty people.

These few, particularly those who make news choices for nationwide audiences, wield a tremendous amount of political power because their choices determine what will be widely available as "news." This is why in public opinion polls that rank the political influence of various American institutions, the news media routinely rank among the top ten. When pollsters asked a national sample of Americans which telephone call the president should answer first if a topnotch editor, business leader, church figure, and educational leader called simultaneously, most chose the newspaper editor.[12] As we saw in Chapter 1, news stories influence what issues ordinary people as well as political elites will think about. Of course, media gatekeepers are not entirely free in their story choices. Coverage of major events, such as wars, assassinations, and airline hijackings, is almost mandatory. Other events can be included or omitted at will, within the limits set by news conventions. On an average evening somewhat more than half of the stories on each major television network represent unique choices. The figures are slightly lower for print media.[13]

Gatekeepers also select the sources through whose eyes the public views the world. As Table 4-2 shows, government officials are the main source of most political stories reported by the wire services and national and local media. This gives public officials an excellent chance to influence the slant of the news. However, when highly controversial issues are at stake, gatekeepers usually turn to unofficial sources as well.[14] Table 4-2 also shows that private individuals rarely are sources either domestically or abroad.[15] Basing the news on a narrow spectrum of sources can lead to biased reporting. Reporters may give widest publicity to the views of "celebrity" authorities in tangentially related fields and ignore important specialists. Reporters' choices of sources have led to one-sided presentations in stories about genetic engineering (recombinant DNA) research, the swine-flu vaccination program, and the development of an artificial heart.[16]

A study of sources used for stories about welfare reform, consumer issues, the environment, and nuclear energy concluded that journalists favor sources that reflect their own inclinations.

> On welfare reform, liberal sources predominate over conservative ones. On consumer issues they look to Ralph Nader, the public interest movement, and liberal activist groups. On pollution and the environment, they select activist environmental groups and, once again, liberal leaders. On nuclear energy, anti-nuclear sources are the most popular.... Journalists by no means depend exclusively on liberal viewpoints. They cite a mixture of public and private, partisan and nonpartisan, liberal and conservative sources. But the liberal side consistently outweighs the conservative.[17]

Sources who have gained recognition as "experts" through media publicity tend to be used over and over again. Newspeople may neglect other, less publicized sources.

When a variety of media cover the same story, as happens routinely, they often use sources representing different elites. When that happens, the thrust of the story may vary widely even though the underlying facts

TABLE 4-2   Sources of Front-Page News Stories (in percentages)

Source	Times/Post staff stories	Local press staff stories	Wire services staff stories	Total stories
Government officials	56	54	60	56
U.S.	34	14	38	28
State	7	17	6	10
Local	5	17	4	9
Foreign	10	6	12	9
Group-linked person	25	34	18	25
Private person	4	6	4	5
Foreign person	4	5	8	7
Other	11	1	10	7

SOURCE: Author's research.

NOTE: Based on content analysis of news stories attributed to staff or wire services writers and published in the *New York Times, Washington Post,* and *Chicago Tribune* from 1994 to 1995. *N* = 2,362 for *Times/Post* stories, 801 for *Chicago Tribune* stories, and 2,032 for wire service stories, for a total of 5,195 stories. "Group-linked" persons are identified as members of a group but are not necessarily official spokespersons for the group.

are the same. For example, when researchers looked at 167 stories about a major stock market crash in 1987, they found that the causes and effects of the crash were assessed in quite diverse fashion by the "CBS Evening News," *Newsweek,* the *New York Times,* and the *Wall Street Journal.* The three print media had relied most heavily on experts from the financial sector as primary sources, drawing 38, 52, and 65 percent of their sources, respectively, from this sector. Government sources and academics took second and third place but were used far less frequently. For CBS, government sources came first, followed by business sector and financial sector sources. CBS was also unique in drawing heavily (44 percent) on unnamed sources.[18]

The use of different sources led to disparate appraisals of the meaning of the crash and hence different impressions about needed remedies. In *Newsweek,* the national debt and presidential policies were cited as the chief causes; in the *New York Times,* it was the debt and computerized trading. *Wall Street Journal* sources emphasized computerized trading and the foreign trade deficit. On the "CBS Evening News," the national debt was the chief villain, with twice the emphasis it had received by other sources. Presidential policies and partisan politics were other important causes. When it came to estimating the effects of the crash, all but the *Wall Street Journal* mentioned improved cooperation between president and Congress as a likely outcome. Beyond that, speculations about probable effects diverged widely, presenting media audiences with clashing images about the country's economic problems.

A few highly respected national newscasters also are extraordinarily influential in putting their versions of news events on the political agenda. By singling out news events for positive or negative commentary, they may sway public and official opinions. If anchors Peter Jennings, Tom Brokaw, or Dan Rather declare that health care legislation will lower the quality of medical care or that an American military presence along the coast of China will risk war, popular support for these policies may plunge.[19] A sixty-second verbal barrage on the evening news or a few embarrassing questions can destroy programs, politicians, and the reputations of major organizations.

Because Americans like to view their media as effective guardians of the public interest, the positive consequences of news story choices are usually stressed. Negative or questionable consequences should not be overlooked, however. For example, Peter Braestrup, chief of the Saigon bureau of the *Washington Post* during the Vietnam War, argued in his book *Big Story* that unwise story choices and interpretations about the conduct of the war misled the public and government officials.[20] Walter Cronkite and other commentators had used available information to construct a picture of defeat for the South Vietnamese and American forces, ignoring data that indicated a defeat for the North Vietnamese. These erroneous interpretations heightened antiwar pressures and contributed to the collapse of public support for the war. They produced a speedup of troop withdrawal and prompted President Lyndon B. Johnson to abandon a second-term race.[21] The economic collapse of the Soviet Union in the 1980s, which led to the abrupt end of the Cold War, is another example. American journalists had largely ignored Soviet economic news, leaving policy makers and the public uninformed about momentous developments.[22]

General Factors in News Selection

As discussed earlier, what becomes news depends in part on the *demographics, training, personality, and professional socialization* of news personnel. In the United States this means, by and large, upwardly mobile, well-educated white males whose political views are liberal and who subscribe in ever larger numbers to the tenets of social responsibility journalism (discussed in Chapter 2). News selection also hinges on the *intraorganizational norms and professional role conceptions* of newspeople and on *pressures of internal and external competition.*

Within each news organization reporters and editors compete for time, space, and prominence of position for their stories. News organizations also compete with each other for audience attention, for advertisers, and, in the case of the networks, for affiliates. If one station or network has a popular program, others often will copy the format and try to place an equally attractive program into a parallel time slot to capture their competitor's audiences and advertisers. Likewise, papers may feel compelled to carry stories simply because another medium in the same market has carried it. Story choices made by the *Washington Post,* the *New York Times,* or the *Los Angeles Times* become models to be followed.

News personnel operate within *the broad political context of their societies* in general and their circulation communities in particular. Most of them have internalized these contexts so that they become their frames of reference. There is "no fundamentally non-ideological, apolitical, non-partisan news gathering and reporting system."[23] If a reporter's political context demands favorable images of racial minorities, news and entertainment will reflect this outlook most of the time. If adverse criticism of minorities is encouraged, the same stories used elsewhere to praise minorities will be used to defame them.[24]

Political pressures also leave their mark. Media personnel depend on political leaders for much of their information and are therefore subject to manipulation by these sources. Politicians and other powerful elites flood the media with self-serving story materials that are often hard to resist. Intensive, frequent contacts and the desire to keep associations cordial may lead to cozy relationships, which make critical detachment unlikely. The ability to woo reporters and elicit favorable media coverage is the mark of the astute politician. Reporters can rarely resist the blandishments of politicians for fear of alienating powerful and important news sources.

Economic pressures are even more potent than political pressures in molding news and entertainment. Newspapers and magazines need sufficient income to cover their production costs. Except for publications that are subsidized by individual or group sponsors, media enterprises must raise this income from subscriptions, from advertisers, or from a combination of these sources. Most costs for television and radio programming are covered solely by advertising income. Therefore, media offerings must appeal to large numbers of potential customers for the products that advertisers sell. This means that programs and stories must be directed either to general audiences in the prime consumption years of life (roughly twenty-five to forty-five years) or to selected special audiences that are key targets for particular advertiser appeals. For instance, toothpaste, laundry detergent, and breakfast cereals are best marketed to the huge nationwide audiences who watch the regular nighttime situation comedies or detective stories; personal computers, fancy foreign sports cars, and raft trips down the Amazon are most likely to find customers among a select few. Advertisers for these latter products are attracted to upscale circulation journals such as *National Geographic* or *Fortune* or to specialized television documentaries.

Because the bulk of programming is directed to the general public, television and radio must maintain a smooth flow of appealing programs throughout the prime evening hours. Many people watch television indiscriminately. As long as the program is unobjectionable, they will remain with the station. In fact, viewers preselect fewer than half of the shows they watch.[25] If boring or controversial programs come on, a sizable part of the audience will defect to another station and remain tuned to it for the rest of the evening. Such considerations deter producers from mixing serious audience-losing programs with light entertainment in prime time. Fears of losing the audience for an entire evening also are major reasons for opposition to expanding the nightly network news to a full hour.

The desire to keep audiences watching a particular station even affects the format of news and public service programs. Newscasters are selected for their physical attractiveness. Informal banter is encouraged, and nearly every newscast contains some fascinating bits of trivia or a touching yet inconsequential human interest story. The news becomes "info-tainment"—a marriage of information and entertainment values. Complicated stories are avoided for fear of confusing audiences. "Dull" stories, such as budget negotiations, are slighted despite their importance. However, media people occasionally underestimate the public's tastes for serious presentations, as shown by the popularity of the televised congressional debates about American involvement in the Persian Gulf War and by the massive attention given to presidential news conferences and addresses. But these are the exceptions rather than the rule. H. L. Mencken was probably right when he said that "nobody ever went broke by underestimating the public's taste."

Criteria for Choosing Specific Stories

In addition to deciding what is publishable news, gatekeepers must choose particular news items to include in their mix of offerings. The motto of the *New York Times,* "All the News That's Fit to Print," is an impossible myth; there is far more publishable news available to any paper than it can possibly use. Gatekeepers also must decide how they want to frame each item so that it carries a particular message. For instance, the rioters who destroyed Los Angeles neighborhoods in 1992 seemed justified when journalists framed the riots as public revenge for the brutal beating of an African American man by white police officers. They did it by interspersing scenes of the beating with scenes of the riot. A focus on

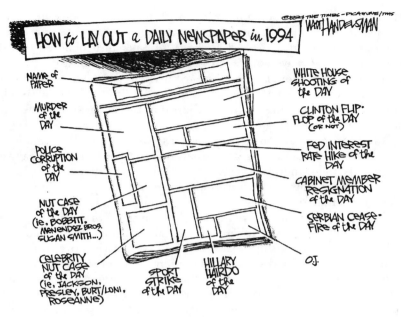

Reprinted by permission: Tribune Media Services.

assaults, looting, and arson committed during the riot would have given the story a different slant.

The criteria newspeople use in story selection relate primarily to audience appeal rather than to the political significance of stories, their educational value, their broad social purposes, or the newspeople's own political views. This holds particularly true for television, where viewer numbers, demographic characteristics, and viewer attitudes are constantly monitored by rating services, such as A. C. Nielsen and the American Research Bureau (ARB). For both radio and television, advertising rates are based on audience size. A 1 percent increase in audience size can mean millions of dollars in additional advertising income. Newspaper advertising rates are also based on paid circulation, which is monitored by an independent agency, the Audit Bureau of Circulation. Audiences are rarely asked if they would prefer different programs to existing fare. The fact that they watch or listen to or purchase papers in large numbers is assumed to certify that they like what they get.

The emphasis on audience appeal, and the economic pressures that mandate it, needs to be kept in mind when the totality of media output is evaluated. They explain why the amount and kind of coverage of important issues often are not commensurate with their significance in the real world at the time of publication. For instance, television news coverage of crime reached record highs in 1995 because journalists believed that the public wanted extensive coverage of the O. J. Simpson murder trial and several other sensational cases. The combined story totals for health issues, the economy, and federal budget talks fell substantially below crime story totals, leaving the impression that these stories mattered less than the various crime sagas.[26]

A ten-year comparison of media stories with statistics on escalation of the Vietnam War, crime rates, and urban riots revealed that the peak year for riots was 1968; the peak year for riot stories was one year earlier. In 1967 the ratio of riots to riot stories was 4 to 1; in 1968 it was 12 to 1. With riots no longer anything "special," the ratio went to 16 to 1 in 1969 and 65 to 1 in 1970.[27] In a similar vein, a twelve-year scan of terrorism stories shown on network television revealed "a cumulative pattern of coverage that bears scant relationship to actual trends of terrorism over time."[28] As shown in Table 4-3, the discrepancy between the frequency of a newsworthy event and its coverage is especially well illustrated by crime news reporting. Of all murders occurring in Chicago, 11 percent were reported by the *Chicago Tribune* compared to .0002 percent of assaults. More than 40,000 assaults were covered by a mere 10 stories compared to 101 stories for 926 murders.

Five criteria are used most often for choosing news stories. First, stories must be likely to have a *strong impact* on readers or listeners. Stories about health hazards, consumer fraud, or pensions for the elderly influence people more than do unfamiliar happenings with which they cannot identify. To make stories attractive, newspeople commonly present them as anecdotes that show their effect on average people. Inflation news becomes the story of the housewife at the supermarket; foreign competition becomes the story of laid-off workers in a local textile plant. In the process of personalization, the broader political significance of the story is often lost, and the news becomes trivialized.

Natural or man-made *violence, conflict, disaster,* or *scandal* are the second criterion of newsworthiness. Wars, murders, strikes, earthquakes, accidents, or sex scandals involving prominent people—these are the kinds of things that excite audiences. In fact, inexpensive mass newspapers became viable business ventures in the United States only when the publishers of the *New York Sun* discovered in 1833 that papers filled with breezy crime and sex stories far outsold their more staid competitors. Mass sales permitted sharp price reductions and allowed the "penny press" to be born.

People remember dramatic behavior better than more standard fare. A story of a toddler rescued from a well has become one of the best-

TABLE 4-3   Police Versus Newspaper Crime Reports: Chicago, 1994

Crime	Police reports of Chicago crime		*Tribune* reports of Chicago crime		*Tribune* reports of all crime	
Murder*	926	(0.3%)	101	(64.9%)	407	(69.9%)
Sexual assault	3,048	(1.1%)	15	(9.7%)	90	(15.4%)
Assault	40,425	(16.6%)	10	(6.4%)	37	(6.3%)
Theft/robbery/ burglary	199,014	(81.7%)	28	(18.1%)	48	(8.2%)
Total	243,413	(99.7%)	154	(99.1%)	582	(99.8%)

SOURCE: Compiled from police crime reports and newspaper index.

* Murder includes attempted murder and manslaughter; sexual assault includes rape; theft includes auto thefts.

remembered events of the past twenty years. The murder of 900 members of an American religious sect in Guyana in 1978 has become equally memorable. Of the respondents to a Gallup Poll 98 percent knew of the event—a number matched only by those who remembered the attack on Pearl Harbor in 1941 and those who recalled the dropping of atomic bombs on Hiroshima and Nagasaki in 1945.

A third element of newsworthiness is *familiarity*. News is attractive if it pertains to well-known people or involves familiar situations of concern to many. This is why newspeople try to cast unfamiliar situations, such as mass famines in Africa, into more familiar stories of individual babies dying from malnutrition. The public's keen interest in celebrities is demonstrated by the amazing amount of detail that people can retain about the powerful and famous. More than three decades after the assassination of President Kennedy in 1963 many Americans still remember details of the funeral ceremony, as well as where they were when they heard the news of the killing. The sense of personal grief and loss has lingered, bridging the gap between the average person's private and public worlds. People value the feeling of personal intimacy that comes from knowing details of a famous person's life. Somewhat similar feelings are harbored even toward the cast members of soap operas. People whose lives are confined largely to their homes often adopt soap opera stars as part of their families. They avidly follow the trials and tribulations of these people and may even try to model themselves after them.

Proximity is the fourth element of newsworthiness. Strong preference for local news rests on the assumption that people are most interested in what happens near them. Local media flourish because they concentrate on local events. Roughly 75 percent of the space in local media is used for local stories.[29] Because national television news must concentrate on matters of interest to viewers throughout the entire country, it cannot depict events close to everyone's home. The public receives so much news from Washington and a few major metropolitan areas that these cities and their newsmakers have become familiar to the nation. This, in a sense, makes them "local" events in what media analyst Marshall McLuhan has called the *global village* created by television.

The fifth element is that news should be *timely* and *novel*. It must be something that has just occurred and is out of the ordinary, either in the sense that it does not happen all the time, such as the regular departure of airplanes or the daily opening of grocery stores, or in the sense that it is not part of the lives of ordinary persons.

Among these five basic criteria, *conflict, proximity,* and *timeliness* are most important, judging from a survey of television and newspaper editors who were given sixty-four fictitious stories by a team of researchers and then asked which they would use and their reasons for using them.[30] Conspicuously absent from their choice criteria was the story's overall significance. Significance does play a part, however, when a major event is communicated, such as the outcome of a national election, the death of a well-known leader, or a calamitous natural disaster. Nevertheless, most stories are selected and framed primarily to satisfy the five criteria.

Gathering the News

News organizations establish regular listening posts, or "beats," in those places in which events of interest to the public are most likely to occur. In the United States, beats at the centers of government cover political executives, legislative bodies, court systems, and international organizations. Places in which deviant behaviors are most apt to be reported, such as police stations and hospitals, are monitored. Fluctuations in economic trends are recorded at stock and commodity markets and at institutions designed to check the pulse of the nation's business. Some beats are functionally defined, such as the health or education beats. Reporters assigned to them generally cover a wider array of institutions on a less regular schedule than is true of the more usual beats.

Stories emanating from the traditional beats at the national level, such as the White House, Capitol, or Pentagon, have an excellent chance of publication, either because of their intrinsic significance, the prominence of their sources, or simply because they have been produced by beat reporters on the regular payroll. In the *New York Times* or *Washington Post,* for instance, stories from regularly covered beats outnumber other stories two to one and capture the bulk of front-page headlines.[31]

All major media tend to monitor the same places. As a result, news patterns are stable and uniform throughout the country. On the nightly news the leading story is shared by at least two of the major networks 91 percent of the time. It is featured on the third network in only a slightly less prominent position.[32] As Table 4-4 documents, the media are "rivals in conformity."[33] The table is based on content analysis of two Chicago newspapers and six nightly television newscasts, half of them local to Chicago for a randomly selected 50-day period from June 1 to July 20, 1995. The table presents striking evidence that the same kinds of stories and story types—although not necessarily identical stories—are reported by all news outlets. When the proportions of various types of news are compared, the similarities are greatest among the members of each of the three types of media. National television patterns show heavier proportionate emphases on stories about the national government and international news and proportionate de-emphases of sports news. Thanks to more available space, newspapers carry more nonpolitical news. In fact, it is noteworthy that they devote nearly half of the newshole—the space available for news stories, rather than advertising, legal announcements, circulation information, and the like—to nonpolitical stories. But, though the proportions vary, the array of topics covered is remarkably uniform. This pattern is typical for media systems throughout the United States.[34]

News, as media scholar Leon Sigal has put it, is always "the standardized exceptional."[35] Each day's or week's news is like a familiar play with slight changes in the scenes and dialogue and with frequent replacements in the cast of minor players (although not of major actors). News is exceptional in the sense that it does not portray ordinary events, such as eating breakfast or washing clothes or taking the bus to work. It is standardized in the sense that it deals with the same types of topics in familiar ways and produces standardized patterns of news and entertainment throughout the country. Repeated coverage of the same familiar scenes conveys to the public the feeling that all is going according to expectations and that, even when the news is bad, there is little to worry about. It has all happened before, and people have managed to cope.

News organizations, including the giants in the business, cannot afford to have full teams of reporters and camera crews dispersed across the country. In fact, economic declines have forced them to contract their bases. Even in good times, national networks generally station teams in only half a dozen cities where the equipment, support staff, and news personnel are good. Locations are not selected with an eye to covering all parts of the nation equally well or to providing diverse settings. Chance thus determines which locations receive coverage for routine stories and which are neglected.

TABLE 4-4 Frequency of Mention of News Topics: June 1, 1995, to July 20, 1995 (in percentages)

News topics	Sun Times (2,777)	Chicago Tribune (2,445)	National TV ABC (440)	National TV CBS (435)	National TV NBC (425)	Local TV ABC (530)	Local TV CBS (555)	Local TV NBC (541)
Government/politics								
National government	3.8	4.5	26.2	24.1	23.3	7.8	8.7	6.2
Elections	1.0	1.3	1.0	2.0	1.0	1.5	1.2	1.5
State government	1.0	1.5	1.5	2.2	0.6	1.3	1.1	0.8
Local government	2.2	2.4	0.4	0.1	0.0	3.7	1.6	2.5
International news	6.1	7.2	19.5	17.5	19.0	7.0	4.5	6.4
National affairs news	2.1	2.7	4.2	7.5	9.1	2.3	3.9	6.3
Local affairs news	3.5	3.7	0.0	0.0	0.0	9.5	8.7	8.0
Total	19.7	23.3	52.8	53.4	53.0	33.1	29.7	31.7
Economic issues								
Economy	1.4	1.9	3.0	5.2	5.4	0.6	0.3	0.5
Business	7.5	9.6	2.4	1.9	1.4	2.4	1.2	1.0
Labor/unemployment	1.5	1.4	3.0	1.9	2.2	0.8	0.8	0.9
Transportation/energy	2.3	2.4	2.1	1.1	2.0	1.5	1.3	2.5
Health care	1.3	1.7	7.0	6.7	5.3	3.7	4.1	3.5
Total	14.0	17.0	17.5	16.8	16.3	9.0	7.7	8.4
Social issues								
Civil rights/deprived groups	0.7	0.9	1.9	2.2	1.8	0.5	1.2	1.2
Education	1.2	1.4	0.9	1.3	1.1	2.2	0.3	0.3
Media	0.6	0.8	0.8	2.2	2.3	2.0	1.7	1.8
Religion	0.4	0.7	1.5	0.3	0.6	0.6	1.2	1.3
Abortion/contraception	0.3	0.4	2.0	1.0	0.8	0.3	0.9	0.3
Disease/Ebola virus	0.6	0.6	4.3	3.7	3.0	2.4	1.8	1.2

Other health issues	1.1	1.7	1.5	1.6	0.8	1.5	2.9	1.6
Disasters/accidents	1.7	1.2	1.2	3.1	3.2	2.7	4.1	6.1
Environment	0.9	1.0	1.1	1.0	1.2	0.6	1.0	1.0
Justice system	0.8	1.3	4.6	4.4	3.7	2.2	1.7	0.9
Individual crime	3.5	4.1	2.5	2.2	1.5	13.1	12.3	7.1
Total	11.8	14.1	22.3	23.0	20.0	28.1	29.1	22.8
Other								
Obituaries	1.8	3.5	0.0	0.0	0.0	0.0	0.0	0.0
Weather	1.3	1.8	1.3	2.3	2.1	6.0	7.5	7.2
Sports	23.6	18.7	3.0	1.2	4.0	18.9	19.8	20.7
Entertainment	28.1	22.2	4.3	4.1	5.1	5.2	6.4	9.1
Total	54.8	46.2	8.6	7.6	11.2	30.1	33.7	37.0

SOURCE: Author's research.

TABLE 4-5   Network Coverage of State News: August 1994 to July 1995

Annual number of stories	States		Percentage of mentions	Percentage of electoral vote
1–24	Alaska	New Hampshire	11.4	27.1
	Arizona	North Dakota		
	Connecticut	New Mexico		
	Delaware	North Carolina		
	Hawaii	Ohio		
	Iowa	South Dakota		
	Kentucky	Utah		
	Maine	Vermont		
	Missouri	West Virginia		
	Montana	Wisconsin		
	Nebraska	Wyoming		
	Nevada			
25–50	Alabama	Massachusetts	27.6	32.9
	Arkansas	Minnesota		
	Georgia	Mississippi		
	Idaho	New Jersey		
	Indiana	Oregon		
	Illinois	Rhode Island		
	Kansas	South Carolina		
	Louisiana	Tennessee		
	Maryland	Washington		
51–100	Colorado	Virginia	14.7	11.6
	Michigan	Washington, D.C.		
	Pennsylvania			
101–200	Florida	Texas	17.5	12.1
	Oklahoma			
201–341	California	New York	28.9	16.3

SOURCE: Data compiled from the Vanderbilt Television News Archives.
NOTE: $N = 2,325$.

Table 4-5 shows the percentage of network news stories devoted to individual American states in broadcasts monitored from August 1994 to July 1995. The table also reports the number of electoral votes to which each state was entitled according to the 1990 census as a rough measure of that state's population and political significance. Coverage of news about the states is extremely uneven. Twenty-three states were covered by fewer than twenty-five stories annually. Such sparse coverage denies their news and their problems a national audience. Overall, the forty-one states covered by up to fifty stories annually represent 60 percent of the country in electoral votes but receive only 39 percent of the state news coverage. At the other end of the spectrum, California, New York, Florida, Texas, and Oklahoma (the victim of a major terrorist attack during the period studied) received more than 46 percent of the national coverage combined but they represent only 28.4 percent of the electoral vote.

Most of the picture coverage comes from East Coast cities, such as Washington, D.C., and New York and from Chicago and Los Angeles. Of course, special events will be covered anywhere in the country. Every network reports presidential nominating conventions, wherever they are held, and routinely follows presidential travels, whether the destination is Hope, Arkansas, President Clinton's home town, or the Great Wall of China. Aside from a few exceptions, events in remote sites are most likely to be covered if they involve prominent people and are scheduled in advance so that plans can be made to have media crews available.

Prior planning is also important for more accessible events. Time is needed to allocate camera crews, move them into position, and process and edit pictures. The necessity of planning ahead leads to an emphasis on the predictable, such as formal visits by dignitaries, legislative hearings, or executive press conferences. The news output reflects this preference for formally scheduled events. The development of portable camera equipment producing videotapes that can be broadcast with little further processing has greatly eased—though not eliminated—this problem. *Spot news* can now be filmed and broadcast fairly rapidly. This is only one example of the profound impact of technological developments on the content of the news.

News Production Constraints

Many news selection criteria reflect the need to process news rapidly and to publish it quickly. Time pressures explain the emphasis on pseudo-events—events created for easy reporting by the media or for the media. Pseudo-events constitute more than half of all television news stories. For example, politicians frequently plan pictorially attractive happenings, such as bridge dedications or county fair visits, to accommodate newspaper or broadcast deadlines. Presidents routinely provide photo opportunities to allow the press to record the many minor events in their schedules. When newspeople need a quick story about an event, such as a revolution in Central America or youth gang violence, they create it by arranging interviews with familiar leaders, whose remarks, knowledgeable or not, then instantly become *the* Central America or *the* youth gang story.

Once stories reach media news offices, selections must be made extremely rapidly. Ben Bagdikian, a former *Washington Post* editor who studied gatekeeping at eight newspapers, found that stories usually are sifted and chosen on the spot.[36] They are not assembled and carefully balanced with an eye to the overall effects. The typical newspaper gatekeeper is able to scan and discard individual stories in one or two seconds. At such speeds, judgments are almost instantaneous. There is no time to reflect or to weigh the merits of one story over another. Stories are judged more by how they balance previously selected stories than by their intrinsic importance. If the gatekeeper has ideological preferences, these are served instinctively, if at all, rather than deliberately. Stories left over at the end of the day ordinarily will not be used on the next day because newer stories will have replaced them. A late-breaking story, therefore, unless it is very unusual or significant, has little chance for publication. Because the network evening news is run on an East Coast schedule, West Coast afternoon stories are frequent casualties because they generally happen too late to be used.

Fewer than 3 percent of the stories in Bagdikian's study were rejected because the editor did not care for the substance of the story or objected to its ideological slant. Twenty-six percent were rejected because of lack of space. The chief reason for other rejections was lack of newsworthiness. The published newspaper usually contains the same proportions of different types of news as the original pool from which the stories were selected.[37] Rejection rates varied for different types of stories. Overall, nearly all wire service, human interest, and crime stories were rejected, along with more than two thirds of farm and science stories. Even though much of the human interest information was rejected, it still constituted the largest single news category—23 percent of total news. By contrast, science news took 5 percent of total space and farm stories 6 percent.[38]

Public relations experts and campaign managers know the deadlines of important publications, such as the *New York Times, Wall Street Journal, Time, Newsweek,* and network television news. They schedule events and news releases to arrive in gatekeepers' offices precisely when needed and in appropriate formats such as computer diskettes, electronic mail, or videotape cassettes. Public relations firms distribute thousands of videotaped releases annually. If they are attractively presented and meet newsworthiness criteria, journalists find it hard to resist using them. This is especially true for smaller organizations that lack adequate resources to produce their own stories. They relish receiving such information subsidies.[39] Publicists for particular causes thus can influence the news production process. Powerful elites in the public and private sector make ample use of these opportunities. Even though the bulk of public relations releases is discarded, a substantial portion of news stories is based on them, usually without identifying the source. If publicists want to stifle publicity that is likely to harm their clients, they can announce news just past the deadlines, preferably on weekends when few newscasts are scheduled.

Publications with less frequent deadlines, such as weekly news magazines, have a lot more time to decide what to publish. That makes it easier to separate the wheat from the chaff. News magazine staffs also have more resources than most daily papers to explore background information and present stories in a context that helps readers to evaluate them. Hence their stories are often far more measured and thoughtful than corresponding stories in the daily press.

Television news staffs have even less time than newspaper staffs to investigate most stories and far less time to provide background and interpretation. This is why background or investigative stories that appear on television frequently originate in the print media. The problem of insufficient time pertains not only to preparing stories but also to presenting them. The average news story on television and radio takes about a minute, just enough time to announce an event and present a fact or two about it. Complex stories may have to be ignored if they cannot be drastically condensed.

Print media have space problems as well, but they are less severe than time constraints faced by electronic media. The average newspaper reserves 55 percent of its space for advertising. Straight news stories account for 27 percent of the space, and the remainder is used for features of various types. Some papers reserve a standardized amount of space for news; others expand or contract the newshole depending on the flow of news and advertising. But whether the paper is a slim eight-page version or five to ten times that size, there is rarely enough space to cover stories as fully as reporters and editors would like.[40]

Besides the need to capsulize news stories, television reporters also want stories with visual appeal. Events that make dull pictures may have to be omitted. Racial violence in South Africa, for example, disappeared from television news after the government had prohibited picture-taking. It is an unfortunate fact for television that what is visually appealing may not be important. For instance, during political campaigns, motorcades, rallies, hecklers, and cheering crowds make good pictures. Candidates delivering speeches are visually dull by comparison. Television cameras therefore concentrate on the colorful scenes rather than on the speech. If interesting pictures are flashed on the screen in competition with the speech, they often distract attention from it.

Because picture production is expensive for television as well as for print, picture stories selected early are likely to be kept even if more important stories break later. Financial considerations, as well as personnel reasons, also favor information originated by staff members. Stories by employees already on the payroll are preferred to wire service stories by unknown reporters or stories from outside sources for which additional fees must be paid. News executives also have personal relationships with their own staff members and do not want to disappoint them by rejecting their stories.

Effects of Gatekeeping

The gatekeeping influences that have been discussed give a distinctive character to the American news product. There are many exceptions, of course, when one looks at individual programs or stories. There are also noticeable differences in emphases among the conservative rural press, more moderate papers in small- and middle-sized towns, and the liberal press in major metropolitan centers. For instance, a study of the lifestyle section of American daily newspapers showed that news about the women's movement and women's careers constituted 20 percent of the coverage in this section in rural papers and nearly double that amount in papers in metropolitan areas.[41] Despite such variations, several shared attributes of American news stand out. They will be discussed under four headings: people in the news, action in the news, info-tainment news, and support for the establishment.[42]

People in the News

The gatekeeping process winnows the group of newsworthy people to a very small cadre of familiar and unfamiliar figures. In print and broadcast news, most stories in news magazines and network television news feature familiar people, predominantly political figures. Fewer than fifty politicians are in the news regularly. The list is headed by the *incumbent president*. Other people receive coverage primarily for unusual or remarkable activities, but incumbent presidents are covered regardless of what they do. News about *leading presidential candidates* ranks next; in presidential election years it often outnumbers stories about the president.[43]

A third well-covered group consists of *major federal officials*, such as political leaders in the House and Senate, the heads of major congressional committees, and cabinet members in active departments. In the post-Watergate period major White House staff members are part of the circle. So are former officials such as secretaries of state and secretaries of defense who are asked to comment on the current scene. The Supreme

Court is in the news only intermittently, generally when important decisions are announced or during confirmation hearings for Supreme Court justices. Agency heads rarely make the news except when they announce new policies or feud with the president. Some people, however, are regularly in the news regardless of their current political status merely because their names are household words. Members of the Kennedy clan and a host of "experts" such as economist Milton Friedman or consumer activist Ralph Nader are prime examples.

Below the federal level, the activities of *governors and mayors from large states and cities* are newsworthy if they involve major public policy issues or if the incumbent is unusual because of race, gender, or prior newsworthy activities. *Notorious individuals* also receive frequent news attention if their deeds have involved well-known people. Presidential assassins, mass murderers, or members of extremist political groups fall into this category. Ample coverage also goes to targets of congressional investigations and politicians indicted for wrongdoing in office.

Among the many powerful people rarely covered in the news are economic leaders (such as the heads of large corporations), financiers, and leaders of organized business (such as the National Association of Manufacturers or the U.S. Chamber of Commerce). A few colorful labor leaders, such as George Meany and James Hoffa, have been news figures in the past, but this was probably due more to their personalities than to their jobs. Important military leaders also remain obscure unless they conduct major military operations, such as Gen. Norman Schwarzkopf in the Persian Gulf War in 1991 or his boss, Gen. Colin Powell. Political party leaders surface during elections but remain in the shadows at other times. Political activists, such as civil rights leaders or the heads of minority parties, or pleaders of special causes, such as right-to-die activist Jack Kevorkian, come and go from the news scene, depending on the amount of visible conflict they are able to produce. The same holds true for the heads of voluntary associations, such as leaders of antiabortion groups or churches.

Most people never make the news because their activities are not unusual enough to command media attention. Ordinary people have their best chance for publicity if they protest or riot or strike, particularly against the government. The next best chance goes to victims of disasters, personal tragedy, and crime, and to the actors who brought about their plight. The grisly nature of crimes, disasters, or other human tragedies, rather than the identity of the people involved, determines their newsworthiness. Ordinary people also make the news if their lifestyles or social activities become highly unusual or if their behavior diverges greatly from the norm for persons of their age, gender, and status. Finally, ordinary people make the news in large numbers as nameless members of groups whose statistical profile is reported or whose opinions have been tapped through polls or elections.

Action in the News

The range of activities reported in the news is quite limited—conflicts and disagreements among government officials (particularly friction between the president and Congress about economic or foreign policies), violent and nonviolent protest (much of it about government activities), crime, scandals and investigations, and impending or actual disasters. When the nation is at war, a large number of war stories are reported.

Government policies also provide frequent story material. These stories generally report the political maneuvers leading to policy decisions rather than the substance of the policy and its likely impact. Government personnel changes, including campaigns for office, are another news focus. Finally, two aspects of the ever-changing societal scene receive substantial coverage from time to time: major national events, such as inaugurations or moon landings, and important social, cultural, or technological developments, such as the 1995 Million-Man March of African American men and their supporters on Washington or advances in the fight against killer diseases such as cancer and AIDS.

Info-tainment News

The criteria for newsworthiness and the constraints on news production shape American news and its impact, regardless of the particular subject under discussion. That means a stress on novel and entertaining events, familiar people and situations, and conflict and violence. Events are described, but their underlying causes and likely consequences and the major issues involved are often slighted.

Novelty and Excitement. Sensational and novel occurrences often drown out news of more lasting significance that lacks excitement. For instance, as Table 4-4 shows, a fairly average newspaper such as the *Chicago Sun Times* devotes more than ten times more news to sports than to local government. Dramatic events, such as airline hijackings or serial murders, preempt more consequential happenings. Preoccupation with a single striking event, such as the stock market crash of October 19, 1987, can shortchange coverage of other news, such as a punitive American airstrike against Iranian targets. Speculations about a religious broadcaster's strong prospects in the 1988 Iowa presidential caucuses drowned out a Soviet leader's announcement of plans to withdraw from the long and bloody war in Afghanistan.

The emphasis on excitement also leads to stress on trivial aspects of serious stories. Inflation becomes a human interest drama about John and Jane Doe, working-class homeowners who are struggling to pay their mortgage. The larger issues involved in inflation are apt to be ignored. But judging from attention patterns, personalized dramatic stories are far more likely to be noticed than learned discussions by economic experts.

The search for novelty and entertainment leads to fragmented discontinuous news that focuses on the present and ignores the past. The here and now is what counts most. When breaking news is published as quickly as possible, the background needed to place a story into context is often missing. Clarifications are usually buried in the back pages. On television, snippets of news may drive home an easily understandable theme, such as "Washington is in a mess" or "The inner city is decaying," whereas individual news items may remain blurred.

Fragmentation makes it difficult for audiences to piece together a coherent narrative of events. More background and interpretation would need to be balanced by reducing the numbers of news items presented to the audience. It would also increase the chance for subjective interpretation by news commentators. A few papers, such as the *Christian Science Monitor,* and a few news programs, such as the "Newshour with Jim Lehrer," cover fewer stories and present them in more detail. People who carefully read *Monitor* stories or watch "Lehrer" acquire a better background for understanding political issues, but they miss out on other news for which there is no space. They may also get skewed information if newspeople misinterpret the significance of complex events.

Familiarity and Similarity. The demand for stories about familiar people and events close to home produces circular effects. Familiar people and situations are covered minutely, which makes them even more familiar and therefore even more worthy of publicity. The reverse is also true. During the 1996 presidential election campaign, speculations about General Powell's entry into the presidential race received more coverage than most of the dozens of actual candidates whose names were doomed to oblivion even when they were still in the running.

Familiar people may become objects of prying curiosity. The details of their private lives may take up an inordinately large amount of time and space in the mass media. The marital trials and tribulations of even distant political figures, such as Princess Diana, wife of the heir to the British throne, may command front-page coverage for extended time periods. Tabloids and serious media alike cover such stories at length. Only rarely do they focus on the potentially significant political consequences that might ensue, such as the political consequences of abandoning the monarchy and turning Britain into a Republic.

The current criteria of newsworthiness have led to news that is very parochial compared with news in other countries. Slim coverage of news about foreign people and cultures leaves Americans deficient in their understanding of international affairs, a subject explored more fully in Chapter 11. The pattern is circular: If events in Peru are rarely covered, stories about Peru will require a lot of background to make sense to Americans. This may take more time and space than the media are willing to give to any story, except during a crisis. Therefore, foreign coverage in American media is usually about people to whom Americans feel culturally close and whose policies are somewhat familiar, such as the English, the Canadians, and the people of Northern European countries. Foreign news concentrates on situations that are easy to report, which often means violent events such as revolutions, major disasters, and the like. This type of coverage conveys the faulty impression that most foreign countries are always in serious disarray.

Conflict and Violence. The heavy news emphases on conflict and bad news, which is most prevalent in big city media, have three major consequences.[44] The first and perhaps most far-reaching consequence is the dangerous distortion of reality that emphasis on negative news events may create. Crime coverage provides examples. Media stories rarely mention that many inner-city neighborhoods are relatively free of crime. Instead they convey the impression that entire cities are dangerous jungles. This impression may become a self-fulfilling prophecy. In the wake of crime publicity, many people avoid the inner city. They even shun comparatively safe neighborhoods after a single, highly publicized crime. The empty streets then make crime more likely.

Studies of people's perceptions of the incidence of crime and the actual chances that they will be victimized indicate that their fears are geared to media realities. In the world of television drama, the average character has a 30 percent to 64 percent chance of being involved in violence; in the real world the average person's chance of becoming a crime victim is a small fraction of that number.[45] In the same way, heavy media emphasis on air crashes and scant coverage of automobile accidents has left the public with distorted notions of the relative dangers of these modes of transportation.

A second consequence is that emphasis on conflict may cause some people to believe that violence is an acceptable way to settle disputes. Even when exposure of the conflict ultimately promotes its resolution, highlighting a violent process often makes it worse. The media usually dramatize and oversimplify conflict, picturing it as a confrontation between two clearly defined sides. It is the hawks against the doves in war, the victors against losers in a legislative battle, the Communists versus anti-Communists in a struggle abroad. Even when a situation is not actually confrontational, the media may present it as a feud or a fight, making agreement more difficult.

Average people, when presented with clashing claims, often feel confused and find it extremely difficult to determine the truth. They have neither the facts nor the time to explore the issues. They are also left with the disquieting sense that conflict and turmoil reign nearly everywhere. This impression is likely to affect people's feelings toward society in general. They may contract "videomalaise," characterized by lack of trust, cynicism, and fear.[46] Many social scientists believe that such feelings undermine support for government, destroy faith in leaders, produce political apathy, and generally sap the vigor of the democratic process.

Finally, the popularity of violence stories has encouraged groups who seek media coverage to behave violently or sensationally to enhance their chances for publicity. One example comes from a lengthy strike by a union of Chicano workers against a Texas furniture company. During the first year, the nonviolent strike received very little publicity. To attract media coverage the leaders decided to stage noisy marches to the Capitol on the first and second anniversaries of the strike. Moderate language in appeals to the company and city authorities was replaced by fighting words. City councilors were called "rednecks" and challenged to stop the union's marches. These inflammatory accusations created a confrontation, brought city police to the scene, and heightened tensions. Celebrities, including Sens. Edmund Muskie (D) of Maine and Birch Bayh (D) of Indiana and farm labor leader Cesar Chavez, were invited to enter the fray. These maneuvers broke the year-long dearth of media coverage. No longer peaceful, the strike finally received ample publicity. In turn, this created sufficient pressure to bring about a settlement.[47]

A taste for conflict is not the same as a taste for controversy, however. Fear of offending members of the mass audience, wire service subscribers, or affiliated station managers often keeps stories dealing with controversial subjects such as abortion or distasteful religious rituals out of the media, especially network television. If such stories are reported, the treatment is ordinarily bland, carefully hedged, and rarely provocative. In fact, the world that television presents to the viewer generally lags behind the real world in its recognition of controversial social changes. The civil rights struggle, women's fight for equality, and changing sexual mores were widespread long before they became common on the television screen or received serious attention in the print media. Compared with television, newspapers can afford to be more daring because normally there is no other daily paper in the same market. Moreover, the nature of the medium makes it easier for the audience to ignore stories they find offensive or distasteful.

Neglect of Major Societal Problems. Despite the ascendancy of social responsibility journalism, the constraints of news production still force the media to neglect serious persistent societal problems, such as alcoholism, truancy, environmental pollution, and care of elderly and disabled individuals. The pattern changes after a dramatic event, such as a rash of deaths in nursing homes or a big welfare fraud case. If a reporter investigates and finds that six elderly people starved to death because of neglect, the spotlighted incident may then lead to a series of reports on food in retirement homes. The shocking deaths provide the element of novelty. After that novelty has worn off, interest dims and media attention flags, even if the problem remains unsolved. One commentator calls it "the Weekend Yawn Rule." When the 1992 Los Angeles riots raised the racism issue, 80 percent of the audience was likely to tune out following a weekend of saturation analytical coverage. When audience boredom sets in, media coverage evaporates.[48] Important stories, such as passage of a major job training bill in 1995, receive scant coverage if they lack the excitement of controversy. The bill in question was passed with nearly unanimous votes.[49]

Inadequate training of media staffs is another reason for neglecting social problems. Proper appraisal of the merits of health care plans, or prison systems, or pollution control programs requires technical knowledge. Specialized reporters with expertise in areas such as urban affairs, science, or finance are available as yet only in large news organizations. Moreover, a science reporter can hardly be expected to be an expert in all fields of science. Nor can a reporter skilled in urban problems be expected simultaneously to master the intricacies of a major city's budget, its transportation system, and its services to juveniles. Because most news organizations throughout the country lack the trained staffs needed to discuss major social problems constructively, politicians and all kinds of "experts" can easily challenge the merits of unpalatable media stories.

Judging from media use patterns, most of the public is not very interested in the intricacies of major societal problems. For those who are interested and might be in a position to find solutions, lack of adequate media coverage makes it more difficult to rouse public support and become newsworthy in the process.

Support for the Establishment

The gatekeeping process also yields news that basically supports political and social institutions in America. Although the media regularly expose the misbehavior and inefficiencies of government officials and routinely disparage politicians, for the most part they display a supportive attitude toward political leaders and the American political system in general. Misconduct and poor policies are treated as deviations, thereby implicitly reaffirming the merit of prevailing norms. Assumptions that underscore the legitimacy of the current political system are routinely embedded in news stories. For instance, when police protect a factory from violence by workers, it is assumed that they are the legitimate guardians of public order engaged in an appropriate government activity. The possibility that workers should own the factories and have a right to wrest them from the control of capitalists is never raised. Similarly, stories discussing the plight of homeless children tacitly assume that they ought to be living in conventional family units. The fact that other arrangements might be preferable is rarely considered.[50]

American political symbols and rituals, such as the presidency, the courts, elections, and patriotic celebrations, are treated with a high degree of respect by the media, enhancing their legitimacy. By contrast, news stories cast a negative light on antiestablishment behavior, such as protest demonstrations that disrupt normal activities, inflammatory speeches by militants, or looting during a riot. Obscenity and profanity in public places usually are edited out of news events. When they are included, they generate floods of complaints about disrespect, prying, and poor taste. This puts dampers on such exposés, at least temporarily.

Explicit and implicit support for the established system, as well as sugar-coating of political reality, sometimes helps and sometimes hurts the public interest. It hurts if faults in the established system and prevailing political ideologies are allowed to persist when publicity might lead to correction. The fear of publicity can also have a salutary effect on errant public figures. There are, however, situations in which shielding the shortcomings of the political system and even individual misconduct may be helpful. For instance, at times of national or international crises, when the nation's prestige is an important political asset, detrimental stories can severely weaken the country. Similarly, the ability of elected leaders to govern effectively can be seriously damaged by focusing disproportionally on failures and slighting successes and by dwelling on irrelevant personal issues that diminish a leader's stature.

Generalized support for the establishment and the status quo is not unique to the media, of course.[51] Most institutions within any particular political system go along with it if they wish to prosper. People on their staffs have been socialized to believe in the merits of their political structures. Moreover, financial concerns make it essential for the media to cater to advertisers and audiences who firmly support the American political system. Staff members whose personal ideologies differ usually conform with established norms to avoid conflict with their bosses, advertisers, or affiliated stations. People are socialized throughout life to support their country and its policies. They want to believe that the people running their government are competent, honest, and working hard to solve the nation's major problems. They often resent exposés that call into question this comfortable sense of security. Media support for the establishment thus helps to maintain respect for it and perpetuate it.[52]

Establishment support is further strengthened by the media's reliance on government information and press releases. As pointed out earlier, in the United States the bulk of news, particularly news pertaining to activities beyond the local community, comes from officials and agencies of the government.[53] Official viewpoints are likely to be particularly dominant when reporters must preserve access to their special beats, such as the Pentagon or Justice Department, or when story production requires government assistance in collecting or gaining access to data. For instance, when military personnel are needed to transport correspondents to war zones or when film producers want demonstrations of moonflight research, the resulting stories are apt to support official views.[54]

Government officials and agencies are also used routinely to verify information. Reporters generally equate official position and rank of sources with accuracy. The higher the official level and rank the better. The assumption that government sources, such as police departments or Department of Agriculture spokespersons or presidential press aides, are reliable is, of course, debatable, especially because the particular thrust given to a story may put agencies into a good or bad light. Many private groups have complained that nearly exclusive reliance on government sources deprives them of the chance to publicize their own, more accurate versions of stories and that it results in one-sided reporting tilted toward support of the establishment.

Appraising the News-Making Process

Do newspeople do a good job in selecting the types of news and entertainment categories they cover? Do they allot appropriate amounts of time and space to each of these categories? Do they fill them with good individual stories? The answers depend on the standards that the analyst is applying. If one contends that news can and should be a mirror of society faithfully reproducing a miniature version of life, the news-making process leaves much to be desired. With their emphasis on the exceptional rather than the ordinary, on a few regular beats rather than a wide range of news sources, and on conflict and bad news rather than the ordinariness of daily life, the media picture a world that is far from reality. Reality becomes further distorted because the process of shaping news events into interesting, cohesive stories often gives these events totally new meanings and significance. This is why critics claim that the news creates reality rather than reports it.[55]

If one adopts the classical albeit debatable American notion that the media should be the eyes and ears of intelligent and aware citizens who are interested primarily in news of major social and political significance to their community and country, one will again find fault with the gatekeeping process. Much space and time are given to trivia, and many interesting developments are ignored or reported so briefly that their meaning is lost. Often the human interest appeal of a story or its sensational aspects distract the audience from recognizing the story's real significance.[56]

Even if one tests the media by their professed story formulas, appraisal scores are not high. An analysis of 350 randomly selected television news reports, which yielded 207 routine average length stories, showed that only four of seven key story elements were well covered. As Table 4-6 indicates, the factual elements of various types of stories were included in most stories. More than 90 percent had adequate information about *who* the important actors in the story were, *what* factual situation was involved, and *where* and *when* the situation had happened. But only half (51 percent) of the stories explained *why* the situation was occurring. In some news categories, such as law enforcement, only one third (30 percent) of the stories provided reasons. On an average only one third (34 percent) of the stories told *how* the situation developed by giving details about the process.

Stories become more meaningful if they are put into an appropriate context, such as comparisons with similar past events or accounts of the impact of the events on various groups. On an average, 65 percent of the stories provided *contextual information.* Unfortunately, contextual data were often scarcest in stories needing them most, such as reports about the economy or America's relations with its Western allies.

To find fault is easy; to suggest realistic remedies is far more difficult. Few critics would agree on what is noteworthy enough to deserve publication. Gradations and ranks in significance depend on the observer's world view and political orientation. Much of the published criticism of the media consists of polemical works that take the media to task for omitting the critic's areas of special concern. But one person's intellectual meat is another's poison. Conservatives would like to see more stories about the misdeeds of America's enemies and about waste and abuse in social service programs. Liberals complain that the media legitimize big business and the military and neglect social reforms and radical perspectives.

TABLE 4-6   Coverage of News Elements in National and Local Broadcasts (in percentages)

News elements	Who	What	Where	When	Why	How	Context	Total number of stories
Events abroad								
East bloc politics	100	100	95	95	30	30	60	(20)
West bloc politics	100	100	90	100	35	20	43	(12)
Mideast problems	100	100	100	95	55	35	72	(15)
Third World unrest	100	100	100	95	52	45	76	(10)
Foreign/defense policies								
Foreign policy	100	100	93	85	60	30	72	(13)
Defense policy	100	100	94	94	62	46	73	(15)
Economic issues								
Economic conditions	80	100	75	80	60	32	48	(15)
Fiscal policies	95	100	90	86	60	5	73	(25)
Noneconomic issues								
Public officials	100	100	100	100	45	48	82	(18)
Law enforcement	100	100	100	100	30	43	65	(15)
Other domestic issues	100	100	90	95	38	45	59	(24)
Private sector news								
Business news	85	100	90	90	68	30	52	(10)
Health/medical news	95	100	90	95	67	32	73	(15)
Average scores	97	100	93	93	51	34	65	(207)

SOURCE: Author's research, based on analysis of 350 randomly selected television news stories in 1991. Feature stories and stories briefer than 20 seconds were omitted.

NOTE: Numbers represent the percentage of stories in each group that covers the question. End column = *N*s.

There is frequently the additional charge that political bias dictates the choices made about inclusion and exclusion of media fare and about story focus and tone. These charges have been particularly common when the media have featured controversial public policy issues, such as the dangers of atomic energy generation or the merits of a new weapons system, or when political campaigns or demonstrations have been covered.

A number of content analyses of such events definitely refute the charges of political bias, if bias is defined as deliberately lopsided coverage or intentional slanting of news. These analyses show instead that most newspeople try to cover a balanced array of issues in a neutral manner and do include at least a few contrasting viewpoints. But given the constraints on the numbers of sources that can be used and the desire to produce exciting stories that top the competition, the end product is rarely a balanced reflection of all elite viewpoints and all shades of public opinion.[57] Moreover, as mentioned, the prevailing political culture colors everything because it provides the standards by which events are judged and interpreted.

When coverage is unbalanced, as happens often, the reasons generally spring from the news-making process itself rather than from politically or ideologically motivated slanting. For instance, the media covered famine conditions in Somalia because that country was fairly accessible. They ignored similar conditions in Sudan because travel was too difficult there. Geography also affects the news-making process. Events happening in Chicago are reported more fully nationwide than are similar events in Denver because the networks have a permanently leased wire from Chicago to New York but not from Denver to New York. The New Hampshire presidential primary receives disproportionate coverage because it happens to be the first one in a presidential election year.

The stories that are publicized inevitably represent a small, unsystematic sample of the news of the day. In this sense every issue of a newspaper or every television newscast is a biased sample of current events. Published stories often generate follow-up coverage, heightening the bias effect. Attempts to be evenhanded may lead to similar coverage for events of dissimilar importance, thereby introducing bias.

News can be evaluated not only as a mirror of society or as a reflection of socially and politically significant events but also from the standpoint of audience preference. By and large the media gatekeepers appear to be doing well by that standard. People like the products of the mass media industry well enough to consume them on a scale unheard of in the past.[58] Three out of every four adults say they read newspapers regularly; nearly all homes have radio and television and use them extensively. In the average household the radio is turned on for three hours a day and television for seven. Millions of viewers, by their own free choice, have switched from other pretelevision sources of diversion to watching shows condemned as trash by social critics and often even by the viewers themselves. These same people ignore shows and newspaper stories with the critics' seal of approval.

If viewed simultaneously from all three perspectives—mirror of society, recorder of significant political events, and journalistic perfectionist—the media overall have developed a balanced approach. Most newspapers and broadcast enterprises try to mirror at least a portion of the world. Most of the large news organizations also see it as their function to present some serious political and social information and analysis. Of the newspeople polled by Wilhout and Weaver, 90 percent reported thinking that their organizations were doing a good to excellent job in these areas.[59] At the same time, most cater to the audience's appetite for easily digested entertainment and diversion. The end product cannot fully satisfy everyone.

Summary

What is news depends on what a particular society deems socially significant or personally satisfying to media audiences. The prevailing political and social ideology therefore determines what type of information will be gathered and the range of meanings that will be given to it. News collection is structured through the beat system to keep in touch with the most prolific sources of political news.

Beyond the larger framework, which is rooted in America's current political ideology, overt political considerations rarely play a major part in news selection. Instead, the profit motive and technical constraints of news production become paramount selection criteria. These criteria impose more stringent constraints on television than on print media because television deals with larger, more heterogeneous audiences and requires pictures to match story texts. Unlike newspapers, which rarely have competition in the local market, television must compete for attention with several other electronic outlets.

The end products of these various constraints on news making are news media that generally support the American political system but emphasize its shortcomings and conflicts because journalists see themselves as watchdogs of public honesty and because conflict is exciting. News is geared primarily to attract and entertain rather than to educate the audience about politically significant events. The pressures to report news rapidly while it is happening often lead to presentation of disjointed fragments and disparate commentary. This leaves the audience with the impossible task of weaving the fragments into a meaningful tapestry of interrelated events.

If judged in terms of the information needs of the ideal citizen in the ideal democracy, the end product of the gatekeeping process is inadequate. This is especially true of television, which provides little more than a headline service for news and which mirrors the world about as much as the curved mirrors at the county fair. Reality is reflected, but it seems badly out of shape and proportion.

Most of us only faintly resemble the ideal citizen, and most of us look to the media for entertainment rather than for enlightenment. From this perspective a different appraisal suggests itself. By and large, American mass media serve the general public about as well as that public wants to be served in practice rather than in theory. Entertainment is interspersed with a smattering of serious information. Breadth of coverage is preferred over narrow depth. In times of acute crisis, as we shall see in the next chapter, the media can and do follow a different pattern. Serious news displaces entertainment, and the broad sweep of events turns into a narrow, in-depth focus on the crisis. But short of acute crisis, superficiality prevails most of the time.

Notes

1. G. Cleveland Wilhoit and David H. Weaver, *The American Journalist in the 1990's* (Mahwah, N.J.: Lawrence Erlbaum, 1996). Some of the data presented here are not included in the published study. For an example of other supportive studies, see S. Robert Lichter, Stanley Rothman, and Linda S. Lichter, *The Media Elite: America's New Powerbrokers* (New York: Adler and Adler, 1986).
2. John Johnstone, Edward J. Slawski, and William T. Bowman, "The Professional Values of American Newsmen," *Public Opinion Quarterly* 36 (Winter 1972–1973): 522–540.
3. Herbert J. Gans, *Deciding What's News: A Study of CBS Evening News, NBC Nightly News, Newsweek, and Time* (New York: Pantheon, 1979), 39–69, 182–213. For a look at the neoprogressive outlook of the press using coverage of campaign finance news as a test case, see Frank J. Sorauf, "Campaign Money and the Press: Three Soundings," *Political Science Quarterly* 102 (Spring 1987): 25–42.
4. C. Richard Hofstetter, *Bias in the News: Network Television Coverage of the 1972 Election Campaign* (Columbus: Ohio State University Press, 1976), 187–207.
5. James Warren, "Survey Finds News Still Has Male Face," *Chicago Tribune,* April 8, 1992; also see Dick Haws, "Minorities in the Newsroom and Community: A Comparison," *Journalism Quarterly* 68 (Winter 1991): 764–771.
6. Herbert J. Gans, *Deciding What's News,* 39–69, 116–145, 182–213; Stanley Rothman, "The Media, the Experts, and Public Opinion," in *The Mass Media in Liberal Democratic Societies,* ed. Stanley Rothman (New York: Paragon House,

1992), chap. 8; Kevin M. Carragee, "News and Ideology: An Analysis of Coverage of the West German Green Party by the *New York Times*," *Journalism Monographs* 128 (August 1991).

7. David Weaver and G. Cleveland Wilhoit, "The U.S. Journalist in the 1990's and the Question of Quality in Journalism" (Paper delivered at the annual meeting of the International Communication Association, Sydney, Australia, July 11–15, 1994).

8. Ibid. Also see Janet A. Bridges, "Daily Newspaper Managing Editors' Perceptions of News Media Functions," *Journalism Quarterly* 68 (Winter 1991): 719–728.

9. Thomas E. Patterson and Ronald P. Abeles, "Mass Communications Research and the 1976 Presidential Election," *Items* 2 (June 1975): 13–18.

10. Thomas E. Patterson, "News Decisions: Journalists as Partisan Actors" (Paper delivered at the annual meeting of the American Political Science Association, Chicago, August 31–September 3, 1995); Holli A. Semetko, "Journalistic Culture in Comparative Perspective: The Concept of 'Balance' in U.S., British and German TV News" (Paper delivered at the annual meeting of the American Political Science Association, Chicago, August 31–September 3, 1995).

11. Arthur Charity, *Doing Public Journalism* (New York: Guilford, 1996).

12. "Mr. President, Ben Bradlee Calling," *Public Opinion* 9 (September/October 1986): 40.

13. See Dominic L. Lasorsa and Stephen D. Reese, "News Source Use in the Crash of 1987: A Study of Four National Media," *Journalism Quarterly* 67 (Spring 1990): 60–63, and sources cited therein.

14. Jane Delano Brown, Carl R. Bybee, Stanley T. Wearden, and Dulcie Murdock Straughan, "Invisible Power: Newspaper News Sources and the Limits of Diversity," *Journalism Quarterly* 64 (Spring 1987): 45–54; and Sharon Dunwoody and Steven Shields, "Accounting for Patterns of Selection of Topics in Statehouse Reporting," *Journalism Quarterly* 63 (Autumn 1986): 488–496.

15. W. Lance Bennett, "Toward a Theory of Press-State Relations in the United States," *Journal of Communication* 40 (Spring 1990): 103–125.

16. R. Gordon Shepherd, "Selectivity of Sources: Reporting the Marijuana Controversy," *Journal of Communication* 31 (Spring 1981): 129–137; Sharon Dunwoody and Michael Ryan, "The Credible Scientific Source," *Journalism Quarterly* 64 (Spring 1987): 21–27; Stanley Rothman and S. Robert Lichter, "Elite Ideology and Risk Perception in Nuclear Energy Policy," *American Political Science Review* 81 (June 1987): 383–404; and Nancy Pfund and Laura Hofstadter, "Biomedical Innovation and the Press," *Journal of Communication* 31 (Spring 1981): 138–154.

17. Lichter et al., *The Media Elite*, 62. The study is reported on 54–71. Also see Hans Mathias Kepplinger, "Artificial Horizons: How the Press Presented and How the Population Received Technology in Germany from 1965–1986," in *The Mass Media in Liberal Democratic Societies*, ed. Rothman, chap. 7.

18. Lasorsa and Reese, "News Source Use in the Crash of 1987."

19. The impact of news stories attributed to highly credible sources is described in Benjamin I. Page, Robert Y. Shapiro, and Glenn R. Dempsey, "What Moves Public Opinion?" *American Journal of Political Science* 81 (March 1987): 23–43.

20. Peter Braestrup, *Big Story* (Garden City, N.Y.: Anchor Books, 1978).

21. Ibid.

22. Doris Graber, "The New Media," in *Understanding Public Opinion,* ed. Barbara Norrander and Clyde Wilcox (Washington, D.C.: CQ Press, 1996).

23. George Gerbner, "Ideological Perspective and Political Tendencies in News Reporting," *Journalism Quarterly* 41 (August 1964): 495–508.

24. For a discussion of the social systems framework for mass communications analysis, see James S. Ettema, "The Organizational Context of Creativity," in *Individuals in Mass Media Organizations: Creativity and Constraint,* ed. James S. Ettema and D. Charles Whitney (Beverly Hills, Calif.: Sage, 1982), 91–106.

25. Ron Powers, *The Newscasters* (New York: St. Martin's, 1977), 30.

26. "1995 Year in Review," *Media Monitor* 10(1) (January–February 1996): 3. Also see Everett M. Rogers, James W. Dearing, and Soonbum Chang, "AIDS in the 1980s: The Agenda-Setting Process for a Public Issue," *Journalism Monographs* 126 (April 1991).

27. G. Ray Funkhouser, "Trends in Media Coverage of the Issues of the '60's," *Journalism Quarterly* 50 (Fall 1973): 533–538.

28. Michael X. Delli Carpini and Bruce A. Williams, "Television and Terrorism: Patterns of Presentation and Occurrence, 1969 to 1980," *Western Political Quarterly* 40 (March 1987): 45–64.

29. A study of 149 small and large newspapers reports the following news space allocations: local = 75 percent; sports = 6 percent; national = 4 percent; women's issues = 4 percent; international = 3 percent; editorial = 3 percent; state = 3 percent; financial = 2 percent. The measurements refer to space in column inches of total newshole. Dan Drew and G. Cleveland Wilhoit, "Newshole Allocation Policies of American Daily Newspapers," *Journalism Quarterly* 53 (Fall 1976): 434–440.

30. Robert W. Clyde and James K. Buckalew, "Inter-Media Standardization: A Q-Analysis of News Editors," *Journalism Quarterly* 46 (Summer 1969): 349–351. Various theories about news selection criteria are summarized and analyzed in Pamela Shoemaker with Elizabeth Kay Mayfield, "Building a Theory of News Content: A Synthesis of Current Approaches," *Journalism Monographs* 103 (June 1987).

31. Leon V. Sigal, *Reporters and Officials: The Organization and Politics of Newsmaking* (Lexington, Mass.: Heath, 1973), 119–130. Also see Leon V. Sigal, "Sources Make the News," in *Reading the News,* ed. Robert Karl Manoff and Michael Schudson (New York: Pantheon, 1987), 9–37.

32. The leading story is shared by all three major networks 43 percent of the time. Joe S. Foote and Michael E. Steele, "Degree of Conformity in Lead Stories in Early Evening Network TV Newscasts," *Journalism Quarterly* 63 (Spring 1986): 19–23. For comparable data on local news, see William R. Davie and Jung-Sook Lee, "Sex, Violence, and Consonance/Differentiation: An Analysis of Local TV News Values," *Journalism and Mass Communication Quarterly* 72(1) (Spring 1995): 128–138.

33. The phrase is from Stanley K. Bigman, "Rivals in Conformity: A Study of Two Competing Dailies," *Journalism Quarterly* 25 (Autumn 1949): 127–131.

34. Daniel Riffe, Brenda Ellis, Momo K. Rogers, Roger L. Van Ommeren, and Kieran A. Woodman, "Gatekeeping and the Network News Mix," *Journalism Quarterly* 63 (Summer 1986): 315–321. For a discussion of variations in individual stories, see Norman R. Luttbeg, "News Consensus: Do U.S. Newspapers Mirror Society's Happenings?" *Journalism Quarterly* 60 (Autumn 1983): 484–488.

35. Sigal, *Reporters and Officials,* 66.
36. Ben Bagdikian, *The Information Machines* (New York: Harper and Row, 1971), 99–100.
37. Ibid.; Dunwoody and Shields, "Statehouse Reporting," 488–496.
38. David M. White, "The Gatekeeper," *Journalism Quarterly* 27 (Fall 1950): 383–390, replicated by D. Charles Whitney and Lee B. Becker, "'Keeping the Gates' for Gatekeepers: The Effects of Wire News," *Journalism Quarterly* 59 (Spring 1982): 60–65. See also Guido H. Stempel III, "Gatekeeping: The Mix of Topics and the Selection of Stories," *Journalism Quarterly* 62 (Winter 1985): 791–796.
39. Judy Van Slyke Turk, "Information Subsidies and Media Content: A Study of Public Relations Influence on the News," *Journalism Monographs* 100 (December 1986): 1–29.
40. Drew and Wilhoit, "Newshole Allocation Policies," 434–440. Also see Leo Bogart, "How U.S. Newspaper Content Is Changing," *Journal of Communication* 35 (Spring 1985): 82–91.
41. Harriet Engel Gross and Sharyne Merritt, "Effect of Social/Organizational Context on Gatekeeping in Lifestyle Pages," *Journalism Quarterly* 58 (Autumn 1981): 420–427.
42. The first two headings have been adapted from Herbert Gans's study of news magazine and network television news. Herbert J. Gans, *Deciding What's News,* 8–31. See also Gaye Tuchman, *Making News: A Study in the Construction of Reality* (New York: Free Press, 1978); and W. Lance Bennett, *News: The Politics of Illusion,* 2d ed. (New York: Longman, 1988), chaps. 2 and 4.
43. Karen S. Johnson, "The Portrayal of Lame-Duck Presidents by the National Print Media," *Presidential Studies Quarterly* 16 (Winter 1986): 50–65. For a broad discussion of the coverage mix at the federal government level, see Stephen Hess, *The Washington Reporters* (Washington, D.C.: Brookings Institution, 1981), chaps. 3 and 5.
44. Gerald Stone, Barbara Hartung, and Dwight Jensen, "Local TV News and the Good-Bad Dyad," *Journalism Quarterly* 64 (Spring 1987): 37–44.
45. George Gerbner, Larry Gross, Michael Morgan, and Nancy Signorielli, "Charting the Mainstream: Television's Contributions to Political Orientations," *Journal of Communication* 32 (Spring 1982): 106–107. Small-town newspapers are more apt to highlight the positive, telling what is good rather than what is bad, because conflict is less tolerable in social systems in which most of the leaders constantly rub elbows.
46. The term "videomalaise" is Michael J. Robinson's. See Robinson, "American Political Legitimacy in an Era of Electronic Journalism: Reflections on the Evening News," in *Television as a Social Force: New Approaches to TV Criticism,* ed. Richard Adler (New York: Praeger, 1975), 97–139. Gerald C. Stone and Elinor Grusin report that only 25 percent of nightly television news is "good news"; "Network TV as the Bad News Bearer," *Journalism Quarterly* 61 (Autumn 1984): 521.
47. Stephen E. Rada, "Manipulating the Media: A Case Study of a Chicano Strike in Texas," *Journalism Quarterly* 54 (Spring 1977): 109–113. Also see Gadi Wolfsfeld, "Symbiosis of Press and Protest: An Exchange Analysis," *Journalism Quarterly* 61 (Autumn 1984): 550–555.
48. Mike Royko, "Fire Is Going Out of Los Angeles Riot Story," *Chicago Tribune,* May 8, 1992.

49. William Raspberry, "When the Media Misses the Point," *Chicago Tribune*, October 31, 1995.
50. Klaus Bruhn Jensen, "News as Ideology: Economics Statistics and Political Ritual in Television Network News," *Journal of Communication* 37 (Winter 1987): 8–27; Bennett, *News*.
51. For a strong attack on status quo support, see Claus Mueller, *The Politics of Communication* (London: Oxford University Press, 1973); see also Edward S. Herman and Noam Chomsky, *Manufacturing Consent: The Political Economy of the Mass Media* (New York: Pantheon, 1988).
52. There is resistance to change, even in entertainment program formats. See Jay G. Blumler and Carolynn Martin Spicer, "Prospects for Creativity in the New Television Marketplace: Evidence from Program-Makers," *Journal of Communication* 40 (Autumn 1990): 78–101.
53. Sigal, *Reporters and Officials*, 119–130. On government sources for economic news, see Stephen D. Reese, John A. Daly, and Andrew P. Hardy, "Economic News on Network Television," *Journalism Quarterly* 64 (Spring 1987): 137–144; also see Jarol B. Manheim, *All of the People All the Time: Strategic Communication and American Politics* (Armonk, N.Y.: M. E. Sharpe, 1991), 27–35.
54. A comparison of war movies made with and without Pentagon aid showed that aided movies depicted the military in a more favorable light. Russell E. Shain, "Effects of Pentagon Influence on War Movies, 1948–70," *Public Opinion Quarterly* 38 (Fall 1972): 641–647.
55. For a fuller exploration of this issue, see David L. Altheide, *Creating Reality: How T. V. News Distorts Events* (Beverly Hills, Calif.: Sage, 1976); Tuchman, *Making News*; Mark Fishman, *Manufacturing the News* (Austin: University of Texas Press, 1980); and Bennett, *News*, chaps. 3 and 5.
56. But sensational news often contains a great deal of information. See C. Richard Hofstetter and David M. Dozier, "Useful News, Sensational News: Quality, Sensationalism, and Local TV News," *Journalism Quarterly* 63 (Winter 1986): 815–820; and Dan Nimmo and James E. Combs, *Nightly Horrors: Crisis Coverage in Television Network News* (Knoxville: University of Tennessee Press, 1985).
57. Frederick Fico and Stan Soffin, "Fairness and Balance of Selected Newspaper Coverage of Controversial National, State and Local Issues," *Journalism and Mass Communication Quarterly* 72(3) (Autumn 1995): 621–633; Neil J. Kressel, "Biased Judgments of Media Bias: A Case Study of the Arab-Israeli Dispute," *Political Psychology* 8 (June 1987): 211–226; and Lichter et al., *The Media Elite*, 293–301. The difficulties of defining "bias" are explained in Stephen Lacy, Frederick Fico, and Todd F. Simon, "Fairness and Balance in the Prestige Press," *Journalism Quarterly* 68 (Fall 1991): 363–370. Also see Todd F. Simon, Frederick Fico, and Stephen Lacy, "Covering Conflict and Controversy: Measuring Balance, Fairness, Defamation," *Journalism Quarterly* 62 (Summer 1989): 427–434.
58. William Schneider and I. A. Lewis, "Views on the News," *Public Opinion* 8 (August/September 1985): 8–11, 58–59. The authors report the results of a *Los Angeles Times* nationwide survey in 1985 in which the public gave their newspapers a 96 percent positive rating when "very good" and "fairly good" ratings are combined. Local television received a 95 percent positive rating, and network television news ratings were 91 percent positive.
59. Wilhoit and Weaver, *The American Journalist*, 11.

Readings

Emery, Michael, and Edwin Emery. *The Press and America: An Interpretive History of the Mass Media.* Englewood Cliffs, N.J.: Prentice Hall, 1992.

Frank, Reuven. *Out of Thin Air: The Brief Wonderful Life of Network News.* New York: Simon and Schuster, 1991.

Gaunt, Philip. *Choosing the News: The Profit Factor in News Selection.* New York: Greenwood, 1990.

Hallin, Daniel C. *We Keep America on Top of the World: Television Journalism and the Public Sphere.* New York, Routledge, 1994.

Iyengar, Shanto. *Is Anyone Responsible: How Television Frames Political Issues.* Chicago: University of Chicago Press, 1991.

Schudson, Michael. *The Power of News.* Cambridge, Mass.: Harvard University Press, 1995.

Shoemaker, Pamela J. *Gatekeeping.* Newbury Park, Calif.: Sage, 1991.

Shoemaker, Pamela J., and Stephen D. Reese. *Mediating the Message: Theories of Influences on Mass Media Content.* New York: Longman, 1991.

Wilhoit, G. Cleveland, and David H. Weaver. *The American Journalist in the 1990's: U.S. News People at the End of an Era.* Mahwah, N.J.: Lawrence Erlbaum, 1996.

chapter   five

Reporting Extraordinary Events

WHAT COMMON THREAD JOINS the Gulf War, the bombing of a federal building in Oklahoma City, the 1994 earthquake in southern California, and the Los Angeles riots of 1992? The answer is that all are *extraordinary natural or man-made events*. Such events happen rarely. They are dramatic and rich in pictures that tug at human heart strings. And they seem salient to the lives of media audiences because they threaten their shared values and peace of mind and for some, their lives and property. Such events receive an extraordinary amount of sustained media coverage and an extraordinary amount of audience attention because people expect to be informed and to be protected by the appropriate government agencies.

What politically significant roles do media play when such extraordinary events occur, and how do they go about playing them? To answer these questions, we will take a close look at the four situations just mentioned, along with brief glances at related events. Once the broad coverage principles have been explained and illustrated, we will turn to a number of pseudo-crises. These are events when crisis-type coverage has elevated a comparatively normal event to the status of an extraordinary one.

In times of crisis the media, particularly radio and, in recent years, television, become vital arms of government. As usual, they select, shape, and report the news to people in and out of government. But in addition, they provide government officials quick access to the public directly or indirectly through media personnel. Messages from government officials keep endangered communities in touch with essential information and instructions. They also allow government authorities to shape perceptions of the crisis and its causes and appropriate remedies.

Besides its intrinsic importance, coverage of extraordinary events highlights major philosophical and policy issues concerning the government-media relationship. In times of crises, citizens pay close attention to media messages. The media's responsibility to serve public needs becomes exceptionally acute as does the government's responsibility to control, direct, and even manipulate the flow of news for public purposes. The Olympian view of media performance yields to a vision of danger at eyeball distance.

Four Crises

In this chapter we will examine media coverage of four crises: the war against Iraq in the Persian Gulf area in January and February 1991; the riots in Los Angeles that started April 30, 1992; the earthquake that hit southern California on January 17, 1994; and the bombing of a midtown federal building in Oklahoma City on April 19, 1995.

War in the Persian Gulf

In the summer of 1990, hostilities erupted in the Persian Gulf region when Iraq invaded neighboring Kuwait. After economic sanctions failed to bring a withdrawal, the United Nations community, with the United States in the lead, started military operations. The war lasted forty-four days. It began with bombing attacks on Iraq on January 16, followed by a ground attack on February 23. Half a million American troops were sent to the Gulf and a similar number were mobilized on the home front. Although most people assumed that Iraq would lose the war, the outcome and the ultimate cost of the war in terms of people and property losses on both sides were uncertain. Scud missile attacks on Israel raised the possibility of large scale losses by Iraq's enemies.[1]

Los Angeles Riots

On March 3, 1991, after a high-speed chase, several officers of the Los Angeles police stopped an African American motorist for traffic violations. An angry confrontation ensued that ended with the white officers severely beating the motorist. A resident of a nearby apartment building, alerted by the noise, videotaped scenes of the beating. Over the course of the next year, the shocking footage was broadcast thousands of times throughout the nation, creating a widespread consensus among citizens of all races that the police had used excessive force. Police brutality and racism became simmering public issues, kept near the boiling point by the repeated airing of the taped scenes.

When news reports informed Americans at the end of April 1992 that an all-white jury had exonerated all but one of the Los Angeles officers on the charges of brutality, protest demonstrations pockmarked the country. In Los Angeles these demonstrations turned into one of the ugliest urban riots in decades, complete with shootings, beatings, massive arson, and looting. Fifty-three people were killed, and more than 2,000 were injured. Millions of dollars worth of property was destroyed, leaving sections of the city an economic wasteland. In the wake of the rioting, the focus of the ongoing presidential campaign turned to the hitherto neglected problems of urban decay, the alienated, impoverished underclass, and deepening tension between races.[2]

Major Earthquake in Southern California

On January 17, 1994, in the predawn hours, the strongest earthquake in southern California's history left 55 people dead, hundreds injured, and thousands homeless. The main shock lasted for 30 seconds and reached a magnitude of 6.6 on the Richter scale. Numerous severe aftershocks followed. The earthquake and the subsequent aftershocks ignited fires from ruptured gas lines and propane tanks, caused landslides and floods, crumpled highways and overpasses, and toppled buildings, burying victims under tons of debris. Survivors were left without electric power, gas, water, and telephone services and many were isolated for days because of impassable roads. Property damage amounted to billions of dollars.[3]

Oklahoma City Bombing

On April 19, 1995, a car bomb gouged a nine-story hole in a federal office building in downtown Oklahoma City. The explosion left 168 people dead, including many young children in a daycare center located in the building. More than 300 people were missing immediately after the blast, though most of them were later found. More than 460 people were injured, many of them critically. The blast was felt as far as 50 miles away, and nearby buildings were destroyed or damaged. Rescue forces had to crawl over debris and corpses for days to try to extricate survivors trapped in the collapsed building. The explosion reminded observers of the terrorist car bombing that killed 6 people and injured 1,000 in 1993 at the World Trade Center in New York City.[4]

TABLE 5-1   Principal Sources of Disaster Information
(in percentage of responses)

Sources of information	Site A	Site B	Site C	Site D
Electronic media	66	59	75	75
Newspapers	24	20	40	64
Magazines	3	7	8	15
Nonfiction books	10	10	11	4
Other persons	17	12	14	9
Direct experience	37	32	20	6
Public education	9	6	5	—

SOURCE: Dennis E. Wenger, "A Few Empirical Observations Concerning the Relationship between the Mass Media and Disaster Knowledge: A Research Report," in *Disasters and the Mass Media: Proceedings of the Committee on Disasters and the Mass Media Workshop* (Washington, D.C.: National Academy Press, 1980), 244. Reprinted by permission.

NOTE: Multiple answers were permitted. $N = 290$ for Site A, hurricane disasters; 281 for Site B, tornado disasters; 209 for Site C, flood disasters; and 341 for Site D, disaster-free control.

Media Responses and Roles

During crises the public depends almost totally on the media for news and for vital messages from public and private authorities. The mass media are the only institutions equipped to collect this massive amount of information and disseminate it quickly. Therefore, when people become aware of a crisis, they monitor developments through their radios or television sets, often round-the-clock.

Table 5-1 presents data on sources that people used for crisis information in three communities hit by natural disasters. The table demonstrates people's heavy reliance on electronic media, particularly battery-powered radios, and the comparatively small role played by interpersonal communication and direct experience. Community A, located on the Gulf Coast, had experienced numerous hurricanes. Communities B and C in the Midwest had suffered two tornadoes and two major floods, respectively. Community D had no experience with a major natural disaster. A sample of residents in communities A, B, and C was asked, "From what sources have you obtained the greatest amount of information concerning natural disasters?" Several sources could be cited in response.[5] Respondents in the disaster-free control community (D) were asked to speculate about what sources might be most useful.

The audience for crisis information is massive and loyal. For example, 58 percent of the American public closely watched news stories about the Oklahoma City bombing. That was more than twice the number that paid close attention to the heated Medicare debate that had erupted in Congress at that time.[6] When the Gulf War started, television sets everywhere remained turned on throughout the night and into the wee hours of the morning so that people could watch unfolding events. To keep up with the round-the-clock coverage by CNN, all the networks sharply increased news coverage of the war. More than one billion people in 108 nations watched CNN war coverage, making its largely undigested reports of breaking events their leading source of war news. When American audiences were asked in a Gallup Poll about their main source of war news, 89 percent mentioned television, 8 percent mentioned radio, and only 2 percent mentioned newspapers.[7]

Besides information, the public looks to the media for interpretation of the situation, because media personnel are often the first ones on the scene trying to fit events into a coherent story. Official investigations generally come much later. The media also guide the public to appropriate behavior during the crisis. They warn people to retreat to a shelter, announce which areas are unsafe to enter, describe purification of polluted food and water, and supply news of missing persons or schedules to be maintained by schools and workplaces. News stories also explain what immediate steps government authorities are taking to cope with the crisis.

Stages and Patterns of Coverage

Observers of crisis coverage have identified three stages that merge almost seamlessly and often overlap.

Stage One. During the first stage, the crisis or disaster is announced as having just struck or as impending. Media people, officials, and onlookers rush to the scene. A flood of uncoordinated messages is transmitted over the airwaves as radio and television stations interrupt regularly scheduled programs with bulletins announcing the extraordinary event or preempt the entire program for reports from the scene.

Minutes after the start of the Los Angeles riots, television and radio broadcast live from the scene. They showed buildings on fire and beating and looting scenes, usually without a single police officer within camera range. Later, these broadcasts were blamed for tipping off rioters about places where they might assault, burn, and loot with impunity. These same stories also helped police find locations where they were sorely needed. Media offices became information collection centers because people phoned them with reports or called them for information. The most important broadcasts at the start of a disaster are messages describing what is happening, directing people to places of safety, summoning police and military units, and coordinating appeals for relief supplies, such as food, blankets, blood donations, and medical equipment.

In the early phase the number of news broadcasts rises steeply. During the Gulf War and the Los Angeles riots, as well as in the Oklahoma City and southern California disasters, radio and television doubled broadcast time and CNN operated on a twenty-four hour news schedule. Many regular programs were replaced with crisis-related news and interviews. News bulletins were issued throughout the day on radio and television. A steady stream of eyewitnesses was interviewed. With little new to report, the same facts were rehashed endlessly. The initial announcements are relayed to a steadily growing audience by word of mouth, either in person or by telephone. For instance, in 1981 the news of the attempted assassination of President Reagan initially reached a large daytime audience that heard it on radio or television and then, on average, told it to three other people. More than 90 percent of the American public—more than two hundred million people—received the news within ninety minutes after the shooting.[8]

The striking characteristic of initial coverage of extraordinary events is the rapidity of communication. Television and radio, helped by satellite technology, can focus the public's attention almost instantaneously on developing situations. In many cases news about the extraordinary event replaces most other stories. On January 18, 1994, following the southern California earthquake, the *Los Angeles Times* devoted its entire front page, along with many inside pages, to the event. Whatever else happens in the world during crisis periods, regardless of its importance, may be largely blocked out in the affected area or even the entire nation.

During the first stage, the media are the major sources of information, even for public officials concerned with the crisis. Media reports serve to coordinate public activities and to calm the audience. For example, the *Los Angeles Times* carried a special report on "Coping with the Quake" right after it struck. The report gave people tips about temporary housing, health care, and ways to cope with damage in their homes.

Next to reaching the disaster site, the chief problem for newspeople during the first stage is getting accurate information. Rumors abound. During the Gulf War, some of the early information, based on raw, unevaluated data, was incorrect. For example, network reporters told about chemical attacks on Israel and Israeli retaliation that had not occurred. The Oklahoma City blast was immediately dubbed a "terrorist" bombing and false rumors circulated that men of Middle Eastern backgrounds had been sighted near the scene. A connection to Hamas, a terrorist organization, was also reported. The number of dead and the extent of injuries are frequently inflated. Newspeople receive so many conflicting reports that they lack enough time to check their accuracy. The unrelenting pressure for fresh accounts often tempts media personnel to interview inexperienced eyewitnesses and commentators, who may lend a local touch without clarifying the situation. They also may report information that has not been adequately verified or that is atypical.[9] By focusing on the destruction of a small section of Los Angeles during the Los Angeles riots, for instance, the audience was left with the wrong impression that the entire city was in ruins.[10]

If highly technical matters are involved—as happens in explosions, structural failures, and nuclear radiation disasters—it may be impossible to present a coherent story. Government officials, eager to allay the public's fears and prevent panic, usually minimize the dangers when communicating with newspeople. Reporters often lack the expertise to know when officials are concealing the truth. They cannot make sense out of technical jargon into which official messages are couched.

The pressure for news encourages reporters and public officials alike to speculate about what happened and why. At times they spin their own prejudices into a web of scenarios that puts blame for the disaster or its aftermath on socially outcast groups. Blaming Middle Eastern terrorists for the Oklahoma City bombing was a typical response. In the same way, the Los Angeles riots, which occurred during the 1992 presidential campaign, were blamed by Democrats on Republican inattention to urban blight and by Republicans on the welfare programs of the liberal democratic Johnson administration. "Outsiders" in a community (ethnic minorities or political deviants, for example) often become the hapless scapegoats. The racial riots of the 1960s were routinely attributed to "outside agitators" who were depicted as common criminals, bereft of moral dignity and social consciousness.

Stage Two. During the second stage of a crisis, the media try to correct past errors and put the situation into its proper perspective. Enough time generally has elapsed so that the chief dimensions of the crisis have emerged. For instance, in the Oklahoma City bombing, the Los Angeles riots, and the earthquake, the extent of the damage had been ascertained. Names of most victims and their injuries were known. Plans had been made for repairs and reconstruction.

In general, print media are able to do a more thorough job than radio and television in pulling together the various events and fitting them into a coherent story. Print media have larger staffs for investigation and more room to present background details that make the events understandable. For instance, in the months preceding the outbreak of the Gulf War and in the days following the start of the air war and later the ground war, the *New York Times* and the *Washington Post* probed into the reasons for the hostilities, the cost in human lives and property, and ecological damage from oil well fires.

During this second stage, governments and their critics may try to shape political fallout from the event in ways that support their policy preferences. Gulf War coverage, for example, although appearing to present reality sanitized the war. Television showed precision bombings, targeted down chimneys or directly into doors. The air force later admitted that 70 percent of the bombs dropped on Kuwait and Iraq actually missed their targets. The smart bombs shown on television represented only a tiny fraction of the total. Military censorship prevented showing the arrival of dead soldiers in body bags at Dover Air Force base or featuring casualties. Enemy losses were rarely shown.[11] In the disasters in California and Oklahoma political leaders, including the president, earned political plaudits for visiting the affected places and expressing words of sympathy and encouragement as well as announcing emergency aid such as the arrival of Federal Emergency Management Agency (FEMA) personnel.

Stage Three. The third stage overlaps with the first two. It involves attempts by media personnel to place the crisis into a larger, long-range perspective and to prepare people to cope with the aftermath. Steps toward restoration of normal conditions may be discussed. Following the Los Angeles riots, presidential candidates Bill Clinton and George Bush toured the damaged neighborhoods and discussed rebuilding plans. The media also announced restoration of suspended services, such as mail deliveries and bus transportation, and the start of clean-up efforts. Within days of the southern California earthquake, news offerings were peppered with glowing accounts of quick recoveries by California communities struck by previous earthquakes. These stories often supplied detailed accounts of reconstruction efforts.

To cope with long-range post-traumatic shock and to sustain morale when crises are prolonged it may be helpful to describe how some of the hardest hit victims are coping and to give full coverage to healing ceremonies such as memorial church services. The media devoted ample time and resources to this type of coverage in the disasters discussed.

During the Three Mile Island incident in 1979, which involved a potential nuclear disaster, the federal government took unusual measures to calm citizens' fears. It centralized news releases in an attempt to halt disquieting conflicting reports. All information furnished by government and plant officials about the disaster had to be cleared through a press center operated by the Nuclear Regulatory Commission near the site of the accident. Although officials of the damaged plant protested the censorship, they complied with President Jimmy Carter's order. Later a formal investigation of how forty-three newspapers and network evening newscasts reported the accident credited the media with providing balanced treatment in a highly confused and confusing situation.

Positive Effects of Coverage

Information about crises, even if it is bad news, relieves disquieting uncertainty and calms people. The mere activity of watching or listening to familiar reporters and commentators reassures people and keeps them occupied. It gives them a sense of vicarious participation, of "doing something." To maintain this quieting effect, media personnel may avoid showing gruesome details of the crisis. Although this was not true of the Los Angeles riots—during which vivid scenes of assaults and looting were filmed by helicopter crews and broadcast immediately—it was true in Chicago a few weeks later. When rioting youths smashed store windows and looted, causing millions of dollars worth of damage, the front-page headline in the *Chicago Tribune* proclaimed "Two for Two: Bulls Still Champs!" Under the banner-size letters, a much smaller headline noted that "Celebration Breaks Out Repeatedly" and alluded to the disturbances in a single sentence: "In a few areas, victory begat broken windows and uninvited shopping." A few short paragraphs on inside pages carried additional news of the looting.[12]

News stories serve to reassure people that their grief and fears are shared. After seeing the same pictures and listening to the same broadcasts, people can discuss the crisis with neighbors, friends, and coworkers and experience feelings of mutual support. Watching military briefings on television during the Gulf War made Americans feel that they were fully informed about the war's progress and that the authorities were in full control of the situation. Scenes of collapsing buildings or city blocks put to the torch during a riot become less frightening if the news shows that police, firefighters, ambulances, and medical personnel are on the scene. Watching the mayor or governor tour a disaster site provides further reassurance. Finally, directions conveyed by the media about appropriate behavior may save lives and property and ensure that the stricken community continues to function.

Negative Effects of Coverage

Media coverage also may have adverse effects during a crisis, raising serious questions about the responsibility of media personnel to consider the societal consequences of freedom to publish. The government's duty to prevent harm-producing coverage, possibly by strict censorship, may become a major political issue.

News messages may so disturb people that they cannot act rationally. They may panic, endangering themselves and others. For instance, a precipitous mass exodus of frightened people during an impending flood or storm calamity may clog roads and overcrowd shelters; it may lead to injuries and death for those caught beyond the safety of their homes and workplaces. Pictures of violence may lead to a terrifying multiplication effect. Audiences frequently believe that the violent act is merely one of many. One house on fire or the sight of one victim's body may lead to visions of whole neighborhoods on fire and scores of victims killed. Police may be ordered to shoot lawbreakers on sight, and citizens may resort to excessive violence to protect themselves.

Statements provoking unwise reactions are more likely to be publicized in times of crisis because the exceptionally large demand for news and guidance reduces gatekeepers' vigilance. Pack journalism may run rampant when all available news is shared to provide as much coverage as possible. If mistakes are made by news sources or reporters, they are spread by all the media. The rash of erroneous stories linking Middle Eastern terrorists to the Oklahoma City bombing exposed Arab Americans across the United States to hate crimes. After the nuclear mishap at Three Mile Island, workers complained that erroneous media reports, based on conflicting assessments by government officials about the explosiveness of a hydrogen bubble, frightened their families into needless evacuation of the area and threatened the survival of the plant and their job security. Such consequences are commonplace as long as crisis news routinely draws analogies to worst-case scenarios without providing perspectives on their likelihood.[13]

Crisis and disaster news frequently attracts crowds of citizens and reporters to the site, impeding rescue and security operations. News coverage of physical disasters routinely draws looters to the scene. During the Los Angeles riots, police reported that the presence of television cameras seemed to escalate the violence. Rioters actually appeared to perform for the cameras. Sights of looters attracted other looters to the scene, particularly when the pictures revealed that no police officers were present. When violence pits government agents against antigovernment groups, as is often the case in terrorist incidents, ample coverage may incite retaliatory action. The Oklahoma City bombing allegedly was partly revenge by a few members of a right-wing group for government attacks on an antigovernment group in Waco, Texas, two years to the day earlier.

Wide publicity for terrorist acts and heinous crimes (such as airline hijackings, poisoning of food supplies, or serial mass murders) may encourage such acts and lead to copycat crimes. The Los Angeles riots, for example, produced copycat violence in Atlanta, Cleveland, Madison,

Long Beach, and San Jose. The Oklahoma City bombing encouraged bombing threats at many other federal government office buildings. When Los Angeles police were criticized for failure to act decisively to protect the riot-torn areas, police chief Daryl F. Gates told reporters, with camera-equipped helicopters whirring overhead, "We did not want to make it appear that we were overreacting. We were very, very careful not to show that provocativeness."[14] The looters were not so camera shy. Extensive media coverage has been called the lifeblood of terrorism because the perpetrators use their assaults to attract attention to their causes and gain sympathy and support.

Economic crises, too, can escalate as a result of media images. When prices on the financial markets plunged precipitously on October 19, 1987, media accounts used highly alarming language. *Panic, carnage,* and *nightmare selling* were common descriptive terms. Moreover, the media frequently compared the crash to the 1929 stock market calamity and discussed the Great Depression that followed. Such gloomy news apparently fanned the growing panic and further weakened the markets.[15]

Planning Crisis Coverage

Because media play such a crucial role in keeping communities going during crises, most media organizations have plans to cope with crisis coverage problems. This is particularly true for electronic media. In one sample of seventy-two radio and television stations in twelve U.S. cities, 70 percent of the stations had plans for reporting natural disasters, and 73 percent had plans for reporting civil disturbances.[16] The plans generally were more detailed for natural disasters because needs are more predictable, and there is greater consensus about objectives. Nevertheless, much remains to be decided on the spur of the moment. Confusion inevitably reigns at the start of a crisis. Contradictory messages are likely to abound until coordination can be arranged. In addition to media-sponsored plans, most stations are tied into the federal Emergency Broadcast System (EBS), a network for relaying news during emergencies.

Crisis coverage planning has two aspects: preparing for crisis routines and deciding how to present ongoing events. Aside from warning people about impending natural disasters and suggesting preparations, plans to forestall crises are rare, probably because media focus on short-range happenings and because most crises cannot be accurately predicted. Nonetheless, the media often have been blamed for neglecting preventive coverage. The Public's Right to Information Task Force of the President's Commission on the Accident at Three Mile Island blamed the Commonwealth Edison Company, the Nuclear Regulatory Commission, and the media for ignoring problems at the plant prior to the accident and for overemphasizing the safety of nuclear power.[17] In 1968 the Kerner Commission condemned media silence about the plight of African Americans in the United States. Ample early coverage, the members of the commission claimed, might have prevented violence in the mid-1960s. In the same vein, the 1992 Los Angeles riots were blamed in part on inattention to the plight of inner cities and their minority residents by major institutions, including the media.

Coverage to prevent the government from involving the nation in war raises several serious issues. For example, media attention to the Bush administration's support of Iraq's government immediately prior to the Gulf War might have ended support and prevented Iraq's assault on Kuwait that led to the war. Would publication have been a patriotic act or undue interference in the nation's foreign policy? The answer is controversial.

In 1980 columnist Jack Anderson reported that an election-minded Carter administration was planning a military invasion of Iran to counteract the humiliation of the ongoing hostage crisis. The vast majority of papers that normally carry Anderson's column printed it. Most papers also printed government denials. One paper editorialized, "The recklessness of a politically motivated invasion would be far more dangerous than reckless journalism."[18] No major invasion ever took place. Whether one was planned or whether the column thwarted the plans was never clarified.

Natural Disasters. Rodney Kueneman and Joseph Wright, who examined the seventy-two radio and television stations' plans to cover natural disasters, found that the plans were generally predicated on the assumption that people tend to panic and that coverage must be designed to forestall this. Stories that are graphic enough to arouse a lethargic population to prepare for the disaster unfortunately may cause panic or denial. Such "ostrich" inclinations may explain why some residents of southern California have not taken recommended precautions—such as fortifying buildings and storing emergency supplies—despite frequent warnings about the danger of serious earthquakes.[19]

Widespread warnings about an impending disaster may lead to costly, unnecessary preventive measures when the warnings turn out to be false alarms. That happened in the winter of 1990 when warnings about a 50-percent chance of an earthquake in the New Madrid earthquake zone in the Middle West prompted residents to flee, public services to be shut down, and numerous business events to be canceled. The predictions had been made by a climatologist whose credentials had been questioned by a panel of seismologists and geologists. Nonetheless, the story was widely believed. Reporters by the hundreds gathered in the "danger zone" ready to report the event, which did not occur.

Civil Disorders. Most station personnel interviewed for the Kueneman-Wright study assumed that broadcasts about civil disturbances would produce panic among the public and copycat effects. By contrast, social scientists who study disasters deny that panic and contagion occur frequently.[20] Whether or not they are correct, the important fact is that media personnel expect these reactions and act accordingly.

Compared to other types of crises, there has been relatively little advance planning for coverage of civil disturbances, despite their prevalence. From the riots of the 1960s, media personnel learned that it is wise to de-emphasize media presence when violence occurs because the perpetrators are spurred by the chance to have their actions publicized. Media personnel accordingly try to act unobtrusively. For example, they avoid bringing identified television trucks into areas where disturbances are taking place. As mentioned earlier for the Chicago riots in the spring of 1992, newspapers kept stories and pictures about the events off their front pages. However, such precautions are largely wasted when, as in the Chicago case, television reporters broadcast live coverage from the scene.

It also helps to avoid inflammatory details or language in news reports. Milder terms can be substituted for words such as *carnage, holocaust, mob action,* or *massacre.* The general rule is "when in doubt, leave it out." Tempers can be soothed by publicizing interviews with public officials and civic leaders who urge calm behavior and who indicate that the situation is under control. In the Los Angeles riots, Mayor Tom Bradley and Gov. Pete Wilson were shown and quoted repeatedly about progress made in quieting the city. Rodney King, the victim of the police beating that ultimately led to the disturbances, also made an impassioned appeal for ending the violence. Following the Oklahoma City bombing, President Clinton, in a speech at Michigan State University, pleaded for replacing hate talk on radio shows with calmer messages. What he failed to note was that the mainstream media's extensive coverage of the activities of extremist groups, in the wake of the bombing, had riveted the nation's attention on such groups and their rhetoric as never before.[21]

The Problem of News Suppression

In natural as well as man-made crises, suppressing news, either temporarily or permanently, raises major policy questions. How much coverage should be presented immediately, at the risk of telling an inaccurate story, spreading panic, and attracting bystanders and destructive participants to the scene? What facts should be withheld initially or permanently? In the Kueneman-Wright study 80 percent of the newspeople said that they would temporarily withhold information that might provoke troublesome reactions. Some would withhold live coverage entirely, particularly in civil disturbances, believing that it increases the intensity and duration of the crisis. Some news outlets delay live coverage until officials have the situation under control. Others believe that suppression of live coverage will allow the spread of rumors that may be more inciting than judicious reporting of ongoing events. No one knows which of these views is most correct or how different circumstances affect reactions to media coverage of crises.

Deciding whether to suppress coverage becomes particularly difficult when a crisis involves terrorists, prison rioters, assassins of political leaders, or maniacal mass murderers who crave publicity. Live coverage glamorizes their violent acts and may encourage further outrages. "By transforming a killer into a celebrity, the press has not merely encouraged but perhaps driven him to strike again and may have stirred others brooding madly over their grievances to act."[22] As Rep. Edward Feighan (D-Ohio) pointed out after chairing congressional hearings on terrorism and the media, the television age poses new dilemmas for a responsible press. "Terrorism is a new form of symbolic warfare, and the television screen is the battlefield on which these wars will be fought in the future."[23] Even the print media face such dilemmas. The *New York Times* and *Washington Post* reluctantly agreed in 1995 to publish a lengthy tract by a terrorist. The "Unabomber" had threatened to continue his spree of letter bombings unless his manifesto of complaints against society was published.

Publicity does play into the hands of individuals willing to spread terror through indiscriminate killings and other heinous deeds. However, if the press fails to cover the terrorist acts, it can be accused of infringing on the public's right to know. It also forgoes publishing a dramatic event with wide audience appeal and substantial financial rewards. If the press follows the government's official line in describing terrorists and their motives, it becomes a government propaganda tool.[24] If it dwells on either the human strengths or the frightful human frailties of the violent actors, it will be accused of making saints out of villains or villains out of hapless victims of society's malfunctions.

The press faces similar difficult decisions about news suppression during international crises and in time of war. During the Gulf War, the military kept tight control over news stories by escorting small groups of reporters to the battlefront and then requiring that their dispatches be cleared by military censors. A number of reporters resented such constraints and ventured forth on their own in defiance of official rules and at the risk of their personal safety. Although their fellow journalists gener-

Reprinted with special permission of King Features Syndicate.

ally approved, a *Los Angeles Times Mirror* poll showed that 80 percent of the public felt that news censorship by the military was a good idea. When CNN reporter Peter Arnett interviewed President Saddam Hussein during the war and broadcast Hussein's questionable claim that the American air force had bombed an infant formula factory, a number of prominent critics publicly questioned Arnett's patriotism. They felt that in wartime the press ought to avoid publicizing news that might hurt war goals, particularly when the news is broadcast worldwide, as is true of CNN.[25]

Muted coverage is problematic. It generally leads to presentation of the official story only and suppression of unofficial views. The perspectives of civilian and military public security personnel become paramount. As a result security aspects are stressed rather than the causes of violent behavior and the political and social changes, including new public policies, that might prevent future violence. When the press revisited coverage of a tense racial incident involving murder in a New York City neighborhood two years later, they concluded that the facts had been adequately covered without further inflaming the tense public. But crucial details about mistakes made by former public officials in handling the crisis had been omitted, largely because these officials had been the main sources of news. These omissions delayed reforms and deepened the community's racial divisions.[26] In terrorist incidents or prison riots, failure to air the grievances of terrorists and prison inmates deprives them of a public forum for voicing their grievances. Their bottled up anger may lead to more violent explosions. Wartime news suppression may cover up misdeeds and encourage their repetition.

Some observers contend that muted reporting reduces the potential for arousing hatred and creating unbridgeable conflicts. Delayed coverage, these observers argue, can be more analytical and thus more likely to produce reforms. Others contend that the drama of an ongoing crisis raises public consciousness much better and faster than anything else. People will act to remedy injustice only if the situation is acute. If the crisis has already passed, action may seem pointless. A permanent news blackout will make reforms highly unlikely. Those opposed to muted coverage or news suppression are willing to risk paying a high price in lost lives, personal injuries, imprisonment, and property damage in hopes that immediate, complete coverage will shock the community to undertake basic social reforms. Most American political leaders, as well as most newspeople, have hitherto opted for muting violent conflict rather than bringing it to a head.

Finally, there is the unresolved philosophical question about the wisdom and propriety of news suppression in a free society. The true test of genuine press freedom does not come in times of calm. It comes in times of crisis when the costs of freedom may be dear, tempting government and media alike to impose silence. If a free press is a paramount value, then the die must be cast in favor of unrestrained crisis coverage, moderated only by the sense of responsibility of individual journalists.

Covering Pseudo-Crises

Thus far, we have discussed genuinely extraordinary events. But there are many other situations that the press treat like crises because they make interesting news stories. These pseudo-crises become front-page news for days on end, generating many hours of live television and radio coverage. As television critic Rick Kogan put it:

> Real life—not the facsimiles and fantasy versions of it once so persuasively (and successfully) purveyed by entertainment television—gave us the most compelling and, like it or not, engaging TV images of 1991.... The Clarence Thomas hearings, for all their import, also steamed hotter than your favorite

soap. The [William Kennedy] Smith rape trial, even with its numbing forensic details, was more arresting than "L.A. Law." Add to that such almost-surreal details as Los Angeles police officers beating a motorist, a failed coup in the Soviet Union, and Henry Kissinger playing weatherman on "CBS this Morning," and you have the making of a TV mega-hit: "The Real World Show."[27]

The various scenarios that make up this "Real World Show" on television, as well as in the print media, cause two serious problems. They exaggerate the significance of events that are not extraordinary, and they crowd out other events that need coverage. Had the media cut back on overblown coverage, such as the events that Kogan cited, their newshole would have been filled by other, possibly more significant stories.

A brief look at these news stories should be instructive. The Clarence Thomas confirmation hearings were important because they involved questions of fitness of a nominee for a life-long position on the U.S. Supreme Court. Between July 1, 1991, when Thomas was nominated, and October 6, when the hearings took an unexpected turn, the hearings were covered extensively. The networks, for example, ran thirty to forty stories each, collectively taking up more than four hours of airtime.[28] By comparison, in a three-month span, the networks, on average, devote thirty-six stories to the Supreme Court's activities, taking up less than one and a half hours of airtime.

The unexpected turn that was played out for nine days starting on October 6 were charges by Oklahoma University law professor Anita Hill that Thomas had sexually harassed her when she was working in the agency that he headed. Print as well as electronic media featured saturation coverage. Besides reporting the hearings in their entirety, the evening news on ABC, CBS, and NBC carried four hours and eight minutes of reports about the hearings, nearly as much as for the coverage of Thomas's qualifications during the preceding three-month span. The allegations, presented in lurid detail, were the centerpiece of the coverage. Thomas was eloquent in his denials and Hill was equally eloquent in proclaiming that she was telling the truth. The audience was left to judge who should be believed, because neither party could present absolute proof.

The lengthy soap opera undoubtedly deflected attention from more important issues of the candidate's political philosophy and judicial capabilities and it displaced other important news in the print and electronic press. However, the coverage was not without merit. It made voters, particularly women, aware of the fact that the Senate Judiciary Committee was composed entirely of white males and that several members seemed unsympathetic to sexual harassment charges. It consequently contributed to primary election victories of several women candidates for Congress who turned the hearings into a campaign issue.

Although coverage of the Thomas saga thus had redeeming features, this has not generally been common in pseudo-crisis news coverage. The many hours spent on live coverage of the Kennedy Smith rape trial were a sorry loss for news coverage. In the case of the King beating, overly extensive coverage of an important news story contributed to the frustrations that exploded in the Los Angeles riots. The main reason for repeating coverage so frequently was the fact that the pictures were extraordinarily graphic. By contrast, the 1992 trial of mass murderer Jeffrey Dahmer, who told in detail how he drugged, murdered, and cannibalized his young victims, received relatively little coverage, even in the tabloid press, because it offered few good pictures.[29]

Finally, one may take issue with Kogan about whether the failed coup against Soviet President Mikhail Gorbachev received exaggerated, overly dramatic coverage, or whether it was handled properly. These issues are often controversial. As for the entertainment value of Kissinger reporting the weather, this author offers "no comment."

Summary

In American political culture the normal feuds of politics are suspended when major emergencies happen. Although this unwritten rule is mentioned most often in connection with foreign policy, where "politics stops at the water's edge," it applies to the types of domestic crises discussed in this chapter. When life and property are endangered, when sudden death and terror reign, when well-known leaders are assassinated, or when the nation goes to war, normal media coverage practices are suspended. The media largely abandon their adversarial role and become teammates of officialdom in attempts to restore public order, safety, and tranquillity.

The media perform indispensable functions during crises: they diffuse vital information to the public and officials, interpret events, and provide emotional support for troubled communities. Radio is particularly helpful in major disasters because its technical requirements are most adaptable to makeshift arrangements. It can broadcast without regular electric power to isolated people who have only a pocket transistor radio. Round-the-clock radio and television news coverage and satellite transmissions from around the world make it possible to observe extraordinary events wherever they occur.

Because the media play such a large part in public communication during crises, the way they discharge their responsibilities has been of great concern to public officials and to the community at large. Information gaps, misinformation, and the dissemination of information that makes the effects of the crisis worse have led to demands for control of the information flow to better manage each crisis. Many media institutions have formal plans that temporarily set aside the usual criteria for publishing exciting news in the interest of calming the public.

Muted coverage, particularly during civil disturbances and incidents of political terrorism, may be unwise because it may drown out explicit and implicit messages about unmet societal demands. The need to plan for crisis coverage, however, is certain. Modern society faces crises of various sorts so frequently that policy makers in the media and in government would be remiss to make no plans for emergencies. By the same token, they should strive to avoid news distortion and waste when titillating stories tempt them to indulge in excessive coverage.

Notes

1. For details of the Gulf War coverage, see William A. Hachten, *The World News Prism: Changing Media of International Communication,* 3d ed. (Ames: Iowa State University Press, 1992), chap. 9.
2. For details of the Los Angeles riots, see "Rage in L.A.," *Chicago Tribune,* May 1, 1992; Erna Smith, *Transmitting Race: The Los Angeles Riot in Television News* (Cambridge, Mass.: Harvard University Press, May 1994).
3. Compiled from miscellaneous reports in the *Los Angeles Times,* January 17 to January 27, 1994.
4. Compiled from miscellaneous contemporaneous television and newspaper reports.
5. Dennis E. Wenger, "A Few Empirical Observations Concerning the Relationship between the Mass Media and Disaster Knowledge: A Research Report," in *Disasters and the Mass Media: Proceedings of the Committee on Disasters and the Mass Media Workshop* (Washington, D.C.: National Academy Press, 1980), 242–244. For a discussion of news gathering techniques during disasters, see Rahul Sood, Geoffrey Stockdale, and Everett M. Rogers, "How the News Media Operate in Natural Disasters," *Journal of Communication* 37 (Summer 1987): 27–41.
6. Times Mirror Center for the People and the Press, "The GOP Pays the Price." News release, June 14, 1995.
7. *Gallup Poll Monthly,* January 1991, 21.
8. Walter Gantz, "The Diffusion of News about the Attempted Reagan Assassination," *Journal of Communication* 33 (Winter 1983): 56–65.
9. T. Joseph Scanlon, "Media Coverage of Crises: Better than Reported, Worse than Necessary," *Journalism Quarterly* 55 (Spring 1978): 68–72.
10. Wenger, "A Few Empirical Observations," 252–253.
11. Hachten, *World News Prism,* 155–156.
12. Steve Johnson and Susan Kucza, "Two for Two: Bulls Still Champs!" *Chicago Tribune,* June 15, 1992; and Louise Kiernan and John Fountain, "Bulls Fans Stampede over City," *Chicago Tribune,* June 15, 1992.

13. Eleanor Singer and Phyllis Endreny, "Reporting Hazards: Their Benefits and Costs," *Journal of Communication* 37 (Summer 1987): 10–26.
14. Seth Mydans, "Los Angeles Darkness Fell on Neighboring City," *New York Times,* May 20, 1992.
15. John Corry, "Network News Covers the Stock Market Frenzy," *New York Times,* October 21, 1987; and Alex Jones, "Caution in the Press: Was It Really a 'Crash'?" *New York Times,* October 21, 1987.
16. Rodney M. Kueneman and Joseph E. Wright, "News Policies of Broadcast Stations for Civil Disturbances and Disasters," *Journalism Quarterly* 52 (Winter 1975): 670–677.
17. Sharon M. Friedman, "Blueprint for Breakdown: Three Mile Island and the Media before the Accident," *Journal of Communication* 31 (Spring 1981): 116–128.
18. Douglas A. Anderson, "Handling of Controversial 'Merry-Go-Round' Columns," *Journalism Quarterly* 59 (Summer 1982): 295–298.
19. Kueneman and Wright, "News Policies," 671.
20. See the report on the work of the Disaster Research Center at Ohio State University in E. L. Quarantelli and Russell R. Dynes, eds., "Organizational and Group Behavior in Disasters," *American Behavioral Scientist* 13 (January 1970).
21. Robert Reinhold, "Los Angeles Ends Curfew, but Tensions Remain High," *New York Times,* May 5, 1992.
22. *New Yorker,* August 15, 1977, 21.
23. Edward F. Feighan, "After the Hostage Crisis, TV Focuses on Itself," *New York Times,* August 19, 1985.
24. Alex P. Schmid and Janny de Graaf, *Violence as Communication: Insurgent Terrorism and the Western News Media* (Beverly Hills, Calif.: Sage, 1982), 98. For an analysis of the symbiotic relationship of media and sources of crisis news, see Gadi Wolfsfeld, "Symbiosis of Press and Protest: An Exchange Analysis," *Journalism Quarterly* 61 (Autumn 1984): 550–555; Regina G. Lawrence, "Icons, Indexing, and Police Brutality: An Exploration of Journalistic Norms" (Paper delivered at the annual meeting of the International Communication Association, 1995).
25. Hachten, *World News Prism,* 163.
26. William Glaberson, "Press Has Blind Spots, Too," *New York Times,* July 22, 1993.
27. Rick Kogan, "As the World Churns," *Chicago Tribune,* December 19, 1991.
28. S. Robert Lichter and Linda Lichter, eds., "The Trials of Clarence Thomas: Media Coverage of Judge Thomas' Confirmation Battle," *Media Monitor* 5 (October 1991): 1–6.
29. James Warren, "Media Gives Dahmer Trial Mild Coverage," *Chicago Tribune,* February 2, 1992.

Readings

Charters, David A., ed. *The Deadly Sin of Terrorism: Its Effect on Democracy and Civil Liberty in Six Countries.* Westport, Conn.: Greenwood, 1994.

Disasters and the Mass Media: Proceedings of the Committee on Disasters and the Mass Media Workshop. Washington, D.C.: National Academy of Sciences, 1980.

Nimmo, Dan, and James E. Combs. *Nightly Horrors: Crisis Coverage in Television Network News.* Knoxville: University of Tennessee Press, 1985.

Paletz, David, and Alex P. Schmid, eds. *Terrorism and the Media.* Newbury Park, Calif.: Sage, 1992.

Singer, Eleanor, and Phyllis M. Endreny. *Reporting on Risk: How the Mass Media Portray Accidents, Diseases, Disasters, and Other Hazards.* New York: Russell Sage Foundation, 1993.

Taylor, Philip M. *War and the Media: Propaganda and Persuasion in the Gulf War.* New York: St. Martin's, 1992.

Walters, Lynne Masel, Lee Wilkins, and Tim Walters. *Bad Tidings: Communication and Catastrophe.* Hillsdale, N.J.: Lawrence Erlbaum, 1989.

The Media As Policy Makers

IN HIS AUTOBIOGRAPHY LINCOLN STEFFENS, who has been called "America's greatest reporter," tells how a history professor introduced him to an audience as "the first of the muckrakers." Steffens corrected the professor. "I had to answer first that I was not the original muckraker; the prophets of the Old Testament were ahead of me, and to make a big jump in time so were the writers, editors, and reporters (including myself) of the 1890s who were finding fault with 'things as they are' in the pre-muckraking period."[1]

Steffens was right. Public exposés of evil and corruption in high places have been common throughout recorded history. They rest on the assumption that exposure will shame the wrongdoers and lead to public condemnation of their deeds and possibly punishment. Reforms may ultimately ensue.[2] Exposés have always been and always will continue to be an important feature of social responsibility journalism in America. They are a major part of the deliberate manipulation of the political process mentioned in Chapter 1 as one of the media's important functions.

In this chapter muckraking will be examined to show how it really works, with particular attention to public opinion's role. Agenda building, another strategy for manipulating politics, will be examined in situations such as leadership crises driven by political scandal, the development of science policy, and the support of interest group goals. Next we will assess the political impact of nationally broadcast factual and fictional documentaries. The chapter ends with reflections on the responsibility of newspeople to refrain from questionable methods in their zeal to reform society.

Like other manifestations of the social responsibility orientation,

156

manipulative journalism raises philosophical, ethical, and news policy questions. Do newspeople jeopardize important professional values, such as objectivity and neutrality, when they try to influence the events that they report? Do they create a witch-hunting climate that intimidates officeholders and deters capable people from careers in politics? If newspeople fail to objectively report the passing scene, do they sacrifice credibility? Where can media audiences turn for a reasonably unbiased view of the complexities of political life if media sources, such as government officials, are partisans? Claims by newspeople that their political activities reflect the wishes of their audiences are questionable as long as the selection and activities of journalists are not subject to control by the publics that they claim to represent. In fact, public opinion polls show mixed rates of approval for many tactics currently used in investigative journalism.[3]

Despite the concerns it raises, the role of the journalist as political actor is currently popular. The popularity of civic journalism is one example. It has been adapted by newspapers, television, and radio stations in communities throughout the United States, including Chicago; Boston; Miami; Minneapolis; Charlotte, North Carolina; and Wichita, Kansas. *Civic journalists* probe the political concerns of their audiences by arranging town meetings, focus groups, and interviews. Once problems are identified, journalists become actively involved in finding solutions. They have traded their role as neutral observers and critics for the role of activist citizen. In the same way, journalists become participants in the stories they write when they collaborate with policy makers. This happens often when dissatisfied government insiders leak information to journalists. Rather than attempting reforms on their own, they hope to enlist media support to gain their ends. Citizens also routinely contact the media with problems concerning public affairs hoping that media publicity can become a tool to spur government action. Just as the media have taken over many functions formerly performed by political parties during elections, so they have assumed many of the ombudsman, reform, and law enforcement functions traditionally performed by other institutions in society. Whether this is the cause or consequence of the weakening of these other institutions remains a hotly debated question.

Manipulative Journalism in Perspective

The extent of the efforts of newspeople to participate in policy making has fluctuated as philosophies of news making have changed. The turmoil of the 1960s, which raised the public's social consciousness; the Watergate scandal, which forced President Richard Nixon to resign; and the shift toward advocating a social responsibility ethic in journalism schools have once again raised manipulative journalism from a position of disdain to a position of high esteem. Approval is not unanimous, to be sure, but it is widespread, especially in elite media circles. Reporters and media institutions whose investigations have led to important social and political reforms frequently win prizes for high journalistic achievement. Given the prestige accorded to investigative journalists and the political successes attributed to them, it is no surprise that investigative reporting began to thrive in major print and electronic media institutions during the 1970s.

Independent investigative organizations that collaborate with media institutions have flourished as well. The nonprofit, foundation-subsidized Center for Investigative Reporting, established in San Francisco in 1977, is an example. The center uses freelance reporters who collectively conduct investigations and who can be hired by various media to undertake projects that cannot be readily handled internally. The Community Information Project in Los Angeles and the Better Government Association in Chicago are other institutions that do similar investigative work. Investigative Reporters and Editors (IRE), a national organization, has been active in teaching its approaches to mainstream journalists.[4]

Collaboration between independent watchdog organizations and the media is mutually beneficial. It ensures that the investigations of interest to these institutions will be publicized, thereby increasing the chances for corrective action. Tapping into media resources also helps cover the costs of complex investigations that can run into hundreds of thousands of dollars. This added financial support can be crucial. The media, in turn, gain collaborators who are skilled in investigating public issues and who often have excellent connections in government and in the community. The prestige and credibility of the organization may also enhance the credibility of a jointly issued report.

The substance and style of most investigative stories reflect three major objectives. The first objective is to produce exciting stories that will appeal to media audiences. The second objective is that investigative reporters hope to gain plaudits from the journalism profession. The third, in addition to these routine journalistic goals, is that many reporters want to trigger political action or be part of it. Even when political consequences are not initially envisioned, most reporters feel highly gratified when their stories lead to actions that accord with their political and social preferences.

Sometimes the line between deliberate attempts to produce political changes and incidental sparking of reforms is too fine to distinguish. For example, when the media follow up on a report of a series of deaths in nursing homes and discover and describe deplorable conditions that led to these deaths, is this a case of muckraking designed to manipulate political events and bring about reform? Or does the idea that reform is needed arise naturally and purely incidentally from a routine news story? Was Steffens telling the truth when he claimed, "I did not intend to be a muckraker; I did not know that I was one till President Roosevelt picked the name out of Bunyan's *Pilgrim's Progress* and pinned it on us."[5] Could Steffens have specialized in writing sensational exposés of corruption in state and local government and in private business for the sheer joy of delving into the muck, with no thought given to the major reforms that followed in the wake of some of his stories?

From the standpoint of the political reformer, it may not matter whether reform was an intended or unintended byproduct of investigative reporting. The distinction matters to newspeople, however, because it raises controversial issues about the proper role of journalism in American society. Journalists, even when they favor social responsibility journalism in the abstract, do not like to admit that they wrote their stories to produce social and political reforms. Moreover, they do not call attention to the fact that investigative reporting, unlike normal story gathering, is designed to prove a preconceived notion. Sources are carefully selected to gain support for the reporters' hypotheses. Opponents are shunned, except as a counterforce to lend credibility to the investigation.[6]

Muckraking Models

Investigative journalism leads to political action in three ways. Journalists may write stories about public policies in hopes of engendering a massive public reaction that will lead to widespread demands for political remedies.[7] They may write stories to arouse political elites who are officeholders or who have influence with officeholders. These elites, eager to forestall public criticism, then may attempt to resolve the problems, often even before the media report is actually published. Finally, action may ensue from direct collaboration between investigative journalists and public officeholders who coordinate news stories and supportive political activities.

The process can be pictured in the form of three models: the simple muckraking model, the leaping impact model, and the truncated muckraking model. Social scientists Harvey Molotch, David Protess, and Margaret Gordon and their coworkers who developed these models tested them in investigative situations entailing muckraking—sensational exposés of corruption usually involving high status individuals.[8]

The simple muckraking model begins when journalists investigate a serious political problem and the investigation leads to published news that stirs the public. Aroused public opinion then mobilizes policy makers who solve the problem. The process is pictured schematically below, although the sequence of the elements in the model may vary:

Journalistic investigation → Publication → Public opinion → Policy initiatives → Policy consequences

When some elements in the model are skipped entirely, it becomes a leaping impact model. For instance, following investigation and publication of the story, policy initiatives may be taken without prior public opinion pressure. However, a journalistic investigation may have policy consequences even without new initiatives in policy or publication of reports about the investigation. In the truncated muckraking model the sequence is aborted at some point so that the investigation fails to lead to corrective policies. This happens when the investigation does not lead to published stories because the evidence is insufficient or too hot to handle. Published stories may not stir public opinion. An aroused public may not move public officials to act. Policy initiatives may not lead to any symbolic or substantive results.

Several examples of muckraking will illustrate these models. Most of the examples come from intensive studies of muckraking conducted by scholars who had arranged to be alerted to forthcoming media exposés. This permitted them to interview citizens and policy makers concerned with the issue under investigation, both before and after publication of the stories. The impact of the story could then be assessed far more accurately than is usually possible when stories come as a surprise and permit only ex post facto assessment. Actual changes in public policy also were monitored for a period of several months following the exposés. The journalists' motives and methods in conducting the investigations were judged as well.[9]

Simple Muckraking

A story about reform of a school for mentally retarded children in Staten Island, New York, illustrates simple muckraking: the media aroused the public, and the public then demanded and received action. Television commentator Geraldo Rivera presented a seven-minute report about shocking conditions that he had observed during a visit to the Willowbrook State School. After a station near the school had shown the report, some seven hundred viewers called to express their concern. Shocked parents later gathered at the school and solicited promises of help from local public officials. The Staten Island Chapter of the Society for the Prevention of Cruelty to Children began hearings and asked the state and federal governments to investigate.[10] But the flurry of activity was short-lived and largely unproductive. The investigations produced only minor reforms in the school's handling of children.

Modest outcomes are typical in situations that reflect the simple muckraking model. Researchers rarely find solid evidence that media-aroused public opinion is a strong force for change. There are several reasons why. Many Americans are complacent or cynical about the political status quo. It is therefore difficult to spur them to take action on public problems, even those directly affecting them. For example, extensive efforts to arouse public concern about energy shortages and the need for conservation have proved largely futile.[11] Because most Americans' interests lie outside of politics, they ignore or assign little importance to investigative news stories, or forget them quickly, except when they are extraordinarily dramatic and point the finger at identifiable villains. Politicians accordingly often feel safe in ignoring swells in public opinion, believing that they involve relatively few people and that they will soon subside when new issues capture the public's fancy.

On the other end of the interest spectrum, media investigative stories may be about an issue that is already a matter of great concern to the public. Although the investigative story confirms that concern, it does not push the public across the barrier of reluctance to press for political action. For example, a five-part newspaper series in the *Chicago Sun-Times*—"Rape: Every Woman's Nightmare"—dealt with the incidence and consequences of rape in the Chicago area. Interviews conducted prior to the series had shown that the public was already greatly concerned about the problem. The series maintained that concern, but it did little to spur new action to fight crime. An interesting, unexpected byproduct of the rape stories was heightened sensitivity of newspaper staff members to the problem. Following the series, *Sun-Times* stories on rape more than doubled in number, and coverage became more insightful.[12] Investigators rarely notice such unexpected consequences or much-delayed consequences. Hence reports about the effects of investigative stories often understate their impact.

Although it is difficult for the media to arouse public opinion, some investigative stories do. The Willowbrook State School case is an example. The elements that brought about its success included an emotional issue—the treatment of disabled children in the audience's locality; a flamboyant, well-known reporter who dramatized the story; and a local group of citizens directly and profoundly affected by the alleged misbehavior of public officials. When such a story captures people's interest, and they have little prior knowledge about the situation, they may learn much and become highly concerned. As noted, however, major corrective action remains unlikely.[13]

Leaping Impact Muckraking

A media exposé called "Arson for Profit" that was aired by ABC's "20/20" exemplifies the leaping impact model. The investigation indicated that extensive fire damage in Chicago's Uptown neighborhood had been planned by a group of real estate owners. The group bought dilapidated buildings, insured them heavily, and then burned them down to collect the insurance. Following the exposé, government elites voiced concern but failed to act. Nevertheless, the arson stopped because the perpetrators feared further public exposure. In the month following the broadcast, fires declined by 27 percent in the afflicted neighborhood. It was the first decline in five years. Insurance payments for arson also dropped by more than 20 percent in the year following the arson stories. No other metropolitan area showed comparable drops. The Illinois legislature responded belatedly with very minor policy reforms. There were no criminal indictments of the parties implicated in the insurance fraud. This story exemplifies the leaping impact model because the leap was from publication directly to correction; elite arousal and, by and large, elite action and public opinion pressures were nonexistent.

The most common leaping impact situation takes place when newspeople and public officials openly collaborate. This *coalition journalism* may be initiated by media or government personnel, or it may arise by chance without prior formal contacts between media personnel and policy actors. Newspeople are eager to involve government officials in investigative stories because this lends credibility and significance to their stories and increases the chances of substantial policy consequences. Although it may jeopardize the media's zealous pursuit of the watchdog role, coalition journalism gets results.

A good example of coalition journalism concerns the events following an NBC "Newsmagazine" story, "The Home Health Hustle," that exposed fraud and abuse in home health care programs. Public opinion polls showed that the broadcast aroused the concerns of many viewers who previously were unaware of problems with these programs. But public opinion apparently was not instrumental in Congress's decision to introduce appropriate reform legislation. In the fashion of leaping impact models, the legislative results seemed to flow directly from collaboration between investigative reporters and members of the U.S. Senate that preceded airing of the story by several months.

Journalists had met with officials of the Senate's Permanent Subcommittee on Investigations to plan a series of hearings on home health care fraud and to coordinate their broadcasts with the Senate's activities. The hearings were then announced during the broadcast. Senators subsequently credited media personnel with major contributions to the investigation of home health care fraud. However, it is uncertain to what degree the knowledge that television would feature the story spurred the senators to collaborate with the media. The combined investigative activities of the media and the Senate ultimately led to a number of proposals for corrective legislation. Still, in the end, the bills failed to pass. Aside from the effects of increased vigilance by public officials and home health care consumers, there were no major changes that could be directly linked to the investigative stories.[14]

In the same way, when the rape series appeared in the *Chicago Sun-Times,* newspeople had already alerted policy makers. This permitted the policy makers to time announcements of previously planned measures, such as creation of a rape hotline, to coincide with the investigative series. When a story about unnecessary and illegal abortions in state clinics was about to break in Illinois, the governor immediately associated himself with the media investigators prior to publication. This made it possible to make reform proposals part of the original story. It also enhanced the governor's image as an effective leader.

Truncated Muckraking

The truncated muckraking model is well illustrated by the Mirage investigation, conducted jointly by the *Chicago Sun-Times* and CBS's "60 Minutes" program, with the help of Chicago's Better Government Association, a civic watchdog organization. Hoping to demonstrate extensive graft in the city's regulatory agencies, the partners in the investigation opened a bar in Chicago, appropriately named the "Mirage." The bar was wired to record transactions that might take place between its personnel and city officials. In a brief period of time, ample evidence of bribery and fraud was accumulated.[15]

After the story about the illegal transactions was published, public opinion polls recorded that many citizens were outraged. Nonetheless, they took no serious corrective action to prevent similar graft in the future. The model ended with the arousal of public opinion, skipping elite arousal and action and final corrective activities. The failure to produce a correction does not necessarily mean that an official response never occurs. Symbolic responses are common, such as promises of reform by political leaders or studies of the problem, including public hearings, but with no action follow-up. At other times policy makers may punish individual offenders but do nothing to correct the underlying situation.[16]

The Role of Public Opinion

These examples of muckraking suggest that the major role attributed to public opinion in producing political action is greatly exaggerated. More often than not, the media fail to arouse the public, even when investigative stories are written to produce public excitement. When stories do agitate the public, little happens as a rule. Politicians and journalists have learned that public anger is short-lived. It can be safely ignored or channeled to support reform movements that are already under way. Corrective action is more likely to come when publicity-shy wrongdoers mend their ways, when the stories arouse elites, or when journalists and political elites have arranged to collaborate. It also helps when there are follow-ups on the story in different media and over a prolonged period of time.

Even though publicity rarely causes a tidal surge of public opinion, fear that it might do so makes the media more successful than other pressure groups in gaining their reform objectives. Because public opinion is in fact largely irrelevant in generating political reforms, the media's claim that they are handmaidens to the democratic process becomes highly questionable. In fact, the media are using the façade of public opinion support to enhance their already powerful position as political movers and shakers.

The Muddying of Public Figures

Stories about Clinton's philandering, Jesse Jackson's reference to New York City as "Hymietown," Dan Quayle's escape into the National Guard to duck regular Army service, Newt Gingrich's book royalty deals, and Barney Frank's liaison with a male prostitute—all of these are part of the epidemic of mudslinging that mars the American political landscape. In each case, incidents in the lives of these individuals were endlessly examined, interpreted, and judged, regardless of the story's significance, truth, or private nature. It is true that these people are important political figures. At the time the stories broke, Clinton and Jackson were candidates for the presidency, Quayle was running for vice president, Gingrich was Speaker of the House of Representatives, and Frank a congressional representative. Although the American press is entitled to probe the lives and reputations of such public persons, and the American public has a right to know about matters that are politically relevant, there is widespread agreement that the press has become overzealous in such investigations, destroying reputations needlessly.

Political scientist Larry Sabato, who refers to mudslinging episodes as "feeding frenzies," puts the blame on increasingly stiff competition among media for attention and on the need for round-the-clock radio and television enterprises to fill long hours with emotional audience bait.

> In such situations any development is almost inevitably magnified and over-scrutinized; the crush of cameras, microphones, and people combined with the pressure of instant deadlines and live broadcasts hype events and make it difficult to keep them in perspective. When a frenzy begins to gather, the intensity grows exponentially. Major newspapers assign teams of crack reporters and researchers to the frenzy's victims.... Television news time is virtually turned over to the subject of the frenzy. Republican vice-presidential nominee Dan Quayle was the subject of ninety-three network evening news stories over the twelve days of his frenzy in August, 1988—more coverage than twelve of the thirteen presidential candidates had received during all the primaries combined.[17]

By way of contrast, the Reagan-Gorbachev summit meeting eight months before the Quayle story had generated a mere fifty-three stories over a ten-day span.

Such attack journalism—which, as the cartoon shows, does not even exclude fellow journalists—raises a number of important ethical and political issues. From the perspective of the people whose reputations and careers are dragged through the mud and often ruined, it raises questions about the right of privacy of public figures and the ethics of journalists who publish such stories even when they consider them to be politically irrelevant. Some journalists justify giving inordinate amounts of publicity to such incidents by claiming that they might throw some light on the individual's character. But many others, including personnel at elite media, admit that they are merely jumping on the bandwagon of competition. They argue that if others exploit the story, they must feature it as well. That is hardly the epitome of ethical behavior.

Beyond injury to individual public figures, there are broader consequences. The risk of having long-past or more recent indiscretions exposed to public view or having offhand remarks elevated into major pronouncements sharply reduces the pool of people willing to make their careers in politics. Many talented people are likely to prefer the safety of private life over the merciless glare of unstoppable publicity in the public sector. "Gotcha" journalism also contributes to the public's growing cynicism about politics and politicians and erodes its respect for the news profession. Finally, the extraordinary amount of media time and space devoted to mudslinging frenzies comes at the expense of

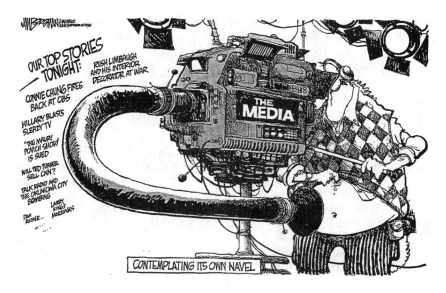

Reprinted with special permission of King Features Syndicate.

other, more worthwhile news that may never be published. The old Greek admonition "everything in moderation" is relevant. Whenever attack journalism seems appropriate, it should be practiced. But there is never a need for feeding frenzies, joined in by journalists in sorry exhibitions of pack journalism.

Beyond Muckraking: Journalists as Political Actors

Direct media intervention in the government process may take a number of forms other than muckraking. Three types of situations are usually involved: fear of adverse publicity, media acting as surrogates for public officials, and media acting as mouthpieces for government officials or interest groups.

Least common are media power plays in which newspeople bully politicians and other public figures into action by threatening to publicize stories that these people would prefer to conceal. For example, tennis star Arthur Ashe decided to announce that he had AIDS when he discovered that the media knew his condition and were prepared to publish it. Unlike overt threats, which are rare, implied or anticipated threats can have major political consequences. Politicians often act or refrain from acting because they know that newspeople might publish damaging information. Adverse publicity from influential columnists is especially feared.

At times, news personnel may act as surrogates for public officials by actively participating in an evolving situation, such as a prison riot or a diplomatic impasse. The solution, developed with the assistance of news personnel or at their initiative, may then significantly shape subsequent government action. Walter Cronkite's impact on relations between Egypt and Israel, by serving as a go-between, is a famous example of diplomacy conducted by journalists. More commonly, reporters frequently spark investigations of illegal activities by alerting law enforcement officials. For example, a Chicago television station alerted city officials to illegal storage of hazardous and flammable chemical waste on the campus of the University of Chicago. Hours later, city fire officials inspected the scene and cited the university for numerous fire code violations.[18]

To prevent impending tragedies and solve existing cases, journalists have also become involved in broadcasts about kidnapped children and in crime-stopper programs that feature reenactments or recountings of unsolved crimes. The programs use media stories, coupled with financial rewards, to elicit information from citizens that may help in solving the crime. They are featured in nearly five hundred communities in the United States and Canada and have helped to clear up thousands of felony cases.[19] In fact, the FBI credits such programs with facilitating the capture of up to 30 percent of the criminals on its Most Wanted List.[20]

A far more common form of interaction occurs when the media become mouthpieces for government officials or interest groups, either because of belief in their causes or in return for attractive stories and other favors. This type of interaction often involves leaks. Government officials who are disgruntled with current policies or practices for personal, professional, or political reasons may leak information to sympathetic journalists to enlist their support. Journalists may cooperate and publish the allegations, or they may investigate the situation, often with the cooperation of the individuals who leaked the information.

When newspeople and officials collaborate, the boundary between ordinary reporting and manipulative journalism can become blurred. It is difficult to tell when one merges into the other because a correct diagnosis of manipulative journalism requires establishing motivations. In many instances the available evidence strongly suggests that newspeople acted as political partisans who used their powers of publicity to foster preferred causes and to harm others. When the *Philadelphia Inquirer* was tipped off by a congressional committee staff member about shoddy treatment of kidney dialysis patients, the paper rushed to the aid of the patients. It was clear from the start that dialysis providers and a negligent federal government would be the outright villains in the news stories.[21] In other cases the main objective in publicizing leaked information is mercenary. Newspeople put their services at the command of anyone who promises to be a fertile source for future news or who can provide an attractive story, no matter what the merits of the story may be. The television networks are particularly eager to obtain exciting scoops during *sweeps,* the periods when audience ratings are measured to determine how much money advertisers will be charged.

Public officials and political interest groups often exploit the media's access to the public to attain their political objectives. Broadcasting the videotaped plea for help by an American hostage in Lebanon in the summer of 1989 is a good example. CBS, CNN, and NBC repeatedly featured a 98-second emotional message by Joseph Cicippo who urged release of an Arab leader kidnapped by Israel in return for his own freedom. Although the networks clearly stated that Cicippo seemed to be reading his plea under duress, they were accused of acting as a willing propaganda conduit for terrorists.[22] Similar charges were made when the *New York Times* and *Washington Post* agreed to publish the Unabomber's rambling, eight-page long ideological tract to forestall further lethal bombings. The papers acted at the request of Attorney General Janet Reno who feared another terrorist attack. Reno's office also hoped that someone would recognize the writing and thus identify the Unabomber.[23]

Although the media are often quite willing to publish stories in compliance with government wishes when they believe that the story serves a good purpose, they are loath to become unwitting government tools. In 1986, for example, officials of the Reagan administration were suspected of spreading false information about Libya in an attempt to forestall terrorist attacks. When rumors about the administration's deception surfaced, news executives expressed outrage. The comment of Roone Arledge, president of ABC News, was typical of the general reaction when he called it "despicable to tinker with the credibility of one of our most sacred and basic institutions, the press, for whatever reason."[24]

Agenda Building

In many instances the media create the climate that shapes political action. This makes them major contributors to agenda building, the process whereby news stories influence how people perceive and evaluate issues and policies. Agenda building goes beyond agenda setting. The media set the public agenda when news stories rivet attention on a problem and make it seem important to many people. Media build the public agenda when they create the political context that shapes public opinions. Agenda building often occurs around a precipitating event such as the Rodney King beating films. The incident became a news icon for dwelling at length on the issues of police brutality and racism and turning them into major foci of public policy.[25]

The breakup of the Soviet Union is another telling case of agenda building. In 1990, during the annual May Day parade, Soviet television, as usual, covered the festivities for the nation. Camera operators had been told to stop filming if protesters against the government made their appearance because Mikhail Gorbachev, the country's leader, did not wish scenes of unrest broadcast. He had given protest groups permission to march to symbolize that he was a more liberal leader than his predecessors. But the television cameras kept filming when protesters came into view carrying banners that asked Gorbachev to resign, condemned the Communist party and the Secret Service (KGB), proclaimed the end of the Red Empire, praised the secession of Lithuania, and carried images of Christ. The huge, nationwide audience, for the first time in recent history, watched a vivid demonstration of opposition to the government. It demonstrated that the country was no longer united behind the leadership and that the voices of protest might not be drowned out by the Soviet state. In the view of many observers, this televised humiliation built the agenda for the imminent revolution that marked the end of the Soviet empire.[26]

Newspeople rarely stir up controversies when established elites agree on matters of public policy, and they have been criticized for timidity on that score.[27] The absence of reported conflict makes it seem, often erroneously, that elites as well as the public approve the unchallenged policies. But when an issue becomes a matter of controversy among political elites, the media frequently zero in on it. They "supply the context that ... gives people reasons for taking sides and converts the problem into a serious political issue. In this sense the public agenda is not so much set by the media as built up through a cycle of media activity that transforms an elite issue into a public controversy."[28] The agenda-building role of the media in policy making thus is symbiotic. The media are an essential part of the operation, but ultimate success hinges on major roles played by other political actors as well.

Molotch, Protess, and Gordon make this clear in the conclusion of their study of the role of investigative journalism in the Watergate scandal. The resolution of the issue was not, as popularly believed, a triumph for unaided media power:

> We therefore disagree with those who would assign "credit" for the Nixon exposures to the media just as we would disagree with those who would assign

it to the Congress. Nor should the credit go, in some acontextual, additive sense, to both of these sectors. Instead, the Watergate "correction" was the result of the ways in which news of the Nixon scandals fit the goals and strategic needs of important media and policy actors. All of these actors, each with some degree of "relative autonomy". . . are part of an evolving "ecology of games," . . . part of a "dance" . . . in which actors have, by virtue of their differential skills and status positions, varying access to participate. Because they so continuously anticipate each other's moves, their activities are, as a matter of course, mutually constituted.[29]

Political Scandal

Sociologists Gladys and Kurt Lang reached similar conclusions. Their study of the role of the media in Watergate traces the precise part played by the media in this "ecology of games" in which the disparate interests of various political actors are blended to create and develop political scenarios. The Langs outlined the steps through which political agendas are usually constructed.[30] A look at the steps makes it clear that there is ample opportunity and often strong temptation for newspeople to guide agenda building deliberately.

Agenda building begins when newspeople decide to publish a particular story. In most instances this is a matter of free choice because few stories are so blatantly significant that omission is unthinkable. The second decision concerns the degree of attention to be given to the story. This is the point where ordinary agenda-setting activities can most readily turn into deliberate agenda building. If newspeople determine that a story should become prominent, they must feature it conspicuously and often enough to arouse the attention of the elite media, including national television, and the attention of political elites. The Watergate story, for instance, received extensive and sustained publicity in the *Washington Post* before it finally caught on and gained nationwide publicity.

Capturing national attention usually requires several other media-controlled steps. Issues must be put into an interpretive frame that will interest media audiences. For instance, as long as the media framed Watergate as an election campaign story, it was discounted by media audiences as just another partisan squabble. Once the media, with the aid of members of Congress, were able to depict it as an issue of pervasive corruption and dishonesty at the highest levels of government, it generated widespread concern. Without this climate of public concern, severe penalties for the Watergate offenders, including President Nixon, would never have been acceptable. In the course of putting issues into a conceptual framework, language becomes an important tool. When newspeople and politicians switched from writing and talking about the Watergate *caper* or the *bugging incident* and began to discuss the Watergate *scandal* and *tragedy,* what had been perceived as a fairly trivial incident became transformed into a very serious matter.

As the Langs noted, the particular sources that the media select to tell a story are important. Skewing inevitably takes place when newspeople tap one human mind, rather than another, for information and interpretation. In the case of major public policy issues, sources become symbols that indicate to media audiences whether a particular position is or is not meritorious. When the media featured prominent Republicans and members of the judiciary acknowledging the gravity of the issues at stake and the need for an investigation, Watergate became a political crisis justifying drastic action.

Scientific and Technological Innovations

Agenda building by the media is not limited to political scandals but includes many other types of issues. We will discuss two areas in which agenda building is of vast importance for American political life: science policy and social movements.

Government support and regulation of science operations have become highly controversial public policy issues in twentieth-century America.[31] Two environmental issues provide particularly interesting examples. The first one has been called the great greenhouse debate and it concerns scientific and political discussions about the threat of global warming.[32] Researchers tracked media coverage of the global warming controversy for an eight-year period from 1985 to 1992 in the television network evening newscasts and the *New York Times, Washington Post, Wall Street Journal, Time, Newsweek,* and *U.S. News & World Report.* They found that coverage was minimal at first, totaling only 25 stories from 1985 through 1987 in all the media combined—not enough to arouse government and public concern. The coverage soared in 1989 and 1990 when the Bush administration sought to defuse growing worldwide pressures for governmental action by expressing its doubts about the seriousness of the situation. Taking their cues from the science community, the thrust of media coverage indicated otherwise. By a margin of nearly nine to one, news coverage suggested that global warming was a major problem that required preventative action by governments throughout the world. News stories also focused the public's attention on specific remedies, such as controlling carbon dioxide emissions, halting or reversing deforestation, and conserving energy. In the end, the media's agenda-building efforts faltered because more controversy emerged in the science community about the ability to keep global warming in check through various government regulation programs. Coupled with the strongly expressed resistance of the Bush administration to undertake major control measures—which could not be ignored by the media—the climate for controls created earlier became far less friendly.

The second tale concerns cancer-causing agents in the environment. Unlike the global warming story, it covers a public policy area in which the government was very active in prevention measures. The main issues related to the question of which pollutants were most dangerous and therefore required regulation. One would expect that views expressed by experts in the field of environmentally caused cancers would be the dominant voices quoted by the media and would provide the information base for government regulators as well as for the general public. However, that is not always the case. When journalists select the sources whose "expert" opinions they quote, they often find that front-line researchers are so deeply involved in their scientific pursuits that they do not wish to talk to the media. When they do, their stories often lack punch because they hedge their claims—as a function of the scientific viewpoint that holds that no truth is absolute—rather than making absolute statements. This is why reporters often turn to less well-qualified sources who are willing and able to express their view strongly and without any doubts. Activists, such as spokespersons for environmental groups, make good story tellers. It also happens not infrequently that reporters have their own views about environmental and other dangers and then seek out spokespersons who share this view. In the words of David Paletz and Robert Entman, "When values are shared by source and press and probably readers too, there is no felt need on the part of reporters to seek countervailing information elsewhere."[33] Widespread opposition by journalists to the use of nuclear power is an example.[34]

In the case of carcinogens in the environment, content analysis of coverage of the issue on the three major television networks, the three major news magazines, and the *New York Times, Washington Post,* and *Wall Street Journal* for the twenty-year period from 1972 to 1992 showed that the media paid more attention to man-made chemicals than any other cancer agent, including tobacco.[35] Judging by the number of stories devoted to each carcinogen, the dangers of tobacco were ranked roughly on a par with those of food additives such as dyes, preservatives and sweeteners, and reproductive hormones such as birth control pills. By contrast, experts rated smoking, overexposure to sunlight, and diet as prime cancer causes and downplayed food additives and preservatives.

Figure 6-1 indicates scientists' appraisals of media portrayals of cancer risks. It shows that half or more of the experts in this field believe that the media distorted the dangers of particular carcinogens in nine out of

FIGURE 6-1 How Scientists Rate Media Portrayals of Cancer Risks

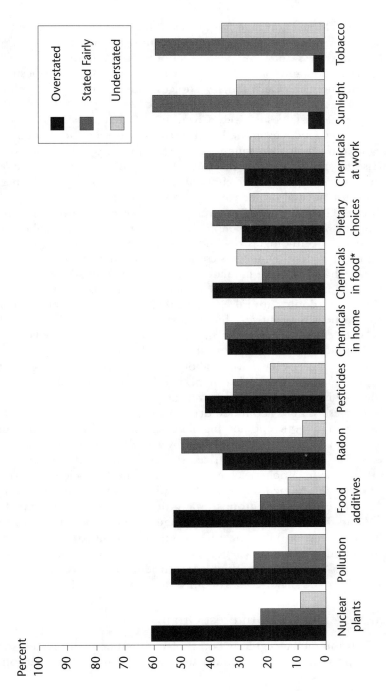

SOURCE: *Media Montior* 7(8) (November/December 1993), 4.

* Naturally occurring.

eleven areas. Media coverage got its best ratings—albeit only 60 percent or less approval—in rating the dangers of sunlight and tobacco. It got its worst ratings (less than 39 percent approval) on naturally occurring chemicals in food and food additives, nuclear plants, pollution, pesticides, household chemicals, and dietary choices. Chemicals in the workplace and radon received rankings of "fairly stated" by 42 percent and 50 percent of the scientists, respectively. Given the fact that news stories, particularly in the key media examined for this study, provided the agenda-building context in which government actions and public opinion flourish, it is a worrisome finding that the media may stray widely from scientific opinions in matters of great public concern. The potential for major damage is great because needed protective measures may be thwarted.

Studies show that media coverage of scientific controversies influences public opinion. For example, when media cover stories about controversial new technologies or medical treatments, public opposition to the highlighted developments is common, even when the coverage is not particularly hostile. When media coverage of the controversy diminishes, opposition diminishes as well. The public, it seems, opts against scientific advances when doubts are raised about their safety. People are especially sensitive to heavily negative safety reports. Political elites, in turn, often are loath to challenge scientific findings that the media have labeled as "expert" opinion or to take actions that may alarm the public.[36]

Similar concerns have arisen about stories in other fields of science. Although some of them are excellent, many are flawed. Only a few scientists, distinguished by their controversial positions on public issues, are steady sources for news about new drugs, new medical procedures, and various aspects of genetic engineering. The rest of the scientific community has remained largely excluded, often by its own choice and sometimes because of its disdain for popularized stories. In the same way, only a few potentially risky technologies have been scrutinized by science reporters, with choices determined haphazardly or with stories mirroring the interests of selected pressure groups. Many other science topics have been ignored and thereby kept off the public agenda, even though they address significant aspects of public health and safety. This situation is improving with the addition of weekly science sections in many newspapers. However, in the process of popularizing highly technical matters, most media reports contain minor and major errors of omission, emphasis, or fact.[37]

Social Movements and Interest Groups

Just as the media regularly boost selected public policy issues, so too can they promote selected groups that are working for specific public causes. Whenever a group needs wide publicity to reach its goals, a decision by media personnel to grant or withhold publicity becomes crucial for the group's success. Many decisions about coverage are made without explicit political motivations to boost a movement or suppress it. But in some instances the sympathies of newspeople for particular causes guide their choices of news content in hopes of influencing the course of politics. This is what happened with Students for a Democratic Society (SDS), part of what came to be known in the 1960s as the *New Left*. The story is particularly interesting because it demonstrates that attention from sympathetic newspeople may boomerang and produce unintended, highly destructive consequences.

SDS had received little media attention for its activities on American campuses until *New York Times* reporter Fred Powledge wrote a long, supportive story in 1965, some five years after the birth of the movement.[38] Coverage by a national news medium amounted to symbolic recognition that student radicalism had become an important political issue. When SDS sponsored a march on Washington to protest the Vietnam War in the spring of 1965, the event received nationwide coverage. Although many newspeople sympathized with the left-liberal reforms advocated by SDS and knew that sensational publicity might be harmful, they focused their stories on the movement's most radical leaders and goals. The framing chosen by the media produced exciting news, but it misled media audiences and affected the self-perceptions of SDS members. The radicals singled out by the media as spokespersons for the organization became celebrities. In turn, this attracted new Leninist and Maoist members who expected the organization to perform as pictured in the media. These new members took over the leadership of the organization and turned it away from its long-range reformist goals to short-range and violent antiwar activities.

Sociologist Todd Gitlin contends that the media's decision in 1965 to give wide publicity to SDS ultimately destroyed the movement and with it much of the power of the New Left. In his vivid metaphor, the media spotlight became a magnifying glass that burned everybody to a crisp. Powledge's efforts to bestow legitimacy on the movement through *New York Times* stories had failed totally. As is often true in agenda building, political forces other than the media contributed to the turn of events. Radicalization of the SDS movement was also enhanced by the Johnson administration's escalation of the Vietnam War and by the growing alienation from mainstream society that it produced among many Americans.[39]

Of course, many movements, interest groups, and lobbies have been helped by media coverage, as long as they did not deviate too far from mainstream values. The civil rights movement is a memorable case. The media framed civil rights protesters as victims of racism rather than as troublemakers and lawbreakers, as their opponents preferred. Sympathetic nationwide coverage of freedom marches and of battles fought for civil rights in Little Rock, Arkansas, Selma, Alabama, and Oxford, Mississippi, helped ready lawmakers and the nation for passage of the Civil Rights Act in 1964.

Support for consumer organizations and environmentalist groups constitutes additional success stories. Media publicity has legitimized these organizations in the eyes of the public and in the eyes of political elites.[40] Their concerns have become the subject of legislation, implemented through newly created public agencies. The benefits of supportive media coverage and the damage done by adverse publicity are well illustrated by two similar rape cases decided in Wisconsin. Citizen groups had organized to recall a judge who, they believed, had unfairly blamed the victim. They succeeded in the case for which they had media support and failed in the other, for which coverage was unfavorable. When the media opposed the protesters, they ruined their public image and credibility by calling them extremists and lynch mobs.[41]

There seems to be a pattern in the role played by media on behalf of successful social movements. That is the conclusion of two German scholars who analyzed how media coverage helped change attitudes and West German laws dealing with conscientious objectors to military service.[42] Their study covered a fifteen-year period from 1961 to 1975. It showed that most media ignored the movement initially, although a few gave it favorable publicity. Uncontested favorable coverage legitimized conscientious objectors and their demands and attracted new supporters. By the time the establishment press began to criticize the movement in the wake of protest activities by conscientious objectors, the movement had become so well accepted that its political demands could not be stopped. The struggle for acceptance of the movement had taken fifteen years, but it seemed much briefer because of sparse coverage by the mainstream press during the initial seven years. Protest actions finally aroused opposition forces and moved the struggle to the center of political attention.

The model illustrated by the case, which appears to be typical for successful social movements, involves four steps. Legitimization of the incipient movement begins with favorable coverage by a few sympathetic journalists. Undisputed media praise then attracts support for the movement among segments of the public. Then the growing movement becomes strong and legitimate enough to make political demands and engage in protest activities. At that time opposing voices are raised in the hitherto silent mainstream media. They come too late, however, to stop the success of the movement in the legislative arena and among important groups within the public.

Protest groups are active partners in the agenda-building game. If they consider publicity essential to the success of their causes, as most of them do, they initiate contacts with potentially sympathetic journalists and create newsworthy events to showcase their objectives. Attracting sustained media attention hinges on the *status* of the group, the perceived *social and political legitimacy* of the group and its goals, the *newsworthiness* of its story, judged by the usual criteria, and the *consonance* of the group's *ideology* with the journalists' inclinations.[43] Journalists prefer to cover high status or otherwise prominent groups that are perceived as legitimate and in pursuit of worthy goals with which the journalists identify and who have interesting stories to tell. When these requirements are met, a transaction takes place, as exchange theorists have pointed out. The journalists' ability to bestow publicity is exchanged for the group's ability to supply newsworthy stories.

Low status organizations whose goals encompass routine human concerns are least likely to attract helpful publicity. Political scientist Edie Goldenberg studied the attempts of four citizen groups in Massachusetts to attract newspaper coverage to the problems of welfare mothers, senior citizens, low-income tenants, and people treated unfairly by the courts. She found that these groups had little success and concluded, "There is bias in the system that consistently favors some and neglects others." The favored groups are "haves," those who possess the resources to make and maintain contact with the press and to arrange their operations so that they complement the needs of the press. The unfavored ones are those "most in need of press attention in order to be heard forcefully in the political arena" yet "least able to command attention and ... least able to use effectively what few resources they do control in seeking and gaining press access." Goldenberg warns, "If intensely felt interests go unarticulated and therefore are unnoticed and unaffected by policy makers, one important aspect of rule of, for, and by the people is weakened."[44] In the eyes of social critics such as Goldenberg, a free press must use its agenda-building powers to benefit all segments of society.

Documentaries and Docudramas

To influence public policy, newspeople are not limited to straight news and feature stories. Fictional productions, such as docudramas shown to millions of viewers on prime-time national television, are used as well. Docudramas are especially compelling because they reconstruct events in highly dramatic, emotional ways. The viewer unfortunately cannot tell what part of the story is real and what part is dramatic frosting.[45]

The political goals of many documentaries and docudramas are obvious. As Oscar Gandy has pointed out, "Too frequently to be mere coincidence, serial dramas, or the made-for-television movies we describe as docudramas, have been aired simultaneously with the discussion of related issues in Congress."[46] An example of a widely publicized docudrama that coincided with related political events was "The Day After," a two-hour ABC dramatization of a nuclear attack on Kansas City and its aftermath. It was broadcast on Sunday, November 20, 1983, following an extensive prebroadcast advertising campaign by the network that included an eight-page viewer's guide. The drama was replete with scenes of burned bodies, faces with blinded eyes rotting from radiation sickness, smoldering rubble, and survivors reduced to preying on each other.

At the time of broadcast, nuclear weapons policy was in the limelight. The Reagan administration was attempting to gain support in the United States and in Europe for deploying American missiles in European NATO countries. Antinuclear groups at home and abroad were working feverishly to stop the deployment. The docudrama was aired a few days before the decision to place the missiles was to be approved by the West German legislature. Excerpts of the docudrama were made available to German television.

Supporters of missile deployment feared that the program would lead to massive public demonstrations designed to force a change in nuclear deployment policies. When the Reagan administration was invited to send a representative to participate in a postbroadcast discussion of the lessons of the docudrama, it showed its profound concern by sending Secretary of State George P. Shultz. Throughout the furor raised by the broadcast, ABC denied that the timing had been politically motivated. The November date was chosen, it claimed, to raise ABC's ratings during a sweeps month, when ratings would be reflected in advertising prices.

What, then, was the political impact of "The Day After," which was viewed by more than 100 million people in homes, schools, churches, and town halls?[47] It appears that the broadcast boosted the activities of antinuclear groups and aroused fears in pronuclear groups that "The Day After" might generate a defeatist attitude among Americans. But public opinion polls after the broadcast did not show massive shifts of public attitudes about nuclear missile policies. In Europe, where immediate drastic political consequences had been expected, the missiles were deployed without major obstacles.

A number of analysts ascribed the lack of impact to flaws in the docudrama, which left the reasons for the nuclear attack uncertain and failed to deal squarely with nuclear policy issues. Others felt that the public had gained knowledge and awareness from the film but had learned to distance itself psychologically from fictional disasters. Therefore, the audience failed to empathize fully with the fictitious stricken residents of Kansas City.

Although the apparent consequences of "The Day After" were less than expected, other docudramas as well as full length motion picture versions of historical events may be more compelling. "J. F. K.," a 1991 movie docudrama, suggested that President Kennedy's assassination sprang from a massive conspiracy that involved the White House, the CIA, and the FBI, among others. Polls subsequently showed that numerous viewers accepted the film's premises.[48] The fictionalized movie reconstruction of President Nixon's life and the false saga of African American soldiers liberating German concentration camps at Dachau and Buchenwald in World War II— broadcast as a PBS documentary "The Liberators" in 1993—found believers who could not tell fact from fiction. Concern or hopes remain high that prime-time broadcasts and the associated media coverage and public discussions may have major political consequences in the long or short run.[49] This potential impact obligates a responsible press to take greater pains to present all sides of an issue and to be more accurate in its depiction, even in a fiction program. Critics of "The Day After" felt that the drama understated the likely consequences of an atomic attack, making it seem less disastrous than the critics' vision. Moreover, the appropriate background for appraising various policy options was lacking. Viewers were not told that the possibility of negotiating a nuclear freeze was severely constricted by the unwillingness of other world powers with nuclear arsenals to reciprocate and to permit verification of compliance.

Methods: Fair and Foul

The fairness and accuracy of news presentations and the appropriateness of news-gathering techniques become important issues when one considers that the media, in combination with other political actors, create the political reality that sets the context for political action.[50] It is a serious matter therefore when the media are accused of frequent resorts to improper methods.

Confirming Prejudgments

A famous $120 million libel suit illustrates concerns about the legitimacy of some media tactics. The suit was brought by Gen. William C. Westmoreland against CBS for statements made about him in a ninety-minute documentary on the Vietnam War called "The Uncounted Enemy: A Vietnam Deception." The principal message of the documentary was that the general, while commander of American forces in Vietnam, had deliberately manipulated information about the strength of enemy troops to show the president and Congress that American troops under his command were winning the war. The Viet Cong offensive in the winter of 1968 demonstrated that the enemy's strength and tenacity had been badly underestimated.

The case is ideal for examining questionable media practices because an internal CBS review of production methods was made public. It indicated that the producers of the documentary believed in Westmoreland's guilt from the very start and organized the production to support their preformed conclusions. The internal report acknowledged that CBS personnel made eleven major errors while putting together the documentary. These included inadequate evidence for charges that a conspiracy was involved, interviewing mostly people who supported the program's overall conclusions, reshooting unsatisfactory testimony after allowing a witness to hear what others had said, and "coddling sympathetic witnesses."[51] The report contained portions of unedited transcripts of interviews in which sources were apparently coached by interviewers. At times interviewers asked loaded questions such as whether the respondent agreed that there had been "a full-fledged conspiracy to fake intelligence reporting." If respondents failed to agree, their remarks were omitted from the final broadcast. Materials that might have undermined the documentary's principal conclusions about General Westmoreland's activities ended up on the cutting room floor.

In the final documentary eight of the ten persons whose testimony was featured disagreed with Westmoreland. One of the two who did not, Lt. Gen. Daniel Graham, was given a mere twenty-one seconds of air time, even though he had been the chief of the army's current intelligence and estimates division in Vietnam in the late 1960s. Overall, Westmoreland and his supporters spoke for only five minutes and fifty-nine seconds, whereas his accusers were given nineteen minutes and nineteen seconds, a ratio of better than three to one for the accusers.

Van Gordon Sauter, then-president of CBS News, acknowledged that CBS policies and standards had been violated during the making of the documentary, but he argued that these flaws did not undermine its editorial integrity. According to him, it was an accurate account of the distorted estimates of enemy strength by the American military in Vietnam.

After several years of legal sparring, Westmoreland dropped his libel suit, leaving the substantive issues unsettled. The issues of media policy are clearer. As acknowledged in the CBS internal report, there is little disagreement about the standards of fairness and accuracy that should be applied in broadcasts on important public issues. But—and this is the disturbing aspect—these standards continue to be breached all too often. Such breaches raise questions about the sense of responsibility of high-level media personnel. When important public matters are at stake, are the media, especially the influential electronic media, exercising sufficient care to make sure that the preconceptions of media personnel do not taint their stories and mislead media audiences?

With investigative journalism growing in popularity, the problem of inaccurate reports has mounted. In 1989, for instance, charges surfaced that a freelance cameraperson had faked and restaged battle scenes in film used in CBS newscasts and documentaries about the war in Afghanistan. Scenes of sabotaging electric supply lines for Kabul, the capital of Afghanistan, allegedly were reenacted days after the event. The location of refugees was misstated to make the story more dramatic, and a Pakistani jet was misidentified as a Soviet plane.[52] In 1993, NBC's "Dateline" program showed how easily General Motors pickup trucks with side saddle gas tanks burst into fire after collision. The problem was that production crews had taped toy rockets to the underside of a truck and had tampered with its gas cap to make sure that the explosion would take place on cue. Caught red-handed in a major deception, NBC quickly settled a suit brought by General Motors.[53]

In many instances inaccurate reports have permanent economic, professional, and social consequences for the individuals and institutions whose stories are told. In the Westmoreland case, for example, the reputation of a prominent general was at stake. In another case, one involving the Kaiser Aluminum and Chemical Corporation, business losses could run into millions of dollars. An investigative report had accused the company of knowingly selling dangerous household electrical wiring under false pretenses. In yet another case a partially fictionalized documentary about the mass murder of African American youths in Atlanta suggested that the killer might still be at large. It raised doubts about the fairness of the trial of the man convicted as the murderer. The broadcast prompted the mayor of Atlanta and civic leaders to launch a public information campaign to blunt the anticipated ill effects.[54]

The serious injuries inflicted when publicity is careless or biased have become a deep concern for civil libertarians. An executive director of the American Civil Liberties Union has warned, "Justice by press release and summary political punishment are methods we should have by now learned to avoid."[55] The problem is made worse by the fact that rebuttals, if permitted at all by the networks, have been subject to their editorial control because, unlike ordinary news, they are considered edited productions so that uncensored rebuttals need not be accommodated.[56]

Entrapment

Serious ethical issues are also raised when newspeople undertake undercover operations or bogus enterprises created to entrap potential and actual wrongdoers. The story told earlier about the Mirage, the tavern set up to elicit and record bribery by city officials, illustrates the practice. So does the preparation of NBC's program "Cataract Cowboys" in 1993. When several Florida eye clinics, contrary to the desired script, turned down the requests of healthy undercover reporters for eye surgery, the producers staged a partly successful entrapment. The "patient" whose requests for surgery had been denied initially, telephoned the clinic to schedule an appointment. The filmed report of her return notes that she "was only a few tests and a half-hour away from surgery." The possibility that the tests might forestall the surgery was never mentioned because it would have ruined the message that NBC's investigative team wanted to convey.[57] A far more massive crime trap was set by Canadian media to expose organized crime in North America. The investigation resulted in a three-and-a-half hour documentary broadcast by the Canadian Broadcasting Company (CBC) on March 27, 1979. CBC reporters and agents who were planted inside organized crime circles used hidden microphones and cameras to obtain dramatic film footage of gangsters discussing their activities. In one instance a reporter arranged meetings with a woman suspected of helping gangsters to buy real estate in Atlantic City. The reporter pretended to represent a person in Italy who wished to export several million dollars from Italy to Canada. The money was then to be funneled into Atlantic City real estate under the guise that it belonged to legitimate Canadian investors. Through this initial contact, another meeting was set up between a disguised reporter, who had had previous experience as an informant for law enforcement agencies and underworld dealers in illegal real estate. All of these meetings were audiotaped and some parts were filmed.[58]

Sting operations like these raise serious civil liberties issues even when they are conducted by regular law enforcement agencies, often under the watchful eyes of the courts.[59] The concerns about protecting the rights of suspects are even greater when the sleuths are acting without an official mandate and without supervision by a responsible public body. Quite aside from civil liberties issues, sting operations raise fundamental questions about the proper functions of the press. Should its watchdog role be carried to the point where it becomes a quasi-police force, tracking down selected offenders whenever a good story promises to be the likely reward?

Summary

In this chapter we examined direct involvement by journalists in the affairs of government. We began with an analysis of muckraking, comparing reality to a series of models of the process. The media's power to arouse public opinion with exposés of corruption is far less than is popularly believed. Even if the public becomes highly concerned, political action is not guaranteed. The belief that muckraking commonly produces reforms when journalists stir the public, and public opinion then pressures for political action, is wrong.

The most propitious road to reform is via direct liaisons between newspeople and government officials. When officials provide story leads in areas in which they would like to produce action, or when newspeople can interest officials in taking action on issues that have come to the media's attention, successful political activities are apt to occur. On rare occasions the media are also able to produce action by participating in political negotiations or by using the club of potential unwanted publicity to force officials to act.

The Watergate scandal illustrates how political action can emerge from the interplay of various political institutions. The media, through a series of agenda-building steps, created the climate in which it became possible to force the resignation of a president. Agenda-building examples from science policy and from the realm of interest group politics demonstrate the impact of the media on developments in these fields. The media serve as catalysts that precipitate the actions of other elements within the society. They enhance the influence of some political forces and weaken others, but the ultimate outcome is beyond their control.

The media's public policy-making roles influence American politics in general as well as the lives of many individuals and institutions. How sensitively and accurately they are performed therefore become matters of grave concern. News gathering and news production frequently are seriously flawed, even when media institutions profess to believe in high standards. How often the ethics and standards of the profession are violated, and what the costs are to people caught in the net of inaccurate publicity, are matters for conjecture.

At the heart of most instances when newspeople become actively involved in politics lies the desire to produce exciting news stories. This is not surprising. Journalism requires telling stories that will attract audiences. That journalists are tempted to be good storytellers above all, even at the expense of other goals, should give pause to those who advocate that those in the media should play the political game actively and regularly. One must ask whether their professional standards equip them to guide politics wisely and well. To put it another way: When issues are put on the crowded political agenda, should their newsworthiness be the controlling factor? If the answer is no, then massive participation by the media in policy making may be quite troubling.

Notes

1. Lincoln Steffens, *The Autobiography of Lincoln Steffens* (New York: Harcourt Brace, 1931), 357.
2. See Larry J. Sabato, *Feeding Frenzy: How Attack Journalism Has Transformed American Politics* (New York: Free Press, 1991), chap. 2; David L. Protess, Fay Lomax Cook, Jack D. Doppelt, James S. Ettema, Margaret T. Gordon, Donna R. Leff, and Peter Miller, *The Journalism of Outrage: Investigative Reporting and Agenda Building* (New York: Guilford Press, 1991), chap. 2.
3. David Weaver and LeAnne Daniels, "Public Opinion on Investigative Reporting in the 1980s," *Journalism Quarterly* 69 (Spring 1992): 146–155.
4. David L. Protess, *Muckraking Matters: The Societal Impact of Investigative Reporting*, Institute for Modern Communications Research Monographs Series (Evanston, Ill.: Northwestern University, 1987), 13.
5. Steffens, *Autobiography*, 357.
6. Protess et al., *Journalism of Outrage*, 214–227.
7. How investigative stories differ from other forms of journalism is described by Matthew C. Ehrlich, "The Journalism of Outrageousness: Tabloid Television News vs. Investigative News," *Journalism and Mass Communication Monographs* 155 (February 1996).
8. Harvey L. Molotch, David L. Protess, and Margaret T. Gordon, "The Media-Policy Connection: Ecologies of News," in *Political Communication Research: Approaches, Studies, Assessments*, ed. David L. Paletz (Norwood, N.J.: Ablex, 1987), 26–48. Protess et al. model the process somewhat differently in their more recent *Journalism of Outrage*. But the earlier version seems more explicit.
9. Protess et al., *Journalism of Outrage*, chaps. 3–6 detail six investigations.
10. Robert Muccigrosso, "Television and the Urban Crisis," in *Screen and Society*, ed. Frank J. Coppa (Chicago: Nelson-Hall, 1979), 44–45.
11. Chris T. Allen and Judith D. Weber, "How Presidential Media Use Affects Individuals' Beliefs about Conservation," *Journalism Quarterly* 60 (Spring 1983): 98–104, 196.
12. Protess et al., *Journalism of Outrage*, chap. 4.
13. Often the chief point of a program is simply to alert the public to a problem; immediate action may not be expected. For example, the PBS documentary "Crisis at General Hospital" was intended to make the public aware of the inequity of a two-tier health system in which people of means are served by excellent private hospitals whereas the remainder of the population receives second-rate care in inferior public hospitals.

14. Protess et al., *Journalism of Outrage,* chap. 3.
15. The full story is told in Zay N. Smith and Pamela Zekman, *The Mirage* (New York: Random House, 1979).
16. Protess et al., *Journalism of Outrage,* 240–244.
17. Sabato, *Feeding Frenzy,* 53.
18. Protess et al., *Journalism of Outrage,* 134–135.
19. Wayne King, "Houston Finds that Dramatizing Crime Does Pay," *New York Times,* January 23, 1984.
20. Michael Killian, "New FBI TV Series Will Seek Viewer Help in Nabbing Criminals," *Chicago Tribune,* February 5, 1988.
21. Protess et al., *Journalism of Outrage,* 179–180.
22. "ABC Refuses to Telecast Taped Plea of U.S. Hostage," *Chicago Tribune,* August 4, 1989.
23. Tim Jones and Gary Marx, "Unabomber Has Media in a Bind," *Chicago Tribune,* September 20, 1995.
24. Robert D. McFadden, "News Executives Express Outrage," *New York Times,* October 3, 1986.
25. Regina Lawrence, *Managing Meaning: Media, Officials, and Police Brutality.* Unpublished Ph.D. dissertation, University of Washington, 1996.
26. Ellen Mickiewicz, *Opening Channels* (New York: Oxford University Press, 1996).
27. W. Lance Bennett, "Toward a Theory of Press-State Relations in the United States," *Journal of Communication* 40 (Spring 1990): 103–125; George A. Donahue, Phillip J. Tichenor, and Clarice N. Olien, "A Guard Dog Perspective on the Role of Media," *Journal of Communication* 45(2) (Spring 1995): 115–132.
28. Gladys Engel Lang and Kurt Lang, *The Battle for Public Opinion: The President, the Press and the Polls during Watergate* (New York: Columbia University Press, 1983), 58.
29. Molotch et al., "The Media-Policy Connection," 45, citing Peter Dreier, "The Position of the Press in the U.S. Power Structure," *Social Problems* 29 (February 1982): 298–310; also see Gadi Wolfsfeld, "Media Protest and Political Violence: A Transactional Analysis," *Journalism Monographs* 127 (June 1991); William A. Gamson, *The Strategy of Social Protest,* 2d ed. (Belmont, Calif.: Wadsworth, 1990); and Clarice N. Olien, Phillip J. Tichenor, and George A. Donahue, "Media Coverage and Social Movements," in *Information Campaigns: Balancing Social Values and Social Change,* ed. Charles T. Salmon (Beverly Hills, Calif.: Sage, 1989), 139–163.
30. Lang and Lang, *Battle for Public Opinion,* 59–60. Also see Michael Schudson, *Watergate in American Memory: How We Remember, Forget, and Reconstruct the Past* (New York: Basic Books, 1992).
31. Oscar H. Gandy, *Beyond Agenda Setting: Information Subsidies and Public Policy* (Norwood, N.J.: Ablex, 1982), 149–162.
32. The title and the information that follows come from "The Great Greenhouse Debate," *Media Monitor* 6(10) (December 1992): 1–6.
33. David L. Paletz and Robert M. Entman, *Media Power Politics* (New York: Free Press, 1981), 144.
34. Stanley Rothman and S. Robert Lichter, "Elite Ideology and Risk Perception in Nuclear Energy Policy," *American Political Science Review* 81 (June 1987): 383–404. For a more general discussion of the problem of sources of science information, see Hans Mathias Kepplinger, "Artificial Horizons: How the

Press Presented and How the Population Received Technology in Germany from 1965–1986," in *The Mass Media in Liberal Democratic Societies,* ed. Stanley Rothman (New York: Paragon House, 1992), 147–176; Kandice L. Salomone, Michael R. Greenberg, Peter M. Sandman, and David B. Sachsman, "A Question of Quality: How Journalists and News Sources Evaluate Coverage of Environmental Risk," *Journal of Communication* 40 (Autumn 1990): 117–130.

35. The information about this case comes from "Is Cancer News a Health Hazard? Media Coverage vs. 'Scientific' Opinion on Environmental Cancer," *Media Monitor* 7(8) (November/December 1993): 1–5.

36. Patrick Leahy and Alan Mazur, "The Rise and Fall of Public Opposition in Specific Social Movements," *Social Studies of Science* 10 (1980): 191–205; and Alan Mazur, "Media Coverage and Public Opinion on Scientific Controversies," *Journal of Communication* 31 (Spring 1981): 106–115.

37. Renate G. Bader, "How Science News Sections Influence Newspaper Science Coverage: A Case Study," *Journalism Quarterly* 67 (Spring 1990): 88–96; Eleanor Singer, "A Question of Accuracy: How Journalists and Scientists Report Research on Hazards," *Journalism Quarterly* 40 (Autumn 1990): 102–116.

38. Todd Gitlin, *The Whole World Is Watching: Media in the Making and Unmaking of the New Left* (Berkeley: University of California Press, 1980), 25–26.

39. For models of the roles played by the media in fostering social movements, see Kevin M. Carragee, "News and Ideology," *Journalism Monographs* 128 (August 1991); Wolfsfeld, "Media Protest and Political Violence"; and Gamson, *The Strategy of Social Protest.*

40. Laura R. Woliver, *From Outrage to Action: The Politics of Grass-Roots Dissent* (Urbana: University of Illinois Press, 1993).

41. Gitlin, *The Whole World,* 284.

42. Hans Mathias Kepplinger and Michael Hachenberg, "Media and Conscientious Objection in the Federal Republic of Germany," in *Political Communication Research,* ed. Paletz, 108–128. Also see Fay Lomax Cook and Wesley G. Skogan, "Convergent and Divergent Voice Models of the Rise and Fall of Policy Issues," *Agenda Setting: Readings on Media, Public Opinion, and Policymaking,* ed. David L. Protess and Maxwell McCombs (Hillsdale, N.J.: Lawrence Erlbaum, 1991), 189–206.

43. Wolfsfeld, "Media Protest and Political Violence," 8–10.

44. Edie Goldenberg, *Making the Papers* (Lexington, Mass.: Heath, 1975), 146–148.

45. The potential impact of docudramas is discussed by William C. Adams, Allison Salzman, William Vantine, Leslie Suelter, Anne Baker, Lucille Bonvouloir, Barbara Brenner, Margaret Ely, Jean Feldman, and Ron Ziegel, "The Power of *The Right Stuff:* A Quasi-Experimental Field Test of the Docudrama Hypothesis," *Public Opinion Quarterly* 49 (Fall 1985): 330–339.

46. Gandy, *Beyond Agenda Setting,* 88.

47. Sally Bedell Smith, "Film on a Nuclear War Already Causing Wide Fallout of Partisan Activity," *New York Times,* November 23, 1983.

48. Bernard Weinraub, "Hollywood Wonders if Warner Brothers Let 'J. F. K.' Go Too Far," *New York Times,* December 24, 1991; Jack R. Payton, "'J. F. K.'s Premise Is Full of Holes—But So Was Warren Report," *Chicago Tribune,* December 24, 1991.

49. For a discussion of the subtle yet significant consequences that are often missed, see Stanley Feldman and Lee Sigelman, "The Political Impact of Prime-Time Television: 'The Day After,'" *Journal of Politics* 47 (May 1985): 556–578.

50. For a full discussion of the role of the media as political actors, see Timothy E. Cook, *Revisiting the Fourth Branch of Government: The News Media as Political Institutions* (Chicago: University of Chicago Press, forthcoming).

51. Richard Bernstein, "CBS Releases Its Study of Vietnam Documentary," *New York Times*, April 27, 1983.

52. Bill Carter, "The Larger Issues Behind the Dan Rather Case," *New York Times*, October 4, 1989.

53. Pat Widder, "Playing with Fire: Blur of Fact and Fiction Costs NBC," *Chicago Tribune*, February 11, 1993.

54. William E. Schmidt, "TV Movie on Atlanta Child Killings Stirs Debate and Casts Doubt on Guilt," *New York Times*, January 31, 1985.

55. Quoted in Deirdre Carmody, "The Role of the Press in the U.S. Corruption Inquiry," *New York Times*, February 5, 1980.

56. For a typical case involving denial of the right to unedited rebuttal, see Sally Bedell, "ABC Backs Off Charge It Made against Mobil," *New York Times*, June 22, 1982.

57. Walter Goodman,"What's News Worthy Is in the Eye of the Beholder," *New York Times*, August 30, 1993.

58. Andrew H. Malcolm, "TV Film Links to Mob in Toronto," *New York Times*, March 28, 1979.

59. Bennett L. Gershman, "Abscam, the Judiciary, and the Ethics of Government," *Yale Law Journal* 91 (July 1982): 1565–1591.

Readings

Charity, Arthur. *Doing Public Journalism*. New York: Guilford, 1996.

Gitlin, Todd. *The Whole World Is Watching: Media in the Making and Unmaking of the New Left*. Berkeley: University of California Press, 1980.

Hallin, Daniel C. *We Keep America on Top of the World: Television Journalism and the Public Sphere*. New York: Routledge, 1994.

Lang, Gladys Engel, and Kurt Lang. *The Battle for Public Opinion: The President, the Press and the Polls during Watergate*. New York: Columbia University Press, 1983.

Popkin, Jeremy D. *Media and Revolution: Comparative Perspectives*. Lexington: University Press of Kentucky, 1995.

Sabato, Larry J., and S. Robert Lichter. *When Should the Watchdogs Bark? Media Coverage of the Clinton Scandals*. Washington, D.C.: Center for Media and Public Affairs, 1994.

Smith, Zay N., and Pamela Zekman. *The Mirage*. New York: Random House, 1979.

Steffens, Lincoln. *The Autobiography of Lincoln Steffens*. New York: Harcourt Brace, 1931.

Media Impact on Attitudes and Behavior

MURPHY BROWN, THE CHARACTER OF A POPULAR prime-time television situation comedy, had a baby out of wedlock in one of the show's episodes, broadcast in May 1992. In this day and age, unmarried motherhood on television is no earth-shaking event—or is it? The story was front-page news for newspapers around the country, including the *New York Times*. There was no dearth of important news at the time that might require filling space with any breaking story, however trivial. As the *New York Times* proclaimed in its story lead: "Thailand is in turmoil, the Federal deficit is ballooning and hot embers of racial resentment still smolder in the ruins of inner-city Los Angeles. But today the high councils of government were preoccupied with a truly vexing question: Is Murphy Brown really against family values?"[1]

Why did Murphy Brown's pregnancy make such big news? The reason was that Vice President Dan Quayle had publicly denounced the show and its story line for eroding family values and glorifying unwed motherhood. President George Bush had been peppered with questions about the make-believe birth during a news conference shared with the Canadian prime minister, who was also asked about it. White House spokesperson Marlin Fitzwater had flip-flopped on the issue in the course of a single day. In the morning, Fitzwater condemned publicity for unwed motherhood; in the afternoon, he praised the fictional mother for foregoing an abortion.

The reason for all the commotion is the widely held belief that factual and fictional media stories shape the thinking and behavior patterns of countless Americans. What would the 38 million Americans of all ages who watched the show learn from it about family values in America? This is just one of the many puzzling questions so often asked about the impact of mass media stories on children and adults. Are people's values and attitudes about society and politics really influenced by what they read and see? Does socially controversial behavior in television fiction and news programs produce imitation in real life? *How much* do people learn from the media and *what* do they learn?

In this chapter we will examine these questions, beginning with the shaping of attitudes that occurs as an unintended byproduct of media exposure. For the most part, newspeople do not try to teach political attitudes and values, nor do people try to learn them. Rather, exposure to individual, dramatic events or the incremental impact of the total flow of information over prolonged periods of time leads to "incidental" learning about the political world. We also will consider the ways in which people choose the media to which they will pay attention and the sorts of things they will learn. Finally, we will address the question posed at the start: To what degree does exposure to the mass media influence behavior in politically significant ways?

Differential Effects of Print and Broadcast News

Most Americans are exposed to combinations of all the media either directly or indirectly through contacts with people who have been exposed. We may know that American troops have been dispatched to Bosnia. We may feel pride or anxiety about the venture and consider it a good or bad foreign policy. But which of these thoughts and feelings come from television, or newspapers, or conversations, or from a combination of media? It is nearly impossible to disentangle such strands of information.[2]

Each medium, however, does make unique contributions to learning. For example, television, because of its visuals, is especially powerful in transmitting realism and emotional appeal. It does less well conveying abstract ideas. In one fairly typical study researchers asked viewers about the main points of specific stories; viewers failed to identify 72 percent of them. Miscomprehension rates for individual stories ranged from 16 percent to 93 percent.[3]

Print media excel in conveying factual details. Because most tests of learning from the media focus on factual learning and rote memory, print media are generally credited with conveying more knowledge than audiovisual media do.[4] In fact, media scholar Neil Postman warns that massive use of television will turn America into a nation of dilettantes who avoid serious thinking because television trivializes the problems of the world. It gives people the illusion of being knowledgeable when, in fact, they are distracted from probing issues in depth.[5]

The claim that the nature of the medium accounts for differences in knowledge gain is not clear-cut, however. Demographic differences may be part of the explanation. Heavy newspaper users tend to be better informed than persons who do not read the paper, but they also generally enjoy higher socioeconomic status and better formal education. Their status in life, therefore, provides above-average incentives for the factual learning that is usually measured. Attitudes toward the media matter as well. Print media are viewed by most people as sources of information, whereas electronic media are viewed as sources of entertainment. These additional differences, rather than the nature of each medium, may explain some of the differences in effects. Television becomes the most instructive medium if one tests for information that is best conveyed audiovisually, such as impressions of people and the inferences they engender or comprehension and long-term memory for highly dramatic events.[6]

Television's greatest political impact, compared with that of other media, is derived from its ability to reach millions of people simultaneously with the same images. Major broadcasts enter nearly every home in the nation instantaneously and simultaneously. Televised events become shared experiences. Millions of Americans were present vicariously when the *Challenger* spacecraft exploded, when a lone student defied armed might at China's Tiananmen Square, and when O. J. Simpson's white Bronco sped along Los Angeles freeways after he had been accused of his ex-wife's murder. America's print media have never attained such a reach and the power that flows from it. Moreover, 23 million American adults are functionally illiterate and therefore are almost entirely beyond the reach of print media. What the poorly educated now learn about politics from television may be fragmentary and hazy, but it represents a quantum leap over their previous exposure and learning.

In short, the research on the differential effects of various types of media reveals that different types present stimuli that vary substantially in nature and content. It would be surprising, therefore, if their impact were identical, even when they deal with the same subjects. However, "there is no evidence of *consistent* significant differences in the ability of different media to persuade, inform, or even to instill an emotional response in audience members."[7] Because current research does not provide adequate answers about the precise effects of these stimulus variations and about the processes by which individuals mesh a variety of media stimuli, we will focus on the end product—the combined impact of all print and electronic media stimuli.

The Role of Media in Political Socialization

Political socialization—the learning about structures and environmental factors and internalizing of customs and rules governing political life—affects the quality of interactions between citizens and their government. Political systems do not operate smoothly without the support of most of their citizens, who must be willing to abide by the laws and to support government through performing duties such as voting, paying taxes, or serving in the military. Support is most readily obtained if citizens are convinced of the legitimacy and capability of their government and if they feel strong emotional ties to it. If political socialization fails to instill such attitudes, policies and laws that depend on public support, such as energy conservation or traffic regulations, may become unenforceable. If political socialization fails to provide citizens with sufficient knowledge, elections may become a sham at best; at worst, they may become a mockery in which clever politicians manipulate an ignorant electorate. Likewise, surveillance of government activities is impossible if people lack a grasp of the nature of government and public policies.

Childhood Socialization

Political socialization starts in childhood. Children usually learn basic attitudes toward authority, property, decision making, and veneration for political symbols from their families, and in recent decades from television. When they enter the more formal school setting, teaching about political values becomes quite systematic. At school, children also learn new factual information about their political and social world, much of it based on mass media information.[8]

Children's direct contacts with the media are equally abundant.[9] Millions of babies watch television. In the winter, young children in the United States spend an average of thirty-one hours a week in front of the television set—more time than in school. Between the ages of twelve and seventeen, this drops to twenty-four hours. Eighty percent of the programs children see are intended for adults and therefore differ substantially from the child's limited personal experiences. Children watch military combat, funerals, rocket launchings, courtships, seductions, and childbirth. If they can understand the message, the impact is likely to be great, because, lacking experience, they are apt to take such presentations at face value.

When asked for the sources of information on which they base their attitudes about the economy or race problems, or war and patriotism, high school students mention the mass media far more often than they mention their families, friends, teachers, or personal experiences.[10] Youngsters who are frequent media users gain substantial information from the media. Compared to infrequent users, they show greater under-standing and support for basic American values, such as the importance of free speech and the right to equal and fair treatment.[11]

The finding that mass media strongly influence socialization runs counter to earlier socialization studies that showed parents and teachers as the chief socializers. Several reasons account for the change. The first is the increasing pervasiveness of television, which makes it easy for even the youngest children to be exposed to mass media images. The second rea-son involves deficiencies in measurement. Much of the early research dis-counted all media influence unless it came through direct contact outside the classroom between the child and the media. That excluded indirect media influence, such as contacts with parents and teachers who convey media information to the child. These exclusions sharply reduced find-ings of media effects. Finally, research designs have become more sophisti-cated. In the early studies children were asked to make their own general appraisal of learning sources. A typical question might be, "From whom do you learn the most: your parents, your school, or newspapers and tele-vision?" The questions used in recent studies have been more specific, inquiring first what children know about particular subjects, such as immi-gration or nuclear energy, and then asking about the sources of their information. In nearly every case the mass media were named as the chief sources of information and evaluations.

What children learn from the mass media and how they evaluate it depends heavily on their stage of mental development. Child psychologist Jean Piaget contended that children between two and seven years of age do not independently perceive the connections among various phenom-ena or draw general conclusions from specific instances. Many of the lessons presumably taught by media stories therefore elude young chil-dren. Complex reasoning skills develop fully only at the teenage level. Children's interests in certain types of stories also change sharply with age, as do their attention and information-retention spans.[12] Most chil-dren strongly support the political system during their early years but often become quite disillusioned about authority figures during their teenage years. This skepticism diminishes as education is completed and the young adult enters the work force. What role the media play in this transformation is unclear.[13] Knowledge is also slim about children's and adolescents' imitation of behavior depicted by media stories, the duration of memories, and the persistence of media effects on learning, behavior, and social relationships.[14]

Adult Socialization

The pattern of heavy media exposure continues into adulthood. The average American adult spends more than four hours a day watching television, well over two hours listening to radio, often while working or traveling by car, eighteen to forty-five minutes reading newspapers, and six to thirty minutes reading a magazine. Time spent with the mass media has jumped 40 percent since the advent of television, mostly at the expense of other leisure activities. Television alone now takes up nearly half of the leisure time of most Americans. On an average day, 80 percent of all Americans are exposed to television and newspapers. On a typical evening, the television audience is close to 100 million people. This can double for extraordinary events when more than 90 percent of the population may gather in front of the nation's television screens.[15]

This massive exposure contributes to the lifelong process of political socialization and learning. The mass media form

> the mainstream of the common symbolic environment that cultivates the most widely shared conceptions of reality. We live in terms of the stories we tell, stories about what things exist, stories about how things work, and stories about what to do.... Increasingly, media-cultivated facts and values become standards by which we judge.[16]

Once basic attitudes toward the political system have been formed, they usually stabilize, and later learning largely supplements and refines earlier notions. The need to cope with information about new events and shifting cultural orientations force the average person into continuous learning and gradual readjustments, although the basic value structure generally remains intact, even when attitudes are modified.[17] However, major personal or societal upheavals may lead to more or less complete resocialization and revised political ideas.

People learn about political norms, rules, values, events, and behaviors largely from the mass media, including fictional as well as factual stories. Personal experiences are severely limited compared with the range of experiences offered to us directly or indirectly by the media about the social order and political activities. An accident report, for example, besides telling what happened, may suggest that police and fire forces respond too slowly and that emergency facilities in the local hospital are inadequate. When societal problems such as poverty or pollution are framed as discrete events, such as one family's starvation or a particular oil spill, attention is likely to be focused on individual solutions, obscuring the larger societal problems.[18] Soap operas on radio and television may persuade audiences that most politicians are corruptible—after all, the majority of those shown on television are.[19] In fact, fictional stories are the most widely used sources for political information. Surveys show that only one half to two thirds of the adult public regularly exposes itself to explicit political news.[20]

People's opinions, feelings, and evaluations about the political system may spring from their own thinking about facts supplied by the media; from attitudes, opinions, and feelings explicitly expressed in news or entertainment programming; or from a combination of the two.[21] Many people who use the media for information, and as a point of departure for formulating their own appraisals, reject or ignore attitudes and evaluations that are supplied explicitly or implicitly by media stories.[22] For example, the fact that independent presidential candidate Ross Perot financed his own campaign in 1992 was condemned by most media as an attempt to "buy" the presidency. Nonetheless, many Americans viewed it as a praiseworthy effort to attain the office without entangling financial supporters.

People are prone to accept newspeople's views about national and international issues whenever they lack personal experience or guidance from social contacts. Even when people think that they are forming their own opinions about familiar issues, they often depend on the media more than they realize. Extensive television exposure has been shown to lead to "mainstreaming," turning people into bland middle-roaders with a basically uniform outlook on political life that is "congruent with television's portrayal of life and society."[23]

When audiences have direct or vicarious experiences to guide them, and particularly when they have already formed opinions grounded firmly in their personal values, they are far less likely to be swayed by the media. In practice, this means that the least informed and least interested are most likely to reflect the viewpoints expressed in the media, particularly television. Parroting of viewpoints espoused by political commentators explains why people uninterested in politics often spout seemingly sophisticated opinions if they have been extensively exposed to news stories.[24]

Media's persuasiveness does not mean that exposure is tantamount to learning and mind changing. Far from it! In fact, two thirds of the people generally do not know their newspaper's preferred position on specific economic, social, and foreign policy issues.[25] Most media stories are promptly forgotten. Stories that become part of an individual's fund of knowledge tend to reinforce existing beliefs and feelings. Acquisition of new knowledge or changes in attitude are the exception rather than the rule. Still, they occur often enough to be highly significant.

Patterns in Socialization

Media exposure patterns may be a partial explanation for knowledge and attitude differences among racial and ethnic groups.[26] For example, African Americans rely less on general mass media for political information than do whites. Accordingly, in a study done in the 1970s, whites in a low-income Los Angeles neighborhood relied on print and electronic political information almost twice as much as their African American neighbors. Hispanics found print and electronic media even less useful for keeping themselves politically informed than did African Americans. Such alienation from major sources of political information, which is persisting, may hamper the political effectiveness of Hispanics and African Americans in dealing with the majority culture.[27]

African Americans and whites extract different information even when they use the same media. African Americans are more apt than whites to believe that factual as well as fictional stories presented by the media are true to life.[28] Therefore, the images that many African Americans form about lifestyles or societal patterns are more likely to mirror the distortions found in media presentations.[29] A study of the diffusion of information about six assassinations showed that each racial group dwelled heavily on news that dealt with its own race. Although all African Americans and whites had heard about the deaths of Martin Luther King, Jr., and President John Kennedy and his brother Robert, many more African Americans than whites (10 percent to 24 percent more) knew about the assassinations of Medgar Evers and Malcolm X. In the same way, many more whites than African Americans knew about the death of white Nazi leader George Lincoln Rockwell.[30]

There are many possible explanations for demographic variations in media use and socialization patterns. Despite the successes of the civil rights movement, most African Americans still belong to different social groups than whites, and they lead lives quite unlike those of the white middle-class to whose tastes most media cater. More African Americans than whites fall into youthful age brackets where readership is generally lower. Fewer African Americans than whites drive to work; hence fewer listen to radio news. For the many African Americans whose schooling has been poor, deficient reading skills make newspaper reading unattractive. Television is an appealing alternative. Accordingly, African Americans on an average watch about 15 percent more television than do whites, albeit different programs.[31]

Some researchers doubt the media and socialization differences between African Americans and whites are based on race-linked cultural differences. Instead they attribute divergences to the fact that the African American population is more frequently poor and educationally deprived and contend that within the subculture of poverty, African Americans and whites use the media in similar ways.[32] Other scholars argue that race and its cultural consequences are indeed important factors in media exposure and impact. Leo Bogart, for example, found racial differences in media-use patterns regardless of socioeconomic status.[33] The unresolved issues thus revolve around the causes of subcultural differences rather than their existence. If differences spring from race-linked cultural differences, they may be resistant to change. If they are linked to socioeconomic status, they may change readily with rising incomes, better education, and improved occupational status.

Gender, age, income, education, region, and city size also generate differences in newspaper reading, radio listening, and television viewing. For instance, men and women differ sharply in daytime television viewing; age has a bearing on newspaper reading; southerners listen to much less radio than do northerners. Program preferences vary as well. Women aged fifty and older are the heaviest viewers of television news, followed by men fifty and older. Twelve- to seventeen-year-olds are the lightest news watchers. Men far exceed women in following sports coverage, whereas women spend more time watching television drama.

Differences in media-use patterns are particularly pronounced between income levels. High-income families, who usually are better educated than poor families, use print media more and television less than the rest of the population. Upper income people also use a greater variety of media: 57 percent are multimedia users compared with 27 percent in the lower economic groups. Thus the well-to-do potentially have much more information and a greater variety of information available to them. This helps them to maintain and increase their influence and power in American society. In part, the poor pay less attention to print media because these media cater to upper income groups rather than the needs and concerns of the poor. Low income audiences prefer television and radio programs, which are easy to grasp and carry a great deal of light entertainment.

The notion of vastly different communications environments for various population groups should not be carried too far, however. The bulk of media entertainment and information is similar throughout the country and is shared by all types of media audiences. The same network television and cable programs are broadcast on the East Coast and the West Coast, in big cities and small towns. Differences among individual media enterprises are slight. Hence television comes close to being a single, nationwide source of news and commentary. Radio is more diverse, but even many radio news programs are little more than national wire service reports. Insofar as newspaper stories are based on wire service information, they, too, are fairly uniform everywhere.

In Chapter 4 we saw that news media cover basically the same categories of stories in the same proportions. Specific stories vary, of course, depending on regional and local interests. Newspapers on the West Coast are more likely to devote their foreign affairs coverage to Asian affairs than are newspapers on the East Coast, which concentrate on Europe and the Middle East. Tabloids put more stress on sensational crime and sex stories than elite papers such as the staid *New York Times*. Nevertheless, news sources everywhere provide a large common core of information and interpretation that imbues their audiences with a shared structure of basic values and information.

Choosing Media Stories

General patterns of media use do not reveal *why* people pay attention to specific stories, but a number of theories have been formulated to help explain how and why such individual choices are made.

Uses and Gratifications Theories

One of the most widely accepted of news choice theories currently is the "uses and gratifications" approach. Put simply, proponents of this approach contend that individuals ignore personally irrelevant and unattractively presented messages and pay attention to the kinds of things that they find useful and intellectually or emotionally gratifying, provided the expenditure of time and effort to digest the material seems reasonable.[34]

Media scholar Lance Bennett groups uses and gratifications into three broad categories: curiosity and surveillance, entertainment and escape, and social and psychological adjustment.[35] For instance, people pay attention to stories that help them in voting or participating in protest demonstrations. They use the media to gain a sense of security and social adequacy from knowing what is happening in their political environment. People feel gratified if the media reinforce what they already know and believe. Finally, the media are used to while away time, reduce loneliness, participate vicariously in exciting ventures, and escape the frustrations of everyday life.[36] People from all walks of life are most likely to view prime-time programs that are action-filled, humorous, and relaxing. They are least likely to choose educational programs, particularly when they involve sophisticated political analysis.[37]

Of course, there is no guarantee that the gratifications that are sought are routinely attained. In fact, media may produce anxieties and fears as well as hatred and alienation. When radio and television were shut down by a long strike in Israel in 1987, the public reacted with relief rather than dismay. Israeli philosopher David Hartman gave this explanation:

> When television and radio become the prisms through which you look at reality, you come away saying, "What an ugly place this is." But when you take away those prisms and people's perceptions of reality are derived exclusively from their own daily experiences, which are for the most part prosaic, they inevitably become more relaxed and stable.[38]

Table 7-1, based on interviews with 6,564 adults in ten small cities throughout the United States, indicates the twenty-five newspaper content areas that are read most widely. People were asked to rate common newspaper topics on a scale of 1 to 5. A score of 1 denoted that they always ignored the topic; a score of 5 denoted that they always read it whenever it appeared. The topics earning the highest scores presumably supply the broadest array of gratifications. Special subcultural needs may lead to significant variations in gratification patterns. For instance, a Jewish person may be particularly eager to receive news from the Middle East and other places that concern Israel. A person of Polish ancestry may look for news about food shortages and political developments in Poland. Women who favor increased job opportunities for women are apt to notice stories about women's expanding presence in the business world. What people actually select depends very much on their lifestyles and the context in which they are exposed to information. What is useful and gratifying in one setting may be less so in another. When people change their lifestyles, such as moving from full-time employment to retirement or trading a desk for a travel job, media patterns may change drastically to bring about closer accord with the people encountered in the new setting.[39]

Table 7-2 shows the kinds of reasons people give when asked why they paid attention or failed to pay attention to particular news stories. Personal, rather then social, gratifications seem most important in choosing stories, whereas lack of interest and casual inattention best explain inattention.

TABLE 7-1 Rankings of Top Twenty-five Content Categories and Average Ratings Across Ten Markets

Rank		Rating
1.	Natural disasters and tragedies	3.93
2.	Stories and columns on the national economy (prices, unemployment, inflation)	3.87
3.	News of the local economy	3.82
4.	Column on local people and events	3.72
5.	Stories about national politics and the president	3.72
6.	Service information (TV listings, weather, movie listings, etc.)	3.71
7.	News of international leaders and events	3.70
8.	Stories on energy, conservation, and the environment	3.67
9.	Stories on things to see and do in the area	3.66
10.	Good Samaritan stories (people helping people)	3.60
11.	Humorous stories and features	3.56
12.	Accident and crime news	3.52
13.	Health and medical advice	3.42
14.	How fast the community is growing	3.33
15.	Editorials and letters to the editor	3.32
16.	Schools and education	3.31
17.	City council and local politicians	3.30
18.	News about the governor and state legislature	3.27
19.	Consumer stories and advice	3.27
20.	Stories about human psychology (the way we think and act)	3.22
21.	Nature and outdoor stories	3.19
22.	How-to advice on such things as crafts, auto and home repairs	3.19
23.	News of record (births, deaths, weddings, etc.)	3.10
24.	Space and exploration	3.10
25.	Science and technology	3.08

SOURCE: Judee K. Burgoon, Michael Burgoon, and Miriam Wilkinson, "Dimensions of Content Readership in 10 Newspaper Markets," *Journalism Quarterly* 60 (Spring 1983): 79. Reprinted by permission of the Association for Education in Journalism and Mass Communication, publishers of *Journalism Quarterly*.

NOTE: Ratings are based on a 1 to 5 scale. A rating of 1 means "never read"; a rating of 5 means "always read."

Other Selective Exposure Theories

Although most of the reasons for missing stories lead to random omissions, systematic omissions occur as well and various cognitive balance theories try to explain them. According to these theories, people avoid information that disturbs their peace of mind, offends their political and social tastes, or conflicts with information, attitudes, and feelings they already hold. Social scientists explain selective exposure by pointing out that peo-

TABLE 7-2   Reasons for Attention or Inattention to News Stories

Reasons for attention	Percent	Reasons for inattention	Percent
Personal relevance	26	Missed the story	47
Emotional appeal	20	No interest	28
Societal importance	19	Too remote	10
Interesting story	15	Too busy	6
Job relevance	12	Doubt media	3
Chance reasons	1	Too complex	3
Miscellaneous	7	Redundant/boring	2
		Doubt story	1

SOURCE: Doris A. Graber, *Processing the News: How People Tame the Information Tide,* 2d ed. (New York: Longman, 1988), 102. Copyright © 1988 by Longman Inc. Reprinted by permission of Longman Inc.

NOTE: $N = 453$ for reasons for attention; 1,493 for reasons of inattention.

ple are uncomfortable when they are exposed to ideas that differ from their own or that question the validity of their ideas. To avoid discomfort, people select information that is congruent with their existing beliefs. Selectivity then lays the groundwork for differential attitudes toward politics. It reduces the already slim chances that an individual's established beliefs, attitudes, and feelings will be altered. Selective exposure therefore helps to explain the considerable stability that exists in cognitions and orientations such as party allegiance or foreign policy preferences.

Scholars now believe that selective exposure occurs to a lesser extent than was thought initially. Many people find it too bothersome to select news stories carefully, particularly when using electronic media. For instance, when television news programs carry stories that are objectionable to a viewer, there is no easy way to screen out the undesired stories and still watch the rest of the broadcast. Many people are actually curious about discrepant information or pride themselves on being open-minded and receptive to all points of view. For instance, Democrats may want to hear what Republicans are saying to find out how the opposition is stating its case. They may also want to determine what counter arguments need to be formulated. Many people actually enjoy hearing news that contradicts their own ideas so that they can refute it. Apparently exposure to discrepant information is not as universally painful as previously thought. News also can be ignored, overlooked, or distorted. The source can be discredited and the message disbelieved.[40]

Much of the evidence for exposure to a highly selective slice of news has come from settings in which available media supported the preferences of the audience. No choice was necessary; selection was de facto rather than deliberate. For example, unionized workers with friends and associates who are also in unions may encounter a lot of prounion information at home and at work. They may not have to make a special effort to seek out only prounion information or reject antiunion opinions. In fact, antiunion information may be unavailable. Genuine rather than de facto selective exposure does occur, of course, but it operates more like a preference than a total exclusion rule. It appears to be most prevalent for those relatively few people who recognize dissonance and find it painful.

Agenda-Setting Theories

If choices of news items were entirely determined by personal needs and pleasures, news selection patterns would show infinite variations. This is not the case. Similarities in the political environment of average Americans and social pressures produce common patterns in the selection of news. As previously mentioned, gatekeeping practices largely account for the similarity in news supply, which is a powerful unifying force. Media also tell people in fairly uniform fashion which individual issues and activities are most significant and deserve to be ranked highly on the public's agenda of concerns.[41] Importance is indicated through cues such as banner headlines or front-page placement in newspapers or first-story placement on television. Frequent and ample coverage also implies significance.

Many people readily adopt the media's agenda of importance, often without being aware of it, rather than selecting or rejecting news on the basis of what is personally gratifying or displeasing. We look at the front page of the newspaper and expect to find the most important stories there. We may watch the opening minutes of a telecast eagerly and then allow our attention to slacken. As a result, agenda setting by the media leads to uniformities in exposure as well as in significance ratings of news items. When the media make events seem important, average people as well as politicians discuss them and form opinions about them. This enhances the perceived importance of these events and ensures even more public attention and, possibly, political action.

Numerous studies confirm the agenda-setting influence of the media.[42] When people are asked which issues are most important to them personally or to their communities, their lists tend to correspond to cues in the news sources that they use in their communities.[43] However, agenda setting varies in potency. Audiences follow media guidance but not slavishly.[44] Past and current experiences, conversations with others, and independent reasoning provide alternatives to media guidance. Comparisons of media agendas with public opinion polls and reports about political and social conditions show that media guidance is most important for new issues that have not been widely discussed and for issues beyond the realm of personal experience.[45] Prominent media coverage does ensure that an issue will be noticed, but it does not guarantee that the audience will assign it the same relative rank of importance that media play has indicated. Likewise, information that is useful or gratifying to the audience will be noted, even if it is on the back pages, receives minuscule headlines, or is briefly reported at the tail end of a newscast.[46] The need for raw material for conversation with friends and associates is a particularly strong force in selecting stories.

Learning Processes

How do audiences process the stories that they have selected? The early models that depicted a straight stimulus-response relationship have been disproven. There is no "hypodermic effect": information presented by the media is not injected unaltered into the minds of audiences. Rather, the images conveyed by the media stimulate perceptions in audience members that reflect the media stimuli as well as each individual's perceptual state at the time the message was received.

Blending New and Old Information

From childhood on people develop ideas and feelings about how the world operates. When these ideas relate to politics, they are usually grounded in information drawn from the mass media. Cognitive psychologists call these mental configurations by various names, including *schemata* and *scripts*.[47] As journalist Walter Lippmann explained seventy-five years ago:

> For the most part we do not first see, and then define, we define first and then see. In the great blooming, buzzing confusion of the outer world, we pick out what our culture has already defined for us, and we tend to perceive that which we have picked out in the form stereotyped for us by our culture.[48]

For instance, Marxists attribute most political events to economic forces. They accordingly interpreted stories about racial rioting in the United States in the late 1960s as signaling proletarian uprisings. Most Americans viewed them as stories about protests against racial injustice and its consequences.

Schemata serve as organizing devices that help people to assimilate new information. If breaking news stories match established schemata, they can be stored easily in memory as another example of a familiar concept. Numerous knowledge-gap studies show that political elites and other well-informed people have developed exceptionally large arrays of schemata allowing them to absorb many stories that are beyond the reach of the poorly informed.[49] The knowledge gap between the privileged and underprivileged widens as a result. Those with the least political knowledge are likely to remain politically unsophisticated and impotent. The knowledge gap between the information-rich and the information-poor also makes mutual understanding of political views more difficult.

Transient Influences

Many transitory factors impinge on news processing. People are intermittently attentive or inattentive and inclined or disinclined to learn. Up to half of the television audience eats dinner, washes dishes, reads, or talks on the telephone while watching television. Examination time at school, illness in the family, or the year-end rush at work may preempt the time normally devoted to media. Researchers cannot predict the effect of media messages without knowing the group context in which exposure or conversation took place. For instance, if one watches or talks about a presidential inauguration with friends who are making fun of the way the president talks and acts, the occasion loses solemnity and becomes banal.[50] How a person interacts with information also depends on the format of that information. If news reports present conflicting facts or opinions, if they are overly long or overly short, if they are repetitious, dull, or offensive, their effect is apt to be diminished. Moreover, the total communications matrix affects the influence of its parts; the impact of print news may be blunted by prior presentations on television and radio that have removed the edge of novelty.[51]

Source credibility and appeal are other significant factors in news processing. People find television news more believable than comparable print news because they tend to trust anchorpersons; seeing them on their living room television screens makes them familiar and trustworthy.[52] Partisanship, too, may play an important role in source appraisal. It may cast a rosy glow over fellow partisans and a pall over the opposition.

Perceptual and Image Factors

When people receive new information they combine it with existing beliefs. But does the new reshape the old or the old reshape the new in the final images? Research shows that images of political candidates are largely perceiver-determined for those aspects for which the audience already has developed complex schemata. For instance, people assume that Democratic presidential candidates will pursue policies typically associated with Democrats. They read or view the news in that vein, picking up bits of information that fit and rejecting, ignoring, or reinterpreting those that do not fit. The same is likely to hold true for information about big business or big labor, Mother Theresa, or England's queen. Average Americans are likely to interpret big business and big labor news negatively. Similarly, if reports about Mother Theresa or Queen Elizabeth permit a choice between favorable and unfavorable interpretations, the favorable image is apt to prevail.

Information about aspects of events or people that are not widely known or stereotyped leads to stimulus-determined images. How the media frame these political issues and depict people largely determines what the audience perceives. The personalities of newcomers to the political scene, assessments of their capabilities, and appraisals of the people with whom they surround themselves, for example, usually are stimulus-determined.[53] Likewise, when the media describe present-day China, when they cast doubt on the safety of nuclear energy production, or when they praise the merits of a newly developed drug, they create images that are apt to dominate people's schemata.

The general rule that media are most influential in areas in which the audience knows least does not apply to specialized publications. Professional journals, for instance, often have a strong impact on their readers' images of professional matters. This happens because of the high credibility of the sources. The professionals who read these publications willingly subordinate their own views to those of the published experts.

Learning Effects: Knowledge and Attitudes

What kinds of politically relevant knowledge, attitudes, feelings, and actions spring from people's contacts with the media? Because of the limitations of measuring instruments, the answer is difficult. In Chapter 1 we pointed out the impossibility of isolating media influence when it is one of many factors in a complex environment. For example, a sample of citizens who were asked why their worries about nuclear war had increased cited the following mixture of reasons: increased media coverage (52%); Reagan administration policies (19%); new weapons/new technology/proliferation (19%); unrest in developing countries (13%); East/West tensions (11%); Soviet belligerence (4%); children/grandchildren's lives (4%); other reasons (2%); don't know/no answer/can't explain (5%).[54] Although these answers tell us which factors played a role, they do not indicate the extent of the role. Until researchers can trace an individual's mental processes and isolate and appraise the significance of each of the components that interact and combine to form mental images, the impact of media on knowledge and attitudes cannot be fully assessed. Nor can researchers understand completely just what is learned from media.

Measurement Problems

Research up to now has focused on very small facets of learning such as testing what specific facts are learned about political candidates or about a few public policies. Even within such narrow areas, testing has been severely limited. It has zeroed in on learning the substance of explicit messages rather than on assessing total knowledge gains. For instance, election coverage of a presidential candidate teaches more than facts about the candidate. It may also inform the audience about the role played by White House correspondents in campaign coverage and about living conditions in other cities. Such ancillary learning, however important it may be, is usually overlooked. Much learning may even be subconscious. People may be unaware that they have learned something new and may not mention it when asked what they have learned. At times new information may be temporarily forgotten, only to reenter consciousness a short while later.[55]

Although many assumptions about learning that seem intuitively correct remain untested, media offerings continue to be judged as if these assumptions were true. The assumption that people deduce important social lessons from specific stories presented by the media is one example. For instance, media researcher Joshua Meyrowitz argues that television has radically changed social roles by stripping them of mystery and holding them up to continuous public scrutiny. Women working in the home who were previously isolated have learned about the attractive roles open only to males in American society, and the successes and failures of the women's movement have affected the behavior of these women. Television allows children to experience the adult world long before they are physically and emotionally prepared to cope with these experiences. In the age of television, political heroes have become ordinary mortals, and authority figures are no longer respected because the mystery of social distance has been stripped away.[56]

We believe that adults as well as children often model their behavior after characters they encounter in the media. We assume that unfavorable stereotypes will hurt the self-esteem of the groups so characterized, and so we urge newspeople to present traditionally adversely stereotyped groups—such as African Americans—in a better light. It is ironic that the improved television image of African Americans has tended to foster new misconceptions, namely that they are an economically privileged group that neither needs nor deserves special assistance.[57] News reports and dramatic shows supposedly teach people how lawyers or police officers or hospitals conduct their business. Impressionable people who watch these shows and like what they see presumably will be motivated to aspire to these professions; conversely, distortions in the portrayal of these roles will mislead inexperienced people who regard them as accurate.

Although we assume these effects, and there is every reason to believe that many are quite common, most of them remain unmeasured. An important exception has been the Cultural Indicators project conducted since the mid-1960s at the University of Pennsylvania's Annenberg School of Communications. Using *cultivation analysis* the investigators studied trends in the dramatic content of network television and the conceptions of social reality produced in viewers. Their findings confirm that heavy viewers of television drama (more than four hours daily) see the world as television paints it and react to that world rather than to reality more than do light viewers of the same demographic background and similar circumstances. For instance, heavy viewers, exposed to large doses of crime in television drama, believe that the dangers of becoming a crime victim are far greater than they actually are.[58] They fear crime more and are more distrustful and suspicious than are persons who view television less often. They also are generally more pessimistic and tend to gravitate toward the middle-of-the-road mainstream politics depicted on television.

Like most research on mass media effects, these findings have been challenged on the grounds that factors other than mass media exposure account for the results. The characteristics of viewers rather than their exposure to television may be responsible for their images of the world and their addiction to television. The technical aspects of the Cultural Indicators project have also been challenged. Such scientific controversies indicate that research on mass media effects needs a lot more refinement before the findings can be considered definitive.

This holds true, too, for a number of experimental studies that have found, for example, that television news coverage of specific events "primes" audiences to appraise politicians in light of these events, narrowing their political perspectives so that single phenomena deflect attention from the broader context.[59] Until such findings have been tested in natural settings to appraise under what conditions and for what length of time they apply, they must be considered tentative and incomplete. For example, it is not surprising that experiments indicate that President Bush's popularity ratings fared better when the audience was primed with questions about Persian Gulf War victories rather than the nation's financial troubles.[60] But thus far experiments have failed to tell us how long the priming effects persist in natural situations and their likely political impact.

A neglected research sphere concerns forgetfulness. Much that is learned from the media is evanescent. When Iran is engulfed by revolution or the mayor of the nation's capital goes to jail, the salient names and facts are on many lips, but after the crisis has passed, this knowledge evaporates rapidly. How rapidly seems to depend on a number of factors, most importantly on people's ability to store and retrieve information. After three months of inattention, most ordinary stories are hard to recall, even by people with good memories. If stories are periodically revived with follow-ups or with closely related stories, memory becomes deepened and prolonged. In fact, a few crucial incidents have been rehearsed so often that they have become permanent memories. The Great Depression, World War II, and the assassination of President Kennedy are examples.[61]

Factual Learning

Given these limitations on initial learning and on remembering, what can be said about the extent of political learning from the mass media? Average people are aware of an impressive array of politically important topics that have been covered by the media. However, they do not master much specific knowledge. They recognize information if it is mentioned to them but fail to recall it without such assistance.[62] When John Robinson and Dennis Davis tested comprehension of the main facts of thirteen television news stories within hours of viewing, comprehension scores hovered around 40 percent, with only minor differences among various age groups. Use of additional media boosted fact retention only slightly. Education and prior information levels produced the largest variations in scores, with the best informed scoring 13.8 percentage points higher than the poorly informed; people whose education terminated in grade school and college graduates' scores were separated by an 11.2 percent gap.

The paucity of factual learning by average individuals has disturbed many people who believe that stories cannot be fully understood without memorizing factual details. Political scientists Scott Keeter and Cliff Zukin, for example, titled their intensive study of voter knowledge gains during the 1976 and 1980 presidential elections *Uninformed Choice*. They argued that most citizens are too uninformed to make intelligent political choices.[63] Earlier studies had registered even less factual knowledge than Keeter and Zukin's research. These judgments may be unduly harsh because knowledge in these studies is gauged solely by a citizen's ability to recall facts such as the names of prominent officeholders and figures about the length of their term of office or the growth rate of budget deficits. Such factual information tests are inappropriate for judging political knowledge and competence. What really matters is that citizens understand what is at stake in major political issues and what policy options are available for coping with various problems. As media scholar Michael Schudson puts it: "There's a difference between the 'informational citizen,' saturated with bits and bytes of information, and the informed citizen, the person who has not only information but a point of view and preferences with which to make sense of it."[64]

Are people aware of major political issues and their significance? Are they able to place them in the general context of current politics? When these genuinely important questions are asked, the picture of the public's political competence brightens considerably. People may not remember the content of political speeches very well, but, as mentioned already, they are aware of a wide range of current issues. Moreover, when interviewers probe for understanding, rather than for knowledge of specific facts, they often discover considerable political insight. For instance, people who cannot define either *price deregulation* or *affirmative action* may have fairly sophisticated notions about these matters. They know about government price controls on some goods and services and fully understand the burdens faced by people hampered in finding a job because of race or gender.[65]

Learning General Orientations

Some media stories leave the audience with politically significant feelings that persist long after facts have faded from memory. Although many details of the 1995 Oklahoma City bomb attack have faded in memory, Americans still retain vivid feelings of horror, sympathy, grief, and disappointment. Often news that etches few facts into people's memories may leave them with generalized feelings of trust or distrust. For instance, prominently featured stories of serious corruption in government may lower the public's esteem for the integrity of government. People who read newspapers severely critical of various actions taken by the government express significantly less trust in government than those exposed to favorable views. People who have not gone beyond grade school seem to be particularly susceptible to erosion of trust in the wake of mass media criticism.[66] Cynical people, in turn, tend to participate less than others in civic activities such as voting and lobbying.[67]

As political scientist Murray Edelman has noted, feelings of both insecurity and security generated by news stories may make people quiescent because they become fearful of interfering with crucial government actions or else complacent about the need for public vigilance. Fear that dissension weakens the government may decrease tolerance for dissidents. Edelman also warns that political quiescence leads to acceptance of faulty public policies, poor laws, and ineffective administrative practices—significant political effects.[68]

On a more personal level, millions of people use the media to keep in touch with their community. This helps to counter feelings of loneliness and alienation because information becomes a bond among individuals who share it.[69] The models of life depicted by the media create wants and expectations as well as dissatisfactions and frustrations. These feelings may become powerful stimulants for social change for the society at large or for selected individuals within it. Alternatively, they may bolster support for the political status quo and generate strong resistance to change. Whether media-induced orientations and actions are considered positive, negative, or a mixture of both depends, of course, on one's sociopolitical preferences.

Deterrents to Learning

Lack of motivation for acquiring political knowledge and distaste for media offerings, as well as deficiencies in the information supply, deter many people from keeping up with politics through media exposure. Rather than discussing politics, which they see as a sensitive topic, they prefer to talk about sports, or the weather, or the local gossip. In fact, as the level of abstract, issue-oriented content of political news rises, the size of the attentive audience shrivels.[70] People scan the news for major crises without trying to remember specific facts. However, when they sense that events will greatly affect their lives, or when they need information for their job or for social or political activities, political interest and learning perk up quickly and often dramatically.[71]

Serious programs on radio and television occasionally become highly popular. Most of them involve themes of corruption, violence, or other wrongdoing, which may account for their popularity. Examples are "60 Minutes," which probes a variety of social ills; "The Winds of War," a made-for-television movie that recapitulated World War II; and documentaries dealing with rape, child-snatching, and prison violence. Broadcasts of congressional hearings on the selection of controversial Supreme Court justices or on the legality of secret activities of the executive branch fall into this category. These are exceptions, however.

Widespread public interest in most political crises flares up like a straw fire and then dies quickly. For instance, interest in the Iran-contra scandal involving the Reagan administration ebbed after a few weeks even though it involved highly dramatic events such as espionage operations, secret weapons deals, and circumvention of congressional mandates. The Republicans' Contract with America in 1994, the 1996 presidential primaries, and the debate over the North American Free Trade Agreement (NAFTA) were stale topics within a few months. Attention spans are erratic and brief, even though most Americans believe that, as good citizens, they ought to be well informed about political news and feel guilty, or at least apologetic, if they are not.

Learning is further inhibited by the alienation of many population groups from the media. Many white ethnics, such as Polish Americans or Italian Americans, and police and union members, for instance, consider most mass media hostile. They often believe that the media lie and distort when they cast police as trigger-happy oppressors of the disadvantaged or unions as corrupt and a barrier to economic progress. Public opinion polls in recent decades show considerable erosion of public confidence in the trustworthiness of the media in general. They now rank near the bottom of trustworthiness, along with Congress and the legal profession.[72]

How media information is presented also affects learning. The public is bombarded daily with more news than it can handle. Most of the news is touted as significant even though much is trivial. The constant crisis atmosphere numbs excitement and produces boredom. The presentation of stories in disconnected snippets further complicates the task of making sense out of them and integrating them with existing knowledge. This is especially true when stories are complex, as is true of most reports about controversial public policies. People who feel that they cannot understand what is happening are discouraged from spending time reading or listening. Featuring conflicting stories and interpretations, without giving guidance to the audience because that might jeopardize objectivity, also hinders learning.[73]

Television news deters the kind of factual and conceptual learning that social scientists measure and prize. Instead, it concentrates on conveying the essence of personalities and a sense of witnessing places and events.[74] Moreover, the average half-hour television news program covers the equivalent in words of only one newspaper page and is designed "to evoke stored information ... in a patterned way" to make use of what the audience already knows.[75] If people watch several newscasts, hoping for an enriched news diet, they find that roughly half the material is repetitive. Even within a single newscast a large proportion of every story is background information that puts the story into perspective for viewers seeing it for the first time.

Viewing purposes are also important. Because most people read newspapers largely to make sure that no unexpected dangers lurk, and because they watch television news to be entertained, audiences are not likely to try

TABLE 7-3 Network Television News Characteristics

Story length (seconds)	Percentage of total stories	Picture exposure (seconds)	Percentage of total stories	Number of pictures	Percentage of total stories
Less than 60	30	1–10	47	1–4	38
60–179	46	11–20	29	5–10	15
180–299	17	21–30	11	11–20	24
300+	7	31+	13	21–54	23

SOURCE: Author's research, based on a sample of 150 news programs from early evening newscasts on ABC, CBS, and NBC.

hard to learn a wealth of factual information. What they actually wish to learn may not match the lessons available from the media, anyway. "Happy-talk" television news formats and exciting film footage encourage the feeling that news should be viewed as a lighthearted diversion.

The internal structure of television newscasts also impedes learning. Three quarters of all news stories take up less than three minutes, yet they are crammed with information that cannot possibly be absorbed in that time. In addition to the abundance of pictures that is noted in Table 7-3, the average news story contains three verbal statements for every two pictorial scenes. For the fifteen to eighteen stories in a typical newscast, viewers are asked to absorb an average of eighteen factual statements and eleven picture scenes per story. That amounts to 324 statements and 198 pictures compressed into 22 minutes of news exposure. Furthermore, in most news programs disparate items are tightly packaged without the pauses that are essential to allow viewers to absorb information. Hence it is not surprising that half the audience after the lapse of a few hours cannot recall a single item from a television newscast. Distracting activities do not help either. Many people watch television while cooking dinner or cleaning house.[76]

Despite all of the deterrents to learning, Americans still attain fairly high political information levels. They also are well socialized into the American system. They may be disappointed and cynical about particular leaders or policies, but relatively few question the legitimacy of the government, object to its basic philosophies, or reject its claims to their support. If one believes in the merits of the system, this finding is, indeed, cause for satisfaction with current political socialization. In this light, the dire predictions about television-induced deterioration of political life and rampant political alienation among citizens have not materialized.[77] If the American population becomes more eager to learn about politics, and if the media improve political reporting, then knowledge levels could rise sharply. However, because television has become the main provider of information, knowledge tests need to be restructured so that they reflect the unique contributions made by audiovisuals to comprehending the world.

Learning Effects: Behavior

Because the media shape people's knowledge, attitudes, and feelings, they obviously can influence behavior. To assess the extent of behavioral effects, two areas that have long been of great political concern will be examined: imitation of crime and violence, particularly among adolescents, and stimulation of economic and political development in underdeveloped regions. In Chapter 8 we will discuss the effects of media coverage on voting behavior and in Chapter 11 the impact of the media on the conduct of foreign affairs.

Crime and Violent Behavior in Children

Many social scientists believe that violence and crime portrayed in the media, particularly on television, lead to imitation. Children and young adults are deemed to be particularly impressionable. Because crime and violence are serious problems in American society, the possible link between television exposure and deviant behavior has been thoroughly investigated. The Surgeon General's office has produced a bookshelf full of information on the topic.[78] Congressional committees have spent countless hours listening to conflicting testimony by social scientists about the impact of television violence. Meanwhile, violent content, particularly in fiction programs, has escalated. A 1996 study that defined *violence* broadly as "any overt depiction of the use of physical force or the credible threat of such force intended to physically harm an animate being or group of beings" found most violence on premium cable channels. Eighty-five percent of programming on HBO and Showtime contained violence. The rate was 59 percent for basic cable channels and 44 percent for broadcast television.[79]

What have studies of the impact of television violence revealed? Despite the strong inclination of many of the researchers to find that crime fiction causes asocial behavior, the evidence is not altogether conclusive. Some children do copy violent behavior, especially when they have watched aggression that was left unpunished or was rewarded and when countervailing influences from parents and teachers are lacking.[80] But, aside from imitating television examples when tempted to do so, children

1985 CHICAGO TRIBUNE

LOCHER

Reprinted by permission: Tribune Media Services.

do not ordinarily become violent after exposure to violence in the mass media. It has been estimated that television-inspired violence accounts for a mere 5 percent of the problem.[81] Most children lack the predisposition and usually the opportunity for violence, and their environment discourages asocial behavior. In fact, exposure to crime makes some children more sympathetic toward the suffering of crime and violence victims.[82] A crude cause and effect model is therefore invalid.

Other confounding factors in assessing the impact of television on children are age-linked comprehension differences. Younger children may not be able to comprehend many of the events presented by the media in the same way that adolescents do. The complex social reasoning that adults often ascribe to even young children does not develop until youngsters reach their teenage years. Although young children often imitate what they have seen, they are rarely able to generalize or respond to implied messages. Several studies of preschool and early grade-school children suggest that much of what adults consider to be violent does not seem so to children. Cartoon violence is an example.[83] Therefore, many of the programs that adults consider to be dangerous actually may be harmless.

The percentage of preadolescents and adolescents in the population who are prone to imitate crime is not known at this time. However, the wide dispersion of television throughout American homes makes it almost certain that the majority of children susceptible to imitating violence will be exposed. Even in the absence of television, many other triggers could arouse these young people to violence. Whatever the source of arousal, even if the actual number of highly susceptible preadolescents and adolescents is tiny and statistically insignificant, the social consequences can be profound. Such considerations prompted Congress to mandate in the 1996 Telecommunications Act that television sets should include a "V-chip" to enable adults to block violent television programs from transmission to their homes. It seems doubtful that the device will be used extensively in the kinds of homes where the most vulnerable youngsters are apt to live, considering the correlation between child delinquency and flawed home environments.

Behavior Change in Adults

What about imitation of socially undesirable behavior by adults? The same broad principles apply. Imitation depends on the setting at the time of media exposure and on the personality and attitudes viewers bring to the situation. Widespread societal norms seem to be particularly important. For instance, the 1970 report of the Presidential Commission on Obscenity and Pornography noted that exposure to aberrant sexual behavior led to comparatively little imitation. In fact, there was some evidence that greater availability of obscene and pornographic materials reduced sex crimes and misdemeanors because vicarious experiences were substituted for actual ones.[84] By comparison, there was a great deal more evidence that exposure to criminal behavior encourages imitation. The difference may be more apparent than real, however, because crime is more likely to be reported, whereas sexual perversions usually remain hidden.

In sum, the precise link between exposure to media images and corresponding behavior remains uncertain. Legislative tampering with media offerings therefore appears premature. It will take a great deal more research and experimentation to determine how media fare can be presented to produce imitation of the many desirable behaviors depicted on television and avoid imitation of undesirable ones. Even assuming that this goal could be reached, it is questionable whether a democratic society should attempt to manipulate the minds of its citizens to protect them from temptations to violate social norms. It may be best to leave control of the content of entertainment programs to widely based informal social pressures. Whether social pressures should be allowed to interfere with reporting real-world violence poses even more difficult dilemmas. The possibly adverse effects on behavior must be balanced against the need to keep informed about the real world.

Socioeconomic and Political Modernization

The assumed potential of the media to guide people's behavior has led to great efforts to use the media as tools for social and political development. The results have been mixed; there have been some successes and many failures.

Psychic Mobility. The hope of using the media to bring about industrialization, improved social services, and democratization ran very high at mid-century. The psychological key to human and material development was then assumed to be a personality characteristic that political scientist Daniel Lerner labeled *empathic capacity*. The media were thought to be the stimuli; when the media present new objects, ideas, and behaviors, they presumably stimulate people to empathize and imagine themselves to be involved with these objects, ideas, and actions. For instance, when the media show how slum dwellers have built new housing, or how flood victims have purified their polluted water supply, audience members presumably wonder, "How could I make this work for me?"

Before mass media became widely available to average people, this "psychic mobility" was generated when people came into direct contact with strangers with different lifestyles and experiences. Because contacts usually were limited to relatively few people, changes spread very slowly. The mass media, however, made it possible for the first time in human history to reach millions of people with comparative ease and to expose them to developmental stimuli, either directly or through contact with others reached by the media. Transistor radios and satellite television and, potentially, the Internet, have opened even remote and inaccessible regions to modern communication and brought news of current lifestyles to isolated communities.

Social scientists who credit the media with a major role in modernization and democratization have made three assumptions. First, the mass media can create interest and empathy for unfamiliar experiences. Second, the mass media provide graphic examples of new practices, which are then readily understood and copied. (For instance, films and videotapes can show people how to build a cinder block house, how to plant potatoes more efficiently, or how to run an honest election.) Third, development, once started, creates an incentive for people to increase their knowledge and skills. Where formal education is not readily accessible, the media provide information and enhance the capacity to learn. Proof of these assumptions is seen in the progress in urbanization, industrialization, living standards, and political advancement that has followed the spread of media to many formerly information-deficient regions.[85]

Psychological Barriers to Modernization. Although many technologically and politically underdeveloped regions have shown measurable progress, with the media apparently serving as catalysts, social and political change has been far slower and more sporadic than development theorists expected. A number of psychological and physical obstacles have kept their dreams from coming true. Most damaging has been outright hostility by individuals or communities to change and unwillingness to alter long-established patterns. Mass media may actually become a negative reference point so that people condemn the lifestyle depicted by the media. The various fundamentalist groups around the world—such as Ayatollah Khomeini's followers in the Middle East or ultra-Orthodox Jews in Israel—that have mobilized to censor mass media offerings and stop social and political changes provide examples.

People who are not overtly hostile to change still may be totally uninterested in altering their lifestyles. They may doubt their ability to cope with new challenges, and they may be reluctant to further complicate a difficult life. People exhibiting such attitudes cannot be persuaded by the mass media without the intervention of a trusted person, such as a priest, physician, or family member. Mass media influence then becomes a "two-step flow" reaching its targets through selected opinion leaders.

Putting unaccustomed behaviors and skills into words and concepts that people with little formal education can understand has also turned out to be exceedingly difficult. For instance, teaching new ways to keep food pure, or to apply for aid from a government agency, or to mark a ballot in a multicandidate election involves concepts that may require formal schooling to grasp. The disparity in social backgrounds between journalists and their audiences may further confound the problem of communication.

Changes that require adopting new social values or abandoning old habits are the most difficult of all and the least likely to occur. For example, people who were taught to abhor capitalism find it difficult to become entrepreneurs even when the media praise new forms of economic enterprise. Ingrained habits, such as driving without seat belts or engaging in unsafe sexual behaviors, are difficult to break despite extensive mass-mediated public education campaigns. Even after people have become aware of the dangers inherent in their behavior, and even when they concede that behavioral change is in their best interests, most still forgo voluntary change.

Adoption of Changes. Despite the difficulties, many mass media campaigns do succeed in bringing about socially desirable changes. How do they do it? We will outline five steps involved in change and indicate how the mass media fit into the picture. First people must become *aware of the possibility for change.* Here the media are especially helpful. Radio can inform people about new energy saving devices or new child-rearing methods. Television and movies can show new technologies and new styles of political participation. Second is *understanding how to accomplish the suggested changes.* For example, people may be aware that public assistance is available, but they may not know how to apply for it. Mass media usually fail to supply detailed information. On the average, only one third of all stories that might inspire action of various types, such as environmental protection or energy conservation, contain implementing information.[86] Unless this gap is filled, the chain leading to the adoption of innovations is broken.

Third is evaluation. People *assess the merits of the innovation* and decide whether they want to adopt it. Innovations often fail to take root because prospective users consider them bad, inappropriate, too risky, or too difficult. Media messages alone may not be persuasive enough. It may be crucial to have a trusted person urge or demonstrate adoption of the innovation. Fourth is trial. The effect of the media in *getting people to try innovations* is limited. Factors beyond media control are more important, such as social and financial costs of the change as well as the audience's willingness to change. In general, young men are most receptive to innovations; older people are most skeptical and cautious. Fifth is adoption. The media contribute most to this phase by *encouraging people to stick with the changes* that they have made part of their life and work styles. For example, adoption of birth control is useless unless it is continuous. The same holds true for many health and sanitation measures or improved work habits. To ensure continuity, mass media must cover a topic regularly, stressing long-range goals and reporting progress.

Predicting which media campaigns designed to change behavior will succeed and which will fail has proven difficult.[87] Douglas S. Solomon, who studied health campaigns conducted by private and public institutions, believes that four factors account for success or failure. To succeed, campaigns must *set well-specified, realistic goals* that are tailored to the needs of various target groups. They must *carefully select appropriate media and media formats* and present them at key times and intervals. *Messages* must be properly *designed for greatest persuasiveness.* There also must be *continuous evaluation and appropriate readjustments.*[88]

In some instances the media's efforts to mobilize people have produced unanticipated attitudes and changes in behavior. For instance, when television was introduced in several Canadian Eskimo communities in the 1970s, programs were designed to show the viewers how to modernize their living conditions and to acquaint them with Canadian affairs generally. Rather than aspiring to modernize their lifestyles, Eskimo adults in the television communities turned their eyes to the past. They wanted to return to traditional Eskimo ways. This attitude was not apparent in localities without television. Whether it sprang from nostalgia for the past or aversion to the lifestyle changes foreshadowed by television is unclear. It is interesting that the adults who yearned for traditional ways aspired to a modern lifestyle for their children following the introduction of television.[89]

Above all, the success of the mass media in bringing about change hinges on the receptivity for change. Ongoing efforts to use the media to modernize developing areas, to turn former Communists into democratic citizens, or to bring socially helpful information to individuals who are poor, elderly, and handicapped must concentrate on identifying the specific circumstances most likely to bring success. Responding to requests initiated locally, rather than designing information campaigns from the outside, and integrating local traditions into new approaches seem to hold the most promise.[90]

Summary

The mass media play a major role in *political socialization,* the learning and accepting of norms and rules, structures, and environmental factors that govern political life. Contrary to earlier findings that indicated limited impact, the media are very influential and consequently a tremendously powerful political force.

However, the impact of the media on political socialization and other aspects of political learning is not uniform for all members of the media audience. The media affect individuals in different ways, depending on lifestyles and circumstances. Psychological, demographic, and situational factors influence perceptions and the ensuing political consequences. So do the manner of news presentation and the perspectives from which news is presented.[91] Although many factors contribute to diversity in socialization and learning, there are also powerful unifying forces. Most Americans are exposed to similar information and develop roughly similar outlooks on what it means and ought to mean to be an American both politically and socially.

Various theories explain why and how individuals select particular information to remember. Learning of specific facts presented by the media is sparse. Nonetheless, people become aware of many political problems and appreciate their basic significance, even without remembering details about them. Equally important, exposure to the media can produce apathy, cynicism, fear, trust, acquiescence, or support—moods that condition participation in the political process, which may range from total abstinence to efforts to overthrow the government by force.

The media may also produce or retard behavior that affects the quality of public life. In this chapter we assessed the role of the media in fostering socially undesirable behaviors, such as crime and violence, and in the political and social development of various population groups. Media influence is greatest in informing people and creating initial attitudes; it is least effective in changing established attitudes and ingrained behaviors.

Given the many largely uncontrollable variables that determine media influence, concerted efforts to manipulate media content to foster societal goals are risky at best. They could set dangerous precedents for inhibiting the free flow of controversial ideas or for using the media as channels for government propaganda.

Notes

1. Michael Wines, "Appeal of 'Murphy Brown' Now Clear at White House," *New York Times,* May 21, 1992.
2. Impact differences between print and electronic media are discussed in W. Russell Neuman, Marion R. Just, and Ann N. Crigler, *Common Knowledge: News and the Construction of Political Meaning* (Chicago: University of Chicago Press, 1992); Marion Just and Ann Crigler, "Learning from the News: Experiments in Media, Modality, and Reporting about Star Wars," *Political Communication and Persuasion* 6 (1989): 109–127.
3. Jacob Jacoby and Wayne D. Hoyer, "Viewer Miscomprehension of Televised Communications: Selected Findings," *Journal of Marketing* 46 (Fall 1982): 12–26.
4. John P. Robinson and Dennis K. Davis, "Television News and the Informed Public: An Information-Processing Approach," *Journal of Communication* 40 (Summer 1990): 106–119.
5. Neil Postman, *Amusing Ourselves to Death: Public Discourse in the Age of Show Business* (New York: Viking Penguin, 1985). For a good discussion of the differences between the effects of print and television news on people's behavior, see Joshua Meyrowitz, *No Sense of Place: The Impact of Electronic Media on Social Behavior* (New York: Oxford University Press, 1985), 94–106.
6. Doris A. Graber, "Seeing Is Remembering: How Visuals Contribute to Learning from Television News," *Journal of Communication* 40 (Summer 1990): 134–155.
7. W. Russell Neuman, *The Future of the Mass Audience* (New York: Cambridge University Press, 1991), 99 (emphasis added). Zhongdang Pan, Ronald E. Ost-

man, Patricia Moy, and Paula Reynolds, "News Media Exposure and Its Learning Effects during the Persian Gulf War," *Journalism Quarterly* 71(1) (Spring 1994): 7–19.

8. John E. Chubb and Terry M. Moe, "Politics, Markets, and the Organization of Schools," *American Political Science Review* 82 (1988): 1065–1088.

9. Bruce Watkins, "Television Viewing as a Dominant Activity of Childhood: A Developmental Theory of Television Effects," *Critical Studies in Mass Communication* 2 (1985): 323–337. Average high school graduates have spent 15,000 hours watching television and 11,000 hours in the classroom. They have seen 350,000 commercials.

10. M. Margaret Conway, Mikel L. Wyckoff, Eleanor Feldbaum, and David Ahern, "The News Media in Children's Political Socialization," *Public Opinion Quarterly* 45 (Summer 1981): 164–178; and Gina M. Garramone and Charles K. Atkin, "Mass Communication and Political Socialization: Specifying the Effects," *Public Opinion Quarterly* 50 (Spring 1986): 76–86.

11. M. Margaret Conway, A. Jay Stevens, and Robert G. Smith, "The Relations between Media Use and Children's Civic Awareness," *Journalism Quarterly* 52 (Autumn 1975): 531–538; Suzanne Pingree, "Children's Cognitive Processes in Constructing Social Reality," *Journalism Quarterly* 60 (Fall 1983): 415–422. Also see Judith Torney-Purta, "From Attitudes and Knowledge to Schemata: Expanding the Outcomes of Political Socialization," in *Political Socialization, Citizenship Education, and Democracy,* ed. Orit Ichilov (New York: Teachers' College, 1990), 98–115; and Judith Torney-Purta, "Cognitive Representations of the Political System in Adolescents: The Continuum from Pre-Novice to Expert" (Paper delivered at the meeting of the International Society for Political Psychology, Helsinki, Finland, 1991).

12. Jean Piaget, *The Language and Thought of the Child,* 3d ed. (New York: Harcourt Brace, 1962). See also Torney-Purta, "From Attitudes and Knowledge to Schemata"; and Pamela Johnston Conover, "Political Socialization: Where's the Politics?" in *Political Science: Looking to the Future; Political Behavior,* Vol. 3, ed. William Crotty (Evanston, Ill.: Northwestern University Press, 1991), 125–152.

13. A study of prime-time values on television showed that fewer than 4 percent concerned citizenship values such as patriotism or citizen duties. Gary W. Selnow, "Values in Prime-Time Television," *Journal of Communication* 40 (Summer 1990): 69.

14. Robert Kubey, "Media Implications for the Quality of Family Life," in *Media, Children, and the Family,* ed. Dolf Zillmann, Jennings Bryant, and Aletha C. Huston (Hillsdale, N.J.: Lawrence Erlbaum, 1994), 61–70.

15. Neuman, *Future of the Mass Audience,* 89–91.

16. George Gerbner, Larry Gross, Marilyn Jackson Beeck, Suzanne Jeffries Fox, and Nancy Signorielli, "Cultural Indicators: Violence Profile No. 9," *Journal of Communication* 28 (Summer 1978): 178, 193. See also George Gerbner, Larry Gross, Michael Morgan, and Nancy Signorielli, "Political Correlates of Television Viewing," *Public Opinion Quarterly* 48 (Summer 1984): 283–300. The media's role in changing social attitudes is discussed in Hans Mathias Kepplinger, "Artificial Horizons: How the Press Presented and How the Population Received Technology in Germany from 1965–1986," in *The Mass Media in Liberal Democratic Societies,* ed. Stanley Rothman (New York: Paragon House, 1992), 147–176.

17. W. Lance Bennett, "Perception and Cognition: An Information-Processing Framework for Politics," in *The Handbook of Political Behavior,* Vol. 1, ed. Samuel L. Long (New York: Plenum Press, 1981), 101. The importance of pre-adult political learning for subsequent political orientations is discussed in Paul Allen Beck and M. Kent Jennings, "Pathways to Participation," *American Political Science Review* 76 (1982): 103–110. Also see Doris A. Graber, *Processing the News: How People Tame the Information Tide,* 2d ed. (Lanham, Md.: University Press of America, 1993), 184–188, 210–213.

18. Shanto Iyengar, *Is Anyone Responsible? How Television Frames Political Issues* (Chicago: University of Chicago Press, 1991), 136–143.

19. Stanley Rothman, S. Robert Lichter, and Linda Lichter, "Television's America," in *The Mass Media in Liberal Democratic Societies,* 221–266.

20. Paula M. Poindexter, "Non-News Viewers," *Journal of Communication* 30 (Autumn 1980): 58–65.

21. For examples of various types of general and specific information supplied by entertainment programming, see Gary W. Selnow, "Solving Problems on Prime-Time Television," *Journal of Communication* 36 (Spring 1986): 63–72; Selnow, "Values in Prime-Time Television"; G. Ray Funkhouser and Eugene F. Shaw, "How Synthetic Experience Shapes Social Reality," *Journal of Communication* 40 (Summer 1990): 75–87; W. James Potter and William Ware, "The Frequency and Context of Prosocial Acts on Primetime TV," *Journalism Quarterly* 66 (Summer 1989): 359–366, 529.

22. Graber, *Processing the News,* 90–93.

23. Gerbner et al., "Political Correlates," 286.

24. Stephen D. Reese and M. Mark Miller, "Political Attitude Holding and Structure: The Effects of Newspaper and Television News," *Communication Research* 8 (April 1981): 182.

25. Reese and Miller, "Political Attitude Holding," 182. For a different perspective, see Donald L. Jordan, "Newspaper Effects on Policy Preferences," *Public Opinion Quarterly* 57 (1993): 191–204; and William Schneider and A. I. Lewis, "Views on the News," *Public Opinion* 8 (August/September 1985): 5–11, 58–59.

26. George Comstock, Steven Chaffee, Natan Katzman, Maxwell McCombs, and Donald Roberts, *Television and Human Behavior* (New York: Columbia University Press, 1978), 307–309. Also see Robert T. Bower, *The Changing Television Audience in America* (New York: Columbia University Press, 1985). The book unfortunately relies on 1980 data. For evidence that similarity in exposure leads to similar socialization, see Alexis S. Tan, "Media Use and Political Orientations of Ethnic Groups," *Journalism Quarterly* 60 (Spring 1983): 126–132.

27. Frederick Williams, Herbert S. Dordick, and Frederick Horstmann, "Where Citizens Go for Information," *Journal of Communication* 27 (Winter 1977): 95–99.

28. Comstock et al., *Television and Human Behavior,* 295–306. Also see Roger D. Masters, "Ethnic and Personality Differences in Response to TV Images of Leaders" (Paper presented at the annual meeting of the American Political Science Association, Washington, D.C., 1991).

29. Ibid.

30. Sheldon G. Levy, "How Population Subgroups Differed in Knowledge of Six Assassinations," *Journalism Quarterly* 46 (Winter 1969): 685–698.

31. Elizabeth Kolbert, "TV Viewing and Selling, by Race," *New York Times*, April 5, 1993.
32. Bradley Greenberg and Brenda Dervin, "Mass Communication among the Urban Poor," *Public Opinion Quarterly* 34 (Summer 1970): 224–235. Also see Bradley S. Greenberg, Michael Burgoon, Judee Burgoon, and Felipe Korzenny, *Mexican Americans and the Mass Media* (Norwood, N.J.: Ablex, 1983). For partly contradictory evidence, see Tan, "Media Use." See also Phyllis A. Katz and Dalman A. Taylor, eds., *Eliminating Racism* (New York: Plenum Press, 1988), 1–16.
33. The statistics in the next three paragraphs are from Leo Bogart, *Press and Public: Who Reads What, When, Where, and Why in American Newspapers* (Hillside, N.J.: Lawrence Erlbaum, 1981), 56, 66, 77. See also Bogart, "Negro and White Media Exposure: New Evidence," *Journalism Quarterly* 49 (Spring 1972): 15–21; and George Comstock and Robin E. Cobbey, "Television and the Children of Ethnic Minorities," *Journal of Communication* 29 (Winter 1979): 104–115.
34. Karl Erik Rosengren, Lawrence A. Wenner, and Philip Palmgreen, eds., *Media Gratifications Research: Current Perspectives* (Beverly Hills, Calif.: Sage, 1985). Also see Gina M. Garramone, "Motivation and Political Information Processing: Extending the Gratifications Approach," in *Mass Media and Political Thought,* ed. Sidney Kraus and Richard Perloff (Beverly Hills, Calif.: Sage, 1985), 201–222; David L. Swanson, "Gratification Seeking, Media Exposure, and Audience Interpretations: Some Directions for Research," *Journal of Broadcasting and Electronic Media* 31 (1987): 237–254.
35. W. Lance Bennett, *News: The Politics of Illusion,* 2d ed. (New York: Longman, 1988), 158–169; and Charles Atkin, "Information Utility and Selective Exposure to Entertainment Media," in *Selective Exposure to Communication,* ed. Dolf Zillman and Jennings Bryant (Hillsdale, N.J.: Lawrence Erlbaum, 1985), 63–92.
36. Michael Morgan, "Heavy Television Viewing and Perceived Quality of Life," *Journalism Quarterly* 61 (Autumn 1984): 499–504; Philip Palmgreen, Lawrence A. Wenner, and J. D. Rayburn II, "Relations between Gratifications Sought and Obtained: A Study of Television News," *Communication Research* 7 (April 1980): 161–192; Robert W. Kubey, "Television Use in Everyday Life: Coping with Unstructured Time," *Journal of Communication* 36 (Summer 1986): 108–123.
37. Neuman, *Future of the Mass Audience,* 122.
38. In Thomas L. Friedman, "No TV? Israel Is Savoring the Silence," *New York Times,* November 6, 1987.
39. Graber, *Processing the News,* 133–136. See also Stuart H. Schwartz, "A General Psychographic Analysis of Newspaper Use and Life Style," *Journalism Quarterly* 57 (Autumn 1980): 392–401.
40. The literature is reviewed in Zillman and Bryant, *Selective Exposure to Communication,* passim.
41. Roy L. Behr and Shanto Iyengar, "Television News, Real-World Cues, and Changes in the Public Agenda," *Public Opinion Quarterly* 49 (Spring 1985): 38–57. For a discussion of replacement of older issues by newer ones, see Hans-Bernd Brosius and Hans Mathias Kepplinger, "Killer and Victim Issues: Issue Competition in the Agenda-Setting Process of German Television," *International Journal of Public Opinion Research* 7(3) (1995): 211–231.

42. Maxwell E. McCombs, "The Agenda-Setting Approach," in *Handbook of Political Communication*, ed. Dan D. Nimmo and Keith Sanders (Beverly Hills, Calif.: Sage, 1981), 121–140; Shanto Iyengar and Donald R. Kinder, *News that Matters: TV and American Opinion* (Chicago: University of Chicago Press, 1987); Benjamin I. Page, Robert Y. Shapiro, and Glenn R. Dempsey, "What Moves Public Opinion?" *American Political Science Review* 81 (March 1987): 23–43; Benjamin I. Page and Robert Y. Shapiro, *The Rational Public: Fifty Years of Trends in Americans' Policy Preferences* (Chicago: University of Chicago Press, 1991); and Donald L. Shaw and Shannon E. Martin, "The Function of Mass Media Agenda Setting," *Journalism Quarterly* 69(4) (1992): 902–920.

43. Doris A. Graber, "Agenda-Setting: Are There Women's Perspectives?" in *Women and the News*, ed. Laurily Keir Epstein (New York: Hastings House, 1978), 15–37.

44. For a relevant case study, see Tony Atwater, Michael B. Salwen, and Ronald B. Anderson, "Media Agenda-Setting with Environmental Issues," *Journalism Quarterly* 62 (Summer 1985): 393–397.

45. Christine R. Ader, "A Longitudinal Study of Agenda Setting for the Issue of Environmental Pollution," *Journalism and Mass Communication Quarterly* 72(2) (Summer 1995): 300–311; Behr and Iyengar, "Television News"; and Michael B. MacKuen and Steven L. Coombs, *More than News: Media Power in Public Affairs* (Beverly Hills, Calif.: Sage, 1981).

46. The importance of personal and contextual factors in news selection and evaluation is discussed in Lutz Erbring, Edie Goldenberg, and Arthur Miller, "Front-Page News and Real World Cues: Another Look at Agenda-Setting by the Media," *American Journal of Political Science* 24 (February 1980): 16–49; David B. Hill, "Viewer Characteristics and Agenda Setting by Television News," *Public Opinion Quarterly* 49 (Fall 1985): 340–350; and Montague Kern and Marion Just, "The Focus Group Method, Political Advertising, Campaign News, and the Construction of Candidate Images," *Political Communication* 12(2) (Summer 1995): 127–145. For a discussion of problems in measuring the relative impact of various factors, see Howard Schuman, Jacob Ludwig, and Jon A. Krosnick, "The Perceived Threat of Nuclear War, Salience, and Open Questions," *Public Opinion Quarterly* 50 (Winter 1986): 519–536.

47. Graber, *Processing the News*, 27–31, and for details on learning processes chaps. 7–9. Also see Robert H. Wicks, "Schema Theory and Measurement in Mass Communication Research: Theoretical and Methodological Issues in News Information Processing," *Communication Yearbook 15* (Newbury Park, Calif.: Sage, 1991), 115–154.

48. Walter Lippmann, *Public Opinion* (New York: Harcourt Brace, 1922), 31.

49. Vincent Price and John Zaller, "Who Gets the News? Alternative Measures of News Reception and Their Implications for Research," *Public Opinion Quarterly* 57(1) (1993): 133–164; and Cecilie Gaziano, "The Knowledge Gap: An Analytical Review of Media Effects," *Communication Research* 10 (October 1983): 447–486. For evidence of shared reactions to television programs, irrespective of educational level, see W. Russell Neuman, "Television and American Culture: The Mass Medium and the Pluralist Audience," *Public Opinion Quarterly* 46 (Winter 1982): 471–487.

50. Eliot Freidson, "Communication Research and the Concept of the Mass," in *The Process and Effects of Mass Communication*, rev. ed., ed. Wilbur Schramm and Donald F. Roberts, 197–208. See also Steven H. Chaffee, "Television and

Social Relations, Introductory Comments," in *Television and Human Behavior,* ed. Comstock et al., 260–263.

51. Larry L. Burriss, "How Anchors, Reporters and Newsmakers Affect Recall and Evaluation of Stories," *Journalism Quarterly* 64 (Summer/Autumn 1987): 514–519. The impact of negative news is discussed in John E. Newhagen and Byron Reeves, "The Evening's Bad News: Effects of Compelling Negative Television News Images on Memory," *Journal of Communication* 42 (Spring 1992): 25–41.

52. Benjamin I. Page and Robert Y. Shapiro, *The Rational Public* (Chicago: University of Chicago Press, 1992), 35.

53. Roberta S. Sigel, "Effects of Partisanship on the Perception of Political Candidates," *Public Opinion Quarterly* 28 (Summer 1964): 488–496. See also Shanto Iyengar, "Television News and Citizens' Explanations of National Affairs," *American Political Science Review* 81 (September 1987): 815–831.

54. Michael A. Milburn, Paul Y. Watanabe, and Bernard M. Kramer, "The Nature and Sources of Attitudes toward a Nuclear Freeze," *Political Psychology* 7 (December 1986): 672.

55. An overview of hypermnesia research is presented in Robert H. Wicks, "Remembering the News: Effects and Message Discrepancy on News Recall over Time," *Journalism and Mass Communication Quarterly* 72(3) (Autumn 1995): 666–682.

56. Meyrowitz, *No Sense of Place.*

57. Robert M. Entman, "Modern Racism and the Images of Blacks in Local Television News," *Critical Studies in Mass Communication* 7 (1990): 332–345; Paula W. Matabane, "Television and the Black Audience: Cultivating Moderate Perspectives on Racial Integration," *Journal of Communication* 38 (Autumn 1988): 21–31; S. Robert Lichter, Linda S. Lichter, Stanley Rothman, and Daniel Amundson, "Prime-Time Prejudice: TV's Images of Blacks and Hispanics," *Public Opinion* 10 (July/August 1987): 13–16. More cynical observers claim that improvement of the images of African Americans reflects the desire to boost audience ratings by tapping the large audience of African American viewers.

58. The chances of becoming a crime victim are small in real life, but in TV life they are 30 percent to 64 percent. See Gerbner et al., "Cultural Indicators," 106–107. For a critique of the work of Gerbner and his associates, see W. James Potter, "Cultivation Theory and Research: A Methodological Critique," *Journalism Monograph* 147 (October 1994). Exposure to news about actual crime predicts salience of crime better than does personal exposure to crime. Edna F. Einsiedel, Kandice L. Salomone, and Frederick P. Schneider, "Crime: Effects of Media Exposure and Personal Experience on Issue Salience," *Journalism Quarterly* 61 (Spring 1984): 131–136. See also Hugh M. Culbertson and Guido H. Stempel III, " 'Media Malaise': Explaining Personal Optimism and Societal Pessimism about Health Care," *Journal of Communication* 35 (Spring 1985): 180–190.

59. Iyengar, *Is Anyone Responsible?;* Iyengar and Kinder, *News that Matters.*

60. An example of corroborative research is Jon A. Krosnick and Donald R. Kinder, "Altering the Foundations of Support for the President through Priming," *American Political Science Review* 84 (June 1990): 497–512.

61. John Stauffer, Richard Frost, and William Rybolt, "The Attention Factor in Recalling Network Television News," *Journal of Communication* 33 (Winter

1983): 29–37. Also see Philip J. Hilts, "A Brain Unit Seen as Index for Recalling Memories," *New York Times,* September 24, 1991.

62. Graber, *Processing the News,* chap. 2; Teun A. Van Dijk, *News as Discourse* (Hillsdale, N.J.: Lawrence Erlbaum, 1988), 139–174; and John P. Robinson and Mark R. Levy, *The Main Source: Learning from Television News* (Beverly Hills, Calif.: Sage, 1986), 57–175. Also see Neuman, *Future of the Mass Audience,* 92, for a brief review of relevant studies.

63. Scott Keeter and Cliff Zukin, *Uninformed Choice: The Failure of the New Presidential Nominating System* (New York: Praeger, 1983). Also see Michael X. Delli Carpini and Scott Keeter, *What Americans Know about Politics and Why It Matters* (New Haven, Conn.: Yale University Press, 1996).

64. Michael Schudson, *The Power of News* (Cambridge, Mass.: Harvard University Press, 1995), 27.

65. V. O. Key, with the assistance of Milton C. Cummings, Jr., *The Responsible Electorate* (Cambridge, Mass.: Harvard University Press, 1965), 7, reached the same conclusion. Also see Page and Shapiro, *Rational Public,* 383–390, regarding the wisdom inherent in public opinion.

66. Arthur H. Miller, Edie N. Goldenberg, and Lutz Erbring, "Type-Set Politics: Impact of Newspapers on Public Confidence," *American Political Science Review* 73 (March 1979): 67–84.

67. Garrett J. O'Keefe, "Political Malaise and Reliance on Media," *Journalism Quarterly* 57 (Spring 1980): 122–128.

68. Murray Edelman, *Politics as Symbolic Action* (New York: Academic Press, 1976); and Murray Edelman, *Constructing the Political Spectacle* (Chicago: University of Chicago Press, 1988).

69. Comstock et al., *Television and Human Behavior,* 289–309.

70. W. Russell Neuman, *The Paradox of Mass Politics: Knowledge and Opinion in the American Electorate* (Cambridge, Mass.: Harvard University Press, 1986), 137.

71. The desire to be politically informed varies widely. For details, see ibid. News selection criteria are discussed in Graber, *Processing the News,* chap. 4.

72. *Public Opinion* 10 (September–October 1987): 25.

73. W. Lance Bennett, *News, The Politics of Illusion,* 3d ed. (White Plains, N.Y.: Longman, 1996), 37–76.

74. Daniel C. Hallin, "We Keep America on Top of the World," in *Watching Television,* ed. Todd Gitlin (New York: Pantheon, 1986), 9–41.

75. Tony Schwartz, *The Responsive Chord* (Garden City, N.Y.: Anchor Press, Doubleday, 1974), 25. For an excellent analysis of learning from television, see Robinson and Levy, *The Main Source,* chaps. 3–7.

76. Richard M. Perloff, Ellen A. Wartella, and Lee B. Becker, "Increasing Learning from TV News," *Journalism Quarterly* 59 (Spring 1982): 83–86.

77. For dire predictions see Jarol B. Manheim, *All of the People All the Time: Strategic Communication and American Politics* (Armonk, N.Y.: M. E. Sharpe, 1991), 204–209; Robert Entman, *Democracy without Citizens: Media and the Decay of American Politics* (New York: Oxford University Press, 1990), chap. 7. For a more positive view see Graber, *Processing the News,* 251–258; and Page and Shapiro, *Rational Public,* 383–390.

78. None of these studies focuses on the effects of exposure to nonfictional violence in the media because the First Amendment would be a strong bar to censorship of news. Surgeon General's Scientific Advisory Committee on Television and Social Behavior, *Television and Growing Up: The Impact of Televised*

Violence (Washington, D.C.: U.S. Government Printing Office, 1971). For a critical review of the follow-up report, see Thomas D. Cook, Deborah A. Kendzierski, and Stephen V. Thomas, "The Implicit Assumptions of Television Research: An Analysis of the 1982 NIMH Report on 'Television and Behavior,'" *Public Opinion Quarterly* 47 (Spring 1983): 161–201.

79. "Violence Dominates on TV, Study Says," *Chicago Tribune,* February 7, 1996.
80. Russell G. Geen, "Television and Aggression: Recent Developments and Theory," in *Media, Children and the Family,* ed. Zillmann et al., 151–162; Jerome L. Singer, Dorothy G. Singer, and Wanda S. Rapaczynski, "Family Patterns and Television Viewing as Predictors of Children's Beliefs and Aggression," *Journal of Communication* 34 (Summer 1984): 73–89. The politics of research on the effects of television violence are discussed by Willard D. Rowland, Jr., *The Politics of TV Violence: Policy Uses of Communication Research* (Beverly Hills, Calif.: Sage, 1983).
81. Elizabeth Kolbert, "Television Gets Closer Look as a Factor in Real Violence," *New York Times,* December 14, 1994.
82. James M. Carlson, *Prime Time Law Enforcement: Crime Show Viewing and Attitudes toward the Criminal Justice System* (New York: Praeger, 1985).
83. Robert P. Snow, "How Children Interpret TV Violence in Play Context," *Journalism Quarterly* 51 (Spring 1974): 13–21.
84. Presidential Commission on Obscenity and Pornography, *Report of the Commission on Obscenity and Pornography* (New York: Bantam Books, 1970). See also the *Attorney General's Commission on Pornography: Final Report,* published in 1986; and Richard A. Dienstbier, "Sex and Violence: Can Research Have It Both Ways?" *Journal of Communication* 27 (Summer 1977): 176–188.
85. David O. Edeani, "Critical Predictors of Orientation to Change in a Developed Society," *Journalism Quarterly* 58 (Spring 1981): 56–64. The carefully measured impact of the introduction of television into a Canadian community is presented in Tannis MacBeth Williams, ed., *The Impact of Television: A Natural Experiment in Three Communities* (Orlando, Fla.: Academic Press, 1985).
86. James B. Lemert, Barry N. Mitzman, Michael A. Seither, Roxana H. Cook, and Regina Hackett, "Journalists and Mobilizing Information," *Journalism Quarterly* 54 (Winter 1977): 721–726.
87. Ronald E. Rice and Charles K. Atkin, eds., *Public Communication Campaigns,* 2d ed. (Newbury Park, Calif.: Sage, 1989).
88. Douglas S. Solomon, "Health Campaigns on Television," in *Television and Human Behavior,* ed. Comstock et al., 316–319.
89. Sheldon O'Connell, "Television and the Canadian Eskimo: The Human Perspective," *Journal of Communication* 27 (Autumn 1977): 140–144; and Gary O. Coldevin, "Anik I and Isolation: Television in the Lives of Canadian Eskimos," *Journal of Communication* 27 (Autumn 1977): 145–153.
90. Everett M. Rogers, "The Rise and Fall of the Dominant Paradigm," *Journal of Communication* 28 (Winter 1978): 64–69; and Wilbur Schramm and Daniel Lerner, eds., *Communication and Change: The Last Ten Years—and the Next* (Honolulu: University Press of Hawaii, 1976).
91. Stuart J. Sigman and Donald L. Fry, "Differential Ideology and Language Use: Readers' Reconstructions and Descriptions of News Events," *Critical Studies in Mass Communication* 2 (December 1985): 307–322.

Readings

Gamson, William A. *Talking Politics*. New York: Cambridge University Press, 1992.

Graber, Doris A. *Processing the News: How People Tame the Information Tide*. Lanham, Md.: University Press of America, 1993.

Gunter, Barrie. *Poor Reception: Misunderstanding and Forgetting Broadcast News*. Hillsdale, N.J.: Lawrence Erlbaum, 1990.

Kubey, Robert, and Mihaly Csikszentmihalyi. *Television and the Quality of Life: How Viewing Shapes Everyday Experience*. Hillsdale, N.J.: Lawrence Erlbaum, 1990.

Lichter, S. Robert, Linda S. Lichter, and Stanley Rothman. *Watching America*. New York: Prentice Hall, 1991.

Meyrowitz, Joshua. *No Sense of Place: The Impact of Electronic Media on Social Behavior*. New York: Oxford University Press, 1985.

Neuman, W. Russell, Marion R. Just, and Ann N. Crigler. *Common Knowledge: News and the Construction of Political Meaning*. Chicago: University of Chicago Press, 1992.

Schudson, Michael. *The Power of News*. Cambridge, Mass.: Harvard University Press, 1995.

Signorielli, Nancy, and Michael Morgan, eds. *Cultivation Analysis: New Directions in Mass Media Effects Research*. Newbury Park, Calif.: Sage, 1990.

Zillmann, Dolf, Jennings Bryant, and Aletha Huston. *Media, Children, and the Family Social Scientific, Psychodynamic, and Clinical Perspectives*. Hillsdale, N.J.: Lawrence Erlbaum, 1994.

c h a p t e r   e i g h t

Elections in the Television Age

WHEN ANCIENT GREEKS WENT TO Apollo's temple at Delphi in search of answers to their questions, the oracle's response was often couched in vague, ambiguous language that lent itself to different interpretations. It was then the inquirer's task to proclaim the oracle's meaning. That meaning would be accepted as truth unless circumstances proved that the interpreter had erred. Modern day interpretations of the messages that voters convey through their votes are not unlike the messages of the ancient oracle: They are based on ambiguous evidence, yet they are widely accepted as truth. They are given sacred status because, in modern democracies, *vox populi, vox Dei*—the voice of the people is the voice of God.

So it happened in the 1992 senatorial primaries when two women won nomination contrary to political expectations. Election gurus interpreted their victories as an outcry by enraged voters against male arrogance and domination as symbolized by the television broadcasts of the confirmation hearings of Clarence Thomas to the U.S. Supreme Court. The surprise victors were Carol Moseley Braun (D-Ill.), who beat a powerful, long-term incumbent, Illinois senator Alan Dixon; and Lynn Yeakel (D-Pa.), a political novice who defeated two strong contenders: Pennsylvania's lieutenant governor, her party's official candidate, and the district attorney of Allegheny County.

Both women maintained that the nationally televised hearings before an all-male committee into charges by Anita Hill, a law professor who claimed she had been sexually harassed by Thomas, convinced them that more women must run for the Senate to correct the gender imbalance.

Yeakel even used advertisements in her campaign that showed Pennsylvania senator Arlen Specter at the hearings imperiously challenging Hill's testimony, followed by Yeakel's question, "Did this make you as angry as it made me?"

The feelings aroused by media coverage of the hearings may well have been the deciding factor, as the victorious women claimed. But, as in most election contests, many other factors could have produced the same outcome. For example, both candidates were involved in multiple-candidate races. Braun is an African American woman whose long-term political career in the state had made her familiar to many Illinois voters. She faced two white candidates, each concentrating on hurting the other's campaign. In such three-way contests in Illinois, victory for the African American candidate has been common. The Yeakel victory also involved a multicandidate race, increasing the chances of an underdog. Five contenders were competing for the Democratic senatorial nomination. Yeakel, like Braun, won by a plurality of the votes. It is doubtful that she could have won in a two-person contest. It is interesting to note that Republican Specter, the chief target of Yeakel's ire, won his primary by a 2 to 1 margin.

Although the link between media and election outcomes has been studied more thoroughly than other media-politics links, the dynamics remain unclear. Definitive answers are lacking for most cause-and-effect questions, such as those posed by the Braun and Yeakel upset victories in the Illinois and Pennsylvania primaries. Speculations about the meanings that citizens express through their votes will continue to be plentiful nonetheless because, like the Delphi oracle, these messages have great symbolic power. They constitute the mandates that politicians claim as justifications for their actions.

The State of Research

Understanding the role of the mass media in elections is hampered by imbalances in research. Presidential elections have been most extensively studied, and congressional elections are drawing increasing attention. Far less is known about the media's role in gubernatorial elections and about their impact in various types of local elections. The limited evidence available suggests that the role of the media varies substantially, depending on the particular office at stake and the news appeal of a campaign. In congressional elections, for example, exciting campaigns are covered whereas routine ones are ignored.

Even at the presidential level little research has been done to explore changes in the role of the media from one election to the next. High costs have discouraged most researchers from studying media influences throughout entire campaigns from the preprimary period to the general election. The crucial early stages in campaigns when candidate selection takes place were largely ignored prior to Ronald Reagan's election in 1980.[1] The influence of factors such as incumbency, three-way competition, or major national crises has not been thoroughly investigated either. It stands to reason that the impact of the media will vary depending on the changing political scene, the type of coverage chosen by newspeople, and the fluctuating interests of voters. Studies of media impact on comparable elections in Canada, Great Britain, France, Germany, and elsewhere have been plagued by similar problems.[2]

Another serious obstacle to understanding is the dearth of media content analyses. Election news content, including commercials, and the context of general news in which it is embedded have been examined in detail only rarely because content analysis is expensive. Without knowing the exact content of election messages, it becomes impossible to test what impact, if any, diverse messages have on viewers' perceptions. Another problem is failure to ascertain media exposure accurately. Investigators frequently assume that people have been exposed to all election stories in a particular news source without checking precisely which stories have come to the attention of various individuals and what these individuals learned from these stories.

A shortage of good data also prevented researchers prior to the Reagan era from isolating the effects of political advertising on political campaigns. Candidates and their supporters spend a large share of their campaign budgets on political advertising displayed on bumper stickers and billboards, printed in newspapers, disseminated through videotapes, or broadcast with clockwork regularity on radio and television. Researchers who now analyze the content and impact of various types of television commercials are finding that these commercials are major factors in campaigns. But the role played by forms of advertising, aside from television, remains largely unexplored. In addition, Internet messages of all types are new territory, waiting to be discovered.

The Consequences of Media Politics

The advent of television and its ready availability in every home, the spread and improvement of public opinion polling, and the use of computers in election data analysis have vastly enhanced the role of the mass media in elections. In this era of media politics, what major changes have been wrought by these technologies? We will consider four major consequences: a sharp decline in party influence, an increase in the power of journalists to influence the selection of candidates, the requirement for candidates to "televise well," and the emergence of made-for-media campaigns.

Decline in Party Influence

Foremost among the changes aided and abetted by the televisual computer age is the declining influence of political parties, particularly in presidential elections. During the 1940s, party allegiance was the most important determinant of the vote. Next in rank were voters' feelings of allegiance to a social group, assessment of the candidate's personality, and consideration of issues, in that order. That ranking has been reversed. The candidate's character has become the prime consideration at the presidential level. Issues associated with the candidate have become intertwined with considerations of character because issues are used to infer character traits.[3] Party affiliation and group membership now are last.[4] When voters base their decisions on a candidate's personality and stand on issues, the media become more important because they are the chief sources of information about these matters.

Political parties correspondingly take on less importance. Voters who can see and hear candidates in their own living rooms can make choices that differ from those made by the party. Split-ticket voting has become common. Rather than voting only for candidates of one party during an election, many voters now choose individuals from opposing parties. Because radio and television give them direct access to voters, candidates can campaign without the assistance of parties, thereby weakening party control. They can raise their own money and build their own organizations. With the aid of the media new candidates can gain a wide following rapidly. This new independence of voters and candidates makes primary and general election races more crowded and less predictable. Party regulars who have groomed themselves for years to attain positions of power may find themselves bypassed.

Party affiliation remains very important at the state and local levels where the average voter knows little about most candidates and media information is scant, particularly on television. This is not true, however, in many local elections when candidates run without overt or covert party designation and endorsement or when candidates of the same party compete against each other in primary elections. When party choice criteria are lacking and personal experience or advice from opinion leaders is unavailable, voters turn to whatever guidance the media may offer. Some will follow expressed or implied media endorsements; others will take them as cues to vote the opposite way. In either case what the media say about the candidates influences voting decisions.

Media as King Makers

More than ever before, journalists can influence the selection of candidates and issues.[5] Candidates, like actors, depend for their success as much on the roles into which they are cast as on their acting ability. In the television age media people usually do the casting for presidential hopefuls, whose performance is then judged according to the assigned role. Strenuous efforts by campaign directors and public relations experts to dominate this aspect of the campaign have been only moderately fruitful.

Casting occurs early in the primaries when newspeople, on the basis of as yet slender evidence, predict winners and losers in order to narrow the field of eligibles who must be covered. Concentrating on the front-runners in public opinion polls makes newspeople's tasks more manageable, but it often forces trailing candidates out of the race prematurely. Early highly speculative calculations become self-fulfilling prophecies because designated "winners" attract supporters whereas "losers" are abandoned.

The 1976 Democratic primaries are an excellent example. Almost a dozen candidates were running, but the media covered Jimmy Carter, the little known former governor of Georgia, far more heavily and favorably than the other contenders. After the New Hampshire primary in February in which Carter received 30 percent of the Democratic vote, NBC's Tom Pettit called Carter "the man to beat." The trailing contenders were largely ignored. *Time* magazine labeled his campaign the only one "with real possibilities of breaking far ahead of the pack."[6] It featured him on its front cover, as did *Newsweek*. Along with the front-cover picture in *Time* went a 2,630-line feature story, compared with 300 lines devoted to all other Democrats in the race.

Primary defeats, such as Carter's poor showing in Massachusetts in early March, were characterized as exceptions that merely slowed his momentum, rather than as disastrous defeats, and poor Gallup Poll ratings were largely ignored. As Figure 8-1 shows, coverage of the Republican contenders in the 1988 election is yet another example of uneven attention. George Bush received twice as much coverage in *Time* and *Newsweek* early in the campaign as Sen. Robert Dole and ten times as much as Rep. Jack Kemp.[7]

Candidates who exceed expectations in garnering votes are declared winners; candidates who fall short are losers.[8] When Pat Buchanan finished 16 points behind Bush in the 1992 New Hampshire primary, the media declared him the winner because he had exceeded their expecta-

FIGURE 8-1   News Coverage of the Republican Contenders in *Time* and *Newsweek* in Early Stages of 1988 Nominating Contest

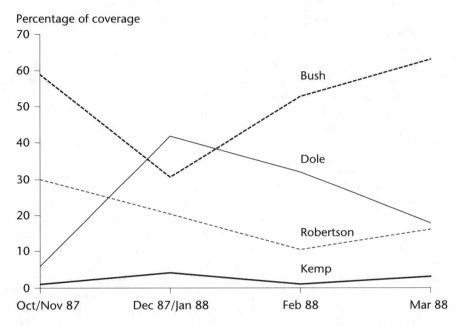

Percentage of coverage

SOURCE: Thomas E. Patterson, "The Press and Its Missed Assignment," in *The Elections of 1988*, Michael Nelson, ed. (Washington, D.C.: CQ Press, 1989), 99.

NOTE: Figure does not show coverage of Pierre DuPont and other possible Republican nominees who, together, received 3 percent or less of the coverage in each time period.

tions. They did the same for Bill Clinton who had trailed Paul Tsongas in New Hampshire in 1992. The Dole candidacy during the 1996 primaries was prematurely declared dead when he finished behind his competitors in a few early and insignificant contests.

Media coverage and public opinion polls tend to move in tandem in the early months of a campaign. Candidates who receive ample media coverage usually do well in the polls. Good poll ratings bring more media coverage. Once the caucus and primary season has started in the spring of the election year, the outcomes of these contests become more important predictors of media attention. The winners and candidates whose scores seem surprisingly good receive heavy media coverage; the media neglect the losers. One other pattern is common, though not universal.

The substance of stories tends to be favorable for trailing candidates in the race and unfavorable for front-runners. Between January and June 1992, for example, more than 60 percent of the television comments about unlikely winners Ross Perot and Tsongas were favorable. That compared to 41 percent for Jerry Brown and Clinton, and 22 percent for President Bush.[9]

The media's role as king maker or killer of the dreams of would-be kings is often played over a long span of time. Image making for presidential elections now begins on a massive scale more than a year before the first primary. The pre-pre-campaign, on a more limited scale, begins shortly after the previous election. By the end of 1981, for instance, thirty Democrats and fourteen Republicans had already been mentioned in newspaper and magazine stories as potential presidential candidates for 1984.[10] Senators and governors who receive favorable publicity over many years may gradually come to be thought of as likely presidential nominees.

In the past, captains of the media industry often used their personal influence and the power of the media under their control to support nominations for their favorites and to harm opponents. The practice has become less overt and may be vanishing. Examples include the efforts of publisher Henry Luce to entice popular war hero Dwight Eisenhower to run for the presidency in 1952. Luce put his publications, such as *Time* and *Life,* at Eisenhower's service. Kyle Palmer and the Chandler family, through their control of the *Los Angeles Times,* were instrumental in getting Richard Nixon a seat in the U.S. House of Representatives in 1946 and a U.S. Senate seat in 1950. Colonel Robert McCormick used the powerful *Chicago Tribune* to defeat policies of Franklin D. Roosevelt and Harry S. Truman and to put Republican politicians into office in Illinois.[11]

The power of the media has also been wielded to destroy candidacies. This happened to two Democratic candidates for the presidency in 1988, Sen. Joseph Biden of Delaware and Sen. Gary Hart of Colorado. Biden was forced out of the campaign by widely publicized charges that his speeches contained plagiarized quotes from other political leaders. As has been discussed in earlier chapters, Hart withdrew after charges of philandering. Recurrent media references to the Chappaquiddick incident, which mentioned Sen. Edward Kennedy (D-Mass.) in conjunction with the drowning of a young woman on his staff, also have dampened efforts by his supporters to draft him as a presidential contender. However, adverse publicity can be overcome. In the 1992 campaign, Clinton was accused of adultery and draft dodging, causing his poll ratings and positive media appraisals to plummet. Despite the bad publicity, he managed to win major primaries and the presidency.

Media images can also become vastly important during the general election campaign. For instance, the Kennedy-Nixon television debates of 1960, the Reagan-Carter debates of 1980, and the Reagan-Mondale debates of 1984 helped to remove public impressions that John F. Kennedy and Ronald Reagan were unsuited for the presidency.[12] Kennedy was able to demonstrate that he was capable of coping with the presidency despite his youth and relative inexperience, and Reagan in 1980 conveyed the impression that he was neither trigger-happy nor physically or mentally decrepit. Four years later, however, his inauspicious start in the opening debate made some viewers wonder whether advancing age had made him unfit for a second term. Demonstration of physical and mental vigor during subsequent debates helped reverse the unfavorable image that could have cost Reagan the election. No other medium could have equaled the reach and impact of television.[13] In fact, the risks of televised debates so awed presidential candidates after the 1960 encounter that a repeat performance did not occur for sixteen years. Since then they have become plentiful, with a veritable flood of debates during the 1988 and 1992 races. Moreover, Congress has considered legislation to make debates mandatory for candidates who are accepting public funding for their campaigns.

Adverse media coverage of policy issues sharply diminished the chances of Presidents Lyndon Johnson, Carter, and Bush for a second term. Disapproval of Bush was directed mainly at his failure to solve major problems in the domestic economy. In Carter's case the media chose to commemorate the anniversary of a major foreign policy failure—the American hostages' prolonged captivity in Iran—just prior to the 1980 presidential election. When major media extracted only unflattering statements from the full record of Johnson's public justifications of his Vietnam policies, they gutted the case the president needed to make in order to become a strong second-term candidate in 1968.[14] Johnson subsequently decided not to seek another term.

Media-operated public opinion polls are yet another weapon in the arsenal for king-making. The CBS-*New York Times* Poll, the NBC-Associated Press Poll, the ABC-*Washington Post* Poll, and the CNN-*USA Today* Poll all conduct popularity ratings and issue polls throughout presidential elections and publicize them extensively. These poll results then become bench marks for voters, telling them who the winners and losers are and what issues should be deemed crucial to the campaign. Depending on the nature and format of the questions asked by the pollsters and the political context in which the story becomes embedded, the responses spell fortune or misfortune for the candidates. Polls may determine which candidates enter the fray and which keep out. In the 1992 presidential campaign, major Democratic politicians chose to keep out of the race because they believed that President Bush's high approval ratings following the Gulf War doomed their candidacies.

Television-Age Recruits

A third important consequence of the new politics is the change it has wrought in the types of candidates likely to be politically successful. Because television can bring the image of candidates for high national and state office directly into the homes of millions of voters, political recruiters have become extremely conscious of a candidate's ability to look impressive and to perform well before the cameras. That requires the flair to act self-confidently and seemingly naturally in front of a bevy of photographers. People who are not telegenic have been eliminated from the pool of available recruits. Abraham Lincoln's rugged face probably would not have passed muster in the television age. President Truman's "Give 'em Hell, Harry" homespun style would have backfired if presented to nationwide groups rather than small gatherings. Franklin D. Roosevelt's wheelchair appearances would have spelled damaging weakness. Roosevelt, in fact, was keenly aware of the likely harmful effects of a picture of him in a wheelchair and never allowed photographs to be taken while he was being lifted to the speaker's rostrum.

Actors and celebrities from other walks of life who are adept at performing before the public now have a much better chance than ever before to be recruited for political office. Reagan, a former actor; Buchanan, a television news commentator; and Pat Robertson, a charismatic preacher, are examples of typical television-age recruits whose chances for public office would have been much smaller in an earlier era. As columnist Marquis Child has put it, candidates no longer "run" for office; they "pose" for office.[15]

In fact, good pictures can counterbalance the effects of unfavorable verbal comments. During the 1984 presidential campaign favorable pictures coincided with favorable poll results despite predominantly negative verbal commentary. When CBS reporter Leslie Stahl verbally attacked President Reagan for falsely posturing as a man of peace and compassion, a Reagan assistant promptly thanked her for showing four-and-a-half minutes of great pictures of the president. He was not in the least concerned about the scathing remarks. The pictures had shown the president

> basking in a sea of flag-waving supporters ... sharing concerns with farmers in a field, picnicking with Mid-Americans, pumping iron ... getting the Olympic torch from a runner ... greeting senior citizens at their housing pro-

By permission of Mike Luckovich and Creators Syndicate.

ject, honoring veterans who landed on Normandy, honoring youths just back from Grenada, countering a heckler ... wooing black inner-city kids....[16]

During the 1996 campaign, President Clinton and his staff members staged an endless series of events designed to capture favorable television coverage around-the-clock, ranging from lengthy Oval Office sessions with teenagers who resisted pressures to smoke to White House meetings with auto-industry representatives to celebrate increased car exports to Japan.[17]

Candidates who perform poorly on television now spend considerable time and money for professional coaching. The results are mixed. Former Senate leader Dole, an experienced politician, for example, was rated as a poor television performer during the 1996 presidential campaign and vastly inferior, on that score, to his rival President Clinton. Television advisers have become year-round regular members of presidential and gubernatorial staffs and their names have become almost as well known as the names of the political bosses of yesteryear. These experts create commercials for the candidates and generate and handle general news coverage of the campaign. Roughly two thirds of the budgets of presidential contenders go for their television contests.

Given the high cost of television commercials and of gaining news exposure, a candidate's personal wealth or ability to raise money remains an important consideration, even when federal funding is available. Activities, statements, and policy proposals likely to alienate donors are shunned. Although there is evidence that the best-financed candidates do not always win, folklore says they do. Hence falling behind in the race for money to finance media exposure is a sharp brake on political aspirations. The political consequences in recruitment and post-election commitments that spring from such financial considerations are enormous.

Campaigning for the Media

A fourth major aspect of the new politics is the fact that mass media coverage has become a pivotal campaign goal. Campaigns are structured to garner the best media exposure before the largest suitable audience and, if possible, with the greatest degree of candidate control over the message. To attract media coverage candidates concentrate on photo opportunities, talk-show appearances, or trips to interesting events and locations.

The New Media. Appearances on various entertainment shows, once considered "unpresidential," have become routine. Maverick candidate Perot started the pattern during the 1992 presidential race by announcing his presidential aspirations on CNN's "Larry King Live" call-in show. The other candidates followed the talk show trek, preferring their lighter banter and the respectful questions of callers to the pointed inquisition in interviews by the national press. Adorned with shades, Governor Clinton played the saxophone on the hip "Arsenio Hall Show"; he even bought television time to stage his own call-in show.

Even when candidates meet voters personally in rallies, parades, or shopping center visits, they generally time and orchestrate these events to attract favorable media coverage. In 1992 candidates also made increasing use of videotapes to supply local television stations and various organizations with messages prepared and transmitted without the intervention of reporters. Given the tight finances of many stations, the expertly prepared tapes were most welcome. Candidate control over messages also increased through satellite interviews in which candidates chatted directly with local correspondents, most of whom were unlikely to ask hostile questions or limit the candidate's speech to sound bites of less than 10 seconds. Even network morning news shows devoted entire hours to conversations with the candidates and arranged for them to answer citizens' telephone calls on the air. All in all, the trend seems to be toward more direct contact by candidates with voters and increased candidate control over campaign messages, all at the expense of campaign message control by the major media.

The political consequences of using these more candidate-centered approaches to campaigning are not entirely clear. They were described as "perhaps the most salutary development of the 1992 campaign" in a major study. "By using an entertainment format, candidates found a way to communicate effectively to audiences they might otherwise miss and to present their views on the topics they wanted to emphasize."[18] The research evidence to support this claim is still quite slim. Political scientist Diana Owen, writing in 1993, called talk radio "one of the most understudied facets of political communication."[19] The same holds true for talk-show television. Nonetheless, the initial claims and findings are intriguing.

For example, a poll conducted in North Carolina in 1992 showed that exposure to MTV (cable's music channel), which had added election news segments to its broadcasts, had no effect on scores on political knowledge tests and responses to political efficacy questions and questions about voting intentions. However, audiences who had paid substantial attention to discussions of voting and elections on talk shows such as "Larry King Live," "Donahue," and "The Rush Limbaugh Show" scored significantly higher on the political knowledge scale than other respondents. Intention to vote increased somewhat. Compared to heavy newspaper readers, talk show devotees knew just as much about the issue positions of presidential candidates, suggesting that interactive communication in an informal setting is an effective way to transmit complex political information.[20]

Information about the demographics of talk show audiences puts these figures into perspective. A 1992 survey of listeners to talk radio programs such as "Larry King Live" or "The Rush Limbaugh Show" demonstrated that this is primarily a "yuppies" audience. Listeners topped general population characteristics in age, income, and maleness. They were a bit more Republican or Independent than Democratic and they leaned toward a Populist political orientation, especially on economic issues. Although they felt alienated from formal political institutions, they were not alienated from the political process. In fact, they had an above average sense of civic duty and believed that their voices could and should be heard. It is therefore not surprising that they rated somewhat above nonlisteners in political knowledge and past voting in elections. Obviously, talk radio—and, probably, talk television as well—has become a major political force, considering its vast audience. The days when talk radio evoked images of an audience of political misfits at the outer edges of the political culture are over, even though such audiences still exist and there are programs that serve their inclinations.

When major candidates campaign extensively on radio talk shows they are addressing a very large—and growing—audience. Ninety-nine percent of American households have one or more radios and 80 percent of the population listen to radio on a daily basis. In fact, during the day-time hours, between 6 A.M. and 6 P.M., radio listening exceeds television watching by substantial numbers (49 percent to 33 percent). Cellular tele-phones make it possible to participate in talk shows during the many hours Americans spend in their cars. There are some 10,000 radio stations in the United States, and call-in radio shows are the fastest growing seg-ment of the market, accounting for nearly 10 percent of all programming. Satellite technology has made it practical to develop network talk radio, which has invigorated AM radio, which had been on the decline.[21] There is a general, as yet unproven perception that talk shows influence politics. Perot's garnering of nearly one fifth of the votes in the 1992 election has been attributed to his talk show appearances. Limbaugh's endorsement of Buchanan before the 1992 New Hampshire primary allegedly under-mined the efforts of President Bush in that key state. Brown's victory in the Connecticut primary and Clinton's political survival of the New York primary have been attributed to talk radio performance.[22]

No discussion of the role of "new" media in campaigns would be com-plete without mentioning the Internet. It promises to be a major campaign factor by the turn of the century. The 1996 campaign provides a glimpse of what we may expect. By 1996 the major parties, as well as some of the minor, had established home pages on the World Wide Web. Most of the presidential contenders had their own official Web sites, which competed for audience attention with the far more numerous unofficial Web sites that supplemented, criticized, and lampooned the official messages. In fact, it was often difficult in 1996 to distinguish the official sites from the parodies, at least initially. Content wise, the range of political information available on the Internet ran from the excellent to the vile. Absent an ethic or other controls, it was a free-for-all, used wisely as well as irresponsibly.

Like talk shows, Web sites permit candidates to broadcast the infor-mation they want the voters to have and even to interact with Web visitors via e-mail or in other electronic formats. Tennessee governor Lamar Alexander (R), for example, announced his 1992 presidency bid in an online "chat session" on America-On-Line. Perot's United We Stand for America organization offered legislative guides and scorecards of votes of members of Congress to its Internet visitors. Other Web sites featured party platforms, speeches, reports, and guides to locations where addi-tional information might be found.

The Internet empowers audiences to interact with politicians directly with comparatively little access restraint by third parties, such as reporters, anchors, or newspaper editors. When it comes to audience reach, however, the Internet is still far less accessible than call shows to the public for sending and receiving messages. For call show access, little more than a telephone is needed. Internet access requires computers connected to the Internet as well as knowledge about using them. Such access and knowledge are currently confined to a small fraction of the population—about 11 percent use the Internet according to 1995 Nielsen Research reports. Mostly, they are young people at the high end of the socioeconomic and educational scale. Similarly, cyberpoliticians who are ready, willing, and able to use the Internet effectively are still in short supply. By the year 2000, this will have changed at all political levels: local, state, national, and international. The problem then will shift from learning how to use this new resource to finding ways of attracting attention in the cacophony of voices in cyberspace and figuring out which niche audiences are the most promising targets for securing votes and campaign resources.

Campaign Tactics. Irrespective of the nature of each medium, candidates must plan their schedules to dovetail with its coverage habits. They spend disproportionate amounts of time campaigning in Iowa and New Hampshire where media coverage is ordinarily heavy, except when these races are essentially uncontested because a native or neighboring son is the candidate, as happened in Iowa in 1992 when Sen. Tom Harkin from Iowa was on the ballot. In 1988 when the outcome of the Iowa race was less certain, Iowa and New Hampshire, which have less than 3 percent of the U.S. population, received more coverage during the primaries than all the other primaries combined.[23] In 1996, each of these states dwarfed news coverage of later primaries by more than a 4 to 1 ratio.[24] Ample media coverage does not guarantee benefits at the polls, however. In 1988 Pete DuPont spent ninety-one days and $560,000 in Iowa, but he received only 7 percent of the Republican vote.

To keep a favorable image of their candidates in front of the public, campaign managers arrange newsworthy events to familiarize potential voters with their candidates' best aspects. Because most television producers do not like "talking heads"—shots of the faces of speakers—candidates may engage in staged activities merely to provide attractive, action-oriented, and symbol-laden pictures. Reporter Leslie Stahl describes how Carter courted the voters in 1980:

> What did President Carter do today in Philadelphia? He posed, with as many different types of symbols as he could possibly find.
> There was a picture at the day care center. And one during the game of bocce ball with the senior citizens. Click, another picture with a group of

teenagers. And then he performed the ultimate media event—a walk through the Italian market.

The point of all this, obviously, to get on the local news broadcasts and in the morning newspapers. It appeared that the President's intention was not to say anything controversial.... Simply the intention was to be seen.[25]

Incumbents have a distinct advantage over challengers. Although they may attract about the same number of campaign stories, incumbents receive additional attention through coverage of their official duties.[26] Incumbents may also be able to dictate time and place for media encounters. When a president schedules a meeting for reporters in the White House Rose Garden, ample coverage is ensured. There even is a quasi-incumbency status for promising challengers. Once they have attained wide recognition as front-runners, newspeople compete for their attention. Their power to grant or withhold it can be translated into influence over quality and quantity of coverage.

The newsworthiness of campaign stories is judged by general news criteria. Therefore minor candidates and newcomers whose chances for success are questionable do not get much coverage. Their efforts to attract the media are apt to fail because they simply are not big news. Lack of coverage, in turn, makes it extremely difficult for them to become well known and increase their chances of winning elections. This is another example of unintentional media bias that redounds to the benefit of established politicians.

Many campaign events are now staged as prime-time, live coverage, television spectacles. Aside from presidential debates, the conventions used to be the biggest single media event of presidential campaigns. Both major parties still select the convention cities with an eye to effective television coverage. Convention managers try to keep a tight rein on speakers and demonstrations to ensure that "good" messages appear in prime time and "bad" ones are banished to off-hours. They want to make certain that desirable images are conveyed and that important speeches are made when the television audience is likely to be at a peak. For their part, media people who cover conventions try to structure the flow of words and pictures to cover unfolding events and still tell a coherent, dramatic story. The difficulty of sustaining interest in nominating conventions when the identity of the nominee has already been firmly established has sharply reduced live prime-time coverage by the major television networks. The gap has been more than filled by gavel-to-gavel coverage by C-SPAN, and extended broadcasts on CNN and PBS and by assorted daytime and night-time programs.

Structuring and staging campaign activities to make them newsworthy has enhanced showmanship at the expense of substance. Because conflict is deemed attractive and memorable, journalists often goad campaigners into confrontations by asking questions that point up existing conflicts or that spur new battles. When journalists select the battlegrounds for presidential contests, they have shaped the political agenda during the campaign as well as afterward. Campaign statements coaxed from unwilling candidates may be subsequently construed as commitments to act.

Media Content

What kinds of newspaper and television coverage have recent elections received? Did the media sufficiently cover the issues that would be likely to require attention from the new president? Were adequate criteria supplied to enable voters to decide which of several policy options would best suit their priorities? Were voters informed about each viable candidate's positions on the issues? Did they receive enough information about each candidate's personality, experience, and ability to evaluate the candidate's likely performance as president? Following some general comments about the media mix, we will address these questions and assess the adequacy of the information supply for making rational voting choices.

Unscrambling the Message Omelet

When Humpty-Dumpty, the egg, fell off the wall in the nursery rhyme, all the king's horses and all the king's men couldn't put him together again. The various components of the media message omelet have had a similar fate. Campaign commercials, for instance, have become a major ingredient of contemporary campaigns and often bestow a distinctive flavor to them. But it is well-nigh impossible to isolate their contribution because all of the ingredients—print and electronic news stories, editorials, talk-show banter and punditry, Internet messages, advertisements, even political jokes and skits on entertainment shows— mix inextricably with each other and become transformed in the process. Ads generate and influence news stories and news stories induce and influence ads that, in turn, lead to other ads and news stories and editorials. And so it goes!

This is why I discuss campaign information as a whole without, in most instances, making distinctions among the unique contributions made by various types of media. Distinctions exist, of course, and become apparent in experimental studies when research participants are exposed to single-format messages so that the impact of various types of formats can be compared. Such studies show, for instance, that television and news magazine formats are superior to newspapers for conveying particular messages to various population groups, and that the content of advertising messages is often discounted because they are regarded as self-serving propaganda.[27]

Distinctive Features of Television Ads. If we single out television commercials for a closer look, what are some of their distinctive features, aside from the fact that their message transmission labors under a cloud of suspicion?

Ads do capture the attention of voters. Uncommitted voters, highly interested voters, and partisans of the advertised candidate are most likely to be influenced by the content of television commercials. But, on the whole commercials, unlike most news stories, are perceiver-determined.[28] People see in them pretty much what they want to see—attractive images for their favorite candidates and unattractive ones for the opponent. Attempts to glamorize political actors and hide their weaknesses may succeed for a while, but the effects last for only a short time. Commercials of opposing candidates, media exposés of deceptive messages, and people's cynicism about campaign propaganda see to that. By and large, commercials have not altered ultimate voting choices in recent presidential campaigns, although they do make significant contributions to voters' images of candidates and policies. Like other persuasive influences, their impact tends to be greatest during early primaries when voters are forming initial opinions about unknown contenders.[29] The claims that television commercials can manufacture fairyland candidates and make them believable to credulous audiences apparently are vastly exaggerated whenever voters have alternative means to know the candidates.[30] Major campaign issues are often covered as extensively in the lengthier television commercials as in network newscasts. Most viewers—particularly those who do not read newspapers and are poorly informed—remember more from the commercials than from television news. Simplicity of content, expert eye-ear appeal, and repetition of the message produce this result.

Whether commercials can inject crucial issues into a campaign remains debated. In the heat of campaigns, wins and losses are often attributed by the candidates to particular commercials or to the ability of the candidates to buy ample television time. The 1988 victory of the Bush campaign, for example, has been attributed to advertisements attacking the environmental and criminal justice policies of Massachusetts governor Michael Dukakis, Bush's opponent. "Boston Harbor," a code word for Dukakis's failure to rid Boston Harbor of pollution, and "Willie Horton," a symbol for coddling of criminals, became famous election battle cries. Scholarly corroborations are lacking for most of the claims that Bush's supposed memorable ads produced election victories and defeats.[31] Most wins and losses spring from a combination of factors. Nevertheless, the battle of the airwaves has become fiercer in recent campaigns, especially during primary contests. It has also begun to branch out from over-the-air television to cable outlets and, during the 1996 presidential campaign, the Internet. Advertising rates are cheaper on cable television—an attractive medium because messages can be more readily tailored to the needs of the smaller cable audiences.

Television commercials often provide the only chance to gain attention for the many candidates who are ignored by the media.[32] That includes the vast majority of also-rans for national office who seem unelectable to major media and most candidates competing for local and even state offices. At the local level, where information is scant, the impact of commercials can be decisive. Indeed, wisely spent advertising funds can buy elections, even for congressional candidates who receive news story coverage.[33] To quote political scientist Michael Robinson, commercials for congressional candidates "can work relative wonders," especially when they are not challenged by the other side. "A well-crafted, heavily financed, and uncontested ad campaign does influence congressional elections."[34] This fact raises the chilling specter that wealthy candidates may be able to buy major public offices by investing their fortunes in expensive advertising campaigns. That fear has escalated with the entry of multimillionaires such as Steve Forbes and Ross Perot into the presidential sweepstakes. Forbes used personal funds to finance an expensive advertising blitz in the 1996 Republican primaries. Perot bought large blocks of television time for infomercials—data-packed commercials—in the 1992 presidential campaign.

Any evaluation of how the media perform their tasks must also take their concerns into consideration. It is extremely difficult for the media to mesh the public's preference for simple, dramatic stories with the need to present sufficient information for issue-based election choices. Information that may be crucial for voting decisions often is too complex and technical to appeal to much of the audience. Hence newspeople feel compelled to feature exciting, humanly touching aspects of the election, even when they are trivial, without totally neglecting essential, unglamorous information useful for more reasoned decision making.

Patterns of Coverage

Prominence of Election Stories. In a presidential election year election stories constitute roughly 13 percent of all newspaper political coverage and 15 percent of television political news. That puts them on a par with foreign affairs news or coverage of crime. Election news receives average attention in terms of headline size, front-page or first-story placement, and inclusion of pictures, but stories are slightly longer than average. Election stories, although quite prominent when primaries, conventions, and significant debates are held, do not dominate the news. Normally, it is quite possible to read the daily paper without noticing election news and to come away from a telecast with the impression that election stories are just a minor part of the day's political developments. Election news competes for audience attention with many other types of stories; this accounts, in part, for its limited impact.

Uniformity of Coverage Patterns. Patterns of presidential election coverage are remarkably uniform, regardless of a newspaper's partisan orientation. Media personnel at highly regarded papers everywhere select the same kinds of stories and emphasize the same types of facts, despite the wealth of diverse materials available to them. The major difference generally is that small newspapers carry fewer election stories and that news stories vary in their evaluation of candidates, issues, and campaign events.[35] Television news patterns are also uniform.

Content analysis studies during congressional, state, and local campaigns show similar patterns. The political portraits that various media paint of each candidate match well in basic outlines and in most details.[36] For example, Table 8-1 shows that the three major local newspapers covered the 1983 mayoral campaign in Chicago in nearly identical fashion. The same held true for Chicago area television. The papers and television stations are owned and operated by different enterprises and appeal to different clienteles. One might expect that the need to compete against each other and the controversial nature of this particular race would have produced more diverse treatment.

Election news patterns are quite stable in successive elections and uniform for all media covering a particular election. Thus Americans receive similar information on which to base their political decisions. Similarity of coverage of election campaigns has benefits as well as drawbacks. The large degree of homogeneity introduced into the electoral process is an advantage in a heterogeneous country, such as the United States, where it can be difficult to develop political consensus. But it also means uniform neglect of many topics and criteria for judging candidates. Shared knowledge is marred by shared ignorance. Uniformity throttles needed diversity.

A uniform information base obviously has not produced totally uniform political views throughout the country. Differences in political evaluations, even among audiences that share the same news, must be attributed to news commentators' varying interpretations of the same facts and

TABLE 8-1   Distribution of Coverage Areas in the 1983 Chicago Mayoral
Primary and General Elections (in percentage of story themes)

Coverage area	Primary election			General election		
	Tribune	*Sun-Times*	*Defender*	*Tribune*	*Sun-Times*	*Defender*
Campaign	43	46	53	42	41	44
Policy	28	24	19	20	21	23
Ethics	13	11	7	8	8	8
Qualities	11	14	19	19	19	14
Party	5	5	3	12	13	11

SOURCE: Doris A. Graber, "Media Magic: Fashioning Characters for the 1983 Mayoral Race," in *The Making of the Mayor: Chicago 1983*, ed. Melvin G. Holli and Paul Green (Grand Rapids, Mich.: Eerdmans, 1984), 84. Reprinted by permission.

NOTE: For primary elections, $N = 639$ for the *Tribune*, 748 for the *Sun-Times*, and 303 for the *Defender*; for general elections, $N = 1,133$ for the *Tribune*, 1,288 for the *Sun-Times*, and 635 for the *Defender*.

to the different outlooks that audiences bring to the news. As pointed out in the previous chapter, the impact of news frequently is perceiver- rather than stimulus-determined.

Of the factors that encourage uniform coverage, the professional socialization that is common to journalists appears to be the most important. As noted in Chapter 4, newspeople share a sense of what is newsworthy and how it should be presented. Pack journalism prevails with reporters covering identical beats in fashions that have become routine for election coverage. That means keeping score about who is winning and losing and reporting dramatic incidents and juicy personal gossip. It means avoiding dull facts as much as possible without totally ignoring essential information.

Coverage does not follow the *campaign model* of reporting.[37] In this model—the utopia of campaign managers—the rhythm of the campaign as produced by the candidates and their staffs determines what is covered. Reporters dutifully take their cues from the candidates. Press coverage conforms instead to an *incentive model*. Whenever exciting stories provide an incentive for coverage, they are published in a rhythm dictated by the needs of the media and the tastes of their audiences. The needs and tastes of the candidates may be ignored unless they manage to generate the kinds of stories and pictures that journalists find irresistible. This is why most campaigns now employ professionals who know how to attract desirable media coverage.

The incentive model is particularly noticeable in election coverage by specialized media. For instance, papers geared to ethnic audiences focus on the aspects of the campaign that are of primary concern to those audiences and slight the rest. Business and labor publications put extraordinary emphasis on the campaign's relation to the economy, featuring stories ignored by general audience publications. In terms of timing of coverage, the incentive model explains why stories abound after the outcomes of contests are known and campaign activities have died down, rather than prior to such events when campaigning peaks.

Political and Structural Bias. Does election coverage give a fair and equal chance for all viewpoints to be expressed so that media audiences can make informed decisions? Are the perennial charges of bias leveled by disappointed candidates evidence that newspeople always show favoritism? Or are they merely reactions to coverage that did not advance their causes? Media people in general try to produce balanced coverage for all major candidates for the same office. This holds true for print journalists, who have no legal obligation to keep coverage balanced, as well as for broadcasters, who are obliged to give equal coverage for special election programs but who are free to indulge in unequal exposure in regular news programs. However, there are no universally accepted standards of fairness and balance.

Newspeople traditionally aim for rough parity in the number of stories about each candidate and rough parity in the balance of overtly favorable and unfavorable stories. However, their choice of story topics may advantage some candidates and disadvantage others. For example, the media stressed the economy in 1992, which put incumbent President Bush into a bad light, rather than foreign policy, which would have given him a very favorable image. Fairness does not mean discussing the candidates from the same perspectives, quoting their friends and enemies in equal proportions, or giving their stories similar time, space, or placement. It does not mean proportionate coverage of major political orientations. For example, during the 1984 Democratic National Convention, 85 percent of the interviews were conducted with liberal Democrats, although they constituted only 56 percent of the Democrats in Congress.[38] An analysis of all sound bites on ABC, CBS, CNN, and NBC during the 1992 campaign found that bias took the form of using quotes from sources hostile to the Bush-Quayle ticket far more often than quotes from enemies of candidates Clinton and Gore.[39]

Table 8-2 demonstrates the unfair imbalance that ensues when the media give the lion's share of coverage to those candidates who have the best chance for election. Republican contender Bernard Epton received practically no coverage during the 1983 Chicago mayoral primary elec-

TABLE 8-2   Source Orientation in the 1983 Chicago Mayoral Primary and
General Elections (in percentage of story themes)

Source orientation	Primary election			General election		
	Tribune	Sun-Times	Defender	Tribune	Sun-Times	Defender
Jane Byrne						
Pro	17	27	12	9	9	2
Anti	29	26	17	11	14	7
Richard Daley						
Pro	23	24	10	1	1	—
Anti	8	2	6	—	—	1
Harold Washington						
Pro	20	21	52	34	38	72
Anti	2	1	3	19	11	2
Bernard Epton						
Pro	1	1	—	18	20	5
Anti	—	—	1	8	8	10

SOURCE: Doris A. Graber, "Media Magic: Fashioning Characters for the 1983 Mayoral Race," in *The Making of the Mayor: Chicago 1983,* ed. Melvin G. Holli and Paul Green (Grand Rapids, Mich.: Eerdmans, 1984), 62. Reprinted by permission.

NOTE: For primary elections, *N* = 639 for the *Tribune,* 748 for the *Sun-Times,* and 303 for the *Defender;* for general elections, N = 714 for the *Tribune,* 828 for the *Sun-Times,* and 508 for the *Defender.*

tions. Most stories discussed Democratic contenders Jane Byrne, the incumbent, Cook County prosecutor Richard M. Daley (the son of the longtime mayor), and U.S. Representative Harold Washington, an African American. Even during the general election, when Epton's chances for victory had risen dramatically because he was running against Washington in a racially polarized city, Epton lagged way behind his opponent. There also was imbalance in the choice of friendly and hostile sources. Incumbents typically receive harsher treatment than challengers because their records in office always provide targets for criticism. In the 1983 mayoral election, for example, the Jane Byrne story, with one minor exception, reflected predominantly the views of her enemies.

Completely fair and balanced reporting may be impossible because candidates' newsworthiness and willingness to talk to reporters vary. Incumbent president Reagan, dubbed "the Great Communicator," was far more newsworthy throughout 1984, because he was the president, than Walter Mondale, his challenger. In the Chicago mayoral campaign, Washington was a charismatic candidate, whereas his Republican challenger was lackluster. There was keen interest in exploring the changes that an African American mayor might bring about for the city. No wonder the media found Washington far more newsworthy than his opponent.

One may even question whether it is fair to attempt to balance coverage when the situation surrounding candidates is not comparable. Reducing an incumbent's coverage to that accorded to a challenger seems unfair and inappropriate because the public needs to know what officeholders are doing. It would be equally inappropriate to automatically expand a challenger's coverage to an incumbent's proportions. Imbalanced coverage in these instances results from *structural bias,* which is caused by the circumstances of news production. This differs from *political bias,* which involves slanting the news for partisan reasons. Structural bias, although devoid of partisan motives, may profoundly affect people's perceptions about campaigns.[40]

At times it may be difficult to judge to what extent structural bias is fueled by political bias. In the Chicago election, for instance, newspeople could argue that the heavy emphasis on negative stories about incumbent Byrne was structural: There were many mayoral failures to cover. One could also claim that newspeople reveled in digging up negative news about her while ignoring her challengers' flaws.

Editorials, of course, are intrinsically biased because their primary purpose is to express opinions. As part of the editorial function, many news media endorse candidates. Republican candidates have received the bulk of endorsements for the presidency in this century; nonetheless, twelve Democrats have succeeded in the twenty-five presidential elections during this period. Endorsements for less exalted offices have been more influential, particularly in elections in which voters had little information to make their own decisions.[41] Influential papers, such as the *Los Angeles Times,* the *Washington Post,* or the late William Loeb's *Manchester Union Leader,* can be extraordinarily successful in promoting the election of candidates they have endorsed and in defeating unacceptable contenders. At the presidential level news coverage tends to be essentially evenhanded, regardless of the candidate endorsed. Below the presidential level the media tend to give more coverage to their endorsed candidates than to those they have not endorsed.

The effort to keep coverage balanced does not extend to third-party candidates. Anyone who runs for the presidency who is not a Republican or Democrat is out of the mainstream of newsworthiness and slighted or even ignored by the news profession. Especially newsworthy third-party candidates, such as George Wallace of the American Independent party in 1968, Robert La Follette of the Progressive party in 1924, John Anderson of the National Unity Campaign in 1980, and Independent Ross Perot in

1992, were notable exceptions. Newsworthiness considerations also account for the sparse coverage of vice-presidential candidates despite the importance of the office. Vice presidents frequently become president, but that possibility always seems remote until it happens. Ninety-five percent of the coverage in a typical presidential election goes to the presidential contenders and only 5 percent to their running mates.

Substance of Coverage: Candidates, Issues, and Events

Content analysis of newspapers and television news broadcasts on the networks, CNN, and local newscasts during the 1992 elections shows that

> the overall pattern of candidate coverage is again very similar on network and local television news and in newspapers. All three kinds of media put the greatest emphasis on the candidates' personal qualities and their chances for election; issue positions come in third, and the campaign factors (finance, staffing, etc.) are last ... candidates were covered the same way across media. Bush was the candidate covered most on personal qualities and issue positions. Perot was covered most in terms of his electoral chances and his campaign organization. The emphasis in Clinton's coverage fell between Bush's and Perot's on every dimension—personal qualities, horse race, campaign organization, and issue positions.[42]

The qualifications highlighted by the media fall into two broad groups: those that are generally important in judging a person's character and those specifically related to the tasks of the office. Included in the first group are personality traits (such as integrity, reliability, and compassion), style characteristics (such as forthrightness or folksiness), and image characteristics (such as the ability to appear productive and level-headed). Professional qualifications at the presidential level include the capacity to conduct foreign and domestic affairs, the ability to mobilize public support, and a flair for administration. The candidate's political philosophy is also a professional criterion. Over the years presidential candidates have been most frequently assessed in terms of their trustworthiness, strength of character, leadership capabilities, and compassion. Professional capacities—the very qualities that deserve the fullest discussion and analysis—have been covered scantily and often vaguely even when an incumbent is running.[43] Only a handful of professional qualifications have been mentioned with any frequency. These include general appraisals of the capacity to handle foreign affairs, which has been deemed crucial throughout the twentieth century, and the capacity to sustain an acceptable quality of life for all citizens by maintaining the economy on an even keel and by controlling crime and internal disorder. The same types of qualities reappear from election to election. Treat-

TABLE 8-3   Candidate Evaluations in Post–Labor Day Network Television
             News: 1984

Candidate	Score	Candidate	Score
Ronald Reagan	−33	Walter Mondale	−10
George Bush	−55	Geraldine Ferraro	−28

SOURCE: Data from Maura Clancey and Michael Robinson, "The Media in Campaign '84: General Election Coverage, Part I," *Public Opinion* 7 (December/January 1985): 53.

NOTE: Scores constitute the balance between all explicitly positive and negative references to the candidate. Neutral comments have been omitted. $N = 625$ news stories from ABC, CBS, and NBC early nightly news.

ment of individual candidates is usually dissimilar. Such disparate coverage makes it very difficult for the electorate to compare and evaluate the candidates on important dimensions. Effective comparisons are also hindered by contradictions in remarks reported about the candidates. Bound by current codes of objective reporting and neutrality in electoral contests, the media rarely give guidance to the audience for judging conflicting claims.

In 1992, as in most recent elections, verbal news commentary about the political candidates was quite negative, especially for the incumbent. On a 5–point favorability scale, the tone of coverage for President Bush generally dropped below the 3–point (neutral) mark, whereas Clinton coverage hovered just above neutral.[44] Journalists speculate about the candidates' venal motivations, flawed characters, and sparse political talents. Choices therefore involve selecting the lesser evil. Table 8-3 shows the typically negative treatment 1984 presidential candidates received on the evening network news between Labor Day and the election. Comparable scores in the 1992 primaries were −56 for Bush and −18 for Clinton. Republican contenders fared equally poorly during the 1996 primaries. In 1988 the chief Democratic contenders were derisively labeled "the seven dwarfs." The lead paragraph in a *Time* magazine story at the end of the 1980 race between Reagan and Carter sums up the typical downbeat mood of recent presidential elections: "For more than a year, two flawed candidates have been floundering toward the final showdown, each unable to give any but his most unquestioning supporters much reason to vote for him except dislike of his opponent."[45] Perot's coverage was in between the major contenders. Such negative characterizations are hardly fair to capable candidates who often possess great personal strengths and skills that should be praised rather than debased.

On the whole, newspaper and television coverage are quite similar, except that the features are starker on television. The usual one- or two-minute television story gives little chance for in-depth reporting and analysis. To conserve their limited time, television newscasters create stereotypes of the various candidates early in the campaign and then build their stories around these stereotypes by merely adding new details to the established image. During the 1980 presidential campaign, Reagan was typecast as an amiable dunce stumbling into the presidency almost by mistake.[46] During the 1992 campaign, Clinton became "slick Willy" and Bush an aimless drifter incapable of guiding the ship of state. Dole's political longevity was satirized by comedian David Letterman, who joked in 1996 that Dole's earliest campaigns had been easy because "there were only thirteen colonies."[47]

The impact of television typecasting is vast because television reaches nearly every voter in national and statewide campaigns. For instance, once Carter had been tagged as "fuzzy" in the 1976 campaign there was, according to his press secretary Jody Powell, "No way on God's earth we could shake the fuzziness question ... no matter what Carter did or said. He could have spent the whole campaign doing nothing but reading substantive speeches ... and still have had the image in the national press."[48] The general feeling in such cases seems to be that leopards do not change their spots.

The overriding consideration in choosing issues, as in other political coverage, is newsworthiness rather than intrinsic importance. This is why the changing record of happenings on the campaign trail, however trivial, receives extended coverage. Rather than exploring serious issues in depth, the emphasis is on brief, rapidly paced, freshly breaking events. In fact, the amount of coverage for particular issues often seems to be in inverse proportion to their significance. For instance, during the 1992 primaries, one out of every six campaign stories on the television networks referred to Governor Clinton's personal life. Sexual foibles, reputed drug use during college days, slips of the tongue, bad jokes, all made headlines and were repeated endlessly on various entertainment programs. The pattern persisted during the 1996 campaign.

Three major features stand out in coverage of issues and events. First and most significantly, the media devote a large amount of attention to hoopla and horse-race aspects of campaigns. By comparison, they slight political, social, and economic problems facing the country and say little about the merits of the solutions proposed, unless these issues can be made exciting and visually dramatic. Second, information about issues is patchy because the candidates and their surrogates try to concentrate on issues that help their campaigns and try to avoid issues likely to alienate any portion of the huge and disparate electorate from which all are seeking support. During the 1992 presidential election for example, news stories concentrated on the economy. Other issues were slighted unless there was a triggering event. For example, news focus turned to race only after the Los Angeles riots and to foreign crises whenever they erupted. Third, there is more issue coverage, albeit unsystematic, than acknowledged in the past. It becomes apparent when *all* issues mentioned in a story are recorded, rather than the main ones only and when one takes note of the frequent coverage of issues in horse-race news and discussions of candidate qualifications. For example, mention that a candidate is compassionate may cite his concern about health care laws as an indication.

Media issue coverage is much narrower than issue coverage in party platforms. In recent elections, some twenty-five issues have usually surfaced intermittently in the press and some twenty on television. Typically, only half of these receive extensive and intensive attention. Many important policy questions likely to arise during the forthcoming presidential term are totally ignored. Although candidates like to talk about broad policy issues, such as war and peace or the health of the economy, newspeople prefer to concentrate on narrower, specific policy positions on which the candidates disagree sharply.[49] Comparisons of candidates' speeches with television newscasts show that two thirds of the issues mentioned by candidates are broad, designed to attract wide support from an anxious electorate. By contrast, only one quarter of the issues featured on television are broad. The rest deal with controversial matters such as abortion, or busing, or military aid for a specific country.[50]

As is the case for coverage of presidential qualifications, issues discussed in connection with individual candidates vary. Voters thus receive little aid from the media in appraising and comparing the candidates on the issues. Compared to print media, television news usually displays more uniform patterns of issue coverage for all the candidates and involves a more limited range of issues. Television stories are briefer, touch on fewer aspects of each issue, and contribute to the stereotypic images developed for particular candidates. Events are often fragmented and barren of context but what is left is dramatized to appeal to the audience. No wonder that most people turn to television for news about the candidates and their campaigns.

Substance of Coverage: "Medialities"

Media coverage should be assessed not only in terms of the numbers of stories devoted to various topics but also in terms of political impact. There are times when election politics is particularly volatile so that a few stories may carry extraordinary weight. Rapid diffusion of these stories throughout the major media enhances their impact. Michael Robinson calls such featured events *medialities*—"events, developments, or situations to which the media have given importance by emphasizing, expanding, or featuring them in such a way that their real significance has been modified, distorted, or obscured."[51]

During the 1988 presidential campaign, for example, medialities included a policy scandal, an economic disaster, and personal foibles:

- The Iran-contra hearings, which suggested that the Reagan administration was inept and contemptuous of the law. They tarnished the luster of several Republican contenders, especially Bush, and their aftereffects lingered throughout Bush's administration.
- The stock market crash of October 19, 1987, which called the capability of the administration into question. American voters are especially sensitive to pocketbook issues.
- The character-tarnishing of several candidates, involving charges of premarital sex (Pat Robertson and Jesse Jackson), philandering (Gary Hart), plagiarism (Joseph Biden and, to a lesser degree, Jackson), and unfair campaign practices (Michael Dukakis, Bush, and others).

Such key stories can have a far more profound impact on the campaign than thousands of routine stories and should be appraised accordingly.

Adequacy of Coverage

How adequate is current election coverage? Do the media help voters enough to make decisions according to commonly accepted democratic criteria? As discussed previously, appraisal of candidates and issues is not made easy for voters. In presidential contests information is ample about the major, mainstream candidates and about day-to-day campaign events. It is sketchy and often confusing about the candidates' professional qualifications and about many important policy issues. Most primary contenders, candidates of minor parties, and vice-presidential candidates are largely ignored. This is not surprising because the field of candidates is usually much larger than most Americans realize. Usually several hundred individuals register as formal candidates for the presidency. The prevalence of negative information makes it seem that all of the candidates are mediocre or even poor choices. This negative cast appears to be a major factor in many voters' decisions to stay home on election day. It also undermines the ability of newly elected officials to command essential support after the election, especially from members of the opposing party.

TABLE 8-4   Median Number of Local Newspaper Paragraphs Mentioning
Selected Themes in Fourteen Tight Congressional Races:
September 27 to November 7, 1978

Themes	Incumbent news	Challenger news
Campaign organization	22	27
Personal characteristics	10	13
Political attributes	49	4
Issues/ideology/group ties	29	12

SOURCE: Peter Clarke and Susan H. Evans, *Covering Campaigns: Journalism in Congressional Elections* (Stanford, Calif.: Stanford University Press, 1983), 61. Reprinted by permission.

Coverage trends in congressional elections are similar to those in presidential contests, though total coverage is minimal by comparison. Challengers receive only a fraction of the coverage bestowed on incumbents. A count of newspaper coverage of forty-one incumbents and forty-one challengers in 1978 congressional races showed that challengers' share of total coverage was 28 percent in discussions of personal and political characteristics and 34 percent in issue discussions. In name mentions, challengers' share was 42 percent and in positive commentary it was 30 percent.[52] As Table 8-4 shows, challengers' coverage is also inferior in quality. The table indicates the major content themes in fourteen tight congressional races in which an incumbent was running. The tone and focus of the stories tend to reflect the incumbents' campaign objectives.[53]

In presidential contests the deficiencies of media coverage are most noticeable during the primary period, when a large slate of same-party candidates is competing in each primary. The media meet this challenge by giving uniformly skimpy treatment to all candidates except those designated as front-runners. It is not uncommon for two or three front-runners to attract 75 percent or more of the coverage, leaving a pack of trailing contenders with hardly any attention at all. As Thomas Patterson has noted, "Issue material is but a rivulet in the news flow during the primaries, and what is there is almost completely diluted by information about the race."[54] Although the quality of coverage during the primaries may be thin, the quantity is substantial, although unequally distributed so that the races in well-covered states become disproportionately influential. By the middle of the primary season, interest in these contests dwindles. Coverage shrivels. It perks up slightly during the conventions and when the final campaign starts following the Labor Day holiday in September.

Media Effects

What do people learn from campaign coverage? It varies, of course, depending on their interest in the campaign, prior political knowledge, desire for certain information, and political sophistication. But several general trends emerge from national surveys, such as those conducted biannually by the Survey Research Center at the University of Michigan, and from intensive interviews of smaller panels of voters, such as those that I have conducted.

Learning about Candidates and Issues

The foremost impression from interviews with voters is that they can recall very little specific campaign information. However, that does not necessarily mean that they have not learned anything. As discussed in the previous chapter, when people are confronted with factual information, such as news about a particular presidential candidate, they assess how it fits into their established view of that candidate. If it is consonant, it strengthens that view and their feelings about the candidate. If it is dissonant, it is likely to be rejected outright, or, possibly, noted as a reasonable exception to their established schema. The least likely approach is a major revision of their established beliefs about the candidate. Once people have processed the news, they forget most of the details and store only their summary impression in memory. When people are later quizzed about these details, they are unlikely to recall them except when they have been frequently repeated in news stories. On-line processing thus creates the false impression that the average person has formed opinions about the candidate without having learned the appropriate facts.[55]

What kinds of information are people likely to select for attention and processing from the vast amounts of presidential campaign information available to most Americans who pay attention to mass media messages? The answer is, "not very much at any one time," except possibly from the debates, which serve as a last-minute cram session for preparing the voting public. Given the length of presidential campaigns, average citizens manage to gather quite substantial amounts of information about the candidates and the issues, nonetheless, especially because many stories are covered repeatedly and often resurface from one election to the next.[56]

Unlike campaigns at state and local levels, which rarely draw a great deal of attention, most citizens are interested in presidential campaigns. Still, interest in the presidential campaign competes with interests in many other events and issues in their public and private lives. This

TABLE 8-5   Presidential Qualities Mentioned by the Public and by Newspapers (in percentages)

| Qualities | Likes | | Dislikes | | |
	Carter	Ford	Carter	Ford	Newspapers
Personal suitability					
Personality traits	49	38	39	18	36
Presidential traits	15	37	21	24	25
Style	5	4	16	10	16
Total	69	79	76	52	77
Professional competence					
Capacities	21	17	16	43	7
Relations with public	1	—	—	—	3
Philosophy	9	4	8	5	12
Total	31	21	24	48	22

SOURCE: Survey data from 1976 Election Survey, Center for Political Studies, Survey Research Center, University of Michigan; newspaper data from author's matching research.

NOTE: The percentages are based on responses to the question, "Now I'd like to ask you about the good and bad points of the two major candidates for president. Is there anything in particular about (name of candidate) that might make you want to vote for him? Is there anything about (name of candidate) that might make you want to vote against him? What is that? Anything else?" $N = 2,182$ for Carter likes, 2,337 for Ford likes, 2,125 for Carter dislikes, and 1,747 for Ford dislikes. $N = 17,423$ mentions of qualities by newspapers.

explains why a panel of voters who kept diaries on the important news stories that came to their attention throughout a presidential election year devoted only 11 percent of their entries to election stories. When asked to name "major current events or issues," 38 percent of the panelists never named the election in four interviews conducted during the primary season.[57] Likewise, during the early months of the 1988 campaign, 69 percent of the respondents to a national Gallup Poll said that they had closely watched news accounts about Jessica McClure, a Texas toddler who was trapped in an abandoned well for several days. Forty percent of the respondents said that they had followed the news of the 1987 stock market plunge avidly, as had 37 percent for accounts about the U.S. Navy's escort of Kuwaiti tankers through the Persian Gulf. The presidential campaign ranked lowest in mention among the prominent news events about which the respondents were questioned. Only 15 percent claimed to have paid close attention to the Democratic race, and only 13 percent claimed close interest in the Republican contest.[58]

A comparison of election information supplied by respondents' newspapers with information mentioned by them reveals roughly similar

TABLE 8-6   Comparison of Percentage of Mention of Issues and Events by Newspapers, Television, and Survey Responses

Issues and events	Newspapers	Television	Survey responses
Campaign events	51	63	0
Domestic politics	19	14	5
Foreign affairs	14	10	5
Economic policy	11	9	75
Social problems	5	4	14

SOURCE: Survey data come from the 1976 Election Survey, Center for Political Studies, Survey Research Center, University of Michigan; media data come from author's research.

NOTE: Survey responses specify the most important national problem. $N = 11,027$ for newspapers, 1,355 for television, and 2,263 for survey responses.

patterns, as Table 8-5 shows. A nationwide sample of people was asked to mention good and bad points about 1976 presidential nominees Gerald Ford and Jimmy Carter that might affect their voting choices. The similarity between media content and the public's views was greatest for heavy users of newspapers. People also remember the content of campaign commercials. In fact, voters who know and care little about the election often have a better grasp of commercials than of the news.[59] Media and public images, however, differ in emphases and richness of detail. The public mentions fewer issues and qualities and describes them less precisely.

Overall, three out of four answers people give when asked what they have learned about candidates and issues or why they would vote or refrain from voting for a certain candidate concern personality traits. People are interested in the human qualities of their elected leaders, particularly their trustworthiness, principled character, strength, and compassion. Their judgments about the extent to which a leader embodies these traits are often based on issue stands. For instance, a presidential candidate who pledges to increase aid for the poor is apt to be characterized as compassionate. The dividing line between knowledge about qualities and knowledge about issues is thus fuzzy.

The issues people typically mention as important in the campaign represent a much abbreviated and imprecise version of media issue coverage. As Table 8-6 indicates, people stress economic and social issues much more than do the media. This is not surprising; these issues are personal. People do not need media coverage to know that inflation, unemployment, poverty, crime, race relations, and environmental pollution are serious problems requiring attention from presidents. Nor is it surprising that people put much less emphasis on campaign hoopla, covered so plentifully by the media. Although they find these fleeting events entertaining, people make little effort to remember them.

Knowledge Base for Voting

Many social scientists accuse the media of providing the public with a flimsy diet of election information, particularly when it comes to policy issues. But the worry and blame are largely misplaced. Although election news definitely stresses personality traits over issues and dwells heavily on day-to-day campaign events and trivia, it does supply a fair amount of issue coverage. Voters who want to know the candidates' stands on specific issues can usually find that information. When voters are poorly informed about issues, it is chiefly because they do not consider elections important enough to take the time to learn about them. Besides, average voters' concentration on personal qualities of the candidates can be defended as sound and rational given the realities of politics. Forming opinions about complex issues such as arms limitation or monetary policies is extraordinarily difficult, particularly when experts' policy recommendations conflict. Therefore voters ignore most issues and pay attention to only a few that are of major interest generally or personally.

The kind of thing that most people can judge best is a candidate's competence and integrity. People have learned through personal experience how to pick a doctor, minister, or mechanic without understanding much about medicine, religion, or machines. They know how to judge others in terms of trustworthiness and general ability. The information that media provide most plentifully facilitates such evaluations of personal character. Even when the details are forgotten, the conclusions drawn from them and stored in memory provide a solid base for voting choices.

Although the media furnish most people with more information than they are willing or able to use, the media fall short of supplying the needs of political elites. Opinion leaders and the mass public that often relies on their guidance would benefit from greater clarity of presentation in the daily press, more point-by-point comparisons of candidates and policies, and more ample evaluations of the political significance of differences in candidates and their programs. Where resources permit, journalists should research important topics neglected by the candidates and make the information available. More coverage should also be given to third-party candidates and vice-presidential contenders and less coverage to often meaningless polls.

Voting Behavior

Does campaigning via the media change votes? The answer to this perennial question so dear to the hearts of campaign managers, public relations experts, and social scientists hinges on the interaction between audiences and messages. Crucial variables include the voter's receptivity to a message urging change, the potency of the message, the appropriateness of its form, and the setting in which it occurs. A vote change is most likely when voters pay fairly close attention to the media and are ambivalent in their attitudes toward the candidates. Messages are most potent if they concern a major and unpredicted event, such as a successful or disastrous foreign policy venture or corruption in high places, and when individuals find themselves in social settings where a change of attitudes will not constitute deviant behavior. This combination of circumstances is fairly rare, which explains why changes of voting intentions are comparatively uncommon. Fears that televised campaigns can easily sway voters and amount to "electronic ballot box stuffing" are therefore unrealistic.

However, even small numbers of media-induced vote changes may be important. Many elections at all levels are decided by tiny percentages of votes, often less than 1 percent. The media may also have a crucial impact on election outcomes whenever they are able to stimulate or depress voter turnout. This is a more likely consequence of media publicity than changes in voting choices. It has led to concern about the changes in turnout that may be produced by broadcasts that predict election results before voting has ended. In the 1980 presidential election, for instance, NBC projected candidate Reagan as the winner at 8:15 P.M. Eastern Standard Time, several hours before the polls closed on the West Coast. This prediction could have reduced the late turnout on the West Coast, affecting presidential, congressional, and state contests. Despite several investigations of the problem, the precise impact of early forecasts of election outcomes remains disputed. Current evidence indicates that the effects, if they do occur, have rarely been substantial.[60]

Attempts to stop immediate dissemination of projections of winners and losers have run afoul of First Amendment free speech guarantees. This may explain why the laws passed in more than half of the states to restrain exit polling are seldom enforced.[61] Congress has tried three times, starting in 1986, to pass a Uniform Poll Closing Act. Although the measure has thus far failed to pass, prospects for ultimate success are good. The major television networks have pledged to refrain from projecting the outcome of a presidential election until the polls have closed. The concern about the impact of exit polls and early forecasts seems overdrawn. Voters are bombarded throughout the election year with informa-

FIGURE 8-2   Issue Focus on ABC and CNN News: January to October 1992
             (in percentages)

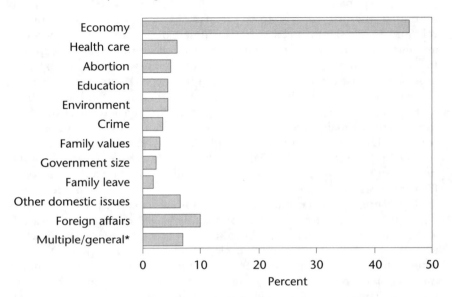

SOURCE: Matthew Robert Kerbel, *Edited for Television: CNN, ABC, and the 1992 Presidential Campaign* (Boulder, Colo.: Westview Press, 1994).

* Domestic or foreign policy items; *N* = 3,028.

tion likely to determine their vote and turnout. Why should there be squeamishness on the very last day of the campaign?

The most important influence of the media on the voter does not lie in changing votes, once predispositions have been formed, but in shaping and reinforcing predispositions and influencing the initial selection of candidates. When newspeople sketched out the Carter image and held him up as a potential winner during the 1976 primaries, ignoring most of his rivals, they made "Jimmy-Who?" into a viable candidate. Millions of voters would never have cast their ballot for the obscure Georgia politician had not the media thrust him into the limelight as a likely winner.

By focusing the voters' attention on selected individuals, their characteristics, and issue stands, the media also determine to a large extent the crucial issues by which the competence of the candidates will be gauged. Very early in the campaign, often long before formal campaigning starts, media interpretations of the significance of issues can shape the political and emotional context of the election. Figure 8-2 illustrates how media coverage can be extraordinarily advantageous for one candidate and damaging to her or his rival. The economy issue, which was heavily covered in the 1992 campaign, favored candidate Clinton and hurt Bush. Bush's strongest issue, foreign affairs, was slighted.

Newspeople shape election outcomes by molding the images of political reality that lead to voting decisions rather than by suggesting voting choices to an electorate that prefers to make up its own mind. As Leon Sigal has noted, they

> play less of an independent part in creating issues, sketching imagery, and coloring perceptions of the candidates than in getting attention for their candidacies. Newsmen do not write the score or play an instrument; they amplify the sounds of the music makers.[62]

Although voters pay most concentrated attention to media coverage just before elections, the crucial attitudes that determine voting choices may already be so firm that the final vote is a foregone conclusion.

Summary

The role played by the media, especially television, in recent campaigns is powerful and pervasive. It has transformed election politics for high offices. Major changes are weakening the influence of political parties and other political actors, dominating the campaign strategies and schedules, and placing the media in the role of king makers in political recruiting and promoting of candidates, particularly at the presidential level.

In this chapter we have scrutinized newspaper and television election coverage throughout the campaign. General coverage patterns, the substance and slant of coverage, and the manner of presentation were considered. The media placed more emphasis on the candidates' personal qualifications for the office and on the ups and downs of the race than on substantive issues. Stories are chosen for their newsworthiness, not their educational value. Structural biases abound and have important political consequences, but outright political bias is rare.

We also examined the effects of media output on the people who are exposed to it. Although the public complains about the skimpiness and shallowness of election coverage, it absorbs only a small portion of the considerable amount of information that is actually available. Nonetheless, the bits of information that people absorb create sufficient political understanding to permit sound voting choices based on appraisal of a chosen candidate's character. Minute changes brought about by the media in final voting decisions or voter turnout may alter the outcome of a close election and the course of political life.

Claims that the media influence elections very little rest on election studies in the 1940s and 1950s that have become obsolete. This early research preceded the age of television dominance and was concerned primarily with massive changes in individual voting decisions. More recent research has cast the net much wider to include media effects on all phases of the election campaign, from the recruitment and nomination stages to the strategies that produce the final outcome. In addition to media impact on the final voting choice, social scientists look at political learning during campaigns and at the information base that supports the voting decision. Television news stories and commercials, in particular, have changed the election game rules, especially at the presidential level. The Internet and its ramifications promise even greater modifications. Candidates and media have become inextricably intertwined. Those who aspire to elective office must play by the evolving new rules of media politics.

Notes

1. For detailed coverage of all phases of the 1992 presidential campaign, see Marion R. Just, Ann N. Crigler, Dean E. Alger, Timothy E. Cook, Montague Kern, and Darrell M. West. *Crosstalk: Citizens, Candidates, and the Media in a Presidential Campaign* (Chicago: University of Chicago Press, 1996).
2. For example, see Winfried Schulz and Klaus Schönbach, eds., *Mass Media and Elections: International Research Perspectives* (Munich: Olschläger, 1983); and Holli A. Semetko, Jay G. Blumler, Michael Gurevitch, David Weaver, with Steve Barkin and G. Cleveland Wilhoit, *The Formation of Campaign Agendas: A Comparative Analysis of Party and Media Roles in Recent American and British Elections* (Hillsdale, N.J.: Lawrence Erlbaum, 1991).
3. Just et al., *Crosstalk,* 151–176.
4. Walter DeVries and V. Lance Tarrance, *The Ticket Splitters* (Grand Rapids, Mich.: Eerdmans, 1972). John H. Kessel, *Presidential Campaign Politics: Coalition Strategies and Citizen Response,* 4th ed. (Homewood, Ill.: Dorsey Press, 1992), 260–266, defines *issues* very broadly. This leads him to the conclusion that issues are most important in voting.
5. For a well-reasoned argument questioning television influence, see Michael J. Robinson, "News Media Myths and Realities: What the Networks Did and Didn't Do in the 1984 General Campaign," in *Elections in America,* ed. Kay Lehman Schlozman (Boston: Allen and Unwin, 1987), 143–170. An equally well-reasoned argument supporting television influence is presented in Dean Alger, "Television, Perceptions of Reality and the Presidential Election of '84," *PS* 20 (Winter 1987): 49–57.
6. F. Christopher Arterton, "Campaign Organizations Confront the Media-Political Environment," in *Race for the Presidency: The Media and the Nominating*

Process, ed. James David Barber (Englewood Cliffs, N.J.: Prentice Hall, 1978), 21–22.

7. Thomas E. Patterson, "The Press and Its Missed Assignment," in *The Elections of 1988,* ed. Michael Nelson (Washington, D.C.: CQ Press, 1989), 93–109.

8. Larry M. Bartels, "Expectations and Preferences in Presidential Nominating Campaigns," *American Political Science Review* 79 (September 1985): 804–815. The importance of the winner image is discussed in Henry E. Brady and Richard Johnston, "What's the Primary Message: Horse Race or Issue Journalism?" in *Media and Momentum: The New Hampshire Primary and Nomination Politics,* ed. Gary R. Orren and Nelson W. Polsby (Chatham, N.J.: Chatham House, 1987), 127–186.

9. "The 1992 Elections—Primary Wrap-Up," *Media Monitor* 6 (June/July 1992): 5.

10. Richard Stout, "The Pre-Pre-Campaign-Campaign," *Public Opinion* 5 (December–January 1983): 17–20, 60.

11. Richard Rubin, *Press, Party and Presidency* (New York: Norton, 1981), 129, 138.

12. For analysis of the impact of debates, see David J. Lanoue and Peter Schrott, *The Joint Press Conference: The History, Impact, and Prospects of American Presidential Debates* (Westport, Conn.: Greenwood, 1991); Sidney Kraus, *Televised Presidential Debates and Public Policy* (Hillsdale, N.J.: Lawrence Erlbaum, 1988); and Kathleen Hall Jamieson and David S. Birdsell, *Presidential Debates: The Challenge of Creating an Informed Electorate* (New York: Oxford University Press, 1988).

13. The potency of visual information is discussed in Doris A. Graber, "Kind Pictures and Harsh Words: How Television Presents the Candidates," in *Elections in America,* ed. Schlozman, 115–141; Shawn W. Rosenberg with Patrick McCafferty, "The Image and the Vote: Manipulating Voters' Preferences," *Public Opinion Quarterly* 51 (Spring 1987): 31–47; Shawn Rosenberg, Lisa Bohan, Patrick McCafferty, and Kevin Harris, "The Image and the Vote: The Effect of Candidate Presentation on Voter Preference," *American Journal of Political Science* 30 (February 1986): 108–127.

14. Walter Bunge, Robert Hudson, and Chung Woo Suh, "Johnson's Information Strategy for Vietnam: An Evaluation," *Journalism Quarterly* 45 (Autumn 1968): 419–425.

15. Quoted in Edwin Diamond, *Sign-Off: The Last Days of Television* (Boston: MIT Press, 1982), 175.

16. Martin Schram, *The Great American Video Game: Presidential Politics in the Television Age* (New York: William Morrow, 1987), 26.

17. William Neikirk, "Clinton Keeping Image Bright," *Chicago Tribune,* April 13, 1996.

18. Just et al., *Crosstalk,* 241.

19. Diana Owen, "Politics and 'The Last Frontier': The Talk Radio Audience and the 1992 Presidential Election" (Paper delivered at the annual meeting of the Midwest Political Science Association, Chicago, 1993), 2.

20. John Bare, "The Role of Non-Traditional News Sources in the 1992 Presidential Campaign" (Paper prepared at the School of Journalism and Mass Communication, University of North Carolina at Chapel Hill, 1992).

21. The figures come from Owen, "Politics and 'The Last Frontier.' "

22. Ibid.

23. Emmett H. Buell, Jr., " 'Locals' and 'Cosmopolitans': National, Regional, and State Newspaper Coverage of the New Hampshire Primary," in *Media and Momentum,* ed. Orren and Polsby, 66.

24. *Media Monitor,* March–April 1996, 2.
25. Michael J. Robinson and Margaret Sheehan, "Traditional Ink vs. Modern Video Versions of Campaign '80," in *Television Coverage of the 1980 Presidential Campaign,* ed. William C. Adams (Norwood, N.J.: Ablex, 1983), 18.
26. James Glen Stovall, "Incumbency and News Coverage of the 1980 Presidential Campaign," *Western Political Quarterly* 37 (December 1984): 628. The effects of incumbency are similar at the congressional level.
27. W. Russell Neuman, Marion Just, and Ann Crigler, *Common Knowledge: News and the Construction of Political Meaning* (Chicago: University of Chicago Press, 1992), 39–59; Just et al., *Crosstalk,* 62–66.
28. Diana Owen, *Media Messages in American Presidential Elections* (Westport, Conn.: Greenwood, 1991), 25–28.
29. Michael Pfau, Tracy Diedrich, Karla M. Larson, and Kim M. Van Winkle, "Influence of Communication Modalities on Voters' Perception of Candidates during Presidential Primary Campaigns," *Journal of Communication* 45(1) (Winter 1995): 122–133.
30. Owen, *Media Messages,* 25–60. For contrary views to this theory, see Joe McGinniss, *The Selling of the President, 1968* (New York: Trident Press, 1969).
31. Darrell M. West contends that ads made Dukakis seem electable and clinched his nomination. See West, "Television Advertising in Senate and Presidential Campaigns" (Paper delivered at the annual meeting of the Midwest Political Science Association, 1992), 9. Also see his larger study, Darrell M. West, *Air Wars: Television Advertising in Election Campaigns, 1952–1992* (Washington, D.C.: Congressional Quarterly, 1993). A second edition is scheduled for 1997 publication.
32. Richard Joslyn, *Mass Media and Elections* (Reading, Mass.: Addison-Wesley, 1984), chap. 7; and Michael J. Robinson, "Three Faces of Congressional Media," in *The New Congress,* ed. Thomas E. Mann and Norman J. Ornstein (Washington, D.C.: American Enterprise Institute, 1981).
33. Bruce E. Gronbeck, "Mythic Portraiture in the 1988 Iowa Presidential Caucus Bio-Ads," *American Behavioral Scientist* 33 (1989): 351–364; J. Gregory Payne, John Marlier, and Robert A. Baucus, "Polispots in the 1988 Presidential Primaries," *American Behavioral Scientist* 33 (1989): 365–381.
34. Michael J. Robinson, "The Media in 1980: Was the Message the Message?" in *The American Elections of 1980,* ed. Austin Ranney (Washington, D.C.: American Enterprise Institute, 1981), 186.
35. For comparisons of coverage in Boston, Los Angeles, Fargo-Moorhead, N.D., and Winston-Salem, N.C., see Just et al., *Crosstalk,* 92–96.
36. See John Carey, "How Media Shape Campaigns," *Journal of Communication* 26 (Spring 1976): 50–57; Windhauser, "Reporting of Campaign Issues"; and Peter Clarke and Susan H. Evans, *Covering Campaigns, Journalism in Congressional Elections* (Stanford, Calif.: Stanford University Press, 1983). For an exception in a senatorial campaign, see Jon F. Hale, "The Scribes of Texas: Newspaper Coverage of the 1984 U.S. Senate Campaign," in *Campaigns in the News: Mass Media and Congressional Elections,* ed. Jan Pons Vermeer (New York: Greenwood, 1987), 91–107.
37. C. Richard Hofstetter, *Bias in the News: Network Television Coverage of the 1972 Election Campaign* (Columbus, Ohio: Ohio State University Press, 1976), 39–41.
38. William C. Adams, "Convention Coverage," *Public Opinion* 7 (December/January 1985): 45.

39. Dennis T. Lowry and Jon A. Shidler, "The Sound Bites, the Biters and the Bitten: An Analysis of Network TV News Bias in Campaign '92," *Journalism and Mass Communication Quarterly* 72(1) (Spring 1995): 33–44.
40. Hofstetter, *Bias in the News*, 32–36. For an interesting discussion of the special concerns involved in covering African American candidates, see Jannette Lake Dates and Oscar H. Gandy, Jr., "How Ideological Constraints Affected Coverage of the Jesse Jackson Campaign," *Journalism Quarterly* 62 (Autumn 1985): 595–600.
41. Byron St. Dizier, "The Effect of Newspaper Endorsements and Party Identification on Voting Choice," *Journalism Quarterly* 62 (Autumn 1985): 589–594.
42. Just et al., *Crosstalk*, 101.
43. Doris A. Graber and David Weaver, "Presidential Performance Criteria: The Missing Element in Election Coverage," *The Harvard International Journal of Press/Politics* 1(1) (Winter 1996): 7–32.
44. Just et al., *Crosstalk,*, 104–112.
45. Quoted in Anthony King, "How Not to Select Presidential Candidates: A View from Europe," in *The American Elections of 1980,* ed. Austin Ranney (Washington, D.C.: American Enterprise Institute, 1981), 305.
46. Typecasts have been extracted from Michael Robinson, "A Statesman Is a Dead Politician, Candidate Images on Network News," in *What's News: The Media in American Society,* ed. Elie Abel (San Francisco: Institute for Contemporary Studies, 1981), 178–182.
47. Quoted in *Media Monitor,* March–April 1996, 6.
48. F. Christopher Arterton, "The Media Politics of Presidential Campaigns," in *Race for the Presidency,* 36.
49. Benjamin I. Page, *Choices and Echoes in Presidential Elections: Rational Man and Electoral Democracy* (Chicago: University of Chicago Press, 1978), chap. 6.
50. Thomas E. Patterson, "Television and Election Strategy," in *The Communications Revolution in Politics,* ed. Gerald Benjamin (New York: Academy of Political Science, 1982), 28.
51. Robinson, "The Media in 1980," 191.
52. Edie N. Goldenberg and Michael W. Traugott, *Campaigning for Congress* (Washington, D.C.: CQ Press, 1984), 127–128. Also see Clarke and Evans, *Covering Campaigns,* 57–72.
53. Timothy E. Cook, *Making Laws and Making News: Media Strategies in the U.S. House of Representatives* (Washington, D.C.: Brookings Institution, 1989), 107.
54. Thomas Patterson, *The Mass Media Election: How Americans Choose Their President,* 3d ed. (New York: Praeger, 1988), 250. Also see Eric R. A. N. Smith, *The Unchanging American Voter* (Berkeley, California: University of California Press, 1989).
55. Milton Lodge and Patrick Stroh, "Inside the Mental Voting Booth: An Impression-Driven Process Model of Candidate Evaluation," in *Explorations in Political Psychology,* ed. Shanto Iyengar and William J. McGuire (Durham, N.C.: Duke University Press, 1993).
56. Michael X. Delli Carpini and Scott Keeter, *What Americans Know about Politics and Why It Matters* (New Haven, Conn.: Yale University Press, 1996), 4.
57. Doris A. Graber, *Processing the News: How People Tame the Information Tide,* 2d ed. (Lanham, Md.: University Press of America, 1993), 140.
58. "The Girl in the Well Outpolls the Men in the Race," *New York Times,* November 19, 1987.

59. Owen reports that more than 90 percent of a sample of sophisticated voters remembered the major 1988 commercials. *Media Messages in American Presidential Elections,* 45.
60. Paul Wilson, "Election Night 1980 and the Controversy over Early Projections," in *Television Coverage,* ed. Adams, 152–153; Percy H. Tannenbaum and Leslie J. Kostrich, *Turned-On TV/Turned-Off Voters: Policy Options for Election Projections* (Beverly Hills, Calif.: Sage, 1983); and Paul J. Lavrakas and Jack K. Holley, eds., *Polls and Presidential Election Campaign News Coverage: 1988* (Evanston, Ill.: Northwestern University Press, 1988).
61. For a discussion of how state laws have fared in the courts, see Stephen Bates, "Lawful Exits: The Court Considers Election Day Polls," *Public Opinion* 8 (Summer 1986): 53–54.
62. Leon V. Sigal, "Newsmen and Campaigners: Organization Men Make the News," *Political Science Quarterly* 93 (Fall 1978): 465–470.

Readings

Arterton, F. Christopher. *Media Politics: The News Strategies of Presidential Campaigns.* Lexington, Mass.: Heath, 1984.
Clarke, Peter, and Susan H. Evans. *Covering Campaigns: Journalism in Congressional Elections.* Stanford, Calif.: Stanford University Press, 1983.
Ferejohn, John A., and James H. Kuklinski. *Information and Democratic Processes.* Urbana: University of Illinois Press, 1990.
Hacker, Kenneth L., ed. *Candidate Images in Presidential Elections.* Westport, Conn.: Praeger, 1995.
Just, Marion R., Ann N. Crigler, Dean E. Alger, Timothy E. Cook, Montague Kern, and Darrell M. West. *Crosstalk: Citizens, Candidates, and the Media in a Presidential Campaign.* Chicago: University of Chicago Press, 1996.
Kerbel, Matthew Robert. *Edited for Television: CNN, ABC, and the 1992 Presidential Campaign.* Boulder, Colo.: Westview Press, 1994.
Kern, Montague. *30–Second Politics: Political Advertising in the Eighties.* New York: Praeger, 1989.
Owen, Diana. *Media Messages in American Presidential Elections.* Westport, Conn.: Greenwood, 1991.
Patterson, Thomas. *Out Of Order.* New York: Alfred A. Knopf, 1993.
Semetko, Holli A., Jay G. Blumler, Michael Gurevitch, David Weaver, with Steve Barkin and G. Cleveland Wilhoit. *The Formation of Campaign Agendas: A Comparative Analysis of Party and Media Roles in Recent American and British Elections.* Hillsdale, N.J.: Lawrence Erlbaum, 1991.
West, Darrell M. *Air Wars: Television Advertising in Election Campaigns, 1952–1992.* Washington, D.C.: Congressional Quarterly, 1993.

The Struggle for Control: News from the Presidency and Congress

SPEAKERS OF THE U.S. HOUSE OF REPRESENTATIVES rarely get much attention from the media. On average, each network mentioned Democratic Speaker Thomas Foley 10.4 times a year, less than once a month from June 1993 to June 1994. The amount of coverage changed dramatically when Republican Newt Gingrich became Speaker of the House in January 1995. Gingrich, a brilliant political strategist, knew the importance of attracting media attention as a propellant to power. *New York Times* reporter Katharine Q. Seelye credits him with having "an astute sense of reporters' needs. He understands the potential of the new technology, including satellites and computers, and enjoys ready access to the levers of the 'alternative' outlets."[1]

Like any ambitious American politician at the turn of the twenty-first century, Gingrich deemed an effective media strategy essential to focus attention on himself and on the agenda of his party. Using high octane, quotable language full of emotional symbolism and unhedged claims assured him a place in the media limelight, which permitted him to put his own spin on issues and set the agenda to which Democrats had to respond. The upshot was that he received more media coverage than any previous Speaker. He even seemed to eclipse the president in media prominence at one time. When the media's love affair with the Speaker cooled and media attacks diminished his stature, his political influence took a nose dive as well.

Why do top level political leaders throughout the world put so much energy into their media strategies when, in the end, the media may be their undoing? Why do they expose themselves to frequently hostile interrogations by journalists who routinely write stories attacking them and their policies? The answer is that politicians desperately need the media to achieve their goals. They know that the media need them as much as or more than the politicians need the media to get information for important stories. They both hope that their interdependence will temper their love-hate relationship. The two institutions have conflicting goals and missions and operate under different constraints. Therefore, they cannot live comfortably with each other, yet they dare not part company.[2]

The Adversarial Relationship

To gain and retain public support and maintain their power, executives and legislators want to influence what information is passed on to the public and to other officials. They want to define situations and project images in their own way to further their objectives. Newspeople, however, have different goals. They feel bound by the economics of the news business to present exciting stories that will attract large audiences. This often means prying into conflict, controversy, or ordinary wheeling and dealing—matters that government officials would like to keep quiet. Government wants its portrait taken from the most flattering angle; at the least it wants to avoid an unflattering picture. The media, eager to maximize audience size, prefer candid shots that show government at its worst.

In this chapter we will take a closer look at the interrelationship of the media and the executive and legislative branches of government at the national level. The interface of the media and the court system and subnational levels of government are targeted in the next chapter. Casual as well as systematic observations readily establish that the media devote a great deal of attention to the affairs of the national government, particularly the presidency. As Table 9-1 shows, during the twelve-month span from August 1994 to July 1995, the early evening news broadcasts of ABC, CBS, and NBC ran an average of 107 network television stories per month about some aspect of the presidency. This amounted to roughly one quarter of all political news stories. The numbers for Congress and the Supreme Court were considerably lower, with a monthly average of 24 congressional stories and a monthly average of 5 stories on the Supreme Court. However, congressional stories would nearly double if stories devoted to individual members, such as former Senate majority leader Bob Dole or Speaker Gingrich, were added.

Table 9-1 indicates that coverage was unevenly distributed with several peaks and valleys for each of the branches of government. Compared

TABLE 9-1   Evening Network News Coverage of the Three Branches of
Government: August 1994 to July 1995 (comparison data
for July 1990 to June 1991)

Month	President		Congress		Supreme Court	
	N	Time	*N*	Time	*N*	Time
1994						
August	69	2:11	42	1:56	1	0:01
September	90	6:00	20	0:57	0	0:00
October	27	0:37	23	1:00	4	0:04
November	103	4:37	21	0:38	8	0:17
December	92	3:47	25	0:57	0	0:00
1995						
January	67	2:46	53	2:11	7	0:05
February	171	4:32	18	0:34	2	0:03
March	116	4:01	11	0:15	2	0:04
April	134	6:05	13	0:37	8	0:10
May	163	6:50	19	0:37	7	0:13
June	131	5:22	20	0:42	16	0:30
July	125	5:29	17	0:45	2	0:03
Total	1,288	52:17	282	11:09	57	1:30
Monthly average	107	4:22	24	0:56	5	0:08
Comparison data	131	8:04	92	3:06	12	0:27

SOURCE: Compiled by the author from the Vanderbilt Television News Archives Indexes.
NOTE: Three major networks have been combined; time is listed in hours and minutes.

to the Bush presidency, the figures for the Clinton presidency represent a
sizable drop in attention to all three branches of government. There are
fewer stories and they are considerably shorter. Differences among the
three networks in number of stories and time allotments were minimal for
the Supreme Court but considerably larger for the president and Congress, as Table 9-2 indicates. The president's share of television time
amounted to roughly 80 percent, compared to 17 percent for Congress
and 2 percent for the Supreme Court.

Newspaper coverage patterns resembled television, but similarity in
patterns does not mean that various media organizations project identical images of public officials. For example, when a local newspaper, an
elite newspaper, and network television covered a proposal by President
Ronald Reagan to cut taxes and the president's 1984 trip to Europe,
three different sets of images emerged from the stories.[3] The *Durham*

TABLE 9-2   Evening Network News Coverage of the Three Branches of
Government in Percentage of Network Time: August 1994
to July 1995

Network	President	Congress	Supreme Court
ABC	75.5	22.0	2.5
CBS	81.1	16.6	2.3
NBC	84.2	13.5	2.3
Average	80.3	17.3	2.4

SOURCE: Compiled by the author from Vanderbilt Television News Archives Indexes.

NOTE: *N* for ABC = 1,350 minutes; *N* for CBS = 1,270 minutes; *N* for NBC = 1,219 minutes.

Morning Herald, a local paper with limited resources for independent
news analysis, presented accounts drawn largely from the wire services.
These stories featured the themes, ideas, and perspectives provided by
the White House and cast the president and the events into a favorable
light. Although the elite *New York Times* reported the White House version of events, it subjected White House reports to critical analysis. The
views of prominent foes of the president and his policies were given
ample space. This created a much less rosy impression of the state of
affairs. The "CBS Evening News" presented a more mixed picture. Verbal
images were predominantly negative, whereas visual images, based on
presidentially controlled photo opportunities, were highly favorable.
Audiences for these three news sources thus were informed about the
same events, but the tint of the interpretive lenses varied.

The Media and the Executive Branch

Four Major Functions

The media perform four major functions for government executives.[4] First, they *inform them about current events,* including developments in other parts of the government. This information sets the scene
for policies. When the media highlight problems such as environmental
hazards or growing homelessness, major or minor executive action often
follows. Not infrequently, media furnish daily news more quickly than
bureaucratic channels. Stories about foreign affairs often reach presidents
faster through the *New York Times* or CNN than through State Department
bulletins that must be coded and then decoded.

Second, the media *keep executive branch officials attuned to the public's major concerns.* They do this directly by reporting on public opinion and indirectly by featuring the stories likely to shape public opinion. Public officials assume that newspeople keep in touch with popular concerns, which are then reflected in their stories. Readers and viewers, in turn, take their cues about what is important from the media.

Third, the media *enable executives to convey their messages to the general public as well as to political elites* within and outside of government. These channels of communication, to which presidents have fairly ready access, provide unparalleled opportunities to explain administration policies. Political elites need them as much as the public does because there is no effective communication system that directly links government officials dispersed throughout the country. As John Kenneth Galbraith has noted:

> Nearly all of our political comment originates in Washington. Washington politicians, after talking things over with each other, relay misinformation to Washington journalists who, after further intramural discussion, print it where it is thoughtfully read by the same politicians. It is the only completely successful system for the recycling of garbage that has yet been devised.[5]

Political elites also use media channels to publicly attack opponents' positions and force them to take stands they may want to avoid.

Fourth, the media *allow chief executives to remain in full public view on the political stage,* keeping their human qualities and professional skills on almost constant display. Newspapers, television, and radio supply a steady stream of commentary about a president's daily routines. Coverage of personal life may be extensive. For instance, when President Reagan was recovering from gunshot wounds in 1981 several daily news briefings kept the public apprised of his progress. The media dutifully reported intimate details of the president's condition, including his mood, his tolerance of various medical procedures, and his daily diet. Beyond providing human interest tidbits, this coverage was intended to reassure the public that it was fully informed about the president's disability and his fitness to continue his official functions. Human interest stories help to forge close personal ties between people and their leaders and may contribute to the relation of trust that turns people into willing followers. They may also diminish the president's stature by making it obvious that he is a quite ordinary human being, despite the majesty of his office.

Media Impact

The political significance of the relationship between the media and the executive branch is much greater than the few functions just described. Media coverage is the very lifeblood of politics because it shapes the perceptions that form the reality on which political action is based. Media do more than depict the political environment; they *are* the political environment. Because direct contact with political actors and situations is limited, media images define people and situations for nearly all participants in the political process. The quantity of such images is rising thanks to new technologies such as e-mail, electronic polls, and Internet discussion groups.

As we saw in previous chapters, the age of television politics that began in the 1950s has vastly enhanced media impact and hence media power. In the past a story might have caused ripples on the political seas when thousands of people in one corner of the country read it in the paper or heard it on the radio. Today that same story can cause political tidal waves when millions worldwide see and hear it simultaneously on television screens so that politicians feel compelled to react to it. Politicians now can visit with millions of potential followers in their living rooms, creating the kinds of emotional ties that hitherto came only from personal contact. Electronic contacts may affect the political future of a member of Congress more than service on an important congressional committee.

Television has tipped the political scales of power among the three branches of government in favor of the presidency, but increased coverage of Congress has begun to reverse the imbalance. We have already described how strongly the news media influence who becomes eligible for presidential office and how profoundly they affect the conduct and outcome of elections. After elections the success of presidential policies, the length, vigor, and effectiveness of a president's political life, and the general level of support for the political system depend heavily on the images that the media convey. Changes in the president's approval ratings are highly correlated with the favorability of news stories.[6] For President Clinton Gallup Polls and good and bad press appraisals showed a correlation.

Support for the Vietnam War ebbed after television news showed and condemned American marines leveling Vietnamese villages and reported massacres of Vietnamese civilians by American troops. Television news generated "greater receptivity to darker news about Vietnam.... It was the end of the myth that we were different, that we were better."[7] Television also bestowed respectability on vocal opponents of the war by publicizing antiwar activities. President Lyndon B. Johnson considered it hopeless to try to recapture public support for the war after Walter Cronkite proclaimed in 1968 that the war could not be won. As David Halberstam put it, "It was the first time in American history a war had been declared over by an anchorman."[8] Although it is difficult to prove conclusively that Vietnam War coverage had the massive effects that Halberstam claims, circumstantial evidence supports his verdict.

The media frequently raise issues that presidents and other public officials would prefer to keep out of the limelight. Budget deficits, crumbling highways and bridges, and inefficient veterans' hospitals are just a few examples. The Watergate scandal, which led to the resignation of President Richard Nixon, demonstrates how constant media prodding can put a damaging issue at the top of the public agenda despite massive presidential efforts to downplay it. The list of major and minor scandals that the media have highlighted to the government's dismay is seemingly endless — President Clinton's questionable real estate deals while he was governor of Arkansas, corruption in regulating savings and loan associations, bounced checks at the congressional bank, tasteless jokes by members of the president's cabinet, and on and on.

Media coverage can increase as well as undermine public support for a president's policies. This is particularly important in national emergencies when backing by Congress and the public is vital. Thanks to war news that highlighted military successes and ignored failures, President George Bush's approval ratings during the Persian Gulf War in the spring of 1991 reached nearly 90 percent. But such steep gains may be short-lived because memories fade quickly and more careful reviews of the war record reveal its flaws. Nine months later, Bush's ratings were below 50 percent and still dropping. Premature predictions that wartime success would sustain his popularity throughout the 1992 election campaign proved incorrect.

Sensational adverse publicity can kill programs. For instance, the publicity following the accident at the Three Mile Island nuclear plant in Pennsylvania in 1979 predictably resulted in sharp curbs in the production of nuclear energy. Welfare programs, such as Head Start's prekindergarten training for underprivileged children or financial aid for minority businesses, were sharply cut in the wake of news about inefficient management and corrupt handling of money in these programs. Media publicity can also be crucial in determining whether a presidential appointee will be confirmed by the Senate. During the Clinton administration, highly unfavorable media publicity was instrumental in killing the nominations of Zoë Baird and Kimba Wood for attorney general. Media stories about womanizing, heavy drinking, and other personal excesses by former senator John Tower were blamed in his failure to gain Senate approval as Secretary of Defense during the Bush administration. As television critic Tom Shales said about the failed Bork Supreme Court nomination, "Television may not have cooked 'his goose' but it certainly did some gourmet basting."[9]

Direct and Mediated Transmission

News about the government is conveyed either directly or indirectly. Direct transmission allows government officials to convey their messages with a minimum of shaping by the media. President Harry S. Truman was the first to use the direct mode by broadcasting his entire State of the Union message in 1947 to a nationwide audience. In January 1961 President John Kennedy further expanded direct coverage by allowing news conferences to be broadcast live. Among public officials, presidents enjoy the greatest opportunities for uncontrolled access to the American people, although C-SPAN's gavel-to-gavel coverage of Congress has leveled the playing field. Other political leaders who are competing with the president for power and public support have tried for matching privileges with only moderate success.

Of course, even live television and radio broadcasts are not totally devoid of media influence because camera angles and other photographic techniques slant all presentations somewhat. For example, in 1985, when President Reagan visited a military cemetery in Bitburg, Germany, to honor the war dead, CBS filmed the president against the backdrop of Nazi storm troopers' graves to suggest that the ceremony could be interpreted as support for the Hitler movement. The White House, disclaiming any intent to honor fallen Nazi soldiers, tried but failed to persuade the network to film the scene from a different angle.[10]

Instant commentary following presidential speeches has often blunted their impact. This happens, for instance, when the State of the Union message is instantly rebutted by a leader from the opposing party. Likewise, print news stories describing a presidential news conference, even when they are followed by the full transcript, involve shaping by media personnel. Compared with the great leeway that newspeople usually have in choosing and interpreting information about the presidency, this type of control is minimal, however.

Indirect or mediated transmission—the shaping of news presentations by media personnel—lies at the heart of the tensions between media and government because it bestows more power on the media than governments like to surrender. Mediated transmission permits journalists to pick and choose from among the facts given to them. They routinely chop lengthy official statements into brief one- or two-sentence quotes and then weave them into an account often supplemented with information gathered from hostile sources. Television sound bites, which used to average forty-five seconds in earlier decades, now average under nine seconds. They rarely exceed twenty seconds. Thus the story is presented in a framework chosen and controlled by the media.

TABLE 9-3   How Network Sources Rated President Clinton's Policies:
January 20, 1993, to June 20, 1994

Policies	Positive	Negative	Number of sources
Foreign policies			
NAFTA	49	51	380
Russia	43	57	81
Korea	31	69	90
Bosnia	26	74	380
Somalia	24	76	98
Haiti	17	83	126
Total foreign policies	31	68	1,155
Domestic policies			
Ethics in government	46	54	147
Economy	43	57	222
Crime	35	65	97
Budget	34	66	313
Health care	33	67	623
Gays in the military	26	74	189
Taxes	18	82	146
Total domestic policies	34	66	1,737

SOURCE: *Media Monitor* 8(4) (July/August 1994): 5.

NOTE: Figures combine ABC, CBS, and NBC nightly news broadcasts.

By judiciously selecting spokespeople for specific points of view, and by structuring questions to elicit answers that fit neatly into the desired scripts, newspeople can control the evaluations of public officials and policies. These appraisals are frequently negative, especially when the popularity of an administration is already falling. Newspeople are often accused of using mediated coverage deliberately, or at the least carelessly, to hurt public officials and their policies. Table 9-3 shows how various news sources quoted on the three major networks appraised President Clinton's foreign and domestic policies during the initial seventeen months of his term. Unlike most of his predecessors, the president received higher marks, albeit still predominantly negative ones, for foreign than for domestic policies. Predictably, Democratic sources were twice as favorable (35 percent) as Republican sources (17 percent).[11]

Media Goals and Tactics

Media personnel refute the charge that they go out of their way to show incumbent administrations in a bad light. They contend that they are looking for lively, significant stories that will earn them the respect of their colleagues and the acclaim of their readers and viewers. They see themselves as guardians of the public interest who help to make government more honest and efficient, and they believe that they have a duty to report the government's problems and wrongdoings. The actors who produced the problematic situation, not the newspeople who reported it, should be blamed, they argue. Politicians who attack the media for focusing on bad news are accused of resembling the ancient Greeks who often killed bearers of bad tidings. This is what reporter William J. Small had in mind when he entitled his book about government and the media *To Kill a Messenger.*[12]

Because news focuses on nonroutine aspects of political life, journalists cover many stories that deal with isolated instances of socially undesirable behavior that reflect badly on government. Media personnel assigned to the presidential beat regularly feature harsh criticism of presidential programs, particularly if it is voiced by politically influential opponents. Minor sins are often blown up as if they were major transgressions. For example, Martin Plissner, the political editor of CBS News, dug out from the back pages of the *New York Daily News* President Carter's racially indelicate remarks that he saw nothing wrong with preserving the ethnic purity of neighborhoods. Then he asked one of his reporters to question the president about them at a press conference. Carter fell into the trap, and the story became front-page news, embarrassing a political leader known for racial tolerance.[13]

Managing a Rocky Marriage

All presidents profess to believe in a free press and to run an open government, but they rapidly develop a distaste for many of the reports about their administration. As President Kennedy told a news conference midway into his term in 1962, "[I am] reading more and enjoying it less."[14]

Presidents' displeasure with media coverage is readily understandable. Media coverage not only embarrasses them regularly and deprives them, to varying degrees, of control over the definition of political situations; it also forces them to talk in sound bites that reporters find attractive and, in the process, to put themselves on record in ways that may narrow their options for future action. Media disclosures of secret activities, such as an impending military intervention or a planned price freeze, may actually force the president's hand. Bargaining advantages may be lost through premature publication of news; trivia, conflict, and public wrongdoing may receive undue emphasis.

In the rocky marriage between the press and the president, open battles are comparatively rare. Despite traded accusations that the government manipulates and lies and the press distorts and entraps, each side is fully aware that it depends on the other. If presidents refuse to talk to reporters, as happened often during the Nixon and Reagan years, or if they instruct their staffs and major departments and agencies to refuse interviews, important stories cannot be covered firsthand. Alienating the prime news maker and source of government news is a major catastrophe for any news organization. Reporters' eagerness to get the news firsthand gives the president a tremendous advantage in influencing the substance and spin of news stories.

The media, for their part, can withhold publicity that the president needs or force publicity that he does not want. They can stress the positive or accent the negative. They can give instantaneous live coverage or delay broadcasts until a time of their choosing. In 1993, for example, NBC broadcast only thirty minutes of President Clinton's first evening news conference. ABC and CBS, despite presidential pleading, refused to carry the event. All of the networks refused to broadcast President Bush's last prime-time news conference in June 1992.

The upshot of interdependence between the press and the government is a good deal of fraternizing and cronyism between these two "enemies," often to the dismay of those who favor an adversarial relationship. Each side works hard to cultivate the other's friendship. They often collaborate in examining political issues and problems. At national party conventions, the leaders regularly provide the networks with live television feeds from different camera angles. Such coziness may reduce journalists' zeal to investigate government's misdeeds. Indeed, charges of collusion have been made particularly when media suppress news at the request of government departments or the White House. Many of these instances have concerned questions of national security. In 1980, for example, the press delayed publicizing plans for a U.S. invasion of Iran to rescue American hostages. In 1987 it suppressed technical data about eavesdropping devices designed to intercept information from Soviet marine cables.

The relationship between the media and the chief executive often displays three distinct phases.[15] Initially, there is a honeymoon period, a time of cooperation when the media convey the president's messages about organization of the new administration, appointment of new officials, and plans and proposals for new policies. At this early stage few policies and proposals have been implemented, so there is little opportunity for adverse criticism. Presidents and their advisers, eager to get their stories across, make themselves readily available to the media and supply them with ample information.

Once the administration embarks on controversial programs and becomes vulnerable to criticism of its record, the honeymoon ends. This seems to be happening earlier and more abruptly now than in the past.[16] (President Clinton had hardly any honeymoon period at all.) Controversies are attractive to the Washington press corps when they involve dramatic conflicts at the highest levels of government. They can be easily covered through interviews with Washington-based sources. The White House may retaliate by withholding news, by restricting presidential contacts with the press, and by increasing public relations activities.

If the rifts between media and the executive branch become exceptionally wide, there may be a third period in which both sides retreat from their mutually hostile behavior to a more moderate stance. This phase frequently coincides with a reelection campaign during which newspeople try harder to provide impartial coverage, and presidents are more eager to keep newspeople happy. The president may also be able to switch the focus of coverage to foreign affairs, knowing that ordinarily this is the area least likely to generate hostile coverage. There is political magic in scenes of American presidents meeting with world leaders in foreign capitals.

The ability of various administrations to get along with the media differs considerably. The president's interpersonal skills as well as the nature of the political problems faced by the administration account for much of the variation. In recent history the Kennedy and Reagan administrations have been particularly good at press relations, whereas the Nixon administration was especially bad. Nixon's Watergate problems might never have developed into a major scandal if he had been able to charm the press.

The relationship between the chief executive and media varies not only from one administration to the next but also from one part of the country to another. Frictions are greatest between the White House and the Washington press corps because they are most interdependent, and familiarity breeds a certain amount of contempt while at the same time dependence breeds resentment. The northeastern seaboard press has a reputation of being more critical than the press in the rest of the country. This is why most presidents occasionally circumvent the Eastern press by scheduling news conferences in other parts of the country and by making major policy announcements away from the East Coast. They may also make concerted efforts to schedule media interviews for cabinet members and other high-level officials away from the Washington area.

In the same way, Presidents Reagan, Bush, and Clinton arranged to visit small communities throughout the country to bask in the adulation of local audiences and local media for the benefit of nationwide television viewers. Taking advantage of new satellite technology, presidents can now be interviewed from the White House television studio by local television and radio stations throughout the country.

Technology permits public officials to tailor their unedited, unfiltered messages for specific demographic groups and to lobby for passage of their causes. The 1991 trade treaty with Mexico is an example. Local anchors in southern California, Texas, and Florida were hooked up with cabinet officials like Labor Secretary Lynn Martin and U.S. Trade Representative Carla Hills to spread President Bush's appeal for support and to counter opposition. All recent presidents have broadcast weekly radio addresses, hoping to bring their unfiltered messages to the attention of the public.

Presidential Communication Strategies

Besides circumventing the Eastern press, presidents use an array of strategies to control the substance and tenor of news. Three approaches are particularly common. First and most important, presidents try to win reporters' favor. This is not difficult because presidents are constantly surrounded by people who must have fresh news to earn their pay. Second, presidents try to shape the flow of news to make good publicity more likely and bad publicity less likely. Third, they pace and arrange their work schedules to produce opportunities for favorable media coverage. Each of these strategies will be discussed in turn.

Winning Favor. To woo reporters, presidents offer good story material as well as occasional scoops that may bring distinction to individual reporters. They cultivate reporters' friendships by being accessible, treating them with respect, and arranging for their creature comforts. To keep reporters in line, presidents may threaten them directly or obliquely with withdrawal of privileges. These may include accommodations in the presidential plane, special interviews, or answers to their questions during news conferences. Presidents may also publicly condemn individual reporters or their organizations for undesirable reporting.

Shaping the News Flow. Presidents try to guide the flow of news by the thrust of their commentary and by controlling contacts with the press. For example, when publicity about illegal transfers of arms to Nicaragua had damaged President Reagan's administration, he managed to divert media attention from the affair by sponsoring a popular Economic Bill of Rights, which included a balanced budget and line-item veto. A monthly economic bulletin was distributed nationwide simultaneously. It included camera-ready copy praising the economic successes of the Reagan administration, such as job growth and lowered inflation.

To avoid questions about embarrassing failures, presidents periodically restrict their contacts with the media largely to picture sessions.

Presidents also may space out releases so that there is a steady, manageable flow of news. If they want emphasis on a particular story, they may withhold competing news that breaks simultaneously. Sometimes a barrage of news is released or even created to distract attention from sensitive developments. Criticism by the Eastern press has been averted by withholding advance copies of speeches or timing them late enough in the evening to preclude adequate coverage in the morning papers in the East.

To control news flow and assure that the administration speaks with a single voice, presidents may prohibit their staffs, on pain of dismissal, from publicly disagreeing with their policies. In addition, they may require administrative departments to clear interviews through the White House to avoid conflicting pronouncements on public policies. Some recent administrations have insisted that officials privy to sensitive information receive approval of their superiors prior to granting interviews to the press.

Orchestrating Coverage. Ways of arranging activities to create favorable publicity are numerous. They include creating newsworthy events, heightening suspense through news blackouts prior to major pronouncements, and staging public ceremonies as media spectacles at times when there are few competing events. Political successes may be coupled with political failures in hopes that publicity for the success will draw attention away from the failure. The Carter administration reportedly timed its announcement of the opening of formal relations with the People's Republic of China late in 1978 to buffer negative publicity if its attempts to clinch a peace settlement between Israel and Egypt failed. In the same way, the Reagan administration hoped that pictures of the American marines' successful military takeover of the tiny island of Grenada would counteract the images of the 1983 bombing of American marines in Lebanon.

Occasionally news management may even go to the point of deceiving the press so that it will convey a smoke-screen message to the public. For instance, in 1961, the Kennedy administration told Miami reporters that five thousand U.S. troops had invaded Cuba's Bay of Pigs. This news was intended to encourage Cubans to rise up in support of a large invasion force. In truth, only one thousand troops had been sent. After the troops ran into trouble, officials admitted that only a few hundred American troops had actually been involved and that their chief mission had been to deliver supplies for anti-Castro guerrillas in Cuba rather than to invade the country. When reporters discovered that they had been used to spread false stories, they were furious. The credibility of the executive branch plummeted.

Institutional Settings

On the President's Side. A president can shape the news indirectly through appointments to the Federal Communications Commission (FCC) and other public agencies concerned with the media and through informal contacts with personnel in these agencies. Financial lifelines can be controlled through the Office of Management and Budget (OMB), which screens the budgetary requests of all federal agencies, including those related to communications. Control can also be wielded through the Justice Department. For instance, the Antitrust Division can challenge the FCC's approval of mergers and can carry appeals through the courts and ultimately to the Supreme Court.

Presidents involve themselves directly in media policy making through various White House organizations, study commissions, and task forces. In 1970 President Nixon created the Office of Telecommunications Policy—the first permanent agency within the White House to plan communications policy. The Carter administration replaced this office with a less powerful organization within the Commerce Department, the National Telecommunications and Information Administration. By downgrading the agency, Carter gave the impression that the White House had distanced itself from communications policy questions and would leave the FCC free from White House pressure. However, a small policy planning staff remained in the White House to advise the president. This divorce of planning from operations still characterizes federal communications policy making and has impeded strong executive leadership.

The White House Press Office and the Office of Communications. The Press Office, staffed by the press secretary and his or her deputies, supplies Washington-based reporters with news about the White House. By custom, the press secretary meets almost daily with the White House press corps to make announcements and take questions. These briefings supply reporters with the president's interpretation of events, which they then cast into perspectives of their own choice.

The Office of Communications, which has existed in various incarnations since the Nixon years, is concerned with long-range public relations management of the presidency. In consultation with the president, it determines the images that the administration needs to convey to gain and retain the approval of important constituencies in the public and private sectors and to win support for desired policies. The office also coordinates the public relations activities of executive branch departments and agencies.

In the Bush administration, the work of the Office of Communications was divided fivefold.[17] Media Relations dealt directly with media for matters such as scheduling public officials for talk-show appearances. Public Affairs coordinated public relations activities throughout the executive branch. Public Liaison set up bimonthly meetings between the president and groups of editors, publishers, and reporters outside Washington. The final two divisions were Speechwriting and Research. The goal was to control, as much as possible, news reports about the administration and its policies. In the Clinton administration, the administrative set-up was enlarged to include a Foreign Affairs and a News Analysis office as well as sections devoted to planning and policy coordination.[18]

Modern public relations activities employ many different techniques. "Focus groups and polling data are used to fashion presidential messages; sound-bites are written into the public pronouncements of the president and his underlings to articulate those messages; public appearances are choreographed so that the messages are reinforced by visual images; and the daily line is enforced to prevent the articulation of conflicting messages."[19] To spread the messages throughout the country, the administration sends cabinet officers and others on speaking tours and arranges satellite interviews in local markets.

It is, of course, essential for presidents to "sell" their policies by soliciting wide support for them and by presenting a united front within their administration. However, in the process democracy may be imperiled because, as John Anthony Maltese says in his book, *Spin Control,* "Style is substituted for substance. Complicated issues are transformed into simple slogans and slick sound-bites … timid, self-interested policymakers … shy away from responsibility for their actions and delude themselves and their constituents with their own symbolic spectacle."[20]

On the Media's Side. The White House press corps consists of fewer than seventy newspeople who cover the president regularly. Many have considerable experience and reputations to match. As a group, they are older and better educated and trained than the average American journalist.[21] The *New York Times, Washington Post, Los Angeles Times, Chicago Tribune, Philadelphia Inquirer,* and other major newspapers have full-time reporters exclusively assigned to the president. So do a number of newspaper chains, such as the Scripps-Howard papers, the Hearst press, and the Newhouse papers. Smaller papers may send their Washington bureau chiefs to the White House whenever there is news of special interest to their region.

Each of the major broadcast networks, as well as CNN, has several reporters at the White House on a regular basis; smaller networks have one. C-SPAN, a twenty-four-hour cable news operation, provides White House coverage as well as gavel-to-gavel coverage of the House of Representatives. The White House is also covered by several other all-news cable services, weekly news magazines, and periodicals, as well as photographers and their supporting staffs. Hard economic times in the 1990s have forced cutbacks in personnel and have increased pooling of resources among media organizations. Even major events, such as presidential trips abroad or the national party conventions, are now often covered by a smaller corps of journalists, whose members report to several major news organizations.

Most of the country's dailies do not have a regular Washington correspondent or part-time "stringer" to cover the White House. The same still holds true for most of the country's television and radio stations. Inexpensive satellite time, however, has lowered news transmission costs and boosted the numbers of stations that can afford direct coverage of the Washington scene. Satellites have enabled many small stations to view the activities of the national government through the prism of local interests. News organizations without Washington staffs rely heavily on wire service news. Major domestic and foreign wire services have full-time reporters accredited to the White House who cover the beat continuously, including presidential trips.

Forms of Contact

Press Releases and News Briefings. The release of news by chief executives or their aides takes a number of routinized forms. Most of these represent a concerted effort to control news output. The most common is the *press release,* a story prepared by government officials and handed to members of the press, usually without an opportunity for questions. It can be used verbatim—and officials hope that it will be. To make sure that the release appears at the most opportune time, it often has a date line that stipulates the earliest time when it may be published. In a *news briefing* reporters have an opportunity to ask the press secretary about the news releases. But because executive officials furnish the news for the briefing, they control the substance and tone of the discussion. Although most press secretaries, as well as members of the press, believe that daily news briefings are unnecessary and could be covered just as well by press releases, the briefings have become traditional.

News Conferences. Although a *news conference* may appear to be a wide-open question period, the official being questioned usually tries to control it tightly. Seemingly spontaneous answers usually have been carefully prepared by experts on the executive's staff and rehearsed during extensive briefings that precede news conferences. Theodore Roosevelt was the first president to summon reporters to the White House regularly. Before Kennedy's presidency, press conferences were not covered live, permitting the White House to make corrections before conference records were published. Kennedy, who was a gifted extemporaneous speaker, stripped away this cloak of protection by allowing live filming of the conference. At the time, press critics called it "goofy" and likened it to "making love in Carnegie Hall."[22]

The live format remains controversial because it leads to posturing by the president as well as by members of the press. It also causes embarrassment for presidents who misspeak or suffer memory lapses. President Bush lowered the risk by mostly holding informal news conferences on short notice, which made it difficult to broadcast the live event without costly interruptions of scheduled programs. The multiplication of media channels has sharply reduced the potential audience for news conferences because the president must compete with more popular entertainment shows. There have been fewer news conferences during the Clinton presidency as a result.

News conferences, as well as press briefings by press secretaries, often begin with a lengthy statement designed to set the tone. There may be advance notice to selected journalists that certain types of queries will receive very interesting answers. Presidents can often control the subject and tone of a news conference by recognizing friendly reporters for questions and avoiding follow-up questions. But no president has been able to squelch embarrassing questions entirely or to deny reporters the chance to use their questions as opportunities to express their own views about controversial issues.[23] Reporters revel in acting like prosecutors trying to extract a confession of major crimes from a hapless subject. Through posing leading questions, they try to force the president or his press secretary into making statements that they may not wish to make.

Backgrounders. Some news conferences are off-the-record *backgrounders* called by high officials to give newspeople important background information that they are honor bound to keep entirely secret or to publish only without revealing its source. Various forms of vague attribution are usually permitted, such as "government sources say," "it has been reported by reliable sources," or even more specifically, "the White House discloses" or the "Defense Department indicates."

Government officials like backgrounders because they are a relatively safe way to "test the waters." They permit officials to bring a variety of policy ideas before their colleagues and the public without openly identifying with them. Secretary of State Henry Kissinger used backgrounders to submit foreign policy options for public debate and to warn foreign countries that their behavior was unacceptable to the United States. To discourage the Soviet Union's support of India in a war with Pakistan, Kissinger told reporters in a backgrounder that Soviet policy might lead President Nixon to cancel a planned trip to Moscow. If the statement had been officially attributed to Kissinger, it would have constituted a threat that might have undermined détente with the Soviet Union. Similarly, Secretary of Defense Caspar Weinberger provided reporters in 1982 with background data on Soviet military capacity to substantiate the administration's claim that the Soviet Union posed a grave military threat to the United States and Europe. Weinberger hoped that the backgrounder would deter reporters from publicly questioning the administration's claims of danger. Public support for the government's defense policies might then increase.

Unlike government officials, reporters are ambivalent about backgrounders. They like having access to news that might otherwise be unavailable, but they dislike being prevented from publishing all aspects of the story or from giving the source of the information so that the story can be placed in its proper perspective. At times reporters have evaded the prohibition on source disclosure by refusing to attend a background briefing and then reporting the story as told to them by reporters who attended. To prevent such leaks, government officials have occasionally solicited written pledges from reporters that they would keep information released during briefings secret. Usually reporters refuse to sign.

Ad Hoc Encounters

In addition to formal encounters, reporters and the president or White House staff meet informally in work or social settings. The most probing stories about White House activities often come from reporters not ordinarily assigned to cover the president. The regulars would be too vulnerable to retaliation by the White House. Top government officials, and occasionally the president, may agree to be interviewed on programs such as "Nightline," "Good Morning America," the "Today" show, "Meet the Press," or "Face the Nation." Questioning on these shows can resemble a no-holds-barred cross-examination. Executive officials participate in this ordeal because these programs provide excellent opportunities to present the administration's position to an interested nationwide audience. Besides, if questioning becomes excessively harsh, the audience often feels sorry for the targets and sides with them.

Leaks. An even less formal release of news occurs through *leaks,* the surreptitious release of information by high- and low-level government sources who wish to remain anonymous or who do not wish to release the information formally. Many leaks are sanctioned at the highest levels. But officials may also leak information that they are not authorized to release.

Sometimes low-level officials leak information to gain attention from top officials.

Leaks are mixed blessings. They can destroy the timing of negotiations, alienate the parties whose secrets have been betrayed, and cause great harm by disclosing politically sensitive matters. They also may bring important suppressed issues to needed public attention, serve as trial balloons, and permit government officials to release information anonymously. Although presidents frequently leak confidential stories, they passionately hate news leaks by others. As long as the source remains hidden, personal confrontation and punishment are impossible. All recent presidents have therefore used federal investigative agencies such as the Federal Bureau of Investigation (FBI) and the Central Intelligence Agency (CIA) to find the sources of news leaks.

A typical leak occurred in 1991 during the Senate confirmation battle over the nomination of Judge Clarence Thomas to the U.S. Supreme Court. Confidential allegations presented to the Senate Judiciary Committee about sexual harassment by the nominee were leaked to the press. The leaks led to a second round of lengthy, acrimonious hearings before the nominee was confirmed. The episode did serious harm to Judge Thomas's reputation and undermined faith in the integrity of the confirmation process.

The harm that leaks cause must be weighed against their benefits. In a system in which the executive maintains tight control over the formal channels of news, leaks provide a valuable counterbalance. President Reagan's controversial budget proposals in 1983 are a case in point. Administration insiders, eager to bring their concerns to the public and Congress, resorted to almost daily leaks of economic appraisals that contradicted the president's views. An irate Reagan proclaimed, "I've had it up to my keister with these leaks," but he modified his budget plans nonetheless.[24]

The Media and Congress

According to political folklore, the television age has permanently altered the balance of political power. The presidency basks in the limelight of publicity at all times while Congress waits in the shadows, making the president dominant and the legislature inferior. As Sen. J. William Fulbright of Arkansas told Congress in 1970, "Television has done as much to expand the powers of the President as would a constitutional amendment formally abolishing the co-equality of the three branches of government."[25]

Image Versus Reality

If one probes beyond these impressions to the underlying facts, the situation appears less clear. When coverage of areas of legislative concerns is added to coverage that mentions Congress explicitly, Congress and the presidency receive roughly the same amount of national news attention. Moreover, it must be remembered that the bulk of coverage of Congress comes through stories about individual members published in their home states. Although local coverage does not generally attract national attention, it is politically crucial for each member.

Table 9-4 presents a comparison of ten issues that emerged for television coverage of the president and Congress when issues were tallied from August 1994 to July 1995. The scores represent a combination of offerings by ABC, CBS, and NBC. Besides showing the number of stories in each category and the length of broadcast time devoted to them, the table also records whether the story appeared in the first, second, or last ten-minute segment of the broadcast. It also indicates the six issues covered prominently for both institutions and the four issues unique to each. The three networks showed almost identical patterns in the types of issues selected for stories about the presidency and Congress and in the placement of stories within broadcast segments. Congress stories generally fared worse in terms of prominent placement and numbers and length of stories than news linked to the presidency. However, the networks differed in the total amounts of time allotted to particular stories. Each network devoted considerably more time to presidential than to congressional stories, confirming that "435 members of the House and 100 members of the Senate compete for the crumbs of network time left after the president has got his share."[26]

Why does Congress fare worse than the presidency? There are several reasons. Most importantly, the presidency makes a better media target because it is a single-headed institution readily personified, filmed, and recorded in the visible person of the chief executive. This gives media audiences a familiar, easily dramatized focus of attention. Even stories originating from congressional sources frequently feature the president as the main actor. A president is like a superstar surrounded by a cast of supporting actors. As the personification of the nation, the president can usually command national television or radio time, often at prime time and simultaneously on all major networks. During a recent ten-year period, three out of eleven congressional requests for television coverage were granted, compared with forty-four out of forty-five for the president.[27]

In contrast to the presidency, Congress is a many-headed Hydra with no single widely familiar personal focus. Its activities are conducted simul-

TABLE 9-4   Top Ten Issues on Network Evening News about the President and
             Congress: August 1994 to July 1995

Issue	Story rank[a] 1	2	3	Time	N	% of N
President						
Bosnia[b]	60	32	8	7:13	142	11.0
Health care	63	22	5	4:20	95	7.4
Crime bill	79	16	6	3:18	77	6.0
Budget	67	16	16	2:47	61	4.9
Russia[b]	44	46	10	2:10	45	3.5
Oklahoma City bombing	76	11	13	2:03	42	3.3
Economy[b]	58	24	18	1:56	41	3.2
Haiti	80	5	15	1:40	36	2.8
U.S. elections	69	28	4	1:39	35	2.7
Welfare reform[b]	64	18	18	0:58	22	1.7
Average (total)	66	22	11	(28:04)	(596)	(46.5)
Congress						
U.S. elections	47	32	21	1:53	34	12.1
Budget	42	46	13	1:04	24	8.5
Crime bill	88	12	0	0:51	17	6.0
Health care	38	31	31	0:44	16	5.7
Oklahoma City bombing	78	14	7	0:40	14	5.0
Contract with America[b]	39	39	22	0:36	13	4.6
Balanced Budget Amendment[b]	50	30	20	0:21	10	3.5
Whitewater scandal[b]	88	11	0	0:20	9	3.2
Haiti	57	29	14	0:17	7	2.5
Unfunded mandates law[b]	33	67	0	0:13	6	2.1
Average (total)	56	31	13	(6:59)	(150)	(53.2)

SOURCE: Compiled by the author from the Vanderbilt Television News Archives.

NOTE: *N* for president = 1,288; *N* for Congress = 282. The numbers are combined monthly scores for ABC, CBS, and NBC early evening newscasts. Stories are rank ordered by time. Time is in hours and minutes. Some percentages have been rounded.

[a] Position of story in first, second, or third ten-minute segment of broadcast; expressed in percentage of number of stories on particular issue.
[b] Top-ranked issues not shared by Congress and the president.

taneously in more than one hundred locations on Capitol Hill. No individual member can command nationwide media coverage at will. Even well-known senators and representatives are viewed as spokespersons for their own or their party's views or as potential presidential candidates, not as spokespersons for Congress as an institution. Their celebrity status often has little to do with their legislative activity in Congress. In fact, there has never been a single spokesperson for Congress in general, or even for the Senate or House, because senators and representatives are loath to designate one of their number as *primus inter pares* (first among equals). Consequently, most stories about Congress deal with individual members or legislative activity on specific issues rather than with the body as a whole.

Another reason why stories on Congress escape wide attention lies in the nature of its work. The legislative branch drafts laws, makes compromises among conflicting interests, forges shifting coalitions, and works out legal details. Stories about the executive branch that describe *what* is actually done are far more memorable than reports about *how* the laborious process of hammering out legislation works. Besides, the most interesting aspect of the legislative process, the shaping of broad guidelines for policy, is usually reported by the media as part of the work of the executive branch. Congress, to quote Chris Matthews, press secretary to Speaker Tip O'Neill, is "the Hamburger Helper to the White House Story."[28]

Congressional coverage is frequently not as useful to the public as it could be because the media concentrate on readily available stories. In the early stages of the legislative process, when there is still time for citizens to influence a bill, congressional coverage has been least ample. Coverage usually focuses on final action that merely ratifies the work of committees and subcommittees.

> Because the legislative truck has so many stops, scheduled and unscheduled, reporters have trouble differentiating them for editors, who are inclined to say, "call me when they finally do something." In the absence of a recognizable news peg—a vote on final passage or an attempted veto override—news organizations rarely expend resources on a pending issue in Congress.[29]

Citizens learn what the new policies are without being exposed to the pros and cons and the political interplay that led to the ultimate compromise.[30] Live television coverage of congressional sessions is changing this and is making Congress more vulnerable to constituent and interest group pressures.

Fearing that legislative floor sessions would present an unedifying, boring spectacle, Congress resisted live radio and television coverage of most sessions until the late 1970s. Prior to 1979 only selected committee hearings were televised, primarily those involving spicy topics such as labor racketeering, Communists in government, or high-level corruption. These televised sessions became highly dramatic morality plays, with casts of sinners brought to justice and congressional knights battling evil before the public. Senators such as Harry Truman and Estes Kefauver and beetle-

YOUR TAX DOLLARS AT WORK : CONGRESS STARTS THE DAY WITH THE PLEDGE.

Reprinted by permission: Tribune Media Services.

browed Sam Ervin were catapulted into the national limelight by these hearings. Many of the targets of the investigations, on the other hand, were harmed by the damaging publicity, even when they were later officially exonerated of any misdeeds. Few ordinary congressional sessions could provide comparable drama. As the *Philadelphia Inquirer* noted after the hearings on organized crime conducted by Senator Kefauver's committee, there is simply "no show like watching people thrown to the lions."[31]

In 1979 the House of Representatives lifted the prohibition on televising its floor sessions. The action was prompted in part by the desire to counterbalance the political advantages reaped by the executive branch from heavy media attention. House sessions began to be telecast by a House-run closed circuit system. The rules for coverage are strict: only the member speaking may be filmed, *not* the listeners unless the Speaker decrees otherwise. This stipulation bars the public from seeing the typically near-empty House chamber and inattentive members. Commercial, cable, and public television systems have access to the House broadcasts but rarely cover them. The broadcasts have received their widest dissemination through live gavel-to-gavel coverage by C-SPAN. Repeated attempts to allow C-SPAN to do its own, more flexible filming have failed.

In 1986 the Senate finally followed suit and permitted live coverage of its proceedings. It was prodded by the concern that the Senate was "fast becoming the invisible half of Congress," in the words of Sen. Robert Byrd (D-W.Va.). Byrd thus phrased the political rationale: "We cannot hold our own with the White House and the House of Representatives when it comes to news coverage of the important issues of the day."[32]

Televised sessions have not changed the publicity balance between the president and Congress. For these reasons, Congress has not become a first-rate "show." A few interesting and unexpected results of congressional coverage have been reported, however. Representatives themselves are apparently among the most avid watchers of House coverage because the television cameras permit them to monitor sessions that they would otherwise miss. Now they can keep up on floor action and issues reported by committees other than their own. Members of Congress are generally unable to edit their videotaped remarks before they are broadcast, unlike their statements in the *Congressional Record*. This has made the legislators more deliberate in their televised utterances. They do not wish to create images that may haunt their careers. Rather they use their appearances to create favorable images for themselves and their pet political projects.

Brief, quotable statements made by members in time to appear on the evening news have multiplied. Some members have claimed that recent sharp increases in the time spent to pass legislation are largely due to television coverage. More members want to be heard and they are likely to take more extreme positions because the media tend to focus on confrontations.[33] The added publicity also may make incumbent representatives even more unbeatable at the polls than they are now. In addition, broadcasting may make it more difficult for congressional leaders to keep the voices of dissident members muffled. It may be harder to reach legislative compromises once representatives have publicly committed themselves to definite positions. However, there is no solid proof thus far that television coverage has harmed consensus-building in the chamber.

Writing Congress Stories

Newspeople assigned to the congressional beat use general criteria of newsworthiness and gatekeeping to decide who and what will be covered and who and what will be ignored. Exciting, novel, or controversial topics that can be made personally relevant to the public and be simply presented have precedence over recurrent complex and mundane problems, such as congressional reorganization or the annual farm bill. Orderly, dispassionate debate usually is passed over in favor of purple rhetoric and wild accusations that can produce catchy headlines. Heated confrontations are more likely to occur in the more intimate committee hearings than in full sessions. Accordingly, committee hearings attract most extensive coverage, particularly on television.

Because Congress is a regular beat, daily press briefings are conducted by the leaders of each chamber. Major media organizations such as the *Washington Post* and the *New York Times,* major newspaper chains such as Gannett, Hearst, and Knight, and the television networks and wire services have full-time reporters covering Congress. Some of these reporters are specialists in various policy areas. Some wire service reporters, for example, concentrate on news of interest to specific regions such as the West or South. There are also Washington "stringer" bureaus whose reporters serve assorted subscriber news services throughout the country. Specialized news services such as Congressional Quarterly cover the congressional beat in detail for professional audiences. In all, more than 7,000 correspondents are accredited to the press galleries in the House and Senate. The ratio of journalists to senators thus is 71 to 1; for representatives it is 16 to 1.[34]

Congressional press releases and written reports provide news sources without a regular reporter on Capitol Hill with much of their information about Congress. These documents are prepared and distributed by congressional press secretaries because wire service reporters are unable to attend the many hearings occurring simultaneously. Press releases enable members of Congress to tell their stories in their own words. They give an advantage to members whose offices can turn out interesting public statements. In 1970 only 16 percent of House offices reported that they had a staffer with press responsibilities; twenty-five years later that figure had risen to nearly 100 percent. Still, only twenty representatives averaged weekly news coverage on national television, and the rest appeared just once every six months.[35]

Senators generally receive considerably more press coverage than do representatives, even though an equal number of reporters cover both houses. On network television, stories about senators outnumber those about representatives almost 7 to 1, probably because senators have greater prominence, prestige, and publicity resources and their larger constituencies make them of interest to a wider audience. In general, high media visibility for senators as well as representatives hinges on serving in important leadership positions and being a congressional veteran. By contrast, sponsoring legislation or service on important committees matters little. *Who* one is obviously counts more than *what* one does. In practice, this means that more than half of the congressional membership receives no national television exposure at all. A mere twenty members of the Senate garner the lion's share of attention.[36]

Unlike the president, neither senators nor representatives enjoy automatic coverage of whatever they say and do, even though they issue frequent press releases and call occasional news conferences. However, on certain topics, such as tax policy or investigation of executive activities, congressional spokespersons, rather than the president, are routinely sought out. In addition, many members of Congress receive regular local coverage through their own news columns or radio or television programs. They usually find their relations with the local media far more congenial than relations with a national press corps, which cares little about focusing on the problems of particular congressional districts. Local media depend on senators and representatives for local angles to national stories because local slants make these stories more attractive to the target audiences. Because their Washington-based senators and representatives are ideal sources, newspeople are loath to criticize them. The Washington press corps lacks such qualms. During the first year and a half of the 103d Congress, 64 percent of all congressional stories broadcast on national news were negative, with the Senate earning a 64 percent negative rating and the House a 61 percent negative rating. Congress as an institution received the most hostile coverage (68 percent), whereas 61 percent of the stories about members were negative. Overall, Congress' press was a shade worse than the president's press during this time period.[37]

Functions of Media

The functions performed by the *national* media for Congress and by Congress for the national media parallel press-presidency relations. However, there are major qualitative differences in the relationship. Neither Congress nor the media need the services of the other as much as the presidency needs the press. The national media can afford to alienate some legislators without losing direct access to congressional news. Similarly, except when passage of major controversial laws is involved, legislators can ignore national publicity and rely instead on publicity in their districts. News about national events and national public opinion is also somewhat less important to most members of Congress than to the president. The home media, rather than national news providers, are particularly important to legislators as sources of news relevant for their own constituents and as channels for transmitting messages to the home district while they are working in Washington.

National as well as local media provide senators and representatives with forums to express their views on political issues and to attract public support for themselves and their causes. Publicity is especially important for minority party leaders, who may need the media to pressure an unresponsive majority to accede to their concerns. However, most members cannot use "outsider strategies" because they rarely receive enough coverage to greatly enhance their legislative effectiveness or reelection chances. In an average year, a third of the Senate and half of the House receives no coverage at all in the national media.[38] Once members achieve visibility, their fame often grows by its own momentum. They become regulars on interview shows, and their opinions are solicited when national issues are debated. Nonetheless, for most members media attention may do little more than make them visible targets for lobby groups. This may lead to reelection support from these groups or research support for pet projects. Publicity also may provide ammunition for rival candidates during the next election campaign.

For members of Congress who are not aspiring to higher office and who do not need nationwide attention to achieve their legislative goals, national publicity may be practically irrelevant. By contrast, favorable media coverage in their districts is essential to let their constituents know what they are doing and to pave the way for reelection. As indicated, local publicity is usually easy for members to obtain. Several members of Congress have even owned mass media outlets, which ensured them ample favorable coverage. Lyndon Johnson is a prominent example. Many members also communicate through newsletters and individual letters sent to selected constituents. Some prepare cable television programs for their district or transmit carefully chosen video excerpts from committee meetings to home district media. Still others, eager to push their legislative agendas, write op-ed pieces for the local and national media. A growing number of Congress members have e-mail addresses and sites on the World Wide Web, but most have not yet learned to use these facilities in novel ways that go beyond the types of communication previously conducted via the older media. For example, most congressional Web sites do not offer constituents opportunities to link to other electronic databases that shed light on the Congress member's work.[39]

A Cautious Relationship

Just as the functions that media perform are similar for the executive and legislative branches, so is the love-hate relationship. But it, too, is less ardent for Congress, even though mutual recriminations are plentiful. Senators and representatives, competing with peers for media attention, bemoan lack of coverage of their pet projects and pronouncements. They complain that reporters treat them as if they were scoundrels conspiring to defraud the public. As Table 9-5 indicates, they have reason to lament the little positive coverage they receive. Members of Congress resent the

TABLE 9-5   An Evaluation of Press Coverage of Congress (in percentage of stories)

Newspaper	Positive	Negative	Neutral	Editorial ratio [a]
Atlanta Constitution	9	34	56	1:2.1
Boston Globe	14	32	53	1:1.8
Chicago Sun-Times	5	26	68	1:3.8
Dallas Morning News	5	18	78	1:1.8
Denver Post	12	32	57	1:1.1
Los Angeles Times	4	20	75	1:10
Miami Herald	6	27	67	1:2.4
Minnesota Star	5	29	66	1:2
Philadelphia Inquirer	8	40	53	1:3
Washington Post	5	21	75	1:2.4

SOURCE: Adapted from Charles M. Tidmarch and John J. Pitney, Jr., "Covering Congress: An Analysis of Reportage and Commentary in Ten Metropolitan Newspapers," *Polity* 17 (Spring 1985): 480. Reprinted by permission.

NOTE: *N* = 2,299 stories, including news, analysis, editorials, op-ed items, and cartoons. The data in the table are based on content analysis of all Congress-related stories that appeared during thirty days spanning July and August 1978.

[a] Ratio of positive to negative editorials with neutral editorials excluded.

cross-examinations that reporters love to conduct with an air of infallibility. They charge and can prove that the media emphasize trivia, scandals, internal dissent, and official misconduct, but often ignore congressional consensus and passage of significant legislation. They blame the media for the declining prestige of Congress.

Journalists, in turn, complain with justification about legislators' efforts to manage the news through their professional publicity staffs. They point to members' lack of candor and to their exclusion of media personnel from many congressional meetings and executive sessions. Broadcasters also resent the strict controls placed on their coverage of congressional sessions. They are barred from taping their own stories and are limited in the subjects they can photograph.

But senators and representatives realize that they need the media for information and for the publicity that is crucial to passing or defeating legislation. They know that the media will discreetly ignore their personal foibles so long as no official wrongdoing is involved. Newspeople, in turn, realize that they need individual legislators for information about congressional activities and as a counterfoil and source of leaks to check the executive branch. Members are valuable for inside comments that can personalize otherwise dull stories. Congress often creates story topics for the media by investigating dramatic ongoing problems like auto or air-craft safety. A congressional inquiry may be the catalyst that turns an everyday event into a newsworthy item. The story then may ride the crest of publicity for quite some time, creating its own fresh and reportable events until it recedes into limbo once more. Newspeople do not want to dry up these sources; nor do media enterprises want to forgo the financial rewards generated by paid campaign commercials.

Congress and Communications Policy

The media, particularly radio and television, are aware of the power Congress has over regulatory legislation. In the past Congress made little use of its power to legislate communications policy, viewing it as a hornet's nest of political conflict best left alone. The major exception was passage of the Communications Act of 1934 and its 1996 sequel and of supple-mentary laws dealing with technical innovations and other changes in the mass communication scene. Whenever strong, unified pressures from industry or consumer groups develop and overcome the strong resistance to change in this controversial policy field with multiple major stake hold-ers, Congress' powers to legislate communications policy become extremely important. As the sixty-two-year time gap between major com-munications laws demonstrates, there usually is a vacuum in both policy formulation and oversight of administration that neither the president nor the FCC has attempted to fill.[40] Communications industry representa-tives occasionally jump into the breach. They are in a strong position to push their ideas because they enjoy a near monopoly over the basic infor-mation needed to make policy.

The communications subcommittees of the Commerce, Science, and Transportation Committee in the Senate and of the Energy and Com-merce Committee in the House also influence communications policy largely through the power of investigation. The FCC has been investigated more frequently than most regulatory bodies. In fact since 1970 more than fifty different congressional committees and subcommittees have reviewed various FCC activities, but there have been few dramatic results. Investigations have included reviews of specific FCC actions, studies of FCC operations and structures, examinations of broad policy issues such as the impact of television's portrayal of the aged or of alcohol and drug abuse, and studies of corruption in television game shows. The appropria-tions committees have wielded their power over the FCC's purse in a desultory way. They occasionally have denied funds for the commission or explicitly directed what particular programs should be funded.[41] However, monetary control became stricter when Congress changed the FCC in

1982 from the status of a permanently authorized agency to one requiring biennial renewal.

Although the Senate has seldom used confirmation hearings to impress its views on new FCC commissioners, this does not mean that the views of powerful senators have been ignored. Prospective commissioners are likely to study past confirmation hearings carefully and take their cues from them. Most presidential nominees have been confirmed. Appointments are usually made to reward the politically faithful.[42] Although congressional control over the FCC has generally been light, there is always the possibility of stricter control. All the parties interested in communications policy, including the White House and the courts, pay deference to that possibility.

Congressional control over the media also includes matters such as postal rates and subsidies, legislation on permissible mergers and chain control of papers, and laws designed to keep failing newspapers alive. Copyright laws, which affect print and electronic media productions, are involved, too. So are policies and regulations about telecommunication satellites, broadcast spectrum allocations, and cable television. The vast, congressionally guided changes in the telephone industry are yet another area of major concern to media interests.

Laws regulating media procedures occasionally have a strong impact on media content and policies. For instance, FCC encouragement of diversification of radio programs was largely responsible for the development of a sizable number of FM rock music stations. These stations were able to provide alternatives to more conventional programs. Congressional scrutiny of documentaries may chill investigative reporting. Congress probed the circumstances surrounding a documentary on drug use at a major university because the events were allegedly staged. It also looked into the accuracy of charges of illicit public relations activity by the Pentagon. Congressional failure to act may also have far-reaching consequences for the mass media. For instance, as long as Congress did not regulate cable television, this medium was left under control of the FCC, the courts, and various state and local governments.

News Impact on Members of Congress

On the whole, despite ample negative coverage, the media treat congressional leaders and Congress with a fair amount of deference and respect. Media critic Ben Bagdikian has even charged that the media are an effective propaganda arm for Congress that virtually guarantees the reelection of any incumbent who is willing to run. "Most of the media are willing conduits for the highly selective information the member of Congress decides to feed the electorate," he argues.[43] This claim is exaggerated; many factors unrelated to media coverage contribute to the high reelection rate of incumbents. Besides, the media often present incumbents in an unfavorable light and do not publicize the bulk of their self-promoting press releases. A study of the Third Congressional District in Wisconsin showed that papers published only 7 percent of the available news release copy from their representative. Senatorial publicity fared even worse. Many papers did not publish any news releases; the most generous papers published no more than 30 percent of the news release copy they received.[44] Nonetheless, there is some truth to Bagdikian's charges of kid-glove treatment.

Michael Robinson's detailed analysis of the impact of media coverage on Congress revealed several major effects. The media have increased the reelection chances of incumbents, but only in the House of Representatives, where local coverage, which is generally favorable, is most important. In the Senate the negative tenor of the national media and the greater attention to challengers seeking Senate seats have reduced the reelection chances of incumbents. Newsletters, direct mail, and campaign brochures and advertisements partially fill gaps left by mass media coverage. They also serve as counterweights to the adverse news coming from newspapers and television. Skill in dealing with the media has become a crucial talent not only for presidents but also for would-be members of Congress. They must know how to "show-boat" to get coverage from newspapers and television.[45]

Compared with the presidency, the institution of Congress has suffered a decline in image and power. This springs partly from stories that usually picture it as lobby-ridden, incompetent, and fragmented and partly from the fact that the White House has provided more exciting copy.[46] However, individual presidents have been more bloodied by adverse publicity than have individual members of the House. Thus the media have fostered a stronger presidency—but weaker presidents—and a weaker Congress—but more durable representatives.

Summary

In this chapter we have examined the relationship between the media and the presidency and Congress. Coverage is ample, but the goals of the media differ from those of government officials. Officials want stories that report them and their work accurately and favorably. They also want to dominate the news-sifting process so that published news mirrors their sense of what is important and unimportant. Newspeople, however, want stories that are newsworthy, judged by the usual criteria. They believe that their publics are more interested in exciting events and human interest tales than in academic discussions of public policies, their historical antecedents, and their projected impact expressed in statistics. Newspeople also feel a special mission, like Shakespeare's Mark Antony, "to bury Caesar, not to praise him." And, like Brutus, they claim that their criticism is not disloyalty. They do not love the government less; they only love the nation more.

Each side in this tug of war uses wiles and ruses as well as clout to have its own way. The outcome is a see-saw contest in which both sides score victories and suffer defeats, but each is most attuned to its own failures rather than to its victories. The public interest is served in equally uneven fashion. If we equate it with a maximum of intelligible information about important issues and events, media presentations fall short. But coverage is good in that it is continuous, often well-informed, with sufficient attention to audience appeal to make dry information palatable. Investigative reporting has brought to light many shortcomings and scandals that otherwise might have remained hidden. The fear of exposure by the media has undoubtedly kept government officials from straying into many questionable ventures, although this effect is hard to document. On the negative side, fear of media coverage and publicity has probably inhibited desirable actions.

Because the contacts between officials of the national government and the media are so constant, a formal institutional structure has been established to handle these interactions. The fairly elaborate setup at the presidential level and the simpler arrangements for Congress have been described. We also have indicated some of the problems that newspeople face in covering a flood tide of complex news expeditiously, accurately, and with a modicum of critical detachment and analysis.

Problems in communications policy making remain. All three branches of government shape communications policy, but there is little coordination among them. Even within the executive and legislative branches control is dispersed among so many different committees and agencies that drift rather than direction has resulted. Few major policy decisions have been made except in times of crisis, and even then the weaknesses of government structures have made it easy for industry spokespersons to dominate decision making.

The government's weakness in this area may be a blessing in disguise and in the spirit of the First Amendment. Because the Constitution commands that Congress shall make no law abridging the freedom of the press, it may be well to keep all communications policy making to the barest minimum. As Chief Justice John Marshall warned early in the nation's history, the power to regulate is the power to destroy.[47] Policy making and regulation overlap. A uniform, well-articulated communications policy, however beneficial it may seem to many people, still puts the government imprint indelibly on the flow of information.

Notes

1. Katharine Q. Seelye, "Gingrich, Now King of the Hill, Used Skill with Media to Climb to the Top," *New York Times,* December 14, 1994.
2. Joe S. Foote, *Television Access and Political Power: The Networks, the Presidency, and the "Loyal Opposition"* (New York: Praeger, 1990), 135, reports that just before President Carter publicly announced that he would recognize the People's Republic of China, he invited the anchors of the three major networks to Washington to break the news to them first. "This incident was tacit recognition that network anchors had assumed a status comparable to congressional leaders for whom this special type of briefing was usually reserved. The media stars had become a powerful force who deserved special handling."
3. David L. Paletz and K. Kendall Guthrie, "The Three Faces of Ronald Reagan," *Journal of Communication* 37 (Autumn 1987): 7–23.
4. Presidential communication in general is discussed by John Tebbel and Sarah Miles Watts, *The Press and the Presidency* (New York: Oxford University Press, 1985); and Barbara Hinckley, *The Symbolic Presidency: How Presidents Portray Themselves* (New York: Routledge, 1990). Also see Samuel Kernell, *Going Public: New Strategies of Presidential Leadership,* 2d ed. (Washington, D.C.: CQ Press, 1992). Books about the relations of individual presidents with the press include Frederic T. Smoller, *The Six O'Clock Presidency: A Theory of Presidential Press Relations in the Age of Television* (New York: Praeger, 1990); and Carolyn Smith, *Presidential Press Conferences: A Critical Approach* (New York: Praeger, 1990). Also see Mark J. Rozell, *The Press and the Carter Presidency* (Boulder, Colo.: Westview, 1989); Mark J. Rozell, *The Press and the Ford Presidency* (Ann Arbor: University of Michigan Press, 1992); and Robert E. Denton, Jr., *The Primetime Presidency of Ronald Reagan: The Era of the Television Presidency* (New York: Praeger, 1988).
5. Quoted in William L. Rivers, *The Other Government: Power and the Washington Media* (New York: University Books, 1982), 19.
6. *Media Monitor,* 8(4) (July/August 1994): 6.
7. David Halberstam, *The Powers That Be* (New York: Alfred A. Knopf, 1979), 49.
8. Ibid., 514. Also see Daniel C. Hallin, *The "Uncensored War": The Media and Vietnam* (New York: Oxford University Press, 1986).
9. Quoted in S. Robert Lichter and Linda S. Lichter, eds., "Bork: Decline and Fall," *Media Monitor* 1 (October 1987): 5.
10. Martin Linsky, *Impact: How the Press Affects Federal Policymaking* (New York: Norton, 1986), 37–38.
11. *Media Monitor,* 8(4) (July/August 1994): 3.
12. William J. Small, *To Kill a Messenger* (New York: Hastings House, 1970).
13. Jules Witcover, *Marathon: The Pursuit of the Presidency, 1972–1976* (New York: Viking, 1977), 302.
14. *Kennedy and the Press: The News Conferences* (New York: Crowell, 1965), 239.

15. Michael Baruch Grossman and Martha Joynt Kumar, "The White House and the News Media: The Phases of Their Relationship," *Political Science Quarterly* 94 (Spring 1979): 37–53.

16. Frederick T. Smoller, *The Six O'Clock Presidency: A Theory of Presidential Press Relations in the Age of Television* (New York: Praeger, 1990), 61–77.

17. John Anthony Maltese, *Spin Control: The White House Office of Communications and the Management of Presidential News* (Chapel Hill: University of North Carolina Press, 1992), 211–213.

18. John Anthony Maltese, *Spin Control: The White House Office of Communications and the Management of Presidential News,* 2d ed. (Chapel Hill: University of North Carolina Press, 1994), 253.

19. Ibid.

20. Ibid., 6.

21. Stephen Hess, "A New Survey of the White House Press Corps," *Presidential Studies Quarterly* 22(2) (Spring 1992): 311–321.

22. Smith, *Presidential Press Conferences,* 41.

23. For a thorough analysis of presidential press conferences, see Smith, *Presidential Press Conferences;* Blaire Atherton French, *The Presidential Press Conference: Its History and Role in the American Political System* (Washington, D.C.: University Press of America, 1982); and Frank Cormier, James Deakin, and Helen Thomas, *The White House Press on the Presidency: News Management and Co-Option* (Lanham, Md.: University Press of America, 1983).

24. Steven R. Weisman, "Reagan, Annoyed by News Leaks, Tells Staff To Limit Press Relations," *New York Times,* January 11, 1983. For a list of measures taken by the Reagan administration to stop leaks, see Ronald Berkman and Laura W. Kitch, *Politics in the Media Age* (New York: McGraw-Hill, 1986), 195–197. The Bush administration tried equally unsuccessfully to stop further leaks following the Thomas affair.

25. Robert O. Blanchard, ed., *Congress and the News Media* (New York: Hastings House, 1974), 105.

26. Kathleen Hall Jamieson, *Eloquence in an Electronic Age: The Transformation of Political Speechmaking* (New York: Oxford University Press, 1988), 14.

27. Stephen Hess, *The Washington Reporters* (Washington, D.C.: Brookings Institution, 1981), 99. The figures are based on 921 newspaper and 87 television stories.

28. Martha Joynt Kumar and Michael Baruch Grossman, "Congress: The Best Beat in Town" (Paper delivered at the annual meeting of the American Political Science Association, Washington, D.C., 1986), 8.

29. Ronald D. Elving, "Making News, Making Law," *Media Studies Journal* 10 (Winter 1996): 50.

30. Hess, *The Washington Reporters,* 104–105; and Michael J. Robinson and Kevin R. Appel, "Network News Coverage of Congress," *Political Science Quarterly* 94 (Fall 1979): 410–411.

31. Gregory C. Lisby, "Early Television on Public Watch: Kefauver and His Crime Investigation," *Journalism Quarterly* 62 (Summer 1985): 242.

32. Quoted in Steven V. Roberts, "Senators Squint into a Future under TV's Gaze," *New York Times,* February 4, 1986.

33. Timothy E. Cook, *Making Laws and Making News: Media Strategies in the U.S. House of Representatives* (Washington, D.C.: Brookings Institution, 1989), provides the most complete analysis of congressional newsmaking.

34. "Media and Congress," *Media Studies Journal,* 10(1) (Winter 1996): 12; and Stephen Hess, *Live from Capitol Hill: Studies of Congress and the Media* (Washington, D.C.: Brookings Institution, 1991), 117. On pages 33–61, Hess presents a content analysis of media coverage of Congress. Also see Cook, *Making Laws and Making News,* 57–70; and Robinson and Appel, "Network News Coverage of Congress," 407–418. For an excellent discussion of congressional press galleries, see Melissa Merson, "Big Picture and Local Angel," *Media Studies Journal* 10(1) (Winter 1996): 55–66.
35. *Media Monitor* 8(5) (September/October 1994): 2.
36. Ibid. Timothy E. Cook, "House Members as National Newsmakers: The Effects of Televising Congress," *Legislative Studies Quarterly* 11 (Summer 1986): 203–226; and Stephen Hess, *The Ultimate Insiders: U.S. Senators and the National Media* (Washington, D.C.: Brookings Institution, 1986). Also see Hess, *Live from Capitol Hill,* 55–58; and Mohamed Wafai, "Senators' Television Visibility and Political Legitimacy," *Journalism Quarterly* 66 (Summer 1989): 323–331, 390.
37. *Media Monitor* 8(5) (September/October 1994): 2.
38. Cook, *Making Laws and Making News,* 59–69.
39. *Media Studies Journal* 10(1) (Winter 1996): 67–74.
40. For a history on the politics of communications policy formulation, see Erwin G. Krasnow, Lawrence D. Longley, and Herbert A. Terry, *The Politics of Broadcast Regulation,* 3d ed. (New York: St. Martin's, 1982), 87–132; and Robert Britt, *The Irony of Regulatory Reform: The Deregulation of American Telecommunications* (New York: Oxford University Press, 1989), chap. 6.
41. Krasnow, Longley, and Terry, *The Politics of Broadcast Regulation,* 99.
42. Ernest Gellhorn, "The Role of Congress," in *Communications for Tomorrow: Policy Perspectives for the 1980's,* ed. Glen O. Robinson (New York: Praeger, 1978), 445–457.
43. Ben H. Bagdikian, "Congress and the Media: Partners in Propaganda," *Columbia Journalism Review* 12 (January–February 1974): 3–10. Also see Lou Cannon's discussion of "the cozy coverage of Congress" in his *Reporting: An Inside View* (Sacramento: California Journal Press, 1977).
44. Leslie D. Polk, John Eddy, and Ann Andre, "Use of Congressional Publicity in Wisconsin District," *Journalism Quarterly* 52 (Autumn 1975): 543–546. Also see Jan Pons Vermeer, *For Immediate Release: Candidate Press Releases in American Political Campaigns* (Westport, Conn.: Greenwood, 1982).
45. Robinson, "Three Faces of Congressional Media."
46. Robinson and Appel, "Network News Coverage," 412. See also David L. Paletz and Robert M. Entman, *Media Power Politics* (New York: Free Press, 1981), 79–98.
47. *McCulloch v. Maryland,* 17 U.S. (4 Wheat.) 316 (1819).

Readings

Cook, Timothy E. *Making Laws and Making News: Media Strategies in the U.S. House of Representatives.* Washington, D.C.: Brookings Institution, 1989.
Hess, Stephen. *The Government/Press Connection.* Washington, D.C.: Brookings Institution, 1984.

___. *Live from Capitol Hill: Studies of Congress and the Media.* Washington, D.C.: Brookings Institution, 1991.

___. *The Ultimate Insiders: U.S. Senators and the National Media.* Washington, D.C.: Brookings Institution, 1986.

Kerbel, Matthew Robert. *Remote & Controlled: Media Politics in a Cynical Age.* Boulder, Colo.: Westview Press, 1995.

Maltese, John Anthony. *Spin Control: The White House Office of Communications and the Management of Presidential News.* Chapel Hill: University of North Carolina Press, 1994.

Mann, Thomas E., and Norman J. Ornstein, eds. *Congress, the Press and the Public.* Washington, D.C.: American Enterprise Institute and Brookings Institution, 1994.

Smith, Carolyn. *Presidential Press Conferences: A Critical Approach.* New York: Praeger, 1990.

Smoller, Frederick T. *The Six O'Clock Presidency: A Theory of Presidential Press Relations in the Age of Television.* New York: Praeger, 1990.

Tebbel, John, and Sarah Miles Watts. *The Press and the Presidency: From George Washington to Ronald Reagan.* New York: Oxford University Press, 1985.

Covering the Justice System and State and Local News

In HIS CLASSIC STUDY OF MEDIA AND PUBLIC OPINION, the renowned American journalist Walter Lippmann likened the performance of the media to "the beam of a searchlight that moves restlessly about, bringing one episode and then another out of darkness into vision." The media were not a "mirror on the world," as others had claimed. Lippmann concluded, "Men cannot do the work of the world by this light alone. They cannot govern society by episodes, incidents, and eruptions."[1]

What Lippmann observed and concluded in 1922 is as true today as it was then. The media provide spotty coverage, leaving much of the political landscape obscured. The institutions that will be covered in this chapter—the criminal justice system, including the courts; state governments and politics; and, to a lesser extent, local politics—have been in the shadows of media coverage. We know too little about them, making informed citizenship difficult. Just like journalists, social scientists have largely ignored these backwaters of politics. Fortunately, that is beginning to change.

The Media and the Courts

Of the three branches of the national government, only the judiciary has been sparsely covered. As Table 9-1 in the previous chapter showed, this is the case even for the highest court in the nation. The pattern of sparse coverage is evident when one looks at individual networks, as Table 9-2 suggested, as well as when one scans major newspapers. For example, between August 1994 and July 1995, ABC devoted roughly 17 hours to presidential stories, 5 hours to congressional stories, and 34 minutes to Supreme Court stories.

At the federal level, judges are rarely in the limelight. They infrequently grant interviews, almost never hold news conferences, and generally do not seek or welcome media attention, primarily because they fear their impartiality and mystique might be compromised. Remoteness enhances the impression that judges are a breed apart, doling out justice to lesser mortals. At the state and local levels, where many judges are elected rather than appointed to office, media coverage is somewhat more common, and the aura of judicial majesty recedes accordingly.

There is one major exception to the immunity from personal media scrutiny that Supreme Court justices enjoy. It is publicity for the hearings conducted prior to their appointment to the Court. At times, these hearings, and the public debate they engender, have been highly acrimonious. Recent examples include the 1987 political battle that scuttled the nomination of conservative judge Robert Bork and the soap opera hearings about alleged sexual improprieties committed by judge Clarence Thomas, whose appointment was ultimately approved in 1991. Because dramatic hearings have great audience appeal, they are now often broadcast live by Court TV, a cable channel that specializes in reporting dramatic judicial proceedings, along with commentary by selected pundits.

Hearings also demonstrate how pressure groups often use the media to influence politics. For instance, during confirmation hearings for Bork and Thomas, liberal as well as conservative groups mounted a massive effort to gain media publicity for their perceptions of the merits of these appointments. Spokespersons for groups such as the American Civil Liberties Union (ACLU), the National Association for the Advancement of Colored People (NAACP), the National Organization for Women (NOW), and the American Federation of Labor and Congress of Industrial Organizations (AFL-CIO) spoke for the liberal camp, and conservatives lobbied through Pat Robertson's Christian Coalition and the Conservative Victory Committee. Tactics included television and radio advertisements, talk-show appearances, essays appearing in the editorial opinion sections of newspapers, wining and dining media personnel, and careful research and coordination work.

The institutional aspects of the courts also receive comparatively little coverage. There are exceptions, of course. The courts' difficulties in coping with the flood of legal actions, the problems of disparate sentencing policies, and the flaws in the correction system have all been the subject of sporadic media investigations. Speeches by Supreme Court justices to public bodies such as the American Bar Association have been telecast and reported nationwide. Chief Justice Warren E. Burger even consented to regular questioning about his annual State of the Judiciary speech. The news conference before the speech remained off the record, however, and the chief justice could not be quoted directly.

Although judges and court systems are not very newsworthy because they generally do not become embroiled in open battles about policies, their work—judicial decisions—does make the news. This is particularly true of U.S. Supreme Court decisions, which frequently have major consequences for the political system. For example, *Brown v. Board of Education* (1954) was widely publicized because it declared unconstitutional the separate schooling of children of different races, and *Roe v. Wade* (1973) and *Planned Parenthood v. Casey* (1992) received ample media attention because they involved the emotional issue of a woman's right to have an abortion.[2] The Court continues to be in the news whenever it rules on issues that are likely to have an immediate pronounced impact on the lives of average Americans. But the focus of news stories is limited to the formal decision. The decision-making process remains largely shrouded in secrecy.[3]

Impact of Coverage

Publicity about Supreme Court decisions informs public officials at all government levels, as well as the general public, about the substance of selected decisions. A small corps of reporters is responsible for choosing the decisions to be covered. At the Supreme Court, full- and part-time reporters combined number about fifty people. Of these only a dozen correspondents for major wire services and for major newspapers are full-time.[4]

Supreme Court coverage is difficult; the reporters must digest voluminous and often contradictory opinions supporting or dissenting from a given decision. This must be done quickly and without help from the justices who authored the opinions. Reporters' deadlines may be only minutes away and the news will be stale after more than twenty-four hours have elapsed. Advice from outside commentators, including legal experts, is usually unavailable initially because such experts are not allowed to preview the opinions. Leaks of advance information are rare. The Supreme Court does have a press office, which provides some reference materials and bare-bones records of the Court's activities. But it refuses to provide interpretations of the justices' decisions in laypersons' terms, fearing entanglement in legal controversies. However, brief analyses of important pending cases are available to the media through publications sponsored by the legal profession.[5]

Because of the shortage of skilled legal reporters, much reporting on the courts, even at the Supreme Court level, is imprecise and sometimes even wrong. Justice Felix Frankfurter once complained that editors who would never consider covering a baseball game through a reporter unfamiliar with the sport regularly assigned reporters unfamiliar with the law to cover the Supreme Court. This situation has improved considerably in recent years, but it is far from cured. Many editors do not want to assign reporters whose knowledge of fine points of the law might make their stories too technical and incomprehensible.

Engel v. Vitale, which outlawed school prayer, and *Baker v. Carr,* which invalidated many electoral district boundaries throughout the United States, provide examples of faulty reporting.[6] Stories about these two decisions in sixty-three metropolitan daily papers featured misleading headlines and sketchy and uninformative coverage.[7] Ill-informed statements by well-known people opposing the Court's decisions made up the major part of the stories. Several stories contained serious errors. For instance, the wrong clause of the Constitution was cited as the basis for the decision outlawing classroom prayer in public schools. Arguments made in lower courts were erroneously attributed to Supreme Court justices. Moreover, the media covered the prayer decision most heavily because it was relatively easy to grasp and presented an emotionally stirring story, although the duller reapportionment decision was of far greater political significance.

Many important decisions are completely ignored. The emphasis is on social policy issues, like civil rights, school prayer, and abortion, and little else.[8] During one typical Supreme Court term even the *New York Times* failed to mention one quarter of all written opinions. In the stories about the remaining 112 opinions, 49 lacked essential information. The *Detroit News* failed to mention 70 percent of the written opinions.[9] However, when the print media decide to focus on a case, coverage can be excellent, including commentary on legal issues and the long-range implications of the case.[10]

The thrust of judicial complaints about sketchy, inaccurate, out-of-context reporting is the same as for coverage of the presidency and Congress. However, reporting of Court activities seems to be more superficial and flawed than its presidential and congressional counterparts.[11] The reasons are not difficult to understand. The volume of decisions is large, frequently clustering near the end of the annual term. The subject matter is often highly technical, hard for reporters to understand and make understandable. With notable exceptions, stories about judicial decisions lack the potential to become exciting, front-page news. They are hard to boil down into catchy phrases and clichés. They rarely lend themselves to exciting visual coverage. The Supreme Court beat tends to be under-staffed. All of these factors make it difficult for assigned reporters to pre-pare interesting, well-researched accounts.

The information supplied to the public, though inadequate for pro-viding important insights into the law and the judicial process, usually sus-tains respect for the judiciary and compliance with its rulings. Most peo-ple are poorly informed about the Supreme Court, but they still hold its work in high esteem.[12] Occasionally Court publicity has the opposite effect, however. For instance, Justice Tom Clark, one of the participants in the 1962 prayer decision, complained that misunderstanding of *Engel v. Vitale* made this ruling unpopular. He blamed inadequate reporting for the misunderstanding and lack of compliance. The decision also led to an abortive movement to pass a constitutional amendment to permit prayers in the public schools.

Public reactions to Supreme Court decisions may affect future deci-sions of the Court because justices are influenced in their work by what they read and hear from the media. Media reports of crime waves, or price gouging by business, or public opposition to aid for parochial schools are likely to set boundaries to judicial policy making.[13] This makes it tragic that much of the reporting leaves the public unprepared to make sound assessments of the Court's rulings. Recent research provides evi-dence that news stories can influence court personnel. For example, the amount of publicity given to a crime influences prosecutors. When there is little publicity, prosecutors are less likely to press for a trial of the case and more likely to agree to a plea-bargain settlement.[14] The effects of media coverage tend to persist for subsequent similar cases.

News about Crime and the Justice System

Publication of decisions by the Supreme Court and lower courts is by no means the only significant news about the judiciary. General news about crime and the work of the justice system is also important in creat-ing images of the quality of public justice. Here a plentiful media diet is available, especially on local television news where nearly 12.5 percent of the coverage is devoted to the topic. Health care issues receive less than one third as much attention. Like stories about other government activi-ties, crime and justice system stories tend to focus on sensational events, often at the expense of significant trends and problems in the legal system that might benefit from greater public attention.[15]

The nature of crime news coverage and its prevalence in the media, particularly television, has long been a matter of concern to public offi-cials and the public. It is widely believed that current coverage practices deflect attention from the social causes of crime and the policies needed to curb it. Sensational stories lead to exaggerated fear of crime because the focus is on the most violent incidents, which in real life constitute only a tiny portion of crime. As Table 4-3 showed earlier, over 64 percent of the crime stories in the *Chicago Tribune* dealt with murder in a year when murder made up three tenths of one percent of the actual crimes in the city. By contrast, white-collar crime, which is widely prevalent and often threatens public health and safety, received little coverage, concealing its seriousness as a social problem. Many experts on criminal behavior contend that extensive graphic coverage of crime can glamorize it and thereby encourage imitation by would-be offenders. News stories that focus selectively on sensational aspects of the case can also mislead the public—and possibly jurors—about who is guilty and who is innocent. When that happens, guilty defendants may escape justice and innocent ones may be convicted.

If there is widespread agreement that current patterns of crime news coverage are excessive and undesirable, why do they continue in daily newspapers and on national and local television throughout the country? There are several reasons. Most importantly, despite their complaints, audiences flock to crime news, partly as an issue of personal security but mostly to satisfy a hunger for excitement. This has been the case since the birth of tabloid newspapers more than 150 years ago. When crime news makes huge front-page headlines, paper sales rise sharply. The local television news, with its heavy crime component, has eclipsed national news, which carries more serious political stories and less crime, in the battle for high audience ratings. In the entertainment world, crime shows are highly popular. Besides audience appeal, crime news has the advantage of ease of coverage. The police beat can supply a steady diet of new crimes for hungry reporters who prefer to mine a news-rich source rather than working leaner beats.

Judicial Censorship

Although news covering all aspects of the U.S. crime and justice system is amply covered by the media, there are important omissions. The Supreme Court bars reporters from all of its deliberations prior to the announcement of decisions. On the few occasions when information about a forthcoming decision has been leaked ahead of time, justices have reacted with great anger and have curtailed the contacts between newspeople and Court personnel. Television cameras are barred from all federal courts, and their proceedings may not be broadcast directly. Federal district and appellate courts allowed cameras in the court room as a three-year experiment in 1991. They ended coverage in 1994 on the grounds that the cameras were distracting to the jurors and witnesses even though appraisals of the experiment had found little or no impact on the administration of justice.

For years many state courts prohibited radio and television reporters from covering trials and other proceedings. This restriction was grounded in fears, spawned by a sensational 1935 kidnapping trial involving the baby of famous transatlantic pilot Charles Lindberg, that electronic equipment might produce a carnival atmosphere that would intimidate participants, endanger witnesses, and harm the fairness of the proceedings. To allow citizens to watch how their courts operate most states have now opened their courts to electronic coverage. Rules about coverage try to protect many of the actors in the judicial drama from undue invasion of their privacy.[16] However, the debate about the wisdom of televising court proceedings reemerged in the wake of the massive media attention to the O. J. Simpson murder trial, which drowned out much other news for nearly a year. Critics of electronic coverage claimed, albeit without firm proof, that showboating by the judge and lawyers distorted and delayed the verdict and diminished the public's regard for the legal system.

Restraints on live audio- and videotape coverage are not the only limitations on judicial publicity. In the interest of ensuring fair trials, courts also limit the information that may be printed about court proceedings. These types of restrictions were discussed in Chapter 3.

Communications Law

Judges' views on communications law are also of interest to newspeople. The FCC's vague legislative mandate has given rise to numerous court battles, as has the interpretation of the First Amendment's free press provisions. From 1986 to 1991, for example, the Supreme Court judged sixty-four free expression cases. Lower courts judged many more.[17] In an average year fifteen to twenty appeals involving FCC decisions about various aspects of communications policy are brought to the courts. Appeals are easy because the law permits any person who is "aggrieved" or whose interests are "adversely affected" by the orders of the FCC to seek a court review. But the courts, including the U.S. Supreme Court, have been sympathetic to the FCC, upholding most of its rulings.

Although the FCC's influence over communications policy thus seems more important for policy impact than the role played by the courts, it is difficult to gauge how much impact the prospects of judicial review have on FCC activities. Agencies frequently modify their behavior to avoid reversals by the judiciary. The vagueness of the power granted to the FCC provides immense leeway to the commission as well as to the courts. As Daniel Polsby and Kim Degnan have observed, "If 'the public interest' leaves the FCC in a trackless normative wilderness in which it is free to make up the rules of the game, the courts' discretion to pass on those rules for reasonable or substantial correspondence with record evidence is not less broad."[18] Interpretation of the scope of the FCC's mandate therefore inevitably involves the courts in shaping communications policy.

Covering State and Local Affairs

It is an axiom of American politics that "all politics is local." Decentralized politics is essential and invigorating in a nation that spans a continent and embodies diverse political cultures and contexts. Because politics at the national level is glamorous and important, it is easy to ignore the grassroots that nourish and shape it. It is therefore not surprising that most research attention has focused on the national level, despite the importance of coverage of local politics and local perspectives on national politics.

The Changing Media Grid

Mirroring the nation's political geography and culture, American newspapers and radio and television stations have been primarily structured to serve a multitude of local markets.[19] At the turn of the century, every large and medium-sized city and even many small towns had at least one newspaper and often more, geared to local political needs. When electronic media made their appearance they, too, were situated in nearly every city to serve local audiences. Technological changes and large-scale migration of former inner-city dwellers to the suburbs have taken their toll on the local focus of many American media enterprises. The numbers of newspapers have shrunk so that most cities are now served by a single newspaper, and many communities no longer have a paper of their own. Electronic media are serving ever larger regions. It is not uncommon for television stations and metropolitan dailies to reach people in fifty counties. Typically their domain then includes some 1,300 governmental units, whose policies should be reported because they involve important public issues, including the power to tax. Numerous state legislators, as well as several national legislators, are elected within these counties. Given the many active political units that require media attention, reporting, of necessity, is highly selective and superficial.

The Vanishing Metropolitan Focus. Because market areas and areas of political interest no longer coincide, reporting has turned away from strictly local problems to more generalized topics of interest to the entire market area. That has meant more focus on soft news like sports and human interest stories. It has also meant less information about important local problems that face citizens as well as more cynical coverage about the human motivations that drive politics.[20] Lack of information about local politics and failure to stress its importance translate into lack of concern and political apathy. As media critic Ben Bagdikian has put it:

> News distribution is no longer designed for individual towns and cities. American politics is organized on the basis of the 20,000 urban and rural places in the country, which is the way citizens vote. But the media have organized on the basis of 210 television "markets," which is the way merchandisers and media corporations sell ads. As a result, the fit between the country's information needs and its information media has become disastrously disjointed.[21]

The disjunction is likely to persist in the future, although the proliferation of audiovisual news programs transmitted via cable, microwave, videotex, and similar technologies may allow some programs to use a narrower focus. Local governments now routinely employ community access cable channels to allow their constituents to watch local government in action. City council meetings, committee hearings, and court procedures have become directly accessible to the public without the intervention of journalists. The suburbs, where such channels have been scarce in the past, are joining the parade, thereby providing more competition for suburban newspapers. However, audiences for broadcasts of local government activities are generally quite small.

Umbrella Competition Patterns. In response to major population shifts from inner cities to sprawling suburbs, print media have developed a structure of "umbrella competition" in which smaller units operate within the area covered simultaneously by the larger units.[22] Suburban newspapers have been thriving, and metropolitan newspapers have developed special sections targeted to different communities in the metropolitan area and suburbs.[23] Nonetheless, metropolitan newspapers have shrunk in circulation. In Philadelphia, for example, the circulation of metropolitan newspapers dropped by nearly 50 percent between 1940 and 1988 (from 1,344,000 to 763,000).[24]

The umbrella pattern consists of four layers. In the first layer, large metropolitan dailies provide substantial amounts of international, national, and regional coverage. In the second layer, smaller satellite dailies resemble their larger cousins but carry more local news. The third layer contains suburban dailies. They emphasize local news, much of it nonpolitical, and are a rapidly growing sector. For example, between 1940 and 1988, suburban newspaper circulation in the Philadelphia area more than tripled (from 147,000 to 461,000).[25] Though still below the metropolitan circulation figures, suburban papers are profitable because they offer an attractive advertising opportunity to the many businesses whose customers now cluster in suburban areas. The fourth layer consists of weekly newspapers and "shoppers" that are distributed free of charge because they contain mostly advertising and only a sprinkling of news and feature stories.

The emphasis on local news increases as one moves through these layers. This has happened because newspapers with a narrower reach try to distinguish themselves from the metropolitan papers and thereby make themselves more attractive to their clientele. But, because of the lack of fit between media markets and political units, most of the local news avoids discussion and analysis of localized public issues, leaving these issues bereft of essential coverage. This explains why citizens who are questioned about their sources of neighborhood news mention personal experience nearly four times as often as either newspapers or local television news.[26] The fact that metropolitan papers now must share the advertising pie with suburban papers, as well as shoppers, has been a major factor in the death of dailies in multipaper cities, leaving most of them without the kind of competition that invigorates political dialogue.

Television stations in smaller markets also tend to feature more local and less national and international news than their larger cousins.[27] More than half of their stories duplicate what other stations are carrying. Duplication is especially common for stories about government and politics, education, crime, and disasters.[28] Most radio news stations, which feature only news or a large amount of news, likewise devote more than half of their airtime to local news. However, stations in smaller radio markets tend to present fewer stories simply because there is less local news available.[29]

The Alternative Press. In addition to the four layers discussed, there is also an alternative press that tends to focus narrowly on issues of interest to people representing minority political cultures or people with distinctive lifestyles and cultural tastes. For example, many specialized media are targeted to various ethnic, racial, and religious groups, as well as media aimed at lesbians and gay men. Some specialized media are published in foreign languages to meet the needs of immigrants. Although they provide in-depth coverage of local, national, and international news of interest to their clientele, they omit news covering broader concerns. Their readers may therefore live in a narrow communications ghetto that keeps them from fully understanding their surroundings.

Specialized media also often try to generate support for issues favored by their audiences and may play a role in influencing local elections. Media serving African American and Hispanic communities are good examples. Besides having their own print media, large subcultural groups in the United States are also served by electronic news media tailored to their special concerns. Television and radio stations geared to the needs of various subcultures exist throughout the country. For example, in 1989 there were 193 radio stations targeted to African American listeners and 108 Spanish-language radio stations in the top 175 radio markets as well as approximately 300 African American newspapers.

For audiences addicted to news broadcasts, there are also all-news cable television stations and all-news radio stations that feature a steady succession of newscasts, many of them repetitive. CNN is a major player in that league. Call-in radio shows, where hosts of varying political persuasions answer all sorts of questions, often engage in spirited discussions with guests and outside callers. In 1989, several call-in shows garnered the political limelight when they successfully campaigned against a proposal for a 51 percent hike in congressional salaries. Talk radio shows have also been able to encourage or discourage the passage of referenda and other important local political issues. Depending on whether listeners agreed or disagreed with the thrust of their advocacy, such political lobbying has been praised or condemned.

Government/Press Relations at Subnational Levels

Subnational news is important for state and local politics for the same reasons that make the media important on the national scene. Subnational news plays a significant role in setting the agenda for public policies. It helps or hinders politicians in achieving their goals. It influences the election and appointment of public officials. It informs the public and officialdom about political affairs and politicians' wrongdoing. However, there are differences in emphasis between national and subnational political coverage, largely because subnational politics operates on a much smaller scale and often performs different functions. Political scientist Delmer D. Dunn, who studied relations between public officials and the press in Wisconsin, identified several important distinctions between the national and subnational levels.[30]

How Officials Use the Press. At the subnational level, it is much easier for public officials to stay in touch with each other about their work without relying on news stories. The fact that officials remain in closer direct contact as well as with a comparatively tiny corps of reporters reduces the need for formal press conferences. Although generally more accessible to reporters, they are therefore less inclined to call press conferences. Moreover, their news is rarely so exciting that they can count on decent attendance at news conferences.

At the subnational level, fewer officials are experts in gaining publicity and using it to advantage. Often their jobs are highly technical and difficult to explain to the lay public in brief news stories. When officials do make the effort to tell their stories, reporters generally lack technical expertise to judge whether they are receiving an accurate or a misleading account. Consequently, they often allow subnational officials to become unchallenged agenda setters. If the story relates to a policy decision involving major issues—for example, whether to start, continue, or stop a project, how to finance it, and similar matters—the official views are likely to define the situation with little media scrutiny. However, lack of skill to use media effectively often prevents state and local officials from benefiting from their control over news stories as much as might otherwise be expected. In fact, the public information and public relations materials they present to the media are often so poorly done that they do more harm than good.

Media scholar Phyllis Kaniss has identified six media styles that are especially common at the subnational level.[31] The *paranoid media-avoider* fears the press and tries to avoid it as much as possible. Information-hungry journalists are likely to retaliate with unfavorable publicity whenever an opportunity to do so presents itself. The *naive professional* supplies the media with information and talks freely with journalists without realizing that uncontrolled release of information empowers reporters to determine what will be published and the perspectives that will be reflected. The *ribbon cutter* is a media junkie who is heavily concerned with initiating events, however trivial, that are likely to attract journalists. The ensuing publicity may have few political payoffs. *Dancing marionettes* take their cues from media editorials and report and take action in areas suggested by newspeople, rather than initiating policies independently. The reward is likely to be favorable coverage, although the policy agenda favored by newspeople may be undesirable from the official's perspective. *Colorful quotables* excel in creating attractive sound bites and making sure that these come to the attention of reporters. Like ribbon cutters, their political rewards are apt to be small. Finally, *liars* conceal or slant information or distort it outright to put themselves in a favorable light.

In place of such unproductive strategies, Kaniss recommends that state and local officials, like their national counterparts, learn to understand the needs of local media so that they can structure the information they supply accordingly. This does not require deferring to journalists' preferences or sensationalizing news. Rather, it requires judicious choices of information for release and careful attention to the framing of stories.[32] For example, Avis LaVelle, press secretary to Chicago's Mayor Richard Daley, always tried to provide reporters with story materials selected and written from a reporter's perspective. In that way, she managed to control news flow in line with the mayor's goals while still pleasing the press.

The era of informal, inexpert handling of the press by subnational officials may be ending. Currently, all governors and most big-city mayors have press secretaries or public information offices. Like their counterparts at the national level, they try to use these offices to push executive programs through recalcitrant legislatures and to disseminate news about their activities to various political elites and interested citizens. However, as on the national level, these efforts often fail. The media may turn out to be powerful enemies rather than friends.

Eagerness for good media coverage is not limited to elected officials. Appointed officials, too, believe that they need good images to help them in their battles for funding and for support of the policies that their agencies try to pursue. A poll of high-level federal officials showed that 79 percent thought that positive coverage increased their chances of achieving major policy goals.[33] Legislatures rarely deny support to seemingly popular agencies. By the same token, bad publicity can hurt. When media frame stories in ways that suit media, rather than official goals, public officials may be forced to recast their own focus of attention. For example, city sanitation departments have been forced to concentrate on cleaning up lesser problems and neglecting more serious ones when publicity highlighted a particular situation.

As on the national level, strategies designed to win media attention from the subnational media include press conferences, press releases, staging events that media are likely to cover, writing op-ed pieces, and writing letters to the editor. Press releases, the most common form of public relations, are also the least productive because they tend to be sparsely used by media. Rates of use may be as low as 5 percent, unless the releases have interesting local angles.[34] Contacting media personnel directly seems to be the best approach, and apparently it is quite successful. Estimates are that more than half of the content of the print and electronic media originates with news sources, rather than springing from questions asked first by journalists. Government officials at all levels provide a large share of these so-called news subsidies.[35]

Most efforts to gain media coverage at the subnational level are directed at the print media, which are generally deemed the most effective transmitters of state and local political news. When governors, lieutenant governors, attorneys general, secretaries of state, and various legislative leaders in all states were polled, a majority named print media as most important in setting the political agenda, with wire services and television following.[36] Television stories are ranked below print press stories in effectiveness because they are too brief and too much skewed toward the sensational. Because state and local political news often lacks visual appeal, local television media tend to relegate such news to the tail end of the broadcast, giving it only cursory treatment.

However, more and more local officials seem to realize that television is the most important medium when it comes to mobilizing public opinion. They therefore watch closely how activities of interest to them are covered on local news to infer from the coverage what public reaction is likely to be. They have also increased their efforts to get television coverage for themselves and the agencies they represent.

How Reporters Operate at Subnational Levels. Reporters are somewhat different at the subnational than the national level, also. Taken as a group, they have less formal education and considerably less job experience. In fact, judging from a comparison of reporters' and officials' level of education in New York's state capital, the officials' level of education may rank considerably above that of reporters and the "locals" may be more informed overall.[37] Turnover rates are high and reporters are often forced to move to a different market when they switch jobs because of clauses in their contracts that forbid them to work for a competitor in the same area, thus making them less likely to be knowledgeable about the localities they cover. Such disparities occasionally contribute to strained relations between reporters and officials when they disagree in their analyses of political events. However, most of the time, personal relations between reporters and officials tend to be more cordial at the subnational level because of their more frequent personal interactions. In fact, ties of friendship have been blamed for the dearth of press criticism of official conduct at subnational levels.

Aside from metropolitan newspapers, news organizations at the subnational level are usually considerably smaller than their national counterparts. It is therefore far less likely that reporters are assigned to a single beat. Rather, general assignment reporters prevail. Although covering a broad range of events and people enhances their understanding of government in general, it also makes it more difficult for them to become experts in particular aspects of politics and to probe deeply into stories. Instead, such roving reporters depend more heavily on routine sources, such as daily inquiries at the police and fire departments, local newspapers, assorted press releases, tips from viewers, wire service stories, and the wire service "day books" that list major local events.[38] Stories with the best pictures and best sound bites tend to become leads, even when they are not necessarily the most important stories. Emphasis on the pictures may even change the thrust of stories and alter their impact.[39]

Because so few state and local stories are intrinsically interesting to media audiences, the pressure to make stories entertaining is heightened. That means featuring colorful, charismatic politicians who speak well in ten-second sound bites or well-known key officials in major cities. It means bypassing opportunities for more ample exposition of problems because carefully calibrated, fact-rich pronouncements are boring for most members of the audience. The hunt for human drama also leads to ambulance chasing by reporters, who haunt victims of various tragedies and their families by intruding into their homes and hospital rooms to get stories.

Because timeliness is deemed so important for American media, late-night newscasts try to present late-breaking events even when they are less important than earlier ones. And because most government business stops in the early evening hours, this means that late night news broadcasts depend even more heavily than earlier ones on the staples supplied by police and fire department records. Kaniss' research showed that the proportion of serious political news on Philadelphia's television stations, on average, was cut in half during the late evening news periods.[40]

Stories about government must compete with heart-wrenching tragedies, heinous crimes, and horrifying disasters. Therefore, local television broadcasts, more so than national ones, concentrate on the sensational aspects of political stories and emphasize personalities. In the process of highlighting people, the importance of events and their broader and long-term consequences may be lost. For example, in a story on city council hearings on subway crime in Philadelphia, the facts and figures provided by various experts and government officials were downplayed compared to conflicting testimony of the Guardian Angels, an out-of-town volunteer patrol organization whose members were unfamiliar with the local scene.[41]

Unlike the much fuller, less sensationalist, and more analytical coverage featured in newspapers, Philadelphia's television stations tended to accept their sources' judgments without question. The views of public officials expressed in press conferences or press releases were often transmitted without passing scrutiny. When criticism was aired, the emphasis was on presenting it as an eye-catching story rather than a full exposition of the facts.

Journalists who work in large metropolitan areas tend to pay more attention to inner-city affairs than to outlying areas. In Philadelphia, the ratio was roughly 2 to 1 for newspapers. On local television, nearly all of the political stories covered inner-city politics, ignoring the suburbs.[42] Unfortunately, suburban reporters did not pick up the slack. A look at the

Reprinted with special permission of King Features Syndicate.

contents of suburban news showed that 73 percent of the stories dealt with crime, accidents, disasters, and the like, slighting stories about other suburban concerns.

There are several reasons for "city myopia" by metropolitan media.[43] Among them is the fact that metropolitan newspaper offices usually are closer to the central city hall than to the suburbs. That makes inner-city officials and other news sources located in the inner city easier to reach. City officials are also more willing to make the trip to newspaper offices and radio and television studios that are located nearby than are their geographically distant suburban colleagues. Inner cities are also more likely to generate the kind of news that political reporters ordinarily cover, such as political wheeling and dealing, an ample dose of corruption, and a heavy slice of crime. Stories of spectacular fires are more common in inner-city neighborhoods, as are stories about ethnic and racial strife and protest demonstrations.[44] Most journalists find the city more exciting and relate its problems to events in the suburbs rather than the other way around. When reporters are assigned to suburban stories on a regular basis, they view it as akin to exile in Siberia. The smaller size of the press

TABLE 10-1   Political News in New York State Papers (in percentages)

Paper locations	Local news	State news	National news	International news	Political news ratio of total
N.Y. State (General)	19	16	45	22	46
Albany	15	45	32	8	42

SOURCE: Adapted from David Morgan, *The Capitol Press Corps: Newsmen and the Governing of New York State* (Westport, Conn.: Greenwood Press, 1978), 20–21.

NOTE: N = 9 general papers, 2 Albany papers.

corps also accounts for the lack of coverage for many important subnational stories and for more pack journalism, generated by the close contacts that often characterize smaller groups.

The Contents of Subnational News

When political scientist David Morgan classified political news in newspapers in New York State, he found that, on average, nine of the eleven papers that he examined devoted the least amount of coverage to state affairs (16 percent), followed by local affairs (19 percent). National news garnered the lion's share of attention (45 percent) and international news took the number two spot (22 percent). The balance between national and international news on one hand and state and local news on the other thus was 2 to 1.[45] Table 10-1 tells the story. The table also shows that the patterns were different for papers in the state's capital, which was the only place where state news predominated (45 percent) and international news was minimal (8 percent). Overall, political news amounted to 46 percent of the newshole in the general press and 42 percent in the Albany papers.

State News: A Neglected Stepchild

Why does state news receive the least attention when states play such important roles in politics? As we have seen, some media specialize in national news, like the national television networks, and other media specialize in local news, like many network affiliates. But few daily publications specialize in state news.

The Local Emphasis. Within states, the major media enterprises that have enough resources to cover more than local news are usually located in the state's most populous cities where local news abounds, rather than in state capitals.

Moreover, most state coverage has traditionally focused on the legislature rather than the governor. Because state legislatures have relatively brief sessions, the flow of news from the capital is intermittent. Many daily papers therefore do not make the state capital a regular full-time beat. In some cases—New Hampshire is an example—the state's media markets overlap state boundaries so that news must appeal to residents of more than one state. That also puts a damper on state news.[46]

The National Emphasis. State news is a double loser. Neglect of the state is even worse at the national level than it is locally. A content analysis of news broadcast on the major networks between August 1994 and July 1995 showed no signs that the vastly expanded national political role of the states is focusing national media attention on state issues. State news was extremely sparse on national television, constituting less than 1.5 percent of all nightly news stories. National television spotlighted a small number of states and neglected the rest. As Table 10-2 shows, some regions of the country received more ample coverage than one might expect, judged by the size of their populations (as reflected in their electoral votes), whereas others received considerably less. The concerns of people in the Middle West rated the least attention relative to their electoral votes, whereas people in the Northeast and Pacific regions dominated. The degree of discrepancy in regional coverage, favorable and unfavorable, is shown in the last column of the table. Table 10-3 provides a closer look at individual states. It shows the ten most covered and the ten least covered states and the degree of favorable and unfavorable imbalance.

From a political perspective, it is impossible to make sense out of the findings: Some comparatively insignificant states, such as Oklahoma and Arkansas, bask in excess coverage whereas more important states, such as Ohio and Illinois, are undercovered. The explanation lies in journalistic criteria. The states with the most ample coverage provided the best story materials at a place and time that was most convenient for the media. Oklahoma was the site of a major bomb disaster, and questionable business deals by the nation's first family were linked to the president's former home in Arkansas. States lacking in such attractions suffered from neglect, which could be costly to the state's economic and political welfare. Compounding such problems, state news coverage on the national networks also lacked political substance, focusing primarily on disaster, crime, and trivia stories. State economic, political, and social conditions and policies were ignored even when they had major national ramifications.

Print media coverage of state news, as judged by the *New York Times,* was considerably better.[47] Even when one excludes coverage of states

TABLE 10-2   Regional Focus of Network News Coverage: August 1994 to July 1995

Regions	Percentage of mentions	Percentage of electoral vote	Discrepancy
Northeast (D.C., Del., Md., N.J., N.Y., Pa.)	22.0	15.6	+6.4
Pacific (Alaska, Calif., Hawaii, Ore., Wash.)	18.5	14.7	+3.8
Southwest (Ark., La., Okla., Texas)	14.0	10.6	+3.4
South (Ala., Fla., Ga., Ky., Miss., Tenn.)	14.2	13.6	+0.6
Mountains (Ariz., Colo., Idaho, Mont., Nev., N.M., Utah, Wyo.)	7.1	7.4	−0.3
Plains (Kan., Neb., N. D., S. D.)	2.5	3.2	−0.7
Middle Atlantic (N.C., S.C., Va., W. Va.)	6.2	7.4	−1.2
New England (Conn., Maine, Mass., N.H., R.I., Vt.)	5.0	6.5	−1.5
Middle West (Ill., Ind., Iowa, Mich., Minn., Mo., Ohio, Wis.)	10.5	20.9	−10.4

SOURCE: Author's research based on the Vanderbilt Television News Archives.

NOTE: $N = 2,325$ mentions in news stories. Figures for the three networks have been combined. The distribution of 538 electoral votes is based on 1990 census figures. Regions have been ranked from most advantaged to least advantaged by network news coverage. Figures are rounded.

within the New York region, more state stories were covered. However, there was regional imbalance as well in *New York Times* stories, with the Pacific area again gaining the lion's share of coverage and the Middle West the least. The fact that the *New York Times* found ample story materials suggests that the networks had the opportunity to report more state news, had they chosen to do so.

Complaints about inadequate coverage must always be tempered by the realization that media space and time are limited. What kinds of stories should the networks have omitted to make room for more news about the states? The answer is painful, given the fact that audiences love the entertainment and trivia stories that should be cut to make room for more politically meaty content. Nonetheless, the growing importance of state politics has made it essential to provide more adequate coverage for the benefit of interested publics, as well as political leaders.

TABLE 10-3   State Distribution of Network News Attention, Ten Leaders and Trailers: August 1994 to July 1995

State	Region	Overcovered States		
		Percentage of mentions	Percentage of electoral vote	Discrepancy
New York	Northeast	14.2	6.1	+8.1
California	Pacific	14.7	10.1	+4.6
Oklahoma	Southwest	5.5	1.5	+4.0
Florida	South	7.1	4.7	+2.4
Colorado	Mountains	2.8	1.5	+1.3
Virginia	Middle Atlantic	3.6	2.4	+1.2
Arkansas	Southwest	2.1	1.1	+1.0
Texas	Southwest	6.9	6.0	+0.9
Rhode Island	New England	1.4	0.7	+0.7
Kansas	Plains	1.7	1.1	+0.6

State	Region	Undercovered States		
		Percentage of mentions	Percentage of electoral vote	Discrepancy
Ohio	Middle West	0.4	3.9	−3.5
Illinois	Middle West	1.6	4.1	−2.5
Pennsylvania	Northeast	2.2	4.3	−2.1
North Carolina	Middle Atlantic	0.7	2.6	−1.9
New Jersey	Northeast	1.3	2.8	−1.5
Missouri	Middle West	0.7	2.1	−1.4
Wisconsin	Middle West	0.8	2.1	−1.3
Connecticut	New England	0.5	1.5	−1.0
Tennessee	South	1.2	2.1	−0.9
West Virginia	Middle Atlantic	0.1	0.9	−0.8

SOURCE: Author's research based on the Vanderbilt Television News Archives.

NOTE: $N = 2,325$ mentions in news stories. Figures for the three networks have been combined. The distribution of the 535 electoral votes (D.C. was excluded) is based on the 1990 census figures.

As Table 10-4 shows, the public does realize the importance of state news, judging from a Middle Western telephone survey conducted in 1987. The respondents were asked to rate the importance of various types of news in their choice of programs. Local news was in first place when one combines "very important" and "important" ratings.[48] State news, including news about the state legislature, although lower on the scale, still was ranked as "very important" or "important" by more than two thirds of the respondents. Unfortunately, deeming it important and paying attention to it are not the same.

TABLE 10-4   News Choice Preferences (in percentages)

News choices	Very important	Important	Somewhat Important	Not important
Local news	44	40	14	3
Weather reports	46	37	15	3
National news	52	31	12	6
World news	47	29	16	8
Statewide news	27	48	20	6
State legislative news	26	39	20	15
Regional news	17	40	31	13
University news	19	37	25	19
Sports reports	15	27	24	34

SOURCE: Adapted from Carolyn A. Lin, "Audience Selectivity of Local Television Newscasts," *Journalism Quarterly* 69 (Summer 1992): 378.

Local News Characteristics

Local television news has become the biggest game in town. Sixty-seven percent of the adult population watches it daily, compared to the 49 percent who watch news on the national networks.[49] That means six million more viewers for local than for national news. Local news has become a huge money maker, generating as much as 40 percent of a station's profits.[50] Stations first started to emphasize local news heavily in the 1970s because they could keep the advertising income. When local stations broadcast national news, most advertising revenue is remitted to the national networks.[51] Production of local news was also attractive because it was popular and far cheaper than most nationally produced entertainment shows. Hence news programs multiplied in numbers as well as length, with some local news programs running as long as ninety minutes.

Primary Concerns. As part of its mandate to ensure that the electronic media serve the public interest, the FCC has urged local television and radio stations to gear their programming to local needs, including coverage of local politics. That mandate has been honored more by lip service than by actual performance. Local stations do carry some local political news, and more than three quarters of their stories originate locally. But the primary emphasis is on local crime and disasters and on entertainment, weather, and sports. This is hardly what the FCC had in mind when it called for "local" programming.

Table 10-5 presents a comparison of national and Chicago-area local television news stories in mid-summer 1995. It shows that 85 percent to 93 percent of national television news dealt with governmental affairs or

TABLE 10-5   Distribution of Television News Story Topics:
June 1, 1995, to July 20, 1995 (in percentages)

	National CBS (435)	National NBC (425)	National ABC (440)	Local CBS (555)	Local NBC (541)	Local ABC (530)
Governmental affairs	58	55	50	30	35	32
Economic issues	10	10	15	4	10	6
Social issues	23	20	28	28	24	28
Total	91	85	93	62	69	66
Sports and entertainment	6	10	6	30	28	26
Miscellaneous	3	5	1	8	3	8
Total	9	15	7	38	31	34

SOURCE: Based on author's content analysis of Chicago stations.

assorted social and economic issues. By contrast, only 62 percent to 69 percent of local news dealt with substantive matters, with sports, entertainment, and a few miscellaneous nonpolitical issues making up the rest. A content analysis of offerings by three local television stations in Philadelphia replicates the Chicago findings. Kaniss found a heavy emphasis on features designed to entertain audiences at the expense of government and public policy stories.[52]

Although these figures show that local news is far fluffier than national news, one must keep in mind that there are generally more local newscasts. With more news time to fill, there is bound to be more filler material. Conversely, although the proportion of serious news may be smaller, the total amount of news may still be greater. But there is another caveat—there may be more stories, but many of them are likely to be updates or outright repetition of earlier news. Moreover, despite the fact that there may be more news available, the majority of viewers are not glued to their television sets, eager to watch successive newscasts as the day develops.

Diversity. Just as one cannot lump all national media together for purposes of analysis, so one must differentiate local media along a number of dimensions. Size is one of them. Stations in the largest markets offered considerably more political news than stations in smaller markets.[53] Likewise, larger television stations devote a smaller percentage of news space to local news. Instead, they pay more attention to national and world events. The difference was roughly 6 percentage points for story count and 9 percentage points for newshole in a study of fourteen stations in Michigan and Oregon when broadcasts were analyzed over a ten-day period.[54] This may mean that stations in larger markets are moving away from emphasizing local news as urged by the FCC's "localism doctrine."

National News on Local Media

One reason for growing attention to national and world news by local stations is greater ease of access. New satellite and microwave technology permits local stations to tap into the pool of national news at will and report it from a local angle. In addition, local stations are increasingly entering into cooperative news-gathering systems, such as Conus and Newsfeed, that allow member stations to send their stories to other members in the system via satellite. Local stations consequently have become less dependent on network coverage for national and world events.

As we saw in Chapter 9, national newsmakers are eager to reach the hinterlands, where coverage tends to be gentler and more in tune with the newsmakers' agendas. Congress members rely heavily on publicity in their home states and make extensive efforts to supply local media with stories and videotapes. Washington also abounds with news bureaus that transmit national news, often presented from local angles, to member organizations or independent local clients.

Content analysis of Washington news gathered by the Washington press corps but presented locally shows that it has a distinctive flavor. With no nationwide audiences to please, local stations can put a more local imprint on the news and thereby make it more relevant to local audiences. Because happy news is preferred to tales of woe, the news can be more upbeat and less critical. Local reporters are also less likely to subject national political leaders to tough questioning because they are more distant from the scene and lack insider knowledge and Washington sources.

In contrast with national news, local newscasts analyzed between 1979 and 1985 covered executive and legislative branches in about equal proportions.[55] However, legislators were more often heard and seen than presidents, who were mentioned more frequently but not actually seen on camera. As is true of national television, senators received considerably more coverage than House members. Compared with national news coverage, they were more likely to be judged favorably. Besides stressing local angles, stories on local television also highlight different organizations and issues. Coverage of Senate committees presented by Table 10-6 is an example that reflects a difference in priorities.[56] The table ranks committees by the number of cameras dispatched by various national and local media organizations to the committee hearings.

TABLE 10-6   Senate Committee Coverage, National Versus Local Priorities: 1979 to 1985

National priorities	Ranking	Local priorities	Ranking
Foreign Relations	1	Foreign Relations	3
Judiciary	2	Judiciary	1
Budget	3	Budget	13
Labor	4	Labor	2
Appropriations	5	Appropriations	8
Finance	6	Finance	4
Governmental Affairs	7	Governmental Affairs	7
Joint Economic	8	Joint Economic	11
Armed Services	9	Armed Services	12
Energy	10	Energy	6
Commerce	11	Commerce	5
Banking	12	Banking	10
Ethics	13	Ethics	15
Environment	14	Environment	9
Agriculture	15	Agriculture	14
Intelligence	16	Intelligence	21
Aging	17	Aging	16
Rules	18	Rules	19
Veterans' Affairs	19	Veterans' Affairs	17
Small Business	20	Small Business	18
Indian Affairs	21	Indian Affairs	20

SOURCE: Adapted from Stephen Hess, *Live from Capitol Hill: Studies of Congress and the Media* (Washington, D.C.: Brookings Institution, 1991), 138.

NOTE: Coverage is based on counts of assigned cameras, February 1979–June 1985.

Election Coverage at the Local Level

The entire American electoral system is organized to reflect local and statewide politics. All national officials—the president, senators, and representatives—are selected from state-based electoral districts, as are state officials and the half million local officials who occupy legislative, executive, judicial, and administrative positions throughout the states. Candidates for most of these offices, including scores of positions on local government boards and committees, are of prime interest to geographically limited constituencies. They rarely attract the attention of nationwide broadcasts or the few newspapers that have a nationwide circulation. Their political fate—and that of the areas that they serve—therefore depends to a major degree on the kind of coverage provided by local media.

News about the Candidates. The role of the local media in promoting candidates in state and local campaigns is similar to what was described in

Chapter 8 for national campaigns. It is a growing role because state officials are spending more money on their media campaigns now than in
earlier years. A large share of campaign spending goes toward efforts to
obtain general media coverage rather than relying only on advertisements. In the past, subnational officials relied heavily on radio coverage
for their advertisements because of the high costs of television. The availability of cable channels is changing this; so is the ability to videotape messages and distribute them directly to interested parties.

Although evidence is still spotty about the quality of election coverage
at the local level, compared to the national level, a study of the 1989 Virginia gubernatorial campaign found that local coverage was superior to
national news media stories. The national media focused on the historic
nature of the campaign, which pitted a white candidate and an African
American gubernatorial candidate against each other in a southern state,
and on the candidates' diverging stands on abortion. Most of the coverage
at the national level related to the African American Democrat; the white
Republican received little attention. The local papers excelled in providing profiles of both candidates and highlighting an array of issues facing
the state.[57] However, both national and local media were one-sided in
painting a highly favorable picture of one candidate (Democrat L. Douglas Wilder, incumbent lieutenant governor) and an unfavorable one of
the other (Republican J. Marshall Coleman, a former state attorney general). In the same way a study of a race for chair of the Fairfax County
(Virginia) Board of Supervisors found, "It appears that a different kind of
press coverage occurs at the 'lower levels' of government—one in which
more serious, substantive reporting is taking place."[58] Other studies have
concluded that coverage characteristics and quality are similar for state
and national coverage of gubernatorial races.[59]

Newspaper endorsements are also more important below the
national level. Most candidates for state and local offices are less familiar
to the voters, who therefore turn more to the news media for guidance.[60]
When viewers were asked to compare debates among presidential contenders at the national level with debates between candidates for state and
local offices, they reported that they found the presidential debates more
important and interesting, but learned more and were influenced more
by the debates at state and local levels.[61] Seventy percent of the viewers in
the local debate were undecided about their voting choices, compared to
40 percent of viewers in the presidential debate. If lack of information is a
disease that plagues national elections, it apparently occurs in a far more
virulent strain at the subnational level.

The fact that news media are now organized to serve larger markets
often makes it difficult for candidates whose districts overlap several mar-

kets, or just a small slice of a large media market, to gain coverage. The media will not report about them as part of regular news coverage because limited time for news is reserved for stories of wider interest. Paid advertising coverage may be too expensive because rates are based on the numbers of people within the market, not on the much smaller numbers that are constituents of the candidate. A state representative who serves a district of 50,000 voters rarely can afford to pay for access to many times that number just because the advertising Area of Dominant Influence in which her or his district is located covers a multitude of urban, suburban, and rural counties.

News about Referenda. Although elections at the national level involve the selection of candidates, albeit often in a context of voting for or against certain issues, elections involving local politics often are completely issue-centered. That happens when various referenda are on the ballot. Although these political contests have low visibility, their impact on the average citizen can dwarf that of the more publicized contests. After studying seventy-two referenda in Massachusetts, Michigan, Oregon, and California between 1976 and 1982, political scientist Betty Zisk concluded that they were impartially covered. Despite the liberal stance of the papers under investigation (the *Boston Globe,* the *Detroit Free Press,* the *Portland Oregonian,* the *Los Angeles Times,* and the *San Francisco Chronicle*), there was little systematic bias in reporting these stories. Several sides of each issue were amply discussed.[62] However, Zisk faults newspeople for merely reporting charges and countercharges rather than analyzing the merits of proposals and unmasking misleading rhetoric and advertisements.[63] When the election was over, voters had agreed with newspaper endorsements about 68 percent of the time.[64] It is impossible to know with certainty whether this indicates media influence or merely an independently occurring concurrence of views.

Zisk reports that the side spending the most money, much of it to gain media coverage, won in three out of four cases (56 of the 72 campaigns—78 percent). She argues that money purchased victory, rather than good causes attracting the most money.

Radio and television, the main sources of political information for average voters, carried little news about the referenda and few editorials. Thirty- and sixty-second television spot advertisements were totally inadequate to cover the important points of most of these complex issues. However, some radio talk shows gave extensive coverage to referenda, albeit often generating more heat than light.[65] Unlike television, major regional newspapers provided comprehensive coverage of referendum issues. They carried extensive background features, pro and con articles and editorials, and news about campaign activities in the major urban centers, though not elsewhere in the jurisdiction covered by the referendum. When a poll tested voter knowledge about a nuclear power proposal for California, results showed that nearly 80 percent of the affected public, which had relied primarily on televised information, fell below the midpoint on a scale measuring knowledge about the proposal. Newspaper-reliant voters fared much better. However, comparisons between learning from newspapers and learning from television may be inappropriate when most survey questions reflect the type of information conveyed by newspapers, rather than television.

The Quality of Local News

Maintaining high-quality coverage is often more difficult for local than for national media. As mentioned, compared to most national television networks, local television has a far greater appetite for news because it usually has three or more daily newscasts. That puts a premium on broadcasting the latest news, rather than repeating more important stories that may have been broadcast earlier in the day. To maintain profitability through a wide audience reach, local television usually pitches its programs to a moderately educated middle-income audience that, presumably, is uninterested in sophisticated political analysis.

It is also more difficult for local newscasters to get high-quality news commentary for local political stories. Many local officials lack the skills and experience required to be good media information sources. Because their jobs are often technical—fire chiefs or health commissioners, for example—they are chosen for their technical abilities and managerial skills, with no regard for public relations expertise. The end result is a dearth of political commentary on local stations. One content analysis of fourteen television stations of assorted sizes from five different markets found that only 43 (1.4 percent) of 3,037 stories that were examined included commentary.[66]

A further problem for local stations, as well as for local newspapers, is their lack of economic resources. This may force them to apply an economy model of news selection. Rather than originating stories on their own and investigating them, they go after the cheapest stories. Usually, that is news based on handouts by various public relations practitioners or news based on rehashed reports by metropolitan newspapers—facetiously dubbed "plagiarism news."[67] In a study of three network affiliates in the western United States, 75 percent of the news at the small, economically weak stations came from handouts, 20 percent started with tips that were investigated, and 5 percent originated with reporters. For the largest, economically soundest station the figures were 50 percent, 36 percent, and 13 percent. As Ben Bagdikian has put it in his inimitable style, journalism is "a daily battle between God and Mammon. Too much of the time, it's Mammon 100 and God 5."[68] Larger local stations and newspapers with greater financial resources do somewhat better in seeking out important news, providing context for their stories, and resisting advertiser pressures.[69] Smaller news outlets cannot afford to antagonize the advertising hand that feeds them.

The difficulties in maintaining high-quality news have serious consequences at the local level because there are few competing information sources for local politics. National problems and national politicians are widely scrutinized by a multitude of media, governmental investigating bodies, interest groups, and academicians. That rarely happens at the local level. Reporting by the local media may be the sole source of information available to interested citizens as well as government officials.

Critics of local news have often charged that it does not perform the important watchdog functions of the press. They complain that reporters are soft on local politicians because they are not comfortable stirring up conflict with people whom they know personally. They are also soft when it comes to local projects and policies out of a sense of local boosterism. Reporters rarely question quantitative estimates of costs and benefits of local development projects. They tend to be upbeat in reporting about local business leaders and economic trends. They may examine local problems and report about the sad consequences, but they rarely turn to genuine investigative reporting. As Kaniss has noted, "While there is much in the news and editorial columns that is critical of local officials, this criticism is limited when compared with the amount of information that is taken directly, and almost unquestioningly, from official bureaucratic sources."[70] There are, of course, major exceptions to these criticisms, particularly in large cities with well-staffed news media. But even there, whenever budgets get tight, investigative reporting is among the first casualties of malnourishment.

Summary

The media spotlight falls unevenly on various features of the body politic. In this chapter, we examined institutions that do not receive sufficient light so that the American public and political leaders can adequately assess these institutions and the roles they play in America's political life. At the national level, the judicial branch suffers from inadequate news coverage. We have explained the reasons for this problem and some of the political consequences, given the federal courts' importance in shaping American political life. We have also noted problems that arise when the crime and justice system is in the news and the focus turns to sensational matters, rather than political substance. The controversy about the appropriateness of allowing cameras in courtrooms during various judicial proceedings highlights many of these issues.

The discussion then turned to media coverage of subnational news. Here we noted that state news is neglected by all media, except those located in state capital cities. Hence most citizens remain ignorant about state politics in their own as well as sister states. However, coverage seems to be adequate for the needs of state-level politicians, who find it easy to work with the local press when needed. We also noted that governmental publicity efforts are becoming more professionalized at the subnational level.

There is far more ample coverage of local than state news. Many regions within metropolitan areas, as well as suburbs and outlying communities, have local newspapers. But the quality of coverage of politics has deteriorated since the turn of the century. Markets reflect technological and merchandising conditions rather than political needs. News media design their offerings accordingly. Fewer cities now have their own daily newspapers, and intracity competition among major dailies has almost vanished. The political dialogue has suffered. However, it seems too early to mourn the death of solid local politics coverage. The new technologies that make it feasible to tailor broadcasts to the needs of small audiences may restore the vigorous publicity that is essential in a democracy.

Notes

1. Walter Lippmann, *Public Opinion* (New York: Free Press, 1965, reissue of 1922 text), 229.
2. 347 U.S. 483 (1954); 410 U.S. 113 (1973); 112 S. Ct. 2791 (1992).
3. Richard Davis, "Lifting the Shroud: News Media Portrayal of the U.S. Supreme Court," *Communications and the Law* 9 (October 1987): 46; and Bob Woodward and Scott Armstrong, *The Brethren* (New York: Simon and Schuster, 1979), claim to present an insider's view of Court proceedings.
4. Richard Davis, *Decisions and Images: The Supreme Court and the Press* (Englewood Cliffs, N.J.: Prentice Hall, 1994), chap. 4.
5. Ibid., chap. 3.
6. *Engel v. Vitale*, 370 U.S. 421 (1962); *Baker v. Carr*, 369 U.S. 186 (1962).
7. Chester A. Newland, "Press Coverage of the United States Supreme Court," *Western Political Quarterly* 17 (1964): 15–36. Also see Kenneth S. Devol, *Mass Media and the Supreme Court*, 2d ed. (New York: Hastings House, 1976).
8. Jerome O'Callaghan and James O. Dukes, "Media Coverage of the Supreme Court's Caseload," *Journalism Quarterly* 69 (Spring 1992): 195–203.
9. David Ericson, "Newspaper Coverage of the Supreme Court: A Case Study," *Journalism Quarterly* 54 (Autumn 1977): 605–607. See also Michael E. Solim-

ine, "Newsmagazine Coverage of the Supreme Court," *Journalism Quarterly* 57 (Winter 1980): 661–664; and Ethan Katsh, "The Supreme Court Beat: How Television Covers the Supreme Court," *Judicature* 67 (1983): 6–12.

10. Stephanie Greco Larson, "How the *New York Times* Covered Discrimination Cases," *Journalism Quarterly* 62 (Winter 1985): 894–896; also see Stephanie Greco Larson, "Supreme Court Coverage and Consequences" (Paper presented at the annual meeting of the Midwest Political Science Association, April 1989).

11. Davis, *Decisions and Imagers,* chaps. 4–6. David L. Grey, *The Supreme Court and the News Media* (Evanston, Ill.: Northwestern University Press, 1968). Also see Frank J. Sorauf, "Campaign Money and the Press: Three Soundings," *Political Science Quarterly* 102 (Spring 1987): 25–42.

12. Gallup Polls taken on July 13, 1987, show that during the 1980s a majority of the public judged the Court's performance as good to excellent. See also Gregory Caldeira, "Neither the Purse Nor the Sword: Dynamics of Public Confidence in the Supreme Court," *American Political Science Review* 80 (December 1986): 1209–1228.

13. Robert E. Drechsel, *News Making in the Trial Courts* (New York: Longman, 1983), 19–22.

14. David Pritchard, "Homicide and Bargained Justice: The Agenda-Setting Effect of Crime News on Prosecutors," *Public Opinion Quarterly* 50 (Spring 1986): 143–159.

15. A detailed account of coverage of crime and justice system news is presented in Doris A. Graber, *Crime News and the Public* (New York: Praeger, 1980). Also see Roy E. Lotz, *Crime and the American Press* (New York: Praeger, 1991); and Gregg Barak, ed., *Media, Process and the Social Construction of Crime: Studies in Newsmaking Criminology* (New York: Garland Publishing, 1994).

16. Susanna Barber, *News Cameras in the Courtroom: A Free Press-Fair Trial Debate* (Norwood, N.J.: Ablex, 1987), especially 18–19.

17. F. Dennis Hale, "Free Expression: The First Five Years of the Rehnquist Court," *Journalism Quarterly* 69 (Spring 1992): 89–103.

18. Daniel D. Polsby and Kim Degnan, "Institutions for Communications Policymaking: A Review," in *Communications for Tomorrow: Policy Perspectives for the 1980s,* ed. Glen O. Robinson (New York: Praeger, 1978), 513.

19. Ben H. Bagdikian, *The Media Monopoly,* 3d ed. (Boston: Beacon Press, 1990), 174.

20. Frederick Fico and Stan Soffin, "Fairness and Balance of Selected Newspaper Coverage of Controversial National, State, and Local Issues," *Journalism and Mass Communication Quarterly* 72(3) (Autumn 1995): 621–633.

21. Bagdikian, *The Media Monopoly,* 288.

22. The term was coined by James N. Rosse. See note 4 in James M. Bernstein, Stephen Lacy, Catherine Cassara, and Tuen-yu Lau, "Geographic Coverage by Local Television News," *Journalism Quarterly* 57 (Winter 1990): 664.

23. Phyllis Kaniss, *Making Local News* (Chicago: University of Chicago Press, 1991), 5.

24. Ibid., 31.

25. Ibid.

26. Paul Lavrakas and Judith Schejbal, "Investigating the Meaning of Responses to the 'Number One Problem' Item" (Paper presented at the annual meeting of the Midwest Association for Public Opinion Research, Chicago, November 1995).

27. See Bernstein et al., "Geographic Coverage by Local Television News," 671.
28. William R. Davie and Jung-Sook Lee, "Sex, Violence and Consonance/Differentiation: An Analysis of Local TV News Values," *Journalism and Mass Communication Quarterly* 72(1) (Spring 1995): 128–138.
29. Daniel Riffe and Eugene F. Shaw, "Ownership, Operating, Staffing and Content Characteristics of 'News Radio' Stations," *Journalism Quarterly* 67 (Winter 1990): 684–691.
30. Delmer Dunn, *Public Officials and the Press* (Reading, Mass.: Addison-Wesley, 1969), 150–163.
31. Kaniss, *Making Local News*, 175–179.
32. Ibid.
33. Martin Linsky, *How the Press Affects Federal Policymaking* (New York: Norton, 1986), 236.
34. Dan Berkowitz and Douglas B. Adams, "Information Subsidy and Agenda-Building in Local Television News," *Journalism Quarterly* 67 (Winter 1990): 725.
35. Judy Van Slyke Turk and Bob Franklin, "Information Subsidies: Agenda-Setting Traditions," *Public Relations Review* 13 (1987): 29–41; Dan Berkowitz, "TV News Sources and News Channels: A Study in Agenda-Building," *Journalism Quarterly* 64 (Autumn 1987): 508–513.
36. Thad Beyle and G. Patrick Lynch, "The Media and State Politics" (Paper presented at the annual meeting of the Midwest Political Science Association, Chicago, April 1991), 5.
37. David Morgan, *The Capitol Press Corps: Newsmen and the Governing of New York State* (Westport, Conn.: Greenwood, 1978), 57–58.
38. Kaniss, *Making Local News*, 107.
39. As Kaniss, *Making Local News*, 108, notes, "Instead of an inverted paragraph order in the newspaper, where the most important information comes first, television news stories have the formula of a mini-drama, with rising action, climax and denouement. Television stories stress action, not background facts."
40. Kaniss, *Making Local News*, 118–120.
41. Ibid., 121.
42. Ibid., 126–127.
43. The term is used in Kaniss, *Making Local News*, 126.
44. Ibid., 76.
45. Morgan, *The Capitol Press Corps*, 20–21.
46. This discussion is based on Stephen Hess, "Levels of the Game: Federalism and the American News System" (Paper presented at the Hofstra University Conference, Hempstead, N.Y., April 1992).
47. For the database used for *New York Times* news, see Doris Graber, "Flashlight Coverage: State News on National Broadcasts," *American Politics Quarterly* 17 (July 1989): 277–290.
48. Carolyn A. Lin, "Audience Selectivity of Local Television Newscasts," *Journalism Quarterly* 69 (Summer 1992): 378.
49. *Washington Post Magazine*, May 13, 1990, 17.
50. Stephen Hess, *Live from Capitol Hill: Studies of Congress and the Media* (Washington, D.C.: Brookings Institution, 1991), 34.
51. Kaniss, *Making Local News*, 102.

52. Ibid., 113–130.
53. Hess, *Live from Capitol Hill*, 49.
54. Bernstein et al., "Geographic Coverage by Local Television News," 668, 670; for similar results, also see Stephen Lacy and James M. Bernstein, "Daily Newspaper Content's Relationship to Publication Cycle and Circulation Size," *Newspaper Research Journal* (Spring 1988): 49–57.
55. Hess, *Live from Capitol Hill*, 53.
56. Ibid., 138.
57. Mark J. Rozell, "Local vs. National Press Assessments of Virginia's 1989 Gubernatorial Campaign," *Polity* 24 (Fall 1991): 75.
58. Mark J. Rozell, "Campaign Press Coverage in the 'New Dominion': The 1991 Fairfax County (Virginia) Board of Supervisors Chairman Election" (Paper presented at the Eighth Citadel Conference on Southern Politics, Charleston, S.C., 1992), 18.
59. For a report on gubernatorial election studies in progress, see Beyle and Lynch, "The Media and State Politics."
60. Byron St. Dizer, "The Effects of Newspaper Endorsements and Party Identification on Voting Choice," *Journalism Quarterly* 62 (Autumn 1985): 589–594.
61. A. Lichtenstein, "Differences in Impact between Local and National Televised Political Candidates' Debates," *Western Journal of Speech Communication* 46 (1982): 291–298; also see Dianne Bystrom, Cindy Roper, Robert Gobetz, Tom Massey, and Carol Beall, "The Effects of a Televised Gubernatorial Debate," *Political Communication Review* 16 (1991): 57–80.
62. Betty H. Zisk, *Money, Media, and the Grassroots: State Ballot Issues and the Electoral Process* (Newbury Park, Calif.: Sage, 1987), 28.
63. Ibid., 246.
64. Ibid., 109.
65. Ibid., 247–248.
66. James M. Bernstein and Stephen Lacy, "Contextual Coverage of Government by Local Television News," *Journalism Quarterly* 69 (Summer 1992): 338.
67. John McManus, "How Local Television Learns What Is News," *Journalism Quarterly* 67 (Winter 1990): 678.
68. Quoted in McManus, "How Local Television Learns What Is News," 672.
69. Bernstein and Lacy, "Contextual Coverage of Government by Local Television News," 339.
70. Kaniss, *Making Local News*, 90–91.

Readings

Barak, Gregg, ed. *Media, Process and the Social Construction of Crime: Studies in Newsmaking Criminology.* New York: Garland Publishing, 1994.

Davis, Richard. *Decisions and Images: The Supreme Court and the Press.* Englewood Cliffs, N.J.: Prentice Hall, 1994.

Hess, Stephen. *Live from Capitol Hill: Studies of Congress and the Media.* Washington, D.C.: Brookings Institution, 1991.

Kaniss, Phyllis. *Making Local News.* Chicago: University of Chicago Press, 1991.

___. *The Media and the Mayor's Race: The Failure of Urban Political Reporting.* Indianapolis: Indiana University Press, 1995.

McManus, John H. *Market-Driven Journalism: Let the Citizen Beware?* Thousand Oaks, Calif.: Sage, 1994.

Surette, Ray. *Media, Crime and Criminal Justice: Images and Realities.* Pacific Grove, Calif.: Brooks/Cole, 1992.

Thaler, Paul. *The Watchful Eye: American Justice in the Age of the Television Trial.* Westport, Conn.: Praeger, 1994.

Foreign Affairs Coverage

WHEN ISRAEL AND JORDAN PREPARED TO SIGN a peace agree-
ment in the fall of 1994, they scheduled the ceremony for midday at a barren desert patch two miles north of the Gulf of Aqaba. The place was subject to sudden desert sandstorms and the appointed hour was at the
hottest time of the day. Why the location and the time? The answer is simple: It provided an excellent photo opportunity. As Israeli officials
explained it, midday at the Arava (near the Jordan border) is time for
morning news in America—just the right time to show Americans that
their president, depicted in a dramatic setting, was the godfather of the
Jordanian-Israeli peace settlement.[1]

Is television coverage really important enough to make major sacrifices to schedule an important diplomatic event to meet television schedules? Do the mass media shape the political dimensions of the world?
What, if any, are the links between the mass media and the process of creating foreign policy and producing policy outputs? How are the media
used by governments to further their policy objectives around the world?
Does television play any active roles separate from those of other media in
the shaping of American foreign policy? In this chapter we will try to
answer such provocative questions, to shed light on the role played by the
mass media in the shaping and conduct of American foreign policy.

We will first focus on the overall significance that American media and
American citizens assign to news about foreign countries. Then we will
point out the significant differences between the production of foreign
and domestic news. We will consider the qualifications of foreign correspondents and the unique problems they face in collecting news and shap-

ing it to meet newsworthiness criteria while heeding the canons of journal-istic ethics and independence. Securing high quality foreign news is an extraordinarily difficult task, and we shall note how well it is currently car-ried out and give examples of past accomplishments and failures.

The Foreign News Niche

Newspeople commonly assume that the American public is interested primarily in what goes on in the United States. Reports about the public's ignorance about foreign countries and foreign affairs lend credence to these assumptions. When asked, Americans themselves profess somewhat greater interest, but when given a choice, they do not seek out foreign news.[2] For example, when NBC news broadcast a prime-time, hour-long interview with Soviet leader Mikhail Gorbachev in December 1987, just prior to a U.S.-Soviet meeting designed to reduce the danger of war, only 15 percent of the national audience tuned in. Half of the viewers who at that time ordinarily watch NBC's entertainment programs switched to other networks. They preferred "Kate and Allie," "Frank's Place," and "The World's Greatest Stuntman" to listening to the leader of a super-power. Public opinion polls have repeatedly shown that two thirds or more of the public is often unaware of important foreign news, even when the situation has received ample and prolonged coverage. Compared to citi-zens of other countries, such as Britain, France, Germany, Italy, Spain, Canada, and Mexico, Americans are least knowledgeable about world events.[3]

Although foreign news lacks attraction for many Americans, it receives a considerable amount of coverage, in print and electronic media. A four-month analysis of coverage in 1995 showed that the *New York Times,* the most ample source of foreign news, averaged 26 stories per day. Regional newspapers, such as the *Buffalo News* or the *Houston Chronicle,* carried an average of twelve foreign stories daily. The television networks, including CNN, averaged between two and three.[4] Compared with major domestic news stories, foreign news normally receives brief space and time and modest display. Elite newspapers like the *New York Times* and the *Washington Post* are exceptions. Selection criteria are also more rigorous. To be published, foreign news must have a more pro-found impact on the political, economic, or cultural concerns of the United States than domestic news. It must involve people of more exalted status, and entail more violence or disaster.[5] During crises, particularly prolonged ones that endanger American lives, foreign coverage often doubles or even triples; it may even drown out most other news. Conversely, the number of stories and their length shrinks when times seem unusually calm, as happened right after the Cold War ended with the collapse of the Soviet Union.[6] Public interest in foreign news fluctuates in similar fashion.

When the spotlight shifts away from foreign news, the number of foreign correspondents usually declines. There were 637 accredited U.S. correspondents in South Vietnam in 1968. When American involvement in the war dwindled, the number dropped to 392 by 1970 and 295 by 1972. By mid-1974 only 33 remained. Even though this small corps of correspondents filed relatively few stories from Vietnam, editors often balked at running them in daily newscasts and papers because the public had presumably lost interest. When this happens, a spiral effect sets in. Presumed lack of interest leads to less coverage. Reduced coverage further lessens interest in foreign news. An upward spiral of domestic news takes up the slack. This pattern prevails in most of the country's newspapers and television newscasts whenever foreign crises subside.

The country's foreign policy elites, including government officials, depend heavily on foreign news covered by prestigious media. As a State Department official attests, "The first thing we do is read the newspaper— *the newspaper*—the *New York Times*. You can't work in the State Department without the *New York Times*."[7] Members of the U.S. Congress, particularly those concerned with foreign affairs, and foreign officials in the United States have made similar comments. All feel that elite newspaper reports keep them informed faster and often better than their own official sources. In fact, the State Department is notorious for slow communications. Its computer and telephone systems date back to the 1970s, so they cannot surf on the Internet, use floppy disks, or interconnect easily with the department's 266 embassies and missions abroad.[8]

Making Foreign News

Although news making for domestic stories and for foreign stories differs substantially, there are many similarities. To make comparisons easier, our discussion of foreign news making will follow the organization of our discussion of domestic news making and news reporting in Chapter 4. First we will consider the gatekeepers—the corps of foreign correspondents who are the front-line echelon among gatherers of foreign affairs news. Then we will discuss the setting for news selection, the criteria for choosing stories and the means of gathering them, the constraints on news production, and finally the effects of gatekeeping on foreign affairs coverage.

The Gatekeepers

Concentration of Control. A striking aspect of foreign news coverage is the high degree of concentration of the news-gathering process. Most news about events happening throughout the world is collected by four major wire services. They are the American-owned Associated Press (AP), the British Reuters, the French Agence France-Presse (AFP), and ITAR, which replaced the Soviet news agency Tass in 1992.[9] Among these world-class wire services, AP is by far the largest. It maintains eighty-four foreign bureaus in seventy countries from which it relays news by modern electronic means to subscribers in all parts of the world. For television, pictorial materials are collected by two television news services: Visnews and WTN. They are owned by British companies, primarily Reuters, the British Broadcasting Corporation (BBC), and Britain's Independent Television News.

The wire services station reporters in nearly half of the countries of the world. North American and Western European countries are most likely to have resident reporters; Africa and the Eastern bloc are least likely to have them—a decidedly uneven distribution. The wire services ferret out the stories that make up the pool from which other gatekeepers select complete reports or find leads to pursue stories more fully. Because wire service reporters work for a vast variety of clients throughout the world, their news must be bland so that it does not offend people whose views span a wide political spectrum. Wire service news therefore emphasizes fast and ample reports of ongoing events, not interpretation, which then falls to other foreign correspondents.

Besides these worldwide organizations, the American market is also served by syndicated news collected by major American papers, like the *New York Times,* the *Washington Post,* and the *Los Angeles Times.* These papers have their own correspondents stationed abroad, a luxury enjoyed by barely 1 percent of all American dailies. Because of the advent of television, the print press foreign correspondent corps has been joined by foreign correspondents from ABC, CBS, NBC, and CNN.

The major recent innovation in collecting and reporting international news is the rise of CNN, the 24-hour Cable News Network. By 1990, ten years after its birth, it had established eighteen overseas news bureaus to collect news round-the-clock, which was then relayed to 53 million homes in the United States and 200 million viewers in more than 100 other countries. The striking feature about CNN, besides the comprehensiveness of its news-gathering apparatus, is its continuous coverage of major crises such as the 1985 hijacking of a TWA jetliner or the 1991 war against Iraq. As is typical of live coverage, the reports are a mixed bag of events and interviews ranging from the trivial to the significant, with less time given to analysis and expert commentary than is typical for network television news.[10] The emphasis is on taping whatever is readily and inexpensively available so that viewers are the first to see a breaking news event at close range. Unique among international news reporting agencies, CNN also collects and broadcasts brief (usually under three minutes) uncensored reports submitted by sources throughout the world. They become part of its weekly two-and-a-half hour "CNN World Report."[11]

The stories gathered by the small corps of initial gatekeepers reach huge audiences. Although subscribers generally use only a limited portion of the coverage made available by these sources, what they do use mirrors the story patterns and interpretation of the initial gatekeepers. As Barry Rubin points out, "Once the main stories of the day have been identified and defined, the media can be like a stampeding herd, hard to turn toward a new interpretation of an issue." The stories chosen set the scene for follow-up stories. "The news of today sequels the news in the news of yesterday. Only a relatively small number of journalists are able or allowed to open up new areas of concern."[12] Stereotypes become fixed; countries and leaders whom gatekeepers depict as friendly or antagonistic to the United States may be characterized that way long after the reality has changed.

Surveillance of the Foreign Scene. The total number of full-time American foreign correspondents has fluctuated over the years, rising during international crises and falling afterward. Overall, the trend has been downward since its peak during World War II. Several reasons account for this. The ability to dispatch correspondents quickly from an American home base to foreign countries is one. Air travel has made it possible for each American correspondent to reach and cover many more countries than ever before. NBC's Andrea Mitchell, for example, between March 1995 and February 1996 has reported from Canada, England, Haiti, China, and Vietnam. Her ABC colleague Sheila MacVicar has covered Iraq, Zaire, Bosnia, and Ireland. But physical mobility is not matched by the psychic mobility that would allow reporters to feel at home in more countries. Nor is it accompanied by sudden spurts in knowledge that would permit such "parachute" reporters to cover a new area with insight.

High costs also have forced a steady decline in the number of foreign correspondents. In the 1990s it cost as much as $300,000 a year to keep one correspondent abroad, a steep price considering the limited demand for foreign affairs stories. Because it is much cheaper, many papers use stringers instead of regular employees and rely on reports produced by local foreign news media. Stringers, who are usually citizens of the country from which they report, are paid for each story a newspaper

TABLE 11-1   Distribution of Foreign Correspondents: 1991 (in percentages)

Major regions	American correspondents abroad		Foreign correspondents in United States[a]		U.S./foreign comparison[b]
Western Europe	777	40%	687	45%	−5%
East Asia	313	16	307	20	−4
Latin America	249	13	140	9	+4
Middle East	187	10	116	8	+2
Southeast Asia and Pacific	125	7	62	4	+3
Soviet Union	90	5	39	3	+2
Sub-Sahara Africa	66	2	27	2	+1
Eastern Europe	50	3	28	2	+1
South Asia	41	2	28	2	0
Canada	28	2	45	3	−1
Other/International agencies	—	—	46	3	—
Total	1,926		1,525		

SOURCE: For U.S. data, Ralph Kliesch, from the E. W. Scripps School of Journalism, Ohio University of Athens, Ohio; for foreign data, *Editor and Publisher International Yearbook, 1991* (New York: Editor & Publisher, 1991).

[a] The figure is for correspondents based in New York and Washington, D.C.
[b] The figure reflects distribution differences between the American and the foreign corps of correspondents, when column four is subtracted from column two.

publishes.[13] At best, they may have keener insight into local problems than American reporters sent to the country. But they often fail to meet the news-gathering standards prized by American media, and they may be unable to tailor news stories to the concerns of American audiences.[14]

U.S. correspondents abroad are unevenly distributed. More are stationed in friendly locations than in neutral or hostile ones. Table 11-1 depicts the regions in which American foreign correspondents were stationed in 1991, and the regions whose correspondents were stationed in New York or Washington to report about the United States. The rank orderings of the two groups are mirror images. Although numbers of correspondents have fluctuated from year to year, the proportions have remained fairly constant for regional distributions as well as locations in particular countries. Table 11-2 shows how three major newspapers and one television organization allocate their correspondents. The table omits figures for ABC, CBS, and NBC, which have 48, 24, and 28 correspondents, respectively. Fewer than ten in each group report on air at least once a month. Clearly, correspondents are thinly spread over relatively few capital cities, leaving huge gaps in coverage. Critics appropriately call this "hopscotch" journalism that leaps over vast, potentially important

TABLE 11-2   Distribution of U.S. Foreign Correspondents Serving Major
             News Outlets

Region	Cities	New York Times	Washington Post	Chicago Tribune	CNN
Asia	Tokyo	3	2	1	3
	Beijing	1	1	1	2
	Hong Kong	1	1	0	0
	Manila	0	0	0	1
	Bangkok	0	0	0	1
	Shanghai	1	0	0	0
Subtotal		6	4	2	7
Middle East	Amman	0	1	0	1
	Beirut	1	0	0	0
	Jerusalem	1	1	1	1
	Cairo	0	1	0	0
Subtotal		2	3	1	2
Europe	London	2	1	1	6
	Paris	4	2	0	2
	Rome	2	1	0	1
	Berlin	1	1	0	0
	Bonn	1	0	0	0
	Frankfurt	1	0	0	0
	Warsaw	2	1	1	0
	Moscow	3	3	1	2
	Geneva	1	0	0	0
	Brussels	1	0	0	1
	Zagreb	1	0	0	0
	Madrid	1	0	0	0
	Ireland	1	0	0	0
Subtotal		21	9	3	12
Africa	Johannesburg	1	1	0	1
	Nairobi	1	1	0	1
Subtotal		2	2	0	2
North America	Toronto	1	2	0	0
	Mexico City	2	1	1	0
Subtotal		3	3	1	0
Central America	San Salvador	0	1	0	0
	Managua	0	0	0	1
Subtotal		0	1	0	1
South America	Buenos Aires	1	1	0	0
	Río de Janeiro	1	0	2	1
Subtotal		2	1	2	1
Total		36	23	9	25

SOURCE: Author's personal communication with newspaper staffs.
NOTE: Figures as of June 1995.

areas. However, the work of American reporters is supplemented through news from Reuters, the British news agency, and Agence France-Presse, the French news agency, which have more ample representation in their former colonial regions where American reporters are especially sparse.

What kinds of people are these journalists who select the foreign news for American elites and publics? What are their biases? And how do they compare with the correspondents who cover the United States for the benefit of foreign nationals?

A typical American journalist abroad is a white male in his forties, college educated, with more than ten years of reporting news under his belt. Like staff people generally in prominent American news organizations, most foreign correspondents are politically liberal, taking positions to the left of mainstream views. Nonetheless, they rarely challenge the government's stance on foreign policy issues, except when major challenges are raised by prominent leaders. When that happens, the media often rush to join the attack on official policies.[15]

Aside from reporters and anchor persons flown in to cover special situations, many foreign correspondents have remained at the same locations for several years, so they are fully familiar with their area of coverage.[16] However, this does not necessarily mean that reporters possess language competence. In one survey, more than 80 percent of American reporters stationed in Western Europe and Latin America claimed to read and speak the native languages fluently or with easy facility. But in Eastern Europe and Africa, these figures were cut in half. The poorest showing was in Central and East Asia, where only 9 percent of American reporters could read the intricate written characters and only 18 percent could speak the languages well. Deficient reading skills hamper American reporters in local interviews and investigations. They must depend on translated newspaper reports and on handouts to the foreign press.[17] This sharply curbs their effectiveness as reporters, especially because contacts with local people and personal ties that may supply good insights also tend to be sparse, judging from survey data. In some countries translators are supplied and controlled by the government. Presence of government officials during interviews dampens the free exchange of ideas that might otherwise take place.

Public relations agencies hired by foreign countries to promote their images provide one very important, usually overlooked, additional source of news about foreign countries. Steadily growing numbers of countries are contracting for professional image management. Citizens for a Free Kuwait, a front organization for the Kuwait government, for example, spent nearly $11 million with just one public relations firm to burnish Kuwait's image in the months after it had been invaded by Iraq.[18] By either stimulating or suppressing media coverage, public relations agencies can improve their client's media image. Presumably this then affects elite and mass opinion so that the country in question enjoys improved relations with American politicians and the American public.[19]

For example, the government of Pakistan in 1989 hired Mark Siegel, a former director of the Democratic National Committee and aide to President Carter, to orchestrate a political visit by Pakistan's new prime minister, Benazir Bhutto. Siegel planned a five-day media blitz around the theme that Pakistan's move toward democracy was a triumph for American political values. He arranged for media exposure for the prime minister on "60 Minutes" and the "McNeil/Lehrer News Hour." During her visit, interviews were also arranged on ABC and NBC news. Bhutto gave a well-publicized address before Congress, a commencement address at Harvard University, and informal remarks at a White House dinner. The publicity was later credited with producing an increase in aid to Pakistan at a time when other foreign aid programs were slashed and with decreasing resistance to supporting Pakistan's defense build-up.[20]

Surveillance of the American Scene. Altogether, 1,525 correspondents from foreign countries covered the United States in 1991. Just as Americans receive the most news about friendly foreign countries, so most news about America goes to its friends.[21] The foreign journalists stationed in the United States represent various regions and countries unevenly. In 1991 the corps included a mere 6 correspondents from Nigeria, Africa's largest nation, compared to 39 from Israel. Japan topped the list with 213 journalists compared to 39 for China and 22 for India, the world's most populous nations. Neighboring Canada had 45 and neighboring Mexico had 9. West Germany sent 129, and East Germany dispatched 5. Italy had a puzzlingly large contingent of 117 correspondents and Belgium made do with 7.[22]

Foreign reporters are an extremely well-educated group. A survey conducted in the mid-1980s found that nine out of ten were university trained, and about half of these had advanced degrees. That included 22 percent who had earned a doctorate. Seventy-eight percent were fluent English speakers, and a majority were fluent in a third language as well. On the average, they spoke three languages. Nevertheless, close contacts with Americans were limited. Only 7 percent said that their best and closest contacts were Americans. In political orientation, foreign newspeople covering the United States were further to the left than most American reporters. Seventy percent claimed to be left-leaning, 14 percent preferred a middle position, and 17 percent leaned to the right.[23]

It is difficult for foreign reporters to cover the whole United States adequately. Most correspondents are kept busy in Washington and New

York. They rarely travel to other parts of the country, except to cover special events such as major sports competitions or presidential nominating conventions. Thus the impressions that foreigners receive about Americans' opinions and politics are largely the views of official Washington. The leftward orientation of most reporters from foreign countries produces a substantial amount of criticism of America's economic, military, and foreign aid policies and often makes the conduct of foreign relations rocky. Hostile coverage is only partially balanced by the influx of news from American media and government broadcasts, such as Voice of America (VOA) or, for several years, WORLDNET, a satellite program sponsored by the U.S. Information Agency (USIA). WORLDNET, which has been stopped for economic reasons, enabled reporters in foreign capitals to have direct access to top administration officials in the United States.

The Setting for News Selection

Cultural Pressures. American correspondents abroad, like domestic journalists, must operate within the context of American politics and American political culture. Besides reflecting the American value structure, stories also must conform to established American stereotypes. Accordingly, when U.S. correspondents in Peru accurately reported about the military government's reforms, the stories were rejected as lies because they contradicted the stereotype that military regimes support the status quo.[24] However, U.S. correspondents abroad have greater leeway than their domestic counterparts to evaluate and interpret news because there is less likelihood that the domestic audience—ordinary citizens or powerful interest groups—will be offended.

Intraorganizational norms and pressures also influence news selection. Foreign news is gathered by a small enough group of reporters to allow for much personal contact and cooperation. Because the wire services perform the initial gatekeeping tasks for most newspapers and electronic media, topic selection is quite uniform. In the U.S., elite papers then take the lead in framing the stories, and editors and reporters throughout the country follow suit.

Political Pressures. Overt and covert political pressures to publish or suppress news stories play a greater role in foreign news production than on the domestic scene. Foreign correspondents often must do their host country's bidding. Many host governments are politically unstable and fear for their survival if they receive unfavorable publicity. Hence, foreign correspondents, like the native newspeople in unstable countries, are heavily censored. If foreign correspondents want to remain in the country, they must write dispatches acceptable to the authorities. Otherwise they face severe penalties—expulsion, confiscation of their notes and pictures, closure of transmission facilities, refusal of contact by public officials, and the like. This has led to a strange phenomenon: The most undemocratic countries often receive the least criticism whereas more open societies are freely reproached.

Scores of countries have barred foreign reporters entirely from entering or have expelled them after entry. Cambodia, Laos, Vietnam, Nicaragua, El Salvador, Albania, the Soviet Union, and South Africa provide vivid examples in recent decades. Britain kept foreign reporters away from the embattled Falkland Islands in 1983. Israel repeatedly imposed tight censorship on coverage of its activities in Lebanon and in the occupied West Bank and Gaza Strip. During the Iran-Iraq hostilities in the early 1980s, reporters were permitted at the front only whenever the host country thought it had won an engagement. Large areas of Central America and of the former Soviet Union have been closed to reporters, making it almost impossible to adequately cover hostilities there. Bureaucratic hurdles abound, ranging from difficult visa requirements, to failure to provide transportation to outlying areas, to hurdles in transmitting the news to one's home base. In some countries reporters face physical danger. Not infrequently, they have been jailed, assaulted, and sometimes murdered. Reporters Without Frontiers, a watchdog organization, warned in 1994 that foreign journalists should keep out of Algeria, then involved in civil war: "Going there is like playing Russian roulette."[25] The Helsinki Accords of 1975, in which many countries promised free and safe access to each other's newspeople, have done little to improve the situation.

When countries previously closed to foreign journalists suddenly open their borders, journalists may be totally unprepared for insightful coverage. The opening of the People's Republic of China in 1972 is an example. Reporters arrived with President Richard Nixon and Secretary of State Henry Kissinger. During their short stay in China, they dutifully reported those stories that the Chinese arranged for them to report. Not surprisingly, their American audiences were treated to a romanticized travelogue rather than solid political analysis.

Media Diplomacy. A recent development in foreign news production is media diplomacy—attempts by correspondents in the United States and abroad to inject themselves directly into the political process and attempts by U.S. and foreign leaders to use news media to further their causes. The Middle East situation presents a number of dramatic examples. CBS anchor Walter Cronkite became a peacemaker in 1977 when he drew from Egypt's president Anwar al-Sadat a promise during a television interview to visit Jerusalem if this would further peace. In a separate interview Cronkite secured a pledge from Israeli prime minister Menachem Begin that he would personally welcome Sadat at Ben Gurion airport. With such mutual commitments, the scene was set for the historic meeting.

When Sadat arrived in Israel, flanked by anchors from the three American networks, two thousand journalists from all over the globe were part of the welcoming crowds. This was media diplomacy in the broadest sense. The event was covered live on American television and radio, giving the principals a chance to woo American audiences. In the weeks that followed, more than thirty million people in America and millions more worldwide watched and judged the peacemaking process. Television alone devoted twenty-four hours of broadcasts to the spectacle, supplemented by radio and print news.

When Arab-Israeli peacemaking moved to the United States the following spring, media diplomacy continued. President Sadat, fully aware of the importance of courting the American public, made himself available for a television interview immediately after arrival for the 1978 Camp David meeting. The next day in his address to the National Press Club, he accused the Israelis of stalling the negotiations. Israel countered this propaganda move by promptly dispatching Foreign Minister Moshe Dayan on a ten-day speaking tour of major American cities to garner favorable publicity for the Israeli side. The media reported it all with relish, proud of the role they had played in bringing about encounters between Israeli and Egyptian officials. Little thought was given to the political ramifications that ensue when foreign heads of state readily use the American press as their public relations tool.

The lessons learned by Sadat and Begin have not been lost on other world leaders. For instance, in 1979 Iran's revolutionary leader, Ayatollah Ruhollah Khomeini, rebuffed official emissaries from the United States who were sent to negotiate the release of the American embassy personnel held hostage by Iranian students. Instead he arranged a series of interviews with American television correspondents, requiring prior approval of questions so that he could control the discussion. To ensure maximum exposure for the Ayatollah's views, Iranian leaders permitted an especially lengthy interview for the popular CBS program "60 Minutes." At the same time they assigned low priority to an interview to be aired on low-audience public television. The Iranian embassy also bought full-page advertisements in the *New York Times* and other American newspapers to offer the American public Iran's version of the hostage story.

For their part, reporters used interviews with Iranian officials to publicize policy proposals for resolving the crisis and to elicit Iranian views and counterproposals. Placing these views before a worldwide audience made them part of the agenda of international politics. Media diplomacy facilitated negotiations that had collapsed at the diplomatic level and aired a number of excellent proposals. Even when normal diplomatic relations exist, reporters often become part of the political process by publicizing interviews with political leaders in which the reporters choose the issues to be discussed and report them from the reporter's perspective.

Although media diplomacy is often helpful, it also is fraught with disadvantages and dangers. Government officials, who have far more foreign policy expertise than journalists, may be maneuvered into untenable positions. They may have to react to unforeseen developments with undue haste or find that broadcasters have aroused interest groups whose demands are troublesome.[26] Also, journalists may inadvertently provide a propaganda forum for foreign leaders. This is why CNN's Peter Arnett was so harshly condemned by many Americans when he engaged Iraqi president Saddam Hussein in a long television interview during the Gulf War. The interview permitted the Iraqi leader to broadcast accusations against his antagonists to a worldwide audience.

Economic Pressures. Economic considerations, like cultural and political factors, strongly influence foreign news selection. First, there is the usual pressure to present appealing stories that attract big audiences and keep the media profitable. This pressure is even more burdensome for foreign correspondents than for their domestic counterparts because their stories must be exceptionally good to attract large audiences. Second, there is the pressure to avoid or minimize huge production costs. Reporting events such as President Nixon's trip to China or Israel's Yom Kippur War cost each network in excess of $3 million per event. Leasing cables for news transmission is expensive and so is telephone communication. Satellite transmission is also costly, especially for short messages. Some stories therefore may be shut out because they cannot be transmitted cheaply, and others may be included merely because transmission is comparatively inexpensive and convenient.

Gathering the News: The Beat

The international beat system is quite similar to local beats. Newspapers initially established their foreign news bureaus in major capitals of the world, primarily in Western Europe. From there correspondents covered entire countries rather than particular types of stories; London, Paris, Bonn, and Rome were the main news-gathering spots. In the wake of the Vietnam War, Saigon, Tokyo, Hong Kong, and other Far Eastern points became important news centers. China moved into focus with the opening of diplomatic relations in 1972.

The average newspaper bureau abroad has one or two correspondents, one or two film crews staffed by foreigners, perhaps a radio correspondent, and a few stringers. Correspondents from these bureaus jet to spots within easy flying range whenever big stories break. For local news they rely heavily on national news services that exist in two thirds of the countries of the world. Countries without such services, and without satellite transmission facilities, are far less likely to receive coverage than countries that have them.

The bulk of foreign affairs news for American media actually originates in Washington from various beats in the executive branch, especially the White House, the State Department, and the Pentagon. The president's views tend to dominate whenever situations are controversial. However, the media put their imprint on the news by deciding which opposition views should be featured and casting them into a favorable or unfavorable light. At times foreign policy stories may be hard to cover because officials are reluctant to talk whenever delicate negotiations or the prestige of the United States is at stake. A further common drawback to Washington stories is their lack of exciting pictures to dramatize them for television. Like domestic newspeople, foreign correspondents prefer to report predictable events, such as elections or summit conferences, so that coverage can be planned well in advance. The decision to film particular foreign stories abroad is usually made in the United States because the media's home offices consider themselves in closer touch with the interests of American audiences. Foreign bureaus do the actual filming.

Foreign news bestows unequal attention on various regions and countries of the world just as domestic news covers regions of the United States unequally. Neither is there any correlation between size of population and amount of coverage. In general, beats cover the countries with which the United States has its most significant diplomatic contacts. In recent years, that has usually meant England, France, West Germany, Italy, and the Soviet Union in Europe; Israel and Egypt in the Middle East; and, more recently, the People's Republic of China and Japan in the Far East. The Western Hemisphere is covered lightly, except when Americans become concerned about humanitarian issues, civil strife, or trade issues. Asian coverage was light until the Vietnam War, when it replaced stories from other parts of the world for several years. Table 11-3 provides data on network television coverage of major regions of the world between March 1993 and February 1994.

As the table illustrates, compared to the 1990–1991 period, attention to Western Europe dropped substantially and attention to Asia rose. In general, stories with visuals are more attractive to television viewers than stories that are purely verbal. Obviously, when one fourth to one third of foreign stories lack pictures, the chances that they will be noticed and remembered diminish considerably. Audiences are more likely to pay

TABLE 11-3   Network Coverage of World Regions: March 1993 to February
1994

Region	Yearly total	Number of stories with visuals	Linkage to the United States
Eastern Europe	399	305	139
Middle East	160	124	47
Asia	152	117	86
Western Europe	145	111	24
Africa	113	89	66
Caribbean	46	28	27
Latin America	26	23	18
North America	5	3	4
Australia	3	3	0

SOURCE: Author's research compiled from Vanderbilt Television News Archives data.

attention to a story that is linked explicitly to U.S. interests. Linkage to a
U.S. concern is especially important for regions with which average Americans are least familiar. It is therefore not unexpected that stories about
Western Europe are less likely to be framed with a U.S. linkage than stories about Africa, Asia, and even Latin America and the Caribbean.

Criteria for Choosing Stories

Foreign news, like domestic news, is selected primarily for audience
appeal rather than for political significance. This means that stories must
have an angle that interests Americans. Sociologist Herbert Gans examined foreign affairs news in television newscasts and in news magazines
and identified seven subjects that are aired frequently.[27] First in order of
frequency of coverage are American activities in foreign countries, particularly when presidents and secretaries of state visit. Second are events that
affect Americans directly in a major way, such as wars, oil embargoes, and
international economic problems. Third are relations of the United States
with Communist and formerly Communist states. Internal political and
military problems of these countries are emphasized. Fourth, elections in
other parts of the world are covered if they involve a change in the head
of state. There also is a sentimental attachment for following the major
(and minor) activities of European royalty. Fifth are stories about dramatic political conflicts. Most wars, coups d'état, and revolutions are
reported; protests, as a rule, are covered only when they are violent. Left-
wing coups receive more attention than right-wing coups. Sixth are disasters, if they involve massive loss of lives and destruction of property. There

is a rough calculus by which severity is measured: "10,000 deaths in Nepal equals 100 deaths in Wales equals 10 deaths in West Virginia equals one death next door."[28] In general, the more distant a nation, the more frequently a newsworthy event must happen to be reported. Seventh are the excesses of foreign dictators, particularly when they involve brutality against political dissidents (for example, the deeds of Uganda's former ruler Idi Amin and genocide in Bosnia). Noticeably absent from American broadcasts and papers are stories about ordinary people and ordinary events abroad. These would be news to Americans, but, except for occasional special features, they are not *news* in the professional dictionary of journalists.

Foreign news stories also must have an appealing format. Emphasis on violence, conflict and disaster, timeliness or novelty, and familiarity of persons or situations are the major selection criteria. For instance, stories from Western Europe and other familiar areas are more likely to be published than stories from other parts of the world. When news from countries with unfamiliar cultures is published, the rule of "uncertainty absorption" comes into play. This unwritten rule requires that gatekeepers avoid foreign news of uncertain accuracy, coming from remote sources. Only plausible stories are acceptable, and they must be cast into a familiar framework, such as the battle against poverty and racism or the moral bankruptcy of military dictators.[29] Such biases make it very difficult to change images of culturally distant countries. Far-off parts of the world are rarely covered except when sensational events such as violence and disaster occur or there is negative news about top-level public officials.[30] Moreover, the high costs of covering news abroad force news organizations to limit the sites where they can maintain full-scale news operations.

The media's preference for news about current happenings has led to concentration on rapidly breaking stories in accessible places. More significant long-range developments, such as programs to improve public health or reduce illiteracy or efforts to create new political parties, do not fill the bill if they lack a recent climax. Pressure for timeliness and novelty also fragments news presentation and usually precludes a follow-up. This gives major events an unwarranted air of suddenness and unpredictability. They have neither a past nor a future—merely a brief presence in the parade of current events.

At times coverage errs in the opposite direction. The story of Americans held hostage in Iran from November 4, 1979, to January 20, 1981, was vastly overcovered. During the first six months of the crisis, nearly one third of each nightly network newscast was devoted to the story.[31] A similar situation developed during the 1991 Gulf War when 57 percent of the foreign news focused on the Middle East. Much of that coverage was repeti-

Reprinted by permission: Tribune Media Services.

tious and uninformative. With media attention riveted on one international trouble spot, most other foreign news is slighted.

News Production Constraints

The problems of producing domestic news are magnified for foreign news making. Staffs are smaller, research facilities are more limited, language barriers are troublesome, and transmission difficulties may be enormous. For television news, which presents the bulk of foreign news for average Americans, the quest for good pictures is often frustrated by restrictions on access or because facilities for taking and processing pictures are inadequate.[32] Pictures are especially important for foreign news because they bring unfamiliar sights, which might be hard to imagine, directly into viewers' homes. Starvation in India or Somalia, the lifestyles of primitive tribes in New Guinea or Australia, or street riots in Spain or China are better understood if they can be visually experienced. However, not even words and pictures combined can tell the whole story if the audience is unfamiliar with the setting in which the reported events are happening. Grisly street scenes of Israeli soldiers chasing and beating Palestinian protesters, rock-throwing youngsters confronted by armed Israelis, and overturned and burning vehicles created the image in 1988 of a brutal military and a country in the throes of an ugly civil war. These pictures profoundly affected the attitude of the American public, including Congress, toward Israel. Most Americans were unaware that the riots were confined to a small section of the country and failed to put Israeli reactions into the appropriate historical perspectives.[33]

The need to keep news stories brief is particularly troubling for foreign correspondents because foreign events are often unintelligible without adequate background information or interpretation. Complexity therefore becomes a major enemy and avoidance or oversimplification the defensive strategy. Stories must be written simply and logically even if the situation defies logic. Usually a single theme must be selected to epitomize the entire complex story. The dominant theme of the Iran hostage stories, for example, was that innocent Americans were imprisoned by irrational anti-American terrorists—a gross oversimplification of a multifaceted situation. The complexities of Iran's internal politics received little attention because they could not be easily incorporated into a dramatic, visually appealing story.

Effects of Gatekeeping

Foreign affairs coverage is ample, dramatic, and up to date, but it lacks depth and breadth. It stereotypes and oversimplifies, and it often distorts facts in the interest of timeliness. Accordingly, a twelve-year study of international terrorism stories led to the conclusion that "network coverage bore little relationship to actual patterns of occurrence. On the whole, the limitations of production and presentation, concerns over audience share, and the narrow focus of journalistic notions of professionalism result in coverage more notable for its erratic nature than for its systematic biases."[34] Officials and publics who rely on foreign affairs news may be misled, and faulty policies may ensue. The news about the Cold War is a good example.

Cold War Perspectives. Because relations between the United States and the Soviet Union were undoubtedly vastly important to Americans, as well as to the world in the period after World War II, one might expect the news media to devote a great deal of attention to the full presentation of all important aspects of the story. What are the facts? Were American government officials and the public offered a broad picture, spanning all aspects of Soviet life and politics? Or was coverage narrowly focused on conflicting interests, provocations, and military power assessments?[35]

To answer these questions, I analyzed every theme in presidential news conferences and in *New York Times* editorials during a forty-six-year period spanning the administrations of presidents Truman, Eisenhower,

TABLE 11-4   Soviet News Story Topics in the U.S. Press: January 1945 to January 1991 (in percentages)

Topic	Press conference themes	Editorial themes
Soviet foreign relations	23	14
Soviet military policy	18	9
U.S. attitude about Soviets	21	33
U.S./Soviet meetings	14	5
U.S. military policy	5	6
Soviet attitudes about United States	4	7
U.S./Soviet comparisons	5	4
Human rights issues	3	11
Soviet leaders' quality	2	4
Communism as ideology	2	3
U.S. policy about Soviet Union	1	2
Soviet technology	1	1

SOURCE: Author's research.

NOTE: N = 2,636 press conference themes and 5,310 editorial themes.

Kennedy, Johnson, Nixon, Ford, Carter, Reagan, and Bush. As Table 11-4 shows, attitudes of American officials regarding the Soviet Union, such as fears about its intentions or the possibility for cooperation (21 percent), and specific events, such as summit meetings (14 percent), were well covered. But only 6 percent of the themes explored during press conferences presented information about the actual status of United States-Soviet relations, mostly about military matters. Trade relations or scientific cooperation were largely ignored.

The Soviet Union's political influence and power were primarily assessed in terms of Soviet relations with other countries (23 percent), such as Vietnam, China, Poland, or regions like Western Europe and the Persian Gulf, or in military terms (18 percent), including defense spending, weapons systems, and troops stationed in satellite countries. Although 41 percent of the themes dealt with these important matters, equally important internal Soviet conditions were slighted. Only 8 percent of the themes covered internal indicators that might have predicted the problems that led to the disintegration of the Soviet Union in the 1990s.

In line with the pattern of highlighting only a few topic areas, the range of internal matters that were covered was also quite limited in scope. It focused on human rights issues (3 percent), such as the plight of dissidents, appraisals of the status of the Communist ideology (2 percent), the quality of the country's political leadership (2 percent), and on Soviet technology (1 percent). Comparisons between the United States and the

Soviet Union were few (5 percent), even though they would have been useful in putting the Cold War into perspective. Though U.S. attitudes toward the Soviet Union were amply discussed (21 percent), there was little reciprocal analysis of Soviet attitudes and fears concerning the United States (4 percent).

One might argue that the topics that received attention seemed to be most important at the time and the ones on which information was most readily available. Still, it is now clear that coverage was inadequate. Unfortunately, the practice of viewing foreign countries with blinders continues. A Times Mirror analysis of foreign news televised in 1995 concluded that the vast majority of news stories (62 percent) dealt with conflicts. Topics like agriculture, demographics, the environment, or education were slighted.[36] Restricted coverage even characterizes the choice of visuals. Pictures of the Gulf War in newsmagazines, for example, focused on showing static pictures of weapons technology and ignored battle scenes, views of Iraq, its people, and leaders other than Saddam Hussein.[37]

Choosing Frames for Friends and Foes. The fact that foreign news reported in the American press is based primarily on American sources who stay closely to the mainstream line explains why pro-American perspectives dominate. As the saying goes, outcomes are judged by whose ox is gored. Coverage of the downing of two planes, one by Soviet fire and the other by American fire, illustrates the principle.

In 1983, a Soviet fighter plane shot down Korean Airlines Flight 007 with a loss of 269 lives. Five years later, in 1988, the *Vincennes,* a U.S. Navy ship, shot down Iran Air Flight 655 with a loss of 290 lives. The Soviets claimed that the shooting was justified because the Korean plane had been identified as a hostile target; the Americans made the same claim for their action. Though the cases differed in detail and in the context in which they occurred, they were sufficiently alike to expect rough similarity in coverage. That did not happen, judging from coverage of the events in *Time, Newsweek,* the *New York Times,* the *Washington Post,* and the "CBS Evening News." The manner in which the news was framed, including the language and pictures used in the stories and the overall context into which the stories were placed, cast the Soviet action as a moral outrage and the American action as a regrettable technological failure.[38]

For example, almost twice as much coverage was given to the tragedy caused by the Soviets than to its American counterpart, even though the loss of life was greater in the Iran Air case. Following the Korean Airlines crash, *Newsweek* proclaimed on its cover "Murder in the Air"; *Time's* cover read "Shooting to Kill: The Soviets Destroy an Airliner." *Newsweek's* cover on the 1988 crash was headlined, "The Gulf Tragedy: Why It Happened," omitting any reference to a suspected villain. In the same way, *Time,* in a small insert on its cover, said innocuously, "What Went Wrong in the Gulf." The stories inside the magazines repeatedly accused the Soviets of knowingly destroying a civilian plane, whereas the Americans' actions were excused as pardonable ignorance. The Soviets' action was characterized as typical behavior for that country and guilt was attributed to its leaders. Not so for the Americans.

The stories about the Korean airliner dwelled on the human tragedy; the Iranian airliner story de-emphasized that aspect. When Soviet actions were described, words like "atrocity," "crime," "massacre," and "murder" abounded. For the Americans, the emphasis was on the accidental nature of the event. When, during the investigation of the action of the *Vincennes*, some doubts were raised about the innocence of the American crew, these facts were mentioned inconspicuously. So was commentary that suggested the Soviet action might have been accidental.

There is no evidence that the distortions that spring from such chauvinistic framing are deliberate. Rather, the framing reflects the actual perspectives of the journalists, based on their choice of sources and the predispositions with which they approach stories involving countries identified as friend or foe. Nonetheless, this type of coverage has political consequences. In 1983, it heightened anti-Soviet feelings among members of Congress and the public, sharply reducing the momentum of the nuclear freeze movement that had been gaining ground.[39] In the Iran Air case in 1988, coverage defused potential pressure for withdrawal of American forces from the Persian Gulf region. Instead of seeing the tragedy as an example of harm caused by America's presence in the area, warranting reconsideration of the policy, the incident consolidated American support behind the Reagan administration's foreign policies in the Gulf.

Wars in the Television Age. In the wake of the Vietnam War, many politicians and other political observers believed that fighting lengthy wars had become nearly impossible for democratic societies in the age of full-color, battle-front television. When battle scenes are broadcast nightly in bloody colors, public support for wars is likely to vanish. The depiction of carnage in a United Nations refugee camp in Lebanon in 1996, after a retaliatory Israeli air raid, presents a case in point. In the wake of showing the torn bodies of the victims, Israel lost measurable amounts of support from its allies. This loss reduced the chances for peace in the Middle East.

To avoid such damages, in the 1982 Falkland Islands War, Great Britain and Argentina both resorted to the kind of censorship usually associated only with authoritarian regimes. Like the Soviets in Afghanistan or the Syrians in Lebanon, the British and the Argentines curbed and delayed pictorial coverage of the war to forestall adverse consequences at home. In the same way, no reporters were permitted to witness the first phases of the U.S. invasion of Grenada in 1983. The military is preoccupied with fighting during these initial stages and disinclined to take time out to deal with reporters. Moreover, it wants to keep its action plans secret. Journalists, on the other hand, want to be at the scene of action from the start with full access to the troops.

The press complained loudly about its exclusion from initial coverage in Grenada. In response to these complaints, a small rotating group of reporters was created that would be alerted about impending military operations so that they could be part of the initial operations. The system failed miserably when it was first tried in Panama in December 1989 in a mission designed to depose Panamanian president Manuel Noriega. The fourteen reporters in the pool reached Panama four hours after the fighting began and were not allowed to file stories until six hours later. Then their movements were restricted to tours under military escort. Government briefings were closely controlled by the military and generally uninformative. Neither the military nor the government was interested in having anyone question the soundness of the Panama intervention and the military phases of its execution. Even the press seemed disinclined to be critical in any way. Public support for the Panama venture, as measured in public opinion polls, may have restrained the press. So may the fact that reporters had previously criticized President Bush for failing to take strong action against President Noriega, who had been accused of a multitude of political misdeeds.[40]

As described in Chapter 5, the situation was not much better during the 1991 Gulf War, even though the rules had been revised again to permit journalists more freedom of movement. The pool system allowed only 100 of the more than 1,600 American reporters in the area access to some 500,000 troops. Reporters who went to the front without authorization were arrested and detained. The upshot was sanitized coverage of the war. Flawlessly executed precision maneuvers were shown but not failures or pictures of the dead and wounded, friend or foe. Although military censorship was to blame for glamorizing the battlefield, journalists must share in the blame for inadequate coverage. Most of them failed to familiarize themselves with the history and politics of the peoples of the region and with the policies of various outside powers interested in the area, including the United States. Had they done so, their coverage could have been far more insightful.[41]

After the war, executives from the major American media filed a report with Defense Secretary Dick Cheney, complaining about the pool system and efforts to sanitize the news and delay it. "By controlling what reporters saw and when they saw it, the military exerted great power to shape and manage the news."[42] The complaints led to yet another revision of the rules, which was endorsed by the journalism community. Under the new rules, pools—which should be as large as possible—will be used only in the initial stages. They will be disbanded within twenty-four to thirty-six hours. The military retains control over the rules, but has promised to facilitate reporting, including facilitating transportation on military vehicles. No agreement was reached on the right of the military to ask to review reporters' work for security purposes.[43]

It is unlikely that the time will ever arrive when the military and the press will be fully satisfied with each other's conduct. Their respective goals are much too antagonistic. War is a dirty business that will never be photogenic when shown in all its brutality. As long as "just" wars for "good causes" (whatever they may be) are condoned and even celebrated by the world community, full coverage remains a sensitive issue. If it does, indeed, discourage military actions, the world community's ability to defend its interests will diminish. Ruthless members of the community can then use the threat of military action to advance their own goals. Peace at any price may be too costly.

Shortcomings and Distortions. Just like domestic news, foreign news neglects major social problems, particularly political and economic development issues. The reasons are readily apparent. Social problems are difficult to describe in brief stories, visual materials are often lacking, and changes come at a glacial pace. Some social problems are extremely complex; most reporters are ill equipped to understand let alone describe them. When they do describe them, the focus is on their dramatic negative aspects: shortages, famines, conflicts, and breakdowns. As Rafael Caldera, former president of Venezuela, told a press conference at the National Press Club in Washington, D.C., "The phrase 'no news is good news' has become 'good news is no news.'... Little or nothing is mentioned about literary or scientific achievements" in American media or "about social achievements and the defense against the dangers which threaten our peace and development." Instead, "only the most deplorable incidents, be they caused by nature or by man, receive prominent attention."[44] It is small consolation for such ruffled feelings that news selection criteria for events in developing nations are typical for news from everywhere.[45]

Negative and conflictual news is more prevalent in the U.S. media than in the media of many other societies. Comparisons of news coverage in the United States and in Canada, societies that are culturally close, furnish examples. The rate of violence on Canadian television news is half the U.S. rate.[46] When the people of Quebec voted in 1980 on the question of separatism from Canada, the *Washington Post* warned that civil war might erupt. American papers featured stories about serious rioting by separatists in English sectors of Montreal. By contrast, the *Toronto Globe and Mail* buried a small story about minor unrest in Quebec in the back pages. The prospect of civil war was never mentioned and was characterized as "ludicrous" by knowledgeable observers.[47] During the Iranian hostage crisis, *New York Times* coverage featured stereotypical portrayals of Muslims and tales of violence. Far more peaceful images emerged from reading the French paper *Le Monde*.[48]

By and large, Western news media feature more conflict than do media in authoritarian and totalitarian societies. In part this happens because government-controlled news organizations find it comparatively easy to shun dramatic negative news, since government subsidies relieve them of the need to secure large audiences. Regardless of the reasons for the difference, the approach used by American news media draws attention to conflict rather than to peaceful settlement and makes much of the world outside of the United States seem chaotic. Ordinary foreign news languishes in the back pages or is condensed into the briefest broadcast accounts, whereas stories concerned with civil disorder and revolutions are featured prominently. Usually they are oversimplified and instead of interpreting what the conflict means to the country and its people, the dominant focus is on what, if anything, the conflict portends for American politics.

Distortions also plague domestic news coverage, but they are less deceptive because American audiences can see the situation more clearly; past experiences and socialization provide corrective lenses.[49] The foreign scene, by contrast, must be viewed without correction for myopia and astigmatism. Americans may be skeptical about the accuracy of the images, but they lack the yardsticks to judge the nature and degree of distortion.

Finally, the thrust of most foreign news stories, like their domestic counterpart, provides support for government policies. The media usually accept official designations of who America's friends and enemies are and interpret these friends' and enemies' motives accordingly. Whenever relationships change, media coverage mirrors the change. Coverage of the Soviet Union's attack on Korean Airlines Flight 007 is a good example of the approach used for disfavored countries. In the same way, a comparison of *New York Times* coverage of strife in Cambodia and East Timor and of elections in Nicaragua and El Salvador showed that "Communist-tainted" Cambodia and Nicaragua were judged unfavorably. By contrast, comparable events in East Timor and El Salvador, countries deemed friendly to the United States, were cast in a favorable light.[50] Because the president and executive branch are the prime sources of foreign affairs news, they can, most of the time, set the agenda of coverage and frame stories to reflect official perspectives.[51]

If the media are generally supportive of government policies, how can their adverse comments about the Vietnam War be explained? The answer is that the media emphasized the government's positions until many respected sources voiced their strong dissent. At that point the media continued to give the administration's views on the war the largest amount of coverage. They coupled it, however, with coverage of the growing dissent in America about the merits of Vietnam policies, giving ample attention to antiadministration voices and to antiwar demonstrations. Even when protest was featured, the media gave voice primarily to "respectable" dissenters, not to political and social outcasts.[52] Other examples of adverse coverage are media opposition to President Reagan's support of the Contras in Nicaragua and opposition to U.S. policies supporting the Marcos regime in the Philippines.

Support of the Status Quo. On the whole, despite some coverage that challenges the official version of international policies and American foreign policies, the tenor of news stories supports prevailing stereotypes about the world. Preoccupation with the developed powers reinforces many Americans' beliefs about the importance of these nations. In the same way, portrayal of less developed countries as incapable of managing their own internal affairs makes it easy to believe that they do not deserve higher status and the media attention that accompanies it.

Newspeople usually are willing to withhold news and commentary when publicity would severely complicate the government's management of foreign policy. For instance, the media refrained from sharply criticizing Iranian leaders during the 1979 hostage crisis to avoid angering them and suppressed information about America's breaking of Japanese military message codes during World War II. Both are examples in which major political interests were at stake. Likewise, news of delicate negotiations among foreign countries may be temporarily withheld to avoid rocking the boat before agreements are reached. When an invasion of Haiti by U.S. troops was in the offing in 1994, CNN and the three major television networks pledged to refrain from showing any pictures that might put the troops at risk.[53]

The Unique Impact of Television

We have already mentioned that television has vastly broadened the American audience for foreign affairs coverage and that television anchors have repeatedly assumed roles formerly reserved for diplomats. But the medium has done even more.[54] With satellite transmission its audience has become global. Millions throughout the world, including government leaders, watched the 1987 hearings on United States-Iranian arms deals and CNN's direct broadcasts from the enemy's capital city during the Gulf War in 1991. The fact that this international audience would be likely to react to these broadcasts constrained the behavior of the actors caught in the publicity glare. The political consequences may have been substantial.

Television changes the substance of important political events in ways that reduce the options of political leaders, as Zbigniew Brzezinski, President Carter's national security adviser, pointed out in a retrospective analysis of the Teheran hostage crisis:

> First, TV transforms essentially a political confrontation into a personal drama. The result is you cannot deal with it coldly in terms of the national interest but you must focus on the personal aspects. Secondly, as the confrontation becomes a personal drama, the bargaining capacity of the kidnappers is enhanced. Concentration on accommodation by the American government becomes more important. Thirdly, it humanizes the enemy. Therefore, you begin to make equations and equivalences, which dulls the sharpness of the possible response.[55]

One can argue that the influence of television in a hostage crisis is benign or that it is harmful. But few would argue with Brzezinski's claim that ample coverage alters the political situation.

Television may do three things in a crisis. First, it may dictate the national agenda by riveting public attention on the crisis to the exclusion of virtually all else. For example, during the stock market crisis of 1987, television slighted news about America's air attack on Iranian bases in the Persian Gulf and news about a domestic airline disaster. These would have been the top stories in calmer times. Second, televised crisis coverage may pressure the president to react hastily so that he does not appear weak and vacillating. As Lloyd Cutler, White House counsel to presidents Carter and Clinton, put it, "If an ominous foreign event is featured on TV news, the President and his advisers feel bound to make a response in time for the next evening news program."[56] This may leave no time for investigation of the news report or for explanation of the event by officials of the foreign country. Normal diplomatic discourse becomes preempted by the media.

Third, television's impact on political elites and mass publics may narrow the president's freedom to bargain and maneuver. This happened during the Iranian hostage crisis. The Carter administration's poorly conducted hostage rescue mission has been attributed to pressures created by the prolonged television coverage of the hostages and publicized charges that President Carter was incompetent to resolve the situation.

Public officials are fully aware that television can affect their actions in major ways. In a survey of 95 officials serving in policy-related jobs, 81 percent indicated that they relied heavily on print and electronic media for policy-relevant information. Fifty-three percent attributed great influence to the media in the early stages of the policy cycle when the issues are initially framed.[57] Whoever controls the agenda during this period—the American government, foreign governments, nongovernmental groups, or media personnel—is apt to have a powerful impact on the definition of the situation. Once the issue has been framed and a policy has been developed, media influence is far less potent.

Among the officials, nearly 80 percent thought that positive and negative media attention enhanced the salience of an issue for the bureaucracy and the public and that it was a bad idea for journalists to act on their own as diplomats.[58] Most (81 percent) agreed that television brings new players into the game of international politics, particularly nongovernmental groups. Most (71 percent) also believed that it speeds up the pace of policy decisions.[59] President Kennedy waited eight days in 1961 before commenting on the erection of the Berlin Wall; President Bush had to respond overnight to its destruction. As Patrick O'Heffernan put it, "Television plays a special role in the American foreign policy process, but that role is limited and diffused. However, when it plays that role ... it exerts a power over events and decisions that surpasses all other media combined."[60] Nonetheless, the public officials cautioned against considering television as omnipotent. Impact hinges on the nature of the issue and the prevailing political environment, including official predisposition to act.[61] Thus pictures of starving Kurdish refugees in the mountains of Iraq would not have spurred relief missions by the Bush administration in 1991 if emergency food aid had not already been a policy alternative.

Appraising Foreign Newsmaking

In 1978, the United States, along with 145 other nations, signed a UNESCO Declaration on the Media. Among other things, the Declaration stated that "the mass media, by disseminating information on the aims, aspirations, cultures and needs of all people, contribute to eliminate ignorance and misunderstanding between peoples." The media also "make nationals of a country sensitive to the needs and desires of others," thereby ensuring "the respect of the rights and dignity of all nations, all peoples and all individuals." The media also foster "the formulation by states of policies best able to promote the reduction of international tension and the peaceful and equitable settlement of international disputes."[62]

Clearly, foreign news in the American press, or in any other press, does not meet the high standards that UNESCO has set for it. It does not "eliminate ignorance and misunderstanding between peoples." It is too sparse and unbalanced, focusing on the wealthier and more powerful countries. It assesses foreign countries largely in terms of U.S. interests, with little attempt to explain their culture and concerns from their own perspective. It does not sensitize Americans to "the needs and desires of others" nor foster "respect of the rights and dignity of all nations." Rather, it reinforces Americans' preexisting assumptions and stereotypes.

These deficiencies must be assessed in light of the basic philosophy of news in a free society. As discussed in Chapter 1, American journalists by and large do not see themselves as extensions of the government, carrying out and keeping in tune with public policies. Although they may sympathize with UNESCO's goals, their first priority is to report exciting news to the American public.[63] In a society that firmly believes in the independence of the press, this is a tolerable consequence.

Just as the press does not serve UNESCO's objectives, it fails to serve many objectives of the American government and many needs of the American public. Reporting of foreign news usually lacks a sense of history and a sense of the meaning of successive events so that it often confuses the public. A good example is the widely believed story that China turned to communism because of failures of American foreign policy. This interpretation ignores the long-range forces that made revolution in China inevitable. It vastly exaggerates the power of the United States to change the course of Chinese politics. The news does not provide sufficient information to permit most Americans to understand the rationale for major foreign policies such as support of the North American Free Trade Agreement (NAFTA) or the limitations of humanitarian interventions.

Some stories, even those directly involving U.S. security, are ignored until events reach crisis proportions or until there is a precipitating incident. *New York Times* correspondent James Reston put the problem this way:

> We are fascinated by events but not by the things that cause the events. We will send 500 correspondents to Vietnam after the war breaks out ... meanwhile ignoring the rest of the world, but we will not send five reporters there when the danger of war is developing.[64]

Phil Foisie, then-assistant managing editor of the *Washington Post,* added, "We are surprised more often than we ought to be and need to be."[65] This leaves the country unprepared for twists and turns in foreign affairs that might have been foreseen.

If one assumes that better information leads to better policies, then deficiencies in news coverage are grave. When President Carter complained that he was ill informed about unrest in Iran prior to the overthrow of the shah in 1979, he intimated that American policy making and public support for policies would have benefited from more accurate news. In this case the CIA was blamed as well as the media, which perform what has been called a "massive overt intelligence operation."[66] Flawed coverage of the Vietnam War also allegedly misled the American public and misdirected foreign policy.[67] The media's stress on conflict—particularly on force as the solution for many international problems—contributes to feelings of insecurity. Although the media are exceedingly important in providing the context for foreign policy and the print media are used widely as the information base for policy formation, their influence is generally weaker than the influence of formal government agencies. When policy failures are not readily apparent and the president alleges that all is going well, contrary media claims are not likely to be believed by officials and the mass public.

Impact on Public Opinion

Because most Americans lack interest and knowledge about foreign affairs, what they see and hear on television, particularly when dramatic pictures are involved, can easily sway them.[68] Viewers are most readily influenced when stories reinforce or sharply challenge stereotypes and when they relate to matters with which average Americans can empathize, such as the suffering of civilians in war-torn areas.[69] In the past, interest in foreign policy was largely confined to a newspaper-reliant elite whose education, interests, and experiences made them far more immune to media influence. Several decades ago, "the public probably would never have heard of El Salvador, much less cared about it. Today the sheer volume of exposure to new information created by television assures a more involved public. Television has created a vast, inadvertent audience for news about foreign policy."[70]

Television coverage has strengthened the president's hand when policies coincide with the tenor of news stories; it limits his options when news and policies conflict. Public support for defense spending more than doubled between 1978 and 1980, jumping from 26 to 90 percent, after television drove home the message that America's foes were gaining power while U.S. power was declining. Scenes of the Iranian hostage crisis, the Soviet assault on Afghanistan, the upheaval in Poland, and the uncontrolled warfare in Central America were powerful messages in this melodrama.[71]

As is true of most media effects, it is difficult to obtain convincing proof that public opinion about foreign countries mirrors the images media stories present. Nonetheless, available data suggest that it does. William C. Adams, after analyzing the content of television coverage of the Arab-Israeli conflict in the 1970s and 1980s, concluded that five important changes should have taken place in public opinion if it, indeed, reflected media coverage. Opinions should have become (1) more favorable to Egypt, (2) more sensitive to differences among Arab nations, (3) less favorable to Israel, (4) more sympathetic to Palestinians, and (5) slightly more pro-Arab overall. All of these changes occurred, some of them dramatically.[72]

Exporting News

Although the American public seems reasonably content with the foreign news it receives, developing nations are unhappy with their coverage by U.S. media. Their disappointment about the world images presented to Americans is compounded by resentment that these images are exported to other countries throughout the globe. In the years since most of these nations gained independence, 80 percent of the non-Communist world's political and economic news has come from only four huge American enterprises: the Associated Press (AP), United Press International (UPI), the *New York Times* News Service, and the *Los Angeles Times-Washington Post* News Service. Most of the remainder has been produced by news agencies based in Britain, France, and Russia. Four countries thus have dominated the world's news supply.[73] However, some confusion in dividing stories by country of origin has arisen from the fact that many developing nation stories are transmitted through communications centers, such as London or New York. For example, most news from Latin America is relayed via New York.

Concentration of international news dissemination has given rise to charges of media imperialism—the dependence of domestic media systems on dominant foreign media systems.[74] Dependence on foreign news resources is particularly galling for developing countries because they believe that the flow of news is primarily one way—into the developing world but not out of it. Western news purveyors slight the happenings and the information needs of people in developing nations. Critics in developing nations also decry the corrupting effects of Western news and entertainment programs that feature violence and sexually explicit episodes. Western programs allegedly damage the cultural identity of developing nations, especially those that are vulnerable because colonialism has sensitized them to foreign values.[75] Imported news and entertainment offerings draw people away from their own heritage and create false expectations that it is easy to become rich. People in developing nations are tempted into materialism for the benefit of industrialists in the United States who are eager to sell their merchandise through television. Buyers of luxury goods then drain the resources of the developing countries.

Such interpretations of the motives and role of Western media are widely believed in developing nations. They seem quite plausible because the international news market is dominated by a few giant Western corporations that sell news, as well as more tangible goods, for profit. However, scientific proof is lacking that Marxist interpretations of the causes and consequences of Western dominance of the news and media entertainment of developing nations are correct. As we noted in Chapter 7, people do not automatically learn new ways of life from the media, even when offerings are designed to educate. Certain relatively rare conditions must first be met to provide an appropriate context. Hence claims that exposure to Western news automatically indoctrinates the audience are false.[76]

Content analyses of Western media, including wire service news, also show that many of the charges of deliberate discrimination against developing nations are either groundless or exaggerated.[77] The emphasis on problems and failures, rather than successes, and lack of attention to many small nations appear to be natural consequences of applying to developing nations the same criteria used for the more developed portions of the world. Although the treatment is the same, its negative impact is likely to be greater in developing than developed nations.[78] The media's emphasis on disasters and conflicts in developing nations reflects the reality that these countries are undergoing major social changes and therefore bear a disproportionate burden of pain and suffering.

Elite newspapers in America, in sharp contrast to smaller, less prominent papers throughout the country, pay considerable attention to the news of developing nations.[79] In the *New York Times, Washington Post,* and *Christian Science Monitor,* for example, an average of 65 percent of foreign news coverage is devoted to developing countries. These nations also fare well in the proportion of front-page stories, editorials, opinion-page articles, and letters to the editor.[80]

Early entry into the media business has given the major news producers an economic edge of size and scale that makes it well-nigh impossible for developing nations to set up viable competing enterprises.[81] Current structures and patterns of telecommunications give price advantages to large producers and consumers. News transmission rates are cheaper when volume is high, making it extremely costly for poor countries to broadcast their messages. It also costs more to transmit news from developing countries than to receive it. In fact, all the economies of scale benefit the rich and hurt the poor.

The high costs of television programming and the comparatively low costs of purchasing foreign television entertainment—roughly one tenth of the cost of original programming—also have discouraged developing countries from creating their own television industries. Many developing countries still lack facilities for producing television shows. Those that have them nonetheless import an average of more than half of their programs, particularly those shown in prime time.[82] That may be changing. In recent years local cultural programs have multiplied in Asia, Latin America, and Africa. They are often exchanged among developing nations.

Because they are dissatisfied with the status quo and see news as a powerful political force, developing countries have lobbied the United Nations Educational, Scientific, and Cultural Organization (UNESCO) to place strict controls on the influx of foreign news. It has been largely a dialogue of the deaf. The United States and other Western countries have strongly resisted these attempts, deeming them infringements of the right to a free press guaranteed by the 1948 Universal Declaration of Human Rights. The trend toward controlled news in the developing world is making headway nonetheless. Even the European Community issued a directive in 1989 urging members to reserve the majority of their airtime for broadcasts originating in Europe.[83] When UNESCO developed a code of journalistic ethics that defined *responsible* reporting and investigated ways to make journalism a government-licensed profession, the United States withdrew from the organization.

Developing countries are also contesting the control of the United States and other Western powers over world radio and satellite facilities. Scarce international frequencies have been allocated on a first-come, first-served basis, giving the developed nations nearly 90 percent of the broadcast spectrum and the bulk of satellite facilities. Developing nations want to change this. They want to divide the spectrum equally among all nations and bar radio and television satellite transmissions across national borders unless the receiving country has given permission. They have also demanded more control over satellites. The U.S. government has resisted demands by the developing nations, believing that countries with current capability to use advanced telecommunications facilities should control these facilities.

The United States has been the world's foremost international broadcaster.[84] The Voice of America broadcasts have been an integral part of the federal government's foreign information program, which is handled by the United States Information Agency (USIA). Broadcasts from short-wave transmitters in the United States and abroad have been beamed in dozens of languages to millions of foreign listeners. The end of the Cold War and economic stringencies have led to sharp curtailments of the scope of these programs, and their institutional structures have been crumbling.[85]

The decline of international broadcasts and other information dissemination activities, such as USIA libraries and sponsorship of visiting scholars, harms U.S. foreign policy objectives. These programs have portrayed American society and its problems and policies abroad and have provided Western news to countries unlikely to receive it in any other way. Iran, Iraq, Cuba, and China are examples. Every major country currently supports institutions that convey information about its policies, its values, and its national life to peoples beyond its borders. Can the United States afford to lag behind and have its image defined in terms of gangsta rap music, crime- and sex-laden movies, and news clips of foreign tourists murdered in Miami or New York?

Summary

The quality of U.S. foreign policy and the effectiveness of U.S. relations with other countries are crucial to the welfare of people throughout the world. Sound policy and relations require a solid information base. As this chapter has shown, the foreign affairs information base on which Americans depend leaves much to be desired. The causes are complex and cannot be changed readily. They involve the structure of the foreign correspondent corps, the sociopolitical setting in which correspondents must work, and the audiences to whose world views and tastes the news must cater.

Foreign correspondents for the most part are well trained and able. But there are too few of them to cover the world. They work within a narrowly controlled organizational structure consisting of a handful of giant news-gathering institutions that supply the news and entertainment needs of the United States and much of the rest of the world. If one distrusts giant information conglomerates that collect and shape the news for much of the world, the present situation is frightening.

Most Americans are reasonably well satisfied with the foreign news produced by these conglomerates. Live satellite television provides vivid images of breaking news, from tanks in Tiananmen Square, to Scud missiles striking Tel Aviv, to Lenin statues toppling in Moscow.[86] Many of the foreign clienteles, particularly political leaders in developing nations, are not. They complain that agents of monopoly capitalism are guilty of "electronic rape" of their people through decadent entertainment and Western political propaganda.

Foreign affairs news often must be produced under trying conditions. Strange locations and inadequate technological facilities can make nightmares of the physical aspects of getting to the scene of the action, collecting information, and transmitting it. These technical difficulties are compounded by political difficulties. They include the reluctance of officials in the United States and abroad to commit themselves publicly on foreign affairs matters and the harassment of correspondents venturing into places where they are unwanted. Expulsion, imprisonment, and physical harm are common. With so much territory to cover and such limited personnel to cover it, newspeople frequently avoid areas where news is hard to get and devote their efforts instead to areas where public attitudes are supportive. This effectively removes many regions from media scrutiny and contributes to unevenness of news flow from various parts of the world.

How good is the foreign affairs news that reaches the United States and other clients of Western international news transmission facilities? The picture is mixed. Foreign correspondents must produce news that is at once timely, exciting, personalized, and brief, yet understandable for an American audience that is not intensely interested in most events abroad. Given the problems of foreign affairs news production, correspondents dwell heavily on negative and sensational news. They write stories from an American perspective and usually follow the current administration's foreign policy assumptions and the American public's stereotyped views of the world. They primarily cover the most important countries, keeping America's national interests and policy objectives in mind. Despite these shortcomings, Americans can obtain a reasonably accurate view of salient political events abroad, particularly if they turn to several elite newspapers that generally give thorough exposure to controversial American foreign policies. However, these papers rarely challenge the objectives of foreign policies, though they may question the effectiveness of executing them.

In recent years television commentators occasionally have become active diplomats through interviews that set the stage for subsequent political developments. Ted Koppel's "Nightline" television program, for example, has regularly featured electronic encounters between opposing leaders such as Philippine president Ferdinand Marcos and his successor Corazón Aquino or South Africa's former president P. W. Botha and Nobel Peace Prize winner Bishop Desmond Tutu. Aside from these adventures, media influence on foreign policy has been largely indirect, exercised primarily through surveillance activities, the power to choose what to report and what to omit, and the ability to interpret the meaning of events. There has been little investigative or adversary journalism except when foreign affairs were obviously going badly and therefore became highly controversial, as happened toward the end of the Vietnam War. Otherwise, political controversy has largely stopped at the water's edge.

Notes

1. Clyde Haberman, "Ceremony Will Be Hot, Windy, and Made for TV," *New York Times,* October 26, 1994.
2. In a nationwide 1990 survey 23 percent of the respondents who read newspapers (62 percent) and 35 percent who watched television news (59 percent) three or more times said that they paid a great deal or a lot of attention to foreign affairs. Holli A. Semetko, Joanne Bay Brzinski, David Weaver, and Lars Willnat, "TV News and U.S. Public Opinion about Foreign Countries: The Impact of Exposure and Attention," *International Journal of Public Opinion Research* 4 (1992): 27.
3. Times Mirror Center for the People and the Press, "Mixed Messages about Press Freedom on Both Sides of the Atlantic," Washington, D.C., March 16, 1994.
4. Times Mirror Center for the People and the Press, "A Content Analysis: International Coverage Fits Public's Ameri-Centric Mood," News Release, June 25, 1995.
5. Pamela J. Shoemaker, Lucig H. Danielian, and Nancy Brendlinger, "Deviant Acts, Risky Business and U.S. Interests: The Newsworthiness of World Events," *Journalism Quarterly* 68 (Winter 1991): 781–795.
6. Pippa Norris, "The Restless Searchlight: Network News Framing of the Post Cold-War World," *Political Communication* 12(4) (1995): 357–370.
7. Bernard C. Cohen, *The Press and Foreign Policy* (Princeton, N.J.: Princeton University Press, 1963), 164–165.
8. Steven Greenhouse, "The State Department: A Snail in Age of E-Mail," *New York Times,* March 6, 1995.
9. William A. Hachten, with the collaboration of Harva Hachten, *The World News Prism: Changing Media of International Communication,* 3d ed. (Ames: Iowa State University Press, 1992), 41–53. Other important international news suppliers are Germany's Deutsche Press Agentur (DPA) and Japan's Kyodo News Service, as well as China's Xinhua News Agency. United Press International, once second only to the Associated Press, has been teetering on the brink of bankruptcy for many years.
10. For an analysis of the contents of "CNN World Report," see Charles Ganzert and Don M. Flournoy, "The Weekly 'World Report' on CNN, an Analysis," *Journalism Quarterly* 69 (Spring 1992): 188–193.
11. Larson, *Television's Window on the World* (Norwood, N.J.: Ablex, 1984), 171–178.
12. Barry Rubin, "International News and the American Media," in *International News: Freedom under Attack,* ed. Dante B. Fascell (Beverly Hills, Calif.: Sage, 1979), 214.
13. Rubin, "International News," 197–198. However, the fact that television news teams generally involve at least three people has produced some increases in the foreign correspondent corps.

14. Daniel Riffe, "International News Borrowing: A Trend Analysis," *Journalism Quarterly* 61 (Spring 1984): 142–148.
15. Nicholas O. Berry, *Foreign Policy and the Press: An Analysis of the* New York Times' *Coverage of U.S. Foreign Policy* (Westport, Conn.: Greenwood Press, 1990), xiii–xiv, 139–151; W. Lance Bennett, "The News about Foreign Policy," in *Taken by Storm: The Media, Public Opinion, and U.S. Foreign Policy in the Gulf War*, ed. W. Lance Bennett and David L. Paletz (Chicago: University of Chicago Press, 1994), 12–40.
16. Leo Bogart, "The Overseas Newsman: A 1967 Profile Study," *Journalism Quarterly* 45 (Summer 1968): 293–306. Judging from more recent profile studies of American journalists in general, these early profiles are still reasonably accurate. See Chapter 4.
17. In the United States, the needs of foreign correspondents are served by the United States Information Agency (USIA). It maintains foreign press centers in major U.S. cities and arranges high-level briefings by government officials and news-gathering tours on major economic, political, and cultural themes. It also provides extensive information services and even helps with arranging appointments and filing facilities at international summits. Washington, D.C., United States Information Agency, *Foreign Press Centers,* January 1996.
18. Jarol B. Manheim, "Strategic Public Diplomacy: Managing Kuwait's Image During the Gulf Conflict," in *Taken by Storm,* 131–148.
19. Jarol B. Manheim and Robert B. Albritton, "Changing National Images: International Public Relations and Media Agenda-Setting," *American Political Science Review* 78 (September 1984): 641–657; Robert B. Albritton and Jarol B. Manheim, "Public Relations Efforts for the Third World: Images in the News," *Journal of Communication* 35 (Spring 1985): 43–59.
20. Jarol B. Manheim, *All of the People All the Time: Strategic Communication and American Politics* (Armonk, N.Y.: M. E. Sharpe, 1991), 125–126.
21. Shailendra Ghorpade, "Foreign Correspondents Cover Washington for World," *Journalism Quarterly* 61 (Autumn 1984): 667–671; and *Editor and Publisher International Yearbook, 1991* (New York: Editor & Publisher, 1991).
22. *Editor and Publisher International Yearbook, 1991.*
23. Ghorpade, "Foreign Correspondents," 667.
24. Sophia Peterson, "International News Selection by the Elite Press: A Case Study," *Public Opinion Quarterly* 45 (Summer 1981): 159.
25. Youssef M. Ibrahim, "As Toll Rises in Algeria's War, a Dearth of News," *New York Times,* December 28, 1994.
26. Patrick O'Heffernan, "Mass Media and U.S. Foreign Policy: A Mutual Exploitation Model of Media Influence in U.S. Foreign Policy," *Media and Public Policy,* ed. Robert J. Spitzer (Westport, Conn.: Praeger, 1993), 187–211.
27. Herbert J. Gans, *Deciding What's News: A Study of CBS Evening News, NBC Nightly News, Newsweek and Time* (New York: Pantheon Books, 1979), 30–36. See also Johan Galtung and Mari H. Ruge, "The Structure of Foreign News," *Journal of Peace Research* 2 (1965): 64–91.
28. Edwin Diamond, *The Tin Kazoo: Television, Politics, and the News* (Cambridge, Mass.: MIT Press, 1975), 94.
29. Daniel C. Hallin, "Hegemony: The American News Media from Vietnam to El Salvador: A Study of Ideological Change and Its Limits," in *Political Communication Research: Approaches, Studies, Assessments,* ed. David L. Paletz (Norwood, N.J.: Ablex, 1987), 17; Robert M. Entman, "Hegemonic Socialization,

Information Processing, and Presidential News Management: Framing the KAL and Iran Air Incidents," in *The Psychology of Political Communication,* ed. Ann Crigler (Ann Arbor: University of Michigan Press, 1996); W. Lance Bennett, "Marginalizing the Majority: Conditioning Public Opinion to Accept Managerial Democracy," in *Manipulating Public Opinion: Essays on Public Opinion as a Dependent Variable,* ed. Michael Margolis and Gary A. Mauser (Pacific Grove, Calif.: Brooks/Cole, 1989), chap. 15; and Hans Mathias Kepplinger, "Put in the Public Spotlight—Instrumental Actualization of Actors, Events, and Aspects in the Coverage on Nicaragua," in *The Mass Media in Liberal Democratic Societies,* ed. Stanley Rothman (New York: Paragon House, 1992), 201–219.

30. See Galtung and Ruge, "The Structure of Foreign News," for their much-quoted scheme for rating the newsworthiness of various types of foreign affairs events. See also Elinar Ostgaard, "Factors Influencing the Flow of News," *Journal of Peace Research* 2 (1965): 39–63.

31. William Adams and Phillip Heyl, "From Cairo to Kabul with the Networks, 1972–1980," in *Television Coverage of the Middle East,* ed. William C. Adams (Norwood, N.J.: Ablex, 1981), 26.

32. Rubin, "International News and the American Media," 227.

33. Francis X. Clines, "In U.S. TV, Israelis Find an Unflattering Mirror," *New York Times,* February 1, 1988; and John Kifner, "Israeli Officials Object to U.S. News Coverage of Riots," *New York Times,* December 29, 1987. Also see Patrick O'Heffernan, *Mass Media and American Foreign Policy: Insider Perspectives on Global Journalism and the Foreign Policy Process* (Norwood, N.J.: Ablex, 1991), 29–36.

34. Michael X. Delli Carpini and Bruce A. Williams, "Television and Terrorism: Patterns of Presentation and Occurrence, 1969 to 1980," *Western Political Quarterly* 40 (March 1987): 45–64.

35. This discussion is patterned on Doris A. Graber, *News and Democracy: Are Their Paths Diverging?* (Bloomington: Indiana University School of Journalism, 1992); also see Norris, "The Restless Searchlight."

36. Times Mirror, "A Content Analysis," 8.

37. Michael Griffin and Jongsoo Lee, "Picturing the Gulf War: Constructing an Image of War in *Time, Newsweek, and U.S. News and World Report,*" *Journalism and Mass Communication Quarterly* 72(4) (1995): 813–825.

38. Robert M. Entman, "Framing U.S. Coverage of International News: Contrasts in Narratives of the KAL and Iran Air Incidents," *Journal of Communication* 41 (Autumn 1991): 6–27.

39. Ibid., 22–23.

40. David R. Gergen, "Diplomacy in a Television Age: The Dangers of Teledemocracy," in *The Media and Foreign Policy,* ed. Simon Serfaty (New York: St. Martin's, 1991), 47–63.

41. Stephen S. Rosenfeld, "In the Gulf: The Wars of the Press," in *The Media and Foreign Policy,* 241–255. For a detailed account of news coverage before and during the war, see Bennett and Paletz, eds., *Taken by Storm.*

42. Hachten, *The World News Prism,* 165–166.

43. Robert Pear, "Military Revises Rules to Assure Reporters Access to Battle Areas," *New York Times,* May 22, 1992.

44. Quoted in Fernando Reyes Matta, "The Latin American Concept of News," *Journal of Communication* 29 (Spring 1979): 169.

45. Gary D. Gaddy and Enoch Tanjong, "Earthquake Coverage by the Western Press," *Journal of Communication* 36 (Spring 1986): 105–112. For a conflicting analysis, see William C. Adams, "Whose Lives Count?: TV Coverage of Natural Disasters," *Journal of Communication* 36 (Spring 1986): 113–122.

46. Benjamin D. Singer, "Violence, Protest, and War in Television News: The U.S. and Canada Compared," *Public Opinion Quarterly* 34 (Winter 1970–1971): 611–616; and Chris J. Scheer and Sam W. Eiler, "A Comparison of Canadian and American Network Television News," *Journal of Broadcasting* 16 (Spring 1972): 156–164.

47. James P. Winter, Pirouz Shoar Ghaffari, and Vernone M. Sparkes, "How Major U.S. Dailies Covered Quebec Separatism Referendum," *Journalism Quarterly* 59 (Winter 1982): 608.

48. Edward W. Said, *Covering Islam: How the Media and the Experts Determine How We See the Rest of the World* (New York: Pantheon Books, 1981), chap. 2.

49. Hanna Adoni and S. Mane, "Media and the Social Construction of Reality: Toward an Integration of Theory and Research," *Communication Research* 11 (July 1984): 323–340.

50. Edward S. Herman, "Diversity of News: 'Marginalizing' the Opposition," *Journal of Communication* 35 (Fall 1985): 135–146. See also W. Lance Bennett, "An Introduction to Journalism Norms and Representations of Politics," *Political Communication* 13(4) (forthcoming, 1996).

51. John A. Lent, "Foreign News in American Media," *Journal of Communication* 27 (Winter 1977): 46–50. See also Jyotika Ramaprasad and Daniel Riffe, "Effect of U.S.-India Relations on *New York Times* Coverage," *Journalism Quarterly* 64 (Summer/Autumn 1987): 537–543; Hallin, "Hegemony"; and David Altheide, "Media Hegemony: A Failure of Perspective," *Public Opinion Quarterly* 48 (Summer 1984): 476–490.

52. Robert M. Entman and David L. Paletz, "The War in Southeast Asia: Tunnel Vision on Television," in *Television Coverage of International Affairs*, ed. William C. Adams (Norwood, N.J.: Ablex, 1982), 181–201; Daniel C. Hallin, "The Media, the War in Vietnam and Political Support: A Critique of the Thesis of an Oppositional Media, *Journal of Politics* 46 (February 1984). Also see Nicholas O. Berry, *Foreign Policy and the Press: An Analysis of the New York Times' Coverage of U.S. Foreign Policy* (Westport, Conn.: Greenwood, 1990), for many examples.

53. "TV Networks Say Coverage Would Not Endanger Troops," *New York Times*, September 19, 1994.

54. The discussion that follows is based on James F. Larson, "Television and U.S. Foreign Policy: The Case of the Iran Hostage Crisis," *Journal of Communication* 36 (Autumn 1986): 108–130; and Joseph Fromm, "TV: Does It Box in President in a Crisis?" *U.S. News & World Report*, July 15, 1985, 23–24. Also see O'Heffernan, "Mass Media and U.S. Foreign Policy," passim.

55. Quoted in John Corry, "The Intrusion of Television in the Hostage Crisis," *New York Times*, June 26, 1985.

56. Quoted in Ibid.

57. O'Heffernan, *Mass Media and American Foreign Policy*, 40.

58. Ibid., 49.

59. Ibid., 75.

60. Ibid., 77.

61. Ibid., 48. Berry, in *Foreign Policy and the Press*, makes the same argument.

62. Article III, UNESCO Declaration on the Media.

63. Timothy E. Cook, "Afterword: Political Values and Production Values," *Political Communication* 13(4) (forthcoming, 1996).

64. James Reston, *Sketches in the Sand* (New York: Knopf, 1967), 195; for supporting evidence in the Gulf War, see Gladys Engel Lang and Kurt Lang, "The Press as Prologue: Media Coverage of Saddam's Iraq, 1979–1990," in *Taken By Storm*, 43–62.

65. Quoted in Rubin, "International News," 216.

66. Ibid., 193.

67. Peter Braestrup, *Big Story: How the American Press and Television Reported and Interpreted the Crisis of Tet 1968 in Vietnam and Washington* (Garden City, N.Y.: Anchor Press/Doubleday, 1978).

68. The influence of television on the perception of unfamiliar issues is discussed in Shanto Iyengar and Donald Kinder, *News That Matters: Television and American Opinion* (Chicago: University of Chicago Press, 1987).

69. William C. Adams, "Mass Media and Public Opinion about Foreign Affairs: A Typology of News Dynamics," *Political Communication and Persuasion* 4 (1987): 263–278.

70. William Schneider, "Bang-Bang Television: The New Superpower," *Public Opinion* 5 (April/May 1982): 13–14.

71. Larson, *Television's Window on the World,* 34–35.

72. William Adams and Phillip Heyl, "From Cairo to Kabul with the Networks, 1972–1980," in *Television Coverage of the Middle East,* ed. William C. Adams (Norwood, N.J.: Ablex, 1981), 16, 19–22. Also see Zhongdang Pan, Ronald E. Ostman, Patricia Moy, and Paula Reynolds, "News Media Exposure and Its Learning Effects during the Persian Gulf War," *Journalism and Mass Communication Quarterly* 71(1) (1994): 7–19; and Semetko et al., "TV News and U.S. Public Opinion," 30. Apparently print news has less impact on opinions than television news.

73. Mustapha Masmoudi, "The New World Information Order," *Journal of Communication* 29 (Spring 1979): 172–185. For an explanation of how international news services function, see Jonathan Fenby, *The International News Services* (New York: Schocken Books, 1986).

74. For a discussion of media imperialism, see Herbert I. Schiller, *Culture, Inc.: The Corporate Takeover of Public Expression* (New York: Oxford University Press, 1989); and René Jean Ravault, "International Information: Bullet or Boomerang?" in *Political Communication Research: Approaches, Studies, Assessments,* ed. David L. Paletz (Norwood, N.J.: Ablex, 1987), 245–265.

75. The impact of foreign television is assessed in Alexis S. Tan, Sarrina Li, and Charles Simpson, "American TV and Social Stereotypes of Americans in Taiwan and Mexico," *Journalism Quarterly* 63 (Winter 1986): 809–814.

76. Ravault, "International Information: Bullet or Boomerang?"; Glen Fisher, *American Communication in a Global Society* (Norwood, N.J.: Ablex, 1987), 15–18; and Michael B. Salwan, "Cultural Imperialism: A Media Effects Approach," *Critical Studies in Mass Communication* 8 (1991): 29–38. For a contrary viewpoint, see Herbert I. Schiller, "Not Yet the Post-Imperialist Era," *Critical Studies in Mass Communication* 8 (1991): 13–28.

77. W. James Potter, "News from Three Worlds in Prestige U.S. Newspapers," *Journalism Quarterly* 64 (Spring 1987): 73–79.

78. Wilbur Schramm and L. Erwin Atwood, *Circulation of News in the Third World: A Study of Asia* (Hong Kong: Chinese University Press, 1981); and David H.

Weaver and G. Cleveland Wilhoit, "Foreign News Coverage in Two U.S. Wire Services," *Journal of Communication* 31 (Spring 1981): 55–63. For a contrary view, see Daniel Riffe and Eugene F. Shaw, "Conflict and Consonance: Coverage of Third World in Two U.S. Papers," *Journalism Quarterly* 59 (Winter 1982): 617–626.

79. Coverage by smaller media is discussed in G. Cleveland Wilhoit and David Weaver, "Foreign News Coverage in Two U.S. Wire Services: An Update," *Journal of Communication* 33 (Spring 1983): 132–148.

80. S. M. Mazharul Haque, "Is U.S. Coverage of News in Third World Imbalanced?" *Journalism Quarterly* 60 (Fall 1983): 523–524. Leonard R. Sussman, "Information Control as an International Issue," in *The Communications Revolution in Politics,* ed. Gerald Benjamin (New York: Academy of Political Science, 1982), 183.

81. Oliver Boyd-Barrett, "Media Imperialism: Towards an International Framework for the Analysis of Media Systems," in *Mass Communication and Society,* ed. James Curran, Michael Gurevitch, and Janet Woolacott (London: Arnold, 1971), 117, 129.

82. One exception is Brazil, which supplies its own domestic market and exports programs worldwide. Omar Souki Oliveira, "Brazilian Media Usage as a Test of Dependency Theory," *Canadian Journal of Communication* 13 (1988): 16–27.

83. Duncan H. Brown, "Citizens or Consumers: U.S. Reactions to the European Community's Directive on Television," *Critical Studies in Mass Communication* 8 (1991): 1–12.

84. Sean Kelly, "Access Denied: The Politics of Press Censorship," in *International News: Freedom Under Attack,* 255.

85. Steven Greenhouse, "Budget Battles Undercut U.S. Information Effort," *New York Times,* July 6, 1995.

86. Timothy J. McNulty, "Decisions at the Speed of Satellite," *Chicago Tribune,* December 22, 1991.

Readings

Bennett, W. Lance, and David L. Paletz. *Taken by Storm: The Media, Public Opinion, and U.S. Foreign Policy in the Gulf War.* Chicago: University of Chicago Press, 1994.

Berry, Nicholas O. *Foreign Policy and the Press: An Analysis of the* New York Times' *Coverage of U.S. Foreign Policy.* Westport, Conn.: Greenwood Press, 1990.

Fortner, Robert S. *Public Diplomacy and International Politics: The Symbolic Constructs of Summits and International Radio News.* Westport, Conn.: Praeger, 1994.

Galtung, Johan, and Richard C. Vincent. *Global Glasnost: Toward a New World Information/Communication Order?* Cresskill, N.J.: Hampton Press, 1992.

Hachten, William A., with Harva Hachten. *The World News Prism: Changing Media of International Communication,* 3d ed. Ames: Iowa State University Press, 1992.

Hallin, Daniel C. *The "Uncensored War": The Media and Vietnam.* New York: Oxford University Press, 1986.

Hess, Stephen. *International News and Foreign Correspondents.* Washington, D.C.: Brookings Institution, 1996.

O'Heffernan, Patrick. *Mass Media and American Foreign Policy: Insider Perspectives on Global Journalism and the Foreign Policy Process.* Norwood, N.J.: Ablex, 1991.

Rotberg, Robert I., and Thomas G. Weiss, eds. *From Massacres to Genocide: The Media, Public Policy, and Humanitarian Crises.* Washington, D.C.: Brookings Institution, 1995.

Trends in Media Policy

I N SHAKESPEARE'S *JULIUS CAESAR* BRUTUS URGES his fellow conspirators to act while the time is ripe:

> There is a tide in the affairs of men
> Which, taken at the flood, leads on to fortune;
> Omitted, all the voyage of their life
> Is bound in shallows and in miseries.
> On such a full sea are we now afloat;
> And we must take the current when it serves
> Or lose our ventures.[1]

Communications policy is standing on just such a threshold in the waning years of the twentieth century. New technologies call for a rethinking of established policy directions, but they must interact with established social structures and cultural patterns. Hence, old policy concepts linger and make the future hostage to the past. With the possible exception of passage of the Telecommunications Act of 1996 that replaced its 1934 predecessor, attempts to take control of the tides of change have faltered thus far, diminishing the chance to reap the full benefits made possible by the communications revolution.

Both the forces pushing for major changes in communications policies and the obstacles that lie in the way will be discussed in this chapter. We will explore some of the areas of disenchantment with mass media performance that have fueled demands for reform and the steps taken by dissatisfied communicators and audiences to improve and supplement the existing information supply. The potential impact of major new technologies on politics and policy alternatives will be examined. Finally, we will

380

peer into the murky crystal ball to try to discern the shape of future communications policies that will affect the interaction between the mass media and the American political system in the twenty-first century.

Dissatisfaction with the Media

Public confidence in the press and regard for its honesty and ethical standards have eroded steadily since their peak in the Watergate era. By 1994, only 10 percent of the respondents to a survey by the National Opinion Research Center expressed "a great deal of confidence" in the people running media institutions. Recent college graduates in the eighteen to twenty-four-year age range were particularly distrustful.[2] When asked to mention specific reasons for mistrusting the media, complaints about sensationalized news headed the list. They were followed by charges that the media often do not tell the whole story but report selectively instead, that they are biased and unfair, and that stories are often inaccurate and full of unverified gossip, rumors, and even lies.

The streams of discontent run sufficiently deep to move sizable numbers of people to lodge formal complaints. More than one hundred thousand complaints about television are registered annually at the Washington Broadcast Bureau of the Federal Communications Commission (FCC).[3] Most complaints concern the display of obscenity, excessive crime and violence, infringement of equal time provisions, unfair portrayals of ethnic and racial minorities and groups outside mainstream society, and dissatisfaction with the substance and amount of advertising.

Besides the formal complaints lodged with the FCC, a host of less formal criticisms have been made as well. Media critics call television a vast intellectual wasteland. They chide the networks for greedy pandering to mass audiences and blame shallow programming, lacking in background and context, and cheap appeals to human emotions on the desire to secure high ratings that will raise advertising income. They complain about the scant denunciation of major malfunctions in American society and politics and about the sneering tone and cynicism that mark coverage of political leaders. Similar complaints are voiced about print media. Newspapers are accused of superficial coverage, toadyish catering to their financial benefactors, and all-too-frequent mean-spirited excursions into sensationalism and sleaze. The press, says *Chicago Tribune* columnist Bill Granger, has become judge, jury, and executioner—the pitbull of politics.[4]

Media orientations toward politics have been criticized as both too liberal and too conservative. Sniping from the left about the media's subservience to the establishment and insensitivity to the concerns of the politically powerless and economically deprived has been balanced by criticism from the middle and the right. Conservatives accuse the media of demeaning the status of American business and industry and of respected professions such as medicine and law. The media, they argue, are unduly romantic about the woes and virtues of the poor, the disadvantaged, and the racially different. In the process the media allegedly undermine the nation's economy and hurt its prestige at home and abroad. Liberals charge that the media perpetuate a society that caters to the interests of economically privileged elites at the expense of the concerns of average Americans. Liberals and conservatives alike accuse the media of invading individual privacy and impairing the fairness of the judicial process. The gist of these charges is that the media do not serve the public interest and that they fail to nourish a viable democratic political order. These elusive concepts are always measured by political yardsticks of questionable accuracy and validity. How valid are the charges that the media fail to nourish democratic life? How do dissatisfied Americans cope with shortcomings in their information supply? What forms do media criticism take and what effects do they produce?

Putting Criticism into Perspective

Most of the charges made by media critics have been echoed in the pages of this book. Nonetheless, a blanket indictment of the media for failure to nourish democratic life adequately is not supported by the evidence. First and foremost, the collective noun *news media* covers a broad range of institutions. It does not refer only to newspapers and news magazines and various forms of television and radio as groupings of news media types; it also refers to individual institutions within these broad categories. In terms of supplying information essential for citizens in a democracy, there is a wide gulf between the *New York Times* on one hand and the scores of tabloids and small town newspapers that highlight local society news on the other. There is a great deal of journalistic wheat as well as chaff in U.S. media, and the proportions of each vary widely in individual media. In fact, I contend that any citizen willing to make the effort to get essential current information about a broad array of major issues of the day can find it in U.S. media, though not necessarily in those most readily available to the average person.

Any fair indictment of the news media must also consider mitigating circumstances. This does not mean that the charges are invalid; it means that they must be put into context to assess the degree of guilt. The pressures under which journalists do their work must be considered. These have been discussed in the chapters dealing with domestic and foreign news production under normal and crisis conditions. Besides the economic constraints to produce profits for the enterprise that account for excesses of negativism and voyeur journalism, they include major journalistic conventions of news production. The zeal to rush to publication with breaking news, for example, fosters mistakes and misinterpretations; the beat system privileges newsworthy events occurring on regular beats over important happenings that occur beyond these beats; pack journalism homogenizes criteria for news selection to make most media rivals in conformity.

Recent economic developments have heightened pressures. The entry of many new enterprises into the field of electronic media has forced electronic as well as print media to compete more fiercely for audiences and for advertisers. Shrinking profit margins in individual enterprises have forced cutbacks in staffs that put additional workloads on the survivors. While databases that could be used to provide context for stories have grown exponentially, the time available to individual reporters to search them has shrunk. Newspaper journalists face the additional problem that the electronic media enjoy the advantage of featuring freshly breaking news so that print must abandon the lure of novelty for other ways to attract audiences. Their solution has been to turn to more analytical and interpretive reporting, which is often indistinguishable from outright editorial commentary. The upshot has been that the public increasingly perceives newspaper reporting as unduly biased.

Finally, one must put complaints about the media into historical perspective. They are occurring at a period in history when regard for most major institutions in the United States is at a low ebb. Moreover, when people are asked to appraise the particular newspaper with which they are most familiar, 80 percent gave it a favorable rating in 1994, a level that has been steady over the past decade. Television networks have had similar ratings, though they plunged by more than 10 percentage points to a 69-percent level in 1994.[5] History also shows that politicians and the general public are fickle in their condemnations as well as their praise. The Founders of our Republic were the first to complain about its venal, lying press on one hand and on the other the first to agree that, warts and all, it was the bedrock on which democratic freedoms rest.

Informal Criticism

Given the public's and politicians' penchant to take the media to task for their many serious shortcomings, what forms do these complaints take? Informal criticism has come from within the journalism profession as well as from the general public. Specialized journals that frequently review media performance, such as the *American Journalism Review* and *Columbia Journalism Review*, publish criticism by media professionals. Many review journals have been short-lived because they could not maintain enough subscribers to pay their expenses. The degree of influence wielded by such journals is a matter of opinion. Within narrow circles, professional reputations may be affected. But the circulation of these reviews is so limited, and the pocketbook effects of adverse criticism are so negligible, that their pressure on the industry to alter journalistic practices is likely to be small.

More robust and probably more influential vehicles of criticism are critical essays by media analysts writing for television networks and high-circulation newspapers and news magazines. Columnists such as *Newsweek*'s Jonathan Alter, reporters such as the *Washington Post*'s Howard Kurtz, and television hosts such as Ted Koppel have become familiar gadflies of the news business and the journalism profession. Their work supplements the efforts of many academic experts who have written critical appraisals of the mass media in recent years. Authors Lance Bennett, Norman Isaacs, Tom Goldstein, Robert Entman, Michael Parenti, and Herbert Schiller belong in this group.[6] They have been joined by a bevy of media insiders such as James Fallows and Leo Bogart.[7] The media also routinely are scanned critically, if informally, at professional conventions of social scientists and journalists. Special workshops, such as the annual Aspen Conference on Communications and Society, have focused narrowly on specific problems of the media and have publicized reform proposals.

Informal criticism has also come from various public interest groups. In many cases these have been institutions organized for other purposes, such as the national Parent and Teacher Association (PTA) or the American Medical Association (AMA). Special media action groups have voiced their concerns publicly. The National Citizens Committee for Broadcasting and Washington-based Center for Media Education are examples. Complaints by public interest and media action groups, like most other forms of informal criticism, have been largely ineffectual. The critics may disturb the news profession momentarily, but they rarely induce major and permanent changes in media policies.

Formal Criticism

Formal protests about media performance can be lodged with the FCC's Broadcast Bureau in Washington or at FCC hearings. The commission holds such hearings before granting broadcast licenses or when licenses have been challenged. They provide opportunities to counter the pressures brought by the media industry and balance the pro-industry biases that public regulatory bodies often develop. For example, in the wake of complaints the FCC has withheld license renewals to stations whose offerings of children's programs fell short of the requirements of the 1990 Children's Television Act.[8]

Formal avenues for criticism and policy suggestions by the public are beneficial. However, a number of serious problems have diminished their usefulness. Most fundamental and least solvable is the problem of making sure that the complaints and suggestions thus aired represent widely shared beliefs. Advocates of mainstream positions are often conspicuously silent. The laudable desire to hear and heed dissenters may lead to inordinate concern about the merits of their claims, to the detriment of more general public interests.

A few examples of vociferous protests illustrate the problem of determining what constitutes the "voice of the people." Some of these protests were ignored; others were heeded. The miniseries "Holocaust" that dramatized Nazi atrocities was loudly opposed by groups claiming that it generated anti-German feelings and hatred between Jews and gentiles. Yet it attracted between 38 and 48 million viewers nightly and was widely acclaimed. In the same way, between 30 and 40 million people watched and praised each episode of the "Godfather" series about Mafia ventures. Yet thousands of Italian Americans denounced the show as slandering Italians. Stories about abortion, homosexuality, drug addiction, the activities of religious cults, or the successful ventures of discredited politicians have often been suppressed or toned down because of the flood of protests they might invite.

Media policies can also be challenged in the nation's courts. However, most lawsuits involving claims about harmful television programming have failed. A widely publicized example is the trial of Ronny Zamora, a teenager who was convicted by a Florida court for murdering an eighty-three-year-old woman. His parents sued the three networks for negligent programming, claiming that television shows had incited and taught their son how to murder. The suit was dismissed by a federal judge who ruled that the media had not been negligent.[9] In 1978 a California court likewise dismissed a negligence suit against NBC brought by the parents of a young rape victim. The rape had mimicked a scene from the movie "Born Innocent," which had been shown on television four days earlier.[10]

To enhance public influence on communications policy, there have been proposals to place ombudsmen—formal advocates of the public's interests—in various bodies that deal with communications policy. Alternatively, a central ombudsman office has been proposed to assist public interest groups and individuals in preparing and presenting their complaints and suggestions. Thus far, these proposals have not been implemented. However, several dozen newspapers have set up ombudsmen facilities to permit readers to challenge news policies.[11] Readers' concerns and ombudsmen's activities are regularly reported by these papers.

Elected or appointed bodies that hear and investigate complaints about mass media output—media councils—are another avenue for channeling criticism. These councils then publicize their findings, using the power of publicity to correct undesirable media practices. Media councils generally lack power to enforce their recommendations. Media councils have been used in Great Britain and in some Middle Western and Western states and cities in the United States. The press has strongly opposed media councils, even though they appear to enhance media credibility and reduce the frequency of libel suits.[12] Journalists fear that councils will impair their editorial independence by publicizing appraisals of the merits of ongoing news policies. When a National News Council was set up in 1973, several news organizations gave space to its activities and reports. But it never became a major force in arbitrating questions of media ethics. It was dissolved in 1984.[13]

Specialized Media

Hundreds of specialized media address information needs neglected or poorly served by the regular media. They are a partial antidote for the general mass media's failure to cover many important groups and issues. Ethnic media, discussed in Chapter 10, are examples. Numerous professional and trade journals and newsletters are devoted to a multitude of concerns such as religion, sports, fine and popular arts, automobiles, health issues, and bird watching. Some specialized media, such as the *New Republic, Mother Jones,* the *National Review,* and, at times, the *New Yorker,* are primarily devoted to political commentary. Recent simple and cheap technologies also enable many interest groups to keep in touch via computer links and to publish and distribute their own magazines, newsletters, and audio- and videotapes on controversial political issues. Antinuclear and environmental groups, for example, have used these means of communication, as have supporters of candidates for political office. If audiences numbering into thousands and even millions of people constitute a "mass," these are, by definition, mass media. Modern means of distributing information bridge the distances that physically separate large but widely dispersed audiences that share specialized interests.

The demand for targeted information has increased in recent years so that more than ten thousand magazines are now published in the

United States, even though the popularity of specialized magazines has led to the demise of broadly oriented publications such as *Look,* the original *Life,* and the *Saturday Evening Post.*[14] Specialized media also encompass the politically radical, iconoclastic, and counterculture media that flourish in times of social and political stress such as the late 1960s and early 1970s. These media feature the flagrant opposition to government policy that is often forbidden in other countries.

In the Vietnam era and its aftermath, some alternative publications went beyond rejecting the current political establishment and attacked the values and culture of American mainstream society. In this they differed from social responsibility journalism that supports basic American values and attacks only their violations. Politically, the underground media were generally left-wing in orientation: Communist, Socialist, or Anarchist. They attracted attention by being totally subjective and visually and verbally shocking. Pornography and profanity abounded because underground journalists felt that their assaults on American society must be sensational to succeed. At the height of underground press popularity, readership was estimated at ten million, with most issues used by several people.

The rise of the underground press demonstrates that mass media can be started and operated with modest means. The media of the 1960s were financed mostly through advertising for things like counterculture records, music productions, pornographic movies, and classified advertisements requesting services such as sex partners, nude models, or hallucinogenic drugs. Staffs were paid meager salaries or no salaries at all.[15]

Underground media in the 1960s were not limited to the comparatively unregulated print realm. They also flourished in the regulated broadcast field. Underground radio stations featured mostly rock music and disc jockeys who commented on society, sexual matters, the drug culture, and other counterculture interests. The FCC rarely interfered with their unconventional activities. The mushrooming of protest media in the 1960s and 1970s—at one time there were nearly one thousand underground newspapers and four hundred counterculture radio stations—attests to the vitality and flexibility of the mass media system.[16] The abrupt decline of underground media with the end of the Vietnam War also shows that the system is able to prune its unneeded branches when the demand ends.

The tolerance of the government for underground media demonstrates that government control over media content, however offensive, has had a light touch. Few countries equal and none exceeds the freedom to express radical viewpoints enjoyed by American media. In fact, some of the causes pressed by underground news sources ultimately became part of mainstream politics. In the end waning public support rather than official censorship led to the steep decline in this genre of journalism. Neither technical nor legal barriers block a revival should social or political conditions provide enough incentives.

The Impact of New Technologies

Marshall McLuhan, the television guru of the 1960s, predicted that the world would become a global village where humanity would partake of a global culture via television.[17] His vision of shared audiovisual news and entertainment has largely come to pass, but reality is quite different and, in many respects, far richer than even McLuhan imagined. The vast amounts of diverse information produced by new technologies permit people to create their own, individualized information diet. The new age of personalized mass media has arrived. Political scientist W. Russell Neuman predicted this development at the start of the 1990s when he pointed out that we now "have the opportunity to design a new electronic and optical network that will blur the distinction between mass and interpersonal communications.... A single high capacity digital network will combine computing, telephony, broadcasting, motion pictures and publishing."[18] The new media confront audiences with growing arrays of choices of program content, format, and timing, and with opportunities for private or public interactive telecommunication.

The new technologies have reduced the public's dependence on traditional media. The store of information made available through new radio, television, and computer channels, through communication satellites, and through round-the-clock news programs has grown by leaps and bounds.[19] Small as well as large communities share in this bounty, reducing the dangers of monopoly control over local information and opening up hitherto closed communication ghettos. Even newspapers can be printed and transmitted electronically, making it easier to bypass local media and rely on distant news sources. Cable television systems now can offer broadcasts from hundreds of separate channels, vastly increasing consumer choices of channels, if not content. The large number of radio and television programs available from satellites can be received by television stations over the air or through cable channels. Individual consumers can tap directly into these offerings through backyard satellite dishes. Space for various types of electronic transmissions, including television, can be rented by public and private parties from the satellites' owners.

Videotape recorders, videotapes, and videodiscs store electronic fare, allowing people to watch broadcasts that they would have missed

Reprinted by permission: Tribune Media Services.

otherwise because of schedule conflicts. Annoying commercials can be readily suppressed. Nearly half of America's 96 million households have at least one video recorder, a phenomenal number considering that it takes a bit of sophistication to operate VCRs. Pay cable and pay over-the-air television provide special entertainment or special interest programs at moderate costs. People pay solely for those programs they choose to watch. Public access cable channels keep citizens in closer touch with various public institutions and political leaders. They also permit these leaders to address the public directly without having their pronouncements mutilated by hostile journalists. Such opportunities slightly tip the scales of editorial power in favor of politicians and away from professional journalists.

When programs are interactive, average people can transform themselves into broadcasters who address their messages to audiences of their choice, including journalists. In addition to flourishing talk shows on radio and television, two-way channels have become commonplace on cable television. Viewers can interact with others while watching the same programs. Two-way communication technologies using radios, telephones, and computers have been useful in integrating outlying areas with social service systems in more populated centers. In Alaska and northern Canada, for example, these technologies deliver educational and health services and give people a greater voice in government.[20]

Thanks to the new technologies the mass media business has made noteworthy advances on three fronts: news gathering, news processing, and news dissemination. Access to computer databases and satellites has put an enormous store of usable information within reach of average newspeople wherever they may be. Even foreign countries kept off-limits by hostile rulers can be explored by satellites, as can remote areas of the globe and even the private retreats of powerful elites. The ability to search databases electronically for specific bits of information and to combine these data in a variety of ways opens up countless new possibilities for creating news stories and providing valuable contextual information for fast-moving current developments.

When it comes to distribution, the array of available channels for immediate or delayed transmission has multiplied far beyond the range deemed possible a scant twenty-five years ago. Stations can even use satellites to supply other stations with live videos of stories that the station has covered locally. These offerings reduce dependence on current network programming, enable local stations to put a local spin on national news, and vastly expand television programming options. The dependence on network programming has been reduced even further by round-the-clock news programming by CNN and its competitors. CNN, in particular, captures large shares of the network audiences whenever there are major continuous news events like the Gulf War or the O. J. Simpson trial.

New broadcasting and narrowcasting technologies usually produce problems along with their benefits and require new policies. High definition television (HDTV) is a case in point. Besides requiring consumers to buy new television sets to receive digital television signals, most television stations will have to spend $8 million to $10 million for new equipment and transmitting towers. In sparsely settled regions, where several towers are required, the costs may run to $25 million. In view of these major and costly changes, the FCC conceived a fifteen-year transition plan. Currently licensed broadcasters would receive a second channel free of charge to duplicate their analog programs in digital versions on this second channel. At the end of the fifteen-year period of airing both analog and digital versions of their programs, the broadcasters would return their original channels to the government while retaining the digital channel as their sole outlet.

The plan, although not abandoned, has run into some powerful political crosscurrents. Although the 1996 Telecommunications Act has embraced the principle of awarding digital channels free of charge, influential members of Congress want the channels auctioned off to the highest bidders. The telephone companies, which pay the government for the right to transmit information over the public airways and who fear potential competition in data transmission from the broadcast industry, are also lobbying against free channels for broadcasters. Naturally, broadcast industry leaders are strongly opposed to any changes in the current rules. They are eager to get high definition television under way, as are the manufacturers of the new television sets. In fact, there are pressures to shorten the transition period to seven years—a window of time that some experts consider far too short to complete the many required equipment changes. Although the technical sophistication of America's engineers may be able to speed up the transition period, it is highly unlikely that the political system will keep pace. The FCC's small staff, which has been chronically overworked, is bogged down with making rules to implement the telephone regulations aspects of the new Telecommunications Act. It has no time to work on rules for high definition television in the foreseeable future. Meanwhile, the broadcast industry, including equipment suppliers, are chomping at the bit. They have been waiting far too long—more than ten years—for this "blessed event." It promises to be a difficult birth.[21]

Another major problem exacerbated by the new technologies concerns safeguarding individual privacy. Ever smaller cameras and microphones permit reporters to spy with little chance for detection. Today reporters and other people can assemble scattered bits of information in seconds to derive a comprehensive portrait of an individual's past. Unless individual privacy becomes more fully protected, the computer age could well turn into an Orwellian nightmare—with individuals living in glass cages and exposed to instant public scrutiny.[22] Likewise, the new information-gathering techniques will make it far more difficult to protect national security information from prying eyes. Congress and the courts will be hard put to strike a sound balance between a free press and a secure society. All this is happening at a time when damaging information can spread through private or public channels faster and more widely than ever before.

The Internet

The technology with potentially the largest impact on the way the traditional media conduct their business is interactive computer communication via the Internet and its components, such as e-mail, Usenets and List-serves, and the World Wide Web. The Internet was created to facilitate communication between defense research centers so that they could survive a nuclear attack. Therefore, it has no central cluster of studios that distribute the bulk of messages. Each unit is equipped to be a broadcaster as well as a receiver. This basic architecture has now been opened to the world's civilian populations, enabling them to broadcast their messages to mass audiences, at costs that are affordable to millions, on a par with the world's journalists.

Faster than rabbits and even fruit flies, various species of broadcasters have multiplied on the Internet, making their messages available to some 30 million viewers and listeners, mostly "white males under 50 with plenty of computer terminal time, great typing skills, high math SAT's, [and] strongly held opinions on just about everything...."[23] The full impact on America's political life in general, and on the news media scene in particular, is as yet unclear. Here are some of the speculations, based on dimly recognizable trends.

The news media's tight control over access to large mass audiences has been sharply diminished. Politicians, for example, who have felt victimized by journalists who paraphrased their comments and boiled them down to meaningless nuggets, can now reach audiences directly. Moreover, they can customize their messages so that they fit the needs of various target populations. Politicians who have found it difficult to win access to a media platform—third-party candidates and candidates for local offices are examples—now have alternative channels at their command.

The Web makes it possible for average individuals, who have long been ignored by the traditional news media, to make their voices heard in the public arena. Individuals and groups with modest intellectual and economic resources can now reach widely dispersed audiences throughout most parts of the world. Their messages can be constructed to inform or deceive, to rally people for good and bad causes, or to entertain them in socially approved or condemned ways. (Censorship has not yet come to the Internet, though it is looming in the wings.) Whether audiences will choose to receive these messages remains to be seen and will probably vary considerably depending on government policies, the identities of the senders and potential receivers, and the contents of these messages. The only thing that seems already clear is that the explosion of easily available information is making the competition for receivers' attention extraordinarily fierce.

There is, as yet, no satisfactory solution to the problem of finding one's way through the Internet's lush jungles of information. It is easy to get lost for hours, sampling usable and unusable intellectual growths without knowing whether one has actually reached the most important specimens. Moreover, the stock of information is doubling every six months! Journalists still remain essential, therefore, because they are trained to ferret out what seems "most important" within their cultural milieu and to present it in language that average people can understand. Unlike the often unknown dispatchers of computerized information, they or their institutions are deemed reasonably trustworthy. This is why most people, for most of their political information, will continue to turn to traditional-style media most of the time. This holds especially true when it comes to general information, beyond specialized concerns, and for the ninety percent of the American public that finds it too difficult, or costly, or inconvenient to use the Internet's sources of political information.

However, information made available through Internet sources is likely to trickle down to the general population through journalists who use the Net and the Web. In fact, journalists are among the elites who stand to gain most from the new riches, and news consumers will profit from it. Information will reach journalists faster, from more diverse sources, and in modes that will allow reporters to question sources quickly with the expectation of a prompt response. The ample competition for audiences by Internet participants as well as the many other new dispensers of political information is apt to raise standards overall—though pessimists might argue that competition will force news quality to drop to the lowest common denominator. Be that as it may, the potential for producing excellent news is growing by leaps and bounds. This is destined to have at least some favorable consequences.

Barriers to Development

A look at technology may tell us what is possible rather than indicate what is likely to happen, particularly in the short run. A number of psychological, political, and economic barriers block the full development of new mass communication technologies. Most people are reluctant to change their media use habits, particularly when there are costs in time, attention, and effort to master new technologies. Computer mandated communication, for example, is unlikely to have wide use in homes where most adults lack a high-school education and have low incomes. By mid-1995, nearly 90 percent of such homes were without computers compared to 44 percent of homes where family income exceeds $50,000.[24]

Many new developments never get off the ground because bureaucracies impose too many regulations to guard against abuses. Unrealistically high standards are frequently prescribed, raising costs beyond economically feasible levels. State and local rules, piled on top of federal regulations, complicate the picture even further. Not only do they add more requirements, but rules issued by various jurisdictions often conflict. Every major technological revolution—and the information transmission revolution is major—has brought about economic and political dislocations. Such massive changes are fought by those whose knowledge and equipment will be made obsolete. Some of the new mass media offerings endanger current jobs. For instance, round-the-clock cable educational programs, structured like regular classrooms, threaten some teachers' jobs. Medical programs that teach people better medical self-care methods may be unwelcome competition for the health profession. Televised programs featuring outstanding practitioners and facilities may establish standards for professional performance that average institutions cannot match.

Communications technologies involve large investments so that their sudden obsolescence becomes a crushing financial blow. Business entrepreneurs often try to derail innovations. Early entrants in a technological field frequently develop a squatter's mentality about rights they have acquired, such as the right to use certain broadcast frequencies or particular technologies. Newcomers, on the other hand, are eager to reallocate facilities in line with their special interests. They want to mandate the use of more advanced technologies, even before they can guarantee that a market for these technologies and services will develop. This could wipe out proven interests in favor of new claimants whose prospects for success are uncertain. Obstacles also arise because competing new technologies benefit various groups unevenly. Power struggles, which may be prolonged, are fiercest before the status quo is determined. Meanwhile, technology continues its advance, raising problems that further delay the green light for implementing new systems.

The Cable Television Case

Cable television's rocky history in the United States, like the HDTV story, illustrates the problems posed by technical innovations. It also illustrates the many political decisions that must be made to fit a new information technology into existing legislative and administrative structures.

When cable television first became available in 1949, established broadcasters viewed it as a serious threat. They feared that the availability of numerous television channels would lead to a large menu of programs similar to the variety then offered by radio shows. This would splinter television audiences. Smaller audiences would mean smaller advertising revenues and smaller profits for existing stations. In turn, this might mean poorer programming because reduced revenue would necessitate curtailment of expenditures. Television networks were also concerned that cable operators would pirate, rather than buy, their signals and broadcast the programs they had produced at high cost. When satellite technology evolved, fears mounted. The networks might be destroyed entirely if stations could pick up programs directly from satellites and broadcast them nationwide via cable television.

The initial response of the FCC to cable technology was typical of regulatory agencies. The commission, prodded by established interests, protected the status quo with regulations that prevented the newcomers from harming these interests. These regulations sharply limited the types of programs that cable television stations could broadcast when they competed with established network services. Consequently, the growth of the cable industry was stunted.

Cable industry groups ultimately persuaded public officials that cable technology was needed because it could reach people in locations inaccessible to regular television signals. The idea of breaking the near monopoly enjoyed by the networks over broadcasting also became attractive. So did the possibility of opening up many new channels for broadcasting to groups hitherto shut out by a limited spectrum. By 1972 these pressures were sufficiently strong to convince the FCC to ease its regulations on the types of programs that cable television could broadcast. The cable system had a new lease on life. However, in what is also a typical move when new technologies arise, the FCC imposed a number of very costly regulations to force cable television to serve public needs that had never been met in the past. A minimum of twenty channels was required, including outlets for the general public, educational institutions, and local governments. There were also requirements for two-way capabilities and for carrying signals of local broadcasters.

When these rules turned out to hamper rapid development of cable television, they were eased in 1976. Service requirements imposed on the new industry were loosened further after successful legal challenges by cable operators who questioned the propriety of regulating cable television as if it were using scarce airwaves when cable transmission channels were plentiful.[25] In 1979 the FCC issued a lengthy research report on the economic impact of cable broadcasting. It concluded—erroneously, as it turned out—that cable was only a minor economic threat to the established television industry and that it did not endanger the industry's "ability to perform in the public interest." In the wake of these findings, the federal shackles were removed from the industry, one by one.[26] With the passage of the Cable Communications Policy Act of 1984, deregulation was complete.[27] The act deregulated rates and made renewal of cable franchises nearly automatic in areas with ready access to over-the-air television—roughly 90 percent of the cabled areas.

FIGURE 12-1   The Cable TV Explosion

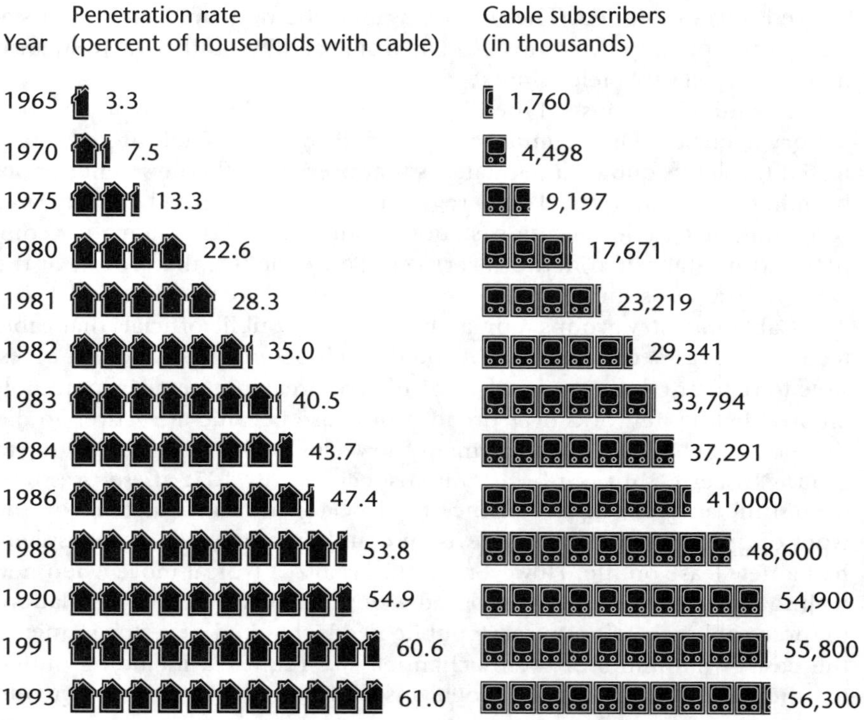

Year	Penetration rate (percent of households with cable)	Cable subscribers (in thousands)
1965	3.3	1,760
1970	7.5	4,498
1975	13.3	9,197
1980	22.6	17,671
1981	28.3	23,219
1982	35.0	29,341
1983	40.5	33,794
1984	43.7	37,291
1986	47.4	41,000
1988	53.8	48,600
1990	54.9	54,900
1991	60.6	55,800
1993	61.0	56,300

SOURCE: Compiled from *The Television and Cable Factbook,* 1994.

Meanwhile, the resistance of the established industries to this new competition had gradually softened. In fact, a number of them, heeding the old adage, "If you can't lick 'em, join 'em," invested heavily in cable facilities once the FCC eased controls regarding cross-ownership and admission of the networks to the cable market. By 1993, broadcasters had full or partial control in nearly half (47%) of the top fifty cable systems; newspaper and magazine publishers participated in one third (34%). These systems reached 56 percent of the nation's cable homes. Fearing that oligopoly might become the dominant cable pattern, Congress provided for cable rate regulation in 1992 to protect consumers from price gouging. Cable rates had risen by more than 60 percent in the preceding five-year period.[28]

Figure 12-1 illustrates the rapid explosion of the cable industry in the 1970s and 1980s and the slower growth thereafter. By 1993, 61 percent of the nation's television households were linked to cable systems, and network television had lost nearly 20 percent of its prime-time television audience. In homes with access to cable as well as network programs, audience figures for these competing systems were on a par.[29]

FCC rules and the opposition of the established industries were not the only hurdles faced by the cable industry. There were and are numerous local political hurdles as well. Laying of cables requires permission from local authorities. To avoid undue duplication of facilities, cable enterprises needed franchises. The franchising process has been highly political, in terms of both the selection of a particular company and the determination of the conditions of the franchise. Many small enterprises were squeezed out because they were unable to pay the costs of bidding for a contract, to grease the wheels of politics, or to finance initial red-ink years.

In the absence of national rules, local franchising policies have been diverse.[30] Franchisers and franchisees had to agree on the time to be allowed for constructing the system and the life of the franchise (usually fifteen years). They also needed agreement on requirements regarding public service and open-access channels and service for outlying areas where costs exceeded profits temporarily or permanently. Service to rural areas posed daunting economic problems, particularly in the western plains and the Rocky Mountain states. Alternatives to cable, such as microwave relays, satellite broadcasts, or transmission over telephone wires, had to be considered. Difficult decisions had to be made in choosing appropriate government agencies to supervise the execution of cable contracts and to ensure that programming serves the public interest. Finally, major controversies had to be settled regarding the nature of the fee structure and the manner in which government would exact its tribute.

Regulatory Options

Governments have several policy options for dealing with emerging broadcast systems. First, they can play a hands-off, *laissez-faire* role, allowing the system to develop as its private owners please.[31] The precedent for this policy is the traditional American stance toward the print media. If one believes that government should regulate information supply only when transmission channels are scarce, as happened with early radio and television, then it makes sense to leave the current rich crop of information transmission systems unregulated. When broadcast and narrowcast outlets are plentiful, market forces presumably come into play so that necessary services will be supplied in a far more flexible way than is possible when government regulations intervene. The only restraints that may be needed are safeguards to protect national security and maintain social norms and privacy.

Second, information transmission systems can be treated as *common carriers,* like the telephone or rail and bus lines. Common carrier status makes transmission facilities available to everyone on a first-come, first-served basis. Under common carrier rules, the owners of cable facilities would not broadcast their own programs as they do now. Instead they would lease their channels to various broadcasters for fees regulated by government or by market forces. As common carriers they would not be allowed to selectively exclude certain programs.

The FCC and many local governments like the common carrier concept. It has been adopted for dealing with communications satellites. But the U.S. Supreme Court decided in 1979 that cable could not be considered a common carrier under federal laws.[32] However, the ruling does not bar state and local authorities from imposing common carrier status on the industry. Congress, too, has repeatedly imposed some common carrier features on the cable television industry. In the mid-1960s, for instance, it ordered cable systems to broadcast all local over-the-air programs. The industry brought suit and won judgments in 1985 and again in 1987 that the "must carry rule" violated the First Amendment rights of cable companies.[33] The victory for cable systems was a defeat for champions of broad public access rights to the media.

Third, the government can confer *public trustee* status on communication enterprises. Owners then have full responsibility for programming but are required to meet certain public service obligations. Examples are adherence to equal time provisions, limitations on materials unsuitable for children or offensive to community standards of morality, and rules about access to broadcast facilities. Access rules are designed to ensure that there are channels available to governments and various publics to broadcast information about public issues such as education, public safety, and medical and social service programs.

The rationale for conferring trustee status on broadcasters has been twofold. In the past, the scarcity argument has been powerful but it has lost validity. The other argument for trustee status is that television is a highly influential medium. There must be assurance that valuable programs are broadcast and harmful ones avoided and that canons of fairness are observed. This is a powerful argument with strong support in much of the world. It is the argument that underlies the treatment of over-the-air television in the 1996 Telecommunications Act. But it is not the primary argument on which the American system was built, and it may clash with the First Amendment.

Paying the Piper

Whether new technologies are treated like any private enterprise, like a common carrier, or like a trustee, their costs have to be paid. There are three possibilities for financing, each with different policy consequences: advertiser support, audience payments, and government subsidies. Various combinations are also possible. Print media, for example, are financed by their audiences, supplemented by advertisements and some mailing subsidies.

Advertiser support requires programming that has mass appeal. Such programming is bound to share the strengths and weaknesses of current mass media. Sponsor influence may increase in the age of medium proliferation because competition for sponsors becomes keener when media multiply. Many outlets—particularly those with small audiences or audiences that lack attraction for advertisers because they represent small markets—may even find it difficult to attract enough sponsors to pay for their operations.

Although advertising revenues have been growing, many new broadcast facilities, such as cable television, rely heavily on *audience payments*. These have generally taken the form of a monthly service charge for the facilities, to which an installation or equipment charge has often been added. Additional programming may be available for a flat monthly rate or on a per-program basis. Service charge financing for broadcasting has been quite popular in many foreign countries. In the United States, however, it initially met with resistance because good broadcast services are available throughout the United States free of charge.

By the mid-1980s much of the initial resistance to paying for television had been overcome. Half of America's households had been cabled, and many were paying for special programs in addition to their standard monthly fees. Although a number of programming services had succumbed to competition and some new cable ventures were in financial difficulties, the industry as a whole was thriving. Some of its services, like around-the-clock live coverage of major news happenings provided by CNN, had become highly influential. These largely unedited broadcasts supplied up-to-the-minute information to mass audiences, as well as to government officials, lobbyists, and to other news professionals. Moreover, the worst fears of old-line broadcasting entrepreneurs had not materialized. The number of viewers had dropped measurably but not catastrophically. The networks were ailing financially, but had high hopes for capturing new audiences and advertisers by tailoring their programs to carefully selected audiences.[34] As had been the case with past innovations, the new media had not mortally wounded their predecessors.

A major social drawback of service charges for broadcasts is that poor families who most need many of the specialized programs are least able to pay. Middle-income families who already enjoy many social advantages benefit most. The information resources made available to them through cable and other programs enhance their status, leaving low income people farther behind.[35] This problem could be reduced through *government subsidies* paid to the cable industry on a basis similar to financing public television or through government subsidies paid to the poor. The latter system seems preferable to avoid making cable financially dependent on the government, thereby endangering cablecasters' freedom of action.

The Shape of the Future

Rather than projecting images of mass communication in the year 2000 and beyond—always a chancy enterprise—I will sketch out areas of likely major changes and identify looming problems. The shape of the future will hinge on how Americans cope with these issues. The here-and-now sets the stage for what will ensue.

Regulation Versus Deregulation

New communications technologies require a complete rethinking of the scope and purpose of federal regulation of broadcast media. The Telecommunications Act of 1996, although moving beyond some of the outdated assumptions of its 1934 predecessor, still falls far short of matching the revolutionary technological changes with appropriate policy innovations. Total deregulation and reliance on traditional First Amendment values are still distant goals. The difference in treatment between the unregulated print media and the regulated electronic media has become highly questionable. Competition has been rising among broadcasters while it has been falling among daily newspapers, and many newspapers are now available in broadcast formats. To bring some logic to the regulatory scheme, proponents of regulation could conceivably include the print media in the future. The price of progress in electronic transmission of printed news may be the loss of freedom from government regulation.

Opponents of extensive deregulation have argued that the age of electronic plenty remains a far-off vision because multiplying broadcast channels does not automatically mean more diversity in programming.[36] They also contend that the impact of television on public life in America is so profound that the public interest requires continued controls. Even when competition is ample, it may be necessary to mandate access to neglected viewpoints and provide programming for ignored audiences, such as children, as well as protecting children from unwholesome information.

Pressures for deregulation have been strong enough to find expression in some aspects of the 1996 Telecommunications Act and in the rules and regulations issued by the FCC, as discussed in Chapter 2. However, counterpressures are strong. Dissatisfaction with the services supplied by private entrepreneurs, including complaints about price gouging, has fueled opposition to deregulation. In fact, current pressures for restoring abandoned controls are strong. The wave of mergers in the 1980s and 1990s, which placed most established and emerging networks under the control of big corporations, rekindled fears that the media might become the mouthpieces of special interests, and that financial returns would be their programming lodestar. Plummeting revenues and sharp cuts in news division staffs heightened these fears. Regulation, rather than deregulation, has once again become the battle cry for champions of a free press:

> The issue is whether there are possible negative effects of failing to regulate expression. If so, maximizing free expression (that is, an absolutist First Amendment stand) becomes a value to weigh against those effects, not the basis for cutting off discussion on the issue.[37]

At the international level pressures are also strong for increasing government control and responsibility for media performance. A great challenge faces broadcast policy makers. They can yield to domestic and international pressures and make government the arbiter of what is good and safe news and entertainment for the public, possibly broadcasting its role, or they can leave that role in private hands, at the mercy of nonelected media tycoons. Given these alternatives, I cast my vote for the latter option, believing with Thomas Jefferson that "error of opinion may be tolerated where reason is left free to combat it."[38]

Two-Way Communication and Televotes

Another important area of public concern is two-way electronic communication. This feature of the communications revolution has been hailed as the gateway to genuine direct democracy, especially at the local level. In the future public business presumably can be conducted in front of the television set. Citizens can watch the proceedings of legislative bodies and cast votes of approval or disapproval. It will no longer be necessary to use public opinion polls or rely on media reports to assess the public's thinking.

Several pilot projects have been conducted in the United States and abroad.[39] In San José, California, for example, school board meetings were televised. All sides of controversial school issues were aired, and the televised discussion was supplemented by newspaper articles. The public was then given a chance to vote on policy suggestions through two-way cable or through ballots printed in the local newspapers. Unfortunately, participation was uneven. In San José, as in most of the other "televote" projects, the bulk of votes came from middle-income people. Most lower-income people, though they liked the idea of interactivity, did not participate.[40]

The possibility of using two-way circuitry for educational programs, particularly those that can improve the status of disadvantaged groups, is less controversial. Available technologies include television and radio call-in shows, electronic computer bulletin boards, and cable public access channels.[41] Their growth rates have been phenomenal. By 1995 11 percent of Americans, 16 years or older, were using the Internet and 21 percent of the group were participating in interactive discussion groups. Again the major obstacle, beyond funding and making new technologies available, is motivating disadvantaged populations to use them. Both successes and failures have been recorded.

Two-way cable has offered a variety of programs to general audiences, but they have been sharply curtailed because they were less popular than expected. Warner Amex Cable Communications' QUBE system, which served 350,000 viewers in Columbus, Cincinnati, Pittsburgh, Dallas, Houston, and St. Louis suburbs, rarely attained more than 2 percent participation for its interactive programs. These included talent contests, astrology shows, exercise classes, interactive games, football games, town meetings, and public hearings involving federal agencies. The reasons for the disappointing results may have been the audience's reluctance to participate, unattractive program formats, and technical difficulties in responding when several viewers were watching one television set.

Fragmentation of the Broadcast Audience

The multitude of broadcast channels and the even broader options created by videotape technology and the Internet have prompted fears that the national political consensus will become fragmented. When people turn to specialized fare in news and entertainment, their attention to politics may diminish. Without national media, there may be no national political consensus.[42] As discussed in Chapter 7, nationwide dissemination of similar news has fostered shared political socialization. When news becomes fragmented, people are likely to be socialized in disparate ways. If political programming becomes available only on channels dedicated to politics, will people choose to watch it? Will government leaders be able to convey their messages to the public? A music fan, tuned in to an all-music station, may watch music programs only; an African American or Hispanic person may tune in only to stations concerned with African American and Hispanic affairs. Many citizens thus may become prisoners of their special interests and may miss out on happenings in the broader culture. The country may be carved up into mutually exclusive, often hostile enclaves.[43]

On the positive side of the ledger, specialization raises the possibility of a better fit between audience needs and public messages. Government programs may operate more successfully, given ampler opportunities for one- and two-way communication with selected audiences. The electoral chances of minority candidates and parties may improve with increased ability to target their messages to selected audiences. The possibilities for change are staggering but too undefined as yet to hazard predictions.

Fears that fragmentation of the broadcast audience will lead to political fragmentation are not shared by everyone, of course.[44] Many people point out that the national consensus was not ruptured when alternative media were used in the past. They argue that fragmented interests create the demand for fragmented media rather than the reverse. If there is political and social consensus, people will seek out information pertaining to the larger community. Others point out that commercially oriented media will always try to attract large audiences by offering programs with wide appeal. That means sticking to the same tried and true formulas. Programming on cable television, which has become uniform and similar to network television, is an example. Even if the new media increase fragmentation, many people do not find this objectionable, believing that pluralism is preferable to the traditional melting-pot ideals.

Media pluralism may herald more local programming. Most local governments are eager to use cable channels to broadcast local political news. Local school systems and police and fire departments have also sought access to cable to air their concerns. If publicity means power, the new communications media may enhance the power of local institutions, possibly at the expense of national ones. The two-way capacity could be used to make programming genuinely attractive to local audiences even when it lacks the polish of professional programs.[45] Although the possibilities for strengthening local communities through increased publicity are good, the new narrowcasting technologies also can deflect interest away from the local scene and produce global villages of like-minded people. National cable television networks, such as CNN and C-SPAN, and the Fox television network, are examples of movement in this direction.

Public Television

Yet another issue brought to the fore by the coming age of broadcast plenty is the fate of public television. As discussed in Chapter 2, public television was organized to provide an alternative to the typical programming available on the commercial networks. It also was intended to be an outlet for programs geared to minorities. These are the very services that cable television and other narrowcasting services presumably will perform on a commercial basis. Because public television has always depended on public subsidies, its audiences, except for children's programs, have been quite limited, and pressures to abandon it may become strong.

Of course, the hitch in this argument is the presumption that the mushrooming commercial television enterprises will be willing and able to fill the niche occupied by the public broadcasting system. A glance at any weekly television schedule raises serious doubts. Most of the new outlets provide clones of the offerings that are familiar from network television.[46] Sophisticated cultural and educational programming is scarce and has not been commercially viable because audiences have remained small. The difficulty of keeping the public broadcasting system solvent may sound its death knell, nonetheless. The European practice of funding public broadcasting principally through consumer fees has never been considered a realistic option in the United States.

The Consequences of Change

The concerns outlined thus far are undoubtedly not the only ones ahead. Many others will require decisions that go far beyond solving technical issues. The direction of communications policy is at stake and with it the tone and possibly the direction of American politics in general. John M. Eger, a former director of the White House Office of Telecommunications Policy, has remarked that this is indeed a time of decision. "For as we are moving into a future rich in innovation and in social change, we are also moving into a storm center of new world problems." The new technologies are "a force for change throughout the world that simply will not be stopped, no matter how it is resisted." And then he asks, "Are we ready for the consequences of this change? Are we prepared to consider the profound social, legal, economic, and political effects of technology around the world?"[47]

Currently, the answer is "no." In the communications field the structure for policy making at all government levels is fragmented and ill-suited to deal with the existing problems, to say nothing of those that must be anticipated.[48] Policies are improvised when pressures become strong, yielding in a crazy quilt pattern to various industry concerns, to public interest groups, to domestic or foreign policy considerations, to the pleas of engineers and lawyers, and to the suggestions of political scientists and economists. Narrow issues are addressed, but the full scope of the situation is ignored.[49] As W. Russell Neuman notes, "the concept of a comprehensive industrial policy or even a broadly focused reformulation of communications policy for the information age is political anathema in the centers of power."[50] The struggle over passage of the 1996 Telecommunications Act, and the compromise measure that is now the law of the land, proves that this assessment is unfortunately correct.

Summary

Many people are dissatisfied with the performance of the mass media, especially television. They can and do air their dissatisfaction through various formal and informal channels, but criticism usually has had limited success in changing media content. To fill the gaps left by the major mass media, many alternative media have been created. These media are organized either to serve demographically distinct populations or to cater to particular substantive concerns or political orientations. The mushrooming of underground print and broadcast media during the Vietnam War era showed that dissent is allowed to flourish in the United States even in war time. It also demonstrated that, in a business dominated by giants, small enterprises can operate successfully on a shoestring budget. The limited demand by the general public for published radical dissent, however, makes it difficult to sustain such publications over long periods of time.

In this chapter we also explored the social and political consequences of technological advances in mass media and outlined the areas in which new public policies are needed. We briefly described some of the new electronic tools and sketched their capabilities in bringing about the age of broadcast plenty and of two-way communication. Their impact on life and politics in the United States could be enormous were it not for the fact that most people, most of the time, are disinclined to spend time and effort to find special-interest information or entertainment. Two-way circuitry has been hailed as the gateway to genuine direct democracy and as a great educational tool. However, electronic plebiscites are as yet too controversial to be adopted widely. Fragmentation of the broadcast audience has raised fears of political fragmentation and breakdown of the national political consensus that has been deemed essential for successful democratic government. But the extent and implications of the danger remain disputed.

Various changes in regulatory policy are in progress to integrate the new broadcast and narrowcast technologies into the existing mass media regulatory structure. But the prospects for a total overhaul of the current policy regime are dim. The forces favoring greater government control of media content are strong at a time when most types of media, including print media, use some form of electronic transmission. Whatever the outcome, the debate needs to be focused more clearly on the merits of the First Amendment in the century that lies ahead. When decisions are made, the perceptive comment of the *Washington Post*'s Alan Barth should be remembered: "If you want a watchdog to warn you of intruders you must put up with a certain amount of mistaken barking."[51]

Notes

1. *Julius Caesar,* act 4, scene 3, line 218.
2. Quoted in Martha Fitzsimon and Lawrence T. McGill, "The Citizen as Media Critic," in *Media Studies Journal* 9(2) (Spring 1995): 91–101.
3. David Gergen, "The Message to the Media," *Public Opinion* 7 (April/May 1984): 5–8; Andrew Randolph, "What Credibility Problem?" *Editor & Publisher* 119 (January 18, 1986): 12–13; Michael Robinson, "Pressing Opinion," *Public Opinion* 9 (September/October 1986): 56–59; and Philip Meyer, "Credibility: And Now the Good News," *Presstime* 7 (June 1985): 26–27.
4. Bill Granger, "Sleazy Does It: Decency and Fair Play Take a Holiday in the New-New Journalism," *Chicago Tribune Magazine,* January 3, 1988, 4. Also see Norman E. Isaacs, *Untended Gates: The Mismanaged Press* (New York: Columbia University Press, 1986).
5. Fitzsimon and McGill, "The Citizen as Media Critic."
6. Isaacs, *Untended Gates;* Tom Goldstein, *Killing the Messenger: 100 Years of Media Criticism* (New York: Columbia University Press, 1989); W. Lance Bennett, *News: The Politics of Illusion,* 3d ed. (New York: Longman, 1996); Robert M. Entman, *Democracy without Citizens: Media and the Decay of American Politics* (New York: Oxford University Press, 1989); Michael Parenti, *Inventing Reality: The Politics of News Media,* 2d ed. (New York: St. Martin's, 1993); and Herbert Schiller, *Communication and Cultural Domination* (New York: International Arts and Sciences Press, 1976).
7. James Fallows, *Breaking the News: How the Media Undermine American Democracy* (New York: Pantheon Books, 1995); Leo Bogart, *Commercial Culture: The Media System and the Public Interest* (New York: Oxford University Press, 1995).
8. Edmund L. Andrews, "Flintstones and Programs Like It Aren't Educational: F.C.C. Says," *New York Times,* March 4, 1993.
9. *Zamora et al. v. Columbia Broadcasting System et al.,* 480 F. Supp. 199 (S.D. Fla. 1979). See also Robert E. Drechsel, "Media Tort Liability for Physical Harm," *Journalism Quarterly* 64 (Spring 1987): 99–105; and Juliet Lusbough Dee, "Media Accountability for Real-Life Violence: A Case of Negligence or Free Speech?" *Journal of Communication* 37 (Spring 1987): 106–138.

10. *Olivia N. (a minor) v. National Broadcasting Company*, 74 Cal. App. 3d 383 (1978), 126 Cal. App. 3d 488 (1981).
11. Donald T. Mogavero, "The American Press Ombudsman," *Journalism Quarterly* 59 (Winter 1982): 548–553, 580.
12. Ronald Farrar, "News Councils and Libel Actions," *Journalism Quarterly* 63 (Autumn 1986): 509–516.
13. Jonathan Friendly, "National News Council Will Dissolve," *New York Times*, March 23, 1984. Media critic Norman Isaacs has proposed ombudsmen as the best alternative to news councils. See Isaacs, *Untended Gates*, 132–146.
14. *Ulrich's International Directory* (New York: Bowker, 1993).
15. John W. Johnstone, Edward J. Slawski, and William W. Bowman, *The Newspeople* (Urbana: University of Illinois Press, 1976), 157–179.
16. They are described more fully in Johnstone, Slawski, and Bowman, *The Newspeople*, 157–181; Laurence Leamer, *The Paper Revolutionaries: The Rise of the Underground Press* (New York: Simon and Schuster, 1972); and Jack A. Nelson, "The Underground Press," in *Readings in Mass Communication*, ed. Michael C. Emery and Ted Curtis Smythe (Dubuque, Iowa: W. C. Brown, 1972), 212–226.
17. Marshall McLuhan, *Understanding Media: The Extensions of Man* (New York: McGraw-Hill, 1964); and Marshall McLuhan and Quentin Fiore, *The Medium Is the Message: An Inventory of Effects* (New York: Bantam Books, 1967).
18. W. Russell Neuman, *The Future of the Mass Audience* (New York: Cambridge University Press, 1991), ix–x.
19. Thomas F. Baldwin, D. Steven McVoy, and Charles Steinfeld, *Convergence: Integrating Media, Information and Communication* (Thousand Oaks, Calif.: Sage, 1996); W. Russell Neuman, Lee McKnight, and Richard Jay Solomon, *The Gordian Knot: Political Gridlock on the Information Highway* (Cambridge, Mass.: MIT Press, 1996).
20. Heather E. Hudson, "Implications for Development Communications," *Journal of Communication* 29 (Winter 1979): 179–186. Also see Bella Mody, Joseph D. Straubhaar, and Johannes M. Bauer, *Telecommunications Politics: Ownership and Control of the Information Highway in Developing Countries* (Hillsdale, N.J.: Lawrence Erlbaum, 1995).
21. Jon Van and Tim Jones, "Digital Promises an Unclear Revolution," *Chicago Tribune*, April 7, 1996.
22. Vincent Mosco, "Une Drôle de Guerre," *Media Studies Journal* 6 (Spring 1992): 57–58.
23. John Perry Barlow, quoted in Bonnie Fisher, Michael Margolis, and David Resnick, "Politics and Civic Life on the Internet" (Paper delivered at the annual meeting of the Midwest Political Science Association, Chicago, April 1995).
24. Times Mirror Center for the People and the Press, "Technology in the American Household," Washington, D.C., October 16, 1995.
25. *Home Box Office, Inc. v. FCC*, 567 F.2d 9 (D.C. Cir.), *cert. denied*, 434 U.S. 829 (1977); and *FCC v. Midwest Video Corp.*, 440 U.S. 689 (1979).
26. Pay television had been freed from federal controls in 1977. Remaining federal controls were dropped by 1979. Benjamin M. Compaine, Christopher H. Sterling, Thomas Guback, and J. Kendrick Noble, Jr., *Who Owns the Media? Concentration and Ownership in the Mass Communications Industry*, 2d ed. (White Plains, N.Y.: Knowledge Industry Publications, 1982), 381, 407.
27. "Cable TV," *Consumer Reports* 52 (September 1987): 547–554.

28. Edmund L. Andrews, "Hopes of Cable Industry Ride on Veto by Bush," *New York Times,* July 25, 1992.
29. Lawrie Mifflin, "Cable Ratings at High, Aided by Simpson Trial," *Chicago Tribune,* March 27, 1995.
30. FCC regulations prevail over conflicting state regulations. *Capital Cities Cable v. Crisp,* 104 U.S. 2694 (1984). Federal law may preempt state laws. See William E. Hanks and Stephen E. Coran, "Federal Preemption of Obscenity Law Applied to Cable Television," *Journalism Quarterly* 63 (Spring 1986): 43–47.
31. Henry Geller, "Mass Communications Policy: Where We Are and Where We Should Be Going," in *Democracy and the Mass Media,* ed. Judith Lichtenberg (New York: Cambridge University Press, 1990), 290–329.
32. *FCC v. Midwest Video Corp.,* 440 U.S. 689 (1979).
33. "Cable TV," *Consumer Reports,* 555.
34. Bill Carter, "Broadcasters Take a Bite Out of Cable in the Ratings," *New York Times,* March 9, 1992.
35. Mosco, "Une Drôle de Guerre," 56–60.
36. Don R. LeDuc, "Deregulation and the Dream of Diversity," *Journal of Communication* 32 (Autumn 1982): 171.
37. Robert M. Entman and Steven S. Wildman, "Reconciling Economic and Non-Economic Perspectives in Media Policy: Transcending the 'Marketplace of Ideas,' " *Journal of Communication* 42 (Winter 1992): 5–19.
38. First inaugural address, March 4, 1801. See Andrew A. Lipscomb, ed., *The Writings of Thomas Jefferson,* Vol. 3 (Washington, D.C.: Thomas Jefferson Memorial Association, 1905), 319.
39. Richard Hollander, *Video Democracy: The Vote-from-Home Revolution* (Mt. Airy, Md.: Lomond, 1985). Public access cable television may also spur political participation. For examples see Patricia Aufderheide, "Cable Television and the Public Interest," *Journal of Communication* 42 (Winter 1992): 52–65.
40. An experiment in Cerritos, California, is described in Lawrence K. Grossman, "Reflecting on Life along the Electronics Superhighway," *Media Studies Journal* 8 (Winter 1994): 27–40.
41. Features of various technologies are discussed by Carrie Heeter, "Implications of New Interactive Technologies for Conceptualizing Communication," in *Media Use in the Information Age: Emerging Patterns of Adoption and Consumer Use,* ed. Jerry L. Salvaggio and Jennings Bryant (Hillsdale, N.J.: Lawrence Erlbaum, 1989).
42. James G. Webster, "Audience Behavior in the New Media Environment," *Journal of Communication* 36 (Summer 1986): 77–91.
43. Lawrence K. Grossman, *The Electronic Republic: Reshaping Democracy in the Information Age* (New York: Viking, 1995).
44. Russell Neuman, *The Future of the Mass Audience* (New York: Cambridge University Press, 1991), 58–63.
45. Use of cable television is compared with use of other media in Gerald L. Grotta and Doug Newsom, "How Does Cable Television in the Home Relate to Other Media Use Patterns?" *Journalism Quarterly* 59 (Winter 1982): 588–591, 609. Also see "Cable TV," *Consumer Reports.*
46. The reasons for this situation are explained by David Waterman, "The Failure of Cultural Programming on Cable TV: An Economic Interpretation," *Journal of Communication* 36 (Summer 1986): 92–107. Also see Robert M. Entman and

Steven S. Wildman, "Reconciling Economic and Non-Economic Perspectives in Media Policy: Transcending the 'Marketplace of Ideas,' " *Journal of Communication* 42 (Winter 1992).

47. John M. Eger, "A Time of Decision," *Journal of Communication* 29 (Winter 1979): 204–207.

48. William A. Lucas, "Telecommunications Technologies and Services," in *Communication for Tomorrow: Policy Perspectives for the 1980s,* ed. Glen O. Robinson (New York: Praeger, 1978).

49. Ithiel de Sola Pool, "The Problems of WARC," *Journal of Communication* 29 (Winter 1979): 187–196.

50. Neuman, "The Future of the Mass Audience," x.

51. Alan Barth, "If the Press Didn't Tell Us, Who Would?" (Chicago: Sigma Delta Chi, 1987).

Readings

Arterton, F. Christopher. *Teledemocracy: Can Technology Protect Democracy?* Beverly Hills, Calif.: Sage, 1987.

Bennett, W. Lance. *News: The Politics of Illusion.* 3d ed. New York: Longman, 1996.

Grossman, Lawrence K. *The Electronic Republic: Reshaping Democracy in the Media Age.* New York: Viking, 1995.

Heap, Nick, Ray Thomas, Geogg Einon, Robin Mason, and Hughie MacKay. *Information Technology and Society.* Beverly Hills, Calif.: Sage, 1995.

Isaacs, Norman E. *Untended Gates: The Mismanaged Press.* New York: Columbia University Press, 1986.

Kessler, Lauren. *The Dissident Press: Alternative Journalism in American History.* Beverly Hills, Calif.: Sage, 1984.

McKibben, Bill. *The Age of Missing Information.* New York: Random House, 1992.

Neuman, W. Russell, Lee McKnight, and Richard Jay Solomon. *The Gordian Knot: Political Gridlock on the Information Highway.* Cambridge, Mass.: MIT Press, 1996.

Newberg, Paula R., ed. *New Directions in Communications Policy.* 2 vols. Durham, N.C.: Duke University Press, 1989.

Pool, Ithiel de Sola. *Technologies without Boundaries: On Telecommunication in a Global Age.* Cambridge, Mass.: Harvard University Press, 1990.

Tehranian, Majid. *Technologies of Power: Information Machines and Democratic Prospects.* Norwood, N.J.: Ablex, 1990.

Index

ABC (American Broadcasting Company). *See* Capital Cities/ABC
Abortion, 10, 308
Access to information, 68–75
  government documents, 70–75
  media rights, 68–69
  private industry documents, 75
Access to media, 59–68
  advertising and, 67
  broadcast media, 60–64
  equal time provision, 61–62
  exclusive broadcast rights, 65
  fairness doctrine, 62–63
  First Amendment and, 59
  interest groups and, 66
  lobby groups and, 67–68
  non-broadcast media, 60
  public office holders, 65–66
  reform proposals, 64
  right of rebuttal, 63–64
Access to news, 25–26
Accuracy in Media (AIM), 53
ACLU. *See* American Civil Liberties Union
Action for Children's Television (ACT), 53
Adams, William C., 368
Adoption, 6–7
Advertising
  access to media and, 67

audience size and, 105
censorship by advertisers, 51–52
in children's television, 49
of cigarettes, 63, 85–86
news selection and, 103–104
political commercials, 244–245
pressures from advertisers, 50–52
rates for, 105
revenues from, 48
support for new technologies, 399
truth-in-advertising laws, 63
withdrawing commercials, 51–52
Afghanistan, 181
AFL-CIO (American Federation of Labor and Congress of Industrial Organizations), 307
African Americans
  news coverage of, 146
  socialization patterns, 195–196
  specialized media for, 316
  stereotypes of, 205–206
  television watching of, 195–196
Agence France-Presse (AFP), 342, 346
Agenda building, 9, 168–177
  freedom of the press and, 9
  interest groups and, 174–177
  political scandal and, 170–171
  science policy and, 171–174
  social movements and, 174–177
  theories of, 201–202

AIDS (acquired immune deficiency syndrome), 52, 65, 77–78, 166
AIM. *See* Accuracy in Media
Alabama Educational Television Commission, 65
Alexander, Lamar, 240
Alter, Jonathan, 384
Alternative press, 315–316, 387
AMA. *See* American Medical Association
America-On-Line, 240
American Civil Liberties Union (ACLU), 181–182, 307
American Express, 51
American Journalism Review, 384
American Journalist in the 1990's, The, 94–96
American Medical Association (AMA), 54, 384
American Newspaper Publishers Association (ANPA), 50
American Voter, The, 13
Anderson, Jack, 146
Anderson, John, 250
Annenberg School of Communications, 206
ANPA. *See* American Newspaper Publishers Association
Antitrust laws, 42, 48
AP. *See* Associated Press
Aquino, Corazón, 372
Arledge, Roone, 168
Arnett, Peter, 149, 351
"Arson for Profit," 162
Ashe, Arthur, 77–78, 166
Aspen Conference on Communications and Society, 384
Assassinations, research on, 195
Associated Press (AP), 43, 342, 368
AT&T, 51
Attack journalism, 164–166
Attention spans, 209–210
Attitudes, media impact on. *See* Behavior and attitudes, media impact on
Audience appeal, 105–106
Audience fragmentation, 402–403
Audience payments, 399
Audience preferences, 127–128
Audience size, 105
Audit Bureau of Circulation, 105

Authoritarian control systems, 19–20, 21, 25–26, 28
Aviation coverage, 93–94

Baby Richard case, 6–7
Backgrounders, 286–287
Bagdikian, Ben, 114, 299–300, 314, 333
Baird, Zoë, 275
Baker v. Carr, 309
Banzhaf, John W., III, 63
Barron, Jerome, 59, 64
Bay of Pigs, 282
Bayh, Birch, 121
BBC. *See* British Broadcasting Corporation
Beats, 108, 351–353
Begin, Menachem, 349–350
Behavior and attitudes, media impact on, 188–189
  behavior effects, 212–218
  broadcast media, 189–191
  learning effects, 204–212
  learning processes, 202–204
  political socialization, 191–195
  print media, 189–191
  socialization patterns, 195–197
  story choices of individuals, 197–202
Behavioral effects, 212–218
  behavior changes in adults, 214–215
  imitation of violent behavior, 212–215
  political modernization, 215–218
  socioeconomic modernization, 215–218
  violent behavior in children, 212–214, 385
Bennett, Lance, 197, 384
Berelson, Bernard, 13
Better Government Association, 158, 163
Bhutto, Benazir, 347
Bias, 95
  effect , 127
  in elections coverage, 248–251
  ideological, 7–8, 19
  political, 250
  structural, 250
Biden, Joseph, 234, 255
Big Story, 102

Blocking devices, 51, 214
Bogart, Leo, 195–196, 384
Bombings. *See* Oklahoma City bombing; World Trade Center bombing
Bombs, making of, 72–73
Boorstin, Daniel, 8
Bork, Robert, 307
Botha, P. W., 372
Bradley, Tom, 147
Braestrup, Peter, 102
Branzburg v. Hayes (1972), 68, 69, 88
Braun, Carol Moseley, 228–229
British Broadcasting Corporation (BBC), 34, 342
Broadcast media
  access to, 60–64
  impact of, 4–5
  impact on behavior and attitudes, 189–191
Broadcasting, 50
Brokaw, Tom, 44, 102
Brown, Jerry, 234, 240
Brown v. Board of Education (1954), 308
Brzezinski, Zbigniew, 364
Buchanan, Pat, 232, 236, 240
Burger, Warren E., 308
Bush, George, 188
  approval ratings, 206, 236, 275
  environmental issues, 171–172
  extraordinary events coverage, 142
  media coverage of campaign, 232, 234–235, 240, 248, 252–253
  Persian Gulf War, 69
  Somalia intervention, 16
  television ads, 244–245
Business control and ownership of media, 34, 39–40, 45–46
Business documents, access to, 75
Byrd, Robert, 293
Byrne, Jane, 249

C-SPAN, 284, 292
Cable Communications Policy Act of 1984, 395
Cable News Network (CNN), 16, 48, 149, 342–343, 363, 390
  "effect," 16
  polls, 235
Cable television, 394–397
  market size, 42, 43

violent programming, 212
Caldera, Rafael, 361
Campaign financing, 238, 244, 245
Campaigns
  campaign model of reporting, 247
  coverage as campaign goal, 238–243
  elections coverage and campaign tactics, 241–243
Canadian Broadcasting Company (CBC), 182
Canadian Eskimos, 218
Canadian media, 182, 361–362
Cancer risks, 172–174
Candidates. *See* Campaigns; Elections coverage; Voting
Capital Cities/ABC (American Broadcasting Company), 17, 40, 42, 48, 52, 178–179
Carcinogens, 172–174
Carter, Jimmy, 367
  campaign tactics, 241–242
  coverage of political elites and, 18
  media coverage of campaign, 17, 235, 252–253, 262
  media embarrassment of, 278
  media influence on candidacy, 232, 262
  speech broadcasts, 66
  suppression of news, 142
"Cataract Cowboys," 182
CAW. *See* Citizens for the American Way
CBC (Canadian Broadcasting Company), 182
CBS (Columbia Broadcasting System), 42, 48, 77, 81, 179–181
  advertising withdrawals, 52
  polls, 235
  stock market coverage, 101
CBTV (Coalition for Better Television), 53
Censorship
  by advertisers, 51–52
  of extraordinary events coverage, 143–144
  of foreign correspondents, 348–349
  by fundamentalist groups, 216
  by government, 26
  judicial censorship, 311–312

military censorship, 142, 148–149, 359–361
  protective censorship, 85–86
  right to know and, 84
  security censorship, 73
  self-censorship, 26, 74
Center for Investigative Reporting, 158
Center for Media Education, 384
Chain ownership, 42–43
Challenger explosion, 190
Chavez, Cesar, 121
Cheney, Dick, 360
Chicago Herald, 99
Chicago Sun-Times, 99, 118, 161, 163–164, 182
Chicago Tribune, 99, 234
  crime coverage, 106, 311
  extraordinary events coverage, 143
  ownership, 40
  wire service, 43–44
Child, Marquis, 236
Children, imitation of violent behavior, 212–214, 385
Children's television, 66
  advertising and, 49
  regulation of, 50
Children's Television Act of 1990, 385
Christian Coalition, 307
Christian Crusade, 63–64
Christian Science Monitor, 119, 369
Cicippo, Joseph, 168
Cigarette advertising, 63, 85–86
Citizen lobbies, 52–54
Citizens for a Free Kuwait, 346
Citizens for the American Way (CAW), 53
Civic journalism, 98, 157
Civil disorder, 147
Civil liberties, 181–183
Civil Rights Act of 1964, 176
Civil rights movement, 176
Clark, Tom, 310
Classified information, 27, 73
Clinton, Bill
  control of media, 26
  extraordinary events coverage, 142
  media coverage of campaign, 233–234, 237–238, 240, 248, 252–253
  mudslinging, 164

Oklahoma City bombing, 147
  policy ratings, 277
CNN. *See* Cable News Network
Coaching, 237–238
Coalition for Better Television (CBTV), 53
Coalition journalism, 162–163
Codes of ethics, 51, 84, 165, 370
Cognitive balance theory, 199–200
Cognitive consistency theories, 15
Cognitive psychology, 202
Cold War coverage, 356–358
Coleman, J. Marshall, 330
Columbia Journalism Review, 384
Combat zone reporting, 69
Common carriers, 398
Communications Act of 1934, 47, 61, 298
Communications law, 312–313
Community Information Project, 158
Competition, 44, 102–103, 314–315
Comprehension of news, 207
Computer Decency Act of 1996, 48
Condoms, 52
Confirmation hearings, 151, 288, 299, 307
Conglomerates, 40
Congressional coverage, 288–300
  adversarial relationship with media, 270–272
  communications policy of Congress, 298–299
  compared with executive branch coverage, 289–293
  congressional elections, 256
  functions of media, 295–296
  impact on members of Congress, 299–300
  relationship between Congress and media, 296–298
  Senate committee coverage, 329
  televised sessions, 292–293
  writing stories about Congress, 293–295
Congressional Quarterly Inc., 294
Congressional Record, 71
Conscientious objectors, 176
Conservative Victory Committee, 307

Consolidation trends, 45
Consumer organizations, 176
Contextual information, 125
Conventions, 242
Cook, Fred, 63–64
Copycat crimes, 144–145
Corporation for Public Broadcasting
  (CPB), 37
Council of Better Business Bureaus, 51
Courts
  communications law and, 312–313
  coverage of, 306–313
  crime coverage and, 310–311
  fair trials, 78–80
  gag rule, 78–80
  impact of coverage, 308–310
  judicial censorship and, 311–312
  media coverage of court cases,
    78–79
  pretrial publicity, 78
  rights of accused persons, 78–80
Cox Broadcasting Corporation, 40
CPB. *See* Corporation for Public Broadcasting
Crime
  copycat, 144–145
  courts and crime coverage, 310–311
  coverage of, 106, 120, 182, 310–311
  imitation of, 212–215, 385
  organized, 182
Crime rates, 106
Crime-stopper programs, 167
Crisis reporting. *See* Extraordinary
  events
Criticism of media, 382–386
Cronkite, Walter, 102, 167, 274,
  349–350
Crossmedia ownership, 39, 396
Cultivation analysis, 206
Cultural Indicators project, 206
Cutler, Lloyd, 364

Dahmer, Jeffrey, 152
Daley, Richard, 249, 318
Davis, Dennis, 207
"Day After, The," 178–179
Dayan, Moshe, 350
Deadlines, 114–115
"Death of a Princess," 65
Debates, 61, 62, 235

Declaration on the Media (UNESCO),
  365–366
Defender, 99
Degnan, Kim, 313
DeLorean, John, 78
Democracies, media role in, 21–23,
  25–28
Democratic National Committee, 64
Democratic National Convention of
  1984, 248
Deregulation, 400–401
Derivative media, 97
Detroit News, 309
Developing nations, 369–370
Dialysis patients, 167–168
Diplomacy by media, 167, 349–351
Disclosure rules, 80–82
Distortion of reality, 120, 125, 206
Dixon, Alan, 228
Docudramas, 177–179
Documentaries, 177–179, 209
Dole, Robert, 232–233, 237, 253
"Donahue," 239
Dow Jones, 42
Dukakis, Michael, 244, 255
Dunn, Delmer D., 316
DuPont, Pete, 241
Durham Morning Herald, 272

Eachus, Todd, 16
Earthquakes, 137
  stages of coverage, 140–142
  warnings of, 146–147
EBS. *See* Emergency Broadcast System
Economic Bill of Rights, 281
Edelman, Murray, 208–209
Edgar, James, 6
Eger, John M., 404
Eisenhower, Dwight D., 234
Elections coverage, 228–229, 243–256.
  See also Voting
  adequacy of, 255–256
  bias in, 248–251
  campaign model of reporting, 247
  campaign tactics and, 241–243
  character of candidates, 231, 251, 255
  congressional races, 256
  consequences of media politics,
    230–243
  coverage as campaign goal, 238–243

decline in party influence and, 231–232
editorial endorsement of candidates, 250
effects of, 257–263
incentive model of reporting, 247–248
issues coverage, 253–254
local coverage, 329–332
medialities, 254–255
patterns of, 245–251
primaries coverage, 256
prominence of election stories, 245–256
public opinion polls and, 233–236
research on elections, 229–230
selection of candidates and, 232–236
substance of, 251–254
talk-show appearances, 238–241
television ads, 244–245
television coverage, 252–253
television presentation of candidates, 236–238
uniformity of, 246–248
women and, 228–229
Electoral district boundaries, 309
Electoral votes, network coverage of state news and, 112–113
Electronic media. *See* Broadcast media
Ellsberg, Daniel, 73–74
Emergency Broadcast System (EBS), 145
Empathic capacity, 215–216
Engel v. Vitale, 309, 310
Entman, Robert, 172, 384
Entrapment, 182–183
Environmental issues, 171–174
Environmentalist groups, 176
Epton, Bernard, 248–249
Equal time provision, 61–62
Ervin, Sam, 292
Eskimos, 218
Espionage, 73
Ethics, 51, 84, 165, 370
Evers, Medgar, 195
Exchange theory, 177
Exclusive broadcast rights, 65
Executive branch coverage, 272–288
ad hoc encounters, 287–288
adversarial relationship with media, 270–272

compared with congressional coverage, 289–293
direct versus mediated transmission, 276–277
forms of contact, 285–287
functions of media, 272–273
impact of, 273–275
institutional settings, 283–285
leaks, 287–288
media goals and tactics, 277–278
president and, 278–281
presidential communication strategies, 281–282
Executive privilege, 74–75
Exit polling, 261–262
Exporting news, 368–371
Exposés, 156. *See also* Muckraking
Extraordinary events, 135–136
accuracy of information, 140–141
audience for crisis information, 138–139
censorship and, 143–144
civil disorder, 147
examples, 136–138
media responses, 138–150
media roles, 138–150
natural disasters, 146–147
negative effects of coverage, 143–145
patterns of coverage, 139–143
planning coverage, 145–147
positive effects of coverage, 143
pseudo-crises, 150–152
sources of disaster information, 138
stages of coverage, 139–143
suppression of news, 147–150
Eye clinics, 182

Factual learning, 207–208
Fairness doctrine, 50, 62–63
Fallows, James, 384
Falwell, Jerry, 77
Family values, 188–189
Fear of offending, 121–122
Federal Communications Commission (FCC), 37, 42, 47–50, 283, 298–299, 391. *See also* Licensing
communications law and, 312–313
complaints filed with, 381, 384–385
local programming regulations, 326
response to cable television, 395–396

Federal officials, news coverage of, 116–117
Feighan, Edward, 148
Finkbine, Sherri, 10
First Amendment, 26–27, 58–59. *See also* Freedom of the press
   access to information and, 68
   access to media and, 59
   commercial messages and, 63
   communications law and, 312
   privacy rights and, 77
   right to know and, 80
   shield laws and, 81–82
Fitzwater, Marlin, 188
Flynt, Larry, 77
Foisie, Phil, 366
Foley, Thomas, 269
Forbes, Steve, 245
Ford, Gerald, 17, 62, 76–77
Foreign affairs coverage, 120, 339–341
   appraisal of, 365–367
   beats, 351–353
   censorship of, 348–349
   Cold War coverage, 356–358
   concentration of control, 342–343
   constraints on news productions, 355–356
   coverage of world regions, 352–353
   criteria for choosing stories, 353–355
   cultural pressures, 348
   distortions of, 361–363
   economic pressures, 351
   effects of gatekeeping, 356–363
   exporting news, 368–371
   foreign correspondents, 343–348
   gatekeepers, 342–348
   impact of television, 363–365
   impact on public opinion, 367–368
   media diplomacy and, 349–351
   news gathering, 351–353
   newsmaking, 341–365
   news selection, 348–351
   political pressures, 348–349
   pro-American perspective of, 358–359
   shortcomings of, 361–363
   surveillance function, 343–348
   television coverage of wars, 359–361
Fox Broadcasting Corporation, 42
Franchises, 25

Frank, Barney, 164
Frankfurter, Felix, 79, 309
Freedom of Information Act, 70, 75
Freedom of speech, 9, 26–27
Freedom of the press, 26–27, 58–59
   access to information, 68–75
   access to media, 59–68
   agenda setting and, 9
   individual rights versus public's right to know, 76–86
   newsmaking control and, 19
   privacy protection and, 76–78
   suppression of news and, 150
Friedman, Milton, 117
Fulbright, J. William, 288
Fundamentalist groups, 52, 53, 216
Future Farmers of America, 62

Gag orders, 78–80
Galbraith, John Kenneth, 273
Gandy, Oscar, 178
Gannett newspaper chain, 39, 42
Gans, Herbert, 353
Gatekeeping, 99–116
   action in the news, 118
   constraints on news production, 113–116
   criteria for choosing specific stories, 104–108
   effects of, 116–124
   foreign affairs coverage, 342–348, 356–363
   gathering news, 108–113
   info-tainment news, 118–122
   news selection factors, 102–104
   newsworthy people, 116–118
   sources for stories, 100–101
   support for the establishment, 122–124
Gates, Daryl F., 145
Gaudet, Hazel, 13
General Electric Company, 40
General Motors, 52, 181
Generative media, 97
Gertz v. Robert Welch (1974), 82
Gingrich, Newt, 164, 269
Gitlin, Todd, 175
Global village, 108, 388
Global warming, 171–172
"Godfather" series, 385

Goldenberg, Edie, 177
Goldman, Ronald, 1–2
Goldstein, Tom, 384
Goldwater, Barry, 63
Gorbachev, Mikhail, 152, 169, 340
Gordon, Margaret, 159, 169
Gossamer Albatross, flight of, 93–94
Government censorship, 26
Government contracts, 72
Government control of media, 34–36
Government/press relations, in local
    coverage, 316–322
Government records, 124
    access to, 70–75
    computerization of, 70–71
    executive privilege and, 74–75
    historical documents, 72–74
    national security documents, 72–74
Government regulation of media. *See*
    Regulation
Government secrets, 27, 73. *See also*
    Government records
Governors, news coverage of, 117
Graham, Daniel, 180
Granger, Bill, 381
Greenhouse effect, 171–172
Grenada, 69, 360
Gulf War, 69, 136, 354
    media response, 139
    neglecting preventive coverage, 146
    positive effects of coverage, 143
    stages of coverage, 140–142
    suppression of news, 148–149, 360
Gun control, 52

Haiti, 363
Halberstam, David, 274
Hall, Arsenio, 238
Hargis, Billy James, 63
Harkin, Tom, 241
Hart, Gary, 11, 234, 255
Hartman, David, 198
"Hate" broadcasters, 86
HBO, 212
Helsinki Accords, 349
High definition television (HDTV),
    390–391
Hijackings, 80
Hill, Anita, 151, 228–229
Hills, Carla, 281

Hispanics
    socialization patterns, 195
    specialized media for, 316
Historical documents, access to, 72–74
Hoffa, James, 117
Holmes, Oliver Wendell, 86
"Holocaust" miniseries, 385
Home health-care programs, 162–163
"Home Health Hustle, The," 162–163
Homosexuality, 76–77
Human interest stories, 114, 273
Hussein, Saddam, 149, 351
Hustler, 77, 83
Hustler v. Falwell, 77, 83

Ideological bias, 7–8, 19
Incentive model of reporting, 247–248
Incumbency, 116, 242, 250
Indecent materials, 48, 51–52, 85
Independent Television News, 342
Independent Television Service, 37
Industry associations, 50–52
Industry documents, access to, 75
Industry lobbies, 50–52
Info-tainment news, 118–122
Informants, 80–82
Information access. *See* Access to infor-
    mation
Insurance fraud, 162
Interest groups. *See also* Lobby groups
    access to media and, 66
    agenda building and, 174–177
    environmentalists, 176
    licensing and, 66
    protest groups, 177
International news. *See* Foreign affairs
    coverage
Internet, 391–393
    access to, 60
    campaign coverage and, 240–241
    hate messages on, 86
    regulation of, 48
Interpretation function of media, 10–11
Intramarket competition, 44
Invasion of privacy, 76–78, 81, 165, 391
Investigative journalism. *See also* Manip-
    ulative journalism; Muckraking
    libel and, 82
    as manipulation function of media, 12
    Watergate scandal, 169–171

Investigative Reporters and Editors
(IRE), 158
Iran Air Flight 655, 358–359
Iran-contra scandal, 209–210, 255
Iran hostage crisis, 74, 146, 350, 354,
364
Isaacs, Norman, 384
Israel, 198, 339, 355–356, 359
ITAR, 342

Jackal syndrome. *See* Pack journalism
Jackson, Jesse, 8, 164, 255
Jackson, Robert H., 78–79
Jefferson, Thomas, 401
Jennings, Peter, 102
"J. F. K.," 179
"Jihad in America," 52
Johnson, Lyndon B., 70, 102, 235,
274
Johnson, Nicholas, 53
Jordan, 339
Journalism. *See also* Investigative journalism
attack journalism, 164–166
civic journalism, 98, 157
coalition journalism, 162–163
codes of ethics, 51, 84, 165, 370
manipulative journalism, 157–159,
166–168
pack journalism, 44–45, 144,
164–166, 247
public journalism, 24, 98, 157
social responsibility journalism,
19–20, 22–23, 98
standards of professionalism, 44–45,
247
Journalists, 94–99
autonomy of, 96–97
background factors, 94–96
demographics, 95–96
as diplomats, 167, 349–351
minorities, 95
organizational factors, 96–98
personality factors, 94–96
as political actors, 166–168
profile of, 94–99
roles of, 98–99
social responsibility role, 98
women, 95–96
Judicial censorship, 311–312

Judicial system. *See* Courts
Judiciary branch. *See* Courts

Kaiser Aluminum and Chemical Corpo-
ration, 181
Kaniss, Phyllis, 317, 320, 327, 333
Keeter, Scott, 207
Kefauver, Estes, 291–292
Kemp, Jack, 232
Kennedy, Edward M., 234
Kennedy, John F.
assassination, 4, 107, 179, 195
debates, 235
news conferences, 276, 278, 285–286
Kennedy, Robert F., 195
Kerner Commission, 146
Kevorkian, Jack, 117
Kidnapping incidents, 74
King, Larry, 238, 239
King, Martin Luther, Jr., 8, 195
King, Rodney, 147, 152, 169. *See also*
Los Angeles riots
Kissinger, Henry, 151, 152, 286–287,
349
Knight Ridder, 42
Kogan, Rick, 150–151, 152
Koppel, Ted, 372, 384
Korean Airlines Flight 007, 358–359,
362
KTTL-FM (Dodge City, Kan.), 86
Kueneman, Rodney, 146, 147, 148
Kurtz, Howard, 384

La Follette, Robert, 250
Lambeth, Edmund, 51
Lang, Gladys, 170–171
Lang, Kurt, 170–171
Language use, 147, 170–171, 216
"Larry King Live," 238, 239
Lasswell, Howard, 5, 11
LaVelle, Avis, 318
Lazarsfeld, Paul, 13
Le Mistral (restaurant), 77
League of Women Voters, 62
Leaks, 73, 79, 157, 167, 168, 287–288
Leaping impact muckraking, 160–163
Learning effects, 204–212
behavioral effects, 212–218
deterrents to learning, 209–212
factual learning, 207–208

general orientations, 208–209
measurement of learned knowledge, 205–207
memory and, 207, 208
Learning processes, 202–204
blending new and old information, 202–203
perceptual and image factors, 203–204
transient influences, 203
Learning theories, 14–15
Lebanon hostage crisis, 168
Legislative branch coverage. *See* Congressional coverage
Lerner, Daniel, 215
Letterman, David, 253
Libel, 82–84, 179–181
Libel Defense Resource Center, 84
Liberalism of journalists, 95
"Liberators, The," 179
Libertarian philosophy, 19–20, 22
Libya, 168
Licensing
interest groups and, 66
performance standards for, 49–50
renewals, 52
withdrawals, 49–50, 86, 385
Life, 387
Lifestyle sections, 116
Limbaugh, Rush, 239, 240
Lincoln, Abraham, 236
Lindberg, Charles, 312
Lippmann, Walter, 202, 306
Livingston, Steven, 16
Lobby groups. *See also* Interest groups
access to media and, 67–68
citizen lobbies, 52–54
industry lobbies, 50–52
public interest lobbies, 52–54
Local coverage
alternative press, 315–316, 387
changes in, 313–316
characteristics of, 326–328
content of, 326–328
diversity of, 327–328
of elections, 329–332
focus of, 314
government/press relations, 316–322
media styles, 317

national news on local media, 328–329
newsmaking, 319–322
print media, 318–319
quality of, 332–333
of referenda, 331–332
regulation of, 50
umbrella competition, 314–315
Loeb, William, 250
Look, 387
Los Angeles riots, 136–137, 152
negative effects of coverage, 144–145
neglecting preventive coverage, 146
positive effects of coverage, 143
stages of coverage, 139–141
Los Angeles Times, 43–44, 80, 140
Los Angeles Times-Washington Post News Service, 368
Luce, Henry, 234

MacVicar, Sheila, 343
Mainstreaming, 194
Maltese, John Anthony, 284
Manchester Union Leader, 250
Manipulation function of media, 12
Manipulative journalism. *See also* Muckraking
journalists as political actors, 166–168
objectives of, 158
policy making and, 157–159
Marcos, Ferdinand, 372
Market, defined, 40
Market size, 40–44
Marshall, John, 301
Martin, Lynn, 281
Mass media. *See* Media
Massachusetts Medical Society, 65
Matthews, Chris, 291
Mayors, news coverage of, 117
McClure, Jessica, 258
McCormick, Robert, 234
McDonald's, 51
McLuhan, Marshall, 6, 108, 388
Meany, George, 117
Media
effects of, 13–18
functions of, 5–12
interpretation function, 10–11
manipulation function, 12

political importance of, 2–5
presentation of information, 210
socialization function, 11–12
surveillance function, 5–10
Media access. *See* Access to media
Media control and ownership, 33–39
   advertiser pressures, 50–52
   business ownership, 39–40
   citizen lobby control, 52–54
   conglomerates, 40
   crossmedia ownership, 39, 396
   forms of control, 34–36
   independents, 39
   industry associations control, 50–52
   intramarket competition, 44
   market size and, 40–44
   multiple owners, 39
   prestige leadership, 44–45
   private ownership patterns, 39–46
   public control, 36
   public versus private control, 34–36
   semipublic control, 36–39
   small business versus big business
      control, 45–46
Media diplomacy, 167, 349–351
Media exposure patterns, 195–197
Media ownership. *See* Media control
  and ownership
Media trends, 380–381
   audience fragmentation, 402–403
   barriers to development, 393–394
   cable television, 394–397
   consequences of change, 404–405
   costs of new technology, 399–400
   criticism of media, 382–386
   dissatisfaction with media, 381–388
   impact of new technologies, 388–400
   Internet, 391–393
   public television, 404
   regulation, 397–398
   regulation versus deregulation,
      400–401
   specialized media, 386–388
   televotes, 401–402
   two-way communication, 401–402
Media use
   agenda-setting theories, 201–202
   demographics of, 195–197
   individual choices of media stories,
      197–202

purposes of, 210–211
racial differences, 196
selective exposure theories, 199–201
use and gratification theories, 97–199
Medialities, 254–255
Memory, effect on learning, 207, 208
Mencken, H. L., 104
Meyrowitz, Joshua, 205
Miami Herald, 11
Miami Herald Publishing Company v.
  Tornillo (1974), 60
Military censorship, 142, 148–149,
  359–361
Million-Man March, 118
Minorities. *See also* African Americans;
  Hispanics; Racial discrimination
   alienation from media, 210
   minority journalists, 95
   racial differences in media use,
      196
"Mirage" investigation, 163–164, 182
Mirror model of newsmaking, 23
Mitchell, Andrea, 343
Mobil Corporation, 67
Modernization
   adoption of changes, 217–218
   political modernization, 215–218
   psychological barriers to, 216
   socioeconomic modernization,
      215–218
Molotch, Harvey, 159, 169
Monopolies, 39, 48
Morgan, David, 322
Morison, Samuel Loring, 73
Mother Jones, 386
MTV, 239
Muckraking, 12, 156
   leaping impact muckraking, 160,
      162–163
   models of, 159–166
   mudslinging of public figures,
      164–166
   public opinion and, 164
   simple muckraking, 160–162
   truncated muckraking, 160, 163–164
Mudslinging, 164–166
Multimedia Company, 39
Murdoch, Rupert, 42
"Murphy Brown," 188–189
Muskie, Edmund, 121

NAACP (National Association for the
Advancement of Colored People), 307
Nader, Ralph, 53, 59, 100, 117
National Association of Broadcasters
(NAB), 50–51
National Black Media Coalition
(NBMC), 53
National Citizens Committee for Broad-
casting (NCCB), 53, 384
National Latino Media Coalition
(NLMC), 53
National News Council, 386
National Opinion Research Center, 381
National Organization for Women
(NOW), 54, 307
National Public Radio (NPR), 37
National Review, 386
National security documents, access to,
72–74
National Telecommunications and
Information Administration, 283
Natural disasters, 146–147
NBC (National Broadcasting Com-
pany), 42, 182, 340
polls, 235
NBMC. *See* National Black Media
Coalition
NCCB. *See* National Citizens Committee
for Broadcasting
Nebraska Press Association v. Stuart
(1976), 79
Negative news, 120–122
Neuman, W. Russell, 388, 405
New England Journal of Medicine, 65
New Left, 175
New Republic, 386
New York Daily News, 278
New York Sun, 106
New York Times Co. v. United States
(1971), 73
New York Times Company, 40
New York Times, 80
  beat coverage, 108
  developing countries coverage, 369
  focus of, 99
  foreign affairs coverage, 340–341
  Gulf War coverage, 141–142
  leadership of, 44
  letters to the editor, 66–67
  Somalia coverage, 16

stock market coverage, 101
Supreme Court coverage, 309
Unabomber tract, 148, 168
wire service, 43–44
New York Times News Service, 368
New York Times v. Sullivan (1964), 82
New Yorker, 386
Newhouse, 42
News blackouts. *See* Suppression of
news
News briefings, 285
News conferences, 285
News gathering, 108–113
  for foreign affairs coverage, 351–353
  improper methods, 179–183
  inaccurate reports, 181
  location of news stories, 109
  picture coverage, 113
  planning, 113
  standardization of, 109
  variety of topics covered, 109–111
"Newshour with Jim Lehrer," 119
Newsmaking, 93–94. *See also* Gatekeeping
  appraisal of, 124–128
  control methods, 25–28
  control of, 18–23
  foreign affairs coverage, 341–365
  gatekeeping, 99–124
  local coverage, 319–322
  mirror model, 23
  models of newsmaking process,
    23–28
  organizational model, 24
  political model, 24
  professional model, 23–24
  profile of American journalists,
    94–99
  public journalism model, 24
  state coverage, 319–322
News media, defined, 382
News selection
  advertisers and, 103–104
  competition and, 102–103
  criteria for choosing stories, 104–108
  criticism of, 7–8
  economic pressures, 103–104
  factors in, 102–104
  foreign affairs coverage, 348–351
  political context, 103

political pressures, 103
production constraints on, 114
programming and, 104
"Newsmagazine," 162–163
Newspaper chains, 42–43
Newspapers
decreasing circulation, 314–315
market size and, 42
most widely read content areas,
198–199
Newsweek, 101
Newsworthiness, 93–94
criteria for choosing specific stories,
104–108
info-tainment news, 118–122
of people, 116–118
Nixon, Richard, 52, 72, 169–170, 234,
349
NLMC. *See* National Latino Media
Coalition
Non-broadcast media. *See* Print media
Nonauthoritarian approaches to con-
trol, 19–23, 27
Noriega, Manuel, 360
Notorious individuals, news coverage of,
117
NOW. *See* National Organization for
Women
NPR. *See* National Public Radio
Nuclear disaster, 142–143, 204–205
Nuclear Regulatory Commission, 142
Nuclear weapons, 178–179

Obscene materials, 48, 51–52, 85
Obscenity rules, 48, 51–52
Office of Communications, 283–284
Office of Management and Budget
(OMB), 283
Office of Telecommunications Policy,
283
O'Heffernan, Patrick, 365
Oklahoma City bombing, 137, 147
media response, 138–139
negative effects of coverage, 144–145
stages of coverage, 140–142
Oligopolies, 44
Onassis, Jacqueline Kennedy, 77
Organization theory, 94
Organizational model of newsmaking,
24

Organized crime, 182
Owen, Diana, 239
Ownership. *See* Media control and own-
ership

Pack journalism, 44–45, 144, 164–166,
247
Pakistan, 347
Paletz, David, 172
Palmer, Kyle, 234
Panama, 360
Parent Teacher Association (PTA), 54,
384
Parenti, Michael, 384
Party affiliation, 231–232
Patterson, Thomas, 256
PBS (Public Broadcasting Service), 37
Pell v. Procunier (1974), 69
Pentagon Papers, 73–74
People's Choice, The, 13
Perot, Ross, 194, 234, 240, 245, 250–252
Persian Gulf War. *See* Gulf War
Personality theory, 94
Persuasion theories, 14
Pettit, Tom, 232
Philadelphia Inquirer, 167–168, 292
Photographs, 113
importance in political campaigns,
236–237
privacy rights and, 77
Piaget, Jean, 192
Planned Parenthood v. Casey (1992), 308
Plissner, Martin, 278
Policy making, 156–157
agenda building, 168–177
confirming prejudgments, 179–182
docudramas and, 177–179
documentaries and, 177–179
entrapment and, 182–183
journalists as political actors,
166–168
manipulative journalism and,
157–159
methods of, 179–183
muckraking models, 159–166
Political bias, 250
Political campaigns. *See* Campaigns
Political elites, 17–18
Political model of newsmaking, 24
Political modernization, 215–218

Political parties, decline in influence, 231–232
Political scandal, 170–171
Political significance, 17
Political socialization, 11–12, 211–212
　adult socialization and, 193–195
　child socialization and, 191–193
　role of media, 191–195
Politics of Broadcast Regulation, The, 47
Polsby, Daniel, 313
Pornography, 48, 51–52, 85, 214
Postman, Neil, 190
Powell, Colin, 117, 119
Powell, Jody, 253
Powledge, Fred, 175
Presidential Commission on Obscenity and Pornography, 85, 214
Presidential coverage. *See* Executive branch coverage
Press passes, 69
Press releases, 124, 285, 318
Pretrial publicity, 78
Primaries coverage, 256
Print media
　access to, 60
　impact of, 4–5
　impact on behavior and attitudes, 189–191
　space problems, 115
　for state and local coverage, 318–319
Prison riots, 150
Privacy Protection Act of 1980, 81
Privacy rights, 76–78, 81, 391
　public figures, 165
Private control of media, 34, 39–40, 45–46
Private surveillance, 5–6, 9–10
Procter and Gamble, 51
Professional model of newsmaking, 23–24
Programming, 35. *See also* Children's television
　indecent and obscene material, 85
　media control and, 46
　news selection and, 104
　protests of programming types, 49–50
　public broadcasting, 38
　for public service, 46
　violence on cable television, 212

Progressive, The, 72–73
Protection of sources, 68, 80–82
Protective censorship, 85–86
Protess, David, 159, 169
Protest groups, 177
Pseudo-crises, 150–152
Pseudo-events, 8, 113
Psychic mobility, 215–216
Public broadcasting system, 37–39, 65, 404
Public control of media, 34–36
Public figures
　libel laws and, 82–84
　mudslinging, 164–166
　privacy rights, 165
Public interest lobby, 52–54
Public journalism, 24, 98, 158
Public opinion
　foreign affairs coverage and, 367–368
　muckraking and, 164
　Somalia intervention and, 16
Public opinion polls, 233–236
Public records access, 70–75
Public relations agencies, 114–115, 346–347
Public service programs, 46, 50
Public surveillance, 5–9
Public Telecommunications Act of 1978, 37
Publicity
　power to produce public action, 6–7
　threats of, 166–167
Pulitzer Prize, 81

Quality of broadcasting, 52–54
Quayle, Dan, 164, 165, 188–189
QUBE system, 402

Racial discrimination, 176. *See also* Minorities
　jury decisions and, 1–2
　license renewals and, 52
Radio
　federal government control of, 36
　market size and, 42
Rape victims, publishing names of, 76
Rather, Dan, 44, 58, 102
Rating services, 105
Reagan, Ronald, 236, 276
　assassination attempt, 4, 140, 273

coverage of political elites and, 18
debates, 235
executive privilege and, 75
Iran-contra scandal, 209–210
leaks, 288
Libya and terrorism, 168
media coverage of campaign, 236–237, 252
military policy, 17
nuclear weapons policy, 178
speech broadcasts, 66
vetoes, 62
Reality distortions, 120, 125, 206
Rebuttals, 63–64, 181–182
Red Lion Broadcasting Co. v. Federal Communications Commission (1969), 63–64
Referenda, local coverage of, 331–332
Regulation, 36, 47–54. *See also* Federal Communications Commission (FCC)
children's television, 50
versus deregulation, 400–401
fair treatment rules, 50
FCC rules, 47–50
licensing as performance control, 49–50
local programming, 50
options for the future, 397–398
public service programs, 50
self-control of media, 51
of station ownership, 48–49
Religious groups, 52, 53, 216
Reno, Janet, 168
Reporters. *See* Journalists
Reporters Committee for Freedom of the Press, 80
Reporters Without Frontiers, 349
Research
on assassinations, 195
early studies, 13–15
effects of media on socialization, 192
on elections, 229–230
lack of research on political elites, 17–18
learning theories and, 14–15
measurement problems, 15–16, 205–207
on nuclear war, 204–205
recent research, 15–18
statistical versus political significance, 17

unanticipated effects, 17
on vote choices, 13–14
Resocialization, 12, 193
Reston, James, 366
Reuters, 342, 346
Richmond Newspapers v. Virginia (1980), 79–80
Right to know
censorship and, 84
fair trials and, 78–80
gag rule and, 78–80
versus individual rights, 76–86
libel laws, 82–84
privacy protection and, 76–78
restrictions on publication, 84–86
shield laws, 80–82
Riots, 80, 104–105, 106, 122, 202. *See also* Los Angeles riots
de-emphasizing media presence, 147
prison riots, 150
Rivera, Geraldo, 160
Robertson, Pat, 236, 255, 307
Robinson, John, 207
Robinson, Michael, 245, 255, 300
Rockwell, George Lincoln, 195
Roe v. Wade (1973), 308
Role theory, 94
Roosevelt, Franklin D., 234, 236
Roosevelt, Theodore, 12, 159, 285
Rubin, Barry, 343
"Rush Limbaugh Show," 239, 240

Sabato, Larry, 165
Sadat, Anwar, 349–350
Satellites, 370
Saturday Evening Post, 387
Sauter, Van Gordon, 180
Saxbe v. Washington Post Co. (1974), 69
Scandals, 170–171
Schemata, 202–204
Schiller, Herbert, 384
School prayer, 309–310
Schudson, Michael, 208
Schwarzkopf, Norman, 117
Science policy, and agenda building, 171–174
Scripts, 202
SDS (Students for a Democratic Society), 175
Sears Roebuck, 51

Security censorship, 73
Sedition laws, 26, 27
Seelye, Katharine Q., 269
Segregation, 308
Selective exposure theories, 199–201
Self-censorship, 26, 74
Self-immolation, 67
Senate committee coverage, 329
Senate hearings, 275, 288
Sensationalism, 67
Sexual harassment, 151
Shakespeare, William, 380
Shales, Tom, 275
Shepherd v. Florida (1951), 78–79
Sheppard v. Maxwell (1966), 78
Shield laws, 80–82
Showtime, 212
Shultz, George P., 178
Siegel, Mark, 347
Sigal, Leon, 109, 263
Simple muckraking model, 160–162
Simpson, Nicole Brown, 1–2
Simpson, O .J., 1–2, 80, 106, 190, 312, 390
Single mothers, 188–189
Sipple, Oliver, 76–77
"60 Minutes," 163–164, 209
Small, William J., 278
Smith, William Kennedy, 151, 152
Soap operas, 107
Social movements, and agenda building, 174–177
Social problems, neglect of, 122
Social responsibility journalism, 19–20, 22–23, 98. *See also* Investigative journalism; Manipulative journalism
Socialization
    of adults, 193–195
    of children, 191–193
    effect of media, 192
    function of media, 11–12
    patterns in, 195–197
    political, 11–12, 191–195, 211–212
    resocialization, 12, 193
Society for the Prevention of Cruelty to Children, 161
Socioeconomic modernization, 215–218
Solomon, Douglas S., 217
Somalia, 16

Source appraisal, by individuals, 203
Source protection, 68, 80–82
Southern California earthquake. *See* Earthquakes
Soviet Union, 33, 102, 169, 286–287
Speaker of the House, 269
Special interest groups. *See* Interest groups
Specialized media, 316, 386–388
Specter, Arlen, 229
Spin Control, 284
Split-ticket voting, 231
Spot news, 113
Stahl, Leslie, 236–237, 241–242
State coverage
    content of, 322–326
    electoral votes and, 112–113
    government/press relations, 316–322
    local emphasis of, 322–323
    media styles, 317
    national emphasis of, 323–326
    network coverage of state news, 112–113
    newsmaking, 319–322
    print media, 318–319
State Department, 341
Statistical significance, 17
Steffens, Lincoln, 156, 159
Stereotypes, 205–206
Stimulus-determined images, 204
Sting operations, 182–183
Stock market coverage, 101, 145, 255
Strikes, 121, 198
Structural bias, 250
Students for a Democratic Society (SDS), 175
Sullivan rule, 82–83
Suppression of news, 22, 69
    extraordinary events, 147–150
    Gulf War, 148–149, 360
Supreme Court. *See* U. S. Supreme Court
Surveillance function of media, 5–10, 343–348
Sweeps periods, 168

Talk shows, 238–241, 316
Technology
    advertising support for, 399

barriers to development, 393–394
costs of, 399–400
impact of, 113, 388–400
Telecommunications Act of 1996, 42,
49–51, 54, 85, 214, 380, 391, 398,
400–401
Television. *See also* Cable television;
Children's television
advisers, 237–238
deterrents to learning and, 210
elections coverage, 252–253
impact on foreign affairs coverage,
363–365
internal structure of television news,
211
market size and, 42
political advertisements, 244–245
presentation of candidates, 236–238
public versus private ownership, 34
violent programming, 212
war coverage, 359–361
watching, 191–192, 193, 195–196
Televotes, 401–402
Terrorism, 106, 140–141, 144–145, 150,
168
Thalidomide, 10
Third-party candidates, 250–251
Thomas, Clarence, 150–152, 228, 288,
307
Thomson Newspapers, 42
Three Mile Island, 142, 144, 145, 275
Tiananmen Square massacre, 67, 190
Time, 232
To Kill a Messenger, 278
Tobacco, 172–174
Tofani, Loretta, 81
Tornillo, Patrick, Jr., 60
Totalitarian ideology, 19, 20–21, 22, 26
Tower, John, 275
Treason laws, 26, 27
Trespass laws, 77
Tribune Company, 40
Truman, Harry S., 234, 236, 276, 291
Truncated muckraking, 160, 163–164
Truth-in-advertising laws, 63
Tsongas, Paul, 233, 234
Turner, Ted, 48
Tutu, Desmond, 372
"20/20," 162
Two-way communication, 401–402

Unabomber, 148, 168
Unbalanced coverage, 127
"Uncounted Enemy, The," 179–181
Underground press, 387–388
UNESCO (United Nations Educational,
Scientific, and Cultural Organization),
20, 365–366, 370
Uniform Poll Closing Act, 261
Uninformed Choice, 207–208
United Church of Christ, 52
United Press International (UPI),
368
U.S. Constitution, 26–27, 59. *See also*
First Amendment; Freedom of the
press
U.S. Department of Justice, 283
U.S. Information Agency (USIA), 348,
370
U.S. Supreme Court. *See also* Courts
access to government documents
and, 73–74
access to information and, 68–69
access to media and, 60, 66
confirmation hearings, 151, 288,
307
impact of media coverage, 308–310
indecent and obscene materials and,
85
libel laws and, 82–83
news coverage of, 117, 270–272
newsworthiness of, 308
privacy rights and, 76–77
right to know and, 78–80
shield laws and, 81
United We Stand for America, 240
Universal Declaration of Human Rights,
370
University of Chicago, 167
University of Houston, 65
University of Pennsylvania, 206
Unwed mothers, 188–189
UPI. *See* United Press International
USA Today, 77–78
Use and gratifications theory, 197–199

"V-chip," 51, 214
Victim names, 76
Videomalaise, 121
Vietnam War, 73, 81, 106, 175, 179–180,
274–275, 363

Violence
  acceptance of, 120–121
  advertiser withdrawals, 51–52
  on cable television, 212
  defined, 212
  imitation of, 212–215, 385
  popularity of stories about, 121
Visnews news service, 342
Visual appeal, 115
Voice of America (VOA), 36, 348, 370
Voter Decides, The, 13
Voting
  behavior of voters, 261–263
  choices based on media coverage,
    13–14
  knowledge base for, 260
  knowledge of candidates and issues,
    257–260
  split-ticket voting, 231
  turnout, 261
  vote changes, 261
  voter knowledge gains, 207–208
*Voting: A Study of Opinion Formation in a
  Presidential Campaign*, 13

W. R. Grace, 67
Wall Street Journal, 99, 101
Wallace, George, 250
Walt Disney Company, 40, 48
War coverage, 359–361
Warner Amex Cable Communications,
  402
Washington, Harold, 249
Washington Post
  beat coverage, 108
  contributions to public broadcasting,
    37
  coverage of political elites, 18
  developing countries coverage, 369
  Gulf War coverage, 141–142
  Somalia coverage, 16
  Unabomber tract, 148, 168
Watchdog role, 98, 158
Watergate scandal, 169–171

Weaver, David H., 94–96, 128
Weekend Yawn Rule, 122
Weinberger, Caspar, 287
Welfare programs, 275
Westinghouse, 48
Westmoreland, William C., 81,
  179–181
White, Byron R., 82, 88
White, Theodore, 18
White House press corps, 284–285
White House Press Office, 283–284
Wilder, L. Douglas, 330
Wilhoit, G. Cleveland, 94–96, 128
Willowbrook State School, 160–162
Wilson, Pete, 147
"Winds of War, The," 209
Wire services, 43–44, 342
WLBT-TV (Jackson, Miss.), 52
Women
  coverage of, 116
  elections coverage and, 228–229
  women journalists, 95–96
Wood, Kimba, 275
World Trade Center bombing, 52, 137
World Wide Web, 391–393
  access to, 60
  advertising on, 67
  campaign coverage and, 240
  hate messages on, 86
  legislators' use of, 296
  regulation of, 48
WORLDNET, 348
Wright, Joseph, 146, 147, 148
Wright, Orville and Wilbur, 93
WTN, 342

X, Malcolm, 195

Yeakel, Lynn, 228–229

Zamora, Ronny, 385
Zemel v. Rusk (1965), 68
Zisk, Betty, 331
Zukin, Cliff, 207